Norway

Deanna Swaney

LONELY PLANET PUBLICATIONS
Melbourne • Oakland • London • Paris

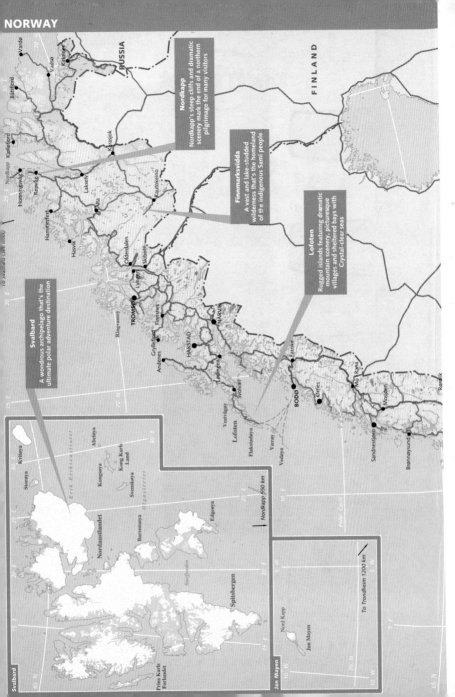

NORWAY

Svalbard

Nordkapp
Nordkapp's steep cliffs and dramatic scenery mark the end of a northern pilgrimage for many visitors

Finnmarksvidda
A vast and lake-studded wilderness that's the homeland of the indigenous Sami people

Lofoten
Rugged islands featuring dramatic mountain scenery, picturesque villages and sheltered bays with crystal-clear seas

Svalbard
A wondrous archipelago that's the ultimate polar adventure destination

RUSSIA

FINLAND

Vardø
Vadsø
Kirkenes
Båtsfjord
Kjøllefjord
Honningsvåg
Nordkapp
Repvåg
Hammerfest
Hasvik
Lakselv
Karasjok
Kautokeino
Alta
Olderdalen
Skibotn
Lyngen
TROMSØ
Finnsnes
Ringvassøy
Gryllefjord
Andenes
HARSTAD
Lødingen
NARVIK
Vesterøy
Svolvær
Lofoten
Flakstadøya
Værøy
Vedøya
Fauske
BODØ
Ørnes
Mo i Rana
Mosjøen
Sandnessjøen
Brønnøysund
Rørvik

To Svalbard (see inset)

Nordkapp 550 km

Polar Circle

To Trondheim 1200 km

Svalbard

Kvitøya
Storøya
Nordaustlandet
Kong Karls Land
Kongsøya
Svenskøya
Abeløya
Barentsøya
Edgeøya
Erik Eriksenstretet
Olgastretet
Storfjorden
Spitsbergen
Prins Karls Forlandet

Jan Mayen
Nord Kapp
Jan Mayen

Norway
1st edition – August 1999

Published by
Lonely Planet Publications Pty Ltd ABN 36 005 607 983
90 Maribyrnong St, Footscray, Victoria 3011, Australia

Lonely Planet Offices
Australia Locked Bag 1, Footscray, Victoria 3011
USA 150 Linden St, Oakland, CA 94607
UK 10a Spring Place, London NW5 3BH
France 1 rue du Dahomey, 75011 Paris

Photographs
All of the images in this guide are available for licensing from
Lonely Planet Images.
email: lpi@lonelyplanet.com.au

Front cover photograph
Norwegian girl at the 1994 Winter Olympics in Lillehammer (José Azel)

ISBN 0 86442 654 2

Although the authors and Lonely Planet try to make the information as accurate as possible, we accept no responsibility for any loss, injury or inconvenience sustained by anyone using this book.

Contents – Text

SOUTHERN NORWAY 154

CENTRAL NORWAY 193

BERGEN & THE SOUTH-WESTERN FJORDS 227

THE WESTERN FJORDS 261

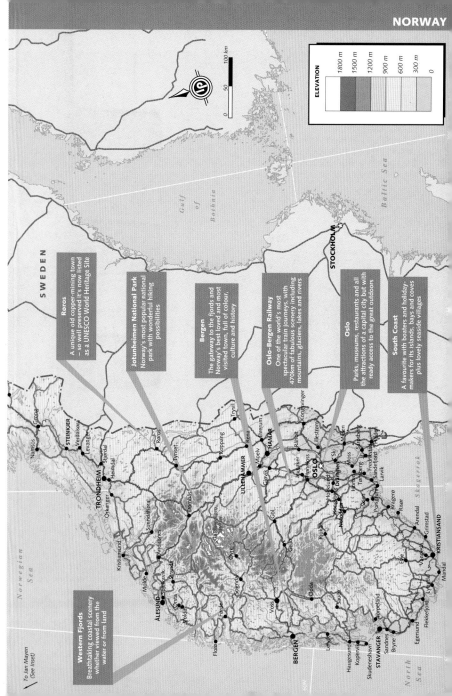

Contents – Maps

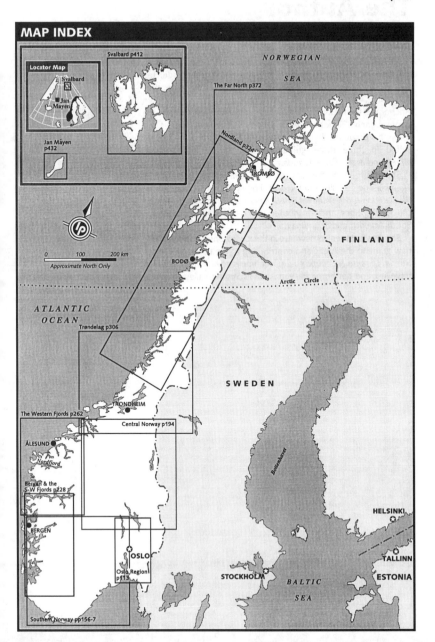

The Author

DEANNA SWANEY

After her university studies, Deanna made a shoestring tour of Europe – including a jaunt into Norway – and has been addicted to travel ever since. Despite an erstwhile career in computer programming, she avoided encroaching yuppiedom in midtown Anchorage by making a break for South America, where she wrote Lonely Planet's *Bolivia* guide. Subsequent travels led through a circuit of island paradises – Arctic and tropical – and resulted in three more guides: *Tonga, Samoa* and *Iceland, Greenland & the Faroe Islands.*

She returned to dry land to write *Zimbabwe, Botswana & Namibia* and has since worked on Lonely Planet's *Brazil, Mauritius, Réunion & Seychelles, Madagascar & Comoros* and *Africa – the South* guides, and contributed to shoestring guides to Africa, South America and Scandinavia.

She was last seen somewhere in the icy regions working on LP's new guide to the Arctic and contributing to the boreal bits of the *Russia, Ukraine & Belarus* guide. Her time is now divided between travelling and her home base in Alaska's Susitna Valley.

FROM THE AUTHOR

First, I must convey boundless thanks to Jens Riis-Næs of NRK and Ingalill Sandal of NORTRA, without whom this project would have been impossible. Just as invaluable was Graeme Cornwallis, whom I must thank for access to his wealth of experience in Norway, his considerable assistance with the intro chapters and his friendship and company for part of my research trip. Norbert Schürer of Duke University drew from his considerable literary expertise to provide the excellent section on Norwegian literature which appears in the Facts about Norway chapter. I'm also indebted to Steinar Lindås and Ulf Prytz of Svalbard Polar Travel for one of the most magical journeys of my life; Svalbard is truly heaven at the top of the earth! Similarly, Andreas Umbreit of Longyearbyen provided a great deal of Svalbard information and improved the book immeasurably with his comments, direction and text checking. Audun Tjomsland at Braathens SAFE graciously helped me more than he probably realises and Kirsti Ramnefjell of Widerøe made possible some of the finest airborne experiences imaginable. I'm also indebted to Trond Kleivdal, of Color Line; Guri Møller, of TFDS; and Steinar Sæterdal, of OVDS, who facilitated my research by organising some superb maritime experiences. As always, I must also convey various warm and fuzzy sentiments to Ernst & Norbert Schürer for great company and fun times, this time in Norway, Sweden and Finland. Heartfelt thanks are also due John & Kari-Anne Bryde of the Røros Tourist Board for the best reception ever in one of Norway's greatest places, and for going the extra mile to help me see the subtler facets of its magic. Thanks also to Glenda Bendure and Ned Friary, who laid the groundwork for this book with their Norway chapter in *Scandinavian & Baltic Europe on a shoestring* – you made this job a hundred times easier. Then there were those folks in Melbourne who rode herd over me and made this job a bit harder – and the results immeasurably better: many thanks to Carolyn Bain, Mark 'Grrrr' Griffiths, Liz Filleul and Jane Fitzpatrick.

There were also many people who went beyond the call of duty and took time from their busy schedules to help me better understand their areas, for which I'm extremely grateful. In no particular order, they include Erling Kjølseth, in Åndalsnes, for a wonderful introduction to Raumadalen and Trollstigen; Torstein Brevik, Finn Viken and Opplev Oppdal, in Oppdal, for good company and a lovely day of rafting on the Driva; Peggy Schlytter of Oslo Promotions, for a warm reception and lots of information, ideas, direction and Oslo Cards; Solveig Barstad in Elverum, for a great day in Elverum and Trysil; Nicklas Fronth of Narvik og Ofoten Reiseliv, Lars Slettjord at the Ofoten Museum and Nils Tyeng at the War Museum, all in Narvik; Anne-Toril Vangberg, Frank Berg Nilssen and Sigbjørn Slåtten in Voss;

Ragnar Heggdal in Molde (thanks especially for the T-shirt); Asbjørn Gabrielsen at Destinasjon Lofoten in Svolvær; Ms Garmo at the Fossheim Steinsenter in Lom; Annebjørg and Anne at Whale Tours in Nyksund, Vesterålen; Torbjørn Evenbye in Kristiansand; Torill Döhl in Mo i Rana; May Britt Hansen at Top of Europe in Alta; Villgunn Celius and Børge in Kirkenes; Rune Rafaelsen of Grenseland in Kirkenes, for his help with the Norway-Russia connections; and Håvard in Kirkenes.

The following people, again in no particular order, also deserve warm thanks: Robert Strauss of Compass-Star Publications, for contact information and the latest from the frog and tamandua press; Bjørn Forbord, for expert dental work; Laurence Fairman, Jacqueline Monica Magi and Roberto Sbenaglia, for happy times in Svalbard; Kari Angelmo in Longyearbyen; Marius Meisfjord, for a long stay in Oslo; Toril Rossaak for helping with Oslo locations; Siri Giil and Halfdan Haukeland in Bergen; Gertrude at NORTRA; Eva Idland in Larvik; Gabrielle Øyen in Kragerø; Elisabeth Bjølstad in Otta; Cecilia at Destinasjon Bodø in Bodø; Karianne Halvorson at DNT in Oslo; Ellen Frisvold in Stavanger; Tonje Sti and Olav at Use-It; Kirsten Brath and Arvid Lyngås, for all their help in Kongsberg; Bjørn Arthur Aadnesen and Eli W Håland, in Egersund; Karl Fredrik Hestbek, Trondheim; Bente Skaarud in Lom; Hilde Mauritzen, Fjærland; Nils Paulsen at the Norsk Bremuseum, Fjærland; Sissel Nerete Ødegård in Stryn; Liv Bodil H Baug in Florø; Eivind Luthen, Oslo, for enthusiasm and information on Norway's pilgrimage routes and movements; Jenny at Mandal; Margot Olsen & Lars Thomas in Dombås; Edith in Kristiansund; Marit Helen Giske in Ålesund; Knut Hansvold and Helga Marie Jønnson in Tromsø; and all the friendly and helpful Norwegians whose names I didn't learn.

Finally, love and best wishes to Earl, Dean, Kim, Jennifer and Lauren Swaney in Fresno and Rodney Leacock in Colorado Springs; to Keith & Holly Hawkings in Anchorage; and to Dave Dault who most admirably held down the fort back home in Alaska. Also a note for Kirsten W – if you see this, please get in touch via Lonely Planet!

This Book

This first edition of *Norway* was written by Deanna Swaney using material from the Norway chapter of *Scandinavian & Baltic Europe on a shoestring* (3rd edition), originally researched by Glenda Bendure and Ned Friary.

From the Publisher

Norway was produced in Lonely Planet's Melbourne office and was coordinated by Mark Griffiths (mapping and design) and Carolyn Bain (editorial).

A big thanks to all who assisted, including Ann Jeffree, Celia Wood, Csanád Csutoros, Joelene Kowalski, Leanne Peake, Lisa Borg and Tony Fankhauser (mapping) and Chris Wyness, Clay Lucas, Helen Yeates, Rebecca Turner, Ron Gallagher, Shelley Muir and Wendy Owen (editing and proofing).

Quentin Frayne produced the Language chapter, Piotr Czajkowski contributed the colour map and Adrian Persoglia created the climate charts. Mick Weldon drew the great cartoons and Martin Harris the illustrations. Sean Pywell helped with flora and fauna advice and Graham Bell wrote the musk ox aside. Thanks also to Tim Uden for Quark expertise and Guillaume Roux for the cover.

And finally, thanks to Deanna herself for her enthusiasm and good humour.

Foreword

ABOUT LONELY PLANET GUIDEBOOKS

The story begins with a classic travel adventure: Tony and Maureen Wheeler's 1972 journey across Europe and Asia to Australia. Useful information about the overland trail did not exist at that time, so Tony and Maureen published the first Lonely Planet guidebook to meet a growing need.

From a kitchen table, then from a tiny office in Melbourne (Australia), Lonely Planet has become the largest independent travel publisher in the world, an international company with offices in Melbourne, Oakland (USA), London (UK) and Paris (France).

Today Lonely Planet guidebooks cover the globe. There is an ever-growing list of books and there's information in a variety of forms and media. Some things haven't changed. The main aim is still to help make it possible for adventurous travellers to get out there – to explore and better understand the world.

At Lonely Planet we believe travellers can make a positive contribution to the countries they visit – if they respect their host communities and spend their money wisely. Since 1986 a percentage of the income from each book has been donated to aid projects and human rights campaigns.

Updates Lonely Planet thoroughly updates each guidebook as often as possible. This usually means there are around two years between editions, although for more unusual or more stable destinations the gap can be longer. Check the imprint page (following the colour map at the beginning of the book) for publication dates.

Between editions up-to-date information is available in two free newsletters – the paper *Planet Talk* and email *Comet* (to subscribe, contact any Lonely Planet office) – and on our Web site at www.lonelyplanet.com. The *Upgrades* section of the Web site covers a number of important and volatile destinations and is regularly updated by Lonely Planet authors. *Scoop* covers news and current affairs relevant to travellers. And, lastly, the *Thorn Tree* bulletin board and *Postcards* section of the site carry unverified, but fascinating, reports from travellers.

Correspondence The process of creating new editions begins with the letters, postcards and emails received from travellers. This correspondence often includes suggestions, criticisms and comments about the current editions. Interesting excerpts are immediately passed on via newsletters and the Web site, and everything goes to our authors to be verified when they're researching on the road. We're keen to get more feedback from organisations or individuals who represent communities visited by travellers.

Lonely Planet gathers information for everyone who's curious about the planet – and especially for those who explore it first-hand. Through guidebooks, phrasebooks, activity guides, maps, literature, newsletters, image library, TV series and Web site we act as an information exchange for a worldwide community of travellers.

Research Authors aim to gather sufficient practical information to enable travellers to make informed choices and to make the mechanics of a journey run smoothly. They also research historical and cultural background to help enrich the travel experience and allow travellers to understand and respond appropriately to cultural and environmental issues.

Authors don't stay in every hotel because that would mean spending a couple of months in each medium-sized city and, no, they don't eat at every restaurant because that would mean stretching belts beyond capacity. They do visit hotels and restaurants to check standards and prices, but feedback based on readers' direct experiences can be very helpful.

Many of our authors work undercover, others aren't so secretive. None of them accept freebies in exchange for positive write-ups. And none of our guidebooks contain any advertising.

Production Authors submit their raw manuscripts and maps to offices in Australia, USA, UK or France. Editors and cartographers – all experienced travellers themselves – then begin the process of assembling the pieces. When the book finally hits the shops, some things are already out of date, we start getting feedback from readers and the process begins again ...

WARNING & REQUEST

Things change – prices go up, schedules change, good places go bad and bad places go bankrupt – nothing stays the same. So, if you find things better or worse, recently opened or long since closed, please tell us and help make the next edition even more accurate and useful. We genuinely value all the feedback we receive. Julie Young coordinates a well travelled team that reads and acknowledges every letter, postcard and email and ensures that every morsel of information finds its way to the appropriate authors, editors and cartographers for verification.

Everyone who writes to us will find their name in the next edition of the appropriate guidebook. They will also receive the latest issue of *Planet Talk*, our quarterly printed newsletter, or *Comet*, our monthly email newsletter. Subscriptions to both newsletters are free. The very best contributions will be rewarded with a free guidebook.

Excerpts from your correspondence may appear in new editions of Lonely Planet guidebooks, the Lonely Planet Web site, *Planet Talk* or *Comet*, so please let us know if you *don't* want your letter published or your name acknowledged.

Send all correspondence to the Lonely Planet office closest to you:

Australia: Locked Bag 1, Footscray, Victoria 3011
USA: 150 Linden St, Oakland, CA 94607
UK: 10A Spring Place, London NW5 3BH
France: 1 rue du Dahomey, 75011 Paris

Or email us at: talk2us@lonelyplanet.com.au

For news, views and updates see our Web site: www.lonelyplanet.com

HOW TO USE A LONELY PLANET GUIDEBOOK

The best way to use a Lonely Planet guidebook is any way you choose. At Lonely Planet we believe the most memorable travel experiences are often those that are unexpected, and the finest discoveries are those you make yourself. Guidebooks are not intended to be used as if they provide a detailed set of infallible instructions!

Contents All Lonely Planet guidebooks follow roughly the same format. The Facts about the Destination chapters or sections give background information ranging from history to weather. Facts for the Visitor gives practical information on issues like visas and health. Getting There & Away gives a brief starting point for re-searching travel to and from the destination. Getting Around gives an overview of the transport options when you arrive.

The peculiar demands of each destination determine how sub-sequent chapters are broken up, but some things remain constant. We always start with background, then proceed to sights, places to stay, places to eat, entertainment, getting there and away, and getting around information – in that order.

Heading Hierarchy Lonely Planet headings are used in a strict hierarchical structure that can be visualised as a set of Russian dolls. Each heading (and its following text) is encompassed by any preceding heading that is higher on the hierarchical ladder.

Entry Points We do not assume guidebooks will be read from beginning to end, but that people will dip into them. The tradi-tional entry points are the list of contents and the index. In addition, however, some books have a complete list of maps and an index map illustrating map coverage.

There may also be a colour map that shows highlights. These highlights are dealt with in greater detail in the Facts for the Visitor chapter, along with planning questions and suggested itin-eraries. Each chapter covering a geographical region usually begins with a locator map and another list of highlights. Once you find something of interest in a list of highlights, turn to the index.

Maps Maps play a crucial role in Lonely Planet guidebooks and include a huge amount of information. A legend is printed on the back page. We seek to have complete consistency between maps and text, and to have every important place in the text captured on a map. Map key numbers usually start in the top left corner.

Although inclusion in a guidebook usually implies a recommen-dation we cannot list every good place. Exclusion does not necessarily imply criticism. In fact there are a number of reasons why we might exclude a place – sometimes it is simply inappropriate to encourage an influx of travellers.

Introduction

Norway (Norge) stretches nearly 3000km from the balmy beach towns of the south to the treeless Arctic archipelago of Svalbard in the north, taking in vast forests, rugged peaks, haunting fjords, dramatic glaciers, expansive icefields and wild Arctic tundra. The country also boasts pleasantly low-key modern cities, rustic fishing villages, hundreds of worthwhile museums and rich historic sites ranging from restored Viking ships to medieval stave churches.

Compared with most of Europe, Norway retains something of a frontier character, and Norwegians value their easy access to wild outdoor country, including the forested green belts that surround even the largest cities. For outdoors enthusiasts, this translates into excellent wilderness hiking, mountaineering and nordic skiing, while the less active can sit back and enjoy some of the most scenic ferry, bus and train rides imaginable.

Most visitors to Norway are struck by its incredible beauty, and nearly every part of the country has inspired poets, artists, composers, photographers and dreamers (well, maybe not the Oslo railyards ...). In the south, this beauty is exemplified by the rolling farmlands of Østfold, the rocky coasts of Rogaland, the enchanted forests of Telemark, the sunny Skagerrak beaches, the bleak alpine plateaux of the interior, the cold coniferous forests along the Swedish border and the dramatic world-renowned landscapes of the Western Fjords.

As one moves north, the population thins and the horizons grow wider. From Trondheim northwards stretch 1500km of vast and varied landscapes, most of which lie within the Arctic Circle. Here the terrain ranges from soaring coastal peaks and tiny fishing villages beside turquoise seas to the vast boreal forests of the Sami country and the barren treeless peninsulas of the Arctic Ocean coast. In addition, Norway also extends to two high Arctic possessions. The small volcanic island of Jan Mayen lies well off the beaten track (or any track) and the indescribable Svalbard archipelago, quite literally one of the planet's most breathtaking places, attracts adventurers who don't mind paying well for exceptional quality.

Summer visitors will be treated to a special high-latitude phenomena, for Norway is the proverbial 'Land of the Midnight Sun'. Between mid-May and early August, the twilight lingers through the night in southern Norway, but in the counties of Nordland, Troms and Finnmark, as well as Svalbard and Jan Mayen, the sun doesn't set for weeks on end. In fact in Longyearbyen, Svalbard, the sun doesn't set between 20 April and 21 August! The down side, of course, is that winters can be oppressively cold and dark, and north of the Arctic Circle the perpetual summer daylight rapidly gives way to the polar night. In Tromsø the sun doesn't rise at all between 25 November and 17 January, and Longyearbyen is gripped by darkness for nearly four months from 26 October to 16 February! Despite the gloom, however, a winter visit to Norway will avail you to several wonderful opportunities, including the chance to ski some of the world's best alpine and nordic venues, to take an adventurous wilderness trip by dogsled or to gaze up in wonder at the mesmerising spectacle of the aurora borealis.

There is, however, a fly in the ointment. Thanks to its official policies, extremely high taxes and relative remoteness, Norway is expensive, to put it mildly, and budget travel will require some effort – as well as a redefinition of the word 'budget'. Fortunately, wild camping is free, rail passes allow relatively inexpensive travel in the southern part of the country, and supermarkets offer some relief from the cost of restaurant meals. If you really want to enjoy the magic of Norway, however, the most important things to do are budget generously, tighten your belt a bit and forget about converting local expenditure into your home currency!

Facts about Norway

HISTORY
Prehistory

Near the end of the last Ice Age around 11,000 years ago, the first humans arrived in the area of modern-day Norway from Siberia. It's thought that this ancient hunting culture – known as the Komsa – was the forerunner of the modern Sami peoples. Regarding the Sami, however, all that's known is that they occupied northern Scandinavia from prior to the Christian era. Also in prehistoric times, the coastal Fosna culture pursued a hunting, fishing and herding lifestyle around the site of Trondheim and the northern end of the Western Fjords.

After the ice had receded from northern Europe, people also began migrating northwards from central Europe and settling in southern Scandinavia, including along the southern Norwegian coast. These early inhabitants, who belonged to the Nøstvet-Økser culture, didn't have access to flint, which meant that most of their tools had to be made from bone. Initially these people followed a nomadic hunter-gatherer lifestyle, and it was several thousand years before they began establishing more permanent settlements. Although Stone Age peoples in southern Norway would have been of mixed European background, it's likely that the predominant type was tall, blonde, blue-eyed and spoke a Germanic language which was the predecessor of modern Scandinavian languages.

Around 2500 BC, the Battle-Axe, Boat-Axe and Funnel-Beaker cultures (named for the various stone tools they used) entered southern Norway from what is present-day Sweden. Thanks to the paucity of naturally occurring metals, relatively few of their tools were made from bronze or other metals, and the most significant Bronze Age relics are rock carvings which portray ships and religious symbols. This indicates that travel and trade were increasing in importance, and that trade links had probably been developed with lands to the south and west. The Scandinavians traded amber for metals, particularly bronze, from mainland Europe.

Rock carvings from the era prior to 500 BC depict agricultural and maritime scenes and indicate improvements in farming and ship-building methods, as well as other technological advances. In addition, the burial customs of this day, which involved mounds, suggest spiritual and temporal leadership by powerful chieftains. Until around 500 BC, the climate in this region remained relatively warm and amenable to agriculture, but then came a cooling trend and people had to refine their agricultural methods to accommodate the changes, as indicated by the ruins of stone and turf dwellings, farms and furnaces from this period.

Although trade between southern Norway and the Mediterranean area was interrupted by Celtic migrations eastward across Europe, it was revived during the later days of the Roman Empire, when Rome provided Norway with such items as fabric, iron implements and pottery. The use of iron tools allowed more land to be cleared of trees, and larger boats were built with the aid of iron axes. By the 5th century, the Norwegians had learned how to smelt their own iron from ore found in the southern Norwegian bogs. The runic alphabet also arrived, probably from a Germanic source, and over the following centuries became a medium of communication, as evidenced by inscriptions found in stone slabs throughout the region. The fall of the Roman Empire, however, saw a 200-year period of migration and fighting between several regions of the country.

Around 700 AD, Irish monks constructed a monastery at Selje, which probably represented the first appearance of Christianity in Norway. At this time, thanks to its difficult geography, much of Norway was divided into small, independent, non-confederated kingdoms ruled by *jarls* (earls). At this time, the only mainland European awareness of Norway was of the road known as the Norovegr ('North Way'), the trade route which led from Oslofjord westward along the southern coast.

The Viking Era

Norway's greatest impact on world history probably occurred during the Viking Age, when the prospect of trade, political stress and an increasingly dense agricultural population inspired many Norwegians to seek out greener pastures abroad. The word 'Viking' is derived from *vik*, which now means 'creek' in Norwegian, but in Old Norse referred to a bay or cove (and still does in Icelandic). The connection probably referred to their anchorages during raids.

The catalyst for the Viking movement was probably overpopulation in western Norway, where polygamy led to an excess of male heirs and too little land to go around. The division of land into ever-smaller plots became intolerable for many, causing young men to migrate abroad to seek their fortunes.

The *Anglo Saxon Chronicle* for 787 quotes that three ships came to Britain from Hordaland (Heredalande), piloted by sailors who were described as Northmen, but there's no indication that they were involved in any sort of warfare. Around this time, Nordic shipbuilders developed a relatively fast and manoeuvrable sailing vessel which had a heavy keel, up to 16 pairs of oars and a large square sail, and was sturdy enough for ocean crossings. It's suspected that Norwegian farmers had peacefully settled in Orkney and Shetland as early as the 780s, but it's generally accepted that the Viking Age didn't begin until 793 with the plundering of St Cuthbert's monastery on the island of Lindisfarne, off the coast of Northumberland, Britain.

This initial attack was followed a year later by the plundering of Jarrow, also in Northumberland, but the movement really took off the following year, when a contingency of 100 Viking ships set their sights on south Wales. However, they were successfully resisted by King Maredydd

Norse Seafaring

Realising the vast distances covered by the early voyagers through difficult seas, one can only wonder what sort of ships and technology the Norse people used to travel so far through uncharted territory. Archaeological evidence suggests that Viking longboats, low vessels over 30m long, were used primarily in war and raiding. The majority of the settlers travelled in smaller cargo boats called *knerrir* (singular *knörr*). These sturdy little craft, scarcely 18m in length with little freeboard, were designed to carry great loads. Journeys in them must have been crowded, uncomfortable and often frightening.

Perhaps the most interesting aspect of these early voyages, however, is the method of navigation employed. The sagas mention a mysterious device known as a *solarsteinn*, or 'sunstone', which allowed navigation even when the sky was overcast or the sun was below the horizon and celestial navigation was impossible.

It is now generally agreed that the solarsteinn was a crystal of cordierite, which is found around Scandinavia and has natural polarising qualities. When observed from below and rotated, light passing through the crystal is polarised blue when the long axis is pointed toward the source of the sunlight.

This same principal is used today. Jet planes flying over the polar regions, where magnetic compasses are unsuitable and celestial navigation is difficult, use a sky compass which determines the position of the sun by filtering sunlight through an artificial polarising lens.

and they next concentrated their efforts on Ireland, where the monasteries presented easy targets and yielded a great deal of loot.

They apparently had no reservations about sacking religious communities and, indeed, many Vikings believed that the Christian monasteries they encountered were a threat to their pantheist traditions. Mainly in the more lawless regions of Britain and Ireland, they destroyed Christian communities and slaughtered monks, who could only wonder what sin they had committed to invite the heathen hordes.

Despite this apparent predilection for warfare, the Vikings' considerable barbarism was probably no greater than the standard of the day, and the colonisation of the Western Isles of Scotland appears to have involved a relatively peaceful coexistence between the Vikings and Celts (although the Northmen did sack monasteries in both Applecross and Iona).

As a result of these initial raids, Viking military forces managed to bring Scandinavia to the attention of the rest of Europe. After the initial raids, they spread across the continent in great fleets, terrorising, murdering, enslaving, assimilating or displacing local populations and capturing many coastal regions of Britain, Ireland, France (Normandy was named for these Northmen), Russia (as far east as the river Volga), Moorish Spain (Seville was raided in 844), and the Middle East (they even reached Baghdad). Constantinople (present-day Istanbul) was attacked six times but never yielded and, ultimately, Vikings actually served as mercenaries with the forces of the Holy Roman Empire. Perhaps lesser known is the Viking presence in northern Norway, which exploited the hunting and fishing communities there.

Viking activities resulted in an increased standard of living at home. Not only did Norway benefit from the emigration, which freed up farmland, but it also fostered the emergence of a new merchant class and an influx of slaves which were captured abroad and brought back to provide farm labour. According to western Norway's *wergild*

system of compensation for murder, a slave was worth only half the value of a peasant, who was worth half that of a landlord. A landlord was valued at 25% of the value of a chieftain and one-eighth that of a king.

During the 9th and 10th centuries, Norwegian farmers also crossed the Atlantic to settle the Faroes, Iceland and Greenland. By the year 1001, according to the Icelandic sagas, Leifur Eiríksson, the son of Eiríkur Rauðe (Eric the Red), had explored the coast of North America, which he named Vinland, or the 'land of wine'.

Partially due to a decisive civil war sea-battle (about the year 900), at Hafrsfjord near Stavanger, as many as 20,000 people emigrated from Norway to Iceland to escape the victorious king Harald Hårfagre (Fair-Hair), son of Svarta-Halvdan (Halvdan the Black), who went on to confederate several separate realms into the Kingdom of Norway. In 997, Trondheim was founded at the mouth of the river Nid and soon thereafter became the first capital of the new kingdom.

The reign of Harald Hårfagre was such an odd and entertaining time that it was recorded for posterity in the *Heimskringla*, the Norwegian Kings Saga, by the Icelander, Snorre Sturluson.

According to Snorre, the first unification of Norway was said to have been inspired by a woman who taunted the king by refusing to have relations with a man whose kingdom wasn't even as large as tiny Denmark. Through a series of confederations and trade agreements, he was able to extend his rule as far north as Trondheim. His foreign policies were equally canny, and he even sent one of his sons, Håkon, to be reared in the court of King Athelstan of England.

After going through 10 wives, the king had fathered countless heirs, and naturally this presented a succession problem. This was solved by his last child, Erik, who was his only son with Ragnhild the Mighty, daughter of the Danish King Erik of Jutland. The ruthless Erik managed to rise to power by murdering all of his legitimate brothers except Håkon (who was safe in England), then together with a host of squabbling illegitimate brothers, proceeded to destroy his father's hard-won Norwegian confederation in what can only be described as a reign of considerable ineptitude. When Håkon returned from England to sort out the mess as King Håkon den Gode (Håkon the Good), Erik was forced to flee to Britain where he took over the throne of York as King Erik Blood-Axe.

The Battle of Stamford Bridge in 1066, when Harald Hardråda (Hard-Ruler; see the discussion of Medieval Norway) was killed by King Harold of England, is generally regarded as the end of the Viking Age and expansionism. However, Viking power abroad didn't begin to wane significantly until the 13th century, with the death of King Haakon IV after the Battle of Largs (Scotland) in 1263. In 1261 and 1262, respectively, Greenland and Iceland voluntarily joined the Kingdom of Norway. The dispute with Scotland was resolved in 1266 when the Western Isles and the Isle of Man were sold to the Scots, marking the beginning of the loss of Norwegian territory.

Medieval Norway

King Håkon the Good, who had been baptised a Christian during his English upbringing, brought the new faith back to Norway and attempted to introduce it into his realm by importing missionaries from Britain, as well as an English bishop. However, he met with limited success, particularly in Trondheim, where the subjects appeared to be utterly preoccupied with drinking and toasting Þór (Thor), Oðinn (Odin) and Freyr. Although these missionaries were eventually able to replace the names of the gods with those of Catholic saints, they failed to control the pagan practice of blood sacrifice and when Håkon the Good was defeated and killed in 960, Norwegian Christianity all but disappeared.

It was revived, however, during the reign of King Olav Tryggvason, or Olav I, a Viking who had been converted to Christianity in England and, being a good Viking, decided that only force would work to convert his countrymen to the truth. His downfall came at the hands of his intended wife, Queen Sigrid of Sweden. When she refused to convert to Christianity, Olav cancelled the marriage contract. Sigrid eventually married the pagan king Svein Forkbeard of Denmark and together they managed to orchestrate Olav's death in a great Baltic seabattle, then take over the rule of Norway.

Christianity was finally cemented in Norway by King Olav Haraldsson, Olav II, who was also converted to the faith in England. There, he and his Vikings allied themselves with King Ethelred and managed to save London from a Danish attack under King Svein Forkbeard by destroying London Bridge (from whence we derive the song 'London Bridge is Falling Down'). He was involved in the construction of Norway's first Christian church, at Mosterhamn on the island of Bømlo, Hardanger, in 995. (The foundations of this church were later incorporated into a 12th century stone church, and the 1000th anniversary of Norwegian Christianity was celebrated here in 1995.) Olav founded the Church of Norway in 1024, and even managed to bring Christianity to recalcitrant Trondheim.

However, King Canute (Knut) of Denmark was eyeing Norway for possible annexation and in 1028 he invaded the country, forcing King Olav to flee. Although Olav returned after the death of Canute's appointed governor, a popular farmers' uprising in Trøndelag led to his death at the decisive Battle of Stiklestad in 1030. For Christians, this amounted to martyrdom and the king was thereafter canonised as a saint. Indeed, the great Nidaros Cathedral in Trondheim stands as a memorial to Olav, and until the Protestant reformation it served as a destination for pilgrims from all over Europe (see the boxed text in the Trøndelag chapter). Olav had also provided a lasting identity for Norway as an independent kingdom.

Canute's brief reign was followed, after his death, by four generations of kings who ruled Norway as a semi-autonomous nation. One of these, Harald III (Harald Hardråda, or Harald 'Hard-Ruler'), half-brother of St Olav, raided throughout the Mediterranean region before mounting a disastrous invasion of England in 1066 and falling at the Battle of Stamford Bridge (interestingly, William the Conqueror succeeded in a similar attempt only months later). During this period, three cities were founded: Oslo by Harald Hardråda in 1043 and Bergen and Stavanger by King Olav Kyrre (Olav the Peaceful) around 1070.

The 12th century also saw increased power among the clergy and both stone and stave churches were constructed throughout the land. (Of the few buildings which are still extant, the oldest is at Urnes, on Lustrafjorden, which dates from 1150.) In 1107, the Viking king, Sigurd I ('the Crusader'), who had converted to Christianity, led an expedition of 60 ships to the Holy Land and was involved in the capture of Sidon three years later. Sigurd died in 1130 and much of the rest of the century was fraught with brutal civil wars regarding succession to the throne. These disputes culminated in a crucial naval battle (1184) at Fimreite, on Sognefjord, where a host of wealthy and influential citizens were slaughtered. The victorious King Sverre, a churchman turned warrior, paved the way for medieval Norway's so-called 'Golden Age', which was characterised by a general decline in civil unrest.

Shortly thereafter, Bergen became the national capital and for awhile Norway experienced a period of relative peace and prosperity resulting from trade between coastal towns – particularly the capital Bergen – and the Hanseatic League, which was based in Germany. Unfortunately, the increasing power of the Hanseatic traders eventually began to erode Norwegian power and control over the region. (For more on the Hanseatic League, see the boxed text in the Bergen & the South-Western Fjords chapter.)

Haakon V built brick and stone forts, one at Vardø to protect the north from the Russians, and another at Akershus in 1308 to defend Oslo harbour. The transfer of the national capital from Bergen to Christiania (Oslo) soon followed. Haakon V's successor

was his grandson Magnus, son of Haakon's daughter and a Swedish duke. In addition, Magnus was elected to the Swedish crown in 1319; the two kingdoms united that year and the royal line of Harald Hårfagre came to an end. At this stage, Norway's status began a decline which would last for 200 years and result in it becoming just another province of Denmark.

In August 1349, Norway's social fabric was torn by the Black Death, a bubonic plague which arrived on an English ship via the trading port at Bergen. (The disease eventually killed one-third of the population of Europe.) During this tragic period, land fell out of cultivation, towns were ruined, the church suffered, trading activities faltered and the national coffers decreased by 65%. In Norway as much as 80% of the nobility perished, and because their peasant workforce had also been decimated, the survivors were forced to return to the land, forever changing the Norwegian power base.

By 1387, Norway had lost both its independence and control of Iceland, and 10 years later, Queen Margaret of Denmark formed the Kalmar Union of Sweden, Denmark and Norway, with Eric of Pomerania as king. Margaret's neglect of Norway continued into the 15th century, when trade links with Iceland were broken and the Greenland colonies mysteriously disappeared without a trace.

Around this time, the North Atlantic climate entered a distinct cooling phase, presenting agricultural difficulties. Increasingly powerful Hanseatic traders created a very lopsided trade situation in favour of the Germans, but they did import vital commodities for Norwegian use, and the port of Bergen was largely sustained by the export of dried cod from Nordland. In 1427, the Hanseatic traders in Bergen got word of an impending pirate raid on the port and cleared out; when the attack came, the Norwegian defences were overwhelmed and it was eight years before the Germans returned to re-establish their trade.

In 1469, Orkney and Shetland were pawned to the Scottish Crown by the Danish-

Norwegian King Christian I, who had to raise money for his daughter's dowry. This was meant only as a temporary measure, but just three years later, the Scots annexed both island groups. In 1523, the Swedes seceded from the Union, installing the first Vasa king and setting the stage for a prolonged period of war.

Reformation, War & Political Union

During the 16th century, the Danes attempted to make Danish the official language of all Scandinavia, which by this time had been thoroughly converted to Christianity. In 1537, however, the Reformation replaced the incumbent Catholic faith with Lutheran Protestantism. In 1559, Christian III broke the Hanseatic grip on trade in Bergen, which spawned a diversification in the mercantile population as Dutch, Danish and Scottish traders brought wealth and expertise to the city and created a comfortable Norwegian middle class.

In the late 16th century, a series of disputes began between the Danish Union and Sweden, including the Seven Years War between 1563 and 1570, and the Kalmar War between 1611 and 1614, both of which affected Norway. Trondheim was repeatedly captured and re-captured by both sides. During the Kalmar War a two-pronged invasion of Norway was mounted from Scotland. In Gudbrandsdalen, a grass-roots effort by local farmers succeeded in defeating one of these expeditions (for more details see the boxed text 'Guri Saves the Day' in the Central Norway chapter).

Meanwhile, the Arctic region was undergoing both exploration and exploitation by whalers, sealers and walrus hunters from various nations, followed closely by trappers in search of fox pelts. Uninhabited Svalbard, which offered rich whaling and sealing grounds, had been 'rediscovered' by the Dutch explorer Willem Barents in 1596, as he searched for a north-east passage to China via the Arctic Ocean.

In two further wars during the mid-17th century, Norway lost a good portion of its territory to Sweden. The Great Nordic War with the expanding Swedish Empire was fought in the early 18th century and in 1716 the Swedes occupied Christiania (formerly Oslo, which was renamed by Christian IV in honour of himself). Trondheim was besieged by the Swedes in the winter of 1718-19, but the effort was abandoned after the death of the Swedish emperor, Charles XII. The Swedes were finally defeated in 1720, ending over 150 years of war.

Also in 1720, a company was formed in Bergen to re-establish the Greenland trade and increase profits from whaling and commerce. A Lofoten missionary, Hans Egede, spent 15 years in Greenland bringing Christianity to the Inuit and in the process he founded the Greenlandic capital, Godthåb (Nuuk). However, the Bergen enterprise was soon abandoned and the missions and trade were taken over by Denmark, which proceeded to impose trade restrictions on the Norwegians. Although they were later loosened – especially on the timber trade – a period of famine at the height of the so-called 'Little Ice Age', from 1738 to 1742, resulted in the failure of crops and the death of one-third of the cattle and thousands of people.

Yet another period of hardship came during the Napoleonic wars when Britain blockaded Norway. After the Danes surrendered on 14 January 1814, the Treaty of Kiel presented Norway to Sweden in a 'Union of the Crowns'. However, the Norwegians didn't take kindly to Swedish rule and a contingent of farmers, businesspeople and politicians gathered at Eidsvoll Verk in April 1814 to draft a new constitution and elect a new Norwegian king. The business was completed on 17 May 1814 (and despite the problems that followed, 17 May is still celebrated as Norway's national day). Sweden would have none of this, and the new king, Christian Frederik, had to give in to Sweden and accept their choice of monarch, Karl Johan. Fortunately, war was averted by a compromise which provided for devolved Swedish power. Disputes between Norway and Denmark ensued over joint debts incurred during their union and over ownership of the colonies of Iceland, Greenland and the Faroe Islands (this issue wasn't resolved until 1931, when the World Court settled in favour of Denmark).

The 19th century saw a national cultural revival, including a flowering of musical and artistic expression led by poet and playwright Henrik Ibsen, composer Edvard Grieg and artist Edvard Munch, and the development of a unique Norwegian dialect known as *landsmål* (or *Nynorsk*). Norway's first railway, from Oslo (King Karl Johan changed the name back from Christiania in order to wipe off that vestige of the Danish union) to Eidsvoll, was completed in 1854, and Norway began looking at increased international trade, particularly of fish and whale products.

A rapidly increasing population combined with an increasingly moneyed populace also brought about a period of mass emigration to North America, and between 1825 and 1925, over 750,000 Norwegians re-settled in the USA and Canada. Technological advances included the development of a telephone exchange in Oslo and electric street lighting in Hammerfest.

In 1905, a constitutional referendum was held and, as expected, virtually no one in the country favoured continued union with Sweden. The Swedish king Oskar II was forced to recognise Norwegian sovereignty, abdicate and re-instate a Norwegian constitutional monarchy, with Haakon VII on the throne. The hereditary royal succession remains under the authority of the Storting (parliament). Oslo was declared the national capital of the new and independent Kingdom of Norway.

The first three decades of the 20th century brought a flurry of innovation and technological advances. In 1911, the Norwegian explorer Roald Amundsen reached the South Pole. In 1913, Norwegian women became among the first in Europe to be given the vote. Prior to 1914, hydroelectric projects sprang up all around the country and prosperous new industries emerged to drive the increasingly healthy export econ-

omy. By the start of WWI, Norway's merchant navy had largely converted from sail to steam. Despite Norway's neutrality during WWI, the German forces sank quite a few Norwegian merchant ships.

Norway's odd attitude toward alcohol was well illustrated in 1919, when prohibition was introduced by referendum. It remained in force until 1927, by which time half the Norwegian population was involved either in smuggling or illegally distilling home brew. At that stage, the state monopoly system emerged as an alternative method of restricting alcohol (but even today, that seems to have little effect on the amount of illicit distilling).

In 1920, Norwegian territory was extended for the first time in several centuries with the signing of the Svalbard Treaty, which took effect in 1925. It granted Norwegian sovereignty over the islands with the provision that mineral residency rights be open to all signatories of the treaty, which included Australia, Canada, China, all EU countries (except Ireland and Luxembourg), India, Japan, New Zealand, South Africa, the USSR (now Russia and the former Soviet republics) and the USA. The 1920s brought new innovations, including the development of factory ships which allowed efficient processing of whales at sea and caused an increase in whaling activities, especially around Svalbard and in the Antarctic.

Also in 1920, the Storting voted to join the newly formed League of Nations, a move which was opposed only by the communist-inspired Labour Party, which advocated central planning and was a growing force in Norwegian politics. By 1927, this increasingly militant and revolutionary party dominated the Storting. In the late 1920s and through the 1930s, the effects of the Great Depression in the USA reverberated around the world and brought economic hardship to Norway. By December 1932, the trade unions were experiencing 42% unemployment and farmers were hit especially hard by the economic downturn.

WWII

Although wages and both industrial and agricultural output generally improved from 1933, Norway continued to be plagued by strikes and industrial disputes. At the same time, the doctrine of fascism began to spread throughout Europe.In 1933 the former Norwegian defence minister Vidkun Quisling formed a Norwegian fascist party, the Nasjonal Samling.

After the Germans invaded Norway on 9 April 1940, King Håkon and the royal family fled to Britain and thence to Washington (where they stayed for the duration of the war), leaving behind British, French, Polish and Norwegian forces to fight a desperate rear-guard action.

Six southern towns were burnt out and, in fact, the first Allied victory of WWII didn't occur until late May, when a British naval force re-took Narvik and won control over this strategic iron ore port. However, the British were out on a limb and they were ordered to abandon Arctic Norway to its fate. On 9 June, Narvik again fell to the Germans.

In Oslo, the Germans established a puppet government under Vidkun Quisling, but over the next five years a resistance network fomented sabotage against the German military regime.

Among the most memorable acts of defiance was the famous commando assault of February 1943 on the heavy water plant at Vemork (near Rjukan in Telemark), which was involved in the German development of an atomic bomb (see the boxed text 'The Heroes of Telemark' in the Southern Norway chapter). Arms were smuggled by sea from Shetland to western Norway and Shetland fishermen were involved in various daring acts to aid the resistance. British commandos also prevailed over the Germans in battles at Måløy and Svolvær.

The Germans exacted bitter revenge on the local populace and 1500 Norwegians died during the period of occupation. Among the civilian casualties were 630 Norwegian Jews who were sent to central European concentration camps.

Those Generous Germans

Shortly following the German invasion of Norway in 1940, the Commander-in-Chief of the occupying forces, General von Falkenhorst, issued the following declaration:

Announcement

- I have been given the task of protecting the land of Norway against attack from the Western powers. The Norwegian government has refused several offers of co-operation. The Norwegian people must now themselves decide over the destiny of their country. If this announcement is complied with, such as it was with great understanding by the Danish people in the same situation, Norway will be spared from the horrors of war.
- If resistance should be offered and the hand offered in peaceful intention should be refused, I shall be forced to proceed with the sharpest and most ruthless means to break the resistance.
- Anyone who supports the issued mobilisation order of the fled former government or spreads false rumours will be court-martialled.
- Every civilian caught with weapon in hand will be SHOT.
- Anyone destroying constructions serving the traffic and military intelligence or municipal devices will be SHOT.
- Anyone using weapons contrary to international law will be SHOT.
- The German army, victorious in many battles, the great and powerful air force and navy will see to it that my announcement will be carried through.

The German Commander-in-Chief von Falkenhorst – Infantry General

On an even larger scale, Serbian and Russian prisoners of war were coerced into slave labour on construction projects, and many perished from the cold and an inadequate diet. In fact, the high number of worker fatalities during the construction of the Arctic Highway through the Saltfjellet inspired its nickname, the *blodveien* (blood road).

Finnmark suffered heavy destruction and casualties during the war. The Germans constructed submarine bases in Altafjorden and elsewhere, which were used to attack convoys headed for Murmansk and Arkhangelsk in Russia, hoping to disrupt the supply of armaments to the Russians.

In early 1945, the Germans faced an escalating two-front war and Hitler went missing. In an attempt to delay the Russian advance into Finnmark, the German forces adopted a scorched-earth policy and utterly devastated northern Norway, burning fields, forests, towns and villages. Shortly after the German surrender of Norway, Quisling was executed by firing squad, other collaborators were packed off to prison and on 7 May, the Russian army withdrew from Arctic Norway.

Although the communist party did well in post-war elections, they never took over the Norwegian government and the Iron Curtain remained in place at the Russian border. Severe wartime rationing ended in 1952, and the late 1940s and early 1950s saw much reconstruction in war-ravaged Arctic Norway. Throughout the country, parts of towns and cities burnt out in 1940 or prior to the German surrender were also rebuilt. In addition, the merchant navy and whaling fleet bounced back.

In 1946, Norway became a founding member of the United Nations. Ever conscious of its proximity to Russia, the country also joined NATO in 1949. Closer links with other Scandinavian countries developed after the formation of the Nordic Council in 1952.

Modern Norway

Oil was discovered in the North Sea in the late 1960s and the economy boomed, bringing greater prosperity and increasingly comfortable living standards. Since then, two decades of socialist Labour government have fostered increased central planning, economic controls, socialised medicine, state-sponsored higher education, and what the government has liked to represent as the 'most egalitarian social democracy in western Europe'.

Having said that, modern Norway is not a classic socialist state, as taxes outstrip individual benefits and users' fees are levied on most services and infrastructure. Although home ownership is still considered a luxury and is taxed accordingly, nearly 80% of Norwegians own their own homes.

In 1960, Norway joined the European Free Trade Association (EFTA), but in 1972, Norwegians narrowly voted against joining the European Economic Community (EEC). Through the 1980s, a strong Norwegian economy prevented increased unemployment and social decay, and the results of 1972 were repeated in 1994 with a vote against joining the EEC's successor, the European Union (EU). The 'no' vote was due especially to the concerns of traditional family farms and fishing interests which hoped to avoid competition with their larger and more technologically advanced EU counterparts.

Despite Norway's strong economy, in 1995 the unemployment rate increased to 5.2% (not including people involved in 'retraining' programs), and the recent trend has been towards increased urbanisation, especially in the north.

Although modern Norway enjoys an EU concession which grants it trading privileges as a member of the EFTA (along with other European non-EU members Iceland, Switzerland and Liechtenstein), it continues to remain outside the EU and has so far refused to compromise its position on fishing, whaling and other economic issues.

While a majority of Norwegian voters remain adverse to taking directives from Brussels and hope to maintain their internal controls and subsidies, many folks – particularly urban-dwellers and people in the southern part of the country – recognise that Norway cannot remain forever isolated from the larger world economy.

CLIMATE

The typically rainy climate of mainland Norway is surprisingly mild for its latitude, and thanks to the Gulf Stream, all its coastal ports remain ice-free throughout the year. The coastal mountain ranges block the moisture-laden prevailing south-westerly winds, and precipitation can reach 5000mm annually. Bergen, on the south-west coast, is the wettest city, with 2250mm of annual precipitation.

The continental influences and their corresponding high pressure zones are most prevalent in the south-east, in central Norway and in the far north. Rondane and Gudbrandsdal are among the driest districts of Norway, with less than 500mm of precipitation annually.

In summer, the average maximum temperatures for July are 16°C in the south and around 11°C in the north. However, summer temperature extremes are also possible, even in the Arctic region; in July 1998, the temperature in Narvik rose to over 30°C and in August of the same year, even Svalbard saw temperatures of over 20°C.

In winter, heavy snowfalls are common, which makes for superb skiing, and snow can accumulate up to 10m in the mountains. However, accumulations of 2m to 3m are more usual in the lower areas. In January, the average maximum temperature in the south is 1°C and, in the north, -3°C. It can get much colder, however; in January 1999, the temperature in Kirkenes dropped for a short time to a decidedly chilly -56°C.

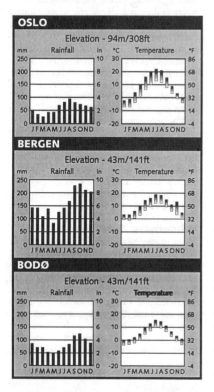

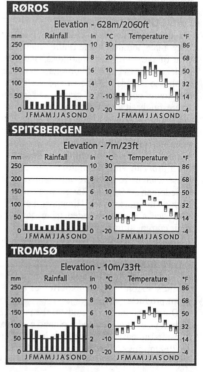

GEOGRAPHY

With a land area of 323,878 sq km, Norway occupies the western part of the Scandinavian peninsula and shares borders with Sweden, Finland and Russia. The country is long and narrow, with a coastline deeply cut by fjords – long, narrow inlets of the sea bordered by high, steep cliffs. Mountain ranges, some capped with Europe's largest glaciers and icefields, cover more than half of the land mass. Only 3% of the country is arable.

The moniker 'Land of the Midnight Sun' is more than just a promotional slogan for the country, as nearly a third of Norway lies north of the Arctic Circle, the point at which there is at least one full day when the sun never sets and one day when it never rises. For more information on this, see the boxed text entitled 'Arctic Phenomena'.

GEOLOGY

The pre-Cambrian rocks in southern Norway were a late addition to the Baltic Shield (the core of the European continent), and date back no more than 1.8 billion years. In the far north, the islands of Lofoten and Vesterålen are largely comprised of granite and gneiss. Interestingly, it's thought that these regions were once attached to the North American crustal plate, as their makeup resembles that of eastern Greenland. When tectonic spreading along the mid-Atlantic Ridge separated the European and North American plates, these ancient rocks were left behind. The Caledonian Mountain Range was once as high as the present-day Himalaya, but with time, ice and water eroded them down to their current altitude.

In the North Sea lie two rift valleys containing upper Jurassic shale bearing rich deposits of oil and gas that are now being exploited. In fact, Norway is now the world's second-largest exporter of petroleum products.

During the glacial periods of the past 1.8 billion years, the elevated highland plateaux subsided at least 700m due to an ice sheet up to 2000m thick. The movement of this ice, which was driven by gravity down former river courses, gouged out the fjords and valleys and created the surrounding mountains by sharpening peaks and exposing high cliffs of bare rock (just a glance at any map of southern Norway will reveal a radiating pattern of slender lakes and fjords). The bulk of the ice melted about 8800 years ago, with the end of the last Ice Age, and Norway is currently experiencing an interglacial period. As a result, only a few remnant icecaps and valley glaciers remain on the mainland.

Svalbard, which is geologically independent of the rest of Europe, sits on the Barents continental plate deep in the polar region and experiences much more dramatic glaciation.

ECOLOGY & ENVIRONMENT

Norwegians appreciate their fresh air, clean water and ample elbow room, and among European nations, Norway has one of the better records when it comes to environmental policies. Industrial waste is highly regulated, recycling is popular, there's little rubbish along the roadsides and general tidiness takes a high priority in both urban and rural environments. On the other hand, loss of habitat has placed 898 species of plants and animals on the endangered or threatened species lists; sport hunting and fishing are more popular here than in most of Europe; the past sin of over-fishing has come back to haunt the economy; and Norway's internationally unpopular stance on whaling and sealing has raised international ire and resulted in boycotts on Norwegian products.

Wilderness Areas

Norway may have one of the lowest population densities in Europe, but thanks to its settlement pattern, which is unique in Europe and favoured scattered farms over villages, even the most remote areas of the country are inhabited and a large proportion of the population is rural. This factor, combined with a national appreciation of fresh air and outdoor recreation, has ensured that most Norwegians have kept some contact with nature.

(continued on page 28)

Glacier & Ice Glossary

Glaciers have forged much of the Norwegian landscape, and even today the country is dotted with remnants of icecaps and valley glaciers, particularly in Svalbard. The following is a list of terms relating to these icy phenomena:

Arête – a sharp ridge between two valley glaciers.
Bergschrund – the crevasse at the top of a valley glacier separating the moving ice from the parent icefield.
Bergy bits – icebergs rising less than 5m above the surface of the sea.
Calving – breaking off of icebergs from tidewater glaciers.
Cirque – an amphitheatre scoured out by a glacier.
Crevasse – a fissure in moving ice, which may be hidden under snow, caused by various strains as the ice flows downhill.
Dead glacier – a valley glacier that stops short of the sea.
Erratic – a stone or boulder which clearly was transported from elsewhere, possibly by a glacier.
Fast ice – solid pack ice.
Firn limit – the highest level on a glacier to which the snow melts each year. The snow that remains above this limit is called firn.
Frazil – needle-shaped ice crystals which form a slush in the sea.
Glacial flour – the fine, talcum-like silt which flows in glacial streams and is deposited in glacial river valley. It is formed by abrasion of ice on rock.
Growler – small iceberg floating just on the surface which is difficult to see, thereby causing a hazard for ships.
Hanging valley – a valley formed when a tributary valley glacier flows into a larger valley glacier.
Horn – the sharp peak that remains after glaciers have scoured all faces of a mountain peak.
Hummock – a place where ice floes have piled atop one another.
Icecap or **icefield** – a stable zone of accumulation and compression of snow and ice, and a source of valley glaciers. An icecap generally covers a larger area than an icefield. When the entire interior of a landmass is covered by an icecap (as in Greenland or Antarctica), it's often called a continental glacier.
Ice floe – a flat chunk of floating sea ice, normally pack ice, but it may also refer to a small iceberg.
Jökulhlaup – Icelandic word meaning 'glacial burst'; refers to a sudden and often catastrophic release of water from a glacier, caused by a broken ice dam or by glacial lifting due to volcanic activity beneath the ice.
Moberg – a mountain created by a volcanic eruption beneath an icecap. A classic moberg appears to have been formed in a jelly mould.
Moraine – deposit of material transported by a glacier. Rock and silt pushed ahead of the glacier is called a terminal moraine, that deposited along the sides is a lateral moraine, and down the centre of a glacier, it's called a medial moraine.
Moulin – French word meaning 'mill'; refers to a pond or stream inside a glacier, often evidenced by a deep round hole in the ice.
Névé – hard granular snow on the upper part of a glacier that hasn't yet turned to ice.
Nilas – thin crust of sea ice that moves up and down with wave action but doesn't break.
Nunatak – Greenlandic word referring to a mountain peak that protrudes through a glacier or icecap.
Pack ice – floating ice formed by frozen seawater, often creating an impenetrable barrier to navigation.
Piedmont glacier – a slumped glacier at the foot of a steep slope, caused by the confluence of two or more valley glaciers.
Polynya – Russian word referring to an area of open water surrounded by pack ice.
Postholing – what hikers do when crossing fields of rotten or melting snow, sinking up to their thighs at every step.
Roche moutonée – French word for 'sheep rock'; a glacier-scoured boulder. They often resemble sheep grazing on the mountainsides.
Sastrugi – Russian word referring to wind-blown furrows in snow.
Suncup – mushroom-shaped snow formation caused by irregular melting on sunny slopes.
Tarn – Gaelic word referring to a lake in a cirque.
Tide crack – a crack separating sea ice from the shore, caused by the rise and fall of tides.
Tidewater glacier – a valley glacier that flows into the sea and calves icebergs.
Valley glacier – a river of ice which flows downward through a valley from an icefield or icecap.

Arctic Phenomena

The Aurora Borealis

There are few sights as mesmerising as an undulating aurora. Although these appear in many forms – pillars, streaks, wisps and haloes of vibrating light – they're most memorable when they take the form of pale curtains, wafting on a gentle breeze. Most often, the Arctic aurora appears as a faint green or light yellow or rose but, in periods of extreme activity, can change to bright yellow or crimson. The visible aurora borealis, or northern lights (in the southern hemisphere, the corresponding phenomenon is called the aurora australis), are caused by streams of charged particles from the sun, the solar winds, flowing past and elongating the earth's magnetic field in the polar regions. Because the field curves downward in a halo surrounding the magnetic poles, the charged particles are drawn earthward. Their interaction with electrons in the upper atmosphere (about 160km above the surface) releases the energy creating the visible aurora. During periods of high activity, a single auroral storm can produce a trillion watts of electricity with a current of one million amps.

The Inuit (Eskimos) call the lights *arsarnerit* ('to play with a ball'), as they were thought to be ancestors playing ball with a walrus skull. It was believed that the lights could be attracted by whistling or repelled by barking like a dog! The Inuit also attach spiritual significance to the lights, and some believe that they represent the capering of unborn children; some consider them gifts from the dead to light the long polar nights and others see them as a storehouse of events, past and future.

Although science dismisses it as imagination, most people report that the aurora is often accompanied by a crackling or whirring sound. Don't feel unbalanced if you hear it – that's the sort of sound you'd expect to hear from such a dramatic display, and if it's an illusion, it's a very convincing one.

The best time of year to catch the northern lights in Norway is from October to March, although you may well see them as early as August in the far south. Oddly enough, Svalbard is actually too far north to catch the greatest activity.

Midnight Sun & Polar Night

Because the earth is tilted on its axis, the polar regions are constantly facing the sun at their respective summer solstices and are tilted away from it in the winter. The Arctic and Antarctic circles, at 66° 30' north and south latitude respectively, are the southern and northern limits of constant daylight on the longest day of the year.

The northern half of mainland Norway, as well as Svalbard and Jan Mayan, lie north of the Arctic Circle, but even in southern Norway, the summer sun is never far below the horizon. Between late May and mid-August, nowhere in the country experiences true darkness and in Trondheim, for example, the first stars aren't visible until mid-August. Although many visitors initially find it difficult to sleep while the sun is shining, most people quickly get used to it, even if that simply means joining the locals in their summer nocturnal hyperactivity.

Conversely, winters here are dark and dreary, with only a few hours of twilight to break the long polar nights. In Svalbard, not even a twilight glow can be seen for over a month, and most northern communities make a ritual of welcoming the sun the first time it peeks above the southern horizon. During this period of darkness, many people suffer from SAD syndrome, or 'seasonally affected depression', which results when they're deprived of the vitamin D provided by sunlight. Its effects may be minimised by using dosages of vitamin D (as found in cod liver oil) or with special solar spectrum light bulbs.

			Arctic Phenomena
Town	**Latitude**	**Midnight Sun**	**Polar Night**
Bodø	67° 18'	4 June to 8 July	15 December to 28 December
Svolvær	68° 15'	28 May to 14 July	5 December to 7 January
Narvik	68° 26'	27 May to 15 July	4 December to 8 January
Tromsø	69° 42'	20 May to 22 July	25 November to 17 January
Alta	70° 00'	16 May to 26 July	24 November to 18 January
Hammerfest	70° 40'	16 May to 27 July	21 November to 21 January
Nordkapp	71° 11'	13 May to 29 July	18 November to 24 January
Longyearbyen	78° 12'	20 April to 21 August	26 October to 16 February
Ny Ålesund	78° 55'	16 April to 25 August	22 October to 20 February

Fata Morgana

If the aurora inspires wonder, the Fata Morgana and related phenomena common in the polar regions may inspire a visit to a shrink. The clear and pure Arctic air does not cause distant features to appear out of focus. As a result, depth perception becomes impossible and the world takes on a strangely two-dimensional aspect in which distances are indeterminable. An amusing example of distance distortion is described in the enigmatic book *Arctic Dreams*, by Barry Lopez:

> A Swedish explorer had all but completed a written description in his notebook of a craggy headland with two unusually symmetrical valley glaciers, the whole of it a part of a large island, when he discovered what he was looking at was a walrus.

Fata Morgana, a special type of mirage, is also common in the vast expanses of sand, ice and tundra found in the Arctic. They are apparently caused by reflections off water, ice and snow, and when combined with temperature inversions, create the illusion of solid, well defined features where there are none. Early explorers laid down on maps and charts careful documentation of islands, headlands and mountain ranges that were never seen again. On clear days off the outermost coasts of Lofoten, Vesterålen, northern Finnmark and Svalbard, you may

well observe inverted mountains or non-existent archipelagos of craggy islands resting on the horizon. It's difficult indeed to convince yourself, even with an accurate map, that they're not really there!

Also unsettling are the sightings of ships, large cities and forests, where there could clearly be none. Normal visibility at sea is just under 18km, but in the Arctic, sightings of islands and features hundreds of kilometres in the distance are frequently reported.

The one that sank the *Titanic*?

(continued from page 24)

It has also meant that the natural element has been greatly altered by human activities. The landscape is crisscrossed by roads which connect remote homes, farmsteads and logging areas to the highway system; all but a couple of major rivers have been dammed for hydroelectric power; most Norwegian families own holiday homes beside lakes, around ski slopes or in areas of natural beauty; and even the wild-looking expanses of Finnmarksvidda and the huge peninsulas that jut into the Arctic Ocean serve as vast reindeer pastures. As a result, apart from the upland icefields and the national parks, real wilderness in Norway is limited to a few forested mountain areas along the Swedish border, scattered parts of Hardangervidda and most of Svalbard.

Recycling

Recycling is gaining popularity and Norwegians strongly support sorting of household waste – paper, glass, plastics, tyres, car batteries and organic matter – for collection. A deposit scheme for glass bottles has been a success and about 96% of glass beer and soft drink bottles is now returned. There is also a pre-paid recycling charge on automobiles sold in Norway, which ensures that they're turned into scrap metal rather than roadside eyesores when their life is over.

Forestry

Although no forestry operation can be entirely environmentally sound, overall, Norway has one of the world's most sustainable forestry policies and much of the current visible damage to the forests is due to agricultural clearing and timber overexploitation between the 17th and 20th centuries.

Today, Norway's extensive forests cover a total of 12 million hectares, or 37% of the national area, of which 2% to 5% is old growth. This amounts to a potential 600 million cubic metres of lumber. Currently, numerous small forestry operations, mostly in eastern Norway, cut about 20 million cubic metres annually. Clear-cutting is prac-

tised in some areas but it's thankfully both rare and on a small scale, and in general, operations employ selective cutting to prevent soil erosion and unsightly landscape degradation. In addition, companies immediately re-seed the cuts, planting a total of around 60 million seedlings annually.

Fishing & Marine Resources

It's a safe bet that Norway's most controversial environmental issues – among both Norwegians and international conservationists – involve marine mammal hunting, fishing rights and declining fish stocks, as well as international opinions and the resulting regulations.

Commercial Fishing Throughout recorded history, the seas off the Norwegian coast have provided bountiful fishing opportunities and, until about 25 years ago, deep-sea fishing in the area was pretty much a free-for-all. During the 1960s, the Norwegian fishing community enjoyed particularly high catches, thanks mainly to the development of sonar which located schools of herring and other commercially valuable fish. As a result of the decreasing stock, the herring fishery declined in productivity, and by the late 1970s, herring stocks were nearly wiped out. Over-fishing also depleted stocks of cod all across the North Atlantic, from Newfoundland's Grand Banks (Canada) to northern Norway.

On 1 January 1977, Norway established a 200 nautical mile offshore economic zone, which was extended to Svalbard later that year and to Jan Mayen in 1980. The country now has agreements with the EU, Russia, the Faroes, Iceland, Greenland and Poland to set quotas. It took 20 years of intensive conservation measures, including strict quotas, before the herring fishery bounced back. Although cod fishing regulations are now in place, it will be many years before the numbers return.

Another major factor in the success of Norwegian offshore fisheries is the amount of warm Gulf Stream water entering the northern seas, which varies from year to year. The larger the volume of warm water, the greater the growth of plankton in the far north and the greater the amounts of food available to fish and marine mammals. Regulations and quotas also take into account these natural fluctuations.

Today, fishing and aquaculture (fish farming) are the backbone of the coastal economy, providing work for over 23,600 people in the fishing fleet, and also providing work in the shipbuilding, fish feed and fishing gear industries and the packaging, processing and transport of fish products. With a catch averaging 2.55 million tonnes annually, Norway is the 11th largest fishing nation, and produces 2.2% of the world's fish.

The aquaculture industry, which has thrived for at least two decades, concentrates mainly on Atlantic salmon and trout, but there has also been experimentation with Arctic charr, halibut, catfish and scallops. Currently, the export of pen-raised salmon and trout constitutes 35% of Norway's fish exports. The main drawback is that diseases in captive stock are spread to wild stock whenever fish escape from the pens. That, plus the perceived need for more government regulation, has brought about restrictions in the growth of this industry, but it still promises to be a major force in the Norwegian economy – and environmental concerns – in coming years.

Whaling No Norwegian environmental issue inspires more international fervour and emotion than that of renewed whaling in the North Atlantic. In 1993 Norway resumed commercial whaling of minke whales in defiance of an international whaling ban. While Norway does support the protection of other threatened species, the government contends that minke whales, with an estimated North Atlantic population of 75,000, can sustain a limited harvest. In 1993, Norwegian hunters were permitted to harpoon a total of 157 minke whales and since then, the quota has doubled. International political circles have reacted apathetically, but conservation groups, especially Greenpeace, have expressed vociferous opposition,

spearheaded protest campaigns and physically challenged whaling ships.

While history indicates that whalers in this region have had no qualms about hunting their prey to the verge of extinction, Norwegians claim that modern whalers have a better and more informed perspective, and that they'd adhere to a more sensible quota system. Most of the pro-whaling ranks feel that conservationists are mainly city folk who have a sentimental relationship with animals and are out of touch with reality. Similarly, they feel that most European and North American city folk have no contact with the land and sea, and that their objections to whaling are irrational and reflect a 'quasi-religious fervour which ... projects human relationships and emotions onto wild sea creatures', or so maintains the Ministry of Foreign Affairs.

For what it's worth, Norwegian whalers work only part time and spend the rest of the year working in the traditional fisheries. To be eligible for whaling, they must own their own boats and be recognised as part of the professional fishing community. They may not use sonar to locate whales and for the kill, they're required to use 50mm or 60mm grenade-powered harpoon guns to ensure that the whale dies as quickly as possible, but rifles may be used as secondary weapons. Each boat is required to carry a trained veterinarian to ensure that all regulations are followed. When a whale is harpooned, it is hauled onto the deck of the boat and flensed (stripped of its blubber), then the meat and blubber are delivered to coastal packing plants. The Norwegians claim that they support only traditional family-owned operations and have no intention or desire to return to industrial whaling.

In addition to hunting, a major threat to Norwegian whales comes from chemical pollution, particularly the PCBs which are suspected of damaging cetacean reproductive and immune systems. This damage has already been observed in baleen whales and in the early 1990s led to numerous deaths from viral infections.

For further information on whales and marine conservation, contact Greenpeace UK (☎ 0171-354 5100, after April 2000 ☎ 020-7354 5100), 30-31 Islington Green, London N1 8XE; or the Whale and Dolphin Conservation Society (☎ 01225-334511), 19A James Street West, Bath, BA1 2BT. In North America, try The American Cetacean Society, National Headquarters, PO Box 2639, San Pedro, CA 90731, USA. The northern Norwegian perspective is available from Høge Nord Alliansen (☎ 76 09 24 14, fax 76 09 24 50), N-8390 Reine. For the Norwegian government's take on the issue, contact the Ministry of Foreign Affairs (☎ 22 34 36 00, fax 22 34 95 80), PO Box 8114 Dep, N-0032 Oslo.

Sealing In Norway, seal hunting is restricted to two species, the harp seal and hooded seal, and the purpose is ostensibly to cull a growing population. This is mainly because the fishing community wishes to restrict the competition between fishing boats and marine mammals who depend on fish and eat up to 2.5kg per day. Secondarily, it provides a livelihood for people in Norway and several other North Atlantic countries.

Sealing occurs only on a very small scale, mainly for fur and meat, but it may successfully be argued that it's a cruel business. To mitigate protests, regulations limit seal hunters to only two tools: a rifle and a *hakapik*, or gaff; the former is for adult seals and the latter for pups (which may not be hunted when they're still suckling). Hunters are also required to take courses and shooting tests before each sealing season.

FLORA & FAUNA

Although Norway's wildlife populations are fairly sparse compared with those of neighbouring Sweden and Finland, its diverse landscapes and altitude ranges mean that it does harbour many different plant communities and a wider variety of species.

In the UK, an excellent source of natural history books and field guides, including some titles on Scandinavia, is Subbuteo Natural History Books Ltd (☎ 01352-756551, fax 01352-756004; sales@subbooks.demon .co.uk), Pistyll Farm, Nercwys, near Mold, Flintshire CH7 4EW (international orders are welcome). In the USA, try the Adventurous Traveler Bookstore (☎ 800-282 3963) or Nature Co (☎ 800-227 1114). In Australia, check out Andrew Isles Natural History Books (☎ 03-9510 5750), 115 Greville St, Prahran 3181, Victoria.

Flora

In general, Norwegian flora is typical of that in temperate climates, and includes around 250 species of flowering plants. In the highlands and northern areas, alpine and Arctic flowers predominate. Mountain avens, large white flowers with eight petals, commonly grow on limey soils. Other attractive mountain species include the long stalked mountain sorrel, which is an unusual source of vitamin C; glacier crowfoot; various saxifrages (livelong, mossy, purple, pyramidal and starry); alpine milk-vetch, trailing azalea, diapensia; alpine gentian; forget-me-nots (myosotis); bearded bellflower; wood anemone; alpine fleabane; and alpine aster. Heather grows mainly in low-lying areas around the coast. For more information, see the book *Mountain Flowers*, available from the DNT (Nkr68), or the Norwegian-language *Norsk Fargeflora* by Finn Winschmann, published by the NKS Forlaget.

Fertile areas at low elevation have well mixed woodland, where the tree species include conifers, ash, elm, lime, oak, beech, Norway maple and alder. Fruit trees, such as apple and plum, are cultivated in sheltered coastal areas, particularly around Hardangerfjord. In mountainous areas of western Norway, the conifer and birch dominated woodlands climb to between 900m and 1200m. Offshore islands are less wooded and in northern Nordland, Troms and southern Finnmark, the tree line may be as low as 200m to 300m.

Around the periphery of the high plateaux and around southern Norway, the forests include scotch pine, Norway spruce, aspen, silver birch, hazel, black alder, mountain ash, and in the higher altitudes, dwarf birch, willow and juniper.

Between the dwarf trees and the snow line, the main vegetation types are mosses, fungi and lichens, such as reindeer moss. Mountain grasses, including sedges, deer grass and Arctic cotton, grow mainly in boggy areas and high in the mountains, near the summer snow line, you'll find saxifrage and a range of smaller tundra plants.

Despite the harsh Arctic conditions, short growing season, severe winters, low precipitation, poor soils and prevailing permafrost, Svalbard has around 165 species of tiny ground-loving plants, including dwarf willow and polar birch and a variety of tundra flowers and lichens.

Hikers will find a profusion of berries, most of which grow low to the ground and ripen between mid-July and early September. The most popular edible varieties are blueberries (huckleberries), which grow on open uplands; blue swamp-loving bilberries; red high-bush and low-bush cranberries; muskeg crowberries and the lovely amber-coloured cloudberries. The last, which are considered a delicacy, are known locally as *moltebær*, and grow one per stalk on open swampy ground. In the Arctic regions of neighbouring Sweden and Finland, nearly everyone takes to the outdoors in droves to pick this delicious bounty, but in Norway, cloudberry patches are zealously guarded. For rules on picking cloudberries, see Food in the Facts for the Visitor chapter.

Fauna

Land Mammals Although Norway does have a variety of European mammal species, as well as many boreal species, Norway's unique settlement pattern, which spreads the human population thinly throughout the country, limits wildlife habitat and restricts numbers.

Rabbits (*kanin*) live in the south and south-west of the country, where they have probably escaped from captivity. Arctic hares (*hare*) are found throughout the country, typically on moors or mountain grassland and sometimes in woodland.

Hedgehogs (*pinnsvin*) occur south of Trøndelag. In southern Norway, forested and lake-studded areas support a good sized beaver (*bever*) population. Badgers (*grevling*) are found in the river valleys and woods of southern Norway and otters (*oter*) are found by wooded watercourses and in the sea (except in north Finnmark).

Weasels (*vesel*) and stoats (*røyskatt*) are widespread in all counties; northern varieties turn white in winter, when they're known as ermine and are trapped for their fur. The more solitary wolverine (*jerv*), a larger cousin of the weasel, inhabits high mountain forests and low alpine areas, mainly near marshes and lakes in Nordland, eastern and central Norway. Pine martens (*skogmår*) are found in many damp forested areas south of Finnmark. Mink also like water and inhabit forested areas as far north as Tromsø.

Red squirrels (*ekorn*) are ubiquitous in coniferous forests throughout Norway, shrews (*spissmus*) are common, and rodents such as the house mouse (*husmus*), brown rat (*rotte*), and voles (*markmus*) are prolific in all counties. Although the Latin name for the brown rat is *Rattus norvegicus*, or 'Norwegian rat', it hails not from Norway (although it has been carried worldwide by Norwegian ships), but from Asia. Some voles, including bank voles, mountain rats and northern water voles, are found as high as 1300m.

Lemmings (*lemen*), which occupy mountain areas through 30% of the country, stay mainly around 800m altitude in the south and lower in the north. They measure up to 10cm and have soft orange-brown and black fur, beady eyes, a short tail and prominent upper incisors. If you encounter a lemming in the mountains, it may become enraged, hissing, squeaking and attempting to attack! There's also a forest-dwelling version (*skoglemen*) which is found near the Swedish border between Hedmark and Finnmark. Most Norwegian bat species (*flaggermus*) favour the south of Norway, but the northern bat flits around throughout the country.

The Truth about Lemmings

If you know anything about lemmings, it's about their penchant for mass suicide, right? Well, we've all heard tales of hundreds of thousands of lemmings diving off cliffs to their deaths. Some people also maintain that their bite is fatal and that they spread disease among the human population. Well those notions may be a bit exaggerated.

Firstly, although lemmings can behave aggressively and ferociously when threatened or cornered, there's no evidence that their bite is any more dangerous than that of other rodents, nor are they particularly prone to spreading any sort of disease.

As for their self-destructive behaviour, things may not be exactly as they seem.

Lemmings are known for their periodic mass movements every five to 20 years, when a particularly productive breeding season results in overpopulation. Thanks to the increased numbers, the vegetation is decimated and food sources grow scarce. As a result, large numbers descend from the high country in a usually futile attempt to find other, less crowded high ground, only to be squashed on roads or eaten by predators and domestic animals. In fact, for a couple of years following a lemming population surge, there will also be an increase in the population of such predators as foxes, buzzards and owls.

Quite often, however, the swarms head for the sea, and often do face high cliffs. When the press of their numbers builds up near the back of the ranks, the leaders may be forced over the edge. Also, inclement weather when crossing fjords or lakes (note, however, that some brighter individuals refuse to enter the water at all) is likely to result in mass drownings. Neither situation is particularly pleasant for either the lemmings or any observers, but it's generally believed that suicide is not the motive!

The good news is that survival of the fittest is busy at work in the high country. The more aggressive individuals who remain in the hills to guard their territories grow fat and happy. They'll live through the winter under the snow and breed the following year. Females as young as 15 days can become pregnant and most individuals give birth to at least two litters of five each year, so the population increases rapidly.

Red deer (*kronhjort*) range as far north as the Arctic Circle and roe deer inhabit the southern and eastern forests. In the forests from the far south to southern Finnmark, moose (*elg*) are fairly common, although they wisely tend to stay clear of people and roads. Wild reindeer (*reinsdyr*) exist in large herds, usually above the tree line and sometimes as high up as 2000m, especially on the Hardangervidda, but also in Jotunheimen, Dovrefjell and inland areas of Trøndelag. The reindeer of Finnmark are owned by the Sami and most are driven to the coast at the start of summer, then back to the interior in winter. The smaller Svalbard caribou (*svalbardrein*) is native only to Svalbard.

In the late 1940s, musk oxen (*moskusokse*) were re-introduced into Dovrefjell National Park from Greenland (for more information, see the boxed text 'Musk Ox' in the Central Norway chapter).

As in most places, wolves (*ulv*) aren't popular with farmers or reindeer herders and hunters, and only a few still exist in the country – some around Hamar, and a few more in Finnmark. They occasionally wander in from Russia and are normally shot due to a perceived risk of rabies. The red fox (*rødrev*) is found in most places although numbers are reducing due to sarcoptic mange, while Arctic foxes (*fjellrev*) are found north of the Oslo-Bergen rail line, mainly above the tree line, and also in Svalbard. A rare forest-dweller is the solitary lynx (*gaupe*), Europe's only large cat.

Brown bears (*bjørn*) have been persecuted for centuries, and while some remain in forested valleys along the Swedish border between Hedmark and Finnmark, Norway's only permanent population is in Øvre Pasvik National Park in eastern Finnmark.

Polar bears (*isbjørn*) are found only in Svalbard, but they aren't strictly land animals and spend much of their time on pack ice or drift ice. Since the ban on hunting came into force in 1973, their numbers have increased to over 5000. They're the world's largest land carnivore, weighing up to 720kg and measuring up to 2.5m long. Despite their size, however, they're swift and manoeuvrable, thanks to the hair on the soles of the their feet which facilitates movement over ice and snow and provides additional insulation. A polar bear's diet consists mostly of seals, beached whales, fish and birds, and only rarely do they eat reindeer or other land mammals (including – ugh – humans). Polar bear milk contains 30% fat and is the richest of any carnivorous land mammal, and allows newborn cubs to grow quickly and survive extremely cold temperatures. Thanks to this rich diet, one polar bear's liver contains enough Vitamin D to kill a human who might eat it.

Marine Mammals The seas around Norway are rich fishing grounds, due to the ideal summer conditions for the growth of plankton. This wealth of nutrients also attracts baleen whales, which eat the plankton, as well as toothed whales and seals, who feed mainly on the fish that eat the plankton. Sadly, many years of whaling in the North Atlantic and Arctic oceans have brought several whale species to the verge of extinction. Apart from the minke whale, there's no sign that the numbers will ever recover in this area.

Minke whales (*minkehval*) measure around 7 to 10m long and weigh between 5 and 10 tonnes. They're baleen whales, which means that they have plates of whalebone baleen rather than teeth, and migrate between the Azores area and Svalbard.

The endangered sei whale (*seihval*), which is also a baleen whale, is found off the coast of Finnmark and is named because its arrival corresponds with that of the *sei* (pollack), which also comes to feast on the seasonal plankton. They measure up to 18m and weigh up to 30 tonnes. The annual migration takes the sei from the seas off north-west Africa and Portugal (winter), up to the Norwegian Sea and southern Barents Sea in summer.

The fin whale (*finhval*) measures 24m and can weigh up to 80 tonnes. These whales were a prime target after the Norwegian Svend Føyn developed the exploding harpoon in 1864, and unregulated whalers left only a few thousand in the North Atlantic. Fin whales are also migratory, wintering between Spain and southern Norway and spending summer in northern Norway, Jan Mayen and Svalbard.

The largest animal on earth, the blue whale (*blåhval*), measures up to 28m and weighs in at a staggering 110 tonnes. Heavily hunted for its oil, the species finally received protection from the International Whaling Commission in 1967 (far too late!). Prior to 1864, there were between 6000 and 9000, but only a few hundred remain in the world's oceans and they haven't been seen in Norwegian waters since the 1960s.

Sperm whales (*spermsetthval*), which measure up to 19m and can weigh up to 50 tonnes, are mainly characterised by their squarish profile. They subsist mainly on fish and squid and usually live in pods of 15 to 20. Their numbers were depleted by whalers after whale oil and the valuable spermaceti wax from their heads. Fortunately, the fish-rich shoals off Vesterålen attract quite a few sperm whales and they're predictably observed on boat tours.

Between Ålesund and Varangerhalvøya, it's possible to see humpback whales (*knolhval*), toothed whales which measure up to 15m and weigh up to 30 tonnes. These are among the most acrobatic whales and often leap about and flap their flukes before sounding. They're also among the most vocal of whales, producing deep songs that can be heard and recorded hundreds of kilometres away.

The bowhead whale (*grønlandshval*), or Greenland right whale, was virtually annihilated by the end of the 19th century for its baleen, which was used in corsets, fans and whips. In 1679, Svalbard had around 25,000 bowheads, but only a handful remain.

Killer whales (*spekkhogger*), or orcas, are the top sea predators and measure up to 7m and weigh 5 tonnes. There are around 1500 off the coast of Norway, swimming in pods of two or three. They eat fish, seals, dolphins, porpoise and whales (such as minke), which may be larger than themselves. The long-finned pilot whale (*grindhval*), about

6m long, may swim in pods of up to several hundred and range as far north as Nordkapp. Belugas (*hvithval*), which are up to 4m long, are found mainly in the Arctic Ocean and travel in pods of five to 10 or more.

The grey and white narwhal (*narhval*), which grows up to 3.5m long, is best recognised by the peculiar 2.7m spiral ivory tusk which projects from the upper lip of the males. This tusk is in fact one of the whale's two teeth and was prized in medieval times. Narwhal live mainly in the Arctic Ocean and occasionally head upstream into freshwater. They live in pods of 15 to 20.

Norway also has bottlenose, white-beaked, Atlantic white-sided and common dolphins.

Seals are often seen near the seashore throughout Norway. The main species include harbour seals (*steinkobbe*), grey seals (*havert*), ringed seals (*ringsel*), harp seals (*grønlandssel*), hooded seals (*klappmyss*) and bearded seals (*blåsel*). The much larger walrus (*hvalross*), which in Norway lives only in Svalbard, measures up to nearly 4m and weighs up to 1300kg. They're best identified by their ivory tusks, which are elongated canine teeth and can measure up to 1m long in the males. Although they were once heavily hunted for their ivory and blubber, since they became a protected species in 1952, their Svalbard population has now reached around 1000.

Fish The variety of fish found in the seas around Norway is quite extensive and some are economically important. The most common are the cod (*torsk*), sprat (*brisling*), haddock (*kolje*), mackerel (*makrell*), capelin (*lodde*), sandeel (*storsil*), ling (*lange*), redfish (or ocean perch – *uer*) and coalfish (or pollock – *sei*). The ugly but rather lovable catfish (*steinbit*) is delicious, as is the blenny (*ålekvabbe*). Herring (*sild*), halibut (*hellefisk*) and hake (*lysing*) have all been overfished and are no longer abundant.

Shrimp (*reker*), crab (*krabbe*) and lobster (*hummer*) are the main edible crustaceans and mussels (*blåskjell*) are also good to eat.

Among freshwater fish, salmon (*laks*) are the most widespread and a large sport

DEANNA SWANEY

Bearded seal

White-tailed eagles are the largest northern Europe raptor, with a wingspan of up to 2.5m

angling community ensures that the stocks are kept as healthy as possible. However, diseases are now spreading from farmed fish to the wild stocks, creating major problems in some areas (see Environment & Ecology, earlier in this chapter). The brown trout (*ørret*) is also popular with anglers, but it's found only in the south. Other common and edible freshwater species include perch (*åbor*), Arctic charr (*røye*), Arctic grayling (*harr*), bream (*brasme*), tench (*suter*) and eel (*ål*).

Birds Norway makes an excellent venue for ornithologists, but the country attracts so many nesting species and permanent residents that it would be quite impossible to discuss them all in detail. The most prominent, as well as a few rarer ones, are discussed in this section.

The best birdwatching sites include Revtangen (coastal Rogaland), Utsira (off the Rogaland coast), Fokstumyra (in Dovrefjell), Femundsmarka National Park (Hedmark), Runde (near Ålesund, with over 150,000 nesting pairs of seabirds), the islands of Nordland (especially Lovund, Træna, Røst, Værøy and Bleiksøya), Øvre Pasvik National Park (eastern Finnmark) and Svalbard (for visiting migratory species in summer).

The greatest bird populations in Norway are along the coastline, where millions of sea birds nest in coastal cliff faces and feed on fish and other sea life. The most prolific species include a number of gulls (*måke*), common tern (*makrellterne*), Arctic tern (*rødnebbterne*), oystercatcher (*tjeld*), cormorant (*skarv*), gannet (*havsule*), razorbill (*alke*), puffin (*lundefugl*), guillemot (*lomvi*), black guillemot (*teist*), shag (*toppskarv*), fulmar (*havhest*), kittiwake (*krykkje*), skuas (*tjuvjo* and *fjelljo*), little auk (*alkekonge*) and European storm-petrel (*storm petrel*).

Among Norway's raptors, the most dramatic and rewarding to see and watch is the lovely white-tailed eagle (*havørn*), of which there are now at least 500 nesting pairs along the Nordland coast, as well as in parts of Troms and Finnmark. The rough-legged buzzard (*fjellvåk*) lives by hunting lemmings and voles in Arctic and alpine tundra areas. There are also about 500 pairs of golden eagle (*kongeørn*) in higher mountain areas. The rare osprey (*fiskeørn*) has a maximum population of 30 pairs and is seen only in heavily forested areas; your best chances of seeing one is in Stabbursdalen and Øvre Pasvik National Parks. You may also see sparrowhawks (*spurvehauk*), merlins (*dvergfalk*), gyrfalcons (*jaktfalk*), peregrine falcons (*vandrefalk*), hen harriers

Norwegian National Parks

Here's a quick rundown of Norway's 21 national parks, with descriptions of what you can expect to find in each:

Børgefjell (1107 sq km; Nord Trøndelag & Nordland)
The boulder-strewn slopes of the Børgefjell massif harbour alpine vegetation in the heights and forested slopes and bogs in lower areas. It's known as a popular birdwatching venue.

Dovrefjell (256 sq km; Oppland, Sør Trøndelag & Møre og Romsdal)
For most Norwegians, Dovrefjell is synonymous with musk oxen, and the hairy beasts attract lots of wildlife buffs. It's also popular with hikers and climbers wanting to tackle Snøhetta (2286m).

Femundsmarka (390 sq km; Hedmark & Sør Trøndelag)
This park, dominated by the lake Femunden, preserves a glaciated highland landscape along the Swedish border.

Forlandet (640 sq km; Svalbard)
This park takes in the 86km-long island, Prins Karls Forlandet, off the west coast of Spitsbergen. It exists mainly to protect breeding grounds for eider ducks, geese and pinnipeds (seals and walruses).

Gressåmoen (182 sq km; Nord Trøndelag)
This park was established to protect one of the country's largest areas of first growth spruce forest. It's also known for boggy areas that attract lots of water-loving birds.

Gutulia (19 sq km; Hedmark)
This tiny park preserves an expanse of primeval old growth forest and is home to numerous bird species.

Hardangervidda (3422 sq km; Oppland, Telemark & Hordaland)
This vast expanse of upland alpine plateau dominates the central portion of southern Norway. It's home to the largest herd of wild reindeer in Europe and is one of Norway's most popular nordic skiing venues.

Jostedalsbreen (1145 sq km; Sogn og Fjordane)
This park takes in the 487 sq km Jostedalsbreen icecap, and its many scenic and impressive valley glaciers provide insight into the natural powers that originally carved out Norway's fjords.

Jotunheimen (1145 sq km; Oppland)
Norway's most popular national park attracts throngs of hikers to its numerous ranges of sharp, scenic and challenging peaks and valleys.

Nordvest Spitsbergen (3560 sq km; Svalbard)
This wild corner of Spitsbergen Island takes in not only the fabulous Kongsbreen icefield but also lovely Magdalenefjord, a number of archaeological sites and some of the world's finest breeding grounds for sea birds, caribou and marine mammals.

Norwegian National Parks

Ormtjernkampen (9 sq km; Oppland)
Norway's smallest national park protects a slice of old growth pine forest, as well as small areas of birch forest and alpine vegetation.

Rago (167 sq km; Nordland)
Lonely and dramatic Rago National Park is characterised by high mountain peaks divided by plunging valleys and waterfalls. It abuts the Padjelanta, Sarek and Stora Sjöfallet National Parks in Sweden, forming a combined protected area of 5700 sq km.

Reisa (803 sq km; Troms)
The most prominent feature of this park is the dramatic Reisa Gorge, its lovely waterfalls, varied wildlife and interesting hiking.

Rondane (580 sq km; Oppland)
Rondane, Norway's first national park, shelters not only herds of wild reindeer but also large areas of stark and inspiring alpine peaks and meadows. It also protects the archaeological remains of ancient hunting cultures.

Saltfjellet-Svartisen (2105 sq km; Nordland)
The two-part Saltfjellet-Svartisen National Park, which straddles the Arctic Circle, combines the upland moors of Saltfjellet with the two vast Svartisen icecaps. It also includes a number of Sami archaeological relics and sacred sites.

Stabbursdalen (98 sq km; Finnmark)
The main reason for preserving Stabbursdalen is its pine forest – the world's most northerly. In addition, it offers excellent wild hiking and broad vistas well off the trodden track.

Sør Spitsbergen (5399 sq km; Svalbard)
By far Norway's largest national park, Sør Spitsbergen takes in Spitsbergen's entire southern peninsula. About 65% is covered in ice, but there are several nesting sites for barnacle geese and eider ducks, and the coastal cliffs attract millions of nesting sea birds.

Øvre Anarjåkka (1399 sq km; Finnmark)
This little known park adjoins Finland's wild Lemmenjoki National Park and protects a vast expanse of birch and pine forests, bogs and lakelands.

Øvre Dividal (743 sq km; Troms)
This lovely, wild park lies at the heart of a complex network of trekking routes in northern Norway, Sweden and Finland. It's known for the Arctic rhododendron and heather, and is also home to the rare wolverine.

Øvre Pasvik (67 sq km; Finnmark)
This park, tucked between Finland and Russia, protects a lovely area of boreal forest as well as large areas of muskeg and the last habitat of the brown bear in Norway.

Ånderdalen (69 sq km; Troms)
This tiny park on the island of Senja protects the bogs and the pine and birch coastal forests typical of Troms county. Some of the trees are over 500 years old.

(*myrhauk*), kestrels (*tørnfalk*) and goshawks (*hønsehauk*). All but the last two are suffering a steep decline in numbers and are rarely observed.

There are also at least four species of owls: short-eared owls (*jordugle*), found on marshy moors; pygmy owls (*spurveugle*), which like coniferous forests; snowy owls (*snøugle*), which like alpine tundra; and eagle owls (*hubro*), which prefer northern and mountain forests.

Especially in southern Norway, you'll also find the usual European variety of woodland birds, including wood pigeons (*rindue*), woodpeckers (*hakkespett*), woodcocks (*rugde*), bullfinches (*dompap*), chaffinches (*bokfink*), cuckoos (*gjøk*), jays (*jayskrike*) and a whole range of tits (chickadees – *meis*). Very few of the spectacular waxwings (*sidensvans*) breed in Norway, but in winter they arrive from Russia in large numbers and may be observed in woods, parks and gardens.

Among the largest woodland birds are the ptarmigan (*fjellrype*) and two other equally tasty species of grouse (*orrfugl* and *jerpe*). The red grouse (*skotsk lirype*) prefers treeless moors and tundra and the bizarre capercaillie (*tiur*), which resembles a wild turkey or a modest peacock, struts around in coniferous forests. Other garden variety birds – crows (*kråke*), blackbirds (*svarttrost*), martins (*taksvale*), ravens (*ravn*), magpies (*skjære*), robins (*rødstrupe*), sparrows (*spurv*) and so on – are quite common.

Norway's host of wading and water birds includes grey herons (*gråhegre*) and numerous sandpiper species – snipe, curlew, ruff, whimbrel, redshanks and so on – as well as godwits (*spove*), plovers (*lo*), turnstone (*steinvender*) and dotterels (*boltit*).

The most prominent ducks are mallard (*stokkand*), eider (*ærfugl*) and red-breasted merganser (*siland*). In marshes, lakes and ponds, you may also observe wildfowl, such as whooper swans (*sangsvane*), bean geese (*sås*), lesser white-fronted geese (*dverggås*), greylag geese (*grågås*) and Canada geese (*canadagås*). Only the greylag is present in large numbers.

Other lovely water birds include the incredible black-throated and red-throated diver (*storlom* and *smålom*, respectively), called 'loons' in North America, and horned grebes (*horndykker*), cranes (*trane*), coots (*sothøne*) and corncrakes (*åkerrikse*). The last two are species of rail. Norway's national bird, the dipper (*fossekall*), lives near and makes its living by diving into mountain streams.

National Parks

Norway's 21 national parks (see the boxed text) have been established to preserve wilderness areas and to protect wildlife and distinctive natural features of the landscape. In many cases, they don't protect any specific features, but rather, attempt to prevent development of remaining wild areas. As a result, park boundaries don't necessarily coincide with the incidence of spectacular natural features or ecosystem boundaries, but simply follow contour lines around uninhabited areas.

Compared to their counterparts in the USA, Britain and elsewhere, Norwegian national parks are very low profile and pleasantly lack the traffic and overdeveloped tourist facilities which have turned parks in many countries into little more than transplanted (or seasonal) urban areas. Some parks, particularly Jotunheimen and Rondane, are increasingly suffering from overuse, but in most parks, erosion, pollution and distress to wildlife are kept to a minimum.

Nature reserves enjoy an even lower profile, and most are rarely visited, mainly because they're usually closed during wildlife breeding seasons, which normally correspond with the high tourist season between May and July. Fortunately, Norway also enjoys plenty of worthwhile wild areas outside the national parks and reserves, so don't limit your outdoor plans to just the designated areas.

Regulations governing national parks, nature reserves and other protected areas are – not surprisingly in Norway – quite strict. In general, there are no restrictions on entry to the national parks, nor are there any fees, but drivers must nearly always pay a toll to use roads leading into the parks. Dumping rubbish, removing plant, mineral, or fossil specimens, hunting or disturbing wildlife, and using motorised off-road vehicles are all prohibited.

More national park and reserve information is available from local tourist offices or the Miljøverndepartement Informasjonssenteret (Ministry of the Environment Information Centre; ☎ 22 34 57 87, fax 22 34 27 56), Myntgata 2, N-0030 Oslo.

GOVERNMENT & POLITICS

Norway is officially a constitutional monarchy under King Harald V and Queen Sonja, but it also enjoys a parliamentary democratic form of government. Although the monarchy has no real political power, it provides a sense of national identity and is widely respected throughout the country and much of the world. General democratic elections are held every four years for the 165 seats in the Storting, which serves as a national assembly or parliament, and all citizens over the age of 18 are eligible to vote in both local and national elections.

There are few extremes in Norwegian politics. The largest conservative party, Høyre, is moderate by European standards; extreme communist parties have a negligible following; and there are no right-wing neo-fascist movements.

With 65 seats, the Labour party, which promotes social-democratic ideals and supports high taxation to support its extensive social programs, is the largest of the six major parties represented in the Storting. From 1986 to 1995, the party was led by Norway's first woman prime minister, Gro Harlem Brundtland. She was succeeded by Labour party chairman Torbjørn Jagland, who stepped down after just a year due to waning support. The 1997 election resulted in a win for a coalition of the Christian Democrat, Liberal and Centre parties, with Christian Democrat Prime Minister Kjell Magne Bondevik at the helm. The next general election is scheduled to occur in 2001.

The Norwegian prime minister is assisted by 18 government ministers who are responsible for various facets of the government. In addition to the national government, each of the 19 counties and 435 municipalities has its own local government which is responsible for building and maintaining schools, hospitals, roads and other local infrastructure.

As for foreign relations, Norway was a founding member of the League of Nations in 1920 and the United Nations in 1944-45. In 1949, it also became a member of NATO and joined the OECD. It is currently affiliated with the European Free Trade Association, but has resisted joining the EU (see History earlier in this chapter).

ECONOMY

Norway's current prosperity is largely due to the North Sea oil fields, which were discovered on the Norwegian continental shelf in the 1960s. Today, petroleum accounts for Nkr114 billion (or around 16%) of Norway's gross domestic product.

Other economic mainstays include fishing, fish farming, forestry, shipping and shipbuilding, and abundant hydroelectric power provides the basis for a number of industries including aluminium, steel and paper production.

In the late 20th century, tourism has also begun to contribute significantly to the economy and, despite its lofty prices, Norway has experienced a steady increase in visitor numbers. Thanks to convenient summer ferry routes, lots of motorists arrive from Britain and continental Europe, cruise ships call in at coastal ports and many Europeans take day or weekend trips to Oslo, Bergen and Stavanger. In winter, skiers head for the mountains and plateaux. Meanwhile, generous funding and substantial user tolls ensure that the transport infrastructure – new roads, tunnels, bridges and ferries – continues to improve.

While Norwegians enjoy among the world's highest per capita incomes and one of the most developed infrastructures, they must also pay some of the world's highest prices -- and among the world's highest taxes. This is thanks mainly to the country's restrictions on imports, labour costs and the comprehensive cradle-to-grave social welfare system which entitles citizens to a government-sponsored university education, generous holiday leave, socialised medical care and a guaranteed pension, among other things.

In many parts of the country, the number of well compensated government employees exceeds the number employed by the private sector. When you consider that private enterprise must still carry the entire economy, it's easy to work out that entrepreneurial initiative is currently strained to its limit. In fact, it's feared that any liberalisation of trade restrictions – particularly membership of the EU – may well cause the entire system to collapse.

POPULATION

Norway's population of 4,348,500 (as of January 1995) represents among the lowest population densities in Europe, at 13 people per square kilometre. Despite the high taxation, the majority of modern Norwegians sit comfortably in the middle class. To preserve the living standard and low population density, immigration is strictly controlled and only *bona fide* refugees (as opposed to nominal 'asylum seekers') are admitted. Most of these come from Somalia, Bosnia, Sri Lanka and other seriously troubled areas.

The largest cities are Oslo with 483,500 residents, Bergen with 223,000, Trondheim with 144,000 and Stavanger with 104,000. The life expectancy for men is 74.2 years and for women, 80.3 years. Families have an average of two children each and, combined with the negligible immigration, this results in fairly static population numbers.

PEOPLE
Nordic

Most of Norway's population is considered to be of Nordic stock; these people are thought to have descended from central and northern European tribes who migrated northward around 8000 years ago, and modern Nordic peoples are in fact the indigenous peoples of southern and central Scandinavia. The 'Nordic type' is generally characterised by a tall sturdy frame, light hair and blue eyes (although plenty of Nordic individuals do have darker fe...ures).

Sami

Norway's 40,000 to 45,000 indigenous Sami people (formerly known as Lapps) make up the country's largest ethnic minority. This hardy, formerly nomadic people has for centuries occupied northern Scandinavia and north-western Russia, living mainly by herding domestic reindeer. The total population of 70,000 Sami still forms an ethnic minority in four countries – Norway, Sweden, Finland and Russia.

In Norway, the Sami mainly occupy the far northern county of Finnmark, but there are also scattered groups in Nordland, Trøndelag and Hedmark. The Sami themselves refer to their area as Sàpmi, or Samiland.

In 1988, the government passed a constitutional amendment stating: 'It is the responsibility of the authorities of the State to

SAMI CULTURAL AREA AND DIALECTS

Dialects
1 South
2 Ume
3 Pite
4 Lule
5 North
6 Inari
7 Skolt
8 Kildin
9 Ter

NORWAY   SWEDEN   FINLAND   RUSSIA

create conditions enabling the Sami people to preserve and develop its language, culture and way of life.' It also provided for the creation of an elected Sami parliament, or Sameting, to serve as an advisory body to bring Sami issues to the national parliament (similar bodies also exist in Finland and Sweden).

In order to be considered a member of the Sami community, a person must meet one of three criteria: speak Sami as their first language; consider themselves a member of the Sami community and live in accordance with that society; or have a parent who satisfies either of those conditions.

History The oldest written reference to the Sami was written by the Roman historian Tacitus in 98 AD, and in 555 AD the Greek Procopius referred to Scandinavia as Thule, the furthest north, and its peoples as *skridfinns*, who hunted, herded reindeer and travelled about on skis. The medieval Icelandic sagas confirm trading between Nordic peoples and the Sami, and the trader Ottar, who 'lived further north than any other Norseman', served in the court of English King Alfred the Great and wrote extensively about his native country and its indigenous peoples. Sami traditions are also highlighted in the 1673 book *Lapponia* by Johannes Schefferus.

During this era, the Sami lived by hunting and trapping in small communities or bands known as *siida*, which occupied their own designated territory. While 17th and 18th century colonisation of the north by Nordic farmers did present conflicts with this system, many of the newcomers found the Sami way of life better suited to the local conditions and adopted their dress, diet, customs and traditions.

Most early writings about the Sami tended to characterise them as pagans and, although churches were established in their lands as early as the 12th century, the first real mission was founded by Thomas von Westen in 1716. His efforts concentrated mainly on eradicating the practice of shamanism and discouraging the use of the Sami language.

Subsequent missionary efforts, however, reversed this policy and concentrated on translating the Bible into their language. The Lutheran catechism was available in the Fell Sami language as early as 1728, due to the efforts of missionary Morten Lund.

Around 1850, school reforms were introduced which restricted the use of the Sami language in schools. From 1902 it became illegal to sell land to any person who couldn't speak Norwegian, and this policy was practised zealously, particularly in the early 20th century. However, there was an about-face after WWII when official policy began promoting internal multiculturalism, and by the 1960s the Sami's right to preserve and develop their own cultural values and language were enshrined across all government spectra. Increasingly, official policy viewed the Sami as Norwegian subjects but also an ethnic minority and separate people. Their legal status improved considerably and the government formed two committees: the Svamekulturutvalget to deal with Sami cultural issues, and the Samerettsutvalget to determine the legal aspects of the Sami status and resource ownership. In early 1990, the government passed the Sami Language Act, which gave the Sami language equal status as Norwegian, and later the same year Norway ratified the International Labour Organisation proposition No 169, which guaranteed the rights of indigenous and tribal peoples.

Although techniques have undergone a modernisation in recent years, reindeer herding is now a major capital earner and represents 2000 tonnes of meat annually, or about 1% of Norway's meat output. In addition to reindeer herding, modern Sami engage in fishing, agriculture, trade, small industry and the production of handicrafts, as well as most other trades and professions in Norwegian society as a whole.

Culture & Traditions Early Sami life was based on hunting and fishing, but sometime during the 16th century the reindeer was domesticated and the hunting economy developed into a nomadic herding economy.

While the reindeer still figures prominently in Sami life, only about 10% of the Sami people are still involved in reindeer herding and transport by reindeer sledge, and only a handful of traditionalists continue to lead a nomadic lifestyle.

Some major identifying elements of Sami culture include the *joik* (or *yoik*), a rhythmic poem composed for a specific person to describe their innate nature and is considered to be owned by the person it describes (see Religion later in this chapter). Other traditional elements include the use of folk medicine, shamanism, artistic pursuits (especially woodcarving and silversmithing) and striving for ecological harmony.

The Sami national dress is the only genuine folk dress that's still in casual use in Norway, and you'll readily see it on the streets and in the supermarkets of Kautokeino and Karasjok. Each district has its own distinct features, but all include a highly decorated and embroidered combination of red and blue felt shirts or frocks, trousers or skirts, and boots and hats. On special occasions, the women's dress is topped off with a crown of pearls and a garland of silk hair ribbons.

Political Organisations In addition to the Sami parliament, which convenes in Karasjok and is elected by direct ballot, the Norwegian Sami people also belong to the Nordic Sami Council, founded in 1953 to foster cooperation between political organisations in Norway, Sweden and Finland. The Norwegian Sami also participate in the World Council of Indigenous Peoples (WCIP), which encourages solidarity and promotes information exchange between indigenous peoples in the various member countries. The Nordic Sami Institute at Kautokeino was established in 1974 and seeks to promote Sami language, culture and education, as well as promote research, economic activities and environmental protection. It's funded by the Nordic Council of Ministers.

In Tromsø in 1980, the Nordic Sami Council's political program adopted the following principles:

We, the Sami, are one people, whose fellowship must not be divided by national boundaries.

We have our own history, tradition, culture and language. We have inherited from our forebears a right to territories, water and our own economic activities.

We have an inalienable right to preserve and develop our own economic activities and our communities, in accordance with our own circumstances and we will together safeguard our territories, natural resources and national heritage for future generations.

An informative but rather angry treatise on Sami culture is the English-language booklet *The Saami – People of the Sun & Wind*, which is published by Átte, Swedish Mountain and Saami Museum, in Jokkmokk, Sweden. It does a good job of describing Sami traditions in all four countries of the Sàpmi region, and is available at tourist shops around the area.

Other

Apart from the small Jewish community, most members of ethnic minorities in Norway are either married to Norwegians or are refugees from trouble spots. They comprise only a tiny proportion of the population and while most live in Oslo, many smaller communities have also accepted limited numbers of refugees.

EDUCATION

Compulsory education was instituted in Norway in 1889, requiring a minimum of seven years' instruction; this was extended to nine years in 1969 and to 10 years in 1997. Currently, about 7.6% of the national budget is spent on education and 20% of the Norwegian population is involved in some sort of educational program. Private school attendance is discouraged unless it's in addition to instruction at state-sponsored schools. About 80% of residents between the ages of 25 and 64 has completed some education beyond secondary level and 27% hold higher degrees. High school students select their own curriculum, including apprenticeship and vocational programs, and many choose to attend school away from their home towns.

Russing Around

An unusual tradition for students graduating from high school is called *russ*. When a student becomes russ, or *rødruss*, he or she dons red overalls and a red beret and, by virtue of this status, is permitted for a time to raise all sorts of holy hell. Although the line is drawn at actual property damage, other sorts of mischief – unrestrained noise, partying, removable graffiti and general obnoxiousness – are permitted and encouraged. This may go on for several weeks around the end of the school year.

In an effort to assist in maintaining the Sami culture, education of Sami students includes Sami cultural studies and some course work in the Sami language. Foreign language instruction for non-Norwegian speakers, special education programs and after-school day care are also subsidised.

Norway has four universities: the University of Oslo, which is the oldest; the University of Bergen; the Norwegian University of Science & Technology in Trondheim; and the University of Tromsø. There are also 26 regional colleges and eight speciality colleges teaching veterinary medicine, sport, music, architecture, the arts, agriculture and business and economics.

ARTS
Music

The earliest recorded Norwegian musical compositions date back to the early 18th century, when town musicians and travelling performers composed music for dances and chamber music performances. After the union with Sweden in 1814, Oslo saw a boom in musical interest whenever the royal court was in town, and officials, landowners and the wealthier classes sponsored musical events at private gatherings.

By the middle of the 18th century, Norway had produced its first virtuoso, violinist Ole Bull (see the boxed text in the Bergen & South-Western Fjords chapter), who came to be known throughout Europe as the 'Nordic Paganini'. His promotion of Hardanger-area folk fiddlers in Bergen concert halls and the collection of Norwegian folk music by Ludvig Mathias Lindeman brought Norwegian folk music traditions to European attention. Also, Bull's mentoring efforts among aspiring Bergen musicians paved the way for composer Edvard Grieg (see the boxed text in the Bergen & South-Western Fjords chapter).

Thanks to Grieg's musical genius and the considerable talent of his contemporaries Halfdan Kierulf and Johan Svendsen, the 1870s and 1880s have been called the 'Golden Age' of Norwegian music. By 1905, when the union between Norway and Sweden was dissolved, Norway had this body of work to put forward as part of its national identity and, in the same spirit, Norwegian composers also cast back to the medieval traditions that had preceded the country's political unions with both Denmark and Sweden. David Monrad Johansen, Geirr Tveitt, Fartein Valen and Pauline Hall based their works on the late German romantics and French impressionists. While Johansen and Tveitt concentrated more on monumentalism, Valen and Hall embraced a lighter, more impressionistic style. During this period, most serious musicians were employed by cinemas and cafés, while composers were relegated to earning a living as teachers and music critics.

After WWII, however, any former ties with German culture were necessarily broken and the new generation of composers opted to study in Paris or the USA rather than Leipzig. Among the newcomers were Kvandal, Hovland, Nystedt and Hagerup Bull, who no longer sought a national musical identity, but rather, to achieve a more international voice. This was realised through the technological revolutions of the 1950s and 1960s, much to the dismay of traditionalists. Novel experimental and avant garde music, involving electronics and sound effects, made its debut and was mostly met with consternation by the bemused public. In fact, churches refused to hire themselves out for such performances, lest their equipment be damaged or their sanctity profaned! As a result, the avant garde era in Norway was mercifully quite brief.

During the last quarter of the 20th century, things grew less surreal. There was a brief period of politicism, in which composers identified with various causes; Alfred Hanson dedicated a violin concerto to Chilean president Salvador Allende and the *Trauermusik* by Søderlind, was inspired by both the war in Biafra and the Soviet invasion of Czechoslovakia. More recent trends, however, have retreated to a long-standing interest in Norwegian folk music and insistence on cultural preservation, which has dominated most modern works while still integrating computer technology.

Classical music is still alive, however, as evidenced by the popular philharmonic orchestras of Oslo, Bergen (which dates from 1765), Trondheim and Stavanger and the Norwegian Opera Company (established in 1958). Both jazz and pop music have also taken hold in Norway, and Norwegian musicians such as saxophonist Jan Garbarek and Sami singer Mari Boine have attracted international attention (and who could forget A-ha, the big Norwegian band of the 80s?).

The increasing enthusiasm for music in Norway is reflected especially in a growing number of local music festivals springing up throughout the country. The best known is the Bergen International Festival, held in May, followed by the internationally acclaimed jazz festivals in Molde and Kongsberg. Other significant music festivals are held annually in Harstad, Elverum, Kristiansand, Trondheim (during the St Olavsdagene festival), Sarpsborg, Risør, Oslo and at least 40 other locations, and it's safe to say that every weekend you can find a worthwhile musical bash somewhere in Norway.

The haunting music of the Sami people of northern Norway is also enjoying interest among aficionados of more esoteric musical styles. Modern Sami artists such as Aulu Gaup, Mari Boine and Nils Aslak Valkeapääs are also performing and recording popularised versions of the traditional *joik*, or personal songs (see the discussions of People and Religion, both elsewhere in this chapter).

Literature

As a country, Norway is fairly young, but its literature goes back over a thousand years. Around the turn of the previous millennium, the Vikings were producing sagas reflecting their lives and experiences, long before the time of Norway's best known modern writers, Ibsen and Hamsun.

There are two large groups of medieval Norse literature: skaldic poetry and eddic poetry. The *skalds* were the Norwegian court poets of the 9th and 10th centuries; they produced songs organised according to a loose rhyme scheme and used a technique of metaphoric descriptions known as *kenning*, as well as complex alliterative structures. These works, with titles such as *Harald's Song* and *Lack of Gold*, served as celebrations of Norwegian kings and their courts.

Eddic poetry is named after the Edda, the most important collection of medieval Icelandic literature, which means that it's culturally Norwegian. The Edda, which combines Christian with pre-Christian elements, is the most extensive source of information on Norse mythology, but it wasn't written down until Snorre Sturluson recorded it in the 13th century, long after the Christianisation of both Norway and Iceland. Its subject matter includes the story of the origin, history and end of the world, instruction on writing poetry, a series of disconnected aphorisms attributed to the god Oðinn, and an anthology of tales similar to the Germanic *Nibelungenlied*.

Apart from the Edda itself, there are three forms of eddic poetry: legendary sagas, heroes' sagas, and didactic poetry. Titles include the *Hymiskviða* (Hymir-Song), which recounts Þór's legendary battle with the Midgård serpent, the *Volsunga Saga*, in which the heroes coincide with those in the Nibelungenlied, and the *Runatal* (Rune-Song), which tells of Oðinn's sacrifice on the world tree *yggdrasil*.

Around the middle of the 13th century, after half the Norwegian population had succumbed to the Black Death, the Norse literary tradition began to wane, and for several centuries following the union with Denmark in 1380, Norway's language, cultural and literary traditions fell into disuse. An indigenous Norwegian literature wasn't resurrected until the late 17th century with the emergence of writers Petter Dass (1647-1707) and Dorothe Engelbretsdatter (1634-1716). Although Dass was Dano-Norwegian (and actually of Scottish stock), he celebrated northern Norway in his *Nordlands Trompet* (Trumpet of the Northland), and his rhythmic poetry spread around the country in the form of folk songs. Engelbretsdatter's complex baroque poetry was extremely popular in her time, but perhaps because of its overtly Christian content, it has been largely ignored by modern anthologists and literary historians.

Romanticism hit Norway in the works of Henrik Wergeland (1808-45), who in his short life wrote large quantities of ecstatic love poetry, mystical religious works, novellas and non-fiction. Wergeland championed his country's cultural independence from Denmark, and also fought for social justice toward the lower classes, especially farmers and the poor.

Near the end of the 19th century, Norwegian literature gained international prominence with the work of 'four great ones': Henrik Ibsen (1828-1906), Bjørnstjerne Bjørnson (1832-1910), Alexander Kjelland (1849-1906) and Jonas Lie (1833-1908). Ibsen was the quintessential Norwegian dramatist, but spent over 30 years of his life travelling and living in Europe. While he started out writing and directing Bergen theatre pieces, his breakthrough came with the German and Italian-influenced plays *A Doll's House* (1880) and *Ghosts* (1881), both of which created a stir all over Europe for their treatment of the role of women and the tensions of family life. In his subsequent plays, including *The Wild Duck* and *Hedda Gabler* (both 1890), Ibsen shifted his emphasis from social to individual psychol-

ogy. In addition to creating absorbing dramas with interesting subject matter, Ibsen also initiated a new dramatic tradition by abandoning verse in favour of prose.

Less well known today, Bjørnson became hugely popular with his story *Trust and Trial* in 1857. Following in Ibsen's footsteps in Bergen, Bjørnson went on to write short stories, drama, journalism, and around 30,000(!) letters. In his early career, his work concentrated on descriptions of rural life in contemporary Norway, and he was (falsely) accused of romanticising the lot of the rural folk. Later, he focused his attentions on social problems in the hope of promoting industrialisation in Norway. In 1903, he was the first Norwegian writer to be awarded the Nobel Prize in Literature.

Realist and satirist Kjelland, who wrote novels, short stories and dramas, was at the heart of one of Norway's biggest literary controversies in 1885. Recommended to parliament for a government stipend, he was rebuffed for alleged immorality. In his *Gift* trilogy – *Garman & Worse* (1880), *Skipper Worse* (1882) and *Gift* (1883) – Kjelland depicted the transition of a patrician family to modern capitalist entrepreneurs.

A generation after these writers, Sigrid Undset (1882-1949) and Knut Hamsun (1859-1952) both received Nobel Prizes in 1928 and 1920, respectively. Frequently characterised as the most significant female writer in Norwegian literature, Undset began her career with a series of books on the plight of poor and middle-class women. Between 1920 and 1922, she published the *Kristin Lavransdottir* trilogy, a historical novel set in 14th century Scandinavia. Though much more optimistic than her earlier work, Undset continued to criticise the fact that women must subject their will and sexuality to social and religious standards. *Kristin Lavransdottir* was followed by the *Master of Hestviken* series, which was also set in medieval times.

The work of Hamsun can be divided into three periods. Most of his early work, including his great novels *Hunger* (1890) and *Mysteries* (1892), features romantic heroes, tragic love stories and psychological examination. Later, Hamsun wrote a number of social novels which praised rural life and criticised industrialisation and urbanisation. A product of this period was *The Growth of the Soil* (1917), for which Hamsun received the Nobel Prize. His last work, the *Vagabond Trilogy* (1927-34), centred around a less romanticised and more human hero. Because of his elitism, his appreciation of Germanic values and his support of rural life, it's no surprise that Hamsun sided with the Nazis in WWII. Unfortunately, his controversial politics have clouded modern appreciation of his literary work, which stands in the tradition of Dostoevsky and Joyce as a significant contribution to literary modernism.

Contemporary Norwegian literature takes on a variety of forms and genres, but little of it has been translated into English. The works of Dag Solstad espouse ironic socialist realism on documentary topics and attack capitalism, but they are not available in English. In a similar vein, but akin to the Latin American magic realism of Vargas Llosa and García Márquez, Kjartan Flogstad's *Dollar Road* portrays the changes in a small Norwegian town with the advent of industrialism. More traditionally mainstream, Knud Faldbakken writes dystopian novels. *Twilight Country* and its sequel *Sweetwater* are set in an unnamed country in a near future, where society has collapsed and characters eke out a living in the face of apocalyptic chaos. Fladbakken's *The Sleeping Prince* retells the fairy tale *Sleeping Beauty* from a woman's perspective, and explores male/female relationships and sexuality.

Herrbjørg Wassmo, one of several prominent modern female writers, received the Nordic Prize for Literature in 1987. Her books centre around the plight of women in Norwegian society. *Dina's Book* tells the eponymous heroine's story in 1840s Norway, while *The House with the Blind Glass Windows* is set in and after WWII.

Finally, the most famous contemporary Norwegian author is Jostein Gaarder. Gaarder's first bestseller *Sophie's World* is typical of all of his books: it addresses serious philosophical and religious issues through the eyes of a young adult, employing the narrative technique of a story within a story. In *Sophie's World*, while learning about the history of Western philosophy through a correspondence course she never entered, young Sophie finds out that she is no more than a character in a novel. In *The Solitaire Mystery*, the analogous literary device is a deck of cards, and in *The Christmas Mystery* it's an advent calendar, but in both cases, a child protagonist must solve some riddle or puzzle which will determine their destiny. *Hello, Is Anybody There?* addresses the problem of dealing with the arrival of a younger sibling by making use of an alien figure. Gaarder's most recent book, *That Same Flower*, is somewhat different, purporting to be the translation of a letter from Floria Æmilia to her lover Saint Augustine. In this feminist guise – giving Augustine's asceticism and ideals a distinctly unusual twist – Gaarder raises familiar issues such as the existence of God and the point of human life.

Architecture

Due to Norway's vast timber resources, the use of wood has been a major factor in the country's architectural designs. Because working in wood required less labour (and less expense) than did cutting, shaping and building in stone, the peasants, farmers, hunters and fishing communities enjoyed cosy wooden homes while the wealthier folks displayed their means by constructing palatial but cold and draughty stone dwellings. In the far north, where both wood and stone were in short supply, the early nomadic Sami ingeniously built their homes of turf, which was in ample supply and provided excellent insulation against the cold.

Most larger religious buildings were also constructed in stone and employed strong Anglo-Saxon influences (notable exceptions include the Gothic-style Nidaros Cathedral in Trondheim and the Romanesque Stavanger Cathedral), which isn't surprising when you consider that Norwegian Christianity was actually imported from England. However, many late Viking Age and early medieval churches were built of ornately worked wood, and although those that survive have been heavily restored, these unique stave churches are some of the oldest surviving wooden buildings on earth (see the boxed text in the Western Fjords chapter). Named for their vertical supporting posts, these churches are distinguished by detailed carved designs, dragon-headed gables resembling the prows of classic Viking ships and by their undeniably beautiful, almost Oriental forms. Of the 500 to 600 which were originally built, only about 20 of the remaining ones retain any of their original components.

After the Black Death, the country fell into Danish hands. For nearly four centuries, architectural styles reflected the European Renaissance and baroque traditions which predominated in Denmark and Germany at the time, and they continued to prevail even after the 1814 dissolution of the Danish union. After the largely wooden town of Oslo burned in 1624, King Christian IV determined that the town be rebuilt in brick masonry with broad streets to reduce fire hazards in the future. During the 19th century, however, the need for larger public buildings in the capital – the Royal Palace, the university, the Oslo Stock Exchange, the Norges Bank, the Christiania Theatre and other public structures – coincided with the embracing of the new and trendy neoclassical (Empire) architectural tradition.

Around the middle of the 19th century, Norwegian architects habitually travelled to Italy to gain inspiration and en route they discovered the 'gingerbread' wooden architecture which was characteristic of the Alps. Realising that this style would work readily in timber-rich Norway, they inspired a flurry of wooden spa hotels adorned with Norwegian motifs which eventually came to be known as the Norwegian 'dragon style'. Although many examples have since burned, this tradition is reflected in a number of historic hotels around the country.

In the early 20th century, architect Henrik Bull introduced the German *Jugendstil* (youthful style) or Art Nouveau architecture. This whimsical style is best reflected in the Ministry of Finance, the National Theatre and the Historical Museum, all in Oslo, as well as the entire town of Ålesund, which was completely rebuilt after a devastating fire in 1904.

After all the destruction of WWII, Norway was faced with the task of major reconstruction in most towns. Thanks to the predominant Labour party, Norwegian architecture took a dramatic turn which could best be summed up by the slogan of the day, 'a roof over our heads'. Reflecting the Soviet notion that housing should be functional but equivalent for everyone and not ostentatious, practical high-density housing and bland commercial and public structures sprang up around the country, leaving such towns as Mo i Rana and Honningsvåg with no charm at all. Fortunately, post-modernism took root in the 1980s and most new structures enjoy a bit more originality.

Visual Arts

Although folk art has been part of Norwegian life since the ancient hunters told their stories in carved stone, the stylised Bronze Age artefacts uncovered with the *Oseberg* ship, and the works of the medieval craftspeople who instilled their distinctive religious devotions into their ornate stave churches, it wasn't until the 19th century that painting and sculpture for its own sake entered the Norwegian artistic consciousness. This is partially due to the country's peripheral location, and the fact that Norwegian artists had to go abroad for their training. The result was the late development of a unique Norwegian artistic voice.

Norway's first acclaimed painter was probably the mid to late 19th century artist JC Dahl who, by superimposing European romanticism on his interpretations of the naturally romantic Norwegian landscapes, came to be known as the father of Norwegian painting. During this period, most Norwegian artists reflected the ideals of schools in Düsseldorf and Munich but by the late 19th century, thanks to the Paris realist movements, a Norwegian artistic identity had begun to emerge. Fortunately, most romanticists of this era managed to avoid the clichéd 'tourist views' of the country, and preferred to see the magnificent Norwegian landscape from the inhabitants' viewpoint.

It was during this period that Norway's two best known artists, painter Edvard Munch (1863-1944) and sculptor Gustav Vigeland (1869-1943), produced the body of their work (for more information on these artists, see the boxed texts in the Oslo chapter). However, they were better received abroad than at home and their unique works had little effect on future Norwegian artistic directions.

During the early 20th century, the impressionist Henri Matisse inspired several ardently decorative Norwegian artists, Axel Revold, Per Krohg and Alf Rolfsen, who soon came to be known as the 'fresco brothers'. Another pupil of Matisse, Henrik Sørensen, whose nationalistic tendencies placed him in the same league, served unofficially as the 'club's' fourth member.

Between the world wars, the cubist and constructivist genres were exhibited by Ragnhild Keyser and Charlotte Wankel, as well as Thorvald Hellesen, who chose to work in France rather than at home. During the 1930s, the surrealist idiom emerged in the works of Sigurd Winge and Erik Johannessen. At the same time, the socialist Arne Ekeland produced monumental frescoes, but with little effect because of his then unorthodox political leanings.

During the post-war years, the brooding forests of Jakob Weidemann, the constructivist paintings of Gunnar S Gundersen, and the literal ('non-figurative') sculptures of Arnold Haukeland and Åse Texmon Rygh dominated the era.

Through the 1980s, international interest in Norwegian art grew and the government began funding art programs not only in Oslo, but also in Bergen and Trondheim. As in much of the developed world, the art of this modern era departed dramatically from the protest work of the 1960s and 70s. Throughout the decade and into the 1990s,

the artistic community tended toward naïve depictions and random displays of colour; the most remarkable progenitor of this period was probably Tore Hansen, but Bjørn Carlsen represented a growing consciousness of the worldwide ecological imbalance. Many down-to-earth Norwegians have dismissed this genre as the 'work of children' or likened it to folk art, but the international community has more generously called it 'subtly humorous'.

The 1990s in Norway were best exemplified by the work of sculptor Bård Breivik, who studied the relationships between humans and their tools, and Per Inge Bjørlo, whose woodcuts and linotype prints primitively depicted both people and animals, as well as a host of higher tech artists who used computers to develop post-modernist images. However, Norway's long-standing artistic relationship with nature continues unabated, and it's likely that the wild open spaces will continue to inspire artists for many years to come.

Cinema

Thanks mainly to Norwegian actress Liv Ullman and Swedish director Ingmar Bergman, Norway's first major film success was the screen version of Sigrid Undset's *Kristin Lavransdottir*, the first volume of a medieval tragedy set in Norway. Of Norway's three Nobel Prize-winning authors, Knut Hamsun has been the most appealing to filmmakers. They have brought to the screen such novels as *Hunger, Pan* and *The Telegraphist*, while two films by other authors, *The Case Against Hamsun* and a three-hour biographical documentary of his life, reveal a fascination with this controversial author who supported Hitler during WWII.

The modern Oscar-winning film *Babette's Feast* also has a Norwegian connection; in her novel, author Karen Blixen set the story in northern Norway, but oddly, director Gabriel Axel set the film in much flatter Danish Jutland. On the other hand, the film *Black Eyes*, by Russian director Nikita Michalkhov, was filmed in the spectacular landscapes around Kjerringøy in Nordland.

An Oscar nomination was given to Nils Gaup's *The Pathfinder*, which is based on a medieval legend and presented in the Sami language. So acclaimed was this film that the Disney Corporation invested in Gaup's next film, *Håkon Håkonsson*, about a Norwegian Robinson Crusoe who set off for the South Seas last century. Also nominated was *Nine Lives* by the prolific Arne Skouen, a *Dagbladet* newspaper columnist who made 17 films between 1948 and 1968. The story is set during the German occupation and follows a soldier put ashore on the stormy northern coast of Norway as he attempts to reach neutral Sweden.

Children's films have also featured in Norwegian filmmaking. Erik Gustavson directed a children's comedy entitled *Herman*, about an Oslo 10-year-old with hair problems, and Marius Holst made the 1995 Berlin Festival winner, *Blue Angel*, which also features childhood conflicts in Oslo. Adolescence is explored in Berit Nesheim's *Frida* and Eva Isaksen has made several films in the *Pelle & Proffen* series, about the adventures of two teenage detectives. Ivo Caprino, who specialises in animation and Norwegian fairy tales, created the humorous and acclaimed cartoon film entitled *Pinchcliff Grand Prix*.

The concerns of Norwegian women are probably best explored in the work of Anja Breien, who launched her successful career in the mid-1970s with *Jostedalsrypa*, about a young 14th century girl who was the only survivor of the Black Death in her western Norwegian valley. Over the past 20 years, Breien has also made a trilogy of films, *Wives*, *Wives 10 Years After* and *Wives III*, about a trio of women who return to their school reunions and discuss their lives. A fourth instalment, which hopes to continue tracing Norwegian women's issues into the new millennium, is planned for sometime around 2005.

Breien's most acclaimed films, however, are probably *Next of Kin*, which was featured at the Cannes Film Festival in 1979, and *Witch Hunt*, which took awards at the Venice Film Festival in 1982.

Perhaps the film about Norway that's most familiar to international audiences is the rather trite *Song of Norway*, which is a popularised biographical treatment of the lives and work of Edvard and Nina Grieg. While the landscapes and music are monumental, the film itself is dedicated more to its potential entertainment value than to historical fact.

SOCIETY & CONDUCT

In general, Norwegians are both independent and outdoor-oriented, and on summer weekends they head for the hills and lakes to partake in the country's excellent hiking, fishing and boating opportunities. In winter, they take to the slopes and forests for downhill or cross-country skiing. Thanks to the age-old law known as *Allemansretten* or 'every man's right', public access to wild areas is guaranteed and 'No Trespassing' or 'Keep Out' signs are virtually unknown. For details on wild camping and hiking, see Activities in the Facts for the Visitor chapter.

Traditional Culture

Of all of Norway's cultural traditions, one of the most evident elements is the *bunad*, the elaborate regional folk costumes. Each district has developed its own unique designs which exhibit varying degrees of colour and originality. In such traditional regions as Hallingdal, Hordaland, Setesdal and parts of Telemark, they remained in everyday use until after WWII but they're currently used mainly for weddings and other festive events.

Traditionally, the intricate embroidery work on these lovely creations was performed by shepherdesses and milkmaids while tending their livestock. Nowadays, these elaborate costumes are produced only by a few serious seamstresses and embroiderers, but because modern folk don't have so much time on their hands, today the purchase of a bunad represents a major financial commitment. The folk museum on the

Bygdøy peninsula in Oslo features displays of these memorable costumes, but the best place to observe them is in Oslo during the 17 May National Day celebrations, when men and women from all over the country turn up in the traditional dress of their heritage areas.

Traditional folk dancing and singing is also enjoying a resurgence in popularity and numerous annual music festivals feature these elements. Ring dances such as roundels, pols, reinlenders, polkas and mazurkas fell into disuse in the 1700s, but they re-emerged around the time of independence in 1905, when the country was seeking a distinctive national identity. Today, troupes of *leikarringer* (folk dancers) practise all over the country and compete in *kappleiker* (dance competitions) which attract large audiences. These festivities are increasingly accompanied by traditional instruments such as the unique Hardanger fiddle, which derives its distinctive sound from four or five sympathetic strings stretched out beneath the usual four strings.

Storytelling is another centuries-old tradition, and trolls figure prominently in Norwegian folklore. Although they're best known in the outside world as habitual harassers of billy goats, in Norway they form the basis for the custom of fireside storytelling that historically helped to pass the dark winter months. These relatively antisocial folks were normally associated with mountainous areas, and while some were considered friendly, most were pesky and cosmetically-challenged creatures who lived underground beneath houses and barns and were a convenient target of blame for the average peasant's woes. Trolls live on in Norway's place names, as mascots, as carved figurines and in scores of folk tales.

Dos & Don'ts

Most Norwegians are straightforward and easy-going, with few customs that differ from those of other Europeans, or of North Americans or Australasians. The traditional handshake is used liberally in both business and social circles when greeting friends or meeting strangers. In the latter case, customary introductions will include your full name and perhaps even profession. A ubiquitous greeting uttered constantly in Norway, is *Vær så god* (pronounced roughly 'var sho GOOT'), which carries all sorts of expressions of goodwill: 'Hello', 'Greetings', 'Goodbye', 'Welcome', 'Pleased to meet you', 'I'm happy to serve you', 'Thanks', 'You're welcome,' and a host of other things. There's no equivalent in English, but it roughly approximates the all-purpose *bitte* in German or *aloha* in Hawaiian.

If you're a guest in a Norwegian home, be sure to remove your shoes before entering the living area. It's customary to present your host with a small gift of sweets or flowers and avoid sipping your drink before he or she makes the toast, *Skål*, which you should answer in return. This traditional ritual is most frequently accompanied by direct eye contact with your host, which symbolises respect and the absence of guile.

RELIGION
Christianity

The first Irish monks arrived at Selje and established a monastery around the year 700. Olav Tryggvason is credited with the introduction of Catholic Christianity to Norway around the turn of the last millennium, and Olav Haraldsson became the country's first saint, but modern Norwegian religion has been most influenced by the German reformer Martin Luther, who viewed the Scriptures as the sole authority of God and advocated that only by grace can humankind be saved from its savage nature. His doctrines were adopted in Norway in 1537.

Today, more than 90% of Norwegians belong to the Church of Norway, which is the national denomination of Protestant Evangelical Lutheranism. The Norwegian constitution states: 'All inhabitants of the Realm shall have the right to free exercise of their religion. The Evangelical-Lutheran religion shall remain the official religion of the State.

Revival of the Ancient Ásatrú

Before Christianity was adopted in Norway as the official state religion, most Scandinavian peoples worshipped a pantheon of Norse gods whose strength, courage and typically reckless demeanour would have been the envy of any good Viking. Nowadays, this ancient religion has been reborn in the form of the nature-based religion known as Ásatrú. It first re-surfaced in Iceland and has now spread back to the Scandinavian mainland, as well as continental Europe, North America and Australia.

Ásatrú, which means 'faith in the Æsir', the gods of pre-Christian Scandinavia, has its origins in the ancient religions of most Germanic peoples – Goths, Germans, Dutch, Anglo-Saxons, etc – and also appears as far away as India, as described in the *Rig Veda*. The medieval Icelandic text, the *Galdrabók*, reveals that people were calling upon the Æsir long after Christianity was adopted by most Germanic peoples. As late as the 1800s, the Sami people often venerated the god Þór, to whom they'd been introduced by their Viking neighbours during the pre-Christian era.

Modern Ásatrú, which is open to anyone, regardless of race, ethnic origin or sexual orientation, was organised in the mid-1970s, almost simultaneously in Iceland, the UK and the USA.

The main gods and goddesses of Ásatrú, which are all considered friendly, practicable, dependable and approachable, include Þór, the god of thunder and friend of the common folk; Oðinn (or Allfather), the chief god, poet and wandering wizard; Tyr, the god of war and justice; Ingvi Freyr, the god of peace, fertility and nature (British images of the 'Green Man' are likely linked to Freyr); Baldur, the 'bleeding god'; Heimdall, the Watchman of Ásgard; Frigga, wife of Oðinn and mother of all the gods and humanity; Freya, the goddess of fertility, love, magic and war; Idunna, the goddess of renewal; Hela, who rules over the place between death and rebirth or reincarnation; and Nerthus, the Mother Earth goddess, who is mentioned in Tacitus' *Germania*. Followers of Ásatrú also revere the spirits of nature (*landvættir*) and various guardian spirits, such as the Disir and Álfar (elves).

The two main rituals in Ásatrú are *blót* or 'sacrifice' and *sumbel*, the 'toast'. While scholars debate whether the former is derived from *blóð*, or 'blood', modern Ásatrú followers sacrifice mead (honey-wine), beer or cider. The liquid is consecrated to the god or goddess being honoured, and drinking a portion of it signifies communion with that particular deity. The rest is poured out as a libation. The sumbel, a ritualised toasting to the gods, is made in three rounds. The first goes to the god Oðinn, who won the mead of poetry from the Giant Suttung. It's also wise to pour a few drops for Loki, the trickster, to ward off nasty surprises. The second round is for the ancestors and honourable dead, and the third round is open to whomever one wishes to honour.

Magical work is a part of the spiritual life of many practitioners of Ásatrú. Magic involves working with natural but unseen forces, including those embodied in the runes, the early Germanic alphabet, as well as the *galdra* (spellcraft) and *seiðr* (shamanism). Magic can help foresee the probable course of events, effect healing and assist people in their endeavours, but there is no substitute for more down-to-earth methods.

While devoid of rigid dogma, Ásatrú is by no means amoral. It is founded on the Nine Noble Virtues: courage, truth, honour, loyalty, hospitality, industriousness, perseverance, self-discipline and self-reliance. From these, individuals can decide upon the appropriate course of action in any situation and honour themselves, their families, their communities and their gods by striving to do what is right. The gods organised the universe from chaotic material (represented by the body of the dead giant Ymir). The remaining chaos allows for a random factor, which helps the universe in its evolution. Not even the gods are all-powerful, so perfection is neither required nor respected.

If you're interested in further information on Ásatrú, check out The Troth (asatru.knotwork .com/troth), c/o Diana L Paxson, PO Box 472, Berkeley, CA 94701, USA.

Reverend Patrick Jörðsvin Buck

The inhabitants professing it are bound to bring up their children in the same.'

Officially, the King of Norway also serves as the head of the Church and has the final say in all controversial decisions. This power was dramatically exercised in 1961 when King Olav V appointed the country's first woman priest and again in 1993 when King Harald V sanctioned the first female bishop. Even more controversial was the occasion in the 1970s when a bishop and quite a few priests quit after the Storting, with royal sanction, passed a liberal abortion law. A good proportion of the populace scarcely noticed the issue, but a few more pious parishioners decided that the Church was Christian in name more than practice and withdrew.

While the average Norwegian attends church about twice a year and the organisation funds missions around the world, as many as 5000 Norwegians leave the official church annually, most of them advocating a separation of Church and State.

Other religious groups represented in Norway include several Christian denominations: the Humanist & Ethical Union with over 50,000 members, some 45,000 Pentecostals and 30,000 Roman Catholics, the Lutheran Free Church with 20,000 adherents, 15,000 Jehovah's Witnesses, 15,000 Methodists, 6400 Seventh-Day Adventists and 1500 Anglicans. The country also has approximately 30,000 Muslims and over 1000 Jews.

Sami

Historically, the Sami religious traditions were characterised mainly by a relationship to nature and its inherent god-like archetypes. In sites of special power, particularly at prominent rock formations, people made offerings to their gods and ancestors to ensure success in hunting or other endeavours. Intervention and healing were effected by shamanic specialists, who used drums and small figures to launch themselves onto out-of-body journeys to the ends of the earth in search of answers. Interestingly, as with nearly all indigenous peoples in the north-

ern hemisphere, the bear, as the most powerful creature in nature, was considered a sacred animal.

Historically, another crucial element in the religious tradition was the singing of the *joik* (also spelt *yoik*), or 'song of the plains'. Each person had his or her own melody or song which conveyed not their personality or experiences, but rather their spiritual essence. So powerful and significant was this personal mantra that the early Christian missionaries considered it a threat to their efforts and banned it as sinful.

Although most modern Sami profess Christianity, elements of the old religion have recently made a limited comeback.

LANGUAGE
Norwegian

Norway has two official languages – Bokmål and Nynorsk – which are quite similar and are spoken or understood by all Norwegians.

Bokmål (BM), literally 'book-language' (also known as Riksmål, the 'national language') is the modern urbanites' version of the language of the former Danish rulers. As the predominant language in Norwegian cities, it's used by over 80% of the population. It's also the main language of instruction for most school children and the predominant language of the media.

Nynorsk (NN), or 'New Norwegian' (as opposed to Old Norwegian, the language used prior to Danish rule) predominates in the Western Fjords and parts of central Norway; it also serves as a *lingua franca* (common language) in those regions which may have one or more dialects. Prior to WWII, Nynorsk was the first language of nearly one-third of all Norwegian school children; as a result of growing urbanisation this figure has been reduced to about 15% today.

Perhaps the most striking oddity of Norway's linguistic dichotomy is that many words and place names have two or more authorised spellings. Today, Nynorsk is the official administrative language in the counties of Møre og Romsdal, Sogn og Fjordane, Hordaland and Telemark. Inter-

estingly, the national government has de-
creed that a certain percentage of television
subtitles be translated into Nynorsk, a practice which displeases the majority of Bokmål speakers.

Fortunately for most visitors, English is
also widely spoken in Norway, even in rural
areas. However, it's still a good idea to learn
a few Norwegian phrases to help you establish
contact with people – and if you're having obvious trouble with your Norwegian, most
people will be happy to switch to English.

For more information and a list of useful
Norwegian words and phrases see the Language chapter at the back of this book. For
a more comprehensive guide to the language get a copy of Lonely Planet's *Scandinavian Europe phrasebook*. There are
also a number of different Norwegian language course books available internationally, most with audio cassettes.

If you're interested in learning Bokmål,
the two best Norwegian books are *Ny i
Norge* and *Bo i Norge*; both are available
locally.

Sami

In northern Norway, a good percentage of the
population speaks Sami, a language of the
Finno-Ugric group. It's related to Samoyed
(among other northern Russian ethnic dialects), Finnish, Estonian and Hungarian.

Sami is spoken by around 20,000 people
in Norway (there are also Sami speakers in
Finland, Sweden and Russia). Although
most of them can also communicate in Norwegian (and some even speak English), visitors who know even a few words of the
local language will be able to access this
unique culture more readily.

Three distinct Sami dialects exist in Norway – the Fell (also called Eastern or Northern) Sami, Central Sami and South Sami –
but a total of 10 different dialects are used
within the Sàpmi region: Ume, Pite, Lule,
Inari, Skolt, Kildin and Ter (see the Sami
Cultural Area & Dialects map on page 40).
Fell Sami is considered the standard Sami
language.

For a few useful Sami greetings see the
Language chapter at the back of this book.

Facts for the Visitor

THE BEST & WORST

For most visitors, any list of Norwegian highlights is topped by the clean air and water; the tidiness of the towns; the calm and friendly Norwegians; and of course the magnificent wilderness, which is always readily accessible – even from central Oslo! The following list (in no particular order) includes some of Norway's finest sites and destinations but it is in no way complete. This is one country without a single dull landscape; every corner of it is beautiful and interesting in some way!

The Top 10

The fjords (see all chapters except Central Norway) – Nothing typifies Norway more than its fjords, which are the top attraction for visitors. In the popular Western and South-Western Fjords regions, Geirangerfjord has perhaps the most spectacular waterfalls and Fjærland is known for its valley glaciers. Nærøyfjord (an arm of Sognefjord) is the narrowest and perhaps most imposing, while Lysefjord, near Stavanger, is often regarded as the most beautiful and unusual. Many of the grand and imposing fjords of Arctic Norway dwarf anything in the south and present an entirely different dimension. While all the fjords are scenic from sea level, even more dramatic are the views from the surrounding peaks; the best vantage points are accessed via walking tracks leading up from nearly every fjord-side village and town.

The Oslo-Bergen railway (Central Norway, Bergen & the South-Western Fjords, The Western Fjords) – The 470km route between Oslo and Bergen is one of the world's finest train journeys, passing between snowy peaks and over the bleak Hardangervidda plateau. Don't miss the side trip on the Flåm line, which hairpins its way down the Flåm valley to Aurlandsfjord, stopping midway at the thundering Kjosfossen waterfall.

Røros (Central Norway) – This well preserved historic copper-mining town presents some wonderful historic architecture, superb hiking and readily accessible history.

Bergen (Bergen & the South-Western Fjords) – This colourful and historic town, is Norway's most visited and best loved town.

Vigeland Park (Oslo) – Although many Norwegians are mystified by its attraction for foreigners, few visitors fail to be impressed by Vigeland Park's amazing sculpture garden, created by Gustav Vigeland, one of Norway's best known artists. (Other highly worthwhile Oslo attractions include the Norsk Folkemuseum, Nasjonalgalleriet and Vikingskipshuset.)

Romadalen & the Trollstigen (The Western Fjords) – The Romadalen valley and the hairpin route up the Trollstigen pass present some of Norway's most dramatic vertical walls and fjord views.

Stave churches – Be sure to visit several of Norway's 31 medieval stave churches. The best known and most photographed are at Borgund (The Western Fjords), Heddal (Southern Norway) and Urnes (The Western Fjords).

Finnmarksvidda (The Far North) – The vast forested and lake-studded expanses of Finnmarksvidda are like no other part of Norway, and are the homeland of the indigenous Sami people.

Lofoten (Nordland) – These rugged islands are Norway's premier fishing and whaling ground but they also feature the most dramatic mountain scenery in the country. Don't miss the Viking Museum at Borg or the spectacular peaks of Moskenesøy.

Svalbard (Svalbard & Jan Mayen) – With its walruses, polar bears, whales and icy landscapes, Norway's bit of the high Arctic is the country's ultimate adventure destination.

The Bottom 10

Although Norway offers an abundance of spectacular landscapes and experiences, there are also some recurring annoyances, most of which relate to the country's lofty prices. Here's where I make all sorts of enemies, at least outwardly, but you'd be surprised how many Norwegians silently agree with these assessments!

The price of a beer – This averages Nkr47 for 500ml. While punitive alcohol taxes ostensibly discourage its consumption, they mostly succeed in stoking government coffers, impoverishing local drinkers, frustrating foreign visitors and inspiring risky home-brewing.

A peripheral problem is the price of the national 'upper' drug, coffee, and the fact that they charge for refills!

Parking rates and regulations – These punish anyone who can afford a car and conspire to stifle even the most inspired attempts at creative parking. While it isn't impossible to get around this, you'll have to be especially tuned in to find the one or two spots in each town that have been overlooked!

Bottlenecks – Vehicle ferries allow typically sluggish trucks, buses and caravans off the boat first, holding up cars and other vehicles, which are typically faster. At times you'll spend hours overtaking the resulting highway constipation. The worst I've encountered are the Skarberget-Bognes ferry in Nordland and the Brimnes-Bruravik ferry on Hardangerfjord.

Heating – Even in summer, most homes and businesses are heated to temperatures that would seem uncomfortable even in the tropics.

Fees – Tourists pay admission to churches, even those that are active. This is extremely unpopular with pious citizens of most other countries.

Tunnels – Whenever the view gets truly spectacular, the road or railway dives into a tunnel. If you want to see the best of Norwegian scenery, plan on a few good stiff climbs on foot!

Hidden charges – Visitors must pay relatively high admission charges to museums and sites of interest, and still have to buy brochures and pamphlets to make sense of what they're seeing. That turns an admission fee of Nkr30 into a de facto fee of Nkr75 or more.

Speed limit – The lethargy-inspiring national speed limit of 80km/h tends to turn many compliant drivers into tranced-out zombies – no joking! While it's wise to avoid on-the-spot fines of Nkr700 to Nkr5000 (or more!) by observing the rules, you're also advised to steer clear of anyone who appears to be falling asleep at the wheel.

Caravans – Some camping grounds, especially in the far south, are often chock-a-block with perman-ently moored caravans, forcing tent campers to squeeze in between them. At nearly all camping grounds, patrons who pay extra for cabins must fork over even more for anything that would require the proprietors to spend a krone, including linen, hot water and cleaning services! Any establishment that departs from this practice and offers value for money is commended in this book.

Tolls – Although Norwegian petrol prices are among the world's highest (Nkr7 to Nkr10/L, at least 90% of which is road tax), drivers still pay high tolls to use vehicle ferries, bridges and tunnels. That's not to mention the charges levied on drivers every time they enter Oslo, Bergen, Kristiansand, Trondheim and other towns. This wouldn't be such an annoyance if public transport were more affordable but, as things are, apart from hitching, there's no inexpensive way of getting around in Norway.

SUGGESTED ITINERARIES

Depending on your length of stay, you might like to consider the following suggestions:

Two days
> From Oslo, take the 'Norway in a Nutshell' tour that includes a rail trip to Flåm and then a combination of boat and bus to Bergen. After a day in Bergen, catch an overnight train back to Oslo.

One week
> Spend two days in Oslo, two days in Bergen and take a three-day jaunt through the Western Fjords, including Fjærland and Geiranger. Alternatively, fly straight to Svalbard and take a cruise up the west coast of Spitsbergen.

Two weeks
> As above, plus continue northward through Åndalsnes, Trondheim and Lofoten.

One month
> As above, plus hop on the northbound Hurtigruten coastal steamer in Lofoten and break your trip at Tromsø, Nordkapp and Kirkenes.

Two months
> Explore the country thoroughly and spend some time skiing or hiking around Jotunheimen, Hardangervidda or the far north. Follow the coastal route north through Nordland, make stops in Tromsø, Alta and Finnmarksvidda (Kautokeino and/or Karasjok) and, if possible, include a flight to Longyearbyen in Svalbard and take a cruise up the west coast of Spitsbergen.

PLANNING

Some say that Norway is so well developed you don't have to plan a thing before your trip since anything can be arranged on the spot. This is fine if you've decided to blow the massive inheritance sitting in your bank account, but if your finances are more modest, prior knowledge and careful planning can make your hard-earned travel budget stretch further. You'll also want to make sure that the things you plan to see and do will be possible at the particular time of year when you'll be travelling.

When to Go

Although Norway covers the same latitude range as Alaska (and much farther north when you include Svalbard), most of the country enjoys a surprisingly temperate climate. For this you can thank the Gulf Stream, which flows north along the coast. In Bergen the average monthly temperature in winter never drops below 0°C and in Vardø, in the far north, the average December temperature is only -4°C. In general, the mountainous inland areas experience warmer summers and colder winters than the typically milder coastal areas, and temperatures over 30°C in summer and lower than -30°C in winter aren't uncommon.

Norway is at its best and brightest from May to September. Late May is particularly pleasant – flowers are blooming and fruit trees blossoming, daylight hours are growing longer and most hostels and tourist sites are open but uncrowded. North of the Arctic Circle, the true midnight sun is visible at least one day a year, and at Nordkapp it stays out from 13 May to 29 July. In Lofoten, it's out from 28 May to 14 July, but nowhere in the country – even the far south – experiences true darkness between late May and late July.

In addition to climatic factors, visitors should also consider the tourist season, which coincides with European school holidays and runs roughly from mid-June to mid-August. During this period, public transport runs relatively frequently; tourist offices, hostels, summer hotels and tourist sites are open their longest hours; and most upmarket hotels offer better value summer rates. There's also a 'shoulder' season, running from mid-May to mid-June and mid-August to early September, when these places are open shorter hours. At other times of year, public transport runs infrequently; most hostels and camping grounds are closed; and tourist sites, museums and tourist offices are open only very limited hours, if at all. Unless you're an avid skier or hope to glimpse the aurora borealis, Norway's cold dark winters can be trying for visitors.

What Kind of Trip

If you decide to travel with others, bear in mind that travel can strain relationships as few other experiences can. This can be minimised by either pre-planning a rigid itinerary or agreeing to remain flexible about everything. When planning your itinerary, it's wise to consider the costs of moving around in Norway. Unless you have an unlimited rail pass and its validity is ticking away, you may want to just hole up for awhile in a place you like and spend some time getting to know it well, observing the local way of life and discovering lesser known sites.

The Getting There & Away chapter has information on organised tours. The young, the elderly and the inexperienced tend to appreciate such tours because they minimise hassles and uncertainties. Longer tours, however, can become experiments in social cohesion and friction can develop. Though often ridiculed, the mad dash that crams an entire country into a one or two-week holiday does have its merits. If you've never visited Norway before, you won't know which areas you'll like, and a quick 'scouting tour' will provide an overview. If you're short of time, it's probably worth picking up an unlimited rail pass that will allow you to sample the best of the country with the least possible expense.

Maps

The best road maps for drivers are the Cappelens series, which are sold in Norwegian bookshops. The 1:325,000 series divides the country into five sections: *No1 Sør Norge-sør*, *No2 Sør Norge-nord*, *No3 Møre og Trøndelag*, *No4 Nordland* and *No5 Troms og Finnmark*. Another excellent Cappelens sheet is the 1:700,000 *No20 Nordkalotten*, which covers all of northern Scandinavia, including north-western Russia.

For all travellers, Nortrabooks has produced the colourful and popular *Bilkart over Norge*. This detailed map includes useful topographic shading and depicts the entire country on one sheet at a scale of 1:1,000,000.

Statens Kartverk, the national mapping agency, covers the country in 21 sheets at a scale of 1:250,000, and also produces hiking maps at a scale of 1:50,000. Most local tourist offices distribute free town plans and hikers can pick up topographic sheets at any DNT office (see Hiking under Activities).

In Norway, maps are available in bookshops, rural general stores, DNT offices and most larger tourist offices.

In the UK, good sources of maps include The Map Shop (☎ 01684-593146, fax 01684-594559), 15 High St, Upton-upon-Severn, Worcs, WR8 0HJ; and Stanfords (☎ 0171-836 1321, fax 0171-836 0189, after April 2000 ☎ 020-7836 1321, fax 020-7836 0189), 12-14 Long Acre, London WC2E 9LP. Either can provide detailed listings of available maps and offer mail-order services.

In the US, contact Maplink (☎ 805-965 4402), 25 E Mason Street, Santa Barbara, CA 93101. In Canada, try Worldwide Books & Maps (☎ 416-363 0719), 1247 Granville Street, Vancouver, BC V62 1G3.

In Australia, there's Map Land (☎/fax 03-9670 4383), 372 Little Bourke St, Melbourne 3000; the Melbourne Map Centre (☎ 03-9569 5472), 740 Waverley Road, Chadstone 3148; or the Travel Bookshop (☎ 02-9241 3554), 20 Bridge St, Sydney 2000.

What to Bring

Norwegians normally dress quite casually (although trendily – especially when it comes to shoes!), so travellers need not pack their finest clothes. However, for cultural events and nights out, it's wise to carry an alternative to jeans and trainers (sneakers).

If you're headed for the great outdoors, remember that the weather can change instantly. You'll be happiest with layers of clothing that can be added or removed as necessary, and even in summer you won't regret having a jacket or jersey (sweater) handy, or at least an anorak (windbreaker), especially for visits to the high country or for appreciating that 'sea breeze' on fjord cruises and ferries. Good walking shoes are requisite and hikers will need a strong pair of hiking boots, as well as a mountain stove

for longer hikes. Budget travellers shouldn't be without a tent and a warm sleeping bag.

For shorter visits, you may also want to cut your food costs by bringing along lightweight food items such as trail mix, peanut butter, Marmite, instant coffee and tea bags. Those staying in hostels will save money by bringing their own sleeping sheets, as linen hire adds Nkr30 to Nkr40 per stay.

TOURIST OFFICES
Local Tourist Offices

Tourist offices in Norway play an important role for visitors and serve as a one-stop clearing house for information and bookings for accommodation and activities. Nearly every city and town – even the tiniest places – has its own tourist office and it's most often conveniently located near the train station, docks or town centre. Many offices run their own excursions or have close ties with local companies who fill that gap. Offices in smaller towns may be open only during peak summer months, while in cities they're open year-round but with shorter hours in the off-season.

The Norges Informasjonssenter tourist office (☎ 22 83 00 50, fax 22 83 81 50, www.oslopro.no), Vestbaneplassen 1, N-0250 Oslo, offers nationwide tourist information. For general brochures and books on travel in Norway, contact the Norwegian Tourist Board (NORTRA; ☎ 22 92 52 00, fax 22 56 05 05, webmaster@nortra.no, www.tourist .no), PO Box 2893, Solli, Drammensveien, N-0239 Oslo.

Tourist Offices Abroad

Australia & New Zealand
(☎ 02-6273 3444, fax 02-6273 3669)
Royal Norwegian Embassy, 17 Hunter St, Yarralumla, ACT 2600
France
(☎ 01 47 45 14 90, fax 01 46 41 07 21)
Office National du Tourisme de Norvège, 88 Avenue Charle de Gaulle, Neuilly-sur-Seine, F-792200 Paris
Germany
(☎ 040-2271 0810, fax 040-2271 0815)
Norwegisches Fremdenverkehrsamt, Mundsburger Damm 45, D-22087 Hamburg

Japan
(☎ 3-3580 5030, fax 3-3503 4457)
Scandinavian Tourist Board, Sanno Grand
Building 913, 2-14-2, Nagata-cho Chiyoda-ku,
Tokyo 100-0014
Netherlands
(☎ 20-671 2854, fax 20-679 8886)
Noors Verkeersbureau, Saxen Weimarlaan 58,
NL-1075 CE Amsterdam
UK & Ireland
(☎ 0171-839 6255, ski hotline 0171-321 0666,
fax 0171-839 6014, after April 2000
☎ 020-7839 6255, ski hotline 020-7321 0666,
fax 020-7839 6014)
Norwegian Tourist Board, Charles House, 5
Lower Regent St, London SW1Y 4LR
USA & Canada
(☎ 212-421 7333, fax 212-752 1456)
Norwegian Tourist Board, 825 Third Ave, New
York, NY 10022

VISAS & DOCUMENTS
Passport
Your most important travel document is
your passport, which must be valid at least
for the intended length of your trip. Some
countries insist that your passport remain
valid for a specified minimum period (usually three months but often up to six
months) after your intended departure date.
If it's about to expire, renew it before you
go, as it can be time consuming to do so on
the road. On the trip, carry your passport at
all times and guard it carefully.

Visas
Citizens of Denmark, Finland, Iceland and
Sweden may enter Norway freely without a
passport. Citizens of the USA, Canada, the
UK, Ireland, Australia and New Zealand
need a valid passport to visit Norway, but
do not need a visa for stays of less than
three months. The same is true for EU and
EEA countries, most of Latin America and
most Commonwealth countries (except
South Africa and several other African and
Pacific countries).

Travel Insurance
You should seriously consider taking out
travel insurance that covers not only medical expenses and luggage theft or loss but

also cancellation or delays in your travel
arrangements (due to illness, ticket loss, industrial action etc). It's a good idea to buy
insurance as early as possible, as late purchase may preclude coverage of industrial
action that may have been in force before
you bought the policy. A policy to cover
theft, personal liability, loss and medical
problems is strongly recommended and
often a standard insurer will offer better
deals than companies selling only travel insurance. Note that some policies specifically exclude 'dangerous activities' such as
motorcycling, skiing, mountaineering,
scuba diving or even hiking. Make sure the
policy covers ambulances and an emergency flight home.

Paying for airline tickets with a credit
card often provides limited travel accident
insurance, and you may be able to reclaim
the payment if the operator doesn't deliver.
In the UK, for instance, institutions issuing
credit cards are required by law to reim-
burse consumers if a company goes into li-
quidation and the amount in contention is
more than UK£100. A policy that pays doctors or hospitals directly may be preferable
to one where you pay on the spot and claim
later. If you have to claim later, make sure
you keep all documentation.

In Norway, EU citizens may be required
to pay a service fee for emergency medical
treatment, but presentation of an E111 form
will certainly expedite matters and minimise
paperwork. Inquire about these at your national health service or travel agent well in
advance; you may be able to pick one up
from a local post office. Travel insurance is
still advisable, however, as long as it allows
treatment flexibility and will also cover ambulance and repatriation costs.

Driving Licence & Permits
Short-term visitors may hire a car with only
their home country's driving licence. Also
ask your automobile association for a Letter of Introduction (*Lettre de Recommendation*) that entitles you to services offered by
affiliated organisations in Norway, usually
free of charge. These services may include

touring maps and information, help with breakdowns, technical and legal advice etc. See the Getting Around chapter for more details on driving your own vehicle.

Hostel & Student Cards

The most useful student card is the International Student Identity Card (ISIC), a plastic ID-style card with your photograph. It can provide discounts on many forms of transport (including airlines, international ferries and local public transport), reduced or free admission to museums and sights and cheap meals in some student restaurants – a worthwhile way of cutting costs. Children under 12 and seniors normally also receive the same discounts. In addition, a Hostelling International (IYHF) card will save on hostel rates.

Seniors' Cards

Senior (*honnør*) discounts are the same as those for students and are normally available to those 67 years of age and over for admission to museums, public pools, transport etc. You don't require a special card, but those who look particularly youthful may need proof of their age to qualify, as the ever-proper Norwegian ticket-sellers won't believe you're a day over 39.

Photocopies

While the risk of theft in Norway is minimal, it's wise to carry photocopies of the first few pages of your passport and other essential documents, such as proof of insurance and travellers cheque purchase slips.

EMBASSIES & CONSULATES
Norwegian Embassies & Consulates

Australia
    (☎ 02-6273 3444, fax 02-6273 3669)
    17 Hunter St, Yarralumla 2600, ACT
Canada
    (☎ 613-238 6571, fax 613-238 2765)
    Royal Bank Centre, 90 Sparks St, Suite 532,
    Ottawa, Ontario K1P 5B4
Denmark
    (☎ 33 14 01 24, fax 33 14 06 24)
    Amaliegade 39, DK-1256 Copenhagen K

Finland
    (☎ 09-171234, fax 09-657807)
    Rehbindervägen 17, SF-00150
    Helsinki/ Helsingfors
France
    (☎ 01 53 67 04 00, fax 01 53 67 04 40)
    28 Rue Bayard, 75008 Paris
Germany
    (☎ 0228-819 970, fax 0228-373 498)
    Mittelstrasse 43, D-53175 Bonn
Ireland
    (☎ 1-662 1800, fax 1-662 1890)
    34 Molesworth St, Dublin 2
Japan
    (☎ 3-3440 2611, fax 3-3440 2620)
    5-12-2 Minami Azabu, Minato-ku,
    Tokyo 106-0047
Netherlands
    (☎ 10-414 4488)
    Willemskade 12, NL-3016 DK Rotterdam
    (☎ 70-311 7611)
    Prinsessegracht 6a, NL-2514 AN Den Haag
New Zealand
    (☎ 04-471 2503)
    61 Molesworth St, Wellington
Russia
    (☎ 095-956 2005)
    Ulitsa Povarskaya 7, RU-00940 Moscow
    (☎ 51295-10037, fax 51295-10044)
    Ulitsa Sofji Perovskoj 5, RU-183038 Murmansk
Sweden
    (☎ 08-665 6340, fax 08-782 9899)
    Strandvägen 113, Stockholm
UK
    (☎ 0171-591 5500, fax 0171-245 6993,
    from April 2000 ☎ 020-7591 5500,
    fax 020-7245 6993)
    25 Belgrave Square, London SW1X 8QD
USA
    (☎ 202-333 6000, fax 202-337 0870)
    2720 34th St NW, Washington DC 20008

Embassies & Consulates in Norway

Australia
    (☎ 22 41 44 33, fax 22 42 26 83)
    Jernbanetorget 2, N-0106 Oslo
Canada
    (☎ 22 46 69 55)
    Wergelandsveien 7, N-0244 Oslo
Denmark
    (☎ 22 54 08 00, fax 22 55 46 34)
    Olav Kyrres gate 7, N-0244 Oslo
Finland
    (☎ 22 43 04 00, fax 22 43 06 29)
    Thomas Heftyes gate 1, N-0244 Oslo

France
  (☎ 22 44 18 20, fax 22 56 32 21)
  Drammensveien 69, N-0244 Oslo
Germany
  (☎ 22 55 20 10, fax 22 44 76 72)
  Oscars gate 45, N-0244 Oslo
Ireland
  (☎ 22 12 20 00, fax 22 55 08 10)
  Drammensveien 126A, N-0212 Oslo
Japan
  (☎ 22 55 10 11)
  Parkveien 33B, N-0244 Oslo
Netherlands
  (☎ 22 60 21 93)
  Oscars gate 29, N-0244 Oslo
New Zealand
  (☎ 66 84 95 30, fax 66 84 89 09)
  Billingstadsletta 19B, PO Box 113,
  N-1361 Billingstad, Asker
Russia
  (☎ 22 60 30 35, fax 22 56 58 78)
  Oscarsgata 16, N-0352 Oslo
Sweden
  (☎ 22 44 35 11, fax 22 55 15 96)
  Nobelsgata 16A, N-0268 Oslo
UK
  (☎ 22 55 24 00)
  Thomas Heftyes gate 8, N-0244 Oslo
USA
  (☎ 22 44 85 50)
  Drammensveien 18, N-0244 Oslo

CUSTOMS

Alcohol is extremely expensive in Norway, so it's probably worth importing your duty-free allotment: 1L of spirits and 1L of wine (or 2L of wine), plus 2L of beer. Even if you don't drink, it will normally be a welcome gift for Norwegian friends. European (EEA)/non-European residents may also import 200/400 cigarettes duty-free.

MONEY
Currency

The Norwegian krone is most often represented as Nkr (preceding the number) in northern Europe (and in this book), and NOK (preceding the number) in international money markets, but within Norway, it's often simply kr (following the amount). One Norwegian krone (Nkr) equals 100 øre. Coins come in denominations of 50 øre and Nkr1, 5, 10 and 20, and notes can be worth Nkr50, 100, 200, 500 and 1000.

Exchange Rates

The following currencies convert at these approximate rates:

country	unit		krone
Australia	A$1	=	Nkr4.88
Canada	C$1	=	Nkr5.12
Denmark	Dkr1	=	Nkr1.15
euro	€1	=	Nkr8.56
Finland	1 mk	=	Nkr1.44
France	FF1	=	Nkr1.30
Germany	DM1	=	Nkr4.38
Ireland	IR£1	=	Nkr10.87
Japan	¥100	=	Nkr6.57
Netherlands	f1	=	Nkr3.88
New Zealand	NZ$1	=	Nkr4.10
Russia	R1	=	Nkr0.33
Sweden	Skr1	=	Nkr0.95
UK	UK£1	=	Nkr12.68
USA	US$1	=	Nkr7.79

Exchanging Money

Travellers Cheques Post offices and banks exchange major foreign currencies and accept all brands of travellers cheques, which command a better exchange rate than cash by about 1%. Post offices offer the best exchange rates but charge a service fee of Nkr10 per travellers cheque or Nkr20 per cash transaction. Some banks, including Kreditkassen and Den Norske Bank, match those rates, but others charge a rather steep Nkr20 per travellers cheque (which means you're better off with higher denomination cheques).

ATMs Norwegian ATMs will allow you to access cash in your home account with an ATM card from your home bank. 'Mini-Banks' (the Norwegian name for ATMs) are found adjacent to many banks and around busy public places such as shopping centres. They accept major credit cards as well as Cirrus and/or Plus format bank cards.

Credit Cards Visa, Eurocard, MasterCard, American Express and Diners Club cards are widely accepted throughout Norway and generally you'll be better off using a credit card as you avoid the fees charged for changing cash or travellers cheques. Credit cards can be used to buy train tickets but are not accepted on domestic ferries apart from the coastal steamer.

If your card is lost or stolen in Norway, report it to the appropriate agency: American Express (☎ 80 03 32 44); Diners Club (☎ 22 83 06 91); Eurocard/MasterCard (☎ 80 03 02 50); and Visa (☎ 22 83 03 90).

Costs

Norway is expensive, and while you can avoid some of the sting by tightening your belt, you'll run through money very quickly, so it pays to plan your trip carefully. One thing to remember is that you must pay for practically everything from parking and coffee refills to using bridges, tunnels and public toilets. Museum admissions may not include parking outside and information leaflets are always sold separately. Drivers must even pay a toll to enter major cities!

If you only stay in camping grounds and prepare your own meals, you can squeak by on around Nkr175 per person per day. Staying in hostels that include breakfast (or eating breakfast at a bakery), having lunch at an inexpensive restaurant and picking up supermarket items for dinner, you can probably manage on Nkr275 per day. Staying at a 'cheap' hotel that includes a buffet breakfast, eating a snack for lunch and an evening meal at a moderately priced rest-aurant, you can expect to spend Nkr400 per person per day if you're doubling up and Nkr500 if you're travelling alone. This is still pretty bare-bones, however, and day trips, entertainment, alcohol, and even a couple of soft drinks will blow most careful budgets.

Once your daily needs are met, you need to add transport costs. With a rail pass and an itinerary that sticks to the rail lines – or hitching – this will be relatively inexpensive. However, adding bus or ferry travel, or trips to the far north (unless you're popping into Narvik from Sweden, this region is really off the rails), the expenses will mount quickly.

If you're content to hike and simply gaze at Norway's magnificent landscapes, sightseeing won't be a major expense, but otherwise, it must be part of your budget. In fact, Norway is one of only a few countries that charges admission to churches (drawing a fair measure of criticism, I might add). Fortunately, the tourist offices in Oslo, Bergen, Stavanger and Røros all sell one to three-day tourist cards including unlimited or discounted admission to most sites of interest, access to local transport, swimming pools, municipal parking and cultural programs. Students, seniors over 67 and children under 12 nearly always receive substantial discounts – sometimes as much as 50% – so it pays to have a student card (or proof of your age).

Tipping & Bargaining

Service charges and tips are included in restaurant bills and taxi fares, and no additional gratuity is expected, but there's no problem if you want to reward exceptional service with a tip. As for bargaining, it's as rare in Norway as bargains themselves. However, if you're spending lots of money at a tourist shop, you can reasonably expect some sort of high-volume discount.

Taxes & Refunds

The 20% MVA (the equivalent of Value-Added Tax in many countries or sales tax in the USA), locally known as MOMS, is normally included in marked prices for goods and services, including meals and accommodation. One exception is car hire, where quoted rates may or may not include MVA.

At shops marked 'Tax Free for Tourists', goods exceeding Nkr308 are eligible for an MVA refund, less a service charge, which works out to 10 to 17% of the purchase price. Ask the shop for a 'Tax-Free Shopping Cheque', which should be presented along with your purchases at your departure point from the country (ferry passengers normally collect their refund from the purser during limited hours once the boat has sailed).

POST & COMMUNICATIONS
Post
Norway has an efficient postal service and it's refreshingly no more expensive than any other in Europe. Postcards and letters weighing up to 20g cost Nkr3.80 within Norway, Nkr4.50 to other Nordic countries, Nkr5.50 to elsewhere in Europe and Nkr6 to the rest of the world. For sending larger parcels, the good value economy (semi-surface) rate will provide delivery anywhere in the world within a month. Poste restante services are available at all but a handful of Norwegian post offices.

In most cities and towns, post offices are open from 9 am to 5 pm weekdays and 10 am to 2 pm Saturday. You need not queue at most post offices; just take a number from the queuing machine and when it appears on the digital readout, go to the indicated window. If there are two buttons on the machine, the upper one is for normal postal services and the lower one for foreign exchange transactions.

Telephone
All Norwegian telephone numbers consist of eight digits and there are no regional area codes. Most pay phones accept Nkr1, Nkr5 and Nkr10 coins and will return unused coins but won't give change, so only insert the minimum amount (Nkr2 for local calls) to ensure a connection. For local calls, you'll get a 70% discount on the standard phone rates between 5 pm and 8 am on weekdays, and any time on weekends, and a 50% discount on other domestic calls. Directory assistance (☎ 180) is available throughout the country and costs Nkr8 per minute.

Card phones and coin phones are found at post offices, transport terminals, kiosks and other public places. Local phonecards (telekort) are sold in Nkr35, Nkr98 and Nkr210 denominations and work out a bit cheaper and infinitely more convenient than using coins. The cards can be purchased at post offices and Narvesen kiosks.

Lonely Planet's eKno Communication Card (see the insert at the back of this book) is aimed specifically at travellers and provides cheap international calls, a range of messaging services and free email – for local calls, you're usually better off with a local card. For further information, visit the eKno website at www.ekno.lonelyplanet.com.

To phone Norway from outside the country, preface the telephone number with the country code (47). If you're dialling an outside number from within Norway, preface the number with the international access code (00), followed by the country code, area code and number you're calling.

Fax
Faxes can be received and sent from most hotels for a commercially-minded charge, and telegrams may be sent by dialling ☎ 138. Alternatively, you can send or receive faxes at public telephone offices.

Email & Internet Access
Email and Internet services have taken off in Norway, and most tourism-oriented businesses now have an email address. However, outside of Oslo, there are still few places for travellers to access email or Internet services. Many public libraries now have computers with Internet access but in most cases there are queues of locals waiting to get online, resulting in long waits to check your email. Some larger hotels, especially the Rainbow chain, have credit-card accessed Internet computers in their lobbies that typically cost Nkr20 for six minutes.

If you'd like to set up a free Hotmail account, which provides email access worldwide, stop by the Use-It office in Oslo. For details on this and other Oslo services, see Information in the Oslo chapter. You'll find a partial list of Internet cafés around Norway and all of Europe at www.cyberiacafe.net/cyberia/guide/ccafe.htm.

If you're bringing a laptop and hope to access your home Internet or email accounts, you'll need a telephone adaptor. Both old and new telephone jacks are in use, so universal access will require the old and new adaptors, as well as a PBX adaptor (for use in hotels). A good source of information and plugs is Tele-Adapt (www.teleadapt.com), which has offices at the following locations:

TeleAdapt Ltd (☎ 0181-233 3000, fax 0181-233 3132, after April 2000 ☎ 020-8233 3000, fax 020-8233 3132, info@uk.teleadapt.com), The Technology Park, Colindeep Lane, London NW9 6TA, UK

TeleAdapt Inc (☎ 408-965 1400, fax 408-965 1414, info@us.teleadapt.com), 2151 O'Toole Ave, Suite H, San Jose CA 95131, USA

TeleAdapt Pty Ltd, (☎ 02-9433 8363, fax 02-9433 8369, info@au.teleadapt.com), Locked Bag 5340, Artarmon, Sydney NSW 2064, Australia

INTERNET RESOURCES

If you're looking for general travel information, you can't beat Lonely Planet's own website www.lonelyplanet.com, which is packed with info on destinations worldwide.

General and tourist information about Norway can be accessed on the Internet at www.norway.org. NORTRA, the Norwegian Tourist Board, has a particularly useful website at www.tourist.no. An excellent site for information on Oslo is www.hurra.no, which includes 'virtual sightseeing'.

The Norwegian Ministry of Foreign Affairs website, www.odin.dep.no, provides all sorts of general information and documentation, as well as daily news updates. For the English-language version, go to the bottom of the Norwegian intro page and click on the British flag (this also provides access to the German and French versions).

The Norwegian Yellow Pages has a helpful site at www.gulesider.no (info is available in English).

For a rundown of tourist offices around the world, try www.mbnet.mb.ca/lucas/travel. Pan-European rail info is detailed on www.raileurope.com and airline info is available on www.travelocity.com. If you're coming from the USA and want to bid on airline seats, call up www.priceline.com. You'll get the lowdown on the latest currency exchange rates on www.xe.net/currency/.

Other useful website addresses are provided throughout the text, where they're most relevant.

BOOKS
Lonely Planet

If you're planning a big trip around northern Europe, check out Lonely Planet's *Scandinavian & Baltic Europe*, which covers Sweden, Finland, Denmark, Iceland, the Faroe Islands, Estonia, Latvia, Lithuania, Kaliningrad (Russia) and St Petersburg, as well as Norway. Lonely Planet also offers separate books on *Denmark, Finland, Iceland, Greenland & the Faroe Islands* and *Estonia, Latvia & Lithuania*, as well as *St Petersburg* and *Russia, Ukraine & Belarus*. To help with communication throughout the region, pick up LP's *Scandinavian Europe phrasebook*, which includes sections on Norwegian, Swedish, Danish, Finnish and Icelandic.

Guidebooks

For drivers, Erling Welle-Strand has written the concise *Motoring in Norway* and the flashier *Adventure Roads in Norway*, both of which describe a number of the country's most scenic driving routes.

The same author has also written *Mountain Hiking in Norway*, which outlines wilderness trail information including hiking itineraries, sketch maps and details on trail huts. A better choice for avid hikers is probably *Norwegian Mountains on Foot* by the Norwegian Mountain Touring Association (DNT), which is the English edition of the Norwegian classic, *Til Fjells i Norge*. Another fine hiking book is *Walking in Norway* by Connie Roos. Avid climbers will want to pick up the excellent *Climbing in the Magic Islands*, by Ed Webster, which is a labour of love covering an exhaustive choice of climbing routes in the Lofoten Islands.

A handsome coffee-table production that describes some of Norway's finest attractions is *Highlights of Norway* by Gro Stangeland and Eva Valebrokk. This worthwhile edition is indeed 'Norway in a Nutshell' and includes all sorts of fascinating background information on sites you probably want to see. A concise overview of Lofoten and Vesterålen is provided in the colourful tourist book *Lofoten & Vesterålen – Mountain Kingdom in the Sea* by Leif Ryvarden.

If you're spending a while in Norway, you'll especially appreciate the cultural direction offered in *Culture Shock – Norway: A Guide to Customs & Etiquette* by Elizabeth Su-Dale.

Travel

The earliest 'intrepid English traveller' account of Norway is *Letters Written during a Short Residence in Sweden, Norway & Denmark*, by Mary Wollstonecraft (whose daughter Mary Shelley found fame by producing the monstrous bestseller, *Frankenstein*). It recounts several emotion-filled months in late 18th century Scandinavia. Another compilation of boreal experiences is provided in *Letters from High Latitudes* by Lord Dufferin, which details a mid-19th century sailing trip around Greenland, Iceland, Jan Mayen, Svalbard and mainland Norway, with extensive references to the more romantic aspects of Norwegian history.

Norway has also been a major player in polar exploration, and numerous expeditions have set off from Tromsø, Jan Mayen and Svalbard. Countless works have been written on this subject, including explorers' journals, exposés and histories of success and dashed dreams. An excellent treatment of one of Norway's most intrepid characters is intriguingly covered in *Nansen* by Roland Huntford. Thor Heyerdahl, the slightly quirky modern Norwegian explorer who has postulated ancient sea voyages between the old and new worlds and across the Pacific, is also well represented in print. His most prominent titles include *The Ra Expeditions*, *The Tigris Expedition*, *The Kon-Tiki Expedition* and *Fatu Hiva*.

For an ethereal and haunting treatment of the Arctic regions, which readily applies to Svalbard and includes references to the Sami culture, read Barry Lopez's classic, *Arctic Dreams*.

History & Politics

A Brief History of Norway by John Midgård covers Norwegian history from prehistoric to modern times. Midgård has also written *Norway & the Second World War*, an easily digestible account of the most tumultuous times in modern Norwegian history. Another concise treatment of Norwegian history (at least through its 1972 publication date) is found in the simply titled *Norway* by Ronald Popperwell. One of WWII's most diabolical characters is examined in the biography *Quisling: A Study in Treason* by Oddvar K Hoidal. One of the finest works on Norway's exotic Arctic wonderland is provided in *No Man's Land* by Martin Conway, which details the history of Svalbard from its discovery to the present day.

There are also a number of works on the Viking era, including two books entitled *The Vikings*, one by Else Roesdahl and the other by Johannes Brøndsted, as well as F Donald Logan's *The Vikings in History*. *The Viking World* by James Graham-Campbell traces the history of the Vikings by detailing excavated Viking sites and artefacts.

The country's leading cultural figures are revealed in a number of biographies, including *Edvard Munch* by JP Hodin; *Enigma – The Life of Knut Hamsun* by Robert Ferguson; *Ole Bull: Norway's Romantic Musician & Cosmopolitan Patriot* by Einar Haugen and Camilla Cai; *The Life of Ole Bull* by Mortimer Brewster Smith; *Gustav Vigeland – The Sculptor & His Works*, by Ragna Thus Stang; *Edvard Grieg: The Man & Artist* by Finn Benestad; and *Song of the Waterfall – The Story of Edvard & Nina Grieg* by Elisabeth Kyle.

Fiction & Literature

If you're interested in Norse mythology and folk tales, your best bets are *The Gods & Myths of Northern Europe* by HR Ellis Davidson and the colourful *Norwegian Folk Tales – from the collection of Peter Christen Asbjørnsen and Jørgen Moe*; the same authors have also produced two volumes entitled *East o' the Sun & West o' the Moon*; one includes 21 tales and the other, 59. The classic *Vinland Sagas*, translated by Magnus Magnusson and Hermann Palsson, contains the *Saga of Eric the Red* and the *Saga of the Greenlanders*, two classic medieval literary works that describe the Norse colonisation

Traditional Nordland fishing boats in the harbour at Å, Lofoten Islands

Not all Norwegians are blonde & beautiful...

'Polar Bear Crossing', Svalbard

Puffin paradise, coastal Norway

DEANNA SWANEY

Flying the flag

NED FRIARY

Fishy business, Lofoten Islands

DEANNA SWANEY

Mum, a polar bear took Dad

DEANNA SWANEY

A bloody long way from anywhere

NED FRIARY

Cod drying on racks, Reine, Lofoten Islands

of Greenland and earliest forays into North America. For a rundown on the modern Norwegian literary effort, see Literature in the Facts about Norway chapter.

NEWSPAPERS & MAGAZINES
Domestic newspapers, including the Oslo dailies *Aftenposten* and the tabloids *Dagbladet* and *Verdens Gang* (better known as just *VG*), are available nationwide, but they're published only in Norwegian. The same goes for Bergen's daily, *Bergens Tidende*. The *International Herald-Tribune*, London dailies, and English-language magazines such as *Time*, *Newsweek* and *The Economist* are sold at major transport terminals and at kiosks in larger towns.

RADIO & TV
Norway's national radio and television network, NRK, has historically struggled to remain informational rather than commercial, but competition from the commercial TV2 network has brought about a change in character and a good number of British and US television programs and films are now creeping in. Most TV broadcasts are in Norwegian, though US and British programs are presented in English with Norwegian subtitles. Hotels with cable TV often have CNN and English-language sports channels.

NRK Radio broadcasts the news in English at 9 am and 9 pm weekdays on 88.7 or 93 FM in Oslo and 89.1 FM in Bergen. The BBC World Service broadcasts on 9410 kHz.

PHOTOGRAPHY & VIDEO
Film & Equipment
Although print and slide film are readily available in major cities, prices are high. A 24-exposure roll of Kodacolor Gold 100 costs around Nkr55, plus Nkr120 to process. The best value by far is offered by the chain Japan Photo, which offers superb discounts on bulk orders. If you purchase videos in Norway, note that the usual system is PAL, which is incompatible with the North American NTSC system.

As you'd imagine, import duties make photographic equipment extremely expensive in Norway, and even second-hand equipment prices reflect the scarcity of inexpensive items. It's therefore wise to bring everything you need from elsewhere. If you have a camera problem, Oslo is by far the best place to have it repaired; they not only have the expertise, but also access to parts (which must be imported).

Technical Tips
Photographers worldwide sing the praises of the magical northern light, and the crystalline air combined with the long, red rays cast by a low sun create excellent effects on film. Add a bit of spectacular scenery and a few picturesque fishing villages and you have a photographic paradise. Due to the clear northern light and glare from water, ice and snow, photographers may want to use a UV filter or a skylight filter and a lens shade. In winter, you may want to polar oil your camera so the mechanism doesn't freeze up. In temperatures below around -20°C, electronic cameras may fail altogether.

Photographing People
Finding subjects and taking interesting 'people photos' are always a photographer's greatest challenge but, happily, most Norwegians enjoy being photographed and few are camera-shy. However, it's still a courtesy to ask permission before snapping away. This is especially important in the Sami areas, where you may encounter some camera sensitivity, as well as in villages where whaling is a mainstay, as people may be concerned that the photos will be used against them in environmental pieces.

TIME
Time in Norway is one hour ahead of GMT/UTC, the same as Sweden, Denmark and most of western Europe. When it's noon in Norway, it's 11 am in London, 1 pm in Finland, 6 am in New York and Toronto, 3 am in San Francisco, 9 pm in Sydney and 11 pm in Auckland. Between March and October, Norway observes daylight-savings time. Timetables and business hours are posted using the 24-hour clock.

ELECTRICITY

The electric current in Norway is generally 220 volts AC, at 50Hz. Passenger vessels crossing the North Sea and the Hurtigruten coastal steamers normally use 220 volts DC. On trains, sleeping cars may use either 110 and 220 volts AC, at 50 Hz. Continental two-pin plugs are used throughout the country.

WEIGHTS & MEASURES

Norway uses the metric system; to convert between metric and imperial units, see the table at the back of the book. At delicatessens, the price may be followed by per/hg; that is, per 100g. Fruit and other items are commonly sold by the piece (*stykke,* abbreviation *stk*). Another oddity is the frequent use of *mil* (mile) for distance, which is not 1.6km but rather a Norwegian nautical mile, which is between 10 and 11km.

LAUNDRY

Coin laundries *(myntvaskeri)* are rather expensive and surprisingly rare, though hostels and camping grounds often have coin-operated washers and dryers available to guests. You may want to bring a supply of laundry soap for hand-washing.

TOILETS

Toilets are western style and nearly every town has public facilities. However, at shopping malls, train stations and bus terminals you may have to pay Nkr1 to Nkr5.

HEALTH

Norway is a very healthy place and no special precautions are necessary when visiting. The biggest risks are likely to be viral infections in winter, sunburn and insect bites in summer, and foot blisters from too many happy days of hiking.

For a medical emergency dial ☎ 113; visit a local pharmacy or medical centre if you have a minor medical problem and can explain what it is. Hospital casualty wards will help if the problem is more serious. Nearly all health professionals in Norway speak English; tourist offices and hotels can make recommendations.

Medical Kit Check List

Following is a list of items you should consider including in your medical kit – consult your phamacist for brands available in your country.

☐ **Aspirin** or **paracetamol** (acetaminophen in the US) – for pain or fever.

☐ **Antihistamine** – for allergies, eg hay fever; to ease the itch from insect bites or stings; and to prevent motion sickness.

☐ **Antibiotics** – consider including these if you're travelling well off the beaten track; see your doctor, as they must be prescribed, and carry the prescription with you.

☐ **Loperamide** or **diphenoxylate** – 'blockers' for diarrhoea; **prochlorperazine** or **metaclopramide** for nausea and vomiting.

☐ **Rehydration mixture** – to prevent dehydration, eg due to severe diarrhoea; particularly important when travelling with children.

☐ **Insect repellent, sunscreen, lip balm** and **eye drops.**

☐ **Calamine lotion, sting relief spray** or **aloe vera** – to ease irritation from sunburn and insect bites or stings.

☐ **Antifungal cream** or **powder** – for fungal skin infections and thrush.

☐ **Antiseptic** (such as povidone-iodine) – for cuts and grazes.

☐ **Bandages, Band-Aids (plasters)** and other wound dressings.

☐ **Water purification tablets** or **iodine.**

☐ **Scissors, tweezers** and a **thermometer** (note that mercury thermometers are prohibited by airlines).

☐ **Syringes** and **needles** – in case you need injections in a country with medical hygiene problems. Ask your doctor for a note explaining why you have them.

☐ **Cold** and **flu tablets, throat lozenges** and **nasal decongestant.**

☐ **Multivitamins** – consider for long trips, when dietary vitamin intake may be inadequate.

Pre-departure Planning

If you're reasonably fit, the only things you should organise before departure are a visit to your dentist to get your teeth in order, and travel insurance with good medical cover (see Travel Insurance under Visas & Documents earlier in this chapter).

Jabs are not necessary for travel in the region, unless you have been travelling through a part of the world where yellow fever may be prevalent. Ensure that your normal childhood vaccines (against measles, mumps, rubella, diphtheria, tetanus and polio) are up to date and/or you are still showing immunity. You may also want to have a hepatitis vaccine, as exposure can occur anywhere.

If you wear glasses take a spare pair and a copy of your optical prescription. You will have no problem getting new glasses or contact lenses made up quickly and competently in Norway but you will pay for the privilege. If you require a particular medication, don't forget to carry a copy of your prescription, which will be necessary to get a refill. Most medications are available in Norway, but may go by a different name than at home, so be sure to have the generic name as well as the brand name.

Basic Rules

Food Stomach upsets are as possible in Norway as they are at home and the same rules apply. Take great care with fish or shellfish (for instance, cooked mussels that haven't opened properly can be dangerous). As autumn approaches, collecting mushrooms is a favourite pastime in this part of the world but don't eat any mushrooms until they've been positively identified as safe.

Water Tap water is always safe to drink in Norway but it's wise to beware of drinking from streams, as even the clearest and most inviting water may harbour giardia and other parasites. For extended hikes where you must rely on natural water, the simplest way of purifying water is to boil it thoroughly. Vigorous boiling should be satisfactory; however, at high altitude water boils at a lower temperature, so germs are less likely to be killed. Boil it for longer in these environments.

If you cannot boil water it should be treated chemically. Chlorine tablets (Puritabs, Steritabs or other brands) will kill many pathogens but not some parasites like giardia and amoebic cysts. Iodine is more effective in purifying water and is available in tablet form (such as Potable Aqua). Follow the directions carefully and remember that too much iodine can be harmful.

Environmental Hazards

Hypothermia Hypothermia occurs when the body loses heat faster than it can produce it and the core temperature of the body falls. It is surprisingly easy to progress from very cold to dangerously cold due to a combination of wind, wet clothing, fatigue and hunger, even if the air temperature is above freezing. It is best to dress in layers; silk, wool and artificial fibres like Capilene polyester are all good insulating materials. A hat is important, as a lot of heat is lost through the head. A strong, waterproof outer layer (and a 'space' blanket for emergencies) is essential. Carry basic supplies, including food containing simple sugars to generate heat quickly, and fluids to drink.

Symptoms of hypothermia are exhaustion, numb skin (particularly toes and fingers), shivering, slurred speech, irrational or violent behaviour, lethargy, stumbling, dizzy spells, muscle cramps and violent bursts of energy. Irrationality may take the form of sufferers claiming they are warm and trying to take off their clothes.

To treat mild hypothermia, first get the person out of the wind and/or rain, remove their clothing if it's wet and replace it with dry, warm clothing. Give them hot liquids – not alcohol – and some high-kilojoule, easily digestible food. Do not rub victims: instead, allow them to slowly warm themselves. This should be enough to treat the early stages of hypothermia. The early recognition and treatment of mild hypothermia is the only way to prevent severe hypothermia, which is a critical condition.

Sunburn You can get sunburnt surprisingly quickly, even through cloud. Use a sunscreen, a hat, and a barrier cream for your nose and lips. Calamine lotion or Stingose are good for mild sunburn. Protect your eyes with good quality sunglasses, particularly if you will be near water, sand or snow.

Infectious Diseases

Diarrhoea Simple things like a change of water, food or climate can all cause a mild bout of diarrhoea, but a few rushed toilet trips with no other symptoms is not indicative of a major problem. Dehydration is the main danger with diarrhoea, particularly in children or the elderly as dehydration can occur quite quickly. Under all circumstances fluid replacement (at least equal to the volume being lost) is the most important thing to remember. Stick to a bland diet as you recover.

Giardiasis Another possible concern is the intestinal parasite *Giardia lamblia*, which causes giardiasis, commonly known as giardia. Symptoms include stomach cramps, nausea, a bloated stomach, watery, foul-smelling diarrhoea and frequent gas. Giardiasis can appear several weeks after you have been exposed to the parasite. The symptoms may disappear for a few days and then return; this can go on for several weeks. You should seek medical advice if you think you have giardiasis.

Hepatitis Hepatitis is a general term for inflammation of the liver. Several distinct viruses cause hepatitis, and they differ in the way they're transmitted. All forms of the illness exhibit similar symptoms, including fever, chills, headache, fatigue, feelings of weakness and aches and pains, followed by loss of appetite, nausea, vomiting, abdominal pain, dark urine, light-coloured faeces, jaundiced (yellow) skin and a yellowing of the ocular sclera. After a bout of hepatitis, it's wise to avoid alcohol for several weeks, as the liver needs some time to recover.

Hepatitis A is transmitted by contaminated food and drinking water, but those stricken by this virus can't do much apart from resting, drinking lots of fluids, eating lightly and avoiding fatty foods. Hepatitis B is spread through contact with infected blood, blood products, body fluids or sexual contact, use of unsterilised needles, blood transfusions, or contact with blood through dermal abrasions. It may also be contracted by having a shave, tattoo or body piercing with contaminated equipment. The symptoms of hepatitis B may be more severe than type A and the disease can lead to long-term problems such as chronic liver damage, liver cancer or a chronic infectious status.

Hepatitis A and B may be controlled by vaccine, but following basic sanitation practices will minimise the possibility of contracting hepatitis A and avoiding risky situations will help prevent hepatitis B.

HIV & AIDS Infection with the human immunodeficiency virus (HIV) may lead to acquired immune deficiency syndrome (AIDS), which is fatal. Any exposure to blood, blood products or body fluids may put the individual at risk. It's often transmitted through sexual contact or dirty needles – vaccinations, acupuncture, tattooing and body piercing can be potentially as dangerous as intravenous drug use.

Sexually Transmitted Diseases STD clinics are widespread in Norway, and don't be shy about checking them out if you think you may have contracted something. Gonorrhoea and syphilis are typically treated with antibiotics, but each strain requires a doctor's attention to determine which antibiotic will be most efficacious. At present, there is no cure for herpes or HIV/AIDS.

Cuts, Bites & Stings

Bee and wasp stings are usually more painful than dangerous, but people who are allergic to stings may experience severe breathing difficulties and will require urgent medical care. Midges, small blood-sucking flies related to mosquitoes, are a major annoyance in Arctic regions during summer and also cause an itchy bite. Calamine lotion or Stingose spray will give relief and ice packs will reduce the pain and swelling, but the best preventative repellent is a skin cream known as *Skin-so-Soft*, produced by Avon.

In northern Norway, the greatest nuisance is the plague of mosquitoes that swarms out of tundra bogs and lakes in summer. Fortunately, malaria is unknown, but the mental risks can't be underestimated, as people have literally been driven insane by the ravenous hordes. Midsummer is the worst, and regular mosquito coils and repellents are scarcely effective; hikers must cover exposed skin and may even need head nets to keep the little buggers from making kamikaze attacks on eyes, noses, ears and throats. If you're camping, a tent with mosquito netting is essential. Most people get used to the mosquito bites after a few days as their bodies adjust and the itching and swelling become less severe. An antihistamine cream should help alleviate the symptoms.

Rabies Rabies, caused by a bite or scratch by an infected mammal, is found in parts of Norway and especially Svalbard, and risks have increased since the physical and political barriers were removed between the East and West in 1989. Dogs are a noted carrier, but cats, foxes and bats can also be infected. Any bite, scratch or even lick from a warm-blooded, furry animal should be cleaned immediately and thoroughly. Scrub with soap and running water, and then apply alcohol or iodine solution. Medical help should be sought promptly to receive a course of injections to prevent the onset of symptoms and death.

Ticks Check your body after walking through tick-infested areas, as ticks can cause skin infections and other more serious diseases. If a tick is found, press down around the tick's head with tweezers, grab the head and gently pull upwards. Avoid pulling the rear of the body as this may squeeze the tick's gut contents through the attached mouth parts into the skin, increasing the risk of infection and disease. Smearing chemicals on the tick will not make it let go and is not recommended.

Snakes Snakes tend to keep a very low profile in Norway but to minimise your chances of being bitten always wear boots, socks and long trousers when walking through undergrowth where snakes may be present. Don't put your hands into holes and crevices, and be careful when collecting firewood.

Snake bites do not cause instantaneous death and antivenins are usually available. Immediately wrap the bitten limb tightly, as you would for a sprained ankle, and then attach a splint to immobilise it. Keep the victim still and seek medical help, if possible with the dead snake for identification. Don't attempt to catch the snake if there is a possibility of being bitten again. Tourniquets and sucking out the poison are now comprehensively discredited.

Women's Health

Use of antibiotics, synthetic underwear, sweating and contraceptive pills can lead to fungal vaginal infections, especially when travelling in hot climates. Fungal infections are characterised by a rash, itch and discharge and can be treated with a vinegar or lemon-juice douche, or with yoghurt. Nystatin, miconazole or clotrimazole pessaries or vaginal cream are the usual treatment.

WOMEN TRAVELLERS

Women travellers have few worries in Norway, and sober Norwegian men are normally the very picture of decorum. While alcohol-impaired men may become tiresome or obnoxious, they're still unlikely to press any uncomfortable issues. Norway's main feminist organisation is Kvinnefronten (Women's Front; ☎ 22 37 60 54) at Holsts gate 1, N-0473 Oslo. Women who have been attacked or abused can contact the Krisesenter (☎ 22 37 47 00) in Oslo or dial ☎ 112 nationwide.

Recommended reading for first-time women travellers is the *Handbook for Women Travellers* by Maggie and Gemma Moss, published by Piatkus Books (London, 1994). *Going Solo* by Merran White (Penguin 1998) is also useful (unfortunately it's not available in the USA).

There are some good general websites for women travellers, including www.journeywoman.com and www.passionfruit.com, plus the women's page on LP's website Thorntree (see Internet Resources earlier in this chapter).

GAY & LESBIAN TRAVELLERS

Norwegians are generally tolerant of alternative lifestyles, and Norway, along with several neighbouring countries, allows gay and lesbian couples to form 'registered partnerships' that grant every right of matrimony except access to church weddings, adoption and artificial insemination. However, public displays of affection (regardless of sexual preference) are not common practice.

Gay and lesbian travellers can find gay entertainment spots in larger cities and towns. The Spartacus International Gay Guide, published by Bruno Gmünder Verlag (Berlin), is an excellent international directory of gay entertainment venues, but it's best used in conjunction with up-to-date listings in local papers, as the popular places tend to change quickly.

For local information on gay issues, contact Landsforeningen for Lesbisk og Homofil Frigjøring (LLH; ☎ 22 36 19 48), St Olavs plass 2, N-0165 Oslo. The Oslo gay and lesbian helpline (☎ 22 11 33 60) is available from 7 to 10 pm Wednesday and 7 to 9 pm Sunday.

DISABLED TRAVELLERS

Although Norway is better than most countries in catering for disabled travellers, it can still be a challenging destination, and anyone with special needs should plan ahead. The Norwegian Tourist Board publishes a list of wheelchair-accessible hotels and hostels. Nearly all street crossings are equipped with either a ramp or a very low kerb (curb),

and crossing signals produce an audible signal – longer beeps when it's safe to cross and shorter beeps when the signal is about to change. Most (but not all) trains have carriages with space for wheelchair users.

Sites of special interest to disabled travellers may be the Storedal Cultural Centre, near Sarpsborg in Østfold, which has several features for blind visitors; the Museum of Norwegian Deaf History in Trondheim; and the Beitestølen Health Sports Centre, in Beitestølen near Jotunheimen National Park, which offers sports programs for disabled athletes and sponsors the *Ridderrennet* competition for visually impaired nordic skiers. For information on disabled travel in Norway, contact the Norges Handikapforbund (☎ 22 95 28 60, fax 22 95 21 51), Folke Bernadottes vei 2, N-0862 Oslo.

You may also want to contact your national support organisation to speak with their 'travel officer', if there is one. They often have complete libraries devoted to travel, and they can put you in touch with tour companies who specialise in disabled travel.

The British-based Royal Association for Disability & Rehabilitation (RADAR) produces a useful publication entitled *European Holiday and Travel* (UK£5), which presents an overview of facilities available to disabled travellers in Europe and other parts of the world (published in odd-numbered years). You can contact RADAR (☎ 0171-250 3222, after April 2000 ☎ 020-7250 3222) at Unit 12 City Forum, 250 City Rd, London EC1V 8AF, UK.

In the USA, contact the Society for the Advancement of Travellers with Handicaps (☎ 212-447 7284, www.sitravel.com), 5th Ave, Suite 610, New York, NY 10016. In Canada, call up the website www.cta-otc.gc.ca/eng/acces/aguidee/htm.

An excellent website is www.accessable.com/index.html, which includes links with operators specialising in disabled travel.

SENIOR TRAVELLERS

Seniors are normally entitled to discounts on museum admissions, air tickets and other transport. A few hotels, including the SAS chain, also have senior discount schemes – so be sure to inquire when making a booking. For a small fee, European nationals aged over 60 can get a Rail Europe Senior Card as an add-on to their national rail senior pass. It entitles the holder to reduced fares in some European countries but the savings vary according to the route. See Train in the Getting Around chapter for information on this, as well as details on the ScanRail 55+ pass.

In your home country, a lower age may already entitle you to all sorts of interesting travel packages and discounts (on car hire, for instance) through organisations and travel agents that cater for senior travellers. Start hunting at your local senior citizens advice bureau or larger seniors' organisations, such as the AARP in the USA (www.aarp.org) or Age Concern England (www.ace.org.uk) in the UK.

TRAVEL WITH CHILDREN

Successful travel with young children requires planning and effort. Don't try to overdo things; packing too much into the time available can cause problems even for adults. And make sure the activities include the kids as well; if they've helped to work out where you're going, chances are they'll still be interested when you arrive. Lonely Planet's *Travel with Children* is a useful source of information.

In many ways, Norway is a children's country, and most towns have attractions and museums specifically for the younger set (one of the finest is Dyrepark in Kristiansand, which offers an open-air zoo, pirate ship battles and family accommodation in the fantasy town of Kardamomme By). Domestic tourism is largely organised around children's interests: regional museums invariably have a children's section with toys and activities, and there are also numerous public parks for kids. Most attractions allow free admission for young children up to about six years of age and half-price (or substantially discounted) admission for those up to 16 or so. Hotels and other accommodation options often have 'family rooms' that accommodate up to two adults and two children for little more than the price of a regular double.

Car rental firms hire out children's safety seats at a nominal cost but it is essential that you book them in advance. The same goes for highchairs and cots (cribs); they are standard in many restaurants and hotels but numbers may be limited. Norway offers a relatively wide choice of baby food, infant formulas, soy and cow's milk, disposable nappies (diapers), etc, but remember that supermarket opening hours are generally shorter than they are elsewhere, and after hours, you may have to resort to more expensive convenience stores.

DANGERS & ANNOYANCES

Unless you live in Japan or elsewhere in Scandinavia, your person and belongings are safer in Norway than at home, and the cities – even east Oslo, which has a relatively poor reputation – are reasonably safe at all hours of the night. That's not to say you should tempt fate or become blasé about security, but there's no call for paranoia. The greatest nuisance value will probably come from drug addicts, alcoholics and/or panhandlers – mainly in Oslo – who can spot a naïve tourist a block away.

Oslo and other larger cities suffer from a growing drug problem, and although dope may be readily available in places, it still isn't legal.

BUSINESS HOURS

Business hours are generally from 9 or 10 am to 4 pm Monday to Friday, though some shops stay open until 7 or 8 pm on Thursday and to 2 pm on Saturday. In summer, banks normally open from 8.15 am to 3 pm weekdays (until 5 pm on Thursday) and post offices operate on weekdays from 8 am to 5 pm and on Saturday from 9 am to 1 pm.

Many Rimi supermarkets stay open until 10 pm on weekdays and 8 pm on Saturday, and some larger shopping centres, particularly in Oslo, have extended hours from 10 am to 8 pm on weekdays and 10 am to 6 pm on Saturday. Also in Oslo, many shops in the central area participate in 'Super Saturday' on the first Saturday of the month, and are open until 7 pm or later. Nearly everything closes on Sunday, although shops catering for tourists may be open.

All but the most popular museums have relatively short hours (from 11 am to 3 pm is common), so museum fiends need to plan their day before setting out.

PUBLIC HOLIDAYS & SPECIAL EVENTS
Public Holidays
The following public holidays are observed in Norway:

New Year's Day
  1 January, *Nyttårsdag*
Easter
  March or April – *Skjærtorsdag* (Maundy Thursday), *Langfredag* (Good Friday), *2.Påskedag* (2nd Easter Day, ie Easter Monday)

Labour Day
  1 May
Constitution Day
  17 May
Ascension Day
  The 40th day after Easter, *Kristi Himmelfartsdag*
Whit Monday
  The 8th Monday after Easter, *2. Pinsedag*
Christmas Day
  25 December, *1. Juledag*
Boxing Day
  26 December, *2. Juledag* (literally '2nd Christmas Day')

Norway's national holiday is 17 May, Constitution Day, when people take to the streets in traditional dress and attend celebratory events throughout the country. The biggest bash is in Oslo, where marching bands and thousands of schoolchildren parade down Karl Johans gate to the Royal Palace, to be greeted by the royal family.

Christmas in Norway – Jul Love It!

Christmas, or *jul*, is as much of a holiday in Norway as it is elsewhere in Christendom; the name is derived from *joulu* or *lol*, a pagan fertility feast that was celebrated all over Europe in pre-Christian times and syncretised nicely with the holiday to honour the birth of Christ. Currently, most people celebrate between Christmas Eve and Epiphany, or the 12th night, although some continue until the Feast of St Canute, which is the 20th day of Christmas.

A Christmas tree is a requisite part of the décor in most homes, and gifts are exchanged on Christmas Eve. In the countryside, sheaves of oats known as *julenek* are mounted on a pole and left out for the birds. In gratitude for past blessings, a bowl of porridge is also left out for the *nisse*, the gnome that historically brought good fortune to farmers. This concept has now been merged with the international tradition of Santa Claus in the personage of *Julenissen*, whom Norwegians believe makes his home in Drøbak, south of Oslo (and there's a Santa Crossing road sign there to prove it!).

There are all sorts of special Christmas confections and concoctions. Among them are *rømmegrøt*, an extremely sweet cream porridge; *rupa*, ptarmigan or grouse; *lutefisk*, a glutinous fish dish that's definitely an acquired taste; *pinneribbe*, mutton ribs steamed over birch or juniper branches; and pork roast, which stems from the Viking tradition of sacrificing a pig at yuletide. Children like to munch raisin buns and a variety of biscuits, including *strull*, *krumkake* and *goro*. And then everyone drinks *gløgg*, readily translated as 'grog'. Good gløgg blends cinnamon, raisins, almonds, ginger, cloves, cardamom and other spices with juice, which may or may not be fermented. Many people also imbibe *julaøl*, or 'holiday beer', which dates from the Viking days when it was associated with pagan sacrifices; as with the lutefisk, not all foreigners fully appreciate it. Die-hard alcohol fans celebrate the season with generous quantities of Norway's own potato power brew, *aquavit*.

In Karasjok and Kautokeino, the Sami people hold their most colourful celebrations at Easter, with reindeer races, *joik* concerts and other festivities. Midsummer's Eve, or *Jonsok*, is generally observed on St Hans Day (23 June) and is celebrated with much fanfare and bonfires in every community from Halden to Grense Jakobselv.

On 13 December, Christian children celebrate the feast of Santa Lucia, the Roman Christian martyr, by dressing in white and holding a candlelight procession. Boys generally wear cone-shaped hats and girls put silver tinsel and glitter in their hair.

Special Events

Norway is chock-a-block with special festivals, which take place at all times of year in every city, town and village. Large and popular ones are covered in this book, but for a one-stop listing of recommended events, pick up a copy of the free booklet *Norway Festivals*, which is produced by Norske Festivaler (☎ 22 38 00 66, fax 22 38 11 16, norfest@ online.no, www.norwayfestivals.com), Sagveien 23a, N-0458 Oslo.

ACTIVITIES

Much of Norway's appeal to visitors lies in its wilderness areas. The Western Fjords, Lofoten Islands and Lyngen Alps (in northern Troms) attract throngs of mountaineers and rock climbers; glacier hikes and ice-climbing are available on Jostedalsbreen, Svartisen and other smaller icecaps; birdwatchers flock to the prolific bird cliffs, marshes and forests; skiers will find the world's best nordic skiing and some very respectable downhill slopes; and hikers will never exhaust the range of excellent day hikes and long-distance walking routes.

Thanks to Norway's 1000-year-old *allemannsretten* ('every man's right') tradition and the *Friluftsleven* (Outdoor Recreation Act), anyone is legally entitled to hike or ski across wilderness areas, including outlying fields and pastures; camp anywhere for up to two days, as long as it's more than 150m from a dwelling; cycle or ride horseback on all paths and roads; and canoe, kayak, row

Minimum Impact Camping

Campers taking advantage of the wonderful *allemansretten* in Norway will help to preserve the country's beauty and foster goodwill by heeding the following guidelines:

- Select a well drained camp site and use a waterproof groundsheet to prevent having to dig trenches, if it's raining.
- Along popular routes, particularly in Jotunheimen or Rondane National Parks, set up camp on sites that have been previously used.
- Carry out all your rubbish, including cigarette butts. Biodegradable items may be buried but anything with food residue should be carried out, lest it be dug up and scattered by animals.
- Use established toilet facilities if they're available. Otherwise, select a site at least 50m from water sources and bury waste at least 20cm below the surface. Carry out or bury used toilet paper (it's probably wise to carry a sturdy plastic bag for this purpose).
- Use only biodegradable soap products and use natural temperature water if possible. When washing with hot water, avoid damage to vegetation either by letting the water cool before pouring it out or by dumping it in a gravelly, non-vegetated place.
- In times when you're permitted to build a fire (15 September to 15 April), try to select an established site and keep fires as small as possible. Use only fallen, dead wood and when you're finished, make sure ashes are cool and buried before you leave the site.

and sail on all rivers and lakes. However, these freedoms come with some responsibilities: not to light fires between 15 April and 15 September; not to litter; to avoid damaging plant or animal life; to leave cultural sites perfectly intact; and to leave the countryside as pristine as it was found.

Hiking

Norway has some of Europe's best hiking, including a network of 19,000km of marked trails that range from easy strolls through the green zones around cities to long treks through national parks and wilderness areas. Many of these trails are maintained by DNT and are marked either with cairns or red 'T's at 100 or 200m intervals.

The hiking season runs roughly from late May to early October, with a much shorter season in the higher mountain areas. In the highlands, the snow often remains until June and returns in September. The most popular wilderness hiking areas are the Jotunheimen and Rondane mountains and the Hardangervidda plateau. If you're after a wilder experience, try such national parks as Øvre Dividal, Stabbursdalen, Rago, Reisa, Dovrefjell, or any of the vast number of unprotected areas throughout the country, such as Trollheimen near Oppdal, the fabulous Sunnmøresalpene in the Western Fjords or the extensive Sylenefjell range along the Swedish border. Avid hikers will never run out of options!

DNT Den Norske Turistforening (the Norwegian Mountain Touring Club, or DNT) and its various chapters maintain a network of over 320 mountain huts and lodges throughout the country. For details and prices for the use of these huts, see Accommodation, later in this chapter.

Crossing Streams

Fortunately, most large rivers along major Norwegian hiking routes are bridged, but trekkers and mountaineers are still bound to face the odd swollen stream or unbridged river. In most cases, however, you need not be put off.

Normally, the sun and heat of the day melt the snow and glacial ice in the high country and cause water levels to rise, so the best time to cross is early in the morning, preferably no sooner than 24 hours after a rainstorm. Remember that constricted rivers passing through narrow passages run deep, so the widest ford is likely to be the shallowest. The swiftest and strongest current is normally found near the centre of straight stretches and at the outside of river bends. Observe the character of the water as it flows and choose a spot with as much slack water as possible.

Never try to cross just above a waterfall and avoid crossing streams in flood – identifiable by dirty, smooth-running water carrying lots of debris and vegetation. A smooth surface suggests that the river is too deep to be crossed on foot. Anything over thigh-deep shouldn't be considered 'crossable' without experience and extra equipment.

Before attempting to cross deep or swift-running streams, be sure that you can jettison your pack in midstream if necessary. Put anything that mustn't get wet inside sturdy waterproof bags. Unhitch the waist belt and loosen shoulder straps, remove any bulky clothing that will inhibit swimming, and remove long trousers. Lone hikers should use a hiking staff to probe the river bottom for the best route and to steady themselves in the current.

Never try to cross a stream barefoot. While crossing, face upstream and avoid looking down or you may risk losing your balance. Two hikers can steady each other by resting their arms on each other's shoulders. More than two hikers should cross forming a wedge pointed upstream, with the people behind holding the waist and shoulder of the person at the head of the wedge.

If you do fall while crossing, don't try to stand up. Remove your pack (but don't let go of it), roll over onto your back, and point your feet downstream, then try to work your way to a shallow eddy or to the shore and attempt to regain your footing.

If you're doing lots of hiking, it's certainly worth joining DNT; membership for one calendar year will set you back Nkr325/160 (Nkr385/220 with catalogues and magazines) for people over/under 26 years of age; members' families pay Nkr125 per person. For further information, contact Den Norske Turistforening (☎ 22 82 28 00, fax 22 82 28 01, www.turistforeningen.no), Storgata 3, PO Box 7, Sentrum, N-0101 Oslo. DNT also sells hiking maps and topographic sheets. The latter, which are published by Statens Kartverk, cover the entire country at scales of 1:50,000 and 1:100,000; catalogue maps outlining map titles and sheet numbers are available free of charge.

Rock Climbing & Mountaineering

As one would imagine, a country with the astounding vertical topography of Norway would be a mecca for climbers interested in rock, ice and alpine pursuits. In fact, outside the Alps, Norway is probably Europe's finest climbing venue. However, due to Norway's climatic and topographic extremes, technical climbers face harsher conditions, shorter seasons and many more concerns and restrictions than hikers and backpackers. The most popular alpine venues include the Lyngen Alps, Lofoten and Western Fjords.

In addition to the rock climbers' classic *Climbing in the Magic Islands* by Ed Webster, which describes most of the feasible routes in the Lofoten Islands, prospective climbers may want to look for *Ice Fall in Norway* by Sir Ranulph Feinnes, which describes a 1970 jog around Jostedalsbreen, and the more practical *Scandinavian Mountains* by Peter Lennon, which introduces the country's finest climbing venues.

Skiing

'Ski' is a Norwegian word and thanks to aeons-old rock carvings depicting hunters travelling on skis, Norwegians make a credible claim to having invented the sport. Interest hasn't waned over the years and these days, it's no exaggeration to say it's the national pastime. Most skiing is of the cross-country (nordic) variety, and Norway has thousands of kilometres of maintained cross-country ski trails. However, visitors should only set off after studying the trails/routes (wilderness trails are identified by colour codes on maps and signposts) and ensuring that they have appropriate clothing, sufficient food and water, and emergency supplies such as matches and a source of warmth. You can either bring your own equipment; rely on friendly locals to loan theirs, or purchase skis, poles and boots on site. You'll probably find the best deals on second-hand gear at weekend flea markets.

Most towns and villages provide some illuminated ski trails, but elsewhere it's still worth carrying a good light source, as winter days are very short and in the north there's no daylight at all in December and January. The ski season generally lasts from early December to April. Snow conditions vary greatly from year to year and region to region, but February and March, as well as the Easter holiday period, tend to be the best (and busiest) times. When nature hasn't provided an ideal skiing surface, many areas use snow cannons to produce more amenable conditions.

There are also scores of resorts with downhill runs, but these are quite expensive due to the costs of ski lifts, accommodation and the *aprés-ski* drinking sessions. Popular spots include the Holmenkollen area near Oslo, Geilo on the Oslo-Bergen railway line, Lillehammer and the nearby Gudbrandsdalen region. Summer skiers can head for the glaciers near Finse, Stryn, Folgefonn or Jotunheimen National Park. For general information, DNT produces the pamphlet *Welcome to the Norwegian Mountains in Wintertime*.

River Rafting

Norway's steep slopes and icy, scenic rivers create an ideal environment for avid rafters, and a number of reputable operators offer trips. These range from short, Class II doddles to Class III and IV adventures and rollicking Class V punishment. While these

The Virtues of Skinny Skis

Throughout modern history, skiing athletes have debated the virtues of maximising one's own muscle power versus taking advantage of the natural benefits offered by gravity. Norwegians tend to acknowledge downhill (alpine) skiing as a necessary and indeed rather exciting facet of the sport – at least where Olympic achievement is concerned – but the country's heart still leans toward its good, age-old and self-propelled version of the sport.

If Norway has a national sport, this is it. Not only do nordic skiing and biathlon (skiing and target-shooting) competitions dominate Norwegian Olympic efforts, they also provide a recreational foundation among people for whom winter is the dominant season of the year. If you've never before practised nordic skiing, you'll quickly learn that it's not only a great source of exercise but also a ticket into the wilderness when few folks are prepared to venture far from the home fires.

The concept is easy. Skiers propel themselves forward over the snow on one ski with the ski pole in the opposite hand. That is, you glide forward with your right ski while thrusting backward with your left ski pole, and then reverse the process by gliding forward with your left ski and placing the stress on your right pole. The process is often made easier in popular areas with pre-laid parallel tracks cut into the snow. Once you get into the rhythm of it, nothing could be simpler.

Nordic skis are narrower than downhill skis, and the bottom of most nordic skis include fish-scale formations designed to maximise the grip of the skis on the snow and allow uphill travel. In certain conditions and temperatures, however, you may need to rely on commercial waxes to improve the skis' grip. Waxes, which range from red to blue, depending on the snow conditions, are applied to the middle section of the skis in order to enhance their grip. In extreme cases, you may have to apply skins – strips of furry animal hide that attach to the bottom of the skis and ensure maximum gripping power on ice and snow.

The Telemark region of Norway has lent its name to the graceful turn that has made nordic skiing popular even on alpine slopes around the world. Normally, Telemark skis pin the toes to the ski but allow the heel to float freely; to turn, one knee is dropped to the surface of the ski while the other is kept straight, thus allowing the skier to smoothly glide around the turn in the direction of the dropped knee.

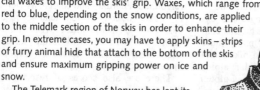

trips aren't especially cheap, most are guaranteed to provide an adrenalin thrill, and the rates include all the requisite equipment and waterproofing. Among the finest venues are Evje (Setesdalen), Sjoa (Heidalen) and Oppdal (Drivadalen). Evje is described in the Southern Norway chapter, and Sjoa and Oppdal in the Central Norway chapter. The Norges Padleforbund (☎ 67 15 46 00, fax 67 13 33 35), Hauger Skoleveien 1, N-1351 Rud, can provide a comprehensive list of rafting operators in Norway.

Dog-Sledding

Although dog-sledding isn't an indigenous Norwegian sport, this Inuit means of transport readily transfers to the Norwegian wilds, and several operators can take you on a range of adventures. While many people are content with just a half-day taster of the sport, keen prospective 'mushers' can jump in the deep end and opt for a two-week dog-sled safari over the Hardangervidda or through Finnmark or Svalbard.

DNT organises several trips through southern Norway. In the north, you'll want to contact Bjørn Klauer in Innset (see Øvre Dividal Nasjonalpark in the Troms & Finnmark chapter) or Sven Engholm in Karasjok (see the Troms & Finnmark chapter). All Svalbard operators can also arrange Svalbard dog-sled tours (see the Svalbard & Jan Mayen chapter) and Arcturus Expeditions in the UK offers extended dog-sledding tours in Norway with operator Odd-Knut Thorsen (see Organised Tours in the Getting There & Away chapter).

Fishing

In the 19th century, Norway was a mecca for wealthy anglers, principally European aristocrats. English lords fished the rivers of western Norway, such as the Lågen (Suldal) and the Rauma (Romsdal). During the 20th century, they were mostly replaced by avid anglers from the USA.

Norway's salmon runs are legendary, and in June and July, you can't beat the streams of Finnmark. In addition to salmon, 41 species of fish inhabit the country's 200,000

rivers and lakes. In the south, you'll normally find the best fishing from June to September, and in the north, in July and August. In Svalbard, the best fishing holes are well kept secrets, but Arctic charr inhabit some rivers and lakes. The 175-page book *Angling in Norway*, available from tourist offices for Nkr130, details the best salmon and trout-fishing areas, fees and regulations. In the UK, it's available from MMW Productions Ltd, 26 Woodsford Sq, London, W14 8DP, UK.

Commandments for Anglers

1. Foreigners may fish on the Norwegian coast but can't sell their catch.
2. Fishing is prohibited less than 100m from fish farms, cables and nets that are anchored or fastened to the shore.
3. Anyone who damages fishing equipment must pay compensation for the damage.
4. Anchoring is prohibited in the vicinity of drift nets or line-fishing sites.
5. It is forbidden to shoot off firearms or make noises that can disturb the fish.
6. Fishing with live bait is prohibited.
7. It's forbidden to abandon fishing tackle or other rubbish that can disturb, delay or damage fish catches or fishing boats.
8. Only Norwegian citizens or permanent residents may catch lobsters.
9. Salmon, trout and charr fishing with a rod is permitted year-round. For rivers with fishing bans, you may still fish within 100m from the river mouth. From 1 June to 4 August, between 6 pm on Friday and 6 pm on Monday, you can fish for salmon, trout and charr with a hook and troll. All anglers for these fish must have a national fishing permit, and must also follow other local fishing regulations.
10. All anglers from boats must wear lifejackets.
11. Don't throw rubbish or pollute the waters in any way.

Regulations vary between rivers but, generally, from mid-September to November, fish under 20cm must be thrown back. At other times between August and May, you can't keep fish less than 30cm in length.

For sea or fjord fishing, no licence is required. All river and lake fishing in Norway requires an annual licence (Nkr180 for salmon, trout and charr and Nkr90 for other fish), which is sold at post offices. A weekly licence is also available for Nkr45. To fish on private land, you must also purchase a local licence, which is available from sports shops, hotels, camp sites and tourist offices. Also see the boxed text 'Commandments for Anglers'.

Tracing Your Ancestors

In the 19th and early 20th centuries, hundreds of thousands of Norwegians migrated westward to settle in the USA and Canada, especially Wisconsin, Minnesota, North Dakota, Utah and Manitoba, and nowadays many of their descendants are returning to the old country to find their roots. To aid them, the Royal Ministry of Foreign Affairs publishes a free booklet, *How to Trace your Ancestors in Norway*. It's available on the Web at www.odin.dep.no; unless you speak Norwegian, be sure to click on the British flag icon to get the English version. Go to the 'About Norway' page to bring up the 'How to trace your ancestors in Norway' option.

Other sources of help include the Norwegian Emigrant Museum (☎ 62 57 85 77, fax 62 57 84 59, knut.djupedal@emigrant .museum.no, www.hamarnett.no/emigrant museum/) in Hamar and the Norwegian Emigration Centre (☎ 51 50 12 67) in Stavanger. A useful website is www.lawzone .com/half-nor/nor-am.htm (the Norwegian-American homepage).

WORK

Because of Norway's relatively low unemployment rate, foreigners can sometimes land a job, particularly in the less desirable service industry, but a command of Norwegian is generally required and preference is typically given to Scandinavians.

As a member of the European Economic Area (EEA), Norway grants citizens of other EEA countries (essentially the EU countries, plus Switzerland, Liechtenstein, Greenland and the Faroe Islands) the right to look for work for a three-month period without obtaining a permit; those who find work have a right to remain in Norway for the duration of their employment.

Other foreigners must apply for work permits through a Norwegian embassy or consulate in their home country before entering Norway. However, a ban on immigration is in effect until further notice, and exceptions are granted only in the case of extenuating circumstances (such as marriage to a Norwegian or valid refugee status) or in cases where highly skilled workers are in demand in a specialised occupation.

ACCOMMODATION
Camping

Norway has nearly 1000 camping grounds. Tent space generally costs from Nkr50 at basic camping grounds to as much as Nkr150 in popular or expensive areas, such as Oslo and Bergen. Most camping grounds also rent simple cabins with cooking facilities starting at around Nkr250 for a very basic two or four-bed bunkhouse. Bring a sleeping bag, as linen and blankets are provided only at an extra charge, which is anywhere from Nkr40 to Nkr60 per visit.

Unless you opt for a more expensive deluxe cabin with shower and toilet facilities, which could range from Nkr400 to Nkr800, you'll normally also have to pay for showers and often for washing water (there are, however, a few enlightened exceptions). Normally, cabin occupants must clean their cabin before leaving or pay an additional cleaning charge, which averages around Nkr90.

Note that although a few complexes remain open year-round, tent and caravan sites are closed in the off-season (normally early September to mid-May).

The allemannsretten (see Activities earlier in this chapter) allows you to pitch a tent anywhere in the wilderness for two nights, as long as you camp at least 150m from the nearest house or cottage and leave no trace of your stay. From 15 April to 15 September, lighting fires anywhere near a woodland is strictly prohibited.

Summer Homes & Cabins

Most tourist offices in popular holiday areas keep lists of private huts, cabins and summer homes that are rented out to holidaymakers when the owners aren't using them. Prices for a week's rental start from around Nkr1300 for a simple place in the off-season to about Nkr5500 for something more elaborate in mid-summer. Most cabins sleep at least four people, and some accommodate as many as 12, so if you have a group and want to spend some time in a certain area, it's a very economical option. Advance booking is normally required, and you'll probably have to pay a deposit of around Nkr500 or 20% of the total fee, whichever is less.

Den Norske Hytteformidling (☎ 55 23 20 80, fax 55 23 24 04, www.hytte.com), Lille Markevei 13, Postboks 103, N-5001 Bergen, publishes an English-language photo catalogue describing hundreds of self-catering cabins and cottages in the Western Fjords area. A similar scheme in Germany is DanCenter (☎ 040-30 97 03, fax 040-32 75 91, www.dancenter.de), Spitalerstrasse 16, D-20095 Hamburg, which makes bookings all over Scandinavia.

DNT & Other Mountain Huts

DNT maintains a network of over 320 mountain huts a day's hike apart all along the country's 19,000km of well marked and maintained wilderness hiking routes. These range from unstaffed huts with two beds to large staffed lodges with more than 100 beds. Nearly all of the huts offer cooking facilities and linen, but in most places, you must also have your own sleeping bag or a hostel-style sheet sleeping bag; these are often sold at staffed huts. (Note that there are also numerous private hikers' huts and lodges peppered around most mountain areas.)

At staffed huts, which are concentrated in the south, you can simply turn up and pay your fees. In compliance with international mountain courtesies, no one is turned away, even if there's only floor space left (however, DNT members over 50 years of age are guaranteed a bed, even if it means displacing a younger hiker!) Nightly fees for DNT members/nonmembers in a room with one to three beds is Nkr150/220; rooms with four to six beds, Nkr105/175; dormitories Nkr75/145; and overflow on the floor, Nkr50/120. Lodging and full board (for DNT members only) ranges from Nkr315 to Nkr365 in the low season, Nkr345 to Nkr385 in high summer and Nkr400 to Nkr430 over Easter week.

Members/nonmembers who prefer to camp outside the huts and use their facilities will pay Nkr35/50. (Otherwise, tenters must camp at least 150m from the hut and may not use the facilities.) Breakfasts are Nkr65/95; a thermos of coffee or tea, Nkr17/27; sandwiches are Nkr9/12; light dinners are Nkr65-80/85-100; and three-course meals, Nkr130/165.

For unstaffed huts, most of which are in the north, you must pick up keys (Nkr100 deposit) in advance from a DNT office or a staffed hut. To pay, fill out a Once-Only Authorisation slip and leave either cash or a valid credit card number in the box provided. There are two classes of unstaffed huts. Self-service chalets are stocked with blankets and pillows and have wood stoves, firewood, gas cookers and a wide range of food supplies for sale (on the honour system). In these, DNT members/nonmembers pay Nkr105/175 for a bed and Nkr50/120 for overflow space on the floor. At other unstaffed huts, users must carry in their own food.

Most DNT huts are closed between 15 October and 15 February. In winter, staffed DNT lodges are open between the Saturday before Palm Sunday and Easter Monday, but huts along the Oslo-Bergen railway and a few others open for the cross-country ski season as early as late February. DNT can provide lists of opening dates for each hut.

Hostels

In Norway, 'youth' hostels are known as *vandrerhjem* and for a reasonable price, they offer a bed for the night, plus use of communal facilities that often include a kitchen where you can prepare meals. Hostels vary widely in character, but increasingly, they're open longer hours, curfews are disappearing and 'wardens' with a sergeant-major mentality are an endangered species (at least outside of Bavaria, Germany!). The trend has also been towards smaller dormitories with just two to six beds. Normally, guests must bring their own sleeping sheet and pillowcase or linen, although you may sometimes be permitted to use your sleeping bag. Most hostels hire sleeping sheets for around Nkr50 for as long as you stay.

Several hostel guides are available, including the HI's annually updated Europe guide. The Norwegian Hostelling Association, Norske Vandrerhjem (☎ 22 42 14 10, fax 22 42 44 76, hostels@sn.no, www .vandrerhjem.no), Dronningensgata 26, N-0154 Oslo, also publishes a free 156-page directory, *Vandrerhjem i Norge*. This publication lists nearly 100 hostels, which are found in just about every city, town or site of interest to visitors.

Some hostels are quite comfortable lodge-style facilities and are open year-round, while others occupy school dorms and are open in summer only. Most have two to six beds per room and cost from Nkr70 to Nkr175. The higher-priced hostels may include a buffet breakfast, while other places may charge from Nkr40 to Nkr60 for breakfast. Some also provide an evening meal for around Nkr80, but nearly all have facilities for cooking your own meals, even it's just a hot plate in your dorm room. Note that the word *lukket* beside a listing doesn't mean 'lock-out', but only indicates when reception is closed (usually from 11 am to 4 pm).

In summer, reservations are recommended, particularly for popular destinations. Most places in Norway accept phone reservations and are normally happy to book beds at your next destination for a small fee (around Nkr20). Note, however, that popular hostels in Oslo and Bergen are often heavily booked in summer.

Prices listed in this book are those for HI members; nonmembers pay an additional Nkr25 per night. Even if you haven't bought a membership in your own country, you can pick up an International Guest Card; after six nights at nonmember prices, you'll qualify for the lower HI member rates. Be sure to request the card on your first night and pick up stamps to fill it on each consecutive night.

Private B&Bs/Pensions

Next to camping and hostels, the cheapest places to sleep are in private rooms booked through tourist offices. These rooms average Nkr150/250 for singles/doubles. Many towns also have pensions and guesthouses in the Nkr250 to Nkr400 range, but linen will only be included at the higher-priced places.

Along the highways, you'll also find lots of *Rom* signs, indicating inexpensive informal accommodation. At these establishments, a basic place to crash for the night will cost from Nkr75 to Nkr200; those who bring their own sheets or sleeping bags may get a discount. For information on farmhouse accommodation in the Western Fjords, contact Fjordtra (☎ 57 67 30 00, fax 57 67 28 06), PO Box 299, N-5801 Sogndal.

Hotels

Although normal hotel prices are high, some hotels offer substantially discounted rates on weekends and in the summer season, which are slow periods for business travel. Nationwide chains offering such deals include the Tulip Inn/Rainbow Hotels, Radisson SAS Hotels and Rica Hotels, all of which maintain high standards. A significant consideration in this land of daunting food prices is that hotels, unlike pensions, normally offer a substantial all-you-can-eat breakfast buffet. If you're travelling with children, ask about family rooms, which accommodate two adults and up to two children for little more than a regular double.

The Norwegian Tourist Board's annually updated accommodation brochure lists most hotels and outlines discount schemes. The Fjord Pass avails you to accommodation at 236 hotels, guesthouses and cabins around the country for Nkr195 to Nkr470 per person. It costs Nkr75 and is valid throughout the summer season. Contact Fjord Tours (☎ 55 32 65 50, fax 55 31 20 60, vibecke @reiselivsutvikling.no), PO Box 1752, N-5024 Bergen. Rainbow's Bonus Pass (☎ 22 01 07 00, www.rainbowhotel.com) costs Nkr175 and provides discounts at Rainbow's 40 hotels around the country. Best Western's Nkr300 Hotel Cheque (☎ 22 55 09 10, fax 22 55 61 23) elicits discounts at 47 Best Western Hotels. A similar scheme is offered by the Rica Hotels (☎ 67 80 72 80, rica@rica.no, www.rica.no), which have a Nkr75 Feriepass that discounts room prices and attractions around Scandinavia.

FOOD

For newly-arrived visitors, the prices of food and drink in Norway may inspire vows to finally begin that diet program they've been planning. The key is to think in krone and avoid converting the Norwegian price into your home currency or you may wind up emaciated. To minimise the sting, you can prepare your own meals, but it's wise to know a few good recipes involving hot dogs and pasta. Most hostels and camping grounds offer cooking facilities but, as an alternative, you may just want to buy a loaf of bread or pack of Ryvita, a slab of Jarlsberg cheese and a tin of smoked fish and enjoy a quiet lunch out in a park somewhere. For other price-conscious ideas, see Budget Options.

By international standards, Norwegian food is fairly bland, and flavourful condiments may be hard to come by, so you may want to carry a supply of your favourite spices from home. However, Norway does have its own culinary tradition, and what Betty Crocker and Julia Child are to the Americans and Delia Smith is to the Brits, Ingrid Espelid is to the Norwegians. Her extremely popular *Fjernsynskjøkkenet* tele-

vision program is the last word in Norwegian cuisine, and for those who want to prepare meals in the local manner, her numerous cookbooks are considered standard works.

Meals

Breakfast or *frokost* is generally a fairly big production, especially at upmarket hotels where you can choose between English, American, Continental and Scandinavian breakfasts. The typical Norwegian breakfast, however, consists of coffee (always!), a boiled egg and some sort of bread or dry biscuits (normally Ryvita) topped with cheese (especially gudbrandsdalsost!), cucumber, tomato and some sort of pickled herring. A basic breakfast is often served at hostels for Nkr50 to Nkr60, and for non-guests, the big hotels offer the whole enchilada for Nkr80 to Nkr90.

For lunch, most people opt for a sandwich or piece of cold *smørbrød*, a slice of bread topped with *pålegg*, which rather recursively refers to 'that which goes on top', be it sardines, shrimp, ham, olives, cucumber, egg or whatever. In the mid-afternoon, Norwegians often break for a snack of coffee and waffles with cream and jam.

The main meal is *middag*, which is eaten anywhere from 4 to 6 pm and is usually the only hot meal of the day. This will normally include some sort of meat, seafood or pasta dish, boiled potatoes, a scoop of vegetables and perhaps even a small salad or green garnish.

Budget Options

There's no such thing as a cheap lunch in Norway, but some supermarkets have reasonably priced delicatessens where you can pick up salads sold by the kilogram or broiled chicken lunches from around Nkr40. At a *konditori*, a bakery with a few tables, you can enjoy relatively inexpensive baked goods, pastries and sandwiches. Cafeterias, which are found everywhere, and university messes (you'll probably need a student card to qualify for discounts) are marginally more expensive but offer better nutritional value, with simple hot dishes starting at around Nkr50. However, they're more popular for a coffee fix and a waffle or quick snack of smørbrød.

Petrol stations normally sell several types of *varm pølse* (hot dogs), which are the cheapest hot meal you can buy, but note that the plumper versions are invariably more palatable than the flavourless slender ones. A basic hot dog without bread costs around Nkr15; with a bun, it ranges from Nkr15 to Nkr20 and with a wrapping of streaky bacon, from Nkr25 to Nkr30. Some places charge an extra Nkr1 or Nkr2 for a garnish of fresh or deep-fried onions.

Other fairly cheap eats are found at a *gatekjøkken* (food wagon or kiosk), which generally serves hot dogs, burgers, chips, previously frozen pizza slices and the like for Nkr30 to Nkr50. Fast-food chains such as McDonald's and Burger King, which do decent-sized burgers for under Nkr20, offer some of the best bulk value around.

Pizzas also feature prominently in the local diet, and it's often cited that *Pizza Grandiosa*, a marginally satisfying brand of frozen pizza, is in fact Norway's national dish. Given its popularity with harried urbanites who lack the time to cook anything elaborate or the money to eat out, that would be difficult to dispute. There are also a couple of pizza chains, notably Peppe's Pizza and Pizza Hut, which offer good value lunch time buffets; all-you-can-eat pizza, bread and salad with a glass of soda costs from Nkr72 to Nkr89.

Meals at moderately priced restaurants start at Nkr90 to Nkr120, though some may feature a *dagens rett* (daily special) for as little as Nkr75. The best value restaurant meals are found around the ethnic areas of Oslo, especially Grønland, which enjoys a range of relatively great value Indian, Bangladeshi and Middle Eastern choices. Open-air markets in the same area offer the country's best deals on fresh produce. Most other towns have at least one Chinese restaurant/takeaway with a good value lunch special for Nkr60 to Nkr80.

Self-caterers will probably be surprised with the lack of variety available in Norwe-gian supermarkets, at least when compared with European, American and Australasian standards. It may also surprise you to see how much processed and chemical-laden convenience food fills the supermarket shelves, and that there's a notable dearth of good, old-fashioned staples (or anything that takes more than 10 minutes to prepare). If you can subsist on bread, pasta, cheese, milk, yoghurt and expensive fresh vegetables, you'll have few worries, but otherwise, you may want to spend some time reading labels.

Note that supermarkets are open on weekdays from around 8 or 9 am to around 6 or 7 pm in smaller towns and 9 or 10 pm in cities. On Saturday, they normally close around 4 pm in towns and 6 pm in cities. Except in very few instances (eg such tourist areas as Geiranger), they're closed on Sunday and holidays.

Meat

While many Norwegians eat meat only in the form of hot dogs and reconstituted meat patties, those who can afford it normally prefer beef, lamb, moose or reindeer. Although few Norwegian meat dishes will knock your socks off, most are quite palatable. Wind-dried meat, or *spekemat*, is a leftover from the days before refrigeration and the ubiquitous *lapskaus* (often called *biddus*, or 'wedding stew', in the Sami areas of the far north) is a hearty meat stew with vegetables.

Seafood

Norwegian seafood specialities include grilled or smoked salmon *(laks)*, boiled shrimp *(reker)*, cod *(torsk)*, catfish *(steinbit)* and other fresh seafood. In summer, you can often buy *ferske reker*, fresh shrimp, from fishing boats for around Nkr60/kg, and it's a real treat. Freshly caught fish are also often sold for relatively good prices around harbourside markets; one of the most popular – and pungent – is at the Torget in Bergen.

Seafood also turns up in an odd array of special dishes that appeal more to die-hard traditionalists than anyone else. *Fiskebollur*, or reconstituted cod, mackerel or saithe balls, are a staple for older folk, and *torsketungur*, cod tongues, are enormously popular in Lofoten. Throughout the country, a favourite is *fiskesuppe*, or fish soup, which is more a thin, creamy and slightly fish-flavoured soup than a hearty stew. It may contain a shrimp or two but is more usually all liquid.

Historically, several creative methods were used to preserve fish, resulting in seafood standards that survive to the present day. *Lutefisk*, which is dried cod made almost gelatinous by soaking it in potash lye, is popular around Christmas but it's definitely an acquired taste, while *rakørret* (also called *rakfisk*), or fermented trout, is considered by many to be utterly disgusting. Herring, or *sild*, which was once the fish of the poor masses, is now considerably more expensive and is normally served pickled in onions, mustard or tomato sauce. *Gravelaks* is a similar item, made by marinating salmon in sugar, salt, brandy and dill. In the north, *torrfisk* (also called *stokkfisk*), or dried cod remains popular and is exported in large quantities to Italy, Spain and Portugal.

Dairy Products

Milk and dairy products are a staple in Norway, and Norwegians of all ages drink milk daily. There's also a range of cheeses, the most renowned of which is the mild but tasty Jarlsberg, a white cheese that has been exported and gained popularity all over the world. It was first produced around 1815 on the Jarlsberg estate in Østfold, east of the Oslofjord. A stronger export cheese is an award-winning continental-style offering known as *ridder*.

Traditional cheeses come in several varieties: *gammelost* has always been considered a 'luxury' cheese, which was suitable for export but not for commoners; *mysost*, or 'whey cheese' was eaten by the masses and *pultost* was a simple cheese made from curdled milk and flavoured with caraway. Although these are no longer the standards, one traditional cheese that's still

ubiquitous, especially on breakfast buffets and in cafeterias, is the sweet caramel-coloured goat cheese known as *geitost* or *gudbrandsdalsost*. This unusual confection is unique to Norway and has now become an integral part of the national culture. It was first made by a milkmaid, Anne Hov, in 1863 at Solbråsetra, above Gudbrandsdalen. She took a notion to add fresh cream to some leftover whey and discovered a new taste treat. Nowadays, it's sliced thinly and eaten on waffles, flatbrød or whole-grain bread, or served as a creamy sweet fondue.

Breads & Pastries

As an accompaniment to cured meats and other hot dishes, many Norwegians like to eat *flatbrød*, a crunchy wafer-like unleavened crispbread that crumbles to the touch. Traditionally it was made from oats and barley and could be stored for many years in a *stabbur* (elevated storage shed). *Lefse*, a light and normally unsweetened griddle cake, which is in fact a leavened version of flatbrød, is often served with sweet condiments. Variations include *lumpe*, which is a potato flour pancake, and *kumpe*, or potato flour dumpling.

In the afternoon, people often eat a snack of waffles, normally with jam and cream. Unlike the firm Belgian waffles, which are better known abroad, Norwegian *vafler*, which are flower-shaped and divided into four or six heart-shaped bits, are soft and normally strongly flavoured with cardamom. Many of the standard European pastries are sold in the konditori all over the country.

Fruit & Vegetables

Fresh vegetables in Norway are almost literally worth their weight in gold; if they're requisite, stock up in the ethnic areas of Oslo, especially around Grønland, where you'll find the best value in the country.

Although it has its origins in South America, the potato features prominently in nearly every Norwegian meal and may be considered a staple in the national diet. Most restaurants serve boiled or roasted potatoes with every dish, and an order of chips is normally twice the size – and three times the price – it would be elsewhere in Europe. Other vegetables that turn up with some regularity are cabbage (*kål*) and turnips (*kålrot*). Carrots, swedes (rutabagas), cauliflower and broccoli also grow fairly well and appear frequently in restaurant meals.

While vegetarianism isn't big in Norway, nearly every restaurant offers some sort of vegetarian dish, even if it's just a cheese and onion omelette or a pasta with cream sauce. Oslo and other larger cities enjoy a choice of trendy but rarely overpriced European-style cafés that will offer a range of creative and inexpensive dishes, normally including several well conceived vegetarian options. At lunch time, you'll normally find something decent for Nkr60 to Nkr100.

The country's main fruit-growing region is around Hardangerfjord, where strawberries, plums, cherries, apples and other orchard fruits proliferate. Although berries are only rarely cultivated, a range of wild berries grow in the forests, mountains, tundra and bogs. Among them are wild strawberries (*ville jordbær*), cranberries (*tyttebær*), black currants (*solbær*), red currants (*rips*), blueberries (*blåbær*), raspberries (*bringbær*) and the most prized, cloudberries (*moltebær*).

The berries, which make excellent snacks and jams, are available to anyone, but there are some restrictions on picking cloudberries, which grow in boggy areas of Nordland, Troms and Finnmark. On private land, they're reserved for the landowners, and on public land in Finnmark, are available only to residents of that county. However, on public land, anyone is welcome to pick them and eat them on the spot.

DRINKS

If Norway has a national drink, it's coffee, and it's drunk in such staggering quantities that one can only wonder how people can remain so calm under the influence of so much caffeine. Coffee first arrived in Norway in the mid-18th century but didn't really take off until a century later, when it was embraced by the upper class. Today its popularity is universal and most Norwegians drink it black and strong, but foreigners who add milk and/or sugar are normally indulged. Unlike in Iceland, however, where coffee enjoys a similarly enthusiastic following, it's not inexpensive and refills aren't free; in bakeries and cafeterias, a small cup normally costs around Nkr14, and refills from Nkr6 to Nkr10.

Teas and infusions are also available all over the country but don't enjoy the same popularity as coffee. The usual range of fizzy drinks (*brus*) and mineral water (*mineralvann*) are available everywhere. Try to buy them at supermarkets rather than kiosks, petrol stations or convenience stores, where they're usually twice the price.

Alcoholic Drinks

Norway's official attitude toward alcohol borders on paranoia, and alcohol sales are strictly controlled and a few towns have implemented virtual prohibition. In some places, including parts of Telemark, drinking beer in public actually calls for a fine of Nkr2000 and/or prison time! The legal drinking age is 18 years for beer (*øl*) and wine (*vin*) and 20 for spirits.

Beer is available in some supermarkets for extortionate prices, but wine and spirits may be purchased only at state monopoly shops known as *Vinmonopolet* (fondly known as just *pole*), which are open until 4, 5 or 6 pm on weekdays and 9 am to 2 pm on Saturday. Unfortunately, only the largest cities and towns actually have a Vinmonopolet and those that would like to have one must apply to the government and face all sorts of scrutiny before a licence will be granted. Generally, the presence of another monopoly shop within a two-hour drive will disqualify any applicant. Fortunately, most of these places are permitted to have an *ølutsalg*, or 'beer outlet', where a range of beers are available in bulk for the most reasonable prices you'll find.

On the mainland, the best value wine is the Spanish vintage, *Amigo*, which costs just Nkr59 for a 750ml bottle. In Svalbard, alcohol is available duty-free, but it's rationed for residents and visitors must present a valid plane ticket in order to purchase it.

Despite its cost, beer is extremely popular, and in bars it's commonly sold in 500ml glasses (about 15% larger than an English pint). The standard Norwegian beer is pils lager, with an alcohol content of around 4%, and it's still brewed in accordance with the 16th century German purity law. The most popular brands are the lagers Ringsnes in the south and Mack in the north. Note that when friends go out drinking, people normally buy their own drinks rather than rounds.

For a powerful dose of Norwegian culture, don't miss the national spirit, *aquavit* (or *akevitt*), which is a potent potato and caraway liquor that dates from the early days of Norwegian trade on the high seas. The name is derived from the Latin *aqua vitae*, the 'living waters'. Although the caraway is an essential ingredient, various modern distilleries augment the spicy flavour with any combination of orange, coriander (cilantro), anise, fennel, sugar and salt! The confection is aged for three to five years in 500L oak barrels that have previously been used to age sherry.

Perhaps the most esteemed version of this libation is Linje Aquavit, or 'line aquavit', which first referred to stores that had crossed the equator. In the early days, ships carried oak barrels of aquavit abroad to trade, but the unsold barrels were returned to Norway and offered for sale. When it was discovered that the product had improved with age and travel, this leftover swill became a highly prized commodity. Today, bottles of Linje Aquavit bear the name of the ship involved, its route and the amount of time the barrels have aged at sea.

Given the prices of beer, wine and spirits, it's probably not surprising that Norwegians do a great deal of illegal distilling and home-brewing. If you're offered any home-made swill, exercise due caution, as things sometimes go wrong and even when they don't, the effects can be mind-numbing!

ENTERTAINMENT

Although Norway isn't known for its awe-inspiring entertainment scene, the larger cities do provide some semblance of nightlife. Film admissions or cover charges in nightclubs average around Nkr50 to Nkr60. Most well known nightspots provide live music performances or dancing on Friday and Saturday night, and may also offer a bit of action on Thursday and Sunday. Norway also has a phenomenal number of music festivals; for more information, see Special Events, earlier in this chapter.

Bars & Clubs

In most bars and nightclubs, a 500ml glass of lager will set you back around Nkr47, but it can be as low as Nkr25 to Nkr35 on the *Børsen* ('stock exchange') system employed in some places, in which the price rises and falls with demand. A glass of house wine starts at around Nkr35 and the cheapest 750ml bottle will cost around Nkr118, but you'll more often pay over Nkr150. Inexpensive spirits average around Nkr40 for a shot.

Other

Most towns have at least one cinema but the offerings are generally about six months behind most of the rest of the world. Oslo, Bergen and other larger towns have theatre, opera and ballet companies, as well as philharmonic orchestras. However, most classical performances take place in winter, when outdoor activities are limited, and few visitors are around to enjoy them.

SPECTATOR SPORTS

For thousands of years, skis were the only practical means of winter transport in much of Norway and, as a result, it is in winter sports that Norwegians have excelled. In fact, the people of Telemark invented the graceful Telemark turn and the word slalom is derived from the Norwegian words *sla låm*, or 'slope track', which originally referred to a nordic ski competition that wove over hill and dale, dodging thickets! In 1928, 1932 and 1936, Sonja Henie was the

Olympic figure skating gold medallist; speed-skater Johann Koss won three gold medals at the Lillehammer Winter Olympics in 1994, and in 1998 in Nagano, Norway finished second on the overall medal table (behind Germany) with 10 gold medals. In winter, big ski-jumping events normally take place at Holmenkollen near Oslo, and other winter events occur at the Olympic venues in Hamar and Lillehammer.

For the past few years the Norwegian men's national football (soccer) team has maintained a top-20 FIFA ranking and a fearsome competitive reputation in world football. The team qualified for the World Cup in 1994 and 1998 and did very well in the 1998 competition, causing a sensation by beating early favourites Brazil in the first round. They were knocked out in the second round by Italy. The bulk of Norway's national team stars play in the English Premier League, notably Manchester United striker Ole Gunnar Solskjær and his Chelsea counterpart Tore Andre Flo. But it's the Norwegian women's national team that has strutted the world stage with most success, clinching the second ever Women's World Cup in 1995 and consistently rating among the best five nations around the globe.

Other sporting successes have been scored by Norwegian women, including long-distance and marathon runners Grete Waitz and Ingrid Kristiansen, and javelin champion Trine Hattestad.

SHOPPING

Given the prices, few people would consider a shopping holiday in Norway. While items in shops are almost always of high quality and shop windows can be veritable works of art, the prices would put off all but the most well heeled visitors. Specialities include wool sweaters and other hand-knitted clothing, pewter ware, intricate silver jewellery, Sami sheath knives, reindeer-leather products, troll figurines, wooden toys and woodwork adorned with *rosemaling* (painted or carved floral motifs). For the best quality Norwegian handicrafts – at corresponding prices – look for the Husfliden shops, which exist in most larger cities and towns.

If you're shipping purchases back home, a good option is the post office's economy option, which is technically surface mail but actually transfers goods overseas by air where possible. For a reasonable price, a parcel may be shipped anywhere in the world in under a month.

Getting There & Away

The first step for anyone headed for Norway is to get to Europe, and in these days of airline competition you'll find plenty of deals to European 'gateway' cities, particularly London, Paris, Frankfurt, Berlin or even Copenhagen. Only a handful of travellers approach Norway and Scandinavia from the east, via Russia, although the trans-Siberian and trans-Mongolian routes offer exceptionally adventurous options.

AIR

Remember to reconfirm your onward or return bookings at least 72 hours before departure for international flights. Otherwise there's a real risk that you'll turn up at the airport only to find that you've missed your flight because it was rescheduled, or that you've been reclassified as a 'no-show' and 'bumped' (see the Air Travel Glossary later in this chapter).

Airports & Airlines

SAS, British Airways, KLM-Royal Dutch Airlines, Air France, Lufthansa Airlines, Sabena, Swissair, Alitalia, Finnair and Icelandair link Oslo's Gardermoen airport with major European and North American cities. Bergen, Stavanger and Trondheim also have direct international flights. If you're flying between the UK and Stavanger (a route used mainly by oil businesspeople) you'll get the best non-business fares by staying at least one Saturday night in Norway.

Braathens SAFE (www.braathens.no) has daily flights between London's Gatwick, Gardermoen and Bergen (☎ 55 23 55 23), and six weekly services between Newcastle, Stavanger (☎ 51 51 10 00), Bergen and Oslo. There are also international daily services between Oslo and Billund (☎ 75 35 33 78), in Denmark, and twice weekly between Tromsø (☎ 77 66 00 00) and Murmansk (☎ 085-10034) in Russia. Note that Braathens SAFE has arrangements with 18 hotels around the country, which offer discounts of up to 20% for holders of Braathens tickets. The best fares are available on super-Apex tickets purchased at least seven days in advance, but you can stay no longer than a month and must spend at least one Saturday night. Baggage limit is normally 30kg per person.

Scandinavian Airlines System, or SAS (☎ 81 00 33 00, www.sas.no), flies daily between London's Heathrow, Gardermoen, Bergen and Stavanger; and twice weekly in summer between Heathrow and Tromsø. It also connects Manchester and Oslo daily except Saturday and flies twice daily between Aberdeen and Stavanger. Its North American hub is New York Newark, with daily flights to and from Oslo and Stockholm. SAS also offers numerous daily

Air Travel Glossary

Baggage Allowance This will be written on your ticket and usually includes one 20kg item to go in the hold, plus one item of hand luggage.

Bucket Shops These are unbonded travel agencies specialising in discounted airline tickets.

Bumped Just because you have a confirmed seat doesn't mean you're going to get on the plane (see Overbooking).

Cancellation Penalties If you have to cancel or change a discounted ticket, there are often heavy penalties involved; insurance can sometimes be taken out against these penalties. Some airlines impose penalties on regular tickets as well, particularly against 'no-show' passengers.

Check-In Airlines ask you to check in a certain time ahead of the flight departure (usually one to two hours on international flights). If you fail to check in on time and the flight is overbooked, the airline can cancel your booking and give your seat to somebody else.

Confirmation Having a ticket written out with the flight and date you want doesn't mean you have a seat until the agent has checked with the airline that your status is 'OK' or confirmed. Meanwhile you could just be 'on request'.

Courier Fares Businesses often need to send urgent documents or freight securely and quickly. Courier companies hire people to accompany the package through customs and, in return, offer a discount ticket which is sometimes a phenomenal bargain. In effect, what the companies do is ship their freight as your luggage on regular commercial flights. This is a legitimate operation, but there are two shortcomings – the short turnaround time of the ticket (usually not longer than a month) and the limitation on your luggage allowance. You may have to surrender all your allowance and take only carry-on luggage.

Full Fares Airlines traditionally offer 1st class (coded F), business class (coded J) and economy class (coded Y) tickets. These days there are so many promotional and discounted fares available that few passengers pay full economy fare.

ITX An ITX, or 'independent inclusive tour excursion', is often available on tickets to popular holiday destinations. Officially it's a package deal combined with hotel accommodation, but many agents will sell you one of these for the flight only and give you phoney hotel vouchers in the unlikely event that you're challenged at the airport.

Lost Tickets If you lose your airline ticket an airline will usually treat it like a travellers cheque and, after inquiries, issue you with another one. Legally, however, an airline is entitled to treat it like cash and if you lose it then it's gone forever. Take good care of your tickets.

MCO An MCO, or 'miscellaneous charge order', is a voucher that looks like an airline ticket but carries no destination or date. It can be exchanged through any International Association of Travel Agents (IATA) airline for a ticket on a specific flight. It's a useful alternative to an onward ticket in those countries that demand one, and is more flexible than an ordinary ticket if you're unsure of your route.

No-Shows No-shows are passengers who fail to show up for their flight. Full-fare passengers who fail to turn up are sometimes entitled to travel on a later flight. The rest are penalised (see Cancellation Penalties).

On Request This is an unconfirmed booking for a flight.

Air Travel Glossary

Onward Tickets An entry requirement for many countries is that you have a ticket out of the country. If you're unsure of your next move, the easiest solution is to buy the cheapest onward ticket to a neighbouring country or a ticket from a reliable airline which can later be refunded if you do not use it.

Open Jaw Tickets These are return tickets where you fly out to one place but return from another. If available, this can save you backtracking to your arrival point.

Overbooking Airlines hate to fly empty seats and since every flight has some passengers who fail to show up, airlines often book more passengers than they have seats. Usually excess passengers make up for the no-shows, but occasionally somebody gets bumped. Guess who it is most likely to be? The passengers who check in late.

Point-to-Point Tickets These are discount tickets that can be bought on some routes in return for passengers waiving their rights to a stopover.

Promotional Fares These are officially discounted fares, available from travel agencies or direct from the airline.

Reconfirmation At least 72 hours prior to departure time of an onward or return flight, you must contact the airline and 'reconfirm' that you intend to be on the flight. If you don't do this the airline can delete your name from the passenger list and you could lose your seat.

Restrictions Discounted tickets often have various restrictions on them – such as needing to be paid for in advance and incurring a penalty to be altered. Others are restrictions on the minimum and maximum period you must be away, such as a minimum of 14 days or a maximum of one year.

Round-the-World Tickets RTW tickets give you a limited period (usually a year) in which to circumnavigate the globe. You can go anywhere the carrying airlines go, as long as you don't backtrack. The number of stopovers or total number of separate flights is decided before you set off and they usually cost a bit more than a basic return flight.

Stand-by This is a discounted ticket where you only fly if there is a seat free at the last moment. Stand-by fares are usually available only on domestic routes.

Transferred Tickets Airline tickets cannot be transferred from one person to another. Travellers sometimes try to sell the return half of their ticket, but officials can ask you to prove that you are the person named on the ticket. This is less likely to happen on domestic flights, but on an international flight tickets are compared with passports.

Travel Agencies Travel agencies vary widely and you should choose one that suits your needs. Some simply handle tours, while full-services agencies handle everything from tours and tickets to car rental and hotel bookings. If all you want is a ticket at the lowest possible price, then go to an agency specialising in discounted tickets.

Travel Periods Ticket prices vary with the time of year. There is a low (off-peak) season and a high (peak) season, and often a low-shoulder season and a high-shoulder season as well. Usually the fare depends on your outward flight – if you depart in the high season and return in the low season, you pay the high-season fare.

services between Oslo and various European capitals, most of which are routed via Copenhagen. Its free baggage allowance is 32kg per person.

Currently, the best deal between the UK and Norway is with Ryanair (Stansted: ☎ 0541-569 569; Torp: ☎ 33 42 75 00), which flies twice daily on weekdays and once daily on weekends between Stansted and Torp airport, 100km south of Oslo. Fares start at £99 (Nkr990) return.

Coast Air (☎ 52 83 41 10, fax 52 84 03 74, www.coastair.no), based in Haugesund, flies daily except Saturday between Bergen, Haugesund, Kristiansand and Aberdeen. British Midland Airways has daily flights between London and Bergen, with occasional special fares. Air UK flies several times daily between Aberdeen and Stavanger and British Airways has five daily flights between Heathrow and Oslo. The Danish airline Maersk (☎ 38 00 80 00, fax 38 02 11 07), with its Norwegian offices in Kristiansand, flies twice weekly between London and Kristiansand, via Copenhagen.

The Norwegian airline Widerøe (☎ 67 11 60 00, fax 67 11 61 95, internetbooking @wideroe.no, www.wideroe.no), based in Lysaker (near Oslo), has services between Kirkenes and Murmansk, Russia, on Monday and Wednesday. In summer, it also flies between Oslo and Berlin (Nkr1850); Oslo and Shetland (Nkr2000); Sandefjord and Copenhagen (Nkr750); and Sandefjord, Stavanger, Bergen and Glasgow (Nkr1450).

Buying Tickets

Your plane ticket will probably be the single most expensive item in your travel budget, and it's worth taking some time to research the current state of the market. Start early: some of the cheapest tickets must be purchased well in advance, and some popular flights sell out early. Have a talk to recent travellers, look at the ads in newspapers and magazines, and watch for special offers. Don't forget to check any Scandinavian or Norwegian newspapers and magazines published in your country of origin.

Inexpensive tickets are available in two distinct categories: official and unofficial. Official ones have a variety of names including advance purchase tickets, advance purchase excursion (Apex) fares, super-Apex and simply budget fares.

Unofficial tickets are discounted tickets that the airlines release through selected travel agents and are usually not sold by the airline offices themselves. Airlines can, however, supply information on routes and timetables and make bookings; their low-season, student and senior citizens' fares can be competitive. Normal, full-fare airline tickets sometimes include one or more side trips in Europe free of charge, which can make them good value.

Return (round-trip) tickets usually work out cheaper than two one-way fares – often much cheaper. Be aware that immigration officials may ask to see return or onward tickets, and that if you can't show either, you might have to provide proof of 'sufficient means of support', which means you have to show a lot of money or, in some cases, valid credit cards.

Round-the-world (RTW) tickets are often real bargains, and can work out to be no more expensive or even cheaper than an ordinary return ticket. The official airline RTW tickets are usually put together by a combination of two or more airlines and permit you to fly anywhere you want on their route systems so long as you don't backtrack. Other restrictions are that you (usually) must book the first sector in advance and cancellation penalties then apply. There may be restrictions on how many stops (or kilometres) you are permitted, and usually the tickets are valid for between 90 days and a year. Prices start at about UK£1000/US$1500, depending on the season and length of validity. An alternative type of RTW ticket is one put together by a travel agent using a combination of discounted tickets. These can be much cheaper than the official ones but usually carry a lot of restrictions.

Generally, you can find discounted tickets at prices as low as, or lower than, advance purchase or budget tickets. Phone around the travel agencies for bargains. You may discover that those impossibly cheap flights are 'fully booked, but we have another one that costs a bit more ...'. Or that the flight is on an airline notorious for its poor safety standards and leaves you in the world's least favourite airport in mid-journey for 14 hours confined to the transit lounge because you don't have a visa. Or the agent claims to have the last two seats available for that country for the whole of August, which he will hold for you for a maximum of two hours as long as you come in and pay cash. Don't panic – keep ringing around.

If you're coming from the USA, South-East Asia or the UK, you'll probably find the cheapest flights are being advertised by obscure agencies. Many such firms are honest and solvent, but there are a few rogues who will take your money and disappear only to reopen elsewhere a month or two later under a new name.

If you feel suspicious about a firm, don't give them all the money at once – leave a deposit of 20% or so and pay the balance when you get the ticket. If they insist on cash in advance, go somewhere else or be prepared to take a very big risk. Once you have the ticket, ring the airline to confirm that you are actually booked onto the flight.

You may decide to pay more than the rock-bottom fare by opting for the safety of a better known travel agent. Firms such as STA Travel, which has offices worldwide, Council Travel in the USA and elsewhere or Travel CUTS in Canada offer good prices to most destinations and won't disappear overnight leaving you clutching a receipt for a nonexistent ticket.

A more novel way of finding inexpensive tickets, especially if you're coming from the USA, is on the website www.price line.com, which tells you when seats are normally available and allows you to name your own price for airline tickets; within an hour, it'll advise you by email whether your bid has been accepted.

Use the fares quoted in this book as a guide only. They are approximate and based on the rates advertised by travel agents at the time of research. Most are likely to have changed by the time you read this.

Travellers with Special Needs

If you have special needs of any sort – you're vegetarian or require a special diet, you're travelling in a wheelchair, taking the baby, terrified of flying, whatever – let the airline people know as soon as possible so that they can make the necessary arrangements. Remind them when you reconfirm your booking (at least 72 hours before departure) and again when you check in at the airport. It may also be worth ringing around the airlines before you make your booking to find out how they can handle your particular requirements.

Children aged under two travel for 10% of the full fare (or free on some airlines) as long as they don't occupy a seat. They don't get a baggage allowance in this case. 'Skycots', baby food and nappies (diapers) should be provided by the airline if requested in advance. Children aged between two and 12 can usually occupy a seat for half to two-thirds of the full fare and get a standard baggage allowance.

Departure Tax

Norway levies a departure tax of Nkr207, which is appended to the price of the airline ticket.

The USA

The North Atlantic is the world's busiest long-haul air corridor and the flight options are bewildering. Larger newspapers such as the *New York Times*, the *Chicago Tribune*, the *San Francisco Chronicle* and the *Los Angeles Times* all produce weekly travel sections in which you'll find any number of travel agents' ads for air fares to Europe.

Thanks to the high ethnic Norwegian population in Minnesota, Wisconsin and North Dakota, you may find small local agencies specialising in travel to Scandinavia and offering good-value charter flights in those areas. Otherwise, you should be able to fly return from New York or Boston to Copenhagen, Oslo or Stockholm for around US$500 in the low season and US$800 in the high season. With most tickets you can usually travel 'open jaws', allowing you to land in one city (Copenhagen, for example) and return from another (such as Oslo) at no extra cost.

Icelandair (☎ 800-223 5500) flies from New York, Boston, Baltimore-Washington, Minneapolis, Fort Lauderdale and Orlando via Reykjavík to many European destinations including Glasgow, Helsinki, Oslo, Stockholm, and Copenhagen. It offers some of the best deals, and on its transatlantic flights it allows a free three-day stopover in Reykjavík – making it a great way to spend a few days in Iceland.

On the other hand, if you're planning on flying within Scandinavian and Baltic Europe, SAS (☎ 800-221 2350) has some interesting regional discounts available to passengers who fly on its transatlantic flights (see Air in the Getting Around chapter).

Airhitch (☎ 800-326 2009 or ☎ 310-394 4215) specialises in stand-by tickets to Europe for US$159/239 one-way from the east coast/west coast, but the destinations are by region (not a specific city or country), so you'll need a flexible schedule.

Another option is a courier flight (see the Air Travel Glossary). They all work slightly differently, so it's best to make your initial contact with the courier services a few months before you plan to travel. Find out more about courier flights from Halbart Express (☎ 718-656 8189) or Now Voyager (☎ 212-431 1616) in New York and IBC in Los Angeles (☎ 310-665 1760). Now Voyager charges a $50 annual registration fee after which flights to Europe (including Copenhagen) cost about US$300 return and allow a stay of seven days.

The Travel Unlimited newsletter, PO Box 1058, Allston, MA 02134, publishes details of the cheapest air fares and courier possibilities for destinations all over the world. It's a treasure trove of information. Another option is the *Air Courier Bulletin* published by the International Association of Air Travel Couriers (☎ 561-582 8320), PO Box 1349, 220 South Dixie Hwy, Lake Worth, FL 33460.

For information on the website www.priceline.com, see Buying Tickets earlier in this chapter.

Discount Travel Agencies North Americans won't get the great deals that are available in London, but a few discount agencies keep a lookout for the best air fare bargains. To comply with regulations, these agencies are sometimes associated with travel clubs.

Airtech
  (☎ 800-575 8324) 584 Broadway, Suite 1007, New York, NY 10012
Cheap Tickets, Inc
  (☎ 800-377 1000)
Council Travel
  (☎ 800-226 8624)
Educational Travel Center
  (☎ 800-747 5551) 438 N Frances St, Madison, WI 53703
High Adventure Travel
  (☎ 800-428 8735 or ☎ 415-912 5600, fax 415-912 5606, airtreks@highadv.com, www.highadv.com) 353 Sacramento St, Suite 600, San Francisco, CA
Interworld Travel
  (☎ 800-468 3796) 800 Douglass Rd, Miami, FL 33134
Last Minute Travel Services
  (☎ 800-527 8646)
Skylink
  (☎ 800-247 6659) 265 Madison Ave, 5th Floor, New York, NY 10014
STA Travel
  (☎ 800-777 0112) 10 Downing St(!), New York, NY 10014
Uni Travel
  (☎ 314-569 2501) PO Box 12485, St Louis, MO 63132

Canada

Travel CUTS has offices in all major Canadian cities. Scan the budget travel agents' ads in the *Globe & Mail*, *Toronto Star* and *Vancouver Sun*.

For courier flights, contact FB on Board Courier Services (☎ 514-631 7925). A return courier flight to London will cost from about C$525 from Toronto or Montreal and C$590 from Vancouver in low season. See the Air Travel Glossary for general information on courier flights. Airhitch (see the USA section) has stand-by fares to Europe from

Toronto, Montreal and Vancouver. You may also find excellent deals to Norway from smaller agencies in parts of Manitoba, where there's a high ethnic Norwegian population.

Icelandair (see the USA section) now has low-cost seasonal flights from Halifax in Nova Scotia to Oslo, Stockholm, Helsinki and Copenhagen via Reykjavík.

Discount Travel Agencies The following sometimes offer good air fare deals:

Flight Centre
   (☎ 604-739 9539) 3030 Granville St, Vancouver, BC V6H 3J8
Nouvelles Frontières
   (☎ 514-526 8444) 1001 Sherbrook East, Suite 720, Montreal, PQ H2L 1L3
Travel CUTS
   (☎ 888-838 2887 or ☎ 416-979 2406) 87 College St, Toronto, Ontario M5T 1P7

The UK

If you're looking for a cheap way into or out of Scandinavia, London is Europe's major centre for discounted fares. You can fly from London to Copenhagen for between UK£99 and £109, to Stockholm for UK£123 to £130, to Riga for UK£258, and to Tallinn for UK£241.

In fact, you can often find air fares from London that either match or beat surface alternatives in terms of cost. A restricted one-month return ticket from London to Copenhagen, for example, is available through discount travel agents for less than UK£100. By comparison, a two-month return by rail between the same cities costs around UK£275. Travelling between airports and city centres is not a problem in Scandinavia thanks to good transport networks.

Those travelling alone may want to consider a courier flight (see the Air Travel Glossary). EU integration and electronic communications means there's increasingly less call for couriers, but you may find something. British Airways, for example, offers courier flights through the Travel Shop (☎ 0181-564 7009, after April 2000 ☎ 020-8564 7009) in London. People taking

flights from Britain pay an Air Passenger Duty; those flying to countries in the EU pay UK£20; those flying beyond it, £10. This may or may not be quoted in the price of your ticket, so check with your travel agent. At present, there is no departure tax if you leave by sea or via the Channel Tunnel.

The entertainment listings magazine *Time Out*, the Sunday papers, the *Exchange & Mart* and *Evening Standard* carry ads for cheap fares. Also look out for the free magazines, such as *TNT*, and newspapers widely available in London. You can often pick them up outside the main train and tube stations.

Discount Travel Agencies Make sure the agent you select belongs to some sort of traveller-protection scheme, such as the Association of British Travel Agents (ABTA). If you have paid for your flight through an ABTA-registered agent who subsequently folds, ABTA guarantees a refund or an alternative. Unregistered bucket shops may be cheaper but are often riskier. The following London agencies offer some of the best discounted deals around:

Bridge the World
   (☎ 0171-209 9000, fax 0171-813 3350, after April 2000 ☎ 020-7209 9000, fax 020-7813 3350) 47 Chalk Farm Rd, London NW1 8AN
STA Travel
   (☎ 0171-581 4132, after April 2000 ☎ 020-7581 4132) 86 Old Brompton Rd, London SW7 3LQ
Trailfinders
   (☎ 0171-937 5400, after April 2000 ☎ 020-7937 5400) 215 Kensington High St, London W8 6BD
Travel Bug
   (☎ 0171-835 2000, after April 2000 ☎ 7835 2000) 125 Gloucester Rd, London SW7 4SF

Continental Europe

Though London is the travel discount capital of Europe, several other cities in the region also provide a wide range of good deals, particularly Amsterdam and Athens. Berlin is also becoming an air hub, especially for connections to Russia. In Germany, individuals who have plane tickets to sell advertise them at good prices in the Urlaub & Reisen (biete) section of major city newspapers.

Discount Travel Agencies Many travel agents in Europe have ties with STA Travel, where you'll find cheap tickets that may be altered once without charge. STA and other discount outlets in important transport hubs include:

Alternativ Tours
(☎ 030-881 2089) Wilmersdorferstrasse 94, Berlin
Council Travel
(☎ 01-42 66 20 87) Rue St Augustine, Paris
(☎ 01-44 55 55 44) 22 Rue des Pyramides, Paris
CTS
(☎ 06-46791) Via Genova 16, off Via Nazionale, Rome
Kilroy Travel
(☎ 030-310 0040) Hardenbergstrasse 9, D-10623 Berlin
International Student & Youth Travel Service
(☎ 01-322 1267) Nikis 11, 10557 Athens
Malibu Travel
(☎ 020-623 6814) Damrak 30, Amsterdam
NBBS
(☎ 020-624 0989) Rokin 38, Amsterdam
SSR
(☎ 01-261 2956) Leonhardstrasse 5-10, Zürich
STA Travel
(☎ 069-70 30 35) Bockenheimer Landstrasse 133, 60325 Frankfurt
USIT
(☎ 01-679 8833) 19 Aston Quay, Dublin
Voyages Wasteel
(☎ 01-43 43 46 10), 2 Rue Michel Charles, 75012 Paris

Australia & New Zealand

STA Travel and Flight Centres International are major dealers in cheap air fares, but it still doesn't hurt to check the travel agents' ads in the Yellow Pages and ring around. The Saturday travel sections of the *Sydney Morning Herald* and Melbourne's *Age* newspapers have many ads offering cheap fares to Europe, but don't be surprised if they happen to be 'sold out' when you contact the agents: they're usually low-season fares on obscure airlines with conditions attached. With Australia's large and well organised ethnic populations, it also pays to check the ethnic press for special deals on flights to Europe.

Discounted return fares to Europe on mainstream airlines through a reputable agent like STA Travel cost between A$1500 (low season) and A$2500 (high season). Flights to/from Perth are usually a few hundred dollars cheaper. The Austrian airline Lauda Air flies from Sydney via Kuala Lumpur to Vienna in the heart of central Europe. In New Zealand, STA Travel and Flight Centres International are popular agencies. A low season return fare from Auckland to Stockholm is around NZ$1185/2049 one-way/return.

Discount Travel Agencies In Australia, the main players in the discount game are Flight Centres International (☎ 131600) and STA Travel (☎ 1300 360 960). STA is represented in most cities (dial ☎ 131 776 for your local branch) and on university campuses. It also has a comprehensive website at www.statravelaus.com.au. New Zealand residents can call STA on ☎ 0800 874 773.

Asia

Singapore and Bangkok are the discount plane-ticket capitals of the region. But be careful: not all agents are reliable. Ask the advice of other travellers before buying tickets. Lauda Air flies direct to Vienna from Hong Kong via Bangkok or Beijing. STA Travel has branches in Tokyo, Singapore, Bangkok and Kuala Lumpur. Mumbai and Delhi are India's air transport hubs but tickets are slightly cheaper in Delhi.

Africa

Nairobi and Johannesburg are the best places in Africa to buy tickets to Europe, thanks to the strong competition between their many bucket shops. Several West African countries offer cheap charter flights to France, and charter fares from Morocco can be incredibly cheap if you're lucky enough to find a seat. From South Africa, Air Namibia and South African Airlines offer particularly inexpensive return youth fares to London. The Student Travel Centre in Johannesburg (☎ 011-447 5414) and the Africa Travel Centre in Cape Town (☎ 021-235 555) are worth trying for cheap tickets.

LAND
Border Crossings

Border crossings between Norway and Sweden or Finland are straightforward; passports are rarely checked and half the time you aren't even aware that you've crossed a border. For Russia, however, everyone needs a visa and travellers are likely to face greater scrutiny.

Note that if you're travelling by rail into Norway, bicycles will be counted as excess baggage and charged accordingly.

Sweden

Bus Nor-Way Bussekspress runs express buses three to four times daily between Oslo, Göteborg (4½ hours, Nkr220) and Malmö (10 hours, Nkr350), with a boat connection to Copenhagen. At 8 am from Monday to Friday, there's a bus from Oslo to Stockholm (nine hours, Nkr320). There are also direct daily buses between Bodø and Skellefteå (8¾ hours, Nkr320) and along the Blå Vägen, or 'Blue Highway', between Mo i Rana and Umeå (7½ hours, Nkr185).

Train There are daily trains between Stockholm and Oslo (seven hours, Nkr675), Trondheim (11 hours, Nkr700) and Narvik (22 hours, Nkr1010). Trains also run daily between Oslo and Helsingborg (7½ hours, Nkr644), via Göteborg (four hours, Nkr409). Note that the Swedish '2000' trains, which leave in the morning and cater to business travellers, tack on a Nkr137 surcharge.

Car & Motorcycle The main highways between Sweden and Norway are the E6 from Göteborg to Oslo, the E18 from Stockholm to Oslo, the E14 from Sundsvall to Trondheim and the E12 from Umeå to Mo i Rana. Many secondary roads also cross the border.

Denmark

Bus To travel by bus to Denmark, take the bus between Oslo and Malmö (see Sweden), then hop on the express boat across the strait to Copenhagen.

Train Trains run three times daily from Oslo to Copenhagen (9½ hours, Nkr790), including a night train which leaves at 10.40 pm. At Helsingborg, Sweden, the train boards a rail ferry across the Øresund to Helsingør, Denmark.

Finland

Bus The E8 highway runs from Tornio, Finland, to Tromsø and secondary highways connect Finland with the northern Sami towns of Karasjok and Kautokeino. Regular buses serve all three routes. In summer, the daily bus run by the Finnish company Eskelisen Lapin Linjat runs between Rovaniemi and Tromsø (11½ hours, Nkr378), via Karesuvanto and Kilpisjärvi. It leaves at 7.10 am southbound and 11.20 am northbound. Also in summer, the company runs daily buses between Rovaniemi and Tana Bru (9¼ hours, Nkr500), via Inari and Ivalo; and between Rovaniemi, Karasjok (6¾ hours, Nkr267) and Lakselv (7¾ hours, Nkr267), with a connection to Nordkapp (11¾ hours, Nkr464). Four times weekly, buses connect Kautokeino with Enontekiö (2¼ hours, Nkr66), with connections to Rovaniemi.

Germany

Bus Twice weekly, Nor-Way Bussekspress buses connect Oslo with Berlin (14¾ hours, Nkr600), via Göteborg, Sweden, and Rostock, Germany. They run on Monday and Thursday southbound and on Tuesday and Friday northbound.

Train Hamburg is the central European gateway for Scandinavia, with several direct trains daily to Copenhagen and a few to Stockholm; in either city, you'll readily find connections into Norway. The train from Hamburg to Copenhagen travels between Puttgarden and Rødby Havn by ferry, which is included in the ticket price; there's also a short ferry segment between Helsingør, Denmark, and Helsingborg, Sweden.

A good train deal to know about in Germany is the Sparpreis fare which allows a 2nd-class, round trip anywhere in Germany within one month for DM209 (an accompanying person pays just DM109). This ticket can be purchased at any German train station and unlimited stopovers along the direct route are allowed, but you are not allowed to complete the return trip within a single Monday-to-Friday period. From northern Germany, you can easily make your way to Denmark and the rest of Scandinavia.

The UK

Bus If you like long and arduous journeys, you can bus it between London and Oslo in about 38 hours, but you may have to change buses as many as four times! The service operates two or three times weekly, all year round, via Amsterdam and Hamburg. Reservations are compulsory. Contact National Express (☎ 01990-505050) in the UK or Nor-Way Bussekspress in Oslo (see Bus in the Getting Around chapter for contact details). The return fare is Nkr2000, so it may well be cheaper to fly!

Train Travelling by train from the UK to Scandinavia can be more expensive than flying. From London a return 2nd-class train ticket will cost UK£228 to Copenhagen, UK£281 to Stockholm and UK£367 to Oslo. Note that the lowest equivalent air fares are UK£94/170/202!

Russia & Asia

Bus Russia has a short border with Norway and buses run three times weekly between Kirkenes and Murmansk. For details on overland travel to and from Russia, see Visiting Russia under Kirkenes in the Troms & Finnmark chapter.

Train To/from Russia and eastern Asia, the rail link can work out at about the same price as flying, depending on how much time and money you spend along the way, and it can be a lot more fun. There are three routes to/from Moscow across Siberia with connections to China, Japan and Korea: the trans-Siberian to/from Vladivostok, and the trans-Mongolian and trans-Manchurian, both to/from Beijing. There's a fourth route

south from Moscow and across Kazakhstan, following part of the old Silk Road to Beijing. These trips take several days and often involve stopovers, and prices vary according to which direction you are travelling, where you buy your ticket and what is included – the prices quoted here are a rough indication only. From Moscow, you must get to St Petersburg and from there either across the Baltic to southern Scandinavia or northward through Karelia to Murmansk and thence to Kirkenes in Norway.

The trans-Siberian takes just under seven days from Moscow via Khabarovsk to Vladivostok, from where there is a boat to Niigata in Japan from May to October. Otherwise you can fly to Niigata as well as to Seattle and Anchorage in the USA. The complete journey between Moscow and Niigata costs from about US$600 per person for a 2nd-class sleeper in a four-berth cabin.

The trans-Mongolian travels via Ulaan Baator, in Mongolia, to Beijing and takes about 5½ days. A hard 2nd-class berth in a four-berth compartment costs from US$195 if purchased in Moscow.

The trans-Manchurian passes through Harbin, in Manchuria, to Beijing, takes 6½ days and costs from US$205.

If you want to stop off along the way or spend some time in Moscow, it will cost more and you'll need 'visa support' – a letter from a travel agent confirming that they're making your travel/accommodation bookings as required in Russia or Mongolia.

Another option transits central Asia and is known as the 'Silk Route'. It runs from Moscow to Almaty in Kazakhstan, crosses the border on the new line to Ürümqi (north-western China), and follows part of the old Silk Road to Beijing. At present there is no direct train, and you must change at Almaty. Moscow to Ürümqi in 2nd class costs about US$300 and takes five or more days, depending on connections.

Locally based companies that offer all-inclusive packages (with visa support) include the Travellers Guest House in Moscow (☎ 7095-971 4059, fax 7095-280 7686, tgh@glas.apc.org); and Monkey Business in

Stave Church, Bygdøy, Oslo

Holmenkollen Ski Jump, Oslo

Stortinget (Parliament), Oslo

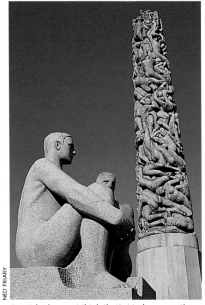

Don't look now, I think that's Medusa over there

I can't do a thing with this hair

Last warning kids!

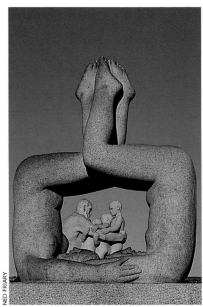

Yoga for beginners…

The granite and bronze sculptures of Gustav Vigeland in Vigeland Park, Oslo

Hong Kong (☎ 852-2723 1376, fax 852-2723 6653, monkeyhk@compuserve.com), with an information centre in Beijing (☎ 8610-6356 2126, fax 8610-6356 2127, monkeychina@compuserve.com) and a useful website for both locations can be found at www.monkeyshrine.com.

In the UK, contact Regent Holidays (☎ 0117-921 1711, fax 0117-925 4866, www.regent-holidays.co.uk) in Bristol, or The Russia Experience (☎ 0181-566 8846, fax 0181-566 8843, after April 2000 ☎ 020-8566 8846, fax 020-8566 8843, www.trans-siberian.co.uk) in London. There are a number of other budget operators.

The *Trans-Siberian Rail Guide* (Compass Star) by Robert Strauss, and *The Trans-Siberian Handbook* (Trailblazer) by Bryn Thomas are comprehensive guides to the route. Lonely Planet's *Russia, Ukraine & Belarus* and *China* guides have detailed information on trans-Siberian travel.

SEA
Transatlantic Passenger Ships & Freighters

Regular, long-distance passenger ships disappeared with the advent of cheap air travel and were replaced by a small number of luxury cruise ships. Cunard Line's *QEII* (US: ☎ 800-728 6273; UK: ☎ 01703-634 166) sails between New York and Southampton 17 times a year, taking five nights/six days each way. The cost of a one-way crossing starts at around US$3000, but they also offer return and 'fly one-way' deals (some include a return on the Concorde). Once a year it does a circuit around the Arctic region, calling in at Iceland as well as several Norwegian ports, including Tromsø and Longyearbyen in Svalbard. Most travel agents can provide the details.

The standard reference for passenger ships is the *OAG Cruise & Ferry Guide* published by the UK-based OAG Worldwide (☎ 01582-600111), Church St, Dunstable, Bedfordshire LU5 4HB, UK.

A more adventurous – but not necessarily cheaper – alternative is as a paying passenger on a freighter. Freighters are far more numerous than cruise ships, and there are many more routes from which to choose. With a bit of homework, you'll be able to sail between Europe and just about anywhere else in the world, with stopovers at exotic little-known ports. Again, the *OAG Cruise & Ferry Guide* is the most comprehensive source of information, although the book *Travel by Cargo Ship* (Cadogan, London) also covers the subject.

Passenger freighters typically carry six to 12 passengers (more than 12 would require a ship's doctor aboard) and although they're less luxurious than dedicated cruise ships, they provide a real taste of life at sea. Schedules tend to be flexible and costs vary, but normally hover around US$100 a day; vehicles can often be included for an additional charge.

Ferry

Ferry connections between Norway and Denmark, Germany, Iceland, the Faroe Islands, Sweden and the UK provide straightforward links, especially for anyone bringing their own vehicle. Note that in most cases, the quoted fares for vehicles also include the driver. Most lines offer substantial discounts for seniors, students and children, so it pays to ask when booking.

If you're travelling by international ferry, particularly from Sweden, Iceland or the Faroes, consider picking up your maximum duty-free alcohol allowance on the boat, as alcohol is prohibitively expensive in Norway and, even if you don't drink, it will make a welcome gift for Norwegian friends.

Denmark DFDS Scandinavian Seaways (☎ 22 41 90 90, bookings ☎ 66 81 66 00) runs daily overnight ferries from Oslo to Copenhagen. Cabin fares start at Nkr415 for Sunday to Wednesday in the low season and climb to Nkr715 on summer weekends. Car fares range from Nkr225 to Nkr330. All cabin categories are quite comfortable and you can take advantage of an excellent dinner buffet en route. The departure in either direction is at 5 pm, arriving at 9 am the following day.

The Color Line (☎ 22 94 44 00, fax 22 83 07 76, colorline@colorline.no) runs three to four ferries daily between Kristiansand and Hirtshals, which takes four hours and is the shortest ferry connection between Norway and Denmark. Fares range from Nkr150 in winter to Nkr370 on weekends from 19 June to 16 August. To transport a vehicle costs from Nkr560 to Nkr1390.

From 19 June to 16 August, Color Line also has one or two daily ferry services on the M/S *Peter Wessel* between Fredrikshavn, Moss and Larvik (once daily the rest of the year). Deck class fares range from Nkr150 on winter weekdays to Nkr370 on summer weekends. Cabins range from Nkr110 per person in a four-bed cabin to Nkr500 for a luxury suite. Their three-hour M/S *Pegasus II* route between Larvik and Skagen runs twice daily and costs from Nkr195 to Nkr250, plus Nkr200 for a car; many people use this route as a duty-free day trip. There are also a number of special discount deals on the Larvik/Moss/Skagen routes.

Stena Line (☎ 22 33 50 00) operates ferries between Oslo and Frederikshavn daily from 19 June to 30 August, and at other times from three to six times weekly. They leave Oslo at 8 pm and Frederikshavn at 10.30 am (6.30 pm on some Mondays) and take 12 hours. Passenger fares cost from Nkr190 at mid-week in winter to Nkr450 on summer weekends. With a car/camper and up to five people, they range from Nkr445/885 to Nkr940/1875.

The Fjord Line (☎ 55 32 37 70) sails from Bergen to Hanstholm on Monday, Wednesday and Friday afternoons, stopping en route in Egersund. It returns from Hanstholm on Tuesday, Thursday and Sunday. From Bergen, deck class fares range from Nkr260 on winter weekdays to Nkr660 on summer weekends. Cabins start at Nkr185 per person. For vehicles, you'll pay from Nkr310 to Nkr515.

The Larvik Line (☎ 22 52 55 00) has a daily ferry from Larvik (via Moss) to Frederikshavn. It takes six hours and costs from Nkr240 to Nkr380 for passengers and Nkr325 to Nkr530 for a car. They also oper-

ate a three-hour daily catamaran service between Larvik and Skagen for the same fares.

Germany The Color Line (☎ 22 94 44 00, fax 22 83 07 76, colorline@colorline.no) has a daily 19-hour ferry link between Oslo and Kiel, departing each city at 2 pm. From 19 June to 16 August, the fare is Nkr600 per person or Nkr1760 for a car and five people. The cheapest two-person cabin ranges from Nkr550 at midweek in the off season to Nkr710 in summer. With a car and cabin for four people, you'll pay from Nkr1430 at midweek in the off season to Nkr1990 in summer.

Iceland & the Faroe Islands The Smyril Line (☎ 55 32 09 70) runs weekly in summer between Bergen and Seyðisfjörður (Iceland), via the Faroe Islands. One-way fares from Bergen begin at Nkr560/780 to Tórshavn in the Faroes and Nkr1190/1710 to Seyðisfjörður, Iceland. These fares are for a couchette, with the lower fares for the first three sailings in June and the last four sailings in August, and the higher fares for midsummer travel. The boat leaves Bergen at 3 pm on Tuesday.

Sweden DFDS Scandinavian Seaways (☎ 22 41 90 90) runs daily overnight ferries between Oslo and Helsingborg, with fares varying according to the season and day of the week, but usually beginning at about Nkr500. The boats leave Oslo at 5 pm southbound and Helsingborg at 7 pm northbound.

From four to six times daily in summer the Scandi Line (☎ 33 42 10 00, fax 33 46 25 08) does the 2½-hour run between Sandefjord (Norway) and Strömstad (Sweden). From 13 June to 14 August passengers pay Nkr135 and a car and driver pay Nkr180. During the rest of the year, passengers pay Nkr98 and cars go for Nkr125.

From early May to mid-September, Fjordlinjen in Sweden (☎ 0526-153 70) sails between Halden and Strömstad three to six times a week. Helminsen Ships (☎ 69 31 60 56) and the M/S *Silverpilen* (☎ 69 32 03 30) – among others – sail daily except Sunday between Fredrikstad and

Strömstad. The one-way/return fares are around Nkr60/95, but they serve more as Swedish and Norwegian 'booze cruises' than real transport links.

The UK Fjord Line (Norway: ☎ 55 54 86 60; UK: ☎ 191-296 1313; fjordline@fjordline.com) sails from Bergen to Newcastle, via Haugesund/Stavanger, twice weekly in winter and thrice weekly in summer. Summer sailings are on Tuesday, Friday and Sunday from Bergen and Monday, Wednesday and Saturday from Newcastle. The trip takes 21 hours. The cheapest fare, for a berth in a four-berth cabin below the car deck, ranges from Nkr410 in midwinter to Nkr1080 on summer weekends. The fare to transport a small car is from Nkr600, a motorcycle from Nkr200.

The affiliated P&O Scottish Ferries and Smyril line run a weekly 'North Atlantic Link' between Bergen and Aberdeen (Scotland) via Lerwick (Shetland) from late May to late September. It leaves Bergen at 3 pm on Tuesday, arriving in Lerwick at 1.30 pm the next day. From there you can make the 14 to 20-hour trip (some sailings go via Orkney) to Aberdeen. Going the other way, the boat leaves Aberdeen for Lerwick every weekday evening. The Bergen ferry leaves Lerwick at 10.30 pm on Monday. Through fares in a reclining seat cost from Nkr1083. Transporting a motorcycle/car costs from Nkr405/1090. Be sure to contact P&O Scottish Ferries in Aberdeen (☎ 0124-572615, fax 0124-574411) or Smyril Line in Bergen (☎ 55 32 09 70, fax 55 96 02 72, office@smyril-line.no) for details well in advance of your trip.

DFDS Scandinavian Seaways has also started up a new service between Harwich and Kristiansund.

ORGANISED TOURS

Given the expenses involved in Norwegian travel, it may be worth looking into an organised tour. Several reputable operators offer affordable itineraries concentrating either on Scandinavia in general or Norway in particular.

North America

Backroads
(☎ 800-462 2848 or ☎ 510-527 1555, fax 510-527 1444, www.backroads.com), 801 Cedar St, Berkeley, CA 94710-1800 – Backroads offers all-inclusive and generally upmarket six-day cycling holidays around Lofoten and Vesterålen (US$2198), and seven-day hiking, rail and ferry tours between Geilo and Bergen, via the Hardangervidda plateau and Sognefjord (US$2598).

Bennett Tours
(☎ 800-221 2420, www.bennett-tours.com) – This company specialises in shorter trips through Scandinavia as well as long-haul trips north to Nordkapp and Hurtigruten cruises.

Borton Overseas
(☎ 800-843 0602, www.borton.com/overseas .html) – Borton's forte is adventure outdoor travel. This agency is also the North American agent for DNT, the Norwegian Mountain Touring Club.

Brekke Tours
(☎ 701-772 8999 or ☎ 800-437 5502, fax 701-780 9352, tours@brekketours.com, www .brekketours.com), 802 N 43rd St, Grand Forks, ND 58203 – This company caters mainly for North Americans of Norwegian descent, and cobbles together a host of Norwegian and Scandinavian options – with the two-week US holiday period in mind. One 10-day tour, entitled the 'Best of Norway', takes in Oslo, Lillehammer, Flåm, Voss, Bergen and Stavanger for US$2470 per person, including air fare from Minneapolis/St Paul. It also offers several other options involving Denmark, Finland, Iceland and Sweden.

Euroseven Tours
(☎ 800-890 3876, www.euroseven.com) – This operator does all-inclusive hotel-based tours from the US east coast.

Scanam World Tours & Cruises
(☎ 800-545 2204, fax 973-835 3030), 922 Hwy 23, Pompton Plains, NJ 07444 – This operator organises cruises and shorter upmarket tours. It's also the North American agent for the Fjord Line ferries.

Scanditours
(☎ 800-432 4176 or ☎ 800-377 9828, fax 416-482 9447 or 416-736 8311, toronto@scand itours.com or vancouver@scanditours.com, www.scanditours.com), 308-191 Eglinton Ave E, Toronto, Ontario M4P 1K1 or 21-1275 W 6th Ave, Vancouver, BC V6H 1A6 – This Canadian company concentrates on northern Norway, as well as historical routes between Oslo and St Petersburg.

Scantours
(☎ 800-223 7226, info@scantours.com, www.scantours.com) – Scantours offers an extensive range of short tours in Norway, from two days around Sognefjord to 14 days aboard the Hurtigruten coastal steamer. Its website includes details and prices for all its offerings.

The UK

Arctic Experience
(☎ 01737-218800, fax 01737-362341, sales@arctic-discover.co.uk, www.arctic-discover.co.uk) 29 Nork Way, Banstead Surrey SM7 1PB – This friendly agency is one of the most popular British tour operators to Scandinavia and the North Atlantic. It offers whale-watching cruises in Nordland and icebreaker cruises in Svalbard.

Arcturus Expeditions
(☎/fax 01389-830204, arcturus@btinternet.com) PO Box 850, Gartocharn, Alexandria, Dumbartonshire G83 8RL – This is one of Britain's most inventive operators and does hiking, trekking, dog-sledding and cruising tours through the furthest reaches of the polar regions. In Norway, it offers hiking and dog-sledding in Finnmark and Dividalen, visits to Jan Mayen and icebreaker cruises and trekking in and around Svalbard. It's highly recommended.

City Breaks
(☎ 0141-951 8411) 2 Blair Ct, North Ave, Strathclyde G81 2LA – Do you have a day or two with nothing to do? How about popping off to Oslo for a day or weekend?

Flying Ghillies
(☎ 01670-789603) PO Box 1, Morpeth, Northumberland NE61 6YX – If you're a fish fan, this is the company to go with. Its speciality in Norway is salmon fishing, combined with other outdoor pursuits.

Mountain & Wildlife Venture
(☎ 015394-33285) Compston Rd, Ambleside, Cumbria LA22 9DJ – This is the British agent for DNT, and can organise a good choice of nordic ski tours and alpine adventures.

Scantours
(☎ 0171-329 2927, after April 2000 ☎ 020-7329 2927, scantoursuk@dial.pipex.com, www.scantours.com) – As with the US branch of this company, the website includes details and prices for a wide range of options throughout Norway, lasting from four to 14 days.

Taber Holidays
(☎ 01274-735611) 126 Sunbridge Rd, Bradford, West Yorks BD1 2SX – Taber offers a range of highlight-oriented, all-inclusive tours around Norway, including cruises, coach tours and self-drive possibilities.

Waymark Holidays
(☎ 01753-516477) 44 Windsor Rd, Slough SL1 2EJ – This company specialises in nordic skiing holidays and other outdoor pursuits.

Wild Oceans
(☎ 0117-984 8040, fax 0117-967 4444) Wildwings, International House, Bank Rd Bristol BS15 2LX – Wild Oceans is a booking agent for Arctic cruises on the *Professor Molchanov*, which does frequent runs to Jan Mayen and Svalbard.

France

Grand Nord Grand Large
(☎ 01-40 46 05 14, fax 01-43 26 73 20) 15 rue du Cardinal Lemoine, F-75005 Paris – As one of the world's most adventurous agencies, GNGL seeks out the locations and activities that are noticed by only a handful of other companies. In Norway, it offers hiking, trekking and kayaking tours in Svalbard and Lofoten.

Australia

Bentours
(☎ 02-9241 1353) Level 11, 2 Bridge St, Sydney – Bentours is the only Australian travel agency specialising exclusively in Scandinavian travel.

Explore Holidays
(☎ 02-9872 6722) 1st Floor, Oasis Centre, Carlingford, Sydney – Explore runs outdoor and adventure-oriented tours in Norway.

Wiltrans/Maupintour
(☎ 02-9255 0899) Level 10, 189 Kent St, Sydney – This company offers a range of pricey luxury tours in Norway and elsewhere in Scandinavia.

Getting Around

Norway's efficient domestic public transport systems include trains, buses and ferries which are often timed to link with each other. The handy *NSB Togruter*, available free at train stations, details rail timetables and includes information on connecting buses. Boat and bus departures vary with the season and the day (services on Saturday are particularly sparse), so pick up the latest timetables *(ruteplan)* from regional tourist offices.

Rail lines extend as far north as Bodø (you can also reach Narvik by rail from Sweden), but beyond the Arctic Circle you're limited to buses and ferries. Thanks to the great distances, bus fares can add up, but InterRail and ScanRail holders are entitled to a 50% discount on express buses between Bodø and Kirkenes. A fine alternative to land travel is the Hurtigruten coastal steamer, which calls in at every sizeable port between Bergen and Kirkenes and provides stunning views of some of Europe's finest coastal scenery.

AIR
Domestic Air Services
Norway has nearly 50 airports with scheduled commercial flights from Kristiansand in the south to Longyearbyen and Ny Ålesund in the north. Thanks to the time and distances involved in overland travel, even budget travellers may want to consider doing some segments by air.

With the main airlines, SAS (www.sas.no) and Braathens SAFE (www.braathens.no), typical one-way fares from Oslo are Nkr1215 to Trondheim and Nkr2305 to Tromsø, but there are several discount programs that make air travel more accessible (see Discounts & Air Passes). With Widerøe (☎ 67 11 60 00, fax 67 11 61 95, internetbooking@wideroe .no, www.wideroe.no), which flies small planes, the flights are more like 'flightseeing' trips than mere transport from A to B, and even standard fares are considerably

lower than on the big airlines. Coast Air (☎ 52 83 41 10, fax 52 84 03 74, www .coastair.no), based in Haugesund, also flies small planes and concentrates on the main airports in southern Norway.

Currently, the best domestic fares come from the upstart Color Air (☎ 81 00 08 11, www.colorair.no), which flies several times daily between Oslo and Bergen, Ålesund and Trondheim for Nkr399 to Nkr699 per segment. In response, Braathens SAFE has introduced its no-frills 'Back' class, with similar fares on the same routes.

Discounts & Air Passes
With Braathens SAFE and SAS, standard 'minipris' return tickets cost only about 10% more than full-fare one-way tickets and there are sometimes promotional fares that make return tickets even cheaper than one-way tickets. In addition, spouses (including gay partners), children aged two to 15 and senior citizens over 67 years of age are eligible for 50% discounts.

Travellers aged under 25 can opt for 'Superhike' and stand-by fares at substantial discounts. On Braathens SAFE, for example, youth stand-by fares from Oslo to Bergen would set you back just Nkr470, and from Oslo to Tromsø, Nkr800. SAS offers its international passengers (who aren't resident in Scandinavia) advance-purchase coupons for Nkr700 to Nkr900, which allow travel on direct flights between any two Scandinavian cities it serves, including several in Norway. Coupons are valid on most SAS flights within the region and must be purchased at least seven days in advance. You can buy up to six coupons, which are good for one segment each. Note that the free baggage limit for economy ticket holders is 20kg.

There are also some good value air passes. Widerøe offers a great value summer ticket (valid from 1 June to 31 August) which costs Nkr385/670 for one-way/return flights within any one of four zones, which are divided at Trondheim, Bodø and Tromsø. Multi-sector flights cost Nkr485/585/885 for two/three/four zones. These tickets must be purchased outside of Norway. Widerøe's *grønn billett*, or 'green ticket', valid for travellers under 25 or over 60, costs Nkr375 on one leg within one of the four zones, plus an additional Nkr100 per extra zone. For its summer 14-day air pass, it has divided the country into three zones, with breaks at Trondheim and Tromsø; 14 days of unlimited travel within one/two/three zones costs Nkr1700/2600/3000, plus an additional Nkr900 per zone for each extra week.

Braathens SAFE's Visit Norway Pass, available between 1 May and 30 September, divides Norway into northern and southern sectors at Trondheim. Flights between any two points in one sector cost Nkr700 (excepting flights between Tromsø and Longyearbyen), and double that when your travel involves two sectors. You can purchase tickets directly from Braathens SAFE after you arrive in Norway, but budget seats are limited and if you're short on time, it's wise to make advance reservations.

Braathens SAFE's 'Back' fares don't include food and drink services; and its Nkr490 domestic one-way fare is available on late bookings if you stay over a Saturday night.

Domestic Departure Taxes

To all domestic fares, add a commuter tax of Nkr71 to fly between any two cities also served by rail (except Bodø).

BUS

Buses on Norway's extensive long-distance bus network are quite comfortable. Tickets are sold on the buses and fares are based on the distance travelled, averaging Nkr112 per 100km. Many bus companies offer student, child, senior and family discounts of 25 to 50%, so it often pays to ask. In northern Norway, holders of InterRail and ScanRail passes are often eligible for discounts.

Nor-Way Bussekspress (☎ 23 00 24 40, within Norway ☎ 81 54 44 44, fax 23 00 24 49, ruteinformasjon@nor-way.no, www.nor-way.no) operates the largest network of express buses in Norway, with routes connecting every main city and extending north all the way to Nordkapp and Kirkenes. There are also a number of independent long-distance companies which provide similar prices and levels of service.

In addition, NSB (Norwegian State Railways) runs several Togbuss ('train-bus') routes. In Nordland, they run between Fauske and Bodø, Narvik, Tromsø, Svolvær and Å, and in the Western Fjords, between Åndalsnes and Ålesund, Dombås and Molde. Holders of Eurail, InterRail and ScanRail passes get half-price on the Nordland routes, but the Western Fjords routes are generally included.

There is also a host of local buses, most of which are confined to a single *fylke* (county). Each of these routes has a number, but quite often it isn't actually marked on the bus, which is more often identified by its destination. To confuse matters even further, some buses also have a second route number, which is used in the specific urban area where it circulates. This number normally does appear on the bus. For information on city and town buses, see Local Transport later in this chapter.

TRAIN

The Norwegian State Railways (Norges Statsbaner or NSB) operates an excellent, though limited, system of lines connecting Oslo with Stavanger, Bergen, Åndalsnes, Trondheim, Fauske and Bodø; there are also lines between Sweden and Oslo, Trondheim and Narvik. For timetable information and bookings phone NSB (☎ 81 50 08 88). Most train stations offer luggage lockers for Nkr10 to Nkr20 and many also have baggage storage rooms.

Most long-distance day trains have 1st and 2nd-class seats and a buffet car or refreshment trolley service. Mobile telephones can be found in all express trains and most Inter-City trains. Doors are wide and there's space for bulky luggage such as backpacks or skis.

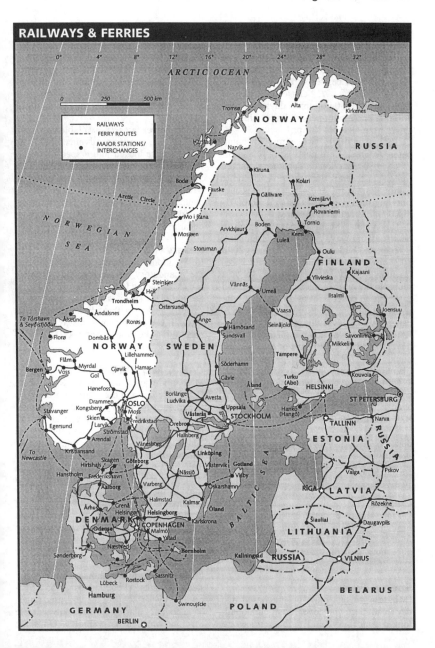

RAILWAYS & FERRIES

Train Passes

The Norway Rail Pass, which allows unlimited travel within the country, can be purchased after you arrive in Norway. High-season prices for 2nd-class travel are Nkr1260/1700 for 7/14 consecutive days of travel or Nkr900 for three days of travel within a one-month period. Prices are 20% lower from October to April.

NSB also offers two annual discount cards. A Green Card costs Nkr280 and offers a 50% reduction on departures marked 'green' in the rail timetables. A Customer Card costs Nkr360 and offers a 50% reduction on green departures as well as a 20% discount on regular departures.

The popular ScanRail pass is valid on nearly all railways in Norway, Denmark, Sweden and Finland and also includes 20 to 50% discounts on many ferries and buses (including a 50% discount on the Togbuss routes in the north). It is an inexpensive and easy way to cover a lot of ground in a relatively short time. The ScanRail Consecutive pass allows 21 days of travel. With the ScanRail Flexipass, you can opt for five days of travel in 15 days or 10 days of travel in one month. Note that there's a supplement for the Flåm line and some Inter-City express trains.

Children travel at half-price, and discounts apply for seniors over 60 and youths aged 12 to 25. The adult fare for the ScanRail pass is as follows:

duration	2nd class	1st class
21 days	US$348	US$452
5 days/15 days	US$187	US$249
10 days/1 month	US$301	US$400

Classes

On long-distance trains, 2nd-class coaches provide comfortable reclining seats with footrests, and 1st-class coaches, which cost 50% more, generally aren't worth the extra expense.

Special Fares

'Minipris' tickets must be purchased one day in advance and cover most, but not all, long-distance services. Eligible services are indicated by green dots in the *NSB Togruter* timetable. Regular/minipris fares from Oslo are Nkr510/390 to Bergen, Nkr500/320 to Åndalsnes, Nkr580/390 to Stavanger and Trondheim. For the maximum minipris fare of Nkr490, you can travel from Stavanger to Bodø, which is Norway's longest domestic rail route.

Even lower fares are available on tickets booked one week in advance, but with these, you're locked into a specific departure and no refunds are available. There's a 50% discount on rail travel for people aged 67 and older and for children under 16. Students get a 60% discount on departures denoted by green dots and 40% on other departures.

Reservations

Reservations cost an additional Nkr20 and are mandatory on many long-distance routes, including between Oslo and Bergen. Second-class sleepers offer a good cheap sleep: a bed in a three-berth cabin costs Nkr100; two-berth cabins cost Nkr200 per person in old carriages and Nkr250 in new carriages.

CAR & MOTORCYCLE

Main highways, such as the Rv11 from Oslo to Bergen and the entire E6 from Oslo to Kirkenes, are open year-round. The quality of the road network is constantly improving and more bridges and tunnels are constructed every year. The longest tunnels link adjacent valleys while shorter tunnels drill through rocky impediments to straighten routes. Most tunnels are lit and some of the longer ones have exhaust fans to remove fumes, while others are lined with padded insulation to absorb both fumes and sound. Motorcyclists must be wary of fumes in longer tunnels and may want to avoid them.

Older roads and mountain routes are likely to be narrow with hairpin bends and steep gradients. Although most areas are accessible by car, some of the less-used routes have poor or untarred surfaces only suitable for four-wheel drive vehicles. On some mountain roads, caravans and motorhomes are forbidden or advisable only for experienced drivers, as it may be necessary to reverse in order to allow approaching traffic to pass. Restricted roads for caravans are outlined on a map published by Vegdirektoratet, PO Box 8142 Dep, N-0033 Oslo.

In winter, spring or early summer, check beforehand to make sure the passes are open, as many remain closed until May or June. If you're expecting snowy or icy conditions, it's wise to use studded tyres or carry tyre chains. The Vegmeldingssentralen, which is Statens Vegvesen's Road User Information Centre (☎ 22 65 40 40 or ☎ 175), provides up-to-date advice on road closures and conditions throughout the country.

Vehicle Ferries

Travelling along the scenic but mountainous and fjord-studded west coast may be spectacular, but it also requires numerous ferry crossings, which can prove time-consuming and costly. For a complete list of ferry schedules, fares and reservation phone numbers, get hold of the Nkr210 *Rutebok for Norge*, a telephone-book-sized transport guide sold in bookshops and larger Narvesen kiosks. You can also order one from Norsk Reiseinformasjon (☎ 22 33 01 92, fax 22 41 60 04), Tollbugata 32, N-0157 Oslo.

Tolls

One bugbear of driving around Norway is having to pay tolls at every turn, so keep a stack of coins handy. New segments of highway and recently built tunnels and bridges must be paid off in user tolls and these often run as high as Nkr50 or Nkr75 per vehicle and driver, and Nkr15 to Nkr25 per passenger. In theory, the tolls are dropped when the construction project is paid off. Some facilities become quite lucrative so this doesn't always happen, but

Road Distances (km)

	Alta	Bergen	Bodø	Florø	Hammerfest	Harstad	Kautokeino	Kirkenes	Kristiansand	Kristiansund	Lillehammer	Narvik	Odda	Oslo	Røros	Stavanger	Tromsø	Trondheim	Ålesund	Åndalsnes
Alta	---																			
Bergen	2176	---																		
Bodø	818	1488	---																	
Florø	2059	253	1365	---																
Hammerfest	144	2318	963	2201	---															
Harstad	581	1649	293	1532	723	---														
Kautokeino	132	2308	950	2191	317	713	---													
Kirkenes	527	2701	1345	2584	497	1108	434	---												
Kristiansand	2266	411	1572	657	2408	1739	2398	2791	---											
Kristiansund	1619	519	925	402	1761	1092	1751	2144	884	---										
Lillehammer	1791	452	1097	483	1933	1264	1923	2316	484	400	---									
Narvik	522	1652	296	1535	666	121	654	1049	1742	1095	1267	---								
Odda	2154	162	1460	320	2269	1627	2286	2679	337	566	363	1630	---							
Oslo	1928	486	1234	541	2070	1401	2050	2453	329	570	170	1404	362	---						
Røros	1589	717	895	600	1731	1062	1721	2114	715	310	331	1065	671	386	---					
Stavanger	2337	157	1643	414	2479	1810	2469	2862	250	680	546	1813	183	574	854	---				
Tromsø	270	1913	556	1796	442	318	402	797	2003	1356	1528	261	1891	1665	1326	2074	---			
Trondheim	1432	744	738	627	1574	905	1564	1957	834	187	359	908	722	496	157	905	1169	---		
Ålesund	1792	387	1098	270	1924	1265	1924	2307	771	137	387	1258	450	557	403	603	1519	350	---	
Åndalsnes	1786	495	1092	388	1928	1269	1928	2311	741	101	264	1262	522	434	280	666	1523	354	123	---

normally the tolls do decrease with time. The cities of Oslo, Bergen, Trondheim, Stavanger and Kristiansand impose tolls on drivers every time they cross the city limits and you must also pay tolls to use roads leading into national parks.

Breakdown Services

By reciprocal agreement, members of most national automobile associations are eligible for breakdown recovery assistance from the Norges Automobil Forbund (☎ 22 34 16 00, fax 22 42 88 30) or the Kongelig Norsk Automobilclub (☎ 80 03 29 00 or ☎ 22 08 60 00). NAF patrols ply the main roads from 10 am to 7 pm, 16 June to 14 August. Emergency telephones can be found along motorways, in tunnels and at certain mountain passes.

Petrol

Leaded and unleaded petrol is available at most petrol stations. Regular unleaded fuel costs from around Nkr7/L in the south to over Nkr10 in the north (around Nkr4.6/L in Svalbard); super premium costs at least Nkr1 more and diesel around Nkr1 less. Credit cards are accepted at most places. In towns, petrol stations may be open until 10 pm or midnight, but there are some 24-hour services. In rural areas, many stations close in the early evening and don't open at all on weekends. Most places include a convenience shop selling staples, snacks, newspapers and magazines; some have 24-hour automatic pumps operated with credit cards or cash notes.

Road Rules

In Norway, traffic keeps to the right. On motorways and other main roads the maximum speed is generally 80km/h (a few roads have segments allowing 90km/h), while on roads through built-up areas, it's normally 50 or 60km/h. The speed limit for caravans (cars pulling trailers) is usually 10km/h less than for cars. If you're tempted to drive faster, bear in mind that the speed limits are zealously enforced, and even 5km/hour over the limit will elicit a puni-

tive on-the-spot fine of at least Nkr700. Similarly, watch for signs designating *Automatisk Trafikkontrol*, which means that there's a speed camera ahead; these big and ugly grey boxes have no mercy at all.

The use of seat belts is obligatory at all times and children under the age of four must have their own seat or safety restraint. The use of dipped headlights (including on motorcycles) is required at all times and right-hand drive vehicles must have beam deflectors affixed to their headlights to avoid blinding oncoming traffic. Drivers must carry a red warning triangle to use in the event of a breakdown; motorists must give way to pedestrians at zebra crossings; and vehicles from other countries must bear an oval-shaped nationality sticker on the back. Motorcycles may not be left on the

---

Haste Makes Waste

In Norway, speed limits are set relatively low by international standards but they're taken very seriously (particularly around the Nordland town of Fauske, which is known as the speed trap capital of the country!). The national speed limit is 80km/h on the open road, but pass a house or place of business and the limit drops to 70 or even 60km/h. Through villages, limits range from 50 to 60km/h, and in residential areas they're 30km/h. If those speeds seem laborious by your home standards, avoid the temptation to crank up the revs. You'll be nabbed for even 5km/h over the limit – there's no leniency, no compromises, and fines start at Nkr700. During my latest visit, one lead-foot foreigner was snared at 139km/h on the open highway (just south of Fauske, as it happens). He was fined Nkr14,000 and enjoyed his 15 minutes of fame in the national headlines, but for a similar infraction, a Norwegian would have also lost their driving licence and probably done a month of jail time.

pavement (sidewalk) and are subject to the same parking regulations as cars.

Drunken driving laws are strict in Norway: the maximum permissible blood alcohol content is 0.05% and violators are subject to severe fines. Driving with a blood alcohol level of 0.08% or greater warrants a fine of Nkr10,000 and a 21-day prison sentence. Because establishments serving alcohol may legally share liability in the case of an accident, you may not be served even a small glass of beer if the server or bartender knows you're driving a car.

Third-party auto insurance (unlimited cover for personal injury and Nkr1,000,000 for property damage) is compulsory and if you're bringing a vehicle from abroad, you'll have fewer headaches with an insurance company Green Card. Ensure that your vehicle is insured for ferry crossings.

UK-registered vehicles must carry a vehicle registration document, or a Certificate of Registration (Form V379, available from the DVLA in the UK). For vehicles not registered in the driver's name, you'll require written permission from the registered owner.

Road Signs

Most road signs are international, but a white M on a blue background indicates a passing place on a single-track road (the 'M' stands for *Møteplass*). *All Stans Forbudt* means 'No Stopping', *Enveiskjøring* is 'One Way'; *Kjøring Forbudt* is 'Driving Prohibited' or 'Do Not Enter'; *Parkering Forbudt* is 'No Parking'; and the bizarre *Rekverk Mangler* is 'Guardrail Missing'.

Car Rental

Norwegian car hire is expensive and geared mainly to the expense-account business traveller. Walk-in rates for a compact car with unlimited kilometres start at around Nkr800 per day (including VAT and insurance) Car-rental companies sometimes advertise a more tourist-friendly 'hotel' rate of Nkr600. Generally, you'll find better deals through international agencies outside of Norway, especially if it's clear you're a tourist and not on a business expense account.

One relatively good and readily available deal is the weekend rate offered by major rental agencies, which allows you to pick up a car after noon on Friday and keep it until 10 am on Monday for around Nkr1000 – be sure it includes unlimited kilometres.

All the major firms, such as Hertz, Avis and Europcar, have desks at Oslo's Gardermoen airport, as well as other airports around the country. They are also represented in city centres. The following is a partial list of firms:

Avis
(☎ 22 83 58 00) Munkedamsveien 27, Oslo
(☎ 55 32 01 30) Lars Hilles gate 20, Bergen
Bislet Bilutleie
(☎ 22 60 00 00, fax 22 60 01 19) Pilestredet 70, Oslo
Budget
(☎ 22 17 10 50) Oslo Spektrum, near Oslo S
(☎ 55 90 26 15) Lodin Leppsgate 1, Bergen
Europcar
(☎ 22 70 67 00, fax 22 70 67 01) Hovinveien 43B, Oslo
Hertz
(☎ 22 20 01 21) SAS Hotel, Holbergs gate 30, Oslo
Thrifty
(☎ 55 90 22 50) Jon Smørs gate 8, Bergen

BICYCLE

Given its great distances, hilly terrain and narrow roads, Norway is not ideally suited for extensive cycle touring, but many people still take the challenge. The long-distance cyclist's biggest headache (sometimes literally) will be tunnels, and there are thousands of them. Many of these, especially in the Western Fjords, are closed to non-motorised traffic due to the danger from hydrocarbon emissions and carbon monoxide fumes. This severely limits where cyclists can go, and even when alternative routes are available, they may involve a couple of days pedalling around a long fjord or over a high mountain pass. Statens Vegvesen distributes the comprehensive booklet *Tunnelguide for Syklister*, which lists all the tunnels in Norway, their lengths, whether they have lights and/or fans and whether they're open to cyclists.

For further information on long-distance cycling routes, contact Syklistenes Landsforening (☎ 22 41 50 80), Storgata 23C, N-0184 Oslo. Serious cyclists should check out its *Cycling Holidays in Norway* and the equally useful *Cycling Experiences in Agder & Telemark* by Knut Bjorå.

The good news is that there are lots of regional cycling venues, and bike hire is available at some tourist offices, hostels and camping grounds. All over the country, regional tourist offices have devised suggested cycling tours and most have produced maps of the best routes. The map *Sykkel-Norge*, distributed free by Statens Vegvesen, is available in English and describes 12 of the country's best and most popular cycling areas. Among the most cycle-friendly communities, providing excellent maps and information, are Larvik in the south; Sandnes, just south of Stavanger; and Røros in central Norway.

Rural buses, express ferries and non-express trains carry bikes for an additional Nkr25, but express trains don't allow them at all and international trains treat them as excess baggage. Color Line ferries and Hurtigruten coastal steamers carry passengers' bikes free of charge.

HITCHING

Hitching is never entirely safe in any country, and Lonely Planet does not encourage it. What's more, the Norwegian government generally considers car ownership a luxury and sets up its tax structure accordingly, so motorists may look askance at anyone who can't afford a vehicle. For that reason, hitching isn't especially popular.

That said, if you're determined to hitch, you will find Norwegians generally friendly, and they understand that not all foreigners enjoy an expense-account budget. With a measure of luck and patience, most hitchhikers do manage to find lifts, but the chances of success are unpredictable; they are generally somewhat better on main highways such as the E6, but you still may wait for hours in bad weather. Western Norway is generally the most difficult area for hitching,

while the more laid-back north is probably the best. One good approach is to ask for rides from truck drivers at ferry terminals and petrol stations; that way, you'll normally have a place to keep warm and dry while you wait.

BOAT

Due to Norway's rugged geography, ferry links are crucial, and an extensive network of car ferries and express boats links the country's offshore islands, coastal towns and fjord districts. Most ferries along the highway system accommodate motor vehicles, but express coastal services normally take only foot passengers and cyclists, as do the lake steamers. See specific destinations for details.

Highway ferries are subsidised and therefore aren't overly expensive (this is of course relative ...), but long queues and delays are possible at popular crossings in summer. If you're in a hurry, you may want to reserve space on a particular sailing. Details on schedules and prices for vehicle ferries and lake steamers are provided in the NTB Timetables or *Rutebok for Norge*.

Hurtigruten Coastal Steamer

For more than a century Norway's legendary Hurtigruten coastal steamer route has served as a lifeline linking coastal towns and villages. One ship heads north from Bergen every night of the year, pulling into 33 ports on its six-day journey to Kirkenes, where it then turns around and heads back south. The return journey takes 11 days and covers a distance of 2500 nautical miles. In agreeable weather the fjord and mountain scenery along the way is nothing short of spectacular.

If you're travelling as a deck-class passenger, there are baggage rooms, a shower room, a 24-hour cafeteria and a coin laundry available. Meals are served in the dining room and you can buy snacks and light meals in the cafeteria. At night, you'll have to roll out a sleeping bag on the floor in one of the lounges, but all-night activity will mean short nights of little sleep, especially in the 24-hour summer daylight. Sample deck-class fares from Bergen are Nkr1159 to Trondheim, Nkr1973 to Stamsund, Nkr2374 to Tromsø, Nkr2992 to Honningsvåg and Nkr3685 to Kirkenes. One en route stopover is allowed on these fares. Accompanying spouses, as well as children and seniors over the age of 67, receive a 50% discount on these fares.

There are also some great off-season deals. From 1 September to 30 April, passengers receive a 40% discount off the basic fare for sailings on any day but Tuesday. Between 1 September and 30 April, passengers aged from 16 to 26 years may buy a 21-day coastal pass for Nkr1750. This allows plenty of time for the return trip between Bergen and Kirkenes with time for stops along the way.

If you prefer a cabin – and most people do – you'll pay an additional Nkr250 to Nkr1100 per night in summer and Nkr105 to Nkr525 in the off season; the exact price depends on which boat you're taking and the

The Venerable M/S *Harald Jarl*

While most travellers on the Hurtigruten coastal steamer routes are looking for the luxury offered by the newer cruise-style ships, a growing number also appreciate the rustic charm embodied by the veteran ships. There's no doubt that the finest of these is the fleet's oldest vessel, the venerable M/S *Harald Jarl*, which was built in Trondheim and first launched on 23 June 1960 to replace the old postal steamer that had previously served the route. Built by the Mechanical Workshop of Trondheim, it measures 87.4m in length and 13.3m in breadth. It has an empty displacement of 1850 tonnes with a draught of 4.4m, and with all equipment, 2600 tonnes with a draught of 4.5m. With 90 cabins and 164 berths, it can accommodate a total of 399 deck and cabin passengers. It's powered by a 4400 HP, 170 RPM Aker diesel engine, manufactured in Oslo in 1959, and can reach a speed of 16 knots.

In the media account of its launch, the vessel was promoted as a harbinger of modern times for the business of coastal shipping, with comfortable saloons in which passengers could relax without being disturbed by the grating of the ship's engines. One of these saloons contains a series of fabulous paintings by Lofoten artist Kaare Espolin-Johnson, which are now insured for Nkr12 million – about the same value as the rest of the ship (now all they need to do is ban smoking in that lounge to protect these lovely and valuable works of art!).

Since those early days, the M/S *Harald Jarl* has plied the popular route between Bergen and Kirkenes, with a decade (1972-1982) of summer stints on the tourist-oriented 'Polar Express' route between Bodø, Tromsø, Honningsvåg and Longyearbyen – and as far north along the Svalbard coast as the ice conditions would permit. Nowadays, it also does special Easter cruises to the Orkney Islands, in honour of its namesake, Harald Jarl, Earl of Orkney (who held this position in the mid-13th century).

Although this lovely old ship is slated for retirement in 2002, along with the Hurtigruten's other veteran ship, the M/S *Lofoten*, which is four years newer, a number of M/S *Harald Jarl* fans are currently mounting a vocal campaign to keep this bit of history afloat. The more people who request passage on this particular ship (as well as on the M/S *Lofoten*), the less the chances that these veteran vessels will be taken out of service. Having been fortunate enough to sail on the M/S *Harald Jarl*, I can tell you that it's not only more economical than the more modern ships but also provides a wonderful cultural study and an inspiring glimpse into the past days of Norwegian coastal shipping.

Deanna Swaney

sailing date. They're most expensive in mid-summer and cheapest during the winter and shoulder seasons. In general, the higher rates are for the newer ships, which provide all the comforts of a cruise liner, while the lovelier and more charming traditional ships, such as the *Lofoten* and the *Harald Jarl* (see the boxed text), are happily a bit cheaper. Cabins are extremely popular, so be sure to book well in advance. You can also book the Hurtigruten as an informal cruise. The one-way, six-day journey, including meals and accommodation in a shared double cabin, ranges from Nkr7200 to Nkr13,600 in midwinter and from Nkr9500 to Nkr25,400 between 1 June and 31 August.

You may want to break up the trip with shore excursions, especially if you're travelling the entire route. The possibilities, which are organised by the shipping company, include the following (northbound/southbound excursions are denoted by N/S): an overland tour between Molde and Kristiansund (Nkr340 – N); a short tour of Trondheim (Nkr150 – S); a day trip to Svartisen (Nkr510 – N); spins around Lofoten (Nkr210 – S) and Vesterålen (Nkr325 – S); a haul from Honningsvåg up to Nordkapp (Nkr335 – N); an overland tour between Honningsvåg and Hammerfest, via Nordkapp (Nkr500 – S); and a tour from Kirkenes, at the end of the line, to the Russian border (Nkr120). These offer fairly good value, but in some cases, you'll miss segments of the coastal scenery.

There's a toll-free number for information and bookings (☎ 81 03 00 00), or you can contact either Troms Fylkes Dampskibsselskap (☎ 77 64 81 00, fax 77 64 81 80, booking@tfds.no or gruppebooking@tfds.no, www.monet.no/hr/), PO Box 548, N-9001 Tromsø; or the Ofotens og Vesterålens Dampskibsselskab (☎ 76 96 76 00, fax 76 11 82 01, booking@ovds.no), PO Box 43, N-8501 Narvik. In North America, you can book through the Bergen Line (☎ 212-319 1300); in the UK, contact Norwegian Coastal Voyages (☎ 0171-371 4011, after April 2000 ☎ 020-7371 4011); and in Australia, Bentours (☎ 02-9241 1353).

LOCAL TRANSPORT
Bus, Tram, Underground & Ferry
Nearly every town in Norway supports a network of local buses and ferries, which circulate around the town centre and also connect it with outlying areas. In most smaller towns, the local bus terminal is adjacent to the train station, ferry quay and/or long-distance bus terminal. Fares range from around Nkr12 to Nkr20 per ride, but if you're doing a lot of bus-hopping, it's probably worth buying a 24-hour ticket. In Oslo, these cost Nkr40 and are good on all forms of local public transport, including buses, trams, underground trains and ferries; in most other towns, they range from Nkr30 to Nkr45.

Taxi
Taxis are best hailed around taxi ranks, but you can also reserve one by telephone. If you're phoning for a taxi immediately, charges begin at the moment the call is taken. Daytime fares, which apply on weekdays from 6 am to 7 pm and on Saturday from 6 am to 3 pm, are Nkr24 at flagfall, plus Nkr12 per kilometre. Weekday evening fares are 25% higher and in the early morning, on Saturday afternoon and evening, and on Sunday, they're 32% higher. On holidays, you'll pay 50% more. These fares are good for up to four passengers, but in some places, you may find 'maxi-taxis' which can carry up to eight passengers for about the same price.

ORGANISED TOURS
Numerous local tour companies operate in Norway and in every tourist office you'll find an exhaustive collection of leaflets, folders and brochures outlining their offerings in the immediate area. Typical offerings include bird or whale-watching cruises, lighthouse cruises, mine tours, city and town tours, glacier-walking tours, mountaineering tours, dog-sledding trips, white-water rafting trips and excursions to hard-to-reach sites of interest. Most tourist offices provide a booking service for any tour that may interest you, but many charge a booking fee of around Nkr20. Recommended tours and companies are listed throughout the book.

A very popular option is the so-called 'Norway in a Nutshell' tour, organised through travel agencies, NSB rail services and tourist offices around southern Norway. Itineraries vary, but most involve a one or two-day excursion taking in the rail line between Oslo and Myrdal, the Flåmbanen line to Flåm, a cruise along Nærøyfjord to Gudvangen, a bus to Voss, and then rail trips to Bergen and back to Oslo (overnight or otherwise). Some versions include a guided tour around Bergen. An alternative to this route involves the rail line between Oslo and Stavanger. For details and prices, see Organised Tours under Oslo, Bergen, Flåm, Voss and Stavanger, in the relevant chapters of this book.

Oslo

Oslo (pronounced 'OOS-loo') is Norway's capital and largest city, but with fewer than 500,000 residents it presents a casual, low-key and readily manageable face. Unlike most European cities, it isn't full of architectural wonders, but buildings are neatly kept and some districts, such as Frogner, offer elegant examples of historic architecture.

Oslo sits at the head of the Skagerrak strait inlet known as Oslofjord. The Nordmarka (north woods) to the north of the city provide a green belt for hiking and skiing, and they turn Oslo into a very liveable city for lovers of the outdoors. The city is also replete with notable museums and monuments, as well as plenty of green spaces.

History

The name Oslo is derived from the words *Ás*, the Old Norse name for the Norse godhead, and *lo*, which meant 'pasture', yielding roughly 'the fields of the gods'. It was originally founded in 1048 by King Harald Hardråda (Harald Hard-Ruler), whose son Olav Kyrre (Olav the Peaceful) set up a cathedral and a corresponding bishopric here. In the early 14th century, King Håkon V created a military presence by building the Akershus Festning (Fortress) in the hope of deterring the Swedish threat from the east. After the bubonic plague of the mid-14th century decimated much of the country, Norway united with Denmark, and from 1397 to 1624 Norwegian politics and defence were handled from Copenhagen. As a result, Oslo slid into obscurity, and in 1624 it burned to the ground. Fortunately, it was resurrected by King Christian IV, who rebuilt it on a more easily defended site and renamed it Christiania, after his humble self.

For three centuries, right through WWII, the city held on as a seat of defence. In 1814 the framers of Norway's first constitution designated it the official capital of the new realm but their efforts were effectively nullified by Sweden, which had other ideas about Nor-

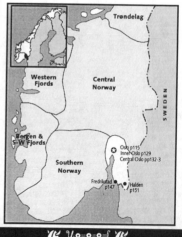

way's future and unified the two countries under Swedish rule. (In the history books, you may occasionally see Oslo at that time referred to as Kristiania, the Swedish spelling of Christiania.) In 1905, when that union was dissolved, the stage was set for Christiania to flourish as the capital of modern Norway. In 1925 it reverted to its original name, Oslo, and the city has never looked back.

OSLO REGION

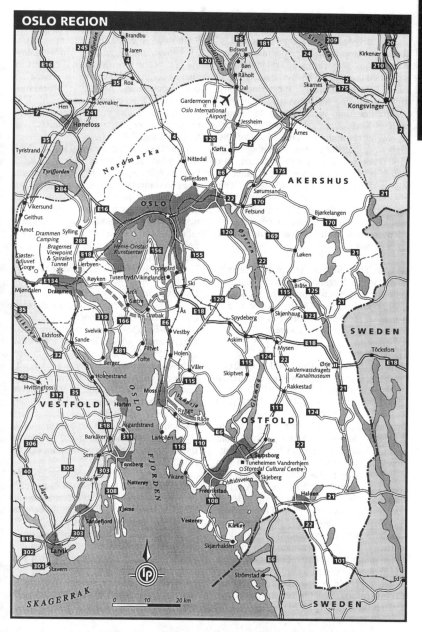

OSLO

Orientation

Oslo's central train station (Oslo Sentral-stasjon or Oslo S) sits at the eastern end of the city centre. From there the main street, Karl Johans gate, forms a ceremonial axis westward through the heart of the city to the Royal Palace. Fortunately, most central city sights, including the harbourfront and Ak-ershus Festning, are within a 15-minute walk of Karl Johans gate, as are the major-ity of hotels and pensions. Many of the sights outside the centre, including Vige-land Park and the Munch Museum, are within relatively easy walking distance or just a short bus or tram ride away. The Bygdøy peninsula is a mere 10-minute ferry ride across the harbour and even the trails and lakes of the Nordmarka wilderness are easily reached on the T-bane (underground train system).

Maps The Norges Informasjonssenter tourist office distributes a free city plan and unless you're heading out to the suburbs, it should be sufficient. On the reverse side is a map of the T-bane system as well as an inset of the Holmenkollen area.

Information

Tourist Offices The well resourced Norges Informasjonssenter tourist office (☎ 22 83 00 50, fax 22 83 81 50, www .oslopro.no), Vestbaneplassen 1, N-0250 Oslo, lies west of the Rådhus (Town Hall), near the harbour. It's open from 9 am to 8 pm daily in July and August; 9 am to 6 pm daily in June; 9 am to 6 pm Monday to Sat-urday in May and September; and 9 am to 4 pm Monday to Saturday the rest of the year. Look for the useful *Oslo Guide* either here or at the Oslo S information office in front of the train station, which is open from 8 am to 11 pm daily. Only the main office can help with information on destinations outside Oslo. For information on events, see the monthly *What's On in Oslo* or check out the above-mentioned website.

The very helpful Ungdomsinformasjonen (Youth Information Office), better known as Use-It (☎ 22 41 51 32, fax 22 42 63 71,

www.unginfo.oslo.no), Møllergata 3, is open from 7.30 am to 6 pm weekdays and 9 am to 2 pm on Saturday from 1 July to 31 August, and 11 am to 5 pm weekdays the rest of the year. Its main functions in-clude booking inexpensive or private ac-commodation and providing information on anything from current events to hitching possibilities. It also publishes *Streetwise*, a comprehensive guide to inexpensive op-tions and nightlife in Oslo.

Den Norske Turistforening (DNT, the Nor-wegian Mountain Touring Club; ☎ 22 82 28 00), Storgata 3, can provide information, maps and brochures on hiking in Norway and sells memberships which include discounted rates on use of its mountain huts along the main hiking routes. You can also book spe-cific huts and pick up keys. Climbers will find information, direction and gear at the Skandinavisk Høyfjellsutstyr (☎ 22 46 90 75), Bogstadveien 1, west of the centre.

Oslo Card To do a circuit of even a few Oslo sites, it's worth picking up the Oslo Card, which covers not only museum ad-missions but also transport on all city buses, ferries, trams, T-bane lines and local NSB trains. It's also valid for a 'mini-cruise' sightseeing boat tour (1 May to 16 August), free parking in city council car parks and admission to the Tøyenbadet and Frogner-badet swimming pools. Card holders are also entitled to Nkr30 cinema tickets and discounts on Bislut car hire (☎ 22 60 00 00), sightseeing bus and boat tours, the Tusen-fryd amusement park, Vikinglandet and the IMAX Media Theatre.

The card costs Nkr150/220/250 for one/two/three days (Nkr50/60/70 for chil-dren under 15); rail pass holders may receive a 20% discount. A one-day family card for two adults and two children costs Nkr350. The card is sold at the tourist offices, hotels and some Narvesen kiosks. It's great value if you're doing a lot of sightseeing, but note that students and senior travellers pay half price at most museums and other sites, and it may be cheaper to buy a public transport pass and pay separate museum admissions.

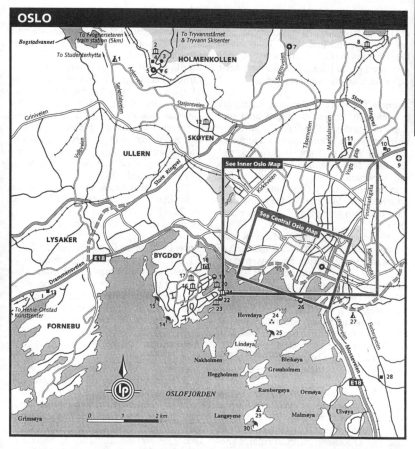

OSLO

PLACES TO STAY
1 Bogstad Camping
4 Holmenkollen Park Hotel Rica
10 Haraldsheim Hostel
11 Sleep-Safe Oslo Vineyard Church Hostel
13 Holtekilen Summerhotel
27 Ekeberg Camping
28 LBM-Ekeberg Hostel
29 Langøyene Camping

PLACES TO EAT
6 Holmenkollen Restaurant

MUSEUMS
2 Holmenkollen Ski Jump & Ski Museum
8 Norsk Teknisk Museum & Telemuseum
12 Emanuel Vigelands Museum
16 Vikingskipshuset
17 Norsk Folkemuseum
18 Oscarshall Slott
20 Kon-Tiki Museum
21 Polarskip Fram
23 Norsk Sjøfartsmuseum

OTHER
3 Skiforeningen Ski Society
5 Holmenkollen T-Bane Station
7 Sognsvann T-Bane Station
9 Aker Sykehus (Hospital)
14 Huk Beach
15 Paradisbukta Beach
19 Dronningen Ferry Terminal
22 Bygdøynes Ferry Terminal
24 Monastery Ruins
25 Hovedøya Beach
26 Vippetangen Quay (Oslofjord Ferries)
30 Langøyene Beach

The Oslo Package (a variation on the card) costs from Nkr370 to Nkr625 per person per day and includes a hotel room, breakfast and the Oslo Card. Up to two children are included free. Contact the tourist office for bookings and restrictions.

Money The bank at Gardermoen airport is open daily from 6.30 am to 8 pm (from 7 am on Sunday). The Oslo S post office changes money from 7 am to 6 pm weekdays and 9 am to 3 pm on Saturday, and also has a 24-hour automatic teller near the rail information desk, which changes foreign currency. You'll find banks scattered all over town, but most of the major ones have branches along Karl Johans gate near Oslo S.

The American Express offices at Karl Johans gate 33 (☎ 22 98 37 20) and north of the Rådhus at Fridtjof Nansens plass 6 (☎ 22 98 37 35) offer the best rates with no commission on most brands of travellers cheques. They're open from 8.30 am to 9 pm weekdays, 10 am to 7 pm on Saturday and 1 to 7 pm on Sunday in summer; the rest of the year, they close at 6 pm on weekdays and 3 pm on Saturday (closed Sunday).

Outside banking hours, the tourist office changes money at a less advantageous rate.

Post The main post office (☎ 22 40 78 23), Dronningens gate 15, is open from 8 am to 6 pm weekdays and 8 am to 3 pm on Saturday. To receive mail, have it sent to Poste Restante, Oslo Sentrum Postkontor, Dronningens gate 15, N-0101 Oslo. There are convenient post office branches at Oslo S, at Solli plass and on Karl Johans gate opposite Stortinget.

Telephone & Fax Telekort card phones and coin phones are found throughout the city. Coin phones take Nkr1 to Nkr20 coins, but you'll need at least Nkr2 for even a local call.

If you need to send faxes or make long-distance calls, use the Tele-Nor telephone office at Kongens gate 21, open from 9 am to 5 pm on weekdays.

Email & Internet Access You can log onto the Internet and send or receive email at the Børsen (Stock Exchange) Internet Café, Nedre Vollgate 19 (entrance is from Stortingsgata). At both Use-It (see Tourist Offices earlier in this section) and Akers Mic, a music shop at Akersgata 9, you can set up Hotmail accounts and access the Internet free of charge. At Akers Mic, however, you must be at least 16 years of age and prepared to get a bit older while you're waiting to get online. It's open daily except Sunday from 10 am to 8 pm (6 pm on Saturday).

You can also access the Internet at the municipal library, Deichmanske Bibliotek (☎ 22 03 29 00), Henrik Ibsens gate 1; phone in advance to book a computer.

Travel Agencies Kilroy Travels (☎ 23 10 23 10), Nedre Slottsgate 23, specialises in student and youth travel and offers discounted stand-by tickets for anyone under 26 and students under 35 with a valid ISIC card. For other options, check out the cluster of agencies near the Rådhus.

Bookshops Tanum Libris at Karl Johans gate 43, Arne Gimnes Bokhandel at Nedre Vollgate 1, Qvist Libris on Drammensveien, and Norli, nearby on Universitetsgata, are large bookshops with comprehensive selections of maps and English-language literature, novels, books on Norway and travel publications. Travel-oriented books, maps and gear are the speciality at Nomaden, Uranienborgsveien 4 (behind the Royal Palace).

For less mainstream publications, including feminist, gay, lesbian and political works, check out Tronsmo, near the National Gallery at Kristian Augusts gate.

Second-hand reading material is found at Ringstrøms, Ullevålsveien 1, which also sells used CDs, and JW Cappelen, Universitetsgata 20 (conveniently opposite the National Gallery).

Libraries The University Library (☎ 22 85 90 11), Drammensveien 42, has a reading room with major foreign-language newspapers. It's open weekdays from 8 am to 6.45 pm, and on Saturday morning. The Deichmanske Bibliotek (☎ 22 03 29 00), Henrik Ibsens gate 1, has a reading room with foreign newspapers and magazines, as well as a good selection of literature.

Laundry Majorstua Myntvaskeri at Vibes gate 15, 1km north of the Royal Palace, is open until 8 pm weekdays and 5 pm on Saturday. A-Snarvask, Thorvald Meyers gate 18, is open until 8 pm weekdays and 3 pm on Saturday; a wash costs Nkr30. Selva As, Ullevålsveien 15, is open daily from 8 am to 9 pm and charges Nkr30 per wash, including soap.

Toilets In this country full of expensive public toilets, there are still several daytime options for free relief: the 3rd floor of the GlasMagasinet arcade on Stortorvet; upstairs in the Paléet arcade at Karl Johans gate 37-43; and in the Deichmanske Bibliotek, Henrik Ibsens gate 1. Alternatively, visit a museum, pop into the Vestbaneplassen tourist office, or buy a drink or fries at any McDonald's or Burger King and you can use their typically clean facilities. Toilets at Oslo S cost Nkr5.

Left Luggage Oslo S has backpack-sized lockers for Nkr20. The left-luggage window, open from 7 am to 11 pm daily, charges Nkr20 per bag per day.

Photography By far the best value for film and processing is Japan Photo, with outlets on the corner of Prinsens gate and Strandgata, and on the corner of Hegdehaugveien and Underhaugsveien. You'll get excellent deals on bulk film orders.

Medical Services For after-hours prescription services, see Jernbanetorget Apotek, the 24-hour pharmacy opposite Oslo S. The Oslo Kommunale Legevakten (☎ 22 11 80 80) casualty medical clinic at Storgata 40 offers 24-hour emergency services. Recommended dental practices are the Majorstuen Tannlegesenter (☎ 22 46 67 54), Kirkeveien 64A, and Tannlegevakten (☎ 22 67 30 00), Tøyen Senter, Kollstadgata 18. The latter is open daily until 10 pm.

Emergency Dial ☎ 112 for police, ☎ 113 for an ambulance and ☎ 110 to report a fire, accident or serious pollution (such as a chemical leak). The central police station (☎ 22 66 90 50) is at Grønlandsleiret 44, with a precinct station (☎ 22 66 86 00) at Kronprinsens gate 8/10.

Walking Tour

Many of Oslo's central sights can be combined in a short walking tour. Starting at Oslo S, head west along Karl Johans gate, the main pedestrian street lined with shops, buskers, panhandlers, fast-food outlets and pavement cafés.

A couple of blocks north-west of the station, you'll reach **Oslo Domkirke**, the city cathedral, which dates from 1697. It's open from 10 am to 4 pm and is worth seeing for its elaborate stained glass by Emanuel Vigeland (son of Gustav Vigeland) and painted ceiling (completed between 1936 and 1950). The exceptional altarpiece, a 1748 model of the Last Supper and the Crucifixion by Michael Rash, was an original feature of the church, but it was moved all over the country before being returned from Prestnes church in Majorstue in 1950. (It was undergoing renovation at the time of researching this book.) The organ front and pulpit were both part of the original construction.

The **Basarhallene** (bazaar halls), around the back of the church, date from 1858 and are currently used as the venue for a summer handicraft market.

Midway along Karl Johans gate rises the yellow-brick parliament building, **Stortinget**, where free tours are conducted during the summer parliamentary recess. Across the street is the stately **Grand Hotel**, constructed in the 1870s.

Eidsvolls plass, a city square filled with fountains and statues, stretches between Stortinget and the **Nasjonalteatret** (National Theatre). The latter, with its lavish rococo hall, was constructed specifically as a venue for the works of Norwegian playwright Henrik Ibsen.

Across Karl Johans gate is the University of Oslo's law and medical campus, and a block north lies the university's **Historisk Museet** (Historical Museum) and the **Nasjonalgalleriet** (National Gallery). Karl Johans gate ends at **Det Kongelige Slott** (the Royal Palace), which is surrounded by a large public park.

Heading down from the National Theatre, Olav V's gate leads to the **Oslo Rådhus** (Town Hall) and the bustling harbourfront. For an good overall view, follow Rådhusgata to Akersgata and turn right to **Akershus Slott** and **Akershus Festning**, where the castle and museums merit a couple of hours of exploration.

Det Kongelige Slott

The Royal Palace, on a hill at the end of Karl Johans gate, is the official residence of the king of Norway. The palace building itself is not open to visitors but the rest of the grounds are a public park. At 1.30 pm, you can watch the changing of the guard, but it's not worth expending much effort to see.

Nasjonalgalleriet

The National Gallery (☎ 22 20 04 04), Universitetsgata 13, houses the nation's largest collection of Norwegian art, including works from the Romantic era and more modern works from 1800 to WWII. Some of Edvard Munch's best known creations are on display, including his most renowned work, *The Scream*, which created quite a stir when it was brazenly stolen (and later recovered) in 1994. There's also a respectable collection of European art, including works by Gauguin, Picasso and many of the impressionists: Manet, Degas, Renoir, Matisse, Cézanne and Monet.

The gallery is open year-round from 10 am to 6 pm on Monday, Wednesday and Friday, until 8 pm on Thursday, 4 pm on Saturday and from 11 am to 4 pm on Sunday. Hours are slightly longer in summer. Admission is free.

Oslo Rådhus

The twin-towered red brick Oslo Town Hall (☎ 22 86 16 00), built in 1950 to commemorate the city's 900th anniversary, houses the city's political administration. Its outside entrance is lined with wooden reliefs from Norse mythology and the interior halls and chambers are decorated with splashy and impressive frescoes and paintings by some of Norway's most prominent artists. It's here that the Nobel prizes are awarded on 10 December each year (see the boxed text 'The Noble Nobels'). From May to September it's open from 9 am to 5 pm daily (from noon on Sunday), with slightly shorter hours the rest of the year. You can view the main hall from the front corridor or pay Nkr15 (free in winter) and tour through it.

Akershus Slott & Festning

Strategically located on the eastern side of the harbour, the medieval Akershus Castle and Fortress dominate the Oslo harbourfront. In 1299, after the coronation of King Håkon V Magnusson, Oslo was named the capital of Norway and a year later, the king ordered the construction of Akershus to protect the city from external threats, such as the one experienced in 1287.

Because it suffered repeated fires and sieges, as well as the 1563 to 1570 War of the North, the fortress was reconstructed to withstand the increased fighting power of the day, including the 1559 addition of the Munk gun tower. Between 1580 and the mid-18th century, it was further fortified with moats and reinforced ramparts.

Oslo was levelled by fire in 1624, but instead of being rebuilt on its original site, the city was renamed Christiania (the name Oslo wasn't re-adopted until 1925) and shifted to the less vulnerable and more defensible site behind the protective fortress walls. In 1818, however, most of the outer rampart was destroyed to accommodate population growth, and much of the castle was subsequently converted into an arsenal and later, a national archive. From 1899 to 1963 it underwent major renovations, and

The Noble Nobels

Each October, in Stockholm, the Nobel Committee announces the winners of its prestigious prizes for physics, chemistry, medicine, literature, peace and economics. One Nobel prize – the lauded Peace Prize – is presented in Oslo, however, and each year on 10 December, the Oslo Rådhus becomes a focus of world attention as it honours individuals who have successfully encouraged or brought peace to tumultuous areas of the world.

Between 1814 and 1905, Norway and Sweden were united as one realm. In his will in 1895, Alfred Nobel, the Swedish founder of the prize (who was also credited with the invention of dynamite), stipulated that the scientific and literary prizes be awarded by Swedish institutions, but that the responsibility for the Peace Prize be delegated to a committee appointed by the Norwegian Storting (Parliament). It's thought that his intentions may have been to foment growing Norwegian agitation against this union, and since 1901, when the first Peace Prize was awarded to Jean Henri Dunant, the Swiss founder of the International Red Cross, the presentation ceremony has been held in Oslo.

Although the Norwegian Storting appoints the five-member committee that determines the winner of the Peace Prize, the parliamentary delegates have no say in the committee's decisions. Instead, nominations are made by such bodies as the executives of the Permanent International Peace Bureau; present and past members of international parliamentary bodies; members of the International Court of Justice in The Hague; university professors of law, political science, history and philosophy; former winners of the Nobel Peace Prize; and the Nobel Committee members themselves. Nominations must be submitted by 1 February each year, and the prize may be awarded to organisations and institutions as well as individuals.

Once the names have been proposed (currently they number around 100 each year) the committee goes to work investigating the merits of each nominee and eventually narrows them down to a shortlist, from which the winner is selected. In recent years, the prize has been awarded to such luminaries as Martin Luther King, Jr (1964); Anwar Sadat and Menachem Begin (1978); Mother Teresa (1979); Lech Walesa (1983); the 14th Dalai Lama, Tenzin Gyatso (1989); Mikhail Gorbachev (1990); Aung San Suu Kyi (1991); Nelson Mandela and FW de Klerk (1993); Yitzhak Rabin, Shimon Perez and Yassir Arafat (1994); the International Campaign to Ban Landmines (1997); and Northern Ireland's John Hume and David Trimble (1998).

Peace, love and explosives?
Bust of Alfred Nobel outside Nobel Institute

DEANNA SWANEY

nowadays, the park-like grounds serve as a venue for concerts, dances and theatrical productions. Note, however, that this complex is a military installation and may be closed to the public whenever there's a state function.

Akershus Slott In the 17th century, Christian IV renovated Akershus Slott (Akershus Castle) into a Renaissance palace, though the front remains decidedly medieval. In its dungeons you'll find dark cubbyholes where outcast nobles were kept under lock and key (one still holds a rather miserable-looking model wrapped in sackcloth), while the upper floors contained banquet halls and staterooms.

The chapel is still used for royal events, and the crypts of King Håkon VII and Olav V lie beneath it. Tours led by university students in period dress provide an entertaining anecdotal history of the place at 11 am and 1 and 3 pm, and are included in the Nkr20 admission fee. However, if you prefer, you can wander through on your own.

The castle is open from 10 am to 4 pm Monday to Saturday and 12.30 to 4 pm on Sunday from May to mid-September. From 16 to 30 April and 16 September to 31 October, it's open only on Sunday afternoons.

Akershus Festning Entry to the fortress is through a gate at the end of Akersgata or over a drawbridge spanning Kongens gate, which is reached from the southern end of Kirkegata. The fortress grounds are open until 9 pm; after 6 pm use the Kirkegata entrance. The Akershus Festning Information Centre (☎ 23 09 39 17, fax 23 09 56 70), inside the main gate, has an exhibit entitled *New Barricades* which recounts the history of the Akershus complex. At 1.15 pm, you can watch the king's guard march off to relieve the morning crew at the Royal Palace, and at 1.30 pm, see the changing of the guard at the fortress itself. Daily from June to August, free guided tours of the castle grounds, in Norwegian and English, leave from the information centre at 10 am (except Sunday), noon and 2 and 4 pm.

Prison Museum The small prison museum, near the information centre, originally served as a powder magazine, but in 1830 it was converted into a prison which held up to 60 people. It was expanded in both 1853 and 1890, and during WWII the Nazis used it as a holding tank for resistance leaders and supporters who had been sentenced to death. Visits may be arranged through the information centre.

Norges Hjemmefront Museet During WWII, the Nazis used Akershus as a prison and execution grounds, and today it's the site of Norway's Resistance Museum (☎ 23 09 31 38). The museum graphically recounts the German occupation of Norway, the murder of half of Norway's 1800 Jews, and the local and Allied resistance movements which published clandestine newspapers, ran a grass-roots weapons industry and sabotaged German installations. It's quite interesting and especially recommended for WWII buffs.

Don't miss the radio receiver used to listen to the BBC's European services, which was rigged up using the dentures of a senior prisoner of war (POW), or the diary of POW Petter Moen, who used a nail to prick his writing into sheets of toilet paper. (Moen was eventually killed, but his diary was later uncovered beneath the prison floorboards.)

The museum is open daily year-round – from 10 am (Sunday from 11 am) to 5 pm in summer, and until 3 pm in mid-winter. Admission is Nkr20.

Forsvarsmuseet The Norwegian Armed Forces Museum (☎ 23 09 35 82), at the fortress parade ground, presents models and dioramas of key moments in Norwegian military history from the Viking age, through the 1814 to 1905 Independence wars, to WWII and the present day. Also on display are the weapons that made it all possible. Admission is free and it's open daily in summer from 10 am to 6 pm, and most days in winter until 3 pm. There's also a small cafeteria.

Christiania Bymodell Of interest to history buffs, the Christiania Bymodell (☎ 22 33 31 47), just outside the northern wall of the fortress, features a 10m by 15m model of old Christiania in 1840, and a multimedia display of its history from its founding in 1624 up until 1900. It's open from 10 am to 4 pm daily except Monday, between 1 June and 31 August. Admission is Nkr30.

Bygdøy

Bygdøy peninsula holds some of Oslo's top attractions: an open-air folk museum; excavated Viking ships; Thor Heyerdahl's raft, the *Kon-Tiki*; and the *Fram* polar exploration ship. You can rush around all the sights in half a day, but allotting a few extra hours will be more enjoyable.

Although only minutes from central Oslo, Bygdøy has a rural character and a couple of good beaches. The royal family maintains a summer home on the peninsula, as do many of Oslo's well-to-do residents.

Ferry No 91 operates from mid-April to late September, making the 10-minute run to Bygdøy (Nkr18) every 40 minutes from 7.45 am (9.05 am on weekends). The last crossing returns from Bygdøy at 6 pm in April and September, 9.20 pm in summer. The ferries leave from Rådhusbrygge 3 (opposite the Rådhus) and stop first at Dronningen ferry terminal, from where it's a 10-minute walk to the folk museum. The ferry continues to Bygdøynes, where the *Kon-Tiki*, *Fram* and maritime museums are clustered. You can also take bus No 30 to the folk museum from Jernbanetorget. From the folk museum it's a five-minute walk to the Viking ships and 15 minutes to Bygdøynes. The route is signposted and makes a pleasant walk.

If you're hungry, there's a fruit stand opposite the folk museum entrance and simple cafés at the folk and maritime museums.

Norsk Folkemuseum The Norwegian Folk Museum (☎ 22 12 37 00) is Norway's largest open-air museum and one of Oslo's finest attractions. More than 140 buildings, mostly from the 17th and 18th centuries, have been gathered from around the country and are clustered according to region of origin. Paths wind past old barns, elevated storehouses *(stabbur)* and rough-timbered farmhouses with sod roofs sprouting wildflowers. The Gamlebyen (Old Town) section is a reproduction of an early 20th century Norwegian town and includes a village shop and old petrol station, and in summer you can see weaving and pottery-making demonstrations. Another highlight is the restored stave church, built around 1200 in Gol and shifted to Bygdøy in 1885.

The exhibition hall near the main entrance includes exhaustive displays on historic toys, festive costumes from around the country (including dress for weddings, christenings and burials), the Sami culture of Finnmark, domestic and farming tools and appliances, as well as visiting exhibits.

It's open from 10 am to 6 pm daily from 15 June to 31 August; 10 am to 5 pm from late May to mid-June and in September, and until 3 or 4 pm the rest of the year. Sunday is a good day to visit, as folk music and dancing is often staged. Admission, including entry to all sights and demonstrations, is Nkr50.

Vikingskipshuset The captivating Viking Ship Museum (☎ 22 12 37 00) houses three Viking ships excavated from the Oslofjord region. The ships had been drawn ashore and used as tombs for nobility, who were buried with all they expected to need in the hereafter: jewels, furniture, food, servants, intricately carved sleighs and fierce-looking figures. Because such burial practices were the exception rather than the rule in Viking society, these graves clearly held nobles of high status. Built of oak in the 9th century, these Viking ships were buried in blue clay, which preserved them amazingly well.

The impressive *Oseberg*, festooned with elaborate dragon and serpent carvings, measures 22m and required 30 oarsmen. The burial chamber beneath it held the largest collection of Viking-age artefacts ever uncovered in Scandinavia. The sturdier 24m-long *Gokstad* is the finest remaining example of a Viking longship, but when it was unearthed, its corresponding burial chamber had already been looted and only a few artefacts were uncovered. Of the third ship, the *Tune*, only a few boards and fragments remain.

The museum is open from 9 am to 6 pm daily from May to August, and the rest of the year from 11 am to at least 3 pm. Admission is Nkr30.

Kon-Tiki Museum The *Kon-Tiki* Museum (☎ 22 43 80 50) is dedicated to the balsa raft which Norwegian explorer Thor Heyerdahl sailed from Peru to Polynesia in 1947. The aim of his journey was to prove that Polynesia's first settlers could have originated in South America. The museum also displays the totora reed boat *Ra II*, built by Aymara people on the Bolivian island of Suriqui in Lake Titicaca. Heyerdahl used it to cross the Atlantic in 1970, to demonstrate the possibility that ancient North Africans and Middle Easterners could have reached the Americas long before the Europeans. The museum is open daily from 9.30 am to 5.45 pm from June to August, 10.30 am to 4 or 5 pm the rest of the year. Admission is Nkr30.

Polarskip Fram Opposite the *Kon-Tiki* Museum lies the 39m rigged schooner *Fram* (meaning 'forward'), launched in 1892. From 1893 to 1896 Fridtjof Nansen's North Pole expedition took *Fram* to Russia's New Siberian Islands, and en route back to Norway the team passed within only a few degrees of the North Pole itself. It was also used by Roald Amundsen in 1911 to land on the Ross Ice Shelf before he struck out on foot for the South Pole, and by Otto Sverdrup who sailed it around southern Greenland to Canada's Ellesmere Island between 1898 and 1902.

You can clamber around inside the boat and imagine how it must have felt to be trapped in the polar ice. The museum also includes an interesting rundown on the history of Arctic exploration. Opening hours are from 9 am to 6.45 pm daily from mid-June to 31 August, with shorter off-season hours. Admission is Nkr25.

Norsk Sjøfartsmuseum The Norwegian Maritime Museum (☎ 22 43 82 40) is dedicated to the numerous aspects of Norway's relationship with the sea, including the fishing industry, shipbuilding and wreck salvaging. Outside the museum there's a seamen's memorial commemorating the 4700 Norwegian sailors killed in WWII, and alongside is Roald Amundsen's ship *Gjøa*, the first ship to completely transit the North-West Passage (from 1903 to 1906). Other features of the museum include a dried cod display, a film with scenic footage of the Norwegian coastline and the underwater realm, lots of figureheads and traditional fishing craft, and an abundance of model ships. These models include the ocean liner *Stavangerfjord*, the *Gibraltar* (used by Norwegians sailing from Morocco to Gibraltar to escape Vichy forces), and the naval frigate *Kong Sverre*. The top-floor balcony of the larger wing opens onto a view over the islands of Oslofjord.

The museum is open daily from 10 am to 7 pm from mid-May to 30 September, and from 10.30 am to 4 or 7 pm the rest of the year. Admission costs Nkr60.

Oscarshall Slott Oscarshall Castle, designed by Johan Henrik Nebelong to reflect a blend of romantic and English neo-Gothic styles, was constructed as a residence for King Oscar I, who reigned from 1847 to 1852. It's open from noon to 4 pm on Tuesday, Thursday and Saturday from 24 May to 20 September. Admission costs Nkr20.

Other Museums

Barnekunstmuseet If you have a particular affinity for your friends' refrigerator art galleries, visit the Children's Art Museum (☎ 22 46 85 73), Lille Frøens vei 4, near the Frøen T-bane station. Actually, if you're in a certain frame of mind, this collection of children's work from 180 countries – textiles, sculpture, paintings and drawings – can seem pleasantly inspiring. It's open Tuesday to Thursday and on Sunday from 11 am to 4 pm from 26 June to 15 August, and shorter hours the rest of the year (but it's closed from 16 August to 9 September). Admission is Nkr30.

Sporveismuseet Vognhall 5 The Tramhall No 5 Transport Museum (☎ 88 00 21 41), in the 1913 trolley station No 5 at Gardeveien 15, is home to a collection of historic trams and trolleys, including the 1875 horse-drawn *Grønntrikken* tram. Other exhibits deal with over a century of public transport in Oslo. It's open Saturday to Monday from 1 May to 30 September, and the rest of the year on Sunday and Monday only. Admission costs Nkr20.

Det Norske Skøytemuseet The Norwegian Skating Museum (☎ 22 43 49 20), Middelthuns gate 26, is dedicated to speed and figure skating in Norway. Featured are historical skating apparatus and information on such Norwegian champions as speed skater Johann Olav Koss and figure skater Sonja Henie. Admission is Nkr20 and it's open from 10 am to 2.30 pm on Tuesday and Thursday, and from 11 am to 2 pm on Sunday.

Vigeland Museum For an in-depth look at Gustav Vigeland's work, visit Vigeland Museum (☎ 22 54 25 30), Nobels gate 32, opposite the southern entrance to Frognerparken. It was built by the city in the 1920s as a home and workshop for the sculptor, in exchange for the donation of the bulk of his life's work, and it contains his early statuary and monuments to public figures, as well as plaster moulds, woodblock prints and sketches. When he died in 1943, his ashes were deposited in the tower, and four years later the museum was opened to the public.

It's open from 10 am to 6 pm Tuesday to Saturday, and noon to 7 pm on Sunday, from May to September. The rest of the year it's open from noon to 4 pm on weekdays and until 6 pm on Sunday. Admission is Nkr30.

Emanuel Vigelands Museum Few visitors realise that Gustav Vigeland's brother Emanuel was also an accomplished artist,

and many Norwegians feel that he actually produced work superior to that of his better known sibling. For a taste of his efforts, check out the stained glass in the Oslo Domkirke, then visit the museum dedicated to his work at Grimelundsveien 8, open from noon to 3 pm on Sunday only. Admission is free. To get there, take T-bane line 1 to the Slemdal stop.

Historisk Museet The highly recommended Historical Museum (☎ 22 85 99 64, www.sv.uio.no/ima/etm/) of the University of Oslo, Frederiks gate 2, is actually three museums under one roof. Most interesting is the ground floor Oldsaksamlingen (National Antiquities Collection), with exceptional displays of Viking-era coins, jewellery and ornaments. A section on medieval religious art includes the doors and richly painted ceiling of a 13th century stave church. The 2nd level has an Arctic exhibit and the Myntkabinettet, a numismatic collection dating from as early as 995 AD. The top floor holds the Ethnographic Museum with changing exhibitions on Asia and Africa. Hours are from 11 am (noon from mid-September to mid-May) to 3 pm daily except Monday. Admission is free.

Kunstindustrimuseet The unusual Museum of Applied Art (☎ 22 03 65 40), St Olavs gate 1, displays Norwegian and international – mainly East Asian – pictorial tapestries, fashion designs and ceramic, silver and glassware from the 7th century to the present day. It's open from 11 am to 3 pm Tuesday to Friday and from noon to 4 pm on weekends. Admission costs Nkr25.

Norsk Teknisk Museum & Telemuseum The Norwegian Science & Technology Museum (☎ 22 79 60 00, www .norsk-teknisk .museum.no), Kjelsåsveien 143 near lake Maridal, has an extensive technical library and a hands-on 'Teknoteket' (or 'learning centre') for scientific research and experimentation. Displays include information on modern advances in communications, industry and energy production. The adjacent

Norsk Telemuseum (☎ 22 77 90 00, www .telenor .no/telemuseum), or Telecom Museum, reveals the history of communications in Norway from Viking beacons to modern Internet technology.

Both museums are open daily from 10 am to 6 pm from 20 June to 20 August, with shorter hours the rest of the year. Admission is free. To get there, take bus No 22, 25 or 37 to Kjelsås station, or tram No 11 or 12 to Kjelsås Allé.

Munchmuseet Munch fans who didn't get enough of the work of Edvard Munch (1863-1944) in the National Gallery can visit the Munch Museum (☎ 22 67 37 74), Tøyengata 53, which is dedicated to his life's work. It holds over 5000 drawings and paintings bequeathed to the City of Oslo by Munch himself. Despite the artist's tendency towards tormented visions, all is not grey. Yes, you'll see *The Sick Child* and *The Maiden & Death*, but lighter themes, such as *The Sun* and *Spring Ploughing*, are also represented.

It's open from 10 am to 6 pm daily from 1 June to mid-September, with shorter winter hours. Admission is Nkr50. Take the T-bane to Tøyen, from where it's a five-minute signposted walk.

Postmuseet If you're in the main post office at Dronningens gate 15, have a look at the free Post Museum (☎ 23 14 80 59) which lies at the opposite end of the block. Exhibits on Norway's 350 years of postal history include a reindeer sledge once used for mail delivery and Norway's largest stamp collection. It's open from 10 am to 3 pm weekdays, until 2 pm on Saturday and from noon to 4 pm on Sunday.

Teatermuseet The Theatre Museum (☎ 22 42 65 09) in the old 1641 Rådhus, Christiania Torv, is housed in the first public theatre in old Christiania. The exhibits cover the history of Oslo theatre from 1800 to the present day. It's open from 11 am to 3 pm on Wednesday and Thursday, and noon to 4 pm on Sunday. Admission is Nkr25.

Norsk Arkitekturmuseum The Norwegian Museum of Architecture (☎ 22 42 40 80), Kongens gate 4 at Kvadraturen near the Akershus Fortress, contains a permanent exhibition of 1000 years of Norwegian architecture and construction, as well as visiting exhibits. It's open from 10 am to 4 pm Monday to Saturday (from 12.30 pm on Sunday) from 2 May to 15 September; and the rest of the year it opens only on Sunday. Admission is Nkr20.

Astrup Fearnley Museet A block east, at Grev Wedels plass 9 (enter from Dronningens gate), is the Astrup Fearnley Museum (☎ 22 93 60 60, nettvik.no/af_museet/), which presents worthwhile modern Norwegian and international art exhibitions. It's open from noon to 4 pm Tuesday to Sunday (until 7 pm on Thursday and 5 pm on weekends). Admission is Nkr40.

Museet for Samtidskunst The National Museum of Contemporary Art (☎ 22 33 58 20), Bankplassen 4, occupies a classic Art Nouveau building which formerly housed the Central Bank of Norway. It features the National Gallery's collections of post-WWII Scandinavian and international art. It's open Tuesday to Sunday from 10 am (11 am Sunday) to 5 pm (8 pm Thursday and 4 pm Saturday). Admission is free.

Stenersenmuseet The Stenersen Museum (☎ 22 83 95 60), Munkedamsveien 15, contains three formerly private collections of works by Norwegian artists from 1850 to 1970. The museum and much of the art, which includes works by Munch, were a gift to the city by Rolf E Stenersen. Other collections were provided by Oslo residents Amaldus Nielsen and Ludvig O Ravensberg. It's open from 11 am to 5 pm Tuesday to Sunday (until 7 pm on Tuesday and Thursday) and admission costs Nkr30.

Ibsen-museet The Ibsen Museum (☎ 22 55 20 09) on Drammensveien is housed in the last residence of Norwegian playwright Henrik Ibsen. The study remains exactly as

Edvard Munch

Edvard Munch (1863-1944) is Norway's most renowned visual artist. The son of a military doctor, he grew up in Christiania (Oslo) in an environment of illness, death and grief that came to dominate his art. His mother died of tuberculosis when Edvard was only five, his elder sister succumbed to the same disease at the age of 15, and his younger sister was diagnosed with mental illness as a young girl.

After studying at the Technical School in Oslo and the Royal School of Drawing, Munch chose art as his life's work. In 1885 he went to Paris where he was influenced by French Realism, and there he produced his first great work, *The Sick Child*, a portrait of his sister Sophie shortly before her death. So provocative was the painting that professional criticism was largely negative, and in his next works he made an effort to lighten up his style, as shown in the holiday scene *Inger on the Beach*.

After returning to Christiania, however, he fell in with a bohemian element whose influence turned him back to his natural tendency for darker themes. In 1889 Munch exhibited his work and was granted a three-year travel study grant which allowed him to return to Paris and study under Léon Bonnat. He learned of the death of his father while in Paris and in 1890 produced the haunting painting *Night*, which depicts a lonely figure in a dark window. The following year he completed *Melancholy* and began sketches of what would be his best known work, *The Scream*, which unequivocally reveals Munch's own 'inner hell' (as well as the same *fin-de-siècle* anxiety that characterises the atmosphere a century later, at the end of the millennium).

In 1892 Munch exhibited at the Artist's Association of Berlin and was so taken with the city and the welcome it afforded him that he decided to remain there and join the city's vibrant artistic community (which at the time included fellow Norwegian Gustav Vigeland). Here he moved into a cycle of dark atmospheric themes that he would collectively entitle *Frieze of Life – A Poem about Life, Love and Death*, which included *Starry Night, Moonlight, The Storm, Vampire, Ashes, Anxiety* and *Death in the Sickroom*. His obsession with darkness and doom eventually led him to another obsession with alcohol, as well as chronic emotional instability and a tragic love affair that was revealed in the 1907 work *Death of Marat*.

After the death of Henrik Ibsen in 1906, Munch was involved in creating the set for Berlin's Deutsches Theatre production of Ibsen's *Ghosts*. The painting *Self-Portrait with a Bottle of Wine* shows how Munch subsequently identified himself with one of the play's characters, the hopeless Osvald. He then went through a commercial period, painting commissioned portraits of Friedrich Nietzsche and his sister Elizabeth. By 1908, however, he decided to face his personal problems by checking into a Copenhagen mental health clinic for eight months.

After leaving the clinic Munch returned to Norway, where he settled on the coast at Kragerø. There he enthusiastically embraced and reproduced the stark winter scenes of the coastal landscape, otherwise favoured as a summer holiday spot. He also produced a body of work for the newly constructed Aula auditorium at the University of Christiania. These works clearly represented the forces of life, light and hope, and displayed a more positive outlook than ever before. *Alma Mater* depicts a woman at the shore with a child at her breast, and *History* portrays an elderly man beneath a spreading oak tree, relating the history of humanity to a young child.

In 1916 Munch purchased the Ekely estate near Christiania and began producing bright and sunny works dedicated to humans in harmony with their landscape. Before his death in 1944 he bequeathed his body of works to the City of Oslo, and today much of his life's work is displayed in the National Gallery, the Munch Museum and also the Bergen Art Gallery.

he left it and other rooms have been restored in the style and colours popular in Ibsen's day. It's open from noon to 3 pm Tuesday to Sunday year-round. Admission costs Nkr30.

Parks & Gardens

Frognerparken & Vigeland Park

Northwest of the centre is green Frognerparken, which attracts Oslo locals with its broad lawns, ponds, stream and rows of shade trees. On a sunny afternoon it's ideal for picnics, strolling or lounging on the grass. Near the southern entrance to the park lies the Oslo Bymuseum (Oslo City Museum; ☎ 22 42 06 45). Housed in the historic Frogner Manor (the first manor was built here during the Viking era, but the current building was constructed in the 18th century), it presents paintings and other exhibits on the city's history. It's open from 10 am to 4 pm Tuesday to Friday (weekends from 11 am). Admission is Nkr30.

The main Frognerparken attraction is Vigeland Park, brimming with nearly 200 granite and bronze works of Norwegian sculptor Gustav Vigeland (1869-1943). His highly charged work, which takes in the entire range of human emotional extremes – from entwined lovers and tranquil elderly couples to contempt-ridden beggars – also includes some less obvious artistic expressions involving lizards and other creatures. His most renowned work, *Sinataggen* (the 'Little Hot-Head'), portrays a London child in particularly ill humour.

The monolithic granite pillar crowning the park's highest hill portrays a mass of writhing human forms, both entwined with and undermining others in their individual struggle to reach the top. The circle of steps around it supports rows of stone figures. It's a great place to visit in the evening after other city sites have closed. Admission is free. Access from the city centre is on tram No 12 or 15, marked Frogner.

If you wish to see more of Gustav Vigeland's work, check out Vigeland Museum (see Other Museums, earlier), opposite the southern entrance to Frognerparken.

Botanisk Hage & Museums

Oslo's Botanical Garden (☎ 22 85 18 35) on Trondheimsveien features over 1000 alpine plants from around the world as well as sections dedicated to vegetation from both temperate and tropical regions. Specimens in the aromatic garden are accompanied by texts in both print and Braille. From 15 April to 14 September, it's open from 7 am to 8 pm weekdays and 10 am to 8 pm on weekends, with shorter hours the rest of the year. Admission is free.

The university's adjoining Zoological Museum (☎ 22 85 16 00) has well presented displays of stuffed wildlife from Norway and elsewhere, including a special exhibit on Arctic wildlife. The Mineralogical-Geological Museum contains displays on the history of the solar system, Norwegian geology, and examples of myriad minerals, meteorites and moon rocks. The Paleontological Museum is full of bones and fossils, including a megatherium (giant ground sloth), a 10m iguanodon skeleton and a nest of dinosaur eggs.

All three university museums are open from 11 am to 4 pm Tuesday to Sunday. Admission is free.

Gamle Aker Kirke

This medieval stone church, north of the centre on Akersbakken, dates from 1080 and is Oslo's oldest building. Lutheran services are held on Sunday at 11 am, but otherwise it's open from noon to 2 pm Monday to Saturday and 9 am to 1 pm on Sunday. Admission is free. Take bus No 37 from Jernbanetorget, get off at Akersbakken and walk up past the churchyard.

Damstredet

The skewed wooden homes of the Damstredet district, some dating from the early 19th century, add a splash of character amid otherwise ordinary architecture. This rather quirky-looking neighbourhood, north of the city centre, provides a pronounced counterpoint to the deprived and dreary suburb of Akerselva, just east across the river.

Gustav Vigeland

The Norwegian sculptor Gustav Vigeland (1869-1943) was born to a farming family near Mandal in the far south of the country. As a child he became deeply interested in Protestantism and spirituality, and during his teenage years he also expressed interests in woodcarving and drawing. At the age of 14 he was enrolled as an apprentice to a master woodcarver in Oslo, but when his father died two years later, Gustav was forced to return home to care for his family. Even so, he never abandoned his hopes of becoming an artist and read all he could on drama and the arts, especially studying the anatomical sculptures of Danish neoclassicist Bertel Thorvaldsen.

In 1888 Vigeland returned to Oslo and with a great deal of effort secured an apprenticeship to sculptor Brynjulf Bergslien. The following year he exhibited his first work at the State Exhibition of Art, and it wasn't long before his talents were being recognised by the public. In 1891 he travelled to Copenhagen and then to Paris and Italy, where he worked with various masters; he was especially inspired by the work of French sculptor Auguste Rodin. When his public grants ran out he returned to Norway to make a living working on the restoration of the Nidaros Cathedral in Trondheim, producing or revitalising many of its gargoyles and other fantasy figures, and fulfilling commissions to produce portraits of prominent Norwegians.

In 1921 the City of Oslo recognised his talents and built him a spacious studio in which to work; in return, he would bequeath to the city all his subsequent works as well as his original models and sketches. This seemed too good a deal to pass up, and in 1924 Vigeland retired to Oslo and spent the rest of his life producing the sculptures now displayed in the enormously popular Vigeland Park and its adjacent museum.

The highlight of the park is the 14m-high Monolith; this incredible production required three stone carvers working daily from 1929 to 1943. It was carved from a single stone pillar quarried from Iddefjorden in south-eastern Norway and depicts a writhing mass of 121 detailed human figures. The figures, together with the pillar, have been interpreted in many ways: as a phallic representation, the struggle for existence, yearnings for the spiritual spheres and transcendence of cyclic repetition.

Leading down from the plinth bearing this column is a series of steps supporting sculptures depicting people experiencing a range of human emotions and activities, while the numerous sculptures dominating the surrounding park carry the artist's themes from the realist to the ludicrous. The result is truly one of Norway's artistic highlights and, best of all, there are no signs admonishing you to keep off the grass or forbidding picnicking on the lawn, wading in the fountains, feeding the ducks or climbing on the statues!

GUY MOBERLY

On winning the annual Oslo three-legged race

Grønland

Oslo's down-to-earth Grønland district, behind the Oslo S train station, has attracted much of the city's immigrant and refugee population and provides a relatively cosmopolitan flavour, as well as a range of inexpensive grocery stores and restaurants. In case you're unsure about the area's politics, check out the enormous rose-clenching fist which has burst through the pavement at the edge of Grønlandstorg.

Holmenkollen

In summer, the Holmenkollen ski jump – perched on a hilltop overlooking Oslo – offers a panoramic view of the city and doubles as a concert venue. During Oslo's annual ski festival, held in March, it draws the world's top ski jumpers. Part of the route to the top is served by a lift, but you're on your own for the steep 114 steps to the view at the very top (afterwards, you can pay Nkr40 and see how it feels to win the Olympic downhill in the adjacent Ski-Simulator). The tower visit is included in the Nkr50 admission to the Ski Museum (☎ 22 92 32 00), where you're led through the 4000-year history of nordic and downhill skiing in Norway.

Highly worthwhile are the exhibits on the Antarctic expeditions of Amundsen and Scott, and Fridtjof Nansen's slog across the Greenland icecap (you'll see the boat he constructed from his sled and canvas tent to row the final 100km to Nuuk). The remarkable thing was that these guys did it all without the aid of North Face or Patagonia!

From Oslo, take T-bane line 1 west to Holmenkollen station, then wind your way up the hill to the ski jump. It's open from 9 am to 10 pm in July and August; until 8 pm in June; from 10 am to 5 pm in May and September; and until 4 pm in winter. If you intend to also visit Tryvannstårnet, buy a combination ticket, which costs an additional Nkr10.

Tryvannstårnet

The Tryvannstårnet observation tower, north of the ski jump, sits at 538m and overlooks the suburban wilderness of Nordmarka. For Nkr30, a lifts zips you to the top and a 20,000 sq km view as far as snowcapped Mt Gausta to the west, the Oslofjord to the south and the boundless Swedish forests to the east. The opening hours are the same as for Holmenkollen. From the Holmen T-bane station, take the scenic ride to the end of the line at Frognerseteren and look for the signposted walking route to the tower.

Henie-Onstad Kunstsenter

In Høvekodden, west of the centre, lies the low-profile but slightly aristocratic Henie-Onstad Art Centre (☎ 67 54 30 50), founded in the 1960s by Norwegian figure skater Sonja Henie and her husband Niels Onstad. The couple actively sought out collectible works of Joan Miró and Pablo Picasso, as well as assorted impressionist, abstract, expressionist and modern Norwegian works. It all comes together pretty well, and when you've seen enough art you can head downstairs for a look at Sonja's various skating medals and trophies. The centre is open from 11 am to 5 pm on Monday, 9 am to 9 pm from Tuesday to Friday and on weekends from 11 am to 5 pm (until 7 pm in summer). Admission costs Nkr50 (Nkr25 with the Oslo Card). From Jernbanetorget, take any bus towards Sandvika and get off at Høvekodden; the centre lies a few minutes walk from the stop.

Vikinglandet

A recent attraction is Vikingland (☎ 64 94 63 63), 10km south of Oslo (adjacent to its sister operation, the Tusenfryd amusement park, which costs Nkr185 to enter in high season). This child-oriented Viking-era theme park features reconstructed houses, costumed interpreters and craft demonstrations. It's open from 1 to 7 pm, 6 June to 16 August. Admission is Nkr100 (Nkr90 with the Oslo Card). Take bus No 541, marked Drøbak.

Islands & Beaches

If the weather's fine, head to one of Oslo's beaches. Ferries to half a dozen islands in

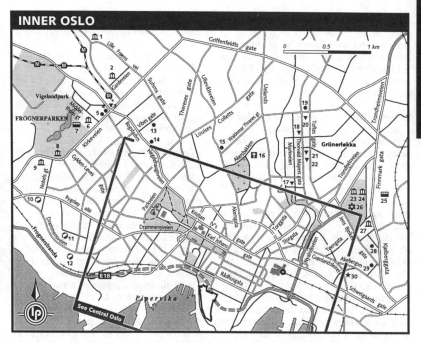

INNER OSLO

PLACES TO EAT
3   Krishna's Cuisine
17 Markveien Mat & Vinhus
18 Olympia Birken
20 Kafe Sult
21 Mucho Mas
22 Café Kjøkkenhagen; Fru
    Hagen

MUSEUMS
1   Barnekunstmuseet
2   Sporveismuseet Vognhall 5
6   Det Norske Skøytemuseet

8   Oslo Bymuseum
9   Vigeland Museum
23 Zoological Museum
24 Mineralogical-Geological
    Museum; Palaeontological
    Museum
27 Munchmuseet

OTHER
4   Vinmonopolet
5   Majorstuen Tannlegesenter
7   Frognerbadet Swimming Pool
10 Swedish Embassy

11 British Embassy
12 Russian Embassy
13 Majorstua Myntvaskeri
14 Skandinavisk Høyfjellsutstyr
15 Ringstrøms
16 Gamle Aker Kirke
19 A-Snarvask
25 Tøyenbadet Swimming Pool
26 Botanisk Hage
28 Tannlegevakten
29 Tyrilikollektivet Climbing
    Centre
30 Central Police Station

the Oslofjord leave from Vippetangen quay, south-east of Akershus Fortress. Boats to Hovedøya and Langøyene are relatively frequent in summer (running at least hourly), while other islands are served less often.

Hovedøya The south-western shore of otherwise rocky Hovedøya, the nearest island to the mainland, is popular with sunbathers. The island is ringed with walking paths to old cannon emplacements and the ruins of a 12th century Cistercian monastery, built by monks from Kirkstead in Britain. Boat Nos 92 and 93 to Hovedøya leave approximately twice hourly between 6.45 am and midnight from late May to mid-August, with much shorter hours the rest of the year.

Langøyene South of Hovedøya lies the undeveloped island of Langøyene, with superb swimming from rocky or sandy beaches (one on the south-eastern shore is designated for nude bathing). Boat No 94 runs hourly to Langøyene from 10.05 am to 7.05 pm, 21 May to 16 August.

Bygdøy Peninsula The Bygdøy peninsula also has two popular beaches, Huk and Paradisbukta, which can be reached on bus No 30A from Jernbanetorget to its last stop. While there are some sandy patches, most of Huk comprises grassy lawns and large smooth rocks which are ideal for sunbathing. It's actually separated into two beaches by a small cove; the beach on the north-western side is open to nude bathing. If Huk seems too crowded, a 10-minute walk through the woods north of the bus stop leads to the more secluded Paradisbukta.

Activities
Hiking A network of trails leads off into the Nordmarka from Frognerseteren (at the end of T-bane line 1), including a good trail down to the lake Sognsvann, 6km northwest of the centre at the end of T-bane line 3. There's also an excellent network of hiking trails around the lake itself; the pleasant route around the lake takes less than an hour. On hot days, the eastern shore offers refreshing swimming, while the wilder western shore is a bit better for relative solitude. Other hiking routes radiate out into the hills beyond.

A more urban but mostly green two-hour walk will take you along the Akerselva river from the Kjelsås tram stop to Vaterlands bru (bridge), right in the heart of Grønland. Other city walks are outlined in the series of maps produced by the Park

og Idrettsvesenet (☎ 22 08 22 00), Kingos gate 17, which covers the entire city in five sheets.

Avid hikers may want to stop by the DNT office (☎ 22 82 28 00), Storgata 3, which maintains several mountain huts in the Nordmarka region (DNT membership is required to use them) and can provide information on longer-distance hiking routes all over Norway.

Climbing The best local climbing is on the pre-bolted faces of Kolsåstoppen, which is accessible on T-bane line 3 to Kolsås. Otherwise, climbers can head for Oslo's two indoor climbing walls. Villmarkshuset (☎ 22 05 05 22), Christian Krohgs gate 16, rises above the urban banks of Akerselva and offers a climbing wall, shooting range and pool diving centre. It also sells a range of outdoor books and equipment. There's another indoor climbing wall at Tyrilikollektivet Climbing Centre (☎ 22 67 58 50), Sverres gate 4.

Cycling Den Rustne Eike (☎ 22 83 72 31), near the harbour by the tourist office, rents seven-speed bicycles for Nkr95 for 24 hours, and mountain bikes for Nkr170 (plus a Nkr1000 deposit). It has information on bike paths and organises cycling tours. Hours are from 10 am to 6.30 pm daily May to October, to 3.30 pm weekdays in winter.

One popular outing is to take the weekend bike train (sykkeltoget) to Stryken, 40km north of Oslo, and cycle back through the Nordmarka. The train leaves Oslo S at 9.15 am on Saturday and Sunday from May to October. For a shorter ride, there's also a bike train that runs from Majorstuen to Frognerseteren on summer weekends at 11 am, noon and 1 pm.

For cycling information contact the local club, Syklistenes Landsforening (☎ 22 41 50 80, fax 22 41 65 65), Storgata 23c.

Horse Riding At Stall Nordbye (☎ 22 14 86 54), Nordre Solberg Gård, you can go riding around the farm for Nkr100 per hour. Take bus No 41 to the Solberg stop.

Skiing Oslo's ski season is roughly from December to March, and the area has over 2400km of prepared nordic tracks (1000km in Nordmarka alone), many of them flood-lit. Easy-access tracks begin right at the end of T-bane lines 1 and 3. Tomm Murstad Skiservice (☎ 22 14 41 24, sdaas@online .no) at the Voksenkollen station, one T-bane stop before Frognerseteren, hires out snow-boards and nordic skis. The downhill slopes at Tryvann Skisenter (☎ 22 14 54 82) are open in the ski season. Skiforeningen (the Ski Society; ☎ 22 92 32 00), Kongeveien 5, N-0390 Oslo, can provide further informa-tion on skiing options.

Ice Skating At the Narvisen outdoor ice rink on Karl Johans gate, you can skate for free whenever it's cold enough to freeze over (it's closed for maintenance from 3 to 4 pm). Skates may be hired for Nkr35.

Swimming Oslo has two municipal swim-ming pools, Frognerbadet (☎ 22 44 74 29) in Frognerparken, and Tøyenbadet (☎ 22 68 24 23) near the Munch Museum. The for-mer is open from 7 am to 7 pm weekdays and from 11 am to 5 pm weekends from 18 May to 20 August. The latter is open vary-ing hours year-round. Admission to either costs Nkr40 (free with the Oslo Card).

Organised Tours

Oslo is so compact that organised city tours aren't really necessary, but they may be an option for anyone short on time.

Båtservice Sightseeing (☎ 22 20 07 15, fax 22 41 64 10) at Pier 3, Rådhusbrygge, does a tidy 7½-hour city tour to the Bygdøy museums, Vigeland Park and the Hol-menkollen ski jump, plus a cruise of the Oslofjord for a reasonable Nkr350, or a three-hour version minus the cruise for Nkr210. Their 50-minute 'mini-cruise' on Oslofjord costs Nkr70 (free with the Oslo Card) and a two-hour cruise costs Nkr140, or Nkr255/325 with lunch/dinner.

HM KristiansenTours (☎ 22 20 82 06, fax 22 36 40 95), Hegdehaugveien 4, offers two-hour tours including a spin around the city centre and visits to Vigeland Park and Holmenkollen for Nkr140; and three-hour versions including a couple of Bygdøy mu-seums for Nkr210.

The popular 'Norway in a Nutshell' day tours start at Nkr1390, and may be booked through any tourist office or travel agency, or directly through NSB. From Oslo, the typi-cal 'Norway in a Nutshell' route includes a rail trip from Oslo across the Hardan-gervidda to Myrdal, a rail descent to Flåm along the dramatic Flåmbanen, a cruise along Nærøyfjord to Gudvangen, a bus to Voss, a connecting train to Bergen for a short visit, then an overnight return rail trip to Oslo (including a 2nd-class sleeper compartment).

Special Events

Oslo's most festive annual event is surely the 17 May Constitution Day celebration, when Oslo residents, whose roots spring from all over Norway, descend on the Royal Palace dressed in the finery of their native districts. It's known mainly as a time for celebration of the family and reverence for child-like fun and children's interests.

In March, the Holmenkollen ski festival attracts nordic skiers and ski jumpers from around the world. August sees the Oslo International Jazz Festival and October, the Scandinavia-oriented Ultima Contempor-ary Music Festival (☎ 22 42 91 20). The former pales in comparison to its counter-parts in Kongsberg and Molde but, thanks to its capital-city location, it does draw a substantial following.

In addition to worldwide millennium festivities, in 2000, Oslo intends to cele-brate its own millennium (celebrating its 1000 year anniversary). Given the fact that the city was founded in 1048, this may seem to be jumping the gun a bit, but recent archaeological finds indicate that the area was settled prior to the city's offi-cial founding, thus justifying (however loosely) the double millennium celebra-tions. Festivities are planned throughout the year – see the tourist offices for further information.

CENTRAL OSLO

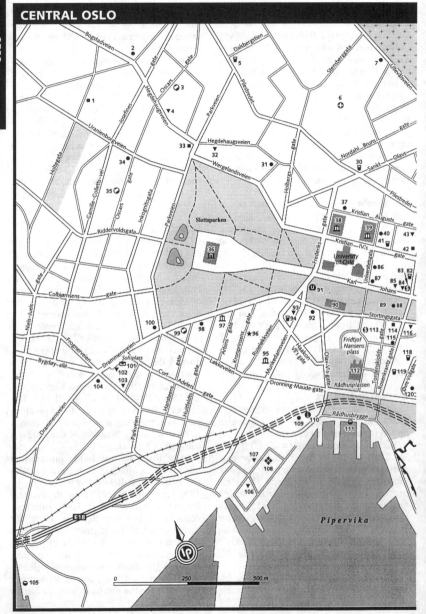

Bogstadveien

Dalbergstien

Sternbergata

Ullevålsveien

Uranienborgveien

Holtegata

Josefines gate

Hegdehaugsveien

Oscars gate

Parkveien

Pilestredet

gate

Nordahl Bruns gate

Olavs

Sankt

Pilestredet

Hegdehaugsveien

Wergelandsveien

Holbergs gate

Camilla Colletts vei

Oscars gate

Inkognitogata

Parkveien

Kristian Augusts gate

Slottsparken

Riddervoldsgata

Frederiks gate

Kristian IV:s gate

University of Oslo

Universitetsgata

Karl Johans

Colbjørnsens gate

Niels Juels gate

Frognerveien

Bygdøy allé

Drammensveien

Drammensveien

Parkveien

Hansteens gate

Huitfeldts gate

Cort Adelers gate

Løkkeveien

Arbins gate

Kronprinsens gate

Ruseløkkveien

Munkedamsveien

Haakon VII:s gate

Dronning Maudes gate

Olav V:s gate

Stortingsgata

Fridtjof Nansens plass

Rosenkrantz' gate

Nordenskiolds gate

Øvre Vollgate

Rådhusplassen

Rådhusbrygge

Solliplass

E18

Pipervika

0   250   500 m

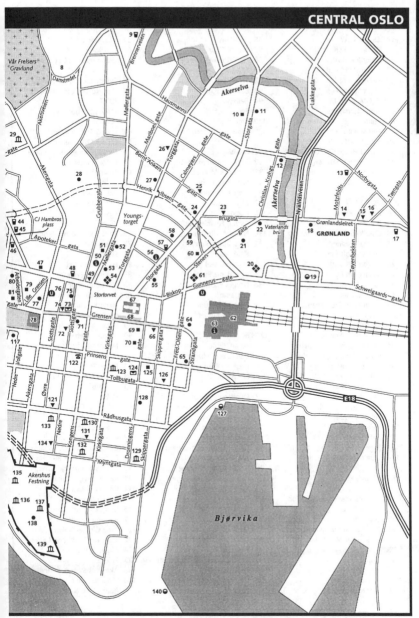

CENTRAL OSLO

CENTRAL OSLO

PLACES TO STAY
1 Ellingsens Pensjonat
10 Albertine Hostel
33 Cochs Pensjonat
42 Hotel Bristol
47 Norrøna Hotel
51 KFUM Sleep-In
60 Hotel Terminus
69 Fønix Hotel
70 Hotell Astoria
79 Rica Travel Hotel
81 Grand Hotel; Grand Café
114 Cecil Hotel; Mr Hong
    Restaurant
125 City Hotel

PLACES TO EAT
4 Peppe's Pizza
14 Punjab Sweet House
15 Oslo Kebab & Pizza House
16 Dhaka Cuisine
23 Teddy's Soft Bar
25 Saigon Lille Café
26 Sushi Nam Hong
32 Tapas
43 Hotel Stefan
49 Stortorvets Gjestgiveri
66 Pizza Hut
72 Tacoland
74 A Touch of France
84 Oluf Loretzen Supermarket
85 Paléet Shopping Complex
93 Vegeta Vertshus
102 Kaffe & Krem
103 Peppe's Pizza
106 La Piazza
107 Smør-Petersen Deli
116 Peppe's Pizza
121 Kafé Celsius
126 Café Sekel
131 Engebret Café
134 Gamle Rådhus

ENTERTAINMENT
5 Underwater Pub
9 Afro International Nightclub
13 Oliven Café
17 Olympen
21 Oslo Spektrum Concert Hall
27 Rockefeller Music Hall
30 Blitz
41 Club Castro
44 Jazid
45 London Pub
46 Herr Nilsens Pub

48 So What
57 Miami Club
58 Den Norske Opera
59 Mars
82 Head On
92 Saga Cinema
94 Belleville
118 Potpurriet
119 Smuget
128 Filmens Hus Café

MUSEUMS
29 Kunstindustrimuseet
38 Historisk Museet
39 Nasjonalgalleriet
95 Stenersenmuseet
97 Ibsen-Museet
123 Postmuseet
129 Astrup Fearnley Museet
130 Norsk Arkitekturmuseum
132 Museet for Samtidskunst &
    Kafé Sesam
133 Teatermuseet
135 Christiania Bymodell
136 Norges Hjemmefront
    Museum
137 Prison Museum
139 Forsvarsmuseet

OTHER
2 Japan Photo
3 Canadian Embassy
6 Rikshospitalet (National
    Hospital)
7 Selva As
8 Damstredet District
11 Oslo Kommunale Legevakten
    (Oslo Emergency Clinic)
12 Villmarkshuset
18 Grønlandstorg
19 Galleri Oslo Long-Distance
    Bus Terminal
20 Galleri Oslo Shopping Centre
22 Clenched Fist Sculpture
24 Kiwi Supermarket
28 Deichmanske Bibliotek
31 HM Kristiansen Tours
34 Nomaden
35 German Embassy
36 Det Kongelige Slott
37 Tronsmo
40 JW Cappelen; Helios Health
    Food Store
50 Ungdomsinformasjonen
    (Use-It)

52 Vinmonopolet
53 Husfliden
54 Glasmagasinet Department
    Store
55 Syklistenes Landsforening
56 Den Norske Turistforening
    (DNT)
61 Oslo City Shopping
    Complex
62 Oslo S Train Station
63 Oslo S Ostbanehallen
64 Jernbanetorget; Stena Line
    & Trafikanten
65 Japan Photo
67 Oslo Domkirke
68 Basarhallene
71 Color Line Ferries
73 Post Office
75 Kilroy Travels
76 Stortinget T-Bane station
77 Akers Mic
78 Stortinget
80 Heimen Husflid
83 American Express
86 Norli Bookshop
87 Tanum Libris Bookshop
88 Narvisen Outdoor
    Ice Rink
89 Eidsvolls Plass
90 Nasjonalteatret
91 Nasjonalteatret T-Bane
    Station
96 Police Station
98 Qvist Libris Bookshop
99 US Embassy
100 Nobel Institute
101 Solli Plass Post Office
104 University Library
105 Hjortneskaia
108 Aker Brygge Shopping
    Complex & IMAX Theatre
109 Den Rustne Eike Bike Hire
110 Norges Informasjonssenter
111 Rådhusbrygge Quay
112 Oslo Rådhus
113 American Express
115 Unique Design
117 Børsen Internet Café
120 Arne Gimnes Bokhandel
122 Tele-Nor Telephone Office
124 Main Post Office
127 Palékaia
138 Akershus Slott & Festning
140 Vippetangen quay No 2
    (Stena Line & DFDS Ferries)

Places to Stay

Camping *Ekeberg Camping (☎ 22 19 85 68, Ekebergveien 65)* occupies a scenic knoll south-east of the city and affords one of the best views over Oslo. Tent sites for one or two people cost Nkr115, with a 10% discount for rail pass holders. It's open from 22 May to 31 August. Take bus No 24 or 46 from Jernbanetorget to the Ekeberg stop (10 minutes).

The enormous *Bogstad Camping (☎ 22 50 76 80, Ankerveien 117)* is open year-round and is situated less than a kilometre from lake Bogstadvannet. Take bus No 32 from Jernbanetorget to the Bogstad Camping stop (30 minutes). Tent sites cost Nkr115 for one or two people, plus Nkr20 for each additional person, plus Nkr40 per vehicle. In summer, four-bed cabins cost from Nkr510 to Nkr810. It has basic kitchen facilities (but no cooking implements) and food is available at the adjacent petrol station.

A good alternative is the more primitive *Langøyene Camping (☎ 22 36 37 98)*, on the Oslofjord island of Langøyene, which charges Nkr60 per person. It's open from 20 May to 20 August. There are showers and a kiosk selling simple snacks. Take boat No 94 from Vippetangen (and take care not to miss the last boat back from Oslo in the evening!).

Those who prefer wild camping can take T-bane line 1 to Frognerseteren at the edge of the Nordmarka or line 3 to Sognsvann. You can't camp at Sognsvann itself, but walk a kilometre or two into the woods and you'll find plenty of natural camp sites.

Hostels Oslo has three HI-affiliated hostels. Rates given here are for members; non-members pay an additional Nkr25, and sheets are an extra Nkr40 per visit.

The year-round *Haraldsheim Hostel (☎ 22 15 50 43 or ☎ 22 22 29 65, Haraldsheimveien 4)* has 270 beds, mostly in four-bed rooms. Rates, breakfast included, are Nkr155/175 in a four-bed dorm without/with bath; Nkr260/330 for a single and Nkr370/450 for a double. There are kitchen

and laundry facilities. It's a busy place so make advance reservations. The hostel is 4km from the city centre; take tram No 10, 11 or 17 or bus No 31 or 32 to Sinsenkrysset, then walk five minutes up the hill.

Holtekilen Summerhotel (☎ 67 53 38 53, Michelets vei 55, Stabekk), 9km west of Oslo, is open from 16 May to 17 August. A bed in a small dorm costs Nkr155, while singles/doubles cost Nkr250/410, with breakfast. Sleeping bags aren't allowed; you must have HI regulation sheets or hire sheets for Nkr40 per visit. Take bus No 151, 161, 251, 252 or 261 to Kveldroveien or catch a local train to Stabekk and cross the footbridge over the E18. It's fairly good value but you'll also have to factor the bus fare into your costs, as the area is too far out to be included in day cards or the Oslo Card.

The third HI hostel is *LBM-Ekeberg (☎ 22 74 18 90, fax 22 74 75 05, Kongsveien 82)*, located in an old house and open from 1 June to 14 August. Beds in dorms cost Nkr165 and single/double rooms are Nkr265/410 (all rates include breakfast). Take tram No 18 or 19 towards Ljarbru and get off at Holtet; from there, it's about 200m along Kongsveien.

KFUM Sleep-In (☎ 22 20 83 97, Møllergata 1), the YMCA summer hostel, is a 10-minute walk from Oslo S (appropriately, the entry is from Grubbegata). Beds cost Nkr100, but it fills up quickly and you need a sleeping bag. Kitchen facilities are available. It's open from early July to mid-August. Reception hours are from 8 to 11 am and 5 pm to midnight. On Thursdays, they sometimes stage musical or cultural events.

If Sleep-In is full, try *Sleep-Safe Oslo Vineyard Church Hostel (☎ 22 15 20 99, fax 22 15 04 99, Lillogata 5)*, with a similar setup, season (from 7 July to 17 August) and reception hours. The cost is Nkr80/110 for a mattress/bed, and breakfast. It's 3km north of the centre via tram No 11, 12 or 17, or bus No 56, to Grefsenveien.

An even simpler place is the *Studenterhytta (☎ 22 49 90 36)*, out of town in the forest at Kjellerberget. This student-oriented mountain hut costs Nkr125; bring your own sleeping bag. Take bus No 41 to Sørkedalen school; it's a 45-minute walk from there. There are also two DNT mountain huts in the Nordmarka above Oslo: *Kikutstua* (☎ *22 42 01 73*), a 15km walk from Frognerseteren; and *Kobberhaughytta* (☎ *22 49 90 14*), 10km from Frognerseteren. Both cost Nkr150 per person and must be booked in advance.

From 8 June to 23 August, *Albertine Hostel* (☎ *22 99 72 00, fax 22 99 72 20, Storgata 55)* boasts an 'international atmosphere' and offers good value at Nkr240/330 for single/double rooms and Nkr135/110 per person in four/six-bed dorms. Breakfast costs Nkr50. Cooking facilities are available and you can hire towels and linen. From Jernbanetorget, take bus No 27, 30 or 31, or tram No 11, 12, 15 or 17 to the Hausmannsgate stop.

Pensions The homy *Ellingsens Pensjonat* (☎ *22 60 03 59, Holtegata 25)*, in a neighbourhood of older homes five blocks north of the Royal Palace, offers the best value in its class. It has 20 small but adequate rooms, each with a desk, chair and sink; toilets and showers are located off the hall. Singles/doubles cost Nkr250/380; reservations are required in summer. Take bus No 1 (towards Majorstuen) from Jernbanetorget and get off at Uranienborgveien.

Somewhat pricey but nearer the centre is *Cochs Pensjonat* (☎ *22 60 48 36, Parkveien 25)*, just north of the Royal Palace. The 65 comfortable but spartan rooms cost Nkr310/420 for singles/doubles with shared bath and Nkr390/530 with a bath and cooking facilities.

Private Homes Staff at the tourist office window at Oslo S book rooms in private homes (two nights minimum stay) for Nkr170 per person. They also book unfilled hotel rooms at slightly discounted rates. The booking fee is Nkr20.

Use-It (☎ *22 41 51 32*), Møllergata 3, books rooms in private homes for Nkr100 to Nkr150 for sleeping bag accommodation and Nkr125 to Nkr150 with bedding.

There's no minimum stay and bookings are free. If you book through this service, either turn up at the appointed time or, if you can't make it, phone the establishment to tell them, so they won't have to wait for you and can give your booking to someone else. From 1 July to 31 August, Use-It is open from 7.30 am to 6 pm weekdays and 9 am to 2 pm on Saturday; the rest of the year, it's open 11 am to 5 pm weekdays. If you're arriving outside of these hours, phone during opening hours and ask for accommodation suggestions and phone numbers so you can book directly.

Hotels The run-down *Fønix Hotel* (☎ *22 42 59 57, fax 22 33 12 10, Dronningens gate 19)*, off Karl Johans gate two blocks from Oslo S, isn't really recommended, but it does offer low standard hotel rates: Nkr375/475 for singles/doubles with shared bath and Nkr495/750 for rooms with bath. All rates include breakfast.

City Hotel (☎ *22 41 36 10, fax 22 42 24 29, Skippergata 19)* is an older hotel with a bit of character, including a front parlour with Victorian furniture. The rooms are quite straightforward and cost Nkr410/590 with shared bath, Nkr495/680 with private bath. Anyone who's sensitive to traffic noise should request a courtyard room.

Rica Travel Hotel (☎ *22 00 33 00, fax 22 33 51 22, Arbeidergata 4)* is a good value business hotel. Rooms are modern and compact yet pleasant, and have private bath, TV, phone and minibar. Standard rates for single rooms range from Nkr485 to Nkr755, doubles from Nkr665 to Nkr895.

Norrøna Hotel (☎ *22 42 64 00, fax 22 33 25 65, Grensen 19)* offers comfortable rooms on a par with those in many of Oslo's better hotels. All rooms have private bath, TV and phone. Rates are Nkr465/625 on weekends from autumn to spring, Nkr600/700 from late June to early August, and Nkr725/850 at other times.

Three members of the Tulip Inn/Rainbow chain of hotels offer reasonably good value on weekend and summer rates. The *Cecil Hotel* (☎ *22 42 70 00, fax 22 42 26 70,*

Stortingsgata 8) has a great location just a stone's throw from Stortinget. Rooms are modern and quiet with private bath, TV, minibar and the like and there's an excellent breakfast buffet. Rates are Nkr460/680 on weekends and throughout July, Nkr775/995 at other times.

Hotell Astoria (☎ 22 42 00 10, fax 22 42 57 65, Dronningens gate 21), west of Oslo S, may not be as spiffy as the Cecil, but the amenities are similar and the rates cheaper at Nkr395/640 on weekends (and during July) and Nkr595/705 on weekdays. Tulip Inn/Rainbow's best summer value is the new *Hotel Terminus (☎ 22 05 60 00, fax 22 17 08 98, Stenersgata 10)*, 200m north of Oslo S. The rooms are comfortable and have full amenities. What's more, the breakfast is above average and complimentary tea and fruit are available throughout the day. The rates are Nkr410/560 from late May through August and on weekends year-round, Nkr610/810 at other times.

The best value of the city's classic hotels is the Inter-Nor *Hotel Bristol (☎ 22 82 60 00, fax 22 82 60 01, Kristian IV's gate 7)*. Rooms are pleasant with cable TV, minibar and bathtub, and the halls and lobby are filled with antiques, chandeliers and old-world charm. The standard rates are Nkr1450/1695, but on weekends they're Nkr620/850. Summer rates are Nkr895/1050.

Another place brimming with period character is the regal *Grand Hotel (☎ 22 42 93 90, fax 22 42 12 25, Karl Johans gate 31)*, with weekday rates of Nkr1520/1920 and weekend rates of Nkr775/990.

For a real splurge, head uphill to the historic *Holmenkollen Park Hotel Rica (☎ 22 92 20 00, fax 22 14 61 92, Kongeveien 26)*, near the Holmenkollen ski jump. In 1891, Dr Ingebrigt Christian Lund Holm opened a castle-like sanatorium here with one of the finest views in Oslo. It subsequently served as a hotel, a military residence and a course centre, but in 1986 it opened under its current name. Rooms range from Nkr845/990 and up to Nkr1195/1290 in summer. The rest of the year, you'll pay from Nkr1345/1440 to Nkr1745/1845.

Places to Eat

Breakfast Nearly all the hotels set up elaborate breakfast buffets for their guests and most of them are open to non-residents for Nkr60 to Nkr90. This is the best option for anyone who wants to start the day with a good value feast. Not even fast-food places have taken up the breakfast challenge; the only *McDonald's* that serves breakfast is at Valkyriegata 13 in Majorstuen.

For something lighter, try one of the ubiquitous bakeries or coffee shops, where you'll find a cup of coffee and a pastry for Nkr25 to Nkr40. You'll find some of the best sticky pastries at *Kaffe & Krem (Drammensveien 30)* on Solli plass.

Snacks Bakeries are an economical option; they normally sell relatively inexpensive sandwiches as well as bread and pastries. The *Baker Hansen* chain has numerous outlets around Oslo.

The fast-food *Tacoland (Nedre Slottsgate 15)* is a good alternative to other nearby fast-food outlets and has reasonable tacos, burritos and fajitas for Nkr20. Pizzerias include the Norwegian chain Peppe's Pizza and the American chain Pizza Hut; both have several branches around the city. The *Pizza Hut* on the corner of Karl Johans gate and Skippergata offers the usual menu, as well as a Nkr74 all-you-can-eat buffet from Sunday to Thursday from 5 pm to midnight. Most *Peppe's Pizza* outlets offer a similar pizza and salad lunchtime buffet for Nkr79 to Nkr89.

Around Oslo S & Grønland Oslo S has a *Café Caroline* with reasonably good cafeteria fare at average prices, a small food mart open till 11 pm daily, hot-dog stands, a sandwich shop and a *Burger King*. The south wing, Østbanehallen, has *McDonald's* and *Tacoland*; the recommended *Rooster Coffee* espresso bar; *Baker Nordby*, with pastries, sandwiches and ice cream; and a grocery store with fruit and a deli. Fruit stalls operate daily except Sunday in front of Oslo S.

The Oslo City shopping complex, opposite the north side of Oslo S, is also packed with eateries: bakeries, a hamburger joint, a pizzeria, and Chinese and Mexican restaurants. The complex is open until 8 pm weekdays and 6 pm on Saturday. At the bus terminal, you'll find a couple of small shops selling fruit and snacks, and a bakery that opens weekdays at 6.30 am.

The nearby *Teddy's Soft Bar (☎ 22 17 64 36, Brugata 3A)* has become a local 1950s institution. For around Nkr60, you'll get a light, typically Norwegian lunch. Try the *pytt i panne*, which is essentially eggs on bread.

The Grønland district north and east of Oslo S is full of great value ethnic eateries. The simple *Punjab Sweet House (☎ 22 17 20 85, Grønlandsleiret 24)*, near the Grønland T-bane station, has simply presented Indian fare – curry, dal, samosas and other light meals. A lunch special including chicken or lamb curry with rice, nan and salad costs Nkr49. A plate of ox keema with nan and salad costs a bargain Nkr25.

At the *Oslo Kebab & Pizza House*, you'll get a kebab and Coke for Nkr40, chicken and chips lunch for Nkr49, falafels for Nkr25 and kebab dinners for Nkr60. There are also a number of little Indian and kebab places along Tøyengata.

A friendly choice is *Dhaka Cuisine (☎ 22 17 22 80)*, which serves good curries from Nkr49 to Nkr59, vegetarian dishes from Nkr35 and tandoori and chicken salad lunches for Nkr30.

Aker Brygge Aker Brygge, the old shipyard turned shopping complex west of the main harbour, has a food court with various eateries including *Chopsticks*, with Chinese dishes for Nkr60; *Bakeriteater*, with good pastries and hearty baguette sandwiches; and a *McDonald's*, a baked-potato stall and hot-dog and ice-cream kiosks.

At the rear of Aker Brygge, just inside the entrance of the Rema 1000 supermarket, is the *Smør-Petersen* deli, which sells delicious salmon quiche, salads and other quality deli foods. You can eat inside, but takeaway works out a bit cheaper. Just south of Rema 1000, the popular Italian restaurant *La Piazza* serves pizza and pasta dishes from Nkr100.

Inside Aker Brygge, the turn-of-the-century design *Albertine (☎ 22 83 00 60)* offers bistro-style food for Nkr15 to Nkr50 for snacks and Nkr50 to Nkr70 for light lunches. The Californian and Hawaiian-themed *Beach Club (☎ 22 83 83 82)* has outdoor seating on the pier and is great for a sunny afternoon, but you'll need patience to wait for a table. This is one of the few places in Oslo which serve full breakfasts. At lunch, burgers range from Nkr50 to Nkr60 and beef and chicken dishes are Nkr85 to Nkr135. The similarly US-style *Big Horn Steak House (☎ 22 83 83 63)* specialises in steaks of various volumes for Nkr100 to Nkr250.

The Central Area The supermarket *Oluf Lorentzen (Karl Johans gate 33)* has chicken for Nkr40 and other deli snacks; it's open until 8 pm on weekdays, 6 pm on Saturday. *Café Sekel (☎ 22 42 42 12, Tollbugata 6)* dishes up generous portions of typical Norwegian cuisine in a country-style atmosphere for Nkr40 to Nkr80.

Egon, in the Paléet complex at Karl Johans gate 37, does pizza, burgers and kebabs; the best deal is the Nkr65 pizza buffet with a simple salad bar from 10 am to 6 pm daily (to 11 pm on Monday and Sunday). In the same complex is *Ma'raja (☎ 22 41 22 63)*, a mainstream Indian restaurant with a typically vast menu. Starters cost from Nkr29 while main dishes range from Nkr89 to Nkr100.

Nearby you'll find the American chain *TGI Friday's (Karl Johans gate 35)*, which sizzles up Oslo's most expensive burgers; for a good sized burger with a choice of relishes, you'll pay Nkr98 to Nkr115. Pasta dishes start at Nkr115 and steaks range from Nkr195 to Nkr245. They also offer US-style Mexican dishes, which range from vegetarian fajitas for Nkr125 to meat-oriented dishes for Nkr185.

Mr Hong (☎ 22 42 20 08), beside the Cecil Hotel on Rosenkrantz gate, has an all-you-can-eat dinner buffet with fresh salad for Nkr105 and a mixed 'Mongolian grill' of meat, seafood and vegetables. Weekdays from 11 am to 3 pm, they serve Nkr49 lunches, including a Chinese main course, rice and coffee. *Sushi Nam Kong (Torggata 24)* is a Japanese-Chinese hybrid which is one of Oslo's best places for a sushi fix. The very simple and good value *Saigon Lille Café (Bernt Ankers gate 7)* conjures up an atmosphere reminiscent of a Saigon back street. Vietnamese main dishes average around Nkr50.

A popular place with art students is *Kafé Celsius (Rådhusgata 19)*, a low-key café with a pleasant courtyard beer garden, and salads and pastas for about Nkr90. It's open from 11.30 am (1 pm on Sunday) to 1 am, closed on Monday.

Kafé Sesam, in Museet for Samtidskunst (the Museum for Contemporary Art), has cheap Chinese food, including a hearty Peking soup with bread for Nkr35 and a selection of filling Chinese dishes with rice and salad for Nkr49. It's open during museum hours. For a sophisticated light meal, there's *Tapas (Hegdehaugveien 22)*, where you'll find light tapas and coffee in a Latin atmosphere.

The *Grand Café* at the Grand Hotel on Karl Johans gate has been serving Oslo's cognoscenti for more than a century – as a reminder, a wall mural depicts the restaurant in the 1890s bustling with the likes of Edvard Munch and Henrik Ibsen. Some of the more affordable dishes range from the light *småretter* menu averaging Nkr100, and the Nkr98 daily special that features a traditional dish and is served weekdays from 3 to 6 pm.

The good value lunch buffet at the *Hotel Stefan (☎ 22 42 92 50, Rosenkrantz gate 1)* comes highly recommended and is generally regarded as the best in town, thanks to chef Morten Myrseth; check it out and judge for yourself! In the evening, superb main courses range from Nkr150 to Nkr170.

If money is no object, you'll find well prepared traditional Norwegian delicacies at the historic *Stortorvets Gjestgiveri*

(☎ 22 42 88 63, Grensen 1), which also has a bar and jazz performances on Friday and Saturday. Alternatively, try *A Touch of France (☎ 22 42 56 97, Øvre Slottsgate 16)*, which serves French-style cuisine and fosters an informal atmosphere with long communal dining tables. Starters range from Nkr55 to Nkr85 and main dishes from Nkr145 for *steinbit* (catfish) fillet to Nkr180 for a mixed fish grill.

The *Engebret Café (☎ 22 22 66 94, Bankplassen 1)* is named for Engebret Christoffersen, who founded the restaurant beside the Christiania Theatre in 1857. It thereby became the city's first 'theatre café' and attracted both actors and writers. Today it's an upmarket place serving Norwegian and international cuisine. It specialises in fish dishes which range from Nkr155 to Nkr230.

The *Gamle Rådhus (☎ 22 42 01 07, Nedre Slottsgate 1)*, housed in a historic 1641 building, is Oslo's oldest restaurant, and has also served as the town hall (hence the name) and a prison. The dark, cosy atmosphere is enhanced by an English-style pub and a roaring fire. If you've always wanted to try the glutinous fish dish *lutefisk*, pop in here in the weeks before Christmas, when they make up big batches of it. For a three-course meal featuring fish or meat, budget for at least Nkr300 per person.

Vegetarians will relish *Krishna's Cuisine (☎ 22 60 62 50, Kirkeveien 59B)*, which offers great value vegetarian buffets for as little as Nkr75, as well as equally appealing à la carte curries and other options.

The popular *Vegeta Vertshus (☎ 22 83 42 32, Munkedamsveien 3B)*, at the top of Stortingsgata near the National Theatre, serves hearty vegetarian buffets, including wholegrain pizza, casseroles and salads. You'll pay Nkr73/83 for a small/large plate and Nkr115 for all you can eat. Hours are from 11 am to 11 pm daily.

Grünerløkka Better known as just 'Løkka', the formerly downmarket workers' district of Grünerløkka has recently become one of Oslo's trendiest neighbourhoods, and the doctors, lawyers and MBAs are filtering in to snap up some of its good value charm. As a result, the restaurant scene presents a range of choices.

The simple but popular **Kafe Sult** (☎ *22 87 04 67, Thorvald Meyers gate 26*) prepares superb fish and pasta dishes, as well as more unusual fare, for Nkr60 to Nkr150. It's always packed so get there early and wait for a table in the attached bar, where the draught beer costs a bargain Nkr33 per 500ml.

At the unassuming **Olympia Birken**, opposite Birkelunden Park, you'll find such Greek specialities as schwarma, souvlaki and moussaka for around Nkr50, as well as lamb curry with rice and salad for Nkr64. It's open weekdays from 10 am to 11.30 pm and on weekends from noon to 10 pm.

One of Europe's best Mexican restaurants is the simple **Mucho Mas** (☎ *22 37 16 09, Thorvald Meyers gate 36*). Starters range from Nkr35 for chips and salsa to Nkr35/60 for a vegetarian/meat taco salad, while vegetarian/meat nachos are Nkr45/65, burritos Nkr55/80 and tacos Nkr25/40. Beans and rice cost an additional Nkr15 each. The beer is also great value at Nkr34 per 500ml. It's open Monday to Saturday from 11 am to 1 am and on Sunday from 1 pm to 1 am. Note that credit cards aren't accepted.

Café Kjøkkenhagen, also on Thorvald Meyers gate, has delicious light lunches for moderate prices. Salads range from Nkr55 to Nkr72, pizzas for around Nkr70, quiche from Nkr44 to Nkr70, pita sandwiches for Nkr40, burgers from Nkr30 and filled pancakes for Nkr50. Next door is the trendy **Fru Hagen** (*Thorvald Meyers gate 40*), which serves Norwegian-style meals until 9.30 pm, then turns into a popular upmarket bar open nightly until 3 am.

Another popular option is the **Markveien Mat & Vinhus** (☎ *22 37 22 97, Torvbakkgata 12*), which is not only a gourmet restaurant but also a bohemian hangout. Starters range from Nkr80 to Nkr100, main courses from Nkr185 to Nkr235. If that's too steep for your budget, drop by late in the evening for a drink and relaxed conversation (its entrance is on Markveien).

Holmenkollen The well known **Holmenkollen Restaurant** (☎ *22 14 62 26*), uphill from the Holmenkollen T-bane station, offers a daily *koldtbord* (literally 'cold table') lunch buffet of traditional Norwegian dishes for a rather steep Nkr180. Other meals range from Nkr165 to Nkr210. Alternatively, you can enjoy the same view and the lighter meals at the adjacent cafeteria for Nkr60 to Nkr100.

Self-Catering For self-catering, the **IKA** supermarket in the Østbanehallen at Oslo S provides one of the best selections in town, while the various **Rimi** outlets offer the best value and generally the longest opening hours. The innovative **Kiwi** supermarket at Storgata 33 is open until 11 pm daily except Sunday. The various **7-Eleven** outlets around town are open 24 hours daily and sell light beer, Nkr5 coffee, hot dogs and other light items.

Helios (*Universitetsgata 22*), next door to JW Cappelen bookshop, is a small health-food store which sells organic produce and wholesome snacks.

Fresh shrimp (*reker*) are sold from stalls near Aker Brygge. The best value fresh produce comes from the market stalls on Brugata and around Grønlandstorg; the Grønland district and the back streets west of Storgata are also brimming with inexpensive ethnic supermarkets where you'll find otherwise unavailable items such as fresh herbs and African, Asian and Middle Eastern ingredients.

Alcohol Anyone over 18 can buy beer at Oslo supermarkets until 8 pm on weekdays and 6 pm on Saturday, but for wine or spirits, you'll have to be at least 20 years old and visit a Vinmonopolet.

The most convenient Vinmonopolet outlets are at Kirkeveien 64, the Oslo City Shopping Centre, Møllergata 10/12 and Elisenbergveien near Gimleveien. These are open from 10 am to 5 pm Monday to Wednesday, 10 am to 6 pm Thursday, 9 am to 6 pm Friday and from 9 or 10 am to 2 or 3 pm Saturday.

Entertainment

The tourist office's monthly *What's on in Oslo* brochure lists current concerts, theatre and special events, while the free *Natt & Dag* entertainment tabloid (in Norwegian only) covers the nightclub scene. The most useful publication for night owls is *Streetwise*, published annually in English by Use-It (see Information earlier in this chapter).

Note that many Oslo night spots have an unwritten dress code which expects patrons to be relatively well turned out. Although foreigners may be excused, it's still best not to show up in grubby gear and hiking boots. For most bars and clubs which serve beer and wine, you must be 18 years of age, but many places – especially those that serve spirits – impose a higher age limit. On weekends, most Oslo night spots remain open until at least 3 am.

Pubs, Discos & Nightclubs Most bars have a happy hour in the early evening, with 500ml of beer starting at around Nkr25; after 9 pm, the price climbs to around Nkr45. Bars and clubs in the centre tend to be pricey, while those east of the centre and north of Oslo S are generally more downmarket.

Smuget (☎ 22 42 52 62, *Rosenkrantz gate 22*) is a reliable hot spot with a disco and live jazz, rock and blues. On weekdays/ weekends you'll pay a cover charge of Nkr50/70. For a mellower jazz atmosphere, there's the cosy and relaxed *Jazid* (*Pilestredet 17*). The *Underwater Pub* (*Dalsbergstien 4*) is only notable on Tuesday and Thursday, when students of the State School of Opera lubricate their vocal chords and treat patrons to their favourite arias.

A pleasant hangout for the smoking post-30 crowd is *Herr Nilsens Pub* (*CJ Hambros plass 5*). On Saturday afternoons, you can gear up for a night on the town with a dose of smooth live jazz.

The trendy *Belleville* (*Haakon VII's gate 5*) features world music and attracts an international crowd. Just a stone's throw from the KFUM Sleep-In is *So What* (*Grensen 9*), a café and club with alternative music. You'll find the rebellious bohemian scene at

Blitz (*Pilestredet 30*), in an old house near Slottsparken. It also features a book café and live concerts.

Head On (*Rosenkrantz gate 11*) attracts a wealthier and trendier clientele to its lively dance venue. There's a cover charge of Nkr50. As its name suggests, the *Afro International Nightclub* (*Brenneriveien 5*) features reggae, jazz and blues, while the *Miami Club* (*Storgata 25*) attempts Caribbean salsa and other Latin beats.

On Friday and Saturday nights, Grønland's *Oliven Café* (*Norbygata 15*) dishes up inexpensive Middle Eastern meals accompanied by Lebanese belly dancing. If you prefer a down-to-earth drinking-den atmosphere, try *Olympen* (*Grønlandsleiret 15*), which offers the best value beer in town. For those imbibing before the sun goes down, 500ml of draught costs Nkr24; after 5 pm, it's just Nkr29.

The *Børsen Internet Café* (*Nedre Vollgate 19*), with its entrance on Stortingsgata, features the novel stock exchange drinks system; that is, the price rises and falls through the evening, according to demand. To enter, you must be over 25 and pay a cover charge of Nkr50. The music is rarely anything special unless you're a techno fan.

The only club catering specifically to the 18 to 21 set is *Mars* (*Storgata 22*). On weekdays it features 90s disco, with live music on weekends.

The most popular gay bars include *Club Castro* (*Kristian IV's gate 7*), a lively dance venue; *Potpurriet* (*Øvre Vollgate 13*), especially popular with the lesbian crowd; and the *London Pub* (*CJ Hambros Plass 5*), which may be a bit too camp for some.

Concerts The city's largest concert halls, *Oslo Spektrum*, near Oslo S, and *Rockefeller Music Hall* (*Torggata 16*), plays host to international musicians. Really big names perform outdoor gigs at Vigeland Park.

Every month but July, Oslo's opera company, *Den Norske Opera* (☎ 22 42 94 75, salg@norskopera.no, *Storgata 23*), stages opera, ballet and classical concerts. Tickets start at Nkr295 per performance.

Cinema The six-screen *Saga cinema (Stortingsgata 28)* shows first-run movies in their original language. Almost daily, the *Filmens Hus café (Dronningens gate 16)* screens old classics and international festival winners. For a more thrilling show, you can check out the new *IMAX Film Theatre (☎ 23 11 66 23)* at Aker Brygge, which presents high-tech productions, including 3D films and simulators.

Other You can take advantage of summer's long daylight hours and spend mellow evenings outdoors – go to the harbour area and listen to live jazz wafting from the floating restaurants, splash out on a beer at one of the outdoor cafés in Vigeland Park, or ride a ferry out to the islands in Oslofjord. If the weather isn't cooperating, you could check out the alternative dance and theatre scene at the café-style *Black Box* in the Aker Brygge complex.

Shopping

Traditional Norwegian sweaters are popular purchases; for good prices and selections, check the Oslo Sweater Shop on Skippergata near Oslo S, and Unique Design at Rosenkrantz gate 13. Husfliden at Møllergata 4 and Heimen Husflid at Rosenkrantz gate 8 are larger shops selling quality Norwegian clothing and crafts, with items ranging from carved wooden trolls to elaborate folk costumes.

If you're happy with pot luck, take a chance at the Vestkanttorget flea market, held on Saturday from 10 am to 5 pm. It's on Amaldus Nilsens plass, which intersects Professor Dahls gate, a block east of Vigeland Park.

Getting There & Away

Air Oslo's international airport is at Gardermoen, 50km north of Oslo, which opened in October 1998 upon completion of a motorway and a high-speed rail link to the centre. The old airport at Fornebu, 8km south-west of the centre, has now been decommissioned and there is ongoing discussion about what to do with it.

At Torp, 100km south of town, there is another international airport which is used by the UK-based Ryanair (☎ 33 42 75 00) for its flights to and from London's Stansted airport. An express bus connects it with Oslo S (1¼ hours, Nkr120 for Ryanair passengers).

The SAS ticket office (☎ 22 17 00 20) is in the Oslo City shopping centre. Braathens SAFE (☎ 67 58 60 00) has an office at Haakon VII's gate 2 and Widerøes Flyveselskap (☎ 67 11 14 60, fax 67 11 14 66) is at Vollsveien 6, PB-131, N-1324 Lysaker (a suburb out of the town's centre). Other airlines include Air France (☎ 22 83 56 30), Haakon VII's gate 9; British Airways (☎ 22 82 20 00, fax 67 53 11 97), Karl Johans gate 16B; and Finnair (☎ 67 53 38 90), at Gardermoen airport.

Bus Long-distance buses arrive and depart from Nor-Way Bussekspress (☎ 23 00 24 40, www.nor-way.no), Schweigaardsgate 8, in Galleri Oslo (east of Oslo S). The train and bus stations are linked via an overhead walkway. Some bus services offer discounts to Eurail and ScanRail pass holders, so be sure to ask.

Oslo-Bergen services (11½ hours, Nkr580) depart at 9.30 am daily from Oslo and 7.20 am from Bergen. In summer there are also direct services to and from Trondheim (10½ hours, Nkr520); Stryn (8½ hours, Nkr500); Florø (10½ hours, Nkr570); Måløy (10½ hours, Nkr590); Røros (six hours, Nkr400); Kristiansand (5½ hours, Nkr350); Stavanger (10 hours, Nkr500); and numerous other destinations in southern Norway.

Train All trains arrive and depart from Oslo S in the city centre. The reservation windows are open from 6 am (international from 6.30 am) to 11 pm daily and an information desk (☎ 81 50 08 88) provides details on routes and timetables throughout the country.

In addition to the frequent services around Oslofjord (to Drammen, Skien, Moss, Fredrikstad, Halden, etc), trains connect

Oslo to Bergen (seven to eight hours, Nkr510); Åndalsnes via Dombås (seven to eight hours, Nkr500); Trondheim via Dombås (six to eight hours, Nkr590); Trondheim (10 hours, Nkr590) and Røros (5½ hours, Nkr440) via Hamar (1½ hours, Nkr160); and Stavanger (10 to 14 hours, Nkr610) via Kristiansand (five hours, Nkr400). All fares are in 2nd-class seats. In addition to daytime trains, all these routes except Trondheim via Røros are conveniently served by overnight trains; 2nd-class sleepers cost an additional Nkr100.

Oslo S has backpack-sized lockers for Nkr20. The left-luggage window, open from 7 am to 11 pm daily, charges Nkr20 per bag. The station also has a summer InterRail Centre where rail pass travellers can shower and await trains.

Car & Motorcycle The main highways into the city are the E6 from the north and south, and the E18 from the east and west. Each time you enter Oslo, you must pass through one of 19 toll stations and pay Nkr12. Note that there's a Nkr250 fine if you use a lane reserved for vehicles with subscription (*abonnement*) passes. Motorcycles aren't subject to the tolls.

If money is no object and you plan to hire a car, see the Getting Around chapter for a list of car rental companies.

Hitching When leaving Oslo it's generally best to take a train to the outskirts of the city in your direction of travel and start hitching from there. The ride board at Use-It (see Information earlier in this chapter) is worth checking, though far more people need rides than offer them.

For hitching to Bergen, take bus No 161 to its final stop and wait beside the E16 towards Hønefoss; from there, follow Rv7 to Hol, Rv50 to Aurland and the E16 to Bergen. For Trondheim, take bus No 31 or 32 to Aker Sykehus or T-Bane line 5 (direction Vestli) to Grorud and wait beside Rv4, which connects to the E6 north. For the south coast and Stavanger, take bus No 31 or 32 to the Maritim petrol station or bus

No 151, 161, 251, 252 or 261 to Oksenøyveien, near Lysaker, and hitch from the bus stop. For Göteborg (Sweden) and points south, use bus No 81, 83 or 85 to Bekkelaget or a local train (Ski) to Nordstrand, which both provide access to the E6 south.

Boat Ferries operated by Scandinavian Seaways (☎ 22 41 90 90), Vippetangen 2, and Stena Line AS (☎ 23 17 90 00), Jernbanetorget 2, connect Oslo with Copenhagen and Frederikshavn (Denmark). They use the Vippetangen quay off Skippergata. Bus No 29 stops within a couple of minutes walk of the terminal.

Color Line ferries (☎ 22 94 44 70) to and from Hirtshals (Denmark) and Kiel (Germany) dock at Hjortneskaia, west of the central harbour. From Oslo S, take tram No 10, 11, 12 or 13.

The seven-hour Hurtigbåt (☎ 37 15 85 60) service between Oslo and Arendal (Nkr400), via Stavern (Nkr310), Kragerø (Nkr350), Risør (Nkr370) and Gjeving/Lyngør (Nkr380), docks at Rådhusbrygge, opposite the Rådhus. From 24 June to 10 August, it leaves Oslo/Arendal at 9 am/4.25 pm Sunday to Thursday; from Oslo only on Friday (at 4 pm) and from Arendal only on Saturday (at 9 am). These boats depart from Palékaia, south of Oslo S.

Getting Around

Oslo has an efficient public transport system with an extensive network of buses, trams, underground trains and ferries. A single fare on any of these services costs Nkr18 and includes one transfer within an hour of purchase. An unlimited 24-hour ticket (*dagskort*) costs Nkr40 and a weekly/monthly card is Nkr140/540. A Nkr110 *flexikort* is valid for up to eight trips and may be shared between two or more people. The single and day tickets are sold on buses and trams while other passes are available from Trafikanten, Narvesen kiosks, post offices and staffed underground stations. Children aged four to 16 and seniors over 67 years of age pay half price on all fares; on weekends, adults using a dagskort or flexikort may travel with up to four children for no extra charge.

The Oslo Card includes all public transport options within the city, with the exception of night buses. Bicycles are carried on trams and trains for an additional Nkr18. The automatic fine for travelling without a ticket is a rather punitive Nkr450.

Trafikanten (☎ 177 or ☎ 22 17 70 30), below the Oslo S tower on Jernbanetorget, provides free schedules and a public transport map, *Sporveiskart Oslo*. It's open from 7 am to 8 pm on weekdays, 8 am to 6 pm on weekends.

To/From the Airport The Flybussen (☎ 67 58 38 00) airport shuttle to Oslo International Airport at Gardermoen departs from the bus terminal at Galleri Oslo three times hourly from 4.40 am to 1 am. The trip takes 40 minutes and the fare is Nkr59. Nor-Way Bussekspress (☎ 81 54 44 44) routes No 5 from Asker, No 7 from Ski, No 9 from Galleri Oslo bus terminal and No 12 from Røa each have 25 to 36 daily departures for Gardermoen. The fare is Nkr55.

There are also rail links, but due to a problem with the Romeriksporten tunnel, services will follow the old rail line until the high-speed link can be completed. The temporary services (☎ 81 50 08 88) leave Asker station every half-hour between 4.30 am and 11.30 pm, stopping en route at Skøyen and the National Theatre. To Gardermoen takes about 30 minutes and costs Nkr70. In addition, most northbound NSB intercity and local trains stop at Gardermoen. When the high-speed train opens, it will depart every 10 minutes from Oslo S and take 19 minutes to reach the airport; the fare will be Nkr120.

Bus & Tram Bus and tram lines lace the city and extend into the suburbs. There's no central station but most converge at Jernbanetorget in front of Oslo S. Most westbound buses, including those to Bygdøy and Vigeland Park, also stop immediately south of the National Theatre.

The frequency of service drops dramatically at night, but on weekends, tram

Nos N10, N12 and N19 and bus Nos 201 to 218 continue to run until 4 am or later. These services are called Nattlinjer and cost Nkr36 per ride, and no passes are valid. For details, see Trafikanten's *Sporveiens Nattlinjer* timetable.

T-Bane The eight-line Tunnelbanen underground system, better known as the T-bane, is faster and extends farther from the city centre than most city bus lines. All eight lines pass through the Nasjonalteatret, Stortinget and Jernbanetorget stations.

Taxi Taxis charge Nkr24 (Nkr30 after 7 pm and on weekends) at flagfall and about Nkr12 per kilometre thereafter. There are taxi stands at Oslo S, shopping centres and city squares. Any taxi with a lit sign is available for hire. Otherwise, phone for a taxi (☎ 22 38 80 90, advance booking ☎ 22 38 80 80), but note that the meter starts running at the point of dispatch. Oslo taxis accept major credit cards.

Car & Motorcycle Oslo has its share of one-way streets which can complicate city driving a bit, but the streets are never as congested as in most European cities. A car may be convenient for exploring outlying areas, but the best way to see the central sites of interest is on foot or with local transport.

Metered street parking, identified by a solid blue sign with a white 'P', can be found throughout the city. The hours listed indicate the period in which the meters are in effect, usually from 8 am to 5 pm, with Saturday hours written in brackets. At other times, parking is free unless otherwise posted. Most meters gobble up Nkr5 to Nkr20 per hour, with the highest rates at busy spots such as post offices. The city centre also has a dozen multistorey car parks, including those at Oslo City and Aker Brygge shopping centres.

Note that the Oslo Card includes parking at all municipal car parks; to use it, fill in your vehicle registration number and the date of validity of your Oslo Card (in ink), remove the sticker from the back of the card and display it in the front window. For further parking information, contact the Traffic Manager (☎ 22 08 20 00).

Boat Ferries to Bygdøy leave from Rådhusbrygge once or twice hourly (for the Bygdøy museums, disembark at the Dronningen pier), while ferries to the Oslofjord islands sail from Vippetangen. The express boat *Princessin* (☎ 22 17 70 30) connects Oslo with Drøbak and other Oslofjord stops en route: Ildjernet, Langåra and Håøya (which is a holiday spot offering fine swimming and camping).

Bicycle Bicycles may be carried on public transport which will get you beyond the edge of town and into the forest before you even begin pedalling. You can hire mountain bikes from Den Rustne Eike (☎ 22 83 72 31) at Vestbaneplassen 2, beside the main tourist office. Rates for seven-speed/mountain bikes start at Nkr95/170 for 24 hours, plus a Nkr1000 deposit.

Around Oslo

DRØBAK

Drøbak, the capital city's nearest 'charming village', makes a pleasant day trip. The large number of clapboard timber buildings here, as well as the cosy atmosphere, Father Christmas theme, and several local attractions, are good for a couple of hours of rambling. There's a small tourist office (☎ 64 93 50 87) in the centre.

The **Saltvannsakvarium** (☎ 64 93 50 87), an aquarium featuring the denizens of Oslofjord, is open daily from 11 am to 7 pm in summer and costs Nkr10. There's also the small **Drøbak Båtforenings Maritime Samlinger** (☎ 64 93 50 87), a museum of maritime paraphernalia which includes a number of boat engines. It's also open from 11 am to 7 pm daily in summer and charges Nkr10 admission. The 1845 **Oscarsborg fortress**, where the shots were fired that sunk the German warship *Blücher* on 9 April 1940, is open for tours in summer.

Getting There & Away

From the Galleri Oslo bus terminal, bus No 541 to Drøbak (one hour, Nkr47) leaves approximately hourly. Alternatively, the express boat *Princessin* (☎ 22 17 70 30) operates in summer. It does one trip from Oslo's Aker Brygge pier on weekdays, allowing several hours in Drøbak before returning to Oslo. The one-way fare is Nkr47.

DRAMMEN

Primarily known as a dormitory community for Oslo, Drammen is an industrial centre in its own right and most of the cars imported to Norway are offloaded into vast car parks near the fjord. Not only was Drammen the start of the Royal Road to Bergen, it was also the original home of the potato alcohol Aquavit. In late autumn, Drammen holds a national Aquavit competition in which celebrities judge which is the best brand.

Information

Tourist information is available from the Drammen Turist og Reiselivskontor (☎ 32 80 62 10, fax 32 80 66 31, tourist@drammen.kommune.no), Bragernes Torg 6.

Things to See & Do

Drammen has several buildings of note: the historic **Stock Exchange** (which now houses a McDonald's); the restored **Rådhus** (once a police station); its twin, the **fire station**; the old **Free Masonic lodge**; the lovely 1870 **Drammen Theatre**, which burned down in 1993 and reopened in 1996; and the Gothic-style Bragernes church. You can also see the house where **Aquavit** was first produced in 1804, at Bergstein 75, by merchant Johan Godtfried Schwencke in response to a royal decree that corn not be used to produce spirits. The district along Øvre Storgate and Mossegården is also prominent in Aquavit history.

Worthwhile hikes will take you up into the **Bragernesåsen** woodlands or up the scenic **Kjøsterudjuvet Gorge**, just over 1km north of town. Pick up hiking maps from the tourist office.

Many people believe Drammen's big highlight is the 1650m-long **Spiralen tunnel** to the 150m summit of Bragernes, which affords a fabulous view over the city. The best part, however, is the fact that the tunnel makes six spirals inside the mountain en route to the top. If you don't have a car, go on a summer Sunday, when bus No 151 does the trip at 10.15 and 11 am and 3 and 6 pm (15 minutes, Nkr16).

An interesting day excursion will take you to Åmot, where the **Royal Blåfarveværk** was established by King Christian VII in 1773 to extract cobalt to produce blue pigments for the glass and porcelain industries. You can visit the mines from noon to 6 pm from 30 May to 6 September (and on weekends from 7 to 30 September), either on your own or with a Nkr30 guided tour. It's also worth looking at the large Haugfoss waterfall, the **Mølla** shop (which sells cobalt blue glass work – alas, the pigments weren't mined on site), and the various art exhibitions in the attached museum (☎ 32 78 49 00, www.blaa.no). Take the relatively frequent NSB express bus No 207 from Drammen to Åmot (1½ hours, Nkr48) and walk 2km north-west.

Places to Stay

Camping and cabins are available at *Drammen Camping (☎ 32 82 17 98)*, beside a scenic stretch of the river Drammenselva. If you prefer a roof over your head, try *Hotel Tollboden (☎ 32 89 10 90, fax 32 89 11 35, Tollbugata 1)* in the town centre.

Østfold

The Østfold region, the detached slice of Norway to the east of Oslofjord, is a mix of forest, pastoral farmland and small industrial towns which rely on the timber trade.

MOSS

Although it enjoys a rather scenic setting beside Oslofjord, Moss is mainly a scruffy industrial port with uninspiring architecture and a stinky pulp mill. Visitors may enjoy

the dispersed Moss By og Industrimuseum (☎ 69 24 85 50), with its main building at Henrik Gerners gate 11. It focuses on the historic sawmills, the mid-18th century ironworkers' dwellings, the 1811 brewery and the 1875 waterwheel and pumps. There's little else of tourist interest except for a ferry link to Hirtshals (Denmark), and another across Oslofjord.

FREDRIKSTAD

Fredrikstad (population 65,000) was founded by King Fredrik II as a trading centre between mainland Europe and western Scandinavia. The modern city is dominated by the 1880 cathedral, which contains stained glass work by Emanuel Vigeland, and the delicate silver arch of the 824m long and 40m high Glomma bridge. The Konsten fortress and historic Gamlebyen are most emphatically worth a visit, but thanks to the dearth of decent inexpensive accommodation, many travellers make Fredrikstad a day trip from Oslo.

Information

You may wrest some information out of the Fredrikstad Tourist Office (☎ 69 32 10 60), over the bridge several kilometres from the centre, but don't expect much. Fortunately, they've now opened a new office (☎ 69 32 03 30) at Nygaardsgata 26, north of the cathedral, which is more convenient for tourists but has probably increased the number of pesky visitor queries. You'll probably fare best at the Gamlebyen office (☎ 69 32 05 65), open between 23 June and 17 August.

If you require a doctor after hours, phone ☎ 69 31 33 33.

Gamlebyen

The Fredrikstad Gamlebyen (Old Town), east of the Glomma, was originally constructed in 1663 as a military enclave which could be readily defended against Swedish belligerence with multiple embankments, moats, gates and even a drawbridge. The long arsenal and infantry barracks are also still in use (and off-limits to visitors), but it's pleasant to stroll along the moats and em-

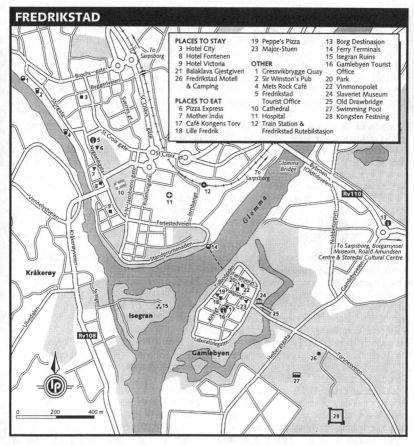

FREDRIKSTAD

PLACES TO STAY
3 Hotel City
8 Hotel Fontenen
9 Hotel Victoria
21 Balaklava Gjestgiveri
26 Fredrikstad Motell & Camping

PLACES TO EAT
6 Pizza Express
7 Mother India
17 Café Kongens Torv
18 Lille Fredrik
19 Peppe's Pizza
23 Major-Stuen

OTHER
1 Gressvikbrygge Quay
2 Sir Winston's Pub
4 Mets Rock Café
5 Fredrikstad Tourist Office
10 Cathedral
11 Hospital
12 Train Station & Fredrikstad Rutebilstasjon
13 Borg Destinasjon
14 Ferry Terminals
15 Isegran Ruins
16 Gamlebyen Tourist Office
20 Park
22 Vinmonopolet
24 Slaveriet Museum
25 Old Drawbridge
27 Swimming Pool
28 Kongsten Festning

bankments and follow the perimeter walls that were once defended by 200 cannons. The narrow cobbled streets have also been preserved and are still lined with picturesque 17th century buildings, many of which remain occupied, and it's by far the best preserved fortress town in Scandinavia. In the Kongens Torv, the central square, you'll find a bank, a café and a rather ludicrous statue of the town founder, King Fredrik II, who appears to be in dire need of a public loo!

From the train station it's a five-minute walk to the riverfront, where a ferry shuttles across the river Glomma to the main gate of Gamlebyen (two minutes, Nkr6). From 23 June to 17 August, the Gamlebyen tourist office (☎ 69 32 05 65) runs Nkr25 guided tours from Kongens Torv. They leave hourly from 11 am to 3 pm weekdays, 11 am to 2 pm Saturday and 1 to 3 pm Sunday.

Fredrikstad Museum

The three-part Fredrikstad Museum (☎ 69 30 68 75) preserves the best of this historic fortress town. Admission costs Nkr30 and includes all three locations.

Gamlebyen The Slaveriet portion of the Fredrikstad Museum in Gamlebyen occupies a 1731 building on the site of the old guard house. It contains a model of the early city and a collection of relics from three centuries of Fredrikstad's civilian, military and industrial activities. It's open daily from 11 am to 5 pm (from noon on Sunday).

Kongsten Festning A 15-minute walk beyond the Gamlebyen drawbridge lies the flower-festooned Kongsten Fort, which dates from 1685 and once served as a lookout and warning post for the troops at nearby Gamlebyen. Little happens here today, but it's fun to scramble around the turrets, embankments, walls and stockade, or just sit in the sun and soak up the silence of this lonely and appealingly unkempt spot.

Isegran The Norse sagas mention the 13th century fortress on the islet of Isegran, which later became a back-row line of defence against Sweden in the mid-17th century. The ruins remain visible at the eastern end of the island. It's also the site of a boathouse containing a sailing exhibit and the modern history of Fredrikstad (1860-1960), as well as visiting exhibitions.

Special Events
The Glomma Festival takes place during the second week in July and features four days of very well attended festivities, including music performances, ritual duels, a 'bathtub regatta' for creative vessels and a veteran sailing ship exhibition.

Places to Stay
The rather scruffy *Fredrikstad Motell & Camping* (☎ 69 32 05 32), in the grounds of the Kongsten Fort, is just about the only choice for budget accommodation. Tent/ caravan camping costs Nkr80/130, single/double motel rooms are Nkr330/420 and cabins cost Nkr240 for two people, Nkr340 for three or four people. From the centre, take bus No 362 towards Torsnes. The nearest youth hostel is *Tuneheimen Vandrerhjem* (☎/fax 69 14 50 01), near lake

Tunevannet, 1km from Sarpsborg, which is in turn a 10km bus ride from Fredrikstad. It's open year-round and beds cost Nkr105/155 without/with breakfast.

Hotel Victoria (☎ 69 31 11 65, fax 69 31 87 55), opposite the cathedral grounds, has single/double rooms for Nkr600/900, and the economic *Hotel Fontenen* (☎ 69 30 05 00, fax 69 31 32 64), beside the cathedral, has rooms starting at Nkr450/650. The upmarket option is *Hotel City* (☎ 69 31 77 50, fax 69 31 30 90, Nygaardsgata 44/46), which charges Nkr675/875 during summer and on weekends at other times. It also includes four eateries: a pub, a casual pizza place, the à la carte Restaurant Frederik and the finer Bourbon St, serving Creole cuisine.

If you're up for a major splurge, you won't regret a night at the atmospheric *Balaklava Gjestgiveri* (☎ 69 32 30 40, fax 69 32 29 40, Færgeportgata 78) in Gamlebyen.

Places to Eat
A good budget option is the *Peppe's Pizza* (☎ 69 32 32 10) in Gamlebyen, which is a great spot to sit along the cobbled street, drink a beer and gaze at the river. In the central area is *Pizza Express*, on Nygaardsgata two blocks north of the cathedral, which does mainly takeaways. For burgers, snacks and coffee in Gamlebyen, there's *Lille Fredrik* (☎ 69 32 17 71), or you can try *Café Kongens Torv*, on the old town square, which is a popular hangout for local youth. It's open daily until 4 pm.

You'll find Indian cuisine at *Mother India* (☎ 69 31 22 00, Nygaardsgata 17), on the corner of Vibes gate. You'll get starters from around Nkr60 and main dishes for Nkr115 to Nkr180. It's open daily in the afternoon and evening.

For a special occasion, you can eat in the outdoor garden at the elegant *Balaklava Gjestgiveri* (☎ 69 32 30 40), in a series of historic buildings in Gamlebyen. It specialises in Norwegian fish and beef dishes, as well as international cuisine. Another fine place in Gamlebyen is *Major-Stuen* (☎ 69 32 15 55), open for lunch daily between noon and 1 pm (2 pm on weekends).

Entertainment

Mets Rock Café (☎ 69 31 78 99), on the river promenade, serves Mexican meals and has a sports bar and rock music nightly from 10 pm. There's no cover charge but you must be over 20 years of age.

Sir Winston's Pub (☎ 69 31 00 80, Storgata 17), beside the river, is in the style of an English pub. It serves pub meals and you can choose between 10 draught beers. On weekends it also offers live music and dancing.

Getting There & Away

Intercity buses arrive and depart from the Fredrikstad Rutebilstasjon (☎ 69 31 37 60) at the train station. Bus No 357 runs to and from Sarpsborg (30 minutes, Nkr37) twice hourly. Nor-Way Bussekspress has at least five daily services between Oslo and nearby Sarpsborg (1¼ hours, Nkr90); four or more of these continue to or originate in Göteborg, Sweden (3¼ hours, Nkr130).

Fredrikstad lies on the rail line between Oslo and Göteborg. Trains to and from Oslo (1¼ hours, Nkr125) run about 10 times daily, but note that southbound international trains require a seat reservation.

Getting Around

For information on city bus routes, phone or visit the Fredrikstad Rutebilstasjon (☎ 69 31 37 60).

To cross the Glomma (the country's longest river) to Gamlebyen, you can either trek over that high and hulking bridge or take the Nkr6 *Go'vakker Randi* ferry (named for a prominent local dance teacher) from Strandpromenaden. It operates from 5.30 am to 11 pm on weekdays; from 7 am on Saturday and from 9.30 am on Sunday. On weekdays from 7 am to 5 pm, a ferry also plies the triangular route between Gressvikbrygge quay (in the town's north-west), the northern end of Kråkerøy and Gressvik.

For a taxi, phone ☎ 69 33 70 11. Bicycle hire is free from Teknisk Etat (☎ 69 30 59 40), with a deposit of Nkr300 per bike.

AROUND FREDRIKSTAD
Hvaler

Norwegian holiday-makers love Hvaler, 'the skerries', an offshore archipelago of 550 forested islands and islets guarding the southern entrance to Oslofjord. The main islands of Kråkerøy, Vesterøy, Spjærøy, Asmaløy and Kirkøy are connected to the mainland by a toll road (Nkr50) and tunnel. In summer, bus No 60 (Nkr50) runs all the way to Skjærhalden, at the far end of Kirkøy, but the best way to explore these quiet islands is by bicycle.

Above the coastline of Akerøy island, accessible only by ferry, clings a well preserved 17th century coastal fortress, renovated in the 1960s. Akerøy holds its local festival on the first Sunday in August.

The mid-11th century stone church on the island of Kirkøy is one of the oldest in Norway and is open to visitors from noon to 4 pm daily between 23 June and 31 August.

From 28 June to 10 August, the M/S *Fredrikshald* sails from Gamlebyen and through the Hvaler skerries at 3 pm daily except Monday and Thursday. Alternatively, you can reach the skerries on the scheduled ferry M/S *Vesleø II* between Fredrikstad and Strömstad (Sweden). From 22 June to 27 August, you can sail from Fredrikstad to Skjærhalden (Nkr60) in the morning and come back on the afternoon boat as it returns from Strömstad.

Also in summer, the M/S *Hvalerfergen II* (☎ 69 37 93 52, fax 69 37 99 00) sails six times daily between Skjærhalden and Sponvika (Nkr60), stopping at several islands en route. It connects with bus No 365 between Fredrikstad and Skjærhalden (Nkr38), which runs more or less hourly.

If you wish to find self-catering accommodation in Hvaler, the tourist office at Fredrikstad has a list of private cottages available by the week for Nkr1500 to Nkr4000. Alternatively, try the guest farm *Sandbrekke Gjestegård (☎ 69 37 94 27, fax 69 37 99 20)* at Skjærhalden on Kirkøy. It charges Nkr490/680 for single/double rooms with breakfast (up to two children may stay for no extra charge).

Roald Amundsen Centre

The renowned polar explorer Roald Amundsen, who in 1911 was the first to reach the South Pole, was born in 1872 at Hvidsten, midway between Fredrikstad and Sarpsborg. Although the family moved to Oslo when Roald was still a small child, the family home in Hvidsten, which was the base for its small shipbuilding and shipping business, is now the Roald Amundsen Centre (☎ 69 34 83 26). It's dedicated to the man's life and expeditions and is open from 10 am to 4 pm daily from May to August. Admission is Nkr25.

Borgarsyssel Museum

Borgarsyssel (☎ 69 15 50 11), the county museum of Østfold, lies immediately east of the scenic river Glomma 2km from the town of Sarpsborg (10km north-east of Fredrikstad) and makes an interesting day visit. This open-air display contains 30 period buildings from various parts of the country and includes a vast collection of cultural art and artefacts. There's also a herbal garden, a petting zoo and the ruins of King Øystein's St Nikolas church, constructed in 1115 and destroyed by the Swedes in 1567. From 18 May to 31 August, the museum is open from 10 am to 5 pm Tuesday to Saturday and from noon to 5 pm on Sunday. From Fredrikstad, trains and buses run many times daily to Sarpsborg.

Storedal Cultural Centre

A unique and worthwhile site is the Storedal Cultural Centre (☎ 69 16 92 67), 8km north-east of Fredrikstad. King Magnus the Blind was born here in 1117; he took the throne at 13 years of age and earned his nickname at 18 when he was blinded by an enemy in Bergen. Coincidentally, a later owner of the farm, Erling Stordahl, also lost his sight at an early age and decided to develop a monument to King Magnus as well as a centre dedicated to blind and other disabled people. In 1970, the Crown Prince Harald opened the centre.

In the botanic garden, which is laid out in the shape of a leaf, the locations of the various plants and herbs are identified by raised areas in the footpath, and are described in both script and Braille. The most intriguing feature is the *Ode til Lyset* (Ode to the Light), a 'sound sculpture' by Arnold Haukeland and Arne Nordheim which translates the fluctuations in natural light into ever-changing music. Erling Stordahl's play *From Darkness to Light*, which is partly a biography of King Magnus and partly a plea for increased human understanding and interaction, is presented in the amphitheatre throughout the summer; contact the centre for specific dates and times.

The centre is open from 10 am to 5 pm daily from 20 May to 31 August. Admission is Nkr10.

Oldtidsveien

People have lived and worked in the Østfold region for thousands of years, and along the 'Oldtidsveien' (the 'old times way', a promotional name for Rv110 – the old sunken road between Fredrikstad and Sarpsborg) lie numerous examples of ancient stone works and rock paintings. At Solberg there are three panels with around 100 figures dating back 3000 years. At Gunnarstorp are several 30m **Bronze Age burial mounds** and several **Iron Age standing stones**. The site at Begby includes well preserved renditions of ships, men and animals, while Hunn has several **stone circles** and a series of rich **burial mounds** dating from 500 BC to 800 AD; they were found to contain jewellery, bronze and glass treasures. The **rock paintings** at Hornes clearly depict 21 ships complete with oarsmen. Access is easiest by car or bus towards Sarpsborg, but all these sites may also be visited on a long day walk or bike ride from Fredrikstad.

HALDEN

The soporific border town of Halden, at the end of Iddefjord between steep rocky headlands, has served as a keystone of Norwegian defence through more than two centuries of Swedish aggression. Locals proudly relate that the two occasions (in 1659 and 1716) on which the Halden resistance resorted to fire to drive out the enemy are commemorated in the Norwegian national anthem by Bjørnsterne Bjørnson, who wrote '... we chose to burn our nation, lest we let it fall'. The fortress crowns the hill behind Halden and makes the town a worthwhile day trip from Oslo or a stop along the rail route between Norway and Göteborg, Sweden.

History

Halden served as a garrison during the Hannibal Wars from 1643 to 1645, and from 1644 it was fortified with a wooden stockade. In 1658, 1659 and 1660, it was attacked by Swedish forces and the need for a better fortification became apparent. In the 1658 Roskilde Treaty between Sweden and Denmark, Norway lost its Bohuslän province (and Bohus fortress), and Halden was left as a border outpost requiring heavy defences. As a result, on 28 July

1660 King Fredrik III of Denmark issued a declaration ordering a stronger fortification on the site.

The pentagonal citadel, as well as the adjoining Gyldenløve fort, Stortårnet and Overberget, was constructed across two parallel hills from 1661 to 1671 (and augmented between 1682 and 1701) from plans drawn up by Dutch architect Willem Coucheron. Between 1716 and 1718, the fort was repeatedly besieged by Swedish forces but the Norwegians managed to resist the onslaught. Its crowning event came on 11 December 1718, when the troublesome Swedish king Charles XII was shot dead on the site (a monument now marks the spot).

Further attacks continued into the 19th century. In the first few years of the 20th century, Fredriksten Fortress was armed with increasingly powerful modern cannons, turret guns and howitzers. However,

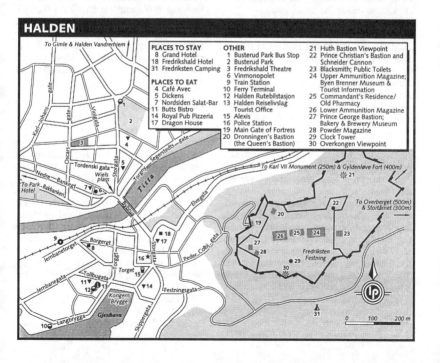

HALDEN

PLACES TO STAY	OTHER	
8 Grand Hotel	1 Busterud Park Bus Stop	21 Huth Bastion Viewpoint
18 Fredrikshald Hotel	2 Busterud Park	22 Prince Christian's Bastion and
31 Fredriksten Camping	3 Fredrikshald Theatre	Schneider Cannon
	6 Vinmonopolet	23 Blacksmith; Public Toilets
PLACES TO EAT	9 Train Station	24 Upper Ammunition Magazine;
4 Café Avec	10 Ferry Terminal	Byen Brenner Museum &
5 Dickens	12 Halden Rutebilstasjon	Tourist Information
7 Nordsiden Salat-Bar	13 Halden Reiselivslag	25 Commandant's Residence/
11 Butts Bistro	Tourist Office	Old Pharmacy
14 Royal Pub Pizzeria	15 Alexis	26 Lower Ammunition Magazine
17 Dragon House	16 Police Station	27 Prince George Bastion;
	19 Main Gate of Fortress	Bakery & Brewery Museum
	20 Dronningen's Bastion	28 Powder Magazine
	(the Queen's Bastion)	29 Clock Tower
		30 Overkongen Viewpoint

To Gimle & Halden Vandrerhjem

To Karl VII Monument (250m) & Gyldenløve Fort (400m)

To Overberget (500m) & Stortårnet (300m)

Fredriksten Festning

To Park Hotel

0   100   200 m

this firepower was removed during the 1906 negotiations for the dissolution of the Swedish-Norwegian union.

Information

The Halden Reiselivslag tourist office (☎ 69 18 01 02, fax 69 18 51 44, llindsko@ sn.no, www.haldentourist.no), at the bus terminal, is open from 9 am to 4.30 pm weekdays from June to August (the rest of the year until 3.30 pm). The information office at the harbour is open from 8 am to 8 pm daily between 1 June and 17 August.

Fredriksten Festning & Museums

Crowning the hilltop behind Halden is the 1661 Fredriksten Fortress, which has resisted six Swedish sieges but never been captured. From the top of Festningsgata in Sørhalden (a neighbourhood of 19th century sea captains' cottages), a half-overgrown cobbled footpath climbs the unkempt lilac-covered slopes to the castle gates.

The museums in the castle grounds cover various facets of the fortress' history. Halden's history is outlined in the Byen Brenner ('the town is on fire') exhibition in the upper part of the fortress. Displays in the old pharmacy describe the history of pharmacology from early Norwegian folk remedies to early 20th century apothecaries. It's housed in the former Commandant's Residence, constructed between 1754 and 1758 and damaged by fire in 1826. After renovation it was used as a powder laboratory, armoury and barracks. Note the Fredrik V monogram over the doorway.

In the former prison building near the entrance is the military section, displaying artefacts and describing the history of military conflict in Halden from the 17th century to WWII. Perhaps the most interesting sites are the brewery, which once produced up to 3000L of beer a day, and the bakery ovens, which baked bread for up to 5000 soldiers.

The fort and museums (☎ 69 18 54 11) are open from 10 am to 5 pm daily from 18 May to 31 August. From 23 June to 23 August, guided tours in Norwegian (or

English, with prior notice) are given daily at noon, 1 and 2 pm (and on Sunday also at 3 pm). Note that the high bastions are unfenced and not particularly safe for children. Admission to the grounds and all museums costs Nkr35.

Fredrikshald Teater

The baroque Fredrikshald Theatre, designed by Balthazar Nicolai Garben, was completed in 1838 and restored in 1982. Guided tours run at noon, 1 and 2 pm from Tuesday to Sunday, from 23 June to 23 August (Nkr35). The Halden Historiske Samlinger (☎ 60 18 54 11) has information on upcoming theatre productions.

Activities

A relaxing but adventurous way to explore the Aremark canals and waterways between Norway and Sweden is on your own by canoe. Canoe hire is available from Haldenvassdragets Kanoutleie (☎ 69 19 72 30), 5km north-east of town in Aremark. You can pick up a boating and recreation map from the tourist office in Halden. For information on canal travel in larger private boats, contact the Båt & Motor a/s (☎ 47 17 58 59) at the Jernbanebrygga in Halden.

Organised Tours

East of Halden, a canal system connects the town with Göteborg, Sweden. The highlight is the Brekke Locks, a system of four locks between Femsøen and Brekke (on the Halden-Strømsfoss run) which raise and lower the boats a total of 26.6m. The region is popular with canoeists and boat owners, but visitors can get a quick taste on the tourist cruise boats *Turisten* and *Fredrikshald* (☎ 90 99 81 11). These small vessels follow the Haldenkanalen between Tistedal (east of Halden) and Strømsfoss (Nkr150/ 225 one-way/return) daily except Monday; and on Thursday, between Strømsfoss and Ørje (Nkr100/150). Either trip takes 3½ hours. To reach Tistedal, take bus No 103, 104 or 106.

On the Thursday trip between mid-June and mid-August, you can visit the Haldenvassdragets Kanalmuseum (Halden Waterways Canal Museum; ☎ 69 81 10 21), beside the canal in Ørje.

Places to Stay

The convenient *Fredriksten Camping* (☎ 69 18 40 32), located in the fortress grounds, offers a quiet green spot to pitch a tent. Sites for a tent and a car cost Nkr100, plus Nkr20 per person. Cabins cost from Nkr235 to Nkr265 for up to four people. The *Halden Vandrerhjem* (☎ 69 18 00 77, fax 69 18 40 05), at the Tosterødberget school on Flinveien in the suburb of Gimle, is open from 21 June to 12 August only. Beds cost Nkr90 and simple single/double rooms are Nkr120/230. Take bus No 104 (marked Gimle) from the Busterud Park bus stop.

The *Fredrikshald Hotel* (☎ 69 18 82 22, fax 69 18 82 29, Ohmes plass 3), near the bridge, has weekend and summer rates of Nkr440/560. The *Grand Hotel* (☎ 69 18 72 00, fax 69 18 79 59, Jernbanetorget 1), opposite the train station, charges Nkr490/690 on weekends and in July. The *Park Hotel* (☎ 69 18 40 44, fax 69 18 45 53, Marcus Tranes gate 30), 1km from the centre, has weekend and summer rates of Nkr645/740.

Places to Eat

If you just want a light sandwich, cakes, Nkr19 milkshakes or a healthy helping of salad, try the *Nordsiden Salat-Bar*, a block north-west of the main bridge. A local favourite is the *Royal Pub Pizzeria*, near the waterfront, with steaks, pizza and à la carte pasta and chicken dishes.

Café Avec (☎ 69 17 80 57), in the historic Borgermestergården, combines a cake and sandwich café with a shop selling ceramic knick-knacks. *Dickens* (☎ 69 18 35 33, Storgata 9) does standard lunches and dinners, with main dishes starting around Nkr70. You can choose between outdoor seating or the dining room in a 17th century cellar.

The unfortunately named *Butts Bistro* (☎ 69 17 20 12), on Tollbugata behind the tourist office, serves Indian-style cuisine, and the *Dragon House*, beside the Fredrikshald Hotel, does Chinese dishes.

Entertainment

According to locals, the best night spot is the *Alexis* (☎ 69 17 51 61, Storgata 2) disco, nightclub and piano bar, open until 3 am on weekends (but may only serve alcohol until 2 am, thanks to an unpopular local ordinance). After 11.30 pm, the cover charge is Nkr60.

Getting There & Away

Trains run every two hours or so between Oslo and Halden (two hours, Nkr170), and an average of four daily trains continue on to Göteborg, Sweden. The long-distance bus terminal sits right at the harbour.

The ferry M/S Linné (Sweden ☎ 0526-153 70) connects Halden with Strömstad (Sweden). From mid-June to mid-August it operates daily except Sunday; and in May, early June, late August and early September it runs on Tuesday, Thursday and Saturday. The fare is Nkr60/95 one-way/return, and staff are quick to point out that duty-free goods are available on board.

Southern Norway

When the weather turns warm, the rocky, island-studded south coast of Sørlandet, with its many bays and coves, becomes a paradisiacal magnet for Norwegian boaters and holiday-makers. The 586km Sørland rail line connecting Stavanger and Oslo (via Kristiansand) keeps mainly inland but buses frequently meet the trains and link the rail line with most south coastal towns. The main highway, the E18, runs inland between Stavanger and Mandal but from there to Oslo it follows a winding route through many lovely coastal towns and villages.

The Coast

TØNSBERG
In the *Saga of Harald Hårfagre*, Snorre Sturluson mentions that the town of Tønsberg existed prior to the Battle of Hafsfjord, which took place in 872. Because of this, as well as the excavation of the medieval St Olav's monastery and the fact that the *Gokstad* and *Oseberg* ships (now in the Viking Ship Museum in Oslo) were discovered nearby, Tønsberg claims to be the oldest town in Norway, and celebrated its 1100-year anniversary in 1971. The name is probably derived from the *tønsberg*, the 'twin hills' on the farm Haugar (now in the centre of town). The farm's name refers to the graves of King Olav of Vestfold and King Sigrød of Trøndelag, both of whom fell in the Battle of Haugar against their brother, Erik Blodøks.

When King Harald Hårfagre divided the kingdom in the 9th century, he appointed his son, Bjørn Farmann, to rule over Vestfold, and the court of Sæheimr, at Tønsberg, became the royal seat. In the late medieval period it served as one of three Hanseatic trading posts in Norway, with ties to Rostock in northern Germany. By the 17th century the town had developed into a major shipping and commercial cen-

HIGHLIGHTS

- Touring the royal silver mines outside the pleasant town of Kongsberg
- Strolling through the narrow streets of the 'white towns' of Risør, Grimstad and Mandal
- Camping, cycling and exploring the beaches and offshore islands of Norway's sunshine coast along the Skagerrak
- Taking a leisurely cruise through the scenic Telemark canal system
- Marvelling at the exquisite roof lines and paintings in the stave church at Heddal
- Scouring the surface of Seljordvatn in search of sea monsters

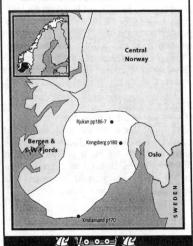

tre, dominated by the timber trade with Dutch and English merchants, and by 1850 it had the largest merchant fleet in Norway. In the mid-19th century Svend Føyn, the 'father' of Norwegian sealing and whaling, turned Tønsberg into a base of operations and source of expertise for whalers in the Arctic and Antarctic waters. This led to the invention of the exploding harpoon at Tønsberg's Henriksen Mechanical Works, which changed the stakes in modern whaling. (The town's next great invention emerged in 1953, when Arne Gravdahl furthered the cause of feminine hygiene by coming up with the sanitary pad.)

In spite of its ample history, modern Tønsberg may not be as exciting as one would expect, as the Sæheimr (now called Jarslberg) Estate is privately owned and not open to the public. You can easily cover the main sites in a couple of hours.

Information
The Tønsberg Turistkonteret (☎ 33 31 02 20, fax 33 31 95 90, toensberg.tourist@ vestfoldnett.no), on the Tønsberg Brygge waterfront, has done an amazing job on its tourist publication detailing the town's history and attractions. The office is open from 10 am to 5 pm Monday to Saturday in June and August; in July, the hours extend to 8 pm. The rest of the year, it's open from 10 am to 3 pm on weekdays only.

Castrum Tunsberghus
The 13th century ruins of Castrum Tunsberghus spread across the 63m hill behind the town, culminating in the modern 17m Slottsfjellstårnet tower, built in 1888. Little remains of the castle itself, which was destroyed by the Swedes in 1503. However, you can still see the 700m long outer wall and poke around the remaining medieval stone foundations, which include King Magnus Lagabøte's Keep, the 1191 Church of St Michael, the hall of King Håkon Håkonsson and various guard towers. Entry to the ruins park is free but admission to the historical exhibits inside the tower is Nkr10.

The tower is open from 11 am to 6 pm daily from late June to mid-August, and shorter hours at other times between late May and mid-September. The rest of the year, it's open Sunday only.

Ruins
Several other interesting ruins are scattered around the town and can be seen on a short walking tour. On the farm Haugar, behind the art museum, see the **Viking-age grave mounds** of kings Olav and Sigrød. In the park off Kongsgaten lie the ruins of **Kongsgården**, the old Royal Court of King Håkon Håkonsson where the kings of Vestfold were elected. From 1987 to 1991, excavations at Storgaten 17 revealed the ruins of the medieval **Church of St Olav**, the largest cylindrical church in Scandinavia, as well as St Olav's monastery and several Viking-age graves.

Historic Buildings
Tønsberg has several interesting old buildings. The most noteworthy include timber homes in **Nordbyen**, and the **Britannia House** (on the waterfront on Nedre Langgate), a 1700 timber building with a Louis XVI façade. Also, take a look at **Svend Foyn's 'arbeiderboliger'**, a self-contained block of 73 flats built by the whaling magnate for his workers.

Vestfold Fylkesmuseum
The Vestfold Folk Museum (☎ 33 31 29 19), along Grev Wedels gate at the foot of Slottsfjellet, presents a large exhibit of model ships, displays on the excavation of the *Oseberg* Viking ship, a host of medieval artefacts from the local district, a collection of historic period-furnished farm buildings, and a section on Tønsberg's whaling history, including skeletons of both a sperm whale and a blue whale. From mid-May to mid-September, it's open from 10 am to 5 pm Monday to Saturday, and noon to 5 pm on Sunday. Admission is Nkr20.

Organised Tours
In July the historic ship D/S *Kysten 1* (☎ 33 31 25 89), built in Trondheim in 1909, operates 3½-hour cruises through the skerries south of Tønsberg. Cruises depart from Honnørbryggen daily at noon and cost Nkr110 (Nkr90 for seniors). Tickets are sold on board.

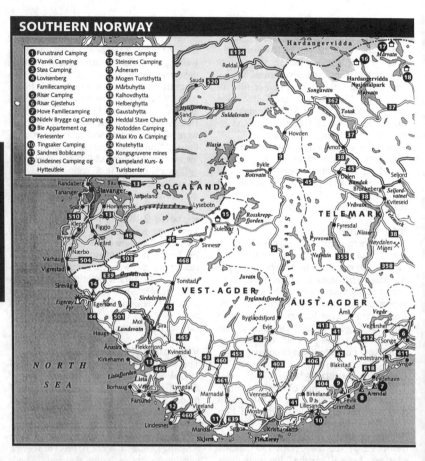

SOUTHERN NORWAY

1 Furustrand Camping
2 Vasvik Camping
3 Støa Camping
4 Lovisenberg Familiecamping
5 Risør Camping
6 Risør Gjestehus
7 Hove Familiecamping
8 Nidelv Brygge og Camping
9 Bie Appartement og Feriesenter
10 Tingsaker Camping
11 Sandnes Bobilcamp
12 Lindesnes Camping og Hytteutleie
13 Egenes Camping
14 Steinsnes Camping
15 Ådneram
16 Mogen Turisthytta
17 Mårbuhytta
18 Kalhovdhytta
19 Helberghytta
20 Gaustahytta
21 Heddal Stave Church
22 Notodden Camping
23 Max Kro & Camping
24 Knutehytta
25 Kongsgruvene mines
26 Lampeland Kurs- & Turistsenter

Places to Stay

The **Tønsberg Vandrerhjem** (☎/fax 33 31 28 48, tonsvand@online.no, Dronning Blancasgata 22), is just a five-minute walk from the train station. Dorm beds cost between Nkr145 and Nkr190, and private singles/doubles are available for Nkr355/476. Prices for all rooms include breakfast. For camping, go to the beachfront **Furustrand Camping** (☎ 33 32 44 02), 5.5km east of the centre. It charges Nkr50 per tent plus Nkr80 per car and Nkr20 per person. The cheapest

huts start at Nkr450. Take bus No 111 or 116 to Tolvsrød (Nkr18).

Hotell Maritim (☎ 33 31 71 00, fax 33 31 72 52, Storgata 17), beside the ruins, offers summer rates starting at Nkr550/700.

From June to August, the **Hotel Borge** (☎ 33 36 74 25), in an 18th century home on the island of Husøy, charges Nkr280/400 for simple rooms without bath, and Nkr340/500 for rooms with private facilities. Take bus No 109 from the centre (Nkr18). If you prefer to stay in the skerries,

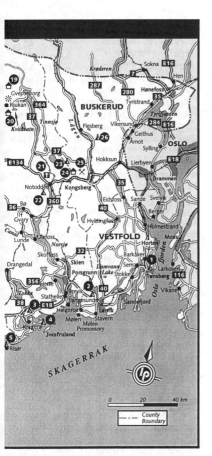

south of town, contact the tourist office for a listing of holiday huts, cabins, cottages, guesthouses and B&Bs.

Places to Eat

For its size, Tønsberg has an unusually large number of restaurants. The small and cosy *Athene* (☎ 33 31 36 66, Øvre Langgate 34) serves up Greek food, music, wine and atmosphere. *Peppe's Pizza* (☎ 33 31 70 71, Nedre Langgate 26B) does its usual inexpensive pizza thing, including a good value pizza buffet. On Monday and Tuesday, *Kong Sverre Pizza Bar* (☎ 33 31 29 03, Tollbodgata 14), in a 300-year-old building, lays on a pizza buffet for a bargain Nkr59. More upmarket is the rustic *Brygga* (☎ 33 31 12 70, Nedre Langgate 35), which has an outdoor terrace and a varied à la carte menu. Nearby *Esmeralda* (☎ 33 31 91 91, Nedre Langgate 26C) serves meals on the terrace, and the attached *Lemon Club og Carlsbar* (☎ 33 31 23 90) features a pub, disco and sports bar, all open to 3 am.

Getting There & Away

The Tønsberg Rutebilstasjon (☎ 33 31 00 20) is on Jernbanegaten, a block south of the train station. Nor-Way Bussekspress buses run at least once daily (except Saturday) between Tønsberg and Kristiansand (five hours, Nkr285), via most coastal towns en route. For an interesting excursion, head out to Verdens Ende (45 minutes, Nkr33) on bus No 351 and see the low-tech and nautically charming fire basket 'lighthouse' that dates from 1932.

Express trains run twice daily between Tønsberg station (☎ 33 37 60 00) and Oslo (1½ hours, Nkr135), while slower local trains run approximately hourly.

Getting Around

City buses cost Nkr18 per ride. The tourist office hires out bicycles for Nkr100/600 per day/week.

LARVIK

When the sun shines, the pleasant little town of Larvik (population 39,000) is an inviting place for travellers to stop for a day or so and explore the surrounding holiday areas.

Larvik's favourite son is Thor Heyerdahl, the quirky scientist and explorer who masterminded the *Ra*, *Ra II* and *Kon-Tiki* expeditions. These voyages were made to demonstrate that the Americas and the South Pacific may well have been settled by migrants from the Middle East rather than Asia, as is conventionally believed. On the occasion of Heyerdahl's 75th birthday in

1989, a statue in his honour was unveiled at Tollerodden, east of the town's harbour. It's sculpted in blue larvikite, a beautiful 50 million-year-old type of granite which is quarried locally. Tollerodden also bears a monument to Colin Archer, who built the polar ship *Fram*.

Oddly enough, Heyerdahl's *Ra* isn't Larvik's only renowned Ra. The other is the great Ice-Age Ra moraine which dammed Farris lake and created the Farris Well; it slips into the sea at Mølen, at the south-western corner of the Brunlanes peninsula (for more about moraines, see the boxed text 'Glacier & Ice Glossary' in the Facts about Norway chapter).

Information

You'll find Larvik town and Kommune information at the helpful Larvik Turistkontor (☎ 33 13 91 00, fax 33 13 91 11), Storgata 48 opposite the ferry dock. From 22 June to 1 August, it's open from 8.30 am to 6 pm Monday to Saturday and 3 to 5 pm on Sunday, with shorter hours the rest of the year.

A coin-operated laundry is available at the Guest Harbour.

Larvik Museum

The three-part Larvik Museum (☎ 33 13 04 04) includes the Herregården (the main building), as well as the Larvik Maritime Museum, immediately east of the harbour, and the Fritzøe Museum.

The **Herregården manor house** was constructed from 1674 to 1677 as the home of the Norwegian Governor General, Ulrik Frederik Gyldenløve, who also served as the Duke of Larvik. As the illegitimate son of King Fredrik IV of Denmark, Gyldenløve was given a dukedom and an estate and sent off to Norway where he wouldn't cause any problems. In the 19th century, this classic baroque timber structure served, in turn, as a town theatre, a vicarage, the town hall and a school. It's currently furnished in the 17th and 18th century mode. Over the road, you can see the inscriptions commemorating royal visits from King Fredrik V of Denmark to King Olav V.

The **Larvik Maritime Museum**, housed in a 1730 brick structure, also served as a vicarage and was later used as a Custom House. The main attractions include a collection of maritime art and artefacts, and a number of model ships.

In the **Fritzøe Museum** at Langestrand, 500m out along the Stavern road, you'll see a collection of tools and implements used in the 17th century sawmill and ironworks that operated here from 1670 to 1870.

Herregården and the Maritime Museum are open from noon to 5 pm daily from 22 June to 15 August. From 24 May to 21 June and 16 August to 20 September, they open from noon to 5 pm on Sunday only. The Fritzøe Museum is open the same hours on Sunday only from 22 June to 15 August but special openings can be arranged through Treschow Fritzøe (☎ 33 12 11 00). Admission to each museum costs Nkr15.

Farris Well

Free guided tours are provided of the Farris Well, at the foot of Bødkerfjellet. Legend has it that this mineral source was used by King Olav in medieval times and it's now the source for Farris-brand mineral water. The plant is open from 10 am to 4 pm daily from 24 June to 2 August.

Bøkeskogen

The 300-hectare Bøkeskogen (beech woods), north of the town centre, form a pleasant green belt for strolling and they contain 80 ancient and Viking-era grave mounds. The highest point affords a fine view over the forest as well as the lake Farrisvatn. The 8km Farris Trail hiking route begins here and passes several waterfalls before it ends at Ono in Vestmarka. On Friday from 6.30 to 10 pm, the *Bøkekroa restaurant* (☎ 33 11 10 53), in the Bøkeskogen park, puts on jazz concerts; on Sunday morning breakfast is served here, accompanied by choir music.

Larvik Kirke

Larvik's Trinity Church was commissioned in 1677 by Duke Gyldenløve for his wedding and was completed in 1763 with the addition of the tower. It's open from 6 to 8 pm weekdays from mid-June to mid-August, and also from 11 am to 1 pm from Tuesday to Friday year-round. Note the elegant baptismal font and Lucas Granagh's altarpiece painting, *Suffer the Little Children to Come Unto Me*, that was probably commissioned by Duke Gyldenløve. The monument outside, by Arne Vigeland, commemorates Norwegians who died in WWII.

Places to Stay

Campers are in luck between 1 June and 1 August, as *Hovlandbanen Camping* (☎ 33 11 44 22), inside a decommissioned race track, lies within easy walking distance of the centre. Tent/caravan sites cost Nkr70/120 and cabins cost from Nkr200 to Nkr220, plus Nkr20 per person for electricity. In August the site is used as an exhibition centre. An alternative is *Vasvik Camping*, beside the lake Farrisvatn. Two people in a tent pay Nkr50/80 without/with a car; caravans pay Nkr100 and cabins range from Nkr300 to Nkr450. Buses between Larvik and Skien or Porsgrunn pass the site every two hours on weekdays and five times daily on weekends; otherwise, it's a 40-minute walk from the centre.

Given its charm, the 1903 *Gyldenløve Hotel* (☎ 33 18 25 26, fax 33 18 79 70, Storgata 26) offers fairly good summer value at Nkr390/550 for singles/doubles without bath. The *Lysko Gjestegård* (☎ 33 18 77 79, fax 33 13 03 30, Kirkestredet 10), opposite the Maritime Museum, has rooms without bath for Nkr350/450.

The tourist office can book holiday cottages on the Brunlanes peninsula (or anywhere in the Larvik Kommune) for Nkr4000 to Nkr8000 per week (plus a booking fee of Nkr20).

Places to Eat

On Monday and Tuesday, *Kong Sverre* (☎ 33 18 53 10, Oscarsgata 4) puts on a pizza buffet for Nkr59, including a soft drink. *Jeppe's* (☎ 33 18 08 08, Storgata 24),

nearer the centre, has a similar set-up on Monday from 7 to 9.30 pm. You'll find steak and seafood dinners nightly at the fully-licensed *Ferdinands Lillekjøkken* (☎ 33 13 05 44, Storgata 32). The *Hansemann Steakhouse* (☎ 33 18 61 48, Kongegata 33) and the adjoining *Kjeller'n* and *Pizza House* restaurants offer meals catering to a range of budgets.

For breakfast, you're limited to the hotels or *Din Baker Konditori-Bakeri*, on Kongensgata just downhill from Øvre Torgata.

If you wish to buy alcohol, the Vinmonopolet is at Nansetveien 36/38.

Getting There & Away

The train and bus stations are side by side on Møllegata. NSB buses (☎ 32 20 30 90) between Larvik and Kongsberg (2¼ hours, Nkr105) run two or three times daily (once on Sunday). Local trains run up to 10 times daily between Oslo S (Central Station) and Larvik (2½ hours, Nkr185). Some of these trains continue from Larvik to Skien (45 minutes, Nkr50), where there are a few daily connections to Nordagutu on the Oslo-Stavanger rail line.

The Hurtigbåt (☎ 37 15 85 60) ferry from Oslo calls in at Stavern (see Around Larvik).

Getting Around

The Vestfold region is fabulous for cycling and bike trails have been meticulously laid out from one end of the county to the other. The tourist office hires bicycles for Nkr75/350 per day/week and sells the indispensable three-part map, *Sykkelkart Vestfold*, for Nkr90. Hedlund Cycle Rental (☎ 33 19 58 08, mobile ☎ 90 62 65 09) in Stavern (see Around Larvik) rents bikes for Nkr75 per day, and is happy to deliver them to you in Larvik.

AROUND LARVIK

Most visitors to the Larvik area head straight for the Brunlanes peninsula, which is a major holiday venue with lots of coastal camping grounds that are chock-a-block with permanently moored caravans.

Some people, however, charge off up the Numendalslågen for a spot of salmon fishing at Holmfoss or Brufoss, or to the lakes and woods for a quieter escape.

Stavern

The appealing little coastal town of Stavern, just a stone's throw south of Larvik, makes a nice stop to stroll around the mid-18th century fort, Fredriksvern Verft, and (if you're there between 11 am and 1 pm Tuesday to Friday) visit the exceptionally colourful 1756 church, which was Norway's first naval house of worship.

Stavern is also the start of the popular 33km Kyststien coastal walk to Ødegården on the western coast of Brunlanes. From mid-June to mid-August, the Stavern Turistkontor (☎ 33 19 73 00), Storgata 27, provides free route maps entitled *Kyststien i Larvik*.

A good mid-range accommodation option is the *Fredtun Folkehøyskole* (☎ 33 19 99 55, fax 33 19 75 15) on Route 301 south of town, which charges Nkr265/450 for simple single/double rooms. The better heeled *Hotel Wassilioff* (☎ 33 19 83 11), on Tollbodgata at the waterfront, has rooms for Nkr650/810.

To get to and from Larvik (15 minutes, Nkr18), use bus No 531, 533 or 535. Note also that the Hurtigbåt ferry between Oslo and Arendal calls in at Stavern (see Getting There & Away in the Oslo chapter).

Helgeroa

The popular and pleasant seaside village of Helgeroa offers little except for some marginal beaches and a sunset view of the sea. Still, in summer it's packed to overflowing with holiday-makers who bet on the odds of fine weather and come looking for a dose of sunshine.

The odd pink-coloured *Helgeroa Hotel* (☎ 33 18 93 00, fax 33 18 83 50), on Krabbegata, charges Nkr650/750 for single/double rooms. Immediately north and south of the village, respectively, are the rather overtaxed camping grounds, *Blokkebukta* (☎ 33 18 89 75) and *Omlid-*

stranda (☎ 33 18 86 00). Neither, however, has any cabins or appealing tent sites – the caravans are just too densely packed. If you do find space, you'll pay around Nkr100 to pitch a tent, plus Nkr10 per person. Try the beach sand!

For meals, you can opt for the informal *Grill Bar* or see the friendly *Vertshuset Syd-Vesten* (☎ 33 18 86 50) at the harbour, which has superb pizzas starting at Nkr119 and fish specialities from around Nkr150. If money is no object, visit the more elegant *Kristinus Bergman* (☎ 33 18 85 33), which specialises in steak and seafood.

You can reach Helgeroa from Larvik (45 minutes, Nkr27), via Stavern, on bus No 531, or directly from Larvik on bus No 532.

Mølen

The Mølen promontory, the end of the Ra moraine which extends from the lake Farrisvatn to the south-western end of Brunlanes, is the only place in this area that experiences big ocean-style waves (and there are postcards to prove it). Most of the time, however, the sea is flat as a millpond. The 230 stone cairns and heaps of boulders, which are laid out in parallel rows, are Iron Age burial mounds. The larger ones – particularly those in the shape of boats – probably honoured nobles, while the nondescript heaps were for those of lower standing. It makes a nice day walk from Helgeroa, about 4km away along the Kyststien coastal walk.

Damvann

When you've had enough of the coast, head north to beautiful, haunting Damvann, a classic 'lake in the woods' and the home of a legendary witch named Huldrene. It's said that any man who looked upon her exquisite beauty was doomed. On Sundays in July, a modern-day version of Huldra (Ellen Dalen), serves meals here from noon to 4 pm. Access is difficult without a car – the nearest bus stop is at Kvelde (about 8km from the lake), 12km north of Larvik on the Numendalslågen road.

KRAGERØ
The popular seaside resort of Kragerø, with its narrow streets and whitewashed houses, has been a market town since 1666 and has long served as a retreat for Norwegian artists. In fact, Edvard Munch spent a few restorative fishing holidays here and, apparently a better painter than author, he wrote 'Many a sleepless night my thoughts and dreams go to Kragerø ... Above blasts the wind from the sea, behind are the fragrant pines, and beyond, the waves breaking over the skerries. My regards to Kragerø, the pearl of the coastal towns.' (In fact, a new statue of Munch has recently been unveiled in the spot where he painted a winter sun over the sea.)

In the early 20th century, Kragerø began attracting Norwegian holiday-makers and today the district boasts at least 3000 summer cottages. For· a great view over the town and its skerries, climb from Kragerø Stadium to the lookout point on Steinmann hill.

Information
The exceptionally helpful Kragerø Fokus Turistkontor (☎ 35 98 23 88, fax 35 98 31 77), Torggata 1, is the place to go for all you need to know about Kragerø and surrounds. It's open from 10 am to 8 pm daily in summer.

If it's time for laundry, head for the coin-operated machines at Havn's Vask og Rens, at the Guest Harbour; free parking is available.

Berg-Kragerø Museum
The Berg-Kragerø Museum on the southern shore of Hellefjord, 3km from the centre, occupies a 120-hectare estate with an 1803 country residence, gardens, walking tracks, a café and a gallery for visiting art and history exhibits. It's open from noon to 6 pm daily from 1 June to 31 August. Admission is Nkr40.

Jomfruland
If you're in Kragerø, chances are you're headed for the offshore island of Jomfru-

land, which is the most popular destination hereabouts. It measures about 7.5km long and 1km wide and is covered largely in forest and encircled by mostly sandy beaches. The landmark old (1869) and new (1937) lighthouses are open to visitors year-round from noon to 6 pm on Sunday only. From early June to late August, they are also open between noon and 4 pm from Monday to Saturday.

In summer, ferries between Kragerø and Jomfruland (20 minutes, Nkr24) are run by Kragerø Fjordbåtselskap (☎ 35 98 58 59) and operate two or three times daily. There's an atmospheric camping ground, *Jomfruland Camping* (☎ 35 99 12 75), beside the lighthouses. Tent camping costs Nkr50 plus Nkr10 per person, caravanners pay Nkr110 (including electricity), and four-bed cabins are Nr350.

Activities
For something totally different, how about a rail-bicycle ride along the 13km railway between Sannidal and Merkebekk. Railbikes (bicycles on bogies) rent for Nkr50/250 per hour/day. Book through Støa Camping (☎ 35 99 02 61) in Sannidal (see Places to Stay & Eat).

Places to Stay & Eat
The summer-only *Kragerø Vandrerhjem* (☎ 35 98 33 33, Lovisenbergveien 20), about 1km from town, has dorm beds/doubles for Nkr195/390, with breakfast. If you don't mind a 4km walk each way, you can camp at *Lovisenberg Familiecamping* (☎ 35 98 87 77), open from 1 May to 1 October. Tent/caravan camping is Nkr90/100 plus Nkr20 per person, and four-bed cabins are Nkr595 to Nkr750. However, there's no bus service yet, so without a vehicle you'd probably do better with *Støa Camping* (☎ 35 99 02 61) in Sannidal, which is readily accessible on bus No 352 (12 minutes, Nkr18). With a tent and car, you'll pay Nkr90 plus Nkr20 per person. Basic cabins are also available.

The *Victoria Hotel* (☎ 35 98 10 66, fax 35 98 29 26, PA Heuchsgata 31) charges

Nkr690/840 for well appointed single/ double rooms.

The rather disoriented *El Paso Western Saloon* (☎ 35 98 15 32) combines the Norwegian seaside with the badlands of West Texas. This is the tourist's choice for steaks, burgers, pizza, attempts at Mexican fare and other non-seafood dishes. Similarly, the attached *Amadeus Musikk Kafe* is a long way from Salzburg but it's not bad on a weekend evening, when live performances are staged.

At *Kafe Edvard* (☎ 35 98 15 50, Edvard Munchsvei 2) you'll find simple Norwegian fare and lunch specials beginning at Nkr55. The prominent *Restaurant Admiralen* (☎ 35 98 31 11, Ytre Strandvei 24) does Norwegian and Chinese specialities. Lunch specials with coffee and a dessert cost Nkr80.

Getting There & Away

Drivers should prepare for headaches in this town of narrow streets, tangled tourist traffic and few parking places. The simplest approach is by rail from Oslo or Kristiansand to Neslandsvatn, where most trains are met by a connecting Tele-Tur bus (☎ 35 53 21 12) to Kragerø. The Hurtigbåt (☎ 37 15 85 60), which sails between Oslo and Arendal daily from 24 June to 10 August, calls in at Kragerø (see Getting There & Away in the Oslo chapter). The fare from Kragerø to Oslo/Arendal is Nkr350/220.

RISØR

Risør, the 'White Town on the Skagerrak', is defined by a cluster of historic white houses (dating from 1650 to 1890) arranged around a busy inner harbour, Indrehavn, which is cluttered with colourful fishing boats and private yachts.

The fact that it's one of the south coast's most picturesque villages hasn't been lost on Norwegian tourists, and it's also the haunt of artists who make it their summer hang-out. You can see what sort of inspiration it has provided at the Risør Kunstpark gallery, at the museum on Prestegata.

Information

Given the town's appeal to visitors, Risør's tourist office (☎ 37 15 22 70), in the library/cinema complex on upper Kragsgata, has little to recommend it. It's open only from 13 June to 16 August; from 9 am to 4 pm weekdays, 10 am to 2 pm Saturday and noon to 6 pm Sunday. For tourist information, you'd do better at the enormous Info-Sør complex (☎ 37 15 85 60, fax 37 15 85 65), on the E18 near the Telemark boundary.

Risør Saltvannsakvariet

The Risør Saltwater Aquarium (☎ 37 14 32 82), on the quay in front of the Risør Hotel, houses examples of saltwater fish, crustaceans and shellfish common to Norway's south coast. It's open from 11 am to 7 pm daily from 20 June to 9 August; and noon to 4 pm from 10 to 30 August. Admission costs Nkr30.

Risør Museum

For the lowdown on the geology, fishing economy and 275-year history of Risør, rather pretentiously divided into 'earth, air, fire and water' exhibits, you can check out the Risør Museum (☎ 37 15 30 85) at Prestegata 9. The museum also includes the WWII fortification and memorial at the Urheia viewpoint, north of the centre. It's open from 11 am to 3 pm daily (from noon on Sunday) from 23 June to 9 August, and on Sunday only from 7 May to 23 June. Admission to both costs Nkr30.

The Skerries

In addition to wandering around the harbour area soaking up the rustic charm, visitors also like to visit the offshore skerries, which are accessed by scheduled ferries and inexpensive water taxis. The most frequented island, Stangholmen, sports the requisite lighthouse; this one dates from 1855 and contains *Stangholmen Fyr restaurant and bar* (☎ 37 15 24 50). In summer, ferries (☎ 37 15 24 50, mobile ☎ 94 29 34 00) leave Tollbubrygga hourly from 10 am and cost Nkr20.

Special Events

Over one weekend in August, Risør hosts the Risør International Wooden Boat Festival, that attracts old salts and other boat people from all over Norway. In early September you can catch Risør's annual Shanty-festival, which features four days of – you guessed it – sea shanties. In fact, it's unique and people really do get into this sort of thing. For specific dates, contact Info-Sør (☎ 37 15 85 60, fax 37 15 85 65).

Places to Stay & Eat

The closest camping ground, *Risør Camping* (☎ 37 15 02 67), is on Sundsveien at Sundet, about 3km from the centre. Bus Nos 103, 104, 105 and 107 will get you to the junction of the Rv416 and Furumoveien (seven minutes, Nkr18), about 1km south of the camping ground. *Risør Gjestehus* (☎ 37 15 50 02, fax 37 15 52 74), 9km west of town at Bossvika, charges a reasonable Nkr350/500 for singles/doubles. Take bus No 103, 104, 105 or 107 (20 minutes, Nkr19). At the only in-town option, the *Risør Hotel* (☎ 37 15 07 00), prices start at a rather steep Nkr795/990, but you will have a nice sea view.

Around the harbour and along Kragsgata, you'll find several moderately priced cafés and restaurants, such as *D/S Excellensen* (☎ 37 15 30 50) on Torvet. Ice-cream shops abound and you'll find inexpensive produce at the *harbourside market*. For coffee and sweet snacks, there's *Karl Broms Bakery*, one block west on Kragsgata.

Getting There & Away

Local buses link Risør with the rail line at Gjerstad (45 minutes, Nkr44) several times daily. Nor-Way Bussekspress buses between Kristiansand (two hours, Nkr120) and Oslo (3¼ hours, Nkr290) connect at Vinterkjær with local buses to and from Risør (30 minutes, Nkr23).

The summer Hurtigbåt between Oslo (5½ hours, Nkr370) and Arendal (1¾ hours, Nkr170) calls in at Risør's Dampskipsbrygga. From Sunday to Thursday, southbound boats arrive at 2.25 pm, and

northbound, at 6.15 pm. On Friday there is only one boat – southbound arriving 9.25 pm. Saturday's boat is northbound, arriving at 10.45 am. They depart shortly thereafter.

LYNGØR

Tiny Lyngør, an offshore islet near the ready-made village of Gjeving, doesn't hide the fact that it won the 1991 European competition for the tidiest town on the continent. Even if it weren't for that distinction, this picturesque little settlement would be worth a visit – largely because visitors can't bring their vehicles across on the ferry.

Places to Stay & Eat

If you want to soak up Lyngør's atmosphere after the day-trippers head back to the mainland, you can hole up in the *Lyngør Appartement-Hotell* (☎ 37 16 65 66, fax 37 16 66 66). In the high season, from 30 June to 28 July, you'll get a self-catering four/six-person hut for Nkr1000/1100. From 28 April to 29 June and 29 July to 8 September, you'll pay Nkr700/800.

Norwegians, it seems, regard Lyngør as a place to spend a few hours for a meal and, considering the islet's small size, there's a boggling choice of eateries. Simple fare is represented at the *Sunniva Kafé* (☎ 37 16 67 48), while more serious dishes are served up at the atmospheric *Den Blå Lanterne* (☎ 37 16 64 80). The *Seilmakerfruens Kro* (☎ 37 16 64 00) dishes up pizza and à la carte specialities.

Getting There & Away

Ferry The Lyngør Båtselskap ferry (☎ 37 16 68 88 or ☎ 94 29 20 43) between Gjeving and Lyngør leaves every one or two hours on weekdays between 7.30 am and 9 pm, and on weekends roughly from 9 am to 4 pm. The fare is Nkr20/25 before/after 5 pm.

Car & Motorcycle You can't drive to Lyngør but if you approach by car from the east, forsake the E18 and follow the slow but lovely coastal route, which winds narrowly over forested peninsulas and past idyllic coves and fishing settlements.

ARENDAL

Arendal, the administrative centre of Aust-Agder county, climbs steeply up the hillsides that surround its harbour area, better known as the Pollen. For swimming and other sorts of communion with the sea, head for the islands of Merdø (accessible by ferry), and Tromøy and Hisøy (both reached by bus).

Information

From mid-June to mid-August, the Arendal Turistkontor (☎ 37 02 21 93, fax 37 02 52 12), Friholmsgate 1, dispenses friendly information and operates town tours. It's open from 9 am to 7 pm Monday to Saturday and noon to 7 pm on Sunday.

The only place in town for laundry is Vaskebaren (☎ 37 02 25 42) at the harbour. It's not self-service, so be sure to ask the price beforehand or you may get a surprise when it comes time to pay! The nearest coin machines are beside the tourist office at Tvedestrand (12km east on Route 410), where you'll pay Nkr20 for a wash.

Tyholmen

A few minutes walk south of the bus station brings you to the old harbourside Tyholmen district, with its 19th century timber buildings featuring neoclassic, rococo and baroque influences. In 1992 it was awarded the Europa Nostra prize for its expert restoration. Predictably, the district is also home to a host of skilled (and often nautically-oriented) artists and craftspeople. Originally, Tyholmen was separated from the mainland by a canal which connected Pollen and Kittelsbukt (the industrial harbour west of the town centre), but it was filled in after the great sailing era. Today, workers are restoring the canal so Tyholmen will again be an island.

You may want to check out the unusual Rådhus, which is actually a shipowner's home dating from 1815. The original star-spangled dome gave way to a flat ceiling and modern tastes in the late 19th century but the elegant original staircase remains. Upstairs hang portraits of 20th century Norwegian royalty and former mayors of Arendal.

Aust-Agder Museum

Oddly enough, the Aust-Agder Museum was first conceived in 1832, when the town asked its globetrotting sailors to be on worldwide lookout for items which may be of interest back home. The results of this search are now housed in the county museum, along with relics of Arendal's shipbuilding, timber and import-export trades. There are also decent collections of folk art, farming implements and sailing paraphernalia. It's open from 10 am to 5 pm weekdays, 9 am to 1 pm Saturday and noon to 3 pm Sunday from 20 June to 20 August.

Offshore Islands

The 260-hectare island of Merdø has been inhabited since the 16th century and bears the remnants of vegetable species introduced in the ballast of early sailing vessels. The Merdøgård Museum (☎ 37 02 24 22), housed in a historic 1736 sea captain's residence, is decked out in period furnishings. From 23 June to 15 August, it's open from noon to 4.30 pm daily. Guided tours are available hourly.

Ferry access to Merdø and Hove (on Tromøy) is on the M/S Merdø (☎ 37 02 64 23), which operates from the end of June to mid-August (Nkr25). You can also get to Merdø on the M/F Trau (☎ 37 08 56 09), which runs year-round.

On the islets of Store and Lille Torungene rise two grand lighthouses which have guided ships into Arendal since 1844. They're visible from the coasts of both Hisøy and Tromøy.

Popular beaches on Hisøy include Stølsvigen, Tangen and Vrageviga. However, there's no bus access (bus No 336 runs only as far as Sandvigen), so you'll need a car or bicycle to reach them. The favoured bathing sites are on Tromøy, Spornes and Hove. The nearest access to Spornes is on bus No 334 but you'll still have a couple of kilometres to walk. Alternatively, take a bike on the M/S Skilsøy ferry (☎ 37 00 55 44), which sails frequently between Arendal and the western end of Tromøy (six minutes, Nkr12 – or Nkr35 after midnight on weekends). Kolbjørnsvik, on Hisøy, may be reached from Arendal (six minutes, Nkr10) on the frequent M/S *Kolbjørn III* (☎ 37 00 55 44), and Hove is accessed on the Merdø ferry (Nkr25).

Organised Tours
On Monday, Tuesday and Thursday in summer, the tourist office organises 1½-hour guided walking tours around Tyholmen, the town museum and the town hall. They depart at 4 pm and cost Nkr40, plus Nkr10 for museum admission.

Places to Stay
The Chinese-oriented *Ting Hai Hotel* (☎ 37 02 22 01, fax 37 02 23 25) has single/double rooms starting at Nkr475/700. If budget isn't an issue, the nicest spot is the *Clarion Tyholmen Hotel* (☎ 37 02 68 00, fax 37 02 68 01, Teaterplassen 2), right on the water. The architecture attempts to emulate Tyholmen's historic theme. In summer, you'll get relatively posh accommodation for Nkr695/760. The modern *Phønix Hotel* (☎ 37 02 51 60, fax 37 02 67 07, Friergangen 1), which rises from the Tyholmen historic district, charges Nkr625/900.

For anything less expensive, you'll have to head out of town. One option is *Hove Familiecamping* (☎ 37 08 53 91), at Hove on Tromøy island, which is accessible on the Merdø ferry (Nkr25). Two people in a tent or caravan (with a car) pay Nkr100 and four-person huts cost Nkr300. It's open from 1 June to 31 August.

The *Nidelv Brygge og Camping* (☎ 37 01 14 25) lies on the Nidelv river at Hisøy, 6km west of Arendal. For tent camping, you'll pay Nkr45 per tent plus Nkr15 per person; in a caravan, the price is Nkr90; and cabins start at Nkr250. From town, take any bus headed for Kristiansand or Grimstad; they run approximately every half-hour (Nkr20).

Otherwise, visit the tourist office and arrange accommodation in a private home or holiday cabin; most places are rented only on a weekly basis but there are a few exceptions.

Places to Eat
If you just want a tasty snack, the waterfront *fish market* sells inexpensive fish cakes. The novel *McDonald's* on the nondescript Torvet serves breakfast from 9 am to 11 am and its regular menu thereafter. Believe it or not, there's also a sail-up window from the Pollen, where boaters can pick up burgers without going ashore!

Also on the Torvet is the *Torvcaféen* (☎ 37 02 61 19), which does the usual café range of snacks. The Pollen boasts several atmospheric open-air restaurants and cafés which double as evening drinking spots. The *Sjølofter* (☎ 37 02 46 00), at the northern end of Langebryggen, specialises in pizza, and *Madame Reiersen* (☎ 37 02 19 00, Nedre Tyholmsvei 3) offers more sophisticated fare, with an emphasis on seafood and pasta dishes.

Away from the shore, on the corner of Torvegaten and Østre gate, sits the *Ting Hai* (☎ 37 02 22 01), one of Norway's few recommended Chinese restaurants. It's open daily for lunch and dinner.

Entertainment
Bars and discos in Arendal are open until 2.30 am. The appropriately harbourside *Fishermans Pub* (☎ 37 02 88 70) on Langbryggen opens from Wednesday to Sunday night. The nightly dancing haunt is *Dixon* (☎ 37 02 72 02, Langbryggen 15), while *Rubens Dansebar*, in the Hotel Phønix, operates on Friday and Saturday, and *Stephanie* (☎ 37 02 40 45, Freiergangen 4) has dancing nightly from Tuesday to Saturday.

Getting There & Away
The Nor-Way Bussekspress buses between Kristiansand (1½ hours, Nkr79) and Oslo (four hours, Nkr310) call in several times daily at the Arendal Rutebilstasjon, which is a large square a block west of the Pollen harbour. Local bus Nos 322, 323 and 324 connect Arendal and Grimstad (30 minutes, Nkr27) every few minutes from 5 am to at least 11 pm.

Arendal is connected with the main rail system by a trunk line from Nelaug, but the station (☎ 37 02 20 03) lies a 10-minute walk through the Fløyheia tunnel (the only vehicles using this tunnel are accessing Arendal's underground car park) from the Torvet. If the tunnel still puts you off, you can climb over the hill along Hylleveien and Iuellsklev.

In summer, the Oslo-Arendal Hurtigbåt (☎ 7 15 85 60) leaves Oslo at 9 am daily, Sunday to Thursday, and from Arendal on the same days at 4.25 pm, stopping en route at Risør, Kragerø and several other ports. On Friday it leaves Oslo at 4 pm, and on Saturday it sails from Arendal at 9 am. The full journey takes seven hours and costs Nkr400, with a 10% discount on return tickets.

Getting Around

Town buses in Arendal charge Nkr15. Sykkelsport, on the corner of Nygaten and Vestre gate, rents bicycles for Nkr70 per day. This is a great way to explore the islands and reach the bathing beaches on Hisøy and Tromøy.

GRIMSTAD

The white town of Grimstad is one of the loveliest on the Skagerrak coast, and what it lacks in surrounding scenery it makes up for in the charm of its narrow pedestrianised centre. It's also renowned as the sunniest spot in Norway, with an average of 266 hours of sunshine per month in summer.

Henrik Ibsen

Henrik Johan Ibsen, Norway's most famous playwright, was born in Skien in 1828. He suffered from the financial difficulties of his parents and by the age of 15 was forced to make his own way in the world. He intended to become a doctor, but after failing courses in both Greek and mathematics, he decided that the sciences weren't his lot. He did, however, have a penchant for poetry and drama. The violinist Ole Bull (who was the driving force behind the musical education of Edvard Grieg) was impressed by Ibsen's early poems and sense of drama and steered him in the direction of the theatre.

Early in his career, Ibsen worked for six years with the theatre in Bergen, followed by five years at the theatre in Christiania, and he thereby acquired a sharp eye for theatrical technique. His masterpiece during this period, *The Pretenders* (1863), takes place in 13th century Norway, with the King Håkon Håkonsson expressing anachronistic dreams of national unity.

Between 1864 and 1891, Ibsen lived and studied in Rome, Dresden and Munich, decrying the small-mindedness of the Norwegian society of the day, yet living on an annual pension granted by the Norwegian State (he didn't return home until 1891, at the age of 63). In his later works, notably *Brand* (1866), the enormously popular *Peer Gynt* (1867), *Emperor & Galilean* (1873), *Pillars of Society* (1877), the highly provocative *Ghosts* (1881), *A Doll's House* (1879), *An Enemy of the People* (1882), *The Wild Duck* (1884), and *Hedda Gabler* (1890), he achieved a more realistic dialogue and came to be known as the father of modern Norwegian drama. Most of these works, however, ascribe to their heroes and heroines deeds that are less than universally heroic, at least in the modern sense.

Peer Gynt was Ibsen's most renowned international success, especially when combined with the music of Edvard Grieg. In this epic, an ageing hero returns to his Norwegian roots after wandering around the world and is forced to face his own soul. As he looks back on a wasted life of travel and his fruitless search for truth, his essence peels away like the skin of an onion, revealing ever deeper facets of his personality. In the end, he discovers that when all the layers are peeled away, there's no core to be found. 'So unspeakably poor, then, a soul can return to nothingness, in the misty grey. You beautiful earth, don't be annoyed that I left

However, Grimstad's current low-key atmosphere, peacefulness and charm belies its past importance, for between 1870 and 1890, Grimstad was one of the greatest – if not *the* greatest – shipbuilding centres in the world. The oak forests that grew on the hillsides were chopped down and sawn into timbers to supply the booming industry; at one point the town had 40 shipyards, and 90 ships were under construction simultaneously.

During the same period, a land shortage caused many local farmers to turn to fishing. Many of them set about building their own boats, thereby extending the shipbuilding tradition even to inland farmsteads. By 1875, Grimstad had a home fleet of 193 boats and ships.

Information

The Grimstad Turistkontor (☎ 37 04 40 41, fax 37 04 93 77), near the waterfront at Smith Petersensgata 31, is open from 8.30 am to 4 pm weekdays, with longer hours between 1 June and 31 August.

There is a coin laundry on the ground floor of the Grimstad Kulturhus (that is, the cinema and bowling alley!).

The Café Java (osmund@cafejava.org, www.cafejava.org), at Sebastian's Restaurant, offers Internet access and email services from 11 am to 8 pm daily.

Henrik Ibsen

no sign when I walked your grass. You beautiful sun, in vain, you've shed your glorious light on an empty house. There was no one within to cheer and warm. The owner, they tell me, was never at home.'

In his highly acclaimed *The Doll's House*, he successfully examined the doctrine of critical realism and the experiences of the individual in the face of the majority. As his protagonist Nora puts it, 'I will have to find out who is right, society or myself.' It is a sentiment which echoes loudly in the present day. As a result, Nora has become a symbol for women who sacrifice family life to struggle for equality and liberation.

In his last drama, the semi-autobiographical *When We Dead Awaken*, Ibsen describes the life of the estranged artist, sculptor Professor Rubek, who returns to Norway in his later years but finds no happiness, having forsaken his only love and his youth to misplaced idealism.

Toward the end of his life, Ibsen summed up his philosophy, quoting to a German friend: 'He who wishes to understand me must know Norway. The magnificent but severe natural environment surrounding people up there in the north forces them to keep to their own. That is why they become introspective and serious, they brood and doubt – and they often lose faith. There, the long, dark winters come with their thick fogs enveloping the houses – oh, how they long for the sun!'

Ibsen became a partial invalid after suffering a heart attack in 1901 and died five years later.

Ibsenhuset & Grimstad By Museum

On 3 January 1844, Henrik Ibsen arrived in Grimstad from his home town of Skien on the sailing ship *Lykkens Prøve*. He took a job as an apprentice in the pharmacy of Jens Aarup Riemann, on the corner of Tverrestredet and Vestregata, and when it was sold in 1847, he shifted to the Lars Nielsen pharmacy. Here he lived in a small room, and this was where he cultivated his interest in writing. By the time he left Grimstad for university studies in Christiania (Oslo), he'd qualified as a pharmacist's assistant and was on his way to future renown as a writer. In fact, his 1861 poem *Terje Vigen* and his 1877 drama *Pillars of Society* take place in the skerries offshore from Grimstad. (Oddly enough, another well known Norwegian author, Knut Hamsun, lived at nearby Norholm from 1918 to 1952.)

The Reimann pharmacy and three neighbouring buildings (Haldorsen's House and stable, the Smithy and the Seaman's House) are now collectively known as Reimanngården, and together they constitute the Grimstad Town Museum (☎ 37 04 46 53). The Ibsenhuset museum, in the old Lars Nielsen pharmacy building, contains many of the writer's belongings, which were donated by his widow and son after his death in 1906.

All the buildings are open from 11 am to 5 pm Monday to Saturday and 1 to 5 pm Sunday from 1 May to 15 September. Admission costs Nkr35.

Sjøfartsmuseet

The Grimstad Maritime Museum, housed in the office of the 1842 Hasseldalen shipyard, provides a glimpse into the history of Grimstad's former economic mainstay. It's open the same hours as the Grimstad By Museum. Admission costs Nkr35. While you're there, it's worth climbing the short track from the end of Batteriveien up the hill Binabben for a view over Grimstad.

Organised Tours

Two-hour sailing trips around the outlying skerries on the M/S *Bibben* (☎ 37 04 31 85,

mobile ☎ 94 58 88 46) are offered daily except Saturday from late June to early August. They depart at noon and cost Nkr95. Three-hour fishing trips during the same period are offered at 3 pm on Tuesday and Thursday for Nkr130.

Places to Stay & Eat

For camping, the nearest option is *Bie Appartement og Feriesenter* (☎ 37 04 03 96, fax 37 04 96 88), 800m north-east of the centre along Arendalsveien. Tent/caravan camping costs Nkr150/170 for two people and cabins are Nkr380 to Nkr1000.

One of the most beautiful places around is the Christian-oriented *BIG's Sommerhotel* (☎ 37 04 30 22, fax 37 04 32 63), near the sea about 4km west of the centre. B&B accommodation costs Nkr300/500 for singles/doubles ; tent camping is Nkr75 for two people, and camping in a caravan costs Nkr150. Take bus No 416 and get off at Østerhusveien; from here it's about 1.5km to the hotel.

The odd but cosy *Grimstad Vertshus & Kro* (☎ 37 04 25 00), in the upper part of town, charges a solid mid-range price of Nkr495/580 with shower. The 'Kro' bit refers to an attached restaurant which isn't everyone's favourite.

The only peach-coloured building in this otherwise white town is the *Grimstad Hotel* (☎ 37 04 47 44). Summer rates are Nkr695/780. A fraction cheaper is the *Helmershus Hotel* (☎ 37 04 10 22) at Grømbukt, west of town; here you'll pay Nkr625/750.

Grimstad Hytteutleie (☎ 37 25 10 65, fax 37 25 10 64), Grooseveien 103, can book holiday cabins in the area for one night or one week.

For tasty fish dinners, you can't beat *Dr Berg* (☎ 37 04 44 99, Storgata 2), right at the harbour. Most dishes average around Nkr100 but portions are smaller than a hearty appetite would appreciate. The recommended dining room at the *Helmershus Hotel* (☎ 37 04 10 22, Vesterled 33), west of the centre, serves a well prepared international menu.

Getting There & Away

The Grimstad Rutebilstasjon (☎ 37 04 05 18) is on Storgata at the harbour. The Nor-Way Bussekspress bus between Oslo (4½ hours, Nkr330) and Kristiansand (one hour, Nkr60) calls in at Grimstad one to three times daily. There are buses to and from Arendal (bus Nos 322, 323 and 324) every few minutes (30 minutes, Nkr27).

Getting Around

You can hire bicycles at the Sørlandet Hotell og Kurssenter, Televeien 5, for Nkr90/400 per day/week, or from Sykkelsport, Bergemoveien 15, for Nkr70 per day.

LILLESAND

Between Kristiansand and Arendal you'll pass Lillesand, which has an unspoiled village centre of old whitewashed houses befitting the 'white town' image claimed by so many south-coast towns. The Lillesand Turistkontor (☎ 37 27 23 77, fax 37 27 29 80), Strandgata 14, is open from 9 am to 6 pm weekdays, 10 am to 4 pm Saturday and noon to 4 pm Sunday from 1 May to 31 August.

Places to Stay

The popular *Tingsaker Camping* (☎ 37 27 04 21, fax 37 27 01 47), on the shore 1km east of the centre, is a typical seaside holiday resort with camping, caravans, cabins and occasional crowds. Unfortunately it's rather expensive: for a tent/caravan, car and two people, you'll pay Nkr130; cabins range from Nkr575 for a simple four-person hut to Nkr760 for a plusher affair. At the *Lillesand Vandrerhjem* (☎ 37 27 50 40, fax 37 27 50 40) at Møglestu, beds cost Nkr100 in a dormitory and Nkr150 per person in a double room.

The *Lillesand Hotel Norge* (☎ 37 27 01 44, fax 37 27 30 70, Strandgata 3) considers itself a sort of international relic and is certainly Lillesand's most atmospheric option. It dates from 1837 but has undergone several renovations, the latest of which was in 1964. There are rooms dedicated to King Alfonso XIII of Spain and author Knut Hamsun, both of whom stayed here, and the antiquarian library was inspired by a graphic print by local artist Ferdinand Finne. Single/double rooms cost Nkr595/970.

Getting There & Away

The most pleasant way to reach Lillesand is by boat from Kristiansand (see The Skerries, under Kristiansand). Otherwise, the Nor-Way Bussekspress bus serves Lillesand from Kristiansand (45 minutes, Nkr30) and Arendal (1¼ hours, Nkr50) two to four times daily.

KRISTIANSAND

Busy Kristiansand, the capital of Sørlandet, is Norway's closest port to Denmark and offers the first glimpse of the country for many ferry travellers from the south. As a seaside resort, it's a popular venue for Norwegian families with children but many foreign visitors just pile off the ferries and onto the next train out of town.

Kristiansand's grid-like layout of wide streets was conceived by King Christian IV, who founded the city in 1641. Just a few years ago, the city was known for its polluted air, foul coastline and dying salmon stream, but thanks to local ingenuity, industrial effluent is now cleaned in three massive sewage plants before it's dumped into the sea and the air pollutants are now filtered. The previously choking residue is now sold as concrete strengthener used on offshore oil rigs, netting millions of krona annually. The small boat harbour area has also been nicely spruced up with a fabulous fish market, several upmarket seafood restaurants and a pizza place, and more amenities are planned.

Orientation

Central Kristiansand's locally-termed *kvadraturen*, the square grid pattern measuring six long blocks by nine shorter blocks, is surrounded on two sides by the sea, one side by the river and on the fourth side by a large city park. The rail, bus and ferry terminals form a cluster west of the city centre. Parking is available here and along most city streets. Pedestrianised Markens gate serves as a focus for the central shopping and restaurant district.

Information

The enthusiastic Destinasjon Sørlandet tourist office (☎ 38 12 13 14, fax 38 02 52 55, destsor@online.no, hotell.nextel.no/destinasjon-soerlandet), Dronningens gate 2, is handy to the ferry, rail and bus terminals. From 2 June to 21 August, it's open from 8 am to 7.30 pm weekdays, 8 am to 3 pm Saturday (late June to mid-August until 7.30 pm), and noon to 7.30 pm Sunday. The rest of the year, it's open weekdays from 8 am to 4 pm.

For maps and information on hiking, huts and organised mountain tours in far southern Norway, see the Kristiansand og Oppland Turistforening (☎ 38 02 52 63), Kristian IV gate 12. It's open from 8 am to 3 pm weekdays.

You can change money at the post office at Markens gate 19 or in the bank at the

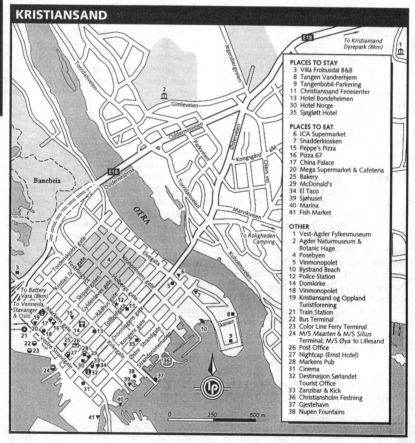

KRISTIANSAND

To Kristiansand Dyrepark (8km)

PLACES TO STAY
3 Villa Frobusdal B&B
8 Tangen Vandrerhjem
9 Tangenbobil-Parkering
11 Christiansand Feriesenter
13 Hotel Bondeheimen
30 Hotel Norge
35 Sjøgløtt Hotel

PLACES TO EAT
6 ICA Supermarket
7 Snadderkiosken
15 Peppe's Pizza
16 Pizza 67
17 China Palace
20 Mega Supermarket & Cafeteria
25 Bakery
29 McDonald's
34 El Taco
39 Sjøhuset
40 Marina
41 Fish Market

OTHER
1 Vest-Agder Fylkesmuseum
2 Agder Naturmuseum & Botanic Hage
4 Posebyen
5 Vinmonopolet
10 Bystrand Beach
12 Police Station
14 Domkirke
18 Vinmonopolet
19 Kristiansand og Oppland Turistforening
21 Train Station
22 Bus Terminal
23 Color Line Ferry Terminal
24 M/S Maarten & M/S Silius Terminal; M/S Øya to Lillesand
26 Post Office
27 Nightcap (Ernst Hotel)
28 Markens Pub
31 Cinema
32 Destinasjon Sørlandet Tourist Office
33 Zanzibar & Kick
36 Christiansholm Festning
37 Gjestehavn
38 Nupen Fountains

0   250   500 m

Color Line ferry terminal, as well as at all the major banks.

Laundry services are available at the Gjestehavn (Guest Harbour), where you'll pay Nkr30 to wash a load and the same to dry.

Christiansholm Festning

The most prominent feature along the Strandepromenaden is Christiansholm Fortress, which was built by royal decree between 1662 and 1672 to keep watch over the strategic Skagerrak straits and protect the city from pirates and rambunctious Swedes. The construction featured walls up to 5m thick and an armoury buried within a concentric inner wall, and was financed by the 1550 local citizens, who were taxed and coerced into labour. Despite – or because of – its strength, the only action it ever experienced was during the Napoleonic Wars in 1807, when soldiers fired on the English ship *Spencer*, whose captain had demanded a handover of the Danish ship *Prins Christian Fredrik*, moored in Kristiansand harbour. The hint was taken and the *Spencer* left without further ado.

In 1872 the structure was damaged when a town fire burned the roof and caused a massive explosion in the powder room. Then during WWII, the occupying Germans plastered over the walls with a layer of concrete, which was subsequently removed. More recently, there have been some major changes, including a new roof with glass clerestory windows, but a ring of eight bronze cannons, cast between 1666 and 1788, still menaces the offshore skerries.

From 15 May to 15 September, the fortress (☎ 38 07 51 50) is open from 9 am to 9 pm daily, with guided tours available at 1 pm daily between 15 June and 15 August. Admission is free.

Nupen Fountain

The rather elaborate three-part fountain near the fortress, which was sculpted by Kjell Nupen, represents the four-masted tall ship of town founder Christian IV, the grid-pattern of the town centre, and the solidity of the modern city. The curious and enormous ceramic jar standing nearby was a gift to the town from the Henning Olsen Is ice-cream factory.

Kristiansand Domkirke

The Kristiansand Cathedral, built in neogothic style in 1885, has seating for 1800 people and is Norway's largest church. It's open to the public from 9 am to 2 pm Monday to Saturday from 1 June to 31 August (until 5 pm from 24 June to 27 July). From 29 June to 8 August, you're welcome to listen to the daily lunch time organ practice. To climb the tower costs Nkr20.

Baneheia & Ravnedalen Parks

Baneheia and Ravnedalen, both north of the city centre, offer wild greenery and a network of lakeside hiking and skiing tracks, some of which are lit up during winter. Both parks were created between 1870 and 1880 by Kristiansand's City Chairman, General Oscar Wergeland. Over a 30-year period, he oversaw the planting of 150,000 coniferous trees and transformed the area into a recreational green belt. From the centre, Baneheia is readily accessed on foot, and is connected to Ravnedalen by a series of pleasant walking tracks.

Agder Naturmuseum & Botaniske Hage

The winding paths through the 50-hectare park at Gimle Estate (☎ 38 09 23 88), Gimleveien 23, will lead you through a botanical garden containing a number of rare (and labelled) trees, shrubs, flowers, rocks, minerals and animals. There's also a historic rose garden dating from 1850. It lies just over 1km from the centre, over the Oddernes bridge. It's open from 10 am to 6 pm Tuesday to Friday and noon to 6 pm Saturday to Monday from 20 June to 20 August, with shorter hours the rest of the year. Admission costs Nkr25.

Posebyen

The Kristiansand Posebyen, or 'Old Town', takes in most of 14 blocks at the northern end of the town's characteristic kvadraturen.

It's worth taking a slow stroll around this enchanting quarter, whose name was given by Norwegian soldiers who came to *reposer* (French for relax). Currently, Kristiansand seniors are constructing a scale model of the city as it appeared when it was designed by Christian IV. Until it's completed, it can be visited only by appointment through the tourist office.

Kristiansand Dyrepark

Over the years, the former Kristiansand zoo gradually expanded into one of Norway's most popular domestic attractions, and is probably *the* favourite holiday destination for children from around the country and other parts of Scandinavia. Although it can't compare with the Disney parks, it also lacks the tackiness of Blackpool, and makes quite a pleasant day out for children and adults. The funfair portion is limited to a log ride and pirate ship cruise, and the zoo portion offers a surprising variety of specimens, including the near-extinct golden lion tamarin. If you want to take advantage of the water park, be sure to bring a swimming costume.

The real highlights, however, are the Nordisk Vilmark (Northern Wilderness), where visitors are transported over the habitat of moose, wolves, lynx and wolverines on elevated boardwalks; and Kardamomme By (Cardamom Town, named for a key ingredient in Scandinavian waffles), a fantasy village based on the popular children's stories of Thorbjørn Egner. The town, which vaguely suggests a setting in northern Africa, has been carefully laid out exactly as it appeared in the illustrated book, and the houses are available as self-catering family accommodation. From 21 May to 16 August, two adults and two children can stay overnight (☎ 38 04 98 00, fax 38 04 33 67) in the charming fantasy houses for Nkr2290 to Nkr3890, including two days' admission to the park.

The park is open from 10 am to 6 pm daily from 20 June to 16 August. Day admission, including all activities, is Nkr175 for adults and Nkr150 for children. To get

there, take the Dyreparkbussen, which operates more or less hourly from 20 June to 16 August.

Vest-Agder Fylkesmuseum

The open-air Vest-Agder folk museum (☎ 38 09 02 28), 4km east of town on the E18, is a collection of farmsteads and hamlets from the Setesdalen region. It also includes displays of traditional costumes, art and children's toys. From 20 June to 20 August, it's open from 10 am to 6 pm daily (from noon on Sunday), and the rest of the year on Sunday only. Admission costs Nkr20.

Setesdalsbanen

The 78km narrow-gauge railway between Kristiansand and Byglandsfjord was opened in 1896 to link Setesdalen with the coast. It was used to transport nickel from the Evje mines and local timber and barrel staves which were used in the salting and export of herring. Although competition from the normal-gauge state railway forced its closure in 1962, the Setesdalsbanen Railway (☎ 38 15 64 82) still runs steam-powered locomotives along the last 20km between Grovane and Kristiansand. In July, trains leave Kristiansand at 6 pm Tuesday to Friday; from 14 to 30 June and 1 to 31 August they run on Sunday only at 11.30 am and 2 pm. The return fare is Nkr50.

Kristiansand Kanonmuseum

The Kristiansand Cannon Museum (☎ 38 08 50 90) at Møvik, 8km south of town, preserves the Germans' heavy Vara Battery which, along with an emplacement at Hanstholm in Denmark, ensured marginal German control of the strategic Skagerrak straits. At each end, four 337-tonne, 38cm cannons with a range of 55km (which was covered in two minutes) controlled traffic along either end of the strait, while the unprotected zone in the middle was heavily mined. In the autumn of 1941, over 1400 soldiers occupied this site.

After the war, the site was renamed Møvik Festning (Møvik Fort) and used by the Norwegian coastal defence forces to keep history from repeating itself. Visitors to the current museum can see the big guns as well as bunkers, barracks, munitions storage (including some daunting 800kg shells), a power generator and all the machinery that accommodated operations there. It's open from 11 am to 6 pm daily from 11 June to 31 August, and Thursday to Sunday only from 1 May to 10 June and 1 to 30 September. Admission costs Nkr40.

The Skerries

In summer, Kristiansand's archipelago of offshore skerries turns into one of the country's greatest sun and sea destinations for Norwegian holiday-makers.

Foreign visitors, who generally spend less time in the area, are normally content with a tourist office cruise either around the islets or a 2½-hour passage along the Blindleia channel to Lillesand. The most popular island, Bragdøy, lies almost within spitting distance of the mainland and boasts a coastal museum, cultural centre and preservation workshop for wooden ships, as well as several nice walks and bathing sites. In the distance, notice the beautiful classic lighthouse Grønningen Fyr, which is still attended by a lighthouse keeper. During school holidays, you can sleep in a dorm bed in the lighthouse for Nkr100; for information, phone Beryl Simonsen (☎ 38 08 55 66).

From 22 June to 16 August, the M/S *Maarten* sails from Kristiansand daily at 11 am and from Lillesand at 2.30 pm. From 29 June to 2 August, the M/S *Silius* does the same trip on Friday and Saturday at 5 pm eastbound and 8.30 pm westbound. Either trip costs Nkr100/150 one-way/return. During the same period, the *Silius* also does two-hour cruises around Randesund, via Bragdøy and several bathing beaches (Nkr90), daily at 11 am and 1.30 pm. (This run can also be used as a ferry service to Bragdøy for Nkr40 return; the last return to the mainland is at 3.15 pm.) On Tuesday and Sunday, there's an evening sightseeing cruise to Ny Hellesund (Nkr120), which was one of 400 Norwegian coastal defences

constructed by the occupying German forces during WWII. For information, contact the Destinasjon Sørlandet tourist office.

Activities

Kristiansand is one of Norway's most popular beach-bathing venues, and if the 15°C waters of the Skagerrak don't put you off, you can join the locals on the sandy Bystrand (town beach). Otherwise, head for the nearby Kristiansand Svømmehall (swimming pool), which charges Nkr35 per session, and then return to the sand to dry off. It's open daily except Sunday in summer.

Kristiansand also caters to scuba divers. Maritime Safaris (☎ 90 76 41 39), Skuteveien 8G, offers diving excursions, scuba diving certification and information on local marine ecology and biology. The tourist office has a list of other companies offering excursions and equipment rental.

Places to Stay

Caravan campers may use the *Tangenbobil-parkering* (☎ 38 12 97 20), not far from the town beach. Tent campers have to go to *Roligheden Camping* (☎ 38 09 67 22, kherlof@online.no), at a popular beach 3km east of the centre on Framnesveien, which also has four-person cabins for Nkr500 to Nkr660. Take bus No 15 from the centre. The Kristiansand youth hostel, *Tangen Vandrerhjem* (☎ 38 02 83 10, fax 38 02 75 05, Skansen 8), lies in a rather bland warehouse landscape, a 10 minute walk northeast of the fortress. It's open year-round and charges Nkr150 for dorm beds and Nkr310/450 for singles/doubles.

In summer, the central *Hotel Bondeheimen* (☎ 38 02 44 40, Kirkegata 15) or 'farmers' home' has rooms starting at Nkr495/690. The small and cosy *Sjøglott Hotel* (☎/fax 38 02 21 20), known as 'det lille hotel' (the little hotel), charges Nkr350/530 for rooms with a toilet but no shower and Nkr490/660 with all facilities. For something a little more rustic, there's the cosy *Villa Frobusdal B&B* (☎ 38 07 05 15, fax 38 07 01 15, Frobusdalen 2), at the edge of Baneheia but within 10 minutes walk of the centre. It's open year-round except in December and rooms start at Nkr490/630.

Small self-catering student flats at *Christiansand Feriesenter (☎ 38 07 98 00, fax 38 07 98 01, Tollbodgata 46)* are centrally located and cost from Nkr600 to Nkr795 per day for up to six people.

The classy *Hotel Norge (☎ 38 02 00 00, fax 38 02 35 30, Dronningens gate 5)* has summer rates of Nkr570/770. Just off the lobby, you can relax amid the shelves of the antiquarian library.

Anker Ferieleiligheter (☎ 38 06 31 61, fax 38 07 07 01, igruppen@online.no) and Holtan Rom & Hytteutleie (☎/fax 38 13 96 16) both book flats, holiday cabins, small guesthouses, B&Bs and rooms in private homes.

Places to Eat

The *Mega* supermarket, opposite the train station, has a cheap cafeteria, and there's a good *bakery* on Rådhus gate near the post office. The large *ICA* supermarket, on the corner of Kongens gate and Elvegata, offers a wide range of groceries and is open until 9 pm weekdays and 6 pm on Saturday.

If you want to follow the locals for a great meal deal, go to the *Snadderkiosken*, near the town beach. It does a relatively vast and great value menu: hot dogs starting at Nkr11, pizzas for Nkr49, cod with mashed potatoes and a green salad for Nkr43 and grilled chicken for Nkr44.

For tacos and burritos in an informal setting, you can't beat *El Taco (☎ 28 07 14 13)*, which serves Mexican-style platters with a drink for Nkr50 to Nkr80. Another popular but more formal Mexican choice is *Amigo's (☎ 38 02 67 60)*, on Vestre Strandgate.

Peppe's Pizza (☎ 38 02 23 22, Gyldenløves gate 7) has pizzas big enough for two people from Nkr114. For a real pizza treat, try *Pizza 67 (☎ 38 02 46 78, Markens gate 35)*, which is actually an Icelandic chain. The counter-cultural theme supports such pizza concoctions as Sergeant Peppers, Flower Power and the throat-searing TNT. *China Palace*, on Markens gate, offers in-expensive lunch specials. You'll find one of the world's most unusual *McDonald's* housed in an 1897 bank building, on the corner of Markens gate and Dronningens gate.

For more of a splurge, join the crowds at the popular harbourside seafood restaurants *Marina (☎ 38 12 07 21)*, at Østre Havn, and *Sjøhuset (☎ 38 02 62 60, Østre Strandgate 12a)*, where you'll pay as much for the setting as for the good meals. For the freshest and best value seafood around, try the *fish market*, where the vendors will cook up the catch of the day for you to enjoy with a beer on the outdoor patio.

Entertainment

The most popular hang-outs for the young include the *Zanzibar* in summer *(☎ 38 02 62 44, Dronningens gate 8)*, which is open year-round, and the attached outdoor café, *Kick*, which presents live music and dancing. *Markens Pub*, on the corner of Markens gate and Tollbodgata, has disco music in the evening from Wednesday to Saturday. *Nightcap (☎ 38 12 86 00, Rådhus gate 2)*, at the Ernst Hotel, is a popular night spot for the 22 to 35-year-old crowd. There's also a large *cinema* on Vestre Strandgate.

Getting There & Away

Nor-Way Bussekspress buses head north at 9 am daily to Voss (11 hours, Nkr480), with connections to Bergen (12 hours, Nkr540). Buses to and from Oslo (5½ hours, Nkr350) run twice daily during the week and once daily on weekends. To and from Stavanger (five hours, Nkr260), they run two or three times daily. Regional buses depart several times daily to Arendal (1¼ hours, Nkr86) and Flekkefjord (three hours, Nkr128). To Evje (one hour, Nkr59), buses run six to eight times a day. All local bus fares are half-price for students and spouses.

There are daily trains to Oslo (five hours, Nkr400) and Stavanger (3¼ hours, Nkr290).

With a vehicle, access to the E18, north of the centre, is via Vestre Strandgate.

For information on ferries to Denmark see the Getting There & Away chapter.

Getting Around

City buses around the centre cost Nkr13 per ride; to the Kristiansand Dyrepark costs Nkr19. In summer, you can get around on the Sykkeltaxi (☎ 91 32 62 64) bicycle rickshaws, which are based on the corner of Markens gate and Rådhus gate. The tourist office loans out simple green bicycles free of charge, with payment of a Nkr200 deposit. For more sophisticated bikes, check out the Sykkelsenter (☎ 38 02 68 35) on Grimtorvet, which charges Nkr130/350 per day/week.

MANDAL

The white town of Mandal, Norway's southernmost town, is best known for Norway's finest bathing beach. The 800m long Sjøsanden, about 1km from the centre, is Norway's Copacabana and the backdrop is as lovely as the sand and sea itself. When the sun isn't cooperating, you can always stroll through the strip of white clapboard buildings of the old town, north of the Mandalselva river. Historically, the town thrived by supplying the timber trade with its ample pine and oak forests.

Information

For queries, TuristInfo Mandal (☎ 38 27 83 00, fax 38 27 83 01, turistkontor@mandalnett .no), Adolf Tidemandsgate 2, is open from 9 am to 4 pm weekdays in summer.

Mandal Museum

On a rainy day, you may want to have a look around the Mandal Museum (☎ 38 27 30 00), Store Elvegata 5/6, which displays a host of historical maritime and fishing artefacts and works by local artists, including Amaldus Nielsen and Adolph Tidemand, and a piece by Mandal's favourite son, Gustav Vigeland. It's open from 11 am to 5 pm Monday to Saturday and 2 to 5 pm Sunday from 1 July to 15 August. Admission costs Nkr10.

Places to Stay & Eat

Campers can stay at the *Sandnes Bobilcamp (☎ 38 26 51 51)*, which lies east of the Mandalselva, 2km north of town. Tent/caravan camping costs Nkr100/120.

Many travellers wind up at the *Købmandsgården Vandrerhjem (☎ 38 26 12 76, fax 38 26 33 02, Store Elvegaten 57)*, which charges Nkr175 per person in a shared double room, including breakfast. If you prefer to stay on the beach, *Sjøsanden Feriesenter (☎ 38 26 60 37, fax 38 26 09 22)*, just a few metres west of its eponymous beach, charges Nkr490 for double rooms and Nkr600 to Nkr750 for a two to six-person self-catering apartment. It also allows tent camping for Nkr60 per tent.

The *First Hotel Solborg (☎ 38 26 66 66, fax 38 26 48 22, Nesveien 1)*, west of the centre, has single/double rooms for Nkr550/800. It's only a 10-minute walk from the beach but on those less-than-optimum days, guests can use the indoor pool. Its dining room is probably the best formal restaurant in town and it also has a bar and weekend disco. For other nightlife possibilities, try the *Soldekket* and *Grand* restaurants. If you just want a good mid-range meal, the *Biffen* and *Dr Nielsen* restaurants serve fish and meat dishes for around Nkr150.

Getting There & Away

The Mandal Rutebilstasjon lies north of the river, just a short walk from the historic district. Bus No 301 connects Mandal with Oslo-Kristiansand-Stavanger trains at Marnardal Station (30 minutes, Nkr29). The Nor-Way Bussekspress coastal route between Stavanger (3½ hours, Nkr230) and Kristiansand (45 minutes, Nkr60) passes through Mandal two to three times daily.

LINDESNES

As the southernmost point in Norway, Lindesnes (literally 'arching land peninsula') provides an occasional glimpse of the power nature can unleash between the Skagerrak and the North Sea and, as the brochures point out, 'the camera angles are better than at Nordkapp (1518km away as the crow flies). However, not only photographers will be inspired by Lindesnes Fyr, the classic lighthouse which rises above the cape.

The first lighthouse on the site was fired up in 1655 using coal and tallow candles to warn ships off the rocks. The current one, built in 1915, has been electrified of course, and is visible up to 19½ nautical miles out to sea.

Also of interest is the Lindesnes District Museum & Gustav Vigeland Gallery, which reveals the history of the Lindesnes district and the inspiration behind the works of sculptor Gustav Vigeland. It's open from 11 am to 4 pm Monday to Saturday and 1 to 5 pm Sunday from 21 June to 9 August.

Places to Stay & Eat

The *Lindesnes Camping og Hytteutleie* (☎ *38 25 88 74, fax 38 25 88 92*), on the shore 3.5km from Lindesnes Fyr, is open year-round (camping vans only in winter). In the high season, tent camping costs under Nkr100 for two people, camping vans can be rented for Nkr350 and cabins range from Nkr200 to Nkr560. About 11km north of the cape lies the simple but cosy *Lindesnes Gjestehus* (☎ *38 25 97 00, fax 38 25 97 65*), which charges Nkr325 per person, including breakfast.

Getting There & Away

Buses from Mandal (one hour, Nkr46) travel the length of the peninsula all the way to the lighthouse.

FLEKKEFJORD

The town of Flekkefjord first emerged as an entity in 1660, but thanks to its competition against royally supported Kristiansand, the Danish king shut it down two years later. Despite that, the fishing industry thrived and by the time it was granted town status in 1842, it was a significant herring fishery and became a major tannery. The town now has a population of 6000.

Information

The Flekkefjord Tourist Office (☎ 38 32 42 54, fax 38 32 12 33), Kirkegata 50, is open from 15 June to 15 August from 10 am to 6 pm weekdays, until 3 pm on Saturday and from noon to 5 pm on Sunday. At other times, it's open weekdays from 9 am to 3 pm.

Things to See

For a view over the town, make the short climb to the top of **Lilleheia**, which is accessed from Dr Kraftsgata. You may also want to stroll through the **Hollenderbyen** (Dutch Town) district, with its narrow streets and old timber buildings. Here you'll find the **Flekkefjord Museum**, which is housed in an 18th century home. Other museum buildings include the **waterfront warehouses** in adjacent Sjøbodene. It's open from 11 am to 5 pm weekdays, noon to 3 pm weekends.

The octagonal **Flekkefjord church**, which was built of logs in 1832, was designed by architect H Lindstow, who also designed the Royal Palace in Oslo. Note that the columns, steeple and baptismal font are also octagonal, as are the tower on the Grand Hotel and numerous public structures around Flekkefjord. The church is open to visitors during the summer months.

Places to Stay & Eat

The nearest camping ground is *Egenes Camping* (☎ *38 32 01 48, fax 38 32 01 11, egenes@online.no*) beside the lake Seluravatnet on the E39, 5km east of Flekkefjord. Tent camping is Nkr50/90 without/with a car, and caravan camping is Nkr100. Campers also pay Nkr15 per person. Four/six-person cabins cost Nkr250/400 and self-catering flats range from Nkr500 to Nkr600. There's also boat and canoe hire and a snack bar, cafeteria and outdoor restaurant. Take bus No 486 (10 minutes, Nkr19) towards Dybvik.

The *Bondeheimen Hotel* (☎ *38 32 21 44, fax 38 32 29 79, Elvegata 7-9*) has simple single/double rooms for Nkr335/490 and an à la carte restaurant and cafeteria. The more upmarket *First Hotel Maritim* (☎ *38 32 33 33, fax 38 32 43 12*) has summer rates of Nkr445/590. The attached bistro serves light meals and the licensed restaurant offers dancing six nights a week.

Getting There & Away

The Nor-Way Bussekspress bus between Kristiansand (two hours, Nkr140) and

Stavanger (2½ hours, Nkr150) passes through Flekkefjord. The nearest train station is at Sira, on the Oslo-Stavanger line, which is accessed by bus No 461 to Gyland (one hour, Nkr27) and bus Nos 480 and 481 to Sira (30 minutes, Nkr26).

EGERSUND

Egersund, arranged around an island-dotted cove amid low hills, was named after the sound which divides it from the offshore island of Eigerøy. The identity of the first known settler in the region, Laithigar, was revealed by an ancient rune stone found in nearby Møgedal, and other sources indicate that there has been a church here since at least 1292. Nearly two-thirds of the original town was gutted by fire in 1843, after which Egersund was reconstructed with wide streets to thwart the spread of future fires. From 1847 to 1979, the local economy was sustained by the pottery and porcelain industry but today Egersund's 8000 people derive most of their income from fishing and the oil and gas industry.

Information

The Egersund Tourist Office (☎ 51 46 82 33, fax 51 46 82 39, bjaadnes@sn.no), Jernbaneveien 2, is open from 20 May to 31 August. The rest of the year, it has a desk at Skrivergården, Strangaten 58.

Dalane Bygdemuseum & Egersund Fayance

The two-part Dalane Folk Museum (☎ 51 49 14 79) features a series of historic timber homes at Slettebø, 4km north of town along the Rv42, and the very worthwhile Egersund Fayance Museum (☎ 51 49 26 40) at Eia, 35km north-east of town. The latter displays the history and wares of Egersund Fayance, the ceramic and porcelain firm which sustained the entire district from 1847 to 1979. The main exhibit is open from 11 am to 5 pm weekdays, mid-June to mid-August, and Sunday from 1 to 6 pm. Egersund Fayance is open the same hours mid-May to mid-August; the rest of the year, both places are open on Sunday

only. Admission to either sector costs Nkr20. For the Dalane Folk Museum, take bus No 233, marked Sirdalsruta (Nkr17); for Egersund Fayance, use bus No 232, marked Lagård or Bybuss (Nkr17).

Historic Buildings

Thanks to a lack of funds for 'modernisation', many historic timber buildings remain. **Strandgaten**, a street of timber houses constructed after the fire of 1843, is worth a stroll. The **Skrivergården** (judicial residence) at Strandgaten 58 was constructed in 1846 as the home of the local magistrate Christian Feyer. The town park along the same street served as his private garden. The **Bilstadhuset** at Nygaten 14 still has its original timberwork, including a sailmaker's loft upstairs; it belongs to the Dalane Folk Museum. Also picturesque are the lovely timber homes and warehouses at **Sogndalsstrand**, south of Hauge, 30km south-east of Egersund. You can get there on bus No 231 from Egersund (30 minutes, Nkr42).

If you're driving along the Rv42, have a look at 19th century **Terland Klopp**, 10km north of town. This lovely 60m bridge is constructed in 21 stone arches and is on UNESCO's list of historical monuments.

Egersund Kirke

The earliest parts of the Egersund Church date from the 1620s but some features are older. The carved altarpiece, a depiction of the baptism and crucifixion of Christ by Stavanger carpenter Thomas Christophersen and painted by artist Peter Reimers, dates back to 1607 and the baptismal font is dated 1583. The church is open from 11 am to 2 pm daily from 20 June to 1 August.

Varberg

You'll get a fine view over the town centre from the summit of Varberg, the hill with the prominent TV mast. The path to the top takes about 15 minutes from the centre of town.

Eigerøy Fyr

Eigerøy Fyr, the majestic 1855 lighthouse on Midbrødøy, near the south-western tip of Eigerøy island, is accessible from the car park by a 2km footpath. There are great views any time (especially on stormy nights!) but the building itself is open only on Sundays in July from 11 am to 4 pm. Take the Nord Eigerøy bus from the Rutebilstasjon and get off at the sign 'Eigerøy fyr' on the Rv502 (15 minutes, Nkr17). From there, it's an hour walk down the Fyrvegen road to the lighthouse.

For a bit more walking, take the Sør Eigerøy bus from the town centre to Augland (15 minutes, Nkr17) and get off at Kværner. From there, it's a 20-minute walk along the road to a lovely area with several short hiking tracks.

Places to Stay & Eat

In summer, the lovely old **Grand Hotell** (☎ 51 49 18 11, fax 51 49 36 46; Johan Feyersgata 3) charges Nkr500/660 for singles/doubles. The most convenient camping ground is **Steinsnes Camping** (☎/fax 51 49 41 36), 3km north of town at Tengs. Campers pay Nkr25 per person; tents without/with a vehicle cost Nkr70/100 and caravan camping is Nkr100. Cabins cost from Nkr220 to Nkr430. To get there, take bus No 241 or 251.

The **Vinstokken** (☎ 51 49 06 60, Strandgaten 60) is a very nice French-style restaurant in the historical district. For something cheaper, try a pizza at **Dolly Dimple's** (☎ 51 49 00 00, Sandakergaten 9).

Getting There & Away

The best way to reach Egersund is by rail. To and from Oslo (eight hours, Nkr540), trains run via Kristiansand three to six times daily. There are also numerous daily services to and from Stavanger (one hour, Nkr100). An international ferry now operates between Bergen and Hanstholm in Denmark, via Egersund (but it's not available for transport between Bergen and Egersund). For details, see the Getting There & Away chapter.

The Interior

Much of the interior portion of southern Norway lies within the sparsely-populated Telemark county (yes, it lends its name to that graceful nordic ski manoeuvre – see the boxed text 'The Virtues of Skinny Skis' in the Facts for the Visitor chapter). This lovely region is characterised by steep forested terrain, high plateaux and countless lakes, and also takes in parts of Buskerud county and the northern portions of Aust-Agder and Vest-Agder.

Public transport in this region isn't particularly convenient; buses run infrequently and the rail lines cover only the area between Bø and Kongsberg, so sightseeing is best done by car. For Telemark tourist information, contact Telemarkreiser (☎ 35 53 03 00), Postboks 2813 Kjørbekk, 3702 Skien.

KONGSBERG

Kongsberg, founded in 1624, owes its existence to the discovery of one of the world's purest silver deposits in the nearby Numedal Valley. In the resulting silver rush, it briefly became the second largest town in Norway, with 8000 inhabitants, including 4000 miners and 2000 farmers. Today, the surrounding hills bear cast-off mining relics and the scars of over 300 shafts. The main shaft of the largest mine, the Kongsgruvene (Royal Silver Mine), plunges 1070m into the mountain, to a depth of 550m below sea level.

History

The history of Kongsberg begins and ends with silver, which was discovered by two children and an ox in 1623. Their father attempted to sell the windfall but the king's soldiers got wind of it and the family was arrested and forced to disclose the site of their discovery. (It's almost certain that silver was discovered earlier, but by wiser individuals who kept it to themselves, lest the peaceful folk and their lands be subject to government interference, pillage, regulation and despoliation.) Between 1623 and 1957, a total of 1.35 million kilograms of pure thread-like 'wire' silver was produced for the royal coffers. Kongsberg is still home to the national mint but the last mine – unable to turn a profit in the modern context – closed in 1957.

Orientation

Kongsberg is neatly split into old and new sections by the falls of the river Numedalslågen. The new eastern section takes in the main shopping district, the tourist office and the rail and bus terminals. In the older section west of the river lie the museum, historic church and youth hostel.

Information

The tourist office (☎ 32 73 50 00, fax 32 73 50 01, office@kongsberg-turistservice.no, www.kongsberg.net), conveniently opposite the train station at Storgata 35, is open from 26 June to 16 August from 9 am to 5 pm weekdays and 10 am to 5 pm on weekends. The rest of the year, hours are from 9 am to 4.30 pm weekdays and 10 am to 2 pm Saturday.

Laundry services are available at Vask & Rens, Nymoens Torg 20, and at Kongsberg Renseri, Schwabesgaten 1. Both lie near the train station.

Kongsberg Domkirke

Norway's largest baroque church, which lies in the Old Town west of the river, was officially opened in 1761. The rococo-style interior features ornate chandeliers and an unusual altar that combines the altarpiece, high pulpit and organ pipes on a single wall.

From 18 May to 31 August, guided tours (Nkr20) are available from 10 am to 4 pm weekdays, 10 am to 1 pm Saturday and 2 to 5 pm Sunday. The rest of the year, the church is open from 10 am to noon Tuesday to Friday.

Norsk Bergwerksmuseum

The worthwhile Norwegian Mining Museum (☎ 32 72 32 00), over the bridge in a 1844 smelter, tells the story of mining in Kongsberg with relics, models and mineral displays, and the old smelting furnaces still survive in the basement. Peripheral sections include the Royal Mint, which was moved from Akershus Fortress in Oslo to the source of silver in 1686, and a ski museum featuring mainly silver trophies won by Norwegian skiers. At certain times, Olympic ski champions Birger Ruud and Petter Hugsted guide visitors around this section.

The museums are open from 10 am to 5 pm daily from 1 July to 15 August, and the rest of the time from mid-May to late September from 10 am or noon until 4 pm (and the rest of the year on Sunday only). Admission is Nkr40.

Lågdalsmuseet

The Lågdal folk museum (☎ 32 73 34 68), with a collection of 32 period farmhouses and miners' cottages, an indoor sampling of recreated 19th century workshops, a local WWII resistance museum, and an optics museum, is a 10 minute walk south-east of the train station. Turn left on Bekkedokk and follow the signposted walkway which parallels the tracks. From 24 June to 18 August, it's open from 11 am to 5 pm daily (later on Wednesdays in July), with guided tours at 11 am and 1.30 and 3.30 pm. In late May and early June, it's open weekends only. Admission costs Nkr25.

Kongsgruvene

Kongsberg's *raison d'être* is the profusion of silver veins in the surrounding district, and in summer, tours into the largest mine, the Kongsgruvene, are available daily. In addition, there are special tours, ranging from easy to mildly adventurous. Information on all tours and times is available through the Norsk Bergverksmuseum (☎ 32 72 32 00, fax 32 72 32 10).

The most frequent and popular mine tour leaves from the signposted Kongsgruvene, which lies about 700m from Saggrenda (8km from Kongsberg). It begins with a 2.3km rail ride along the *stoll*, a tunnel which was painstakingly chipped through

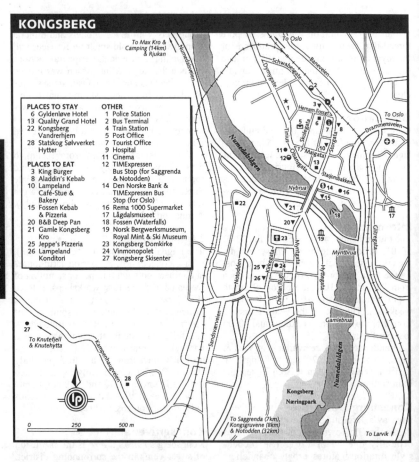

KONGSBERG

PLACES TO STAY
6 Gyldenløve Hotel
13 Quality Grand Hotel
22 Kongsberg Vandrerhjem
28 Statskog Sølvverket Hytter

PLACES TO EAT
3 King Burger
8 Aladdin's Kebab
10 Lampeland Café-Stue & Bakery
15 Fossen Kebab & Pizzeria
20 B&B Deep Pan
21 Gamle Kongsberg Kro
25 Jeppe's Pizzeria
26 Lampeland Konditori

OTHER
1 Police Station
2 Bus Terminal
4 Train Station
5 Post Office
7 Tourist Office
9 Hospital
11 Cinema
12 TIMExpressen Bus Stop (for Saggrenda & Notodden)
14 Den Norske Bank & TIMExpressen Bus Stop (for Oslo)
16 Rema 1000 Supermarket
17 Lågdalsmuseet
18 Fossen (Waterfalls)
19 Norsk Bergwerksmuseum, Royal Mint & Ski Museum
23 Kongsberg Domkirke
24 Vinmonopolet
27 Kongsberg Skisenter

the mountain in order to drain water from the mines. Constructed without machinery or dynamite – the rock was removed by heating it with fire, then throwing water on the rock to crack it – the job progressed at the laborious pace of about 7cm per day and took 73 years (1782 to 1855) to complete its 7km.

Inside, visitors are guided around some of the equipment used in the extraction of silver, including an ingenious creaking and grinding lift which replaced 300m of the

climb between the surface and work area on 65 wet and slippery ladders. Tours run daily in July and early August at 11 am and 12.30, 2 and 3.30 pm. From mid-May to the end of June and in late August, only the first three tours run. In September, they're at 2 pm on Sunday only. Tours cost Nkr55. Be sure to bring warm clothing, as the underground temperatures can be rather chilly.

An alternative is a two-hour walk through the Christian VII mine, which operated between 1843 and 1865, and finishes up in the constricted 'North Passage'. This trip also begins and ends with a 2.3km train ride. It runs on Monday and Thursday at 5 pm, from 1 July to 17 August, and costs Nkr150. If you prefer staying above ground, you can follow the route to work taken by the miners, who left Kongsberg at 4 am to begin their 15-hour work day. The route passes the waterworks which powered the underground machinery and lots of abandoned equipment, finishing up at the Saxony mine. This special tour (Nkr45) operates only once in summer, normally in early to mid-July but can be arranged for groups at any time.

The most exciting option is the 'rope and torch' tour, which begins with a 1km walk through Prince Fredrik's mine. You must then abseil by torchlight down 112m into the mine (after a crash course in abseiling), where you'll see vast mined areas and lots of historical equipment. These tours cost Nkr800, including abseiling instruction, and run three times over summer; contact the Konsberg tourist office for specific dates.

Before or after your mine tour, check out the Sakkerhusene (derived from the German *zechenhäuse*, 'mine houses'), three buildings which were constructed between 1867 and 1874 and served as administrative offices, housing for workers, and areas for washing and leisure. They now house a small museum, a cafeteria and a souvenir shop selling rocks and fashion leather goods.

On the hour on weekdays, bus No 390 links Kongsberg with Sølverket (10 minutes, Nkr20), which is the halt for Kongsgruvene and the other mines. At other times, take the Oslo-Notodden TIMExpress bus to Saggrenda (10 minutes, Nkr20) and walk the 15 minutes from there.

Activities
Kongsberg's best hiking and cross-country skiing is found in the green, forested Knutefjell, immediately west of the town, and the Kongsberg tourist office sells the map *Knutefjell Turkart med Skiløyper*, which

details the maintained hiking and skiing tracks.

From town, the most convenient route heads into the hills from the Kongsberg Skisenter, from where it's a stiff 6km climb to Knutehytta hut, at 695m in the heart of the range. In winter, the steepest part of the climb may be negotiated on the Skisenter's 1700m chairlift. An easier and slightly shorter route to Knutehytta leads north from Meheia, on the Notodden road (accessible on Notodden buses). You can then return to town via the Skisenter. In winter, transport to the Skisenter is by Skitaxi, which costs Nkr25 one-way.

Accommodation at Knutehytta (☎ 32 73 12 83) costs Nkr240/370/465 per person with breakfast/half-board/full board. The Statskog-Sølverket (☎ 32 77 14 00), Kridtmølleveien 20, has 14 cabins scattered around the western part of Knutefjell, with four to 14 beds each. These cost from Nkr250 to Nkr400 per cabin per night.

Special Events
Kongsberg's best known annual event is the famed four-day Kongsberg Jazz Festival (☎ 32 73 31 66, fax 32 73 13 66, www .kongsberg-jazzfestival.no), which takes place in early July and attracts well known artists from around the world.

Places to Stay
Your best accommodation option is probably the *Kongsberg Vandrerhjem* (☎ 32 73 20 24), which bridges the gap between the budget and middle-range. It lies less than 2km from the train station; follow the Storgata shopping street, cross the bridge, turn right and follow the pedestrian walkway over Route 40 to the hostel. Dorm beds cost Nkr185 (including breakfast) and single/double rooms are Nkr400/540 (linen costs Nkr60 extra). Other meals are also available.

The nearest camping ground is at *Max Kro & Camping* (☎ 32 76 44 05, fax 32 76 44 72), 14km north-west of town on Route 37 towards Rjukan. Tent camping costs Nkr50/70 for two people without/with a car, and simple four/six-bed self-catering cabins are Nkr250/300. Use either the once daily (weekdays only) bus No 412 (25 minutes, Nkr22) or the more frequent Kongsberg-Rjukan Nor-Way Bussekspress bus (15 minutes, Nkr22). Nearer to town, *Statskog Sølvverket Hytter* (☎ 32 77 1400, fax 32 77 14 01) offers 14 simple cabins with open fireplaces for Nkr250 to Nkr400.

Of Kongsberg's two finer hotels, the *Gyldenløve Hotel* (☎ 32 73 17 44, fax 32 72 47 80, Hermann Fossgata 1) offers the lowest rates at Nkr520/640 for singles/doubles. Its competitor, the *Quality Grand Hotel* (☎ 32 73 20 29 or ☎ 32 77 28 00, fax 32 73 41 29, Christian Augustsgata 2), near the river, charges Nkr580/800 with breakfast.

About 22km north of town on Rv40 is the *Lampeland Kurs- & Turistsenter* (☎ 32 75 20 46), where single/double rooms cost Nkr495/650 and family rooms for up to four people, with breakfast, start at Nkr700. This outdoor-oriented centre features rustic outdoor barbecues and also hires out canoes and bicycles.

Places to Eat

The popular *Gamle Kongsberg Kro* (☎ 32 73 16 33), south of the river bridge, offers a varied menu, moderate prices and outdoor seating with a fine view of the upper river chutes. More dramatic waterworks are seen – and heard – at the *Fossen Kebab & Pizzeria*, immediately east of the bridge, where you can enjoy pizza, burgers, chicken or light Middle Eastern dishes on a sunny terrace cooled by the spray. Other pizza choices include the *B&B Deep Pan* (☎ 32 72 08 50), immediately south of the bridge, and *Jeppe's Pizza* (☎ 32 73 15 00, Kirkegata 6) in the Old Town. The latter also offers steaks and a few Mexican-style dishes.

The basic *King Burger*, opposite the train station, grills up fast fare, and *Aladdin's Kebab* on Storgata does slightly more sophisticated kebabs, schwarmas and felafels. For coffee and light snacks, try *Lampe-land Café-stue* (☎ 32 73 31 30), on Storgata. However, it's not to be confused with the *Lampe-land Konditori*, on Kirkegata. There's a bakery at the *Rimi* supermarket, west of the train station, and another at Storgata 19. A good grocery selection is available at the *Rema 1000*, east of the bridge, and the Vinmonopolet is just south of the church.

Getting There & Away

By rail, Kongsberg is one to 1½ hours from Oslo (Nkr105); services run four to six times daily. NSB buses between Kongsberg and Larvik (2¼ hours, Nkr105) run two or three times daily (once on Sunday).

Nor-Way Bussekspress TIMExpressen buses (☎ 35 02 60 00) connect Kongsberg with Oslo (Nkr100, 1½ hours), Saggrenda (10 minutes, Nkr20) and Notodden (30 minutes, Nkr40) every half-hour through much of the day. Towards Oslo, they stop at Den Norske Bank; towards Saggrenda and Notodden, in front of the cinema.

Getting Around

The tourist office hires out bicycles for Nkr100 per day.

THE TELEMARK CANAL

The 104km Telemark Canal system, a series of lakes and canals which connect Skien and Dalen (with a branch from Lunde to Notodden), lifts and lowers boats a total of 72m in 18 locks. Most canal travellers bring their own boats (the return trip from Skien to Dalen/Notodden costs Nkr700/300 per boat) but boat-less visitors can choose between popular canal cruises or hiring a canoe and paddling on their own.

Notodden

Industrial Notodden has little to recommend it to tourists but it's still one of Telemark's most visited places, thanks to the impressive Heddal stave church. This lovely and imposing structure, flanked by a tidy churchyard and gentle agricultural land, lies about 5km west of town on the Rv11. For visitor information, contact the Notodden Turistkontor (☎ 35 01 35 20), Birkelandsgata 3.

Heddal Stave Church Heddal, the largest of Norway's 31 remaining stave churches, dates from 1242 but parts of the chancel date from as early as 1147. In 1952 it was heavily restored.

As with all stave churches, it's constructed around Norwegian pine support pillars – in this case, 12 large ones and six smaller ones, all topped by fearsome visages – and has four carved entrance portals. Of special interest are the lovely 1668 'rose' paintings on the rear wall, a runic inscription in the outer passageway (which identifies that construction was completed on 25 October 1242) and the 'Bishop's chair', which was made of an old pillar in the 13th century. Its ornate carvings relate the pagan tale of the Viking, Sigurd the Dragon-slayer, which has been reworked into a Christian parable involving Jesus Christ and the devil. The altarpiece originally dates from 1667 but was restored in 1908, and the exterior bell tower was added in 1850.

The displays in the adjacent building describe the history of the church and its carvings and reveal the finer points of general stave church construction. There's also a cafeteria.

The church and exhibits are open from 10 am to 5 pm, 15 May to 19 June and 21 August to 15 September, and from 9 am to 7 pm between 20 June and 20 August. On Saturdays, when weddings are held, it may be closed to the public. On Sundays from Easter to November, services are held at 11 am (visitors are welcome but to avoid disruption, they must remain for the entire one-hour service); after 1 pm, the church is again open to the public. Admission (except for the Sunday services) costs Nkr25. From Notodden, take bus No 301.

Heddal Bygdetun The Heddal Rural Museum (☎ 35 02 08 40), near the stave church, includes a collection of houses from rural Telemark. It's open from 11 am to 5 pm daily from 8 June to 18 August.

Hydro Notodden Daily from 1 June to 31 May, noon to 4 pm, you can visit the historic Hydro Notodden complex (☎ 35 01 71 00) in the Hydro industrial park. This interesting museum is in the furnace house of the old 1907 potassium nitrate (saltpeter) factory and includes historic industrial exhibits and paintings by Norwegian fairy-tale illustrator Theodor Kittelsen. Admission costs Nkr20.

Special Events In early August, Notodden hosts a well attended blues festival. For programs and information, contact the organising committee, Notodden Blues Festival (☎ 35 02 76 50, fax 35 02 76 51, nbf@bluesfest.no, www.bluesfest.no), PO Box 211, N-3671 Notodden.

Places to Stay The cheapest option in town is the *Nordlandia Telemark Hotel* (☎ 35 01 20 80, fax 35 01 40 60), on the Torget, which has summer single/double rates of Nkr440/580. *Notodden Camping* (☎ 35 01 33 10), 3km out along the Rv11 then 200m south on the Reshjemveien, has tent and caravan sites, plus cabins for rent (Nkr290 to Nkr390). From the centre, take bus No 301 and get off at the Reshjemveien.

Getting There & Away Between Kongsberg and Notodden (30 minutes, Nkr40), TIMExpressen buses run approximately every half-hour. The Oslo-Stavanger rail line also passes through Notodden.

Skien

Industrial Skien is visited mainly by travellers along the Telemark Canal. For tourist information, see the Skien Turistkontor (☎ 35 58 19 10, fax 35 52 26 61), Nedre Hjellegata 18.

Venstøp Museum Author and playwright Henrik Ibsen was born in Skien on 20 March 1828, the son of a local shopkeeper and owner of a spirit distillery. In 1835, the family fell on hard times and moved out to the farm Venstøp, where they stayed for seven years. The 1815 farmhouse, along with the brewery, servants' quarters, storehouse, barn and English-style gardens, has now been converted into a worthwhile museum (☎ 35 52 57 49). It's open from 10 am to 6 pm daily from 15 May to 31 August. From town, take bus No 255 (five minutes, Nkr18).

Places to Stay The year-round hostel *Skien Vandrerhjem (☎ 35 59 95 51, Moflatvien 67)* has dorm beds for Nkr120, singles/doubles for Nkr280/400 and breakfast for Nkr40. There's also a relatively cheap hotel, *Nye Herkules* (☎ 35 59 63 11, fax 35 59 65 88, Moflatvien 59), where rooms cost Nkr400/560.

Kjeldal

Telemark Vannsport (summer ☎/fax 35 94 74 05; winter ☎ 33 44 16 43, fax 33 44 16 97), at the Kjeldal locks, hires out canoes, kayaks and equipment. An organised tour including a two-person canoe with paddles and life jackets, one-way boat transport from Kjeldal to Kviteseid and, two days later, a taxi from Ulefoss back to Kjeldal, costs Nkr770. The handy *Kjeldal Vandrerhjem (☎/fax 35 94 74 05)*, at the locks, makes a great base for operations. Dorm beds cost Nkr90 and rooms are Nkr130/210.

Kviteseid

There's another useful hostel at Kviteseid, on the lake Sundkilen. The *Kviteseid Vandrerhjem (☎ 35 05 32 61, fax 35 05 37 36)* charges Nkr110 for dorm beds and Nkr200/300 for single/double rooms.

Dalen

Visitor information for the beautifully located town of Dalen is dispensed by the Tokke Turistkontor (☎ 35 07 70 65, fax 35 07 73 41). If you're there for a while, you may want to visit the nearby Åmdalsverk mines (☎ 35 07 79 30), which are open from 1 June to 1 September.

Dalen has a *camping ground (☎ 35 07 75 87)* with hostel-style rooms for Nkr130 and cabins for Nkr300. The ornate *Dalen Hotell (☎ 35 53 03 00)*, which first opened in 1894, lies 1km from Dalen Brygge. For a night of soaking up its historic atmosphere, you'll pay a rather hefty Nkr980/1560.

Organised Tours

Daily from early June to early August, the ferry M/S *Telemarken* plies the Øst-Telemark Canal system between Notodden and Lunde (4¾ hours, Nkr190). It leaves Notodden/Lunde at 9 am/2 pm. If you only want to sail one way, buses leave from Notodden to Lunde (one hour, Nkr68) at 11.45 am and from Lunde back to Notodden at 3.45 pm.

Daily from 15 June to 8 August, sightseeing boats dating from the early 1900s, the M/S *Victoria* (built in 1882) and M/S *Henrik Ibsen* (built in 1907), make the leisurely (if not rather sluggish) 11-hour journey between Skien and Dalen. At other times between mid-May and early September, they run six times weekly. The fare is Nkr275. Round-trips, including one-way by boat from Skien to Dalen and a return to Skien by bus, cost a total of Nkr430. In the opposite direction, you can take the Vest-Telemark Bilruter (☎ 35 06 54 00) bus from Skien back to Dalen (3½ hours, Nkr155). For further information, contact Telemarkreiser (☎ 35 53 03 00, *Victoria* mobile ☎ 94 15 25 90, *Henrik Ibsen* mobile ☎ 94 58 00 15, fax 35 52 70 07, destination.telemark@nano.no, www.telemarkskanalen.com).

A great way to see the canal is by canoe, kayak or bicycle, and the ferries will transport your own boat/bicycle for Nkr150/75 between Skien and Dalen. For canoe hire, see Kjeldal, earlier in this section.

RJUKAN

The 6km long industrial town of Rjukan, squeezed into the deep Vestfjorddalen, nestles at the foot of Telemark's highest and most recognisable peak, Gausta (1883m). Thanks to its founders, industrial engineer Sam Eyde and physicist Kristian Birkeland, this hydroelectric company town was aesthetically planned and designed, and in the first 10 years after its founding in 1907, the industry supported 10,000 residents.

In the early days, the administrators' homes occupied the highest slopes, where the sun shone the longest; below them were the homes of office workers

The Heroes of Telemark

In 1933 in the USA, it was discovered that .02% of all water molecules are 'heavy', which means that the hydrogen atoms are actually deuterium, an isotope that contains an extra neutron. Although heavy water looks and tastes like water, it weighs 10% more, boils at 1.4°C higher and freezes at 4°C higher than ordinary water. In the nascent stages of nuclear physics, it was discovered that heavy water serves to stabilise nuclear fission reactions, making it invaluable in the production of the atom bomb.

During WWII in Norway, the occupying Germans were aware that heavy water could be created by the process of electrolysis and, in the hope of eventually building an atom bomb, they set up a heavy water production plant at Vemork, near Rjukan. Had they been allowed to continue, they might well have been successful in achieving their goal and building the bomb, and the war might have ended quite differently. Fortunately, between March and October 1942, Allied insurgents were able to gather intelligence and mount Operation Grouse, which turned out to be one of the most daring sabotage missions of the entire war.

The mission was launched in October 1942 when four Norwegians parachuted into Sognadal, west of Rjukan. They were to be joined a month later by 34 specially trained British saboteurs who would arrive in two gliders. The British insurgents had prepared for their landing at Skoland near the lake Møsvann, but the tow plane and one of the gliders crashed into a mountain, and the other glider crashed on landing. All the British survivors were shot by the Germans.

Undeterred, the Norwegian group changed its mission name to Swallow and retreated to Hardangervidda, where they subsisted through the worst of the winter. On 16 February 1943 a new British-trained group called Gunnerside landed on Hardangervidda. Unfortunately a blizzard was raging and they wound up a long 30km march from their intended drop site. By the evening of 27 February, the saboteurs were all holed up at Fjøsbudalen, north of Vemork, waiting to strike. After descending the steep mountainside along the now-famous Sabotørruta (Saboteurs' Route), they crossed the gorge to the heavy water plant, wire-clipped the perimeter fence and planted the explosives which largely destroyed the facility. Some of the saboteurs retreated on skis to Hardangervidda then fled, in uniform and fully armed, into neutral Sweden, while the rest remained on the plateau, successfully avoiding capture.

The plant was rebuilt by the Germans, but on 16 November 1943, 140 US planes openly bombed Vemork, killing 20 Norwegians in the process. The Germans abandoned any hopes of producing heavy water in Norway and decided to shift their remaining stocks to Germany. However, the remaining saboteurs realised that this relocation procedure involved a ferry across the lake Tinnsjø and on 19 February 1944, the night before the ferry was due to sail, they placed a timed charge on the boat. The following night, the entire project was literally blown out of the water.

In 1965 this intriguing story was made into a dramatic film, *The Heroes of Telemark*, starring Kirk Douglas.

and in the valley's dark depths dwelt the labourers. That segregation has now been eliminated but on the valley floor, daylight remains a premium commodity. Today, tourists can visit several local industries, including the Rjukan Mineralvandfabrik (mineral water plant) and the Mår Kraftverk hydroelectric plant, with its daunting wooden stairway of 3975 steps (it's the world's longest!).

SOUTHERN NORWAY

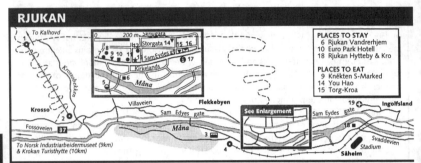

RJUKAN

PLACES TO STAY
6 Rjukan Vandrerhjem
10 Euro Park Hotell
18 Rjukan Hytteby & Kro

PLACES TO EAT
9 Knékten S-Marked
14 You Hao
15 Torg-Kroa

Information

The very helpful Tinn/Rjukan Turist-kontor (☎ 35 09 12 90, fax 35 09 15 75, tinntur@telnett.no), on Torget, can load you up with brochures, information and inspiration. If you need outdoor gear, you'll find a selection at the Fjellsport shop in the centre, and there's a bookshop next door.

Norsk Industriarbeidermuseet

The Norwegian Industrial Workers' Museum (☎ 35 09 51 53), at the Vemork power plant 7km west of Rjukan, honours mainly the Socialist Workers' Party, which reached its height of Norwegian activities in the 1950s. The Soviet-style propaganda may now seem rather ludicrous, but you won't want to miss the exhibit on the events which inspired the 1965 Kirk Douglas film, *The Heroes of Telemark*. It recounts the brave exploits of the Norwegian Resistance movement, which thwarted Hitler's WWII nuclear program with their daring sabotage of the Nazis' heavy water laboratory in the cellar of the hydroelectric power station (see the boxed text 'The Heroes of Telemark'). In the theatre, you can see the short film *If Hitler Had the Bomb*.

The museum is housed in the Vemork power station, which was the largest in the world when it was constructed in 1911. If you're driving, you'll have to park at the swinging bridge and either take the summer shuttle up the hill (Nkr30) or hoof it, which takes about 30 minutes (only disabled travellers and seniors over 65 are permitted to drive up). The museum is open from 10 am to 6 pm daily from 1 May to 30 September. Admission costs Nkr50. Take town bus No 210 westbound (five minutes, Nkr20).

Tinn Museum

This small roadside folk museum (☎ 35 09 41 12) is a collection of houses and furnishings from the 16th to the 20th centuries. It's open daily except Monday from late June to early August; on weekdays it's open 11 am to 5 pm and on weekends from noon to 6 pm. Guided tours run at 11 am and 6 pm. Admission costs Nkr30.

Krossobanen

The Krossobanen cable car was constructed in 1928 by Norsk Hydro to provide its employees with a bit of access to the sun. It has now been renovated and whisks tourists up to Gvepseborg (886m) for a view over the deep dark recesses. It operates from 10 am to 5 pm from 15 June to 5 September (until 6 pm from 2 July to 2 August) and costs Nkr25/50 one-way/return.

Hiking

The popular hiking track up Gausta (1883m)leads to DNT's Gaustahytta (☎ 35 09 41 50) at the summit, which it shares with an enormous radio tower that severely disrupts the mountain's profile. The hut was built in 1893 and provides accommodation for hikers. In former times, hikers had to

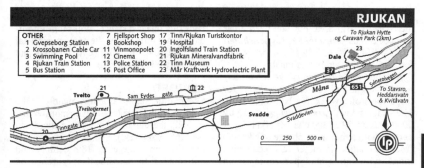

RJUKAN

OTHER
1 Gvepseborg Station
2 Krossobanen Cable Car
3 Swimming Pool
4 Rjukan Train Station
5 Bus Station
7 Fjellsport Shop
8 Bookshop
11 Vinmonopolet
12 Cinema
13 Police Station
16 Post Office
17 Tinn/Rjukan Turistkontor
19 Hospital
20 Ingolfsland Train Station
21 Rjukan Mineralvandfabrik
22 Tinn Museum
23 Mår Kraftverk Hydroelectric Plant

struggle up to the peak all the way from Rjukan, but there's now a road link (the Fv651) to Stavsro at lake Heddersvann, at a height of 1173m. There's no public transport on the 16km route from town but taxis are available for around Nkr150. Allow all day for the hike, which allows plenty of time for exploring the summit. The tourist office distributes a map of the Fv651, which will probably suffice for this hike.

From Gvepseborg, the top station on the Krossobanen cable car, walking tracks strike out onto the expansive Hardangervidda plateau, which is home to Europe's largest herd of wild reindeer. The main route leads north to DNT's Helberghytta and the Kalhovd Turisthytta (☎ 35 09 05 10). An eight-hour walk takes you from Gvepseborg to Kalhovd (where you can catch a bus out or head on to connect with the Nkr75 ferry to Mårbuhytta). From there, it's a two-day walk west to Mogen Turisthytta (☎ 35 07 41 15), where you can catch the Møsvatn ferry (Nkr125) back to Skinnarbu, west of Rjukan on the Rv37.

Alternatively, you can follow the marked route which begins above Rjukan Fjellstue, just north of the Rv37. This historic track follows the Sabotørruta (Saboteurs' Route), the path taken by the members of the Norwegian Resistance as they approached their target, the heavy water laboratory at Vemork. Along the way, several information plaques describe their activities in context. Instead of dropping down from Nystaul,

however, you can also continue 2½ hours farther east to Gvepseborg.

The best map to use for these hikes is Cappelen's *Hardangervidda Øst*, at a scale of 1:100,000.

Places to Stay

Camping is available at *Ryukan Hytte og Caravan Park* (☎/fax 35 09 63 53), about 5km east of the centre. Camping in a small tent costs Nkr50 plus Nkr14 per person and with a car/caravan you'll pay Nkr60/70. Two-bed huts range from Nkr225 to Nkr250, and three/four/six-bed huts are Nkr300/320/600. However, there are all sorts of add-on charges, including Nkr1 for seven seconds of washing up water! From town take bus No 209 (five minutes, Nkr20).

In summer, the year-round *Ryukan Vandrerhjem* (☎/fax 35 09 05 27, Birkelandsgata 2) offers dorm beds for Nkr105 and single/double rooms for Nkr180/250 (off-season rates are lower). At the in-town *Rjukan Hytteby & Kro* (☎ 35 09 01 22), two/four-bed cabins cost Nkr480/690. They're built to emulate the early 20th century hydroelectric workers' cabins.

The more plush *Euro Park Hotell* (☎ 35 09 02 88, fax 35 09 05 05, Sam Eydes gate 67), in the centre, has weekday rates of Nkr690/840, but on weekends, you'll pay just Nkr395/545.

A trio of places at the lake Kvitåvatn, off the Rv651 12km from town, provide a front-row view of Gausta and easy access to the Skipsfjell ski area, but you need a car for access. The *Gaustablikk Høyfjellshotell* (☎ 35 09 14 22, fax 35 09 19 75), has rooms for Nkr750/980 and serves meals.

Kvitåvatn Fjellhytter (☎ 94 32 69 34) rents its eight-bed self-catering cabins for three days/one week for Nkr1605/3500. The simpler *Kvitåvatn Fjellstoge* (☎ 35 09 20 40, fax 35 09 20 95) charges Nkr150 per person, with a minimum charge of Nkr300. Accommodation is either in a cosy pine lodge with six bunks per room or in smaller annexes. Breakfast/lunch/dinner costs Nkr45/45/130.

About 10km west of Rjukan, you can also visit the historic *Krokan Turisthytte* (☎ 35 09 51 31, fax 35 09 01 90), built in 1869 as DNT's first hut and now a museum of sorts. Accommodation is in 15th century log cabins; normal DNT rates apply.

Places to Eat
At the simple but popular *Torg-Kroa* (☎ 35 09 09 30), on the square, you'll get burgers from Nkr55 to Nkr65 and dinners from Nkr75 to Nkr100. The 'Kro' part of the *Rjukan Hytteby & Kro*, a local pizza and fast food hang-out, and there's also a small cafeteria in the *Knékten S-Marked* supermarket. The Chinese-oriented *You Hao* (☎ 35 09 15 85) has daily specials for Nkr72 to Nkr98 and a lunch buffet on Monday to Saturday for Nkr49. The *Euro Park Hotell* has a fine, if expensive, restaurant, as well as a bar and weekend disco.

Entertainment
The bar clientele at the *Euro Park Hotell* is mostly over 30 and the disco attracts the 18 to 25 crowd. Otherwise, you're pretty much limited to the swimming pool or the *cinema*, which changes films weekly.

Getting There & Away
A daily express bus connects Rjukan to Oslo (3¾ hours, Nkr220) via Kongsberg (1¾ hours, Nkr127). If you're driving, there's a shortcut between Rjukan and Geilo over the Tessungdalen toll road (Nkr25 per car).

Getting Around
Rjukan's linear distances will seem intimidating, but fortunately, the convenient local bus Nos 209 and 210 link its far ends and cost only Nkr10 per ride.

SELJORD
Scenic little Seljord is known mainly as the home of Selma, the Nessie-type monster that inhabits the depths of the lake Seljordvatn (see the boxed text). She has been seen on occasion since the early 18th century and still makes an occasional appearance on warm, sunny days. From 10 am to 8 pm, 15 June to 15 August, the Sjøormsenteret (☎ 35 05 10 06), or Sea Serpent Centre, offers the lowdown on Seljord's best known resident.

Hikers can also seek out the area's other enigmatic residents – the feuding troll women, Ljose-Signe, Glima and Tårån, who inhabit the surrounding peaks. Seljord was also the inspiration for some of Norway's best known folk legends, including Asbjørnsen and Moe's *The Three Billy Goats Gruff*, which has been told and re-told around the world.

You may also want to check out the charming 12th century Romanesque stone church, which was built in honour of St Olav. It's open from 10 am to 4 pm Monday to Saturday and 10 am to 1 pm Sunday; admission and guided tours cost Nkr15. In the grounds between the church and its stone wall are two impressions which were reputedly made by two mountain trolls who were so upset by the encroachment of Christianity that they pummelled the site with boulders, hoping to destroy the structure.

Seljord Turistinformasjon (☎ 35 05 10 06) is open from mid-June to mid-August.

Special Events
On the second weekend of September, Seljord holds the Dyrsku'n festival, which started in 1866 and is now Norway's largest traditional market and cattle show, attracting 60,000 visitors annually. If you want to experience the full measure of rural Telemark, don't miss it. Note that it's wise to book accommodation in advance.

Desperately Seeking Selma

The first testimony to the existence of Selma the Sea Monster dates back to the summer of 1750, when Gunleik Andersson-Verpe of nearby Bø was 'attacked by a sea horse' while rowing across the lake. In 1880 Bjørn Bjørge and his mother Gunnhild reported killing a bizarre lizard while doing laundry in the lake. Nearly every summer since, witnesses have sighted the fins and humps of this fast-moving lake creature. According to most observers, the creature measures the size of a large log, or slightly bigger. Some have described it as eel-like while others have likened it to a snail, a lizard or a crocodile and have reported lengths of 25, 30 and even 50m. Amateur videos filmed in 1988 and 1993 reveal a series of humps in the water but their grainy nature renders the evidence inconclusive. Researchers generally remain open-minded but have suggested that the lake is too small to support creatures more than about 7m long.

As with Scotland's famous Nessie, Selma has fuelled local folklore and drawn tourists to search the surface of the deep pine-rimmed lake Seljordvatn (14km long, 2km wide and 157m deep) for signs of the telltale black humps. In 1977 Swedish freelance journalist Jan Sundberg scanned the lake with sonar equipment and detected several large objects moving in unison, then separating in several directions. In the summer of 1998, he returned with an 11-member team and spent 17 days trawling the lake with imaging equipment and even a mini-submarine outfitted with three underwater cameras, sonar and a gripping arm. Sundberg rejects the sceptics who dismiss the sightings and his own sonar evidence as the movements of moose, otters or beavers. According to him, 'The serpent does not fit any species known to humanity. It has several qualities not seen before, such as travelling on the surface at high speed and moving vertically up and down. It shows a back or a head or a neck or all three for long periods above the surface and travels very fast, maybe up to 25 knots.'

The Seljord Council and the lakeside camp site sponsored Sundberg's search for the beast, hoping that the publicity would result in a boost in tourism, and well it might. The village has already cashed in on its monster by setting up a serpent exhibition and changing its coat of arms to depict a yellow Selma on a red background.

In 1992 a 23-member delegation visited Scotland's Loch Ness to determine why Nessie had captured the curiosity of so many people, and to investigate the culture of scepticism that surrounds the reported sightings of these monsters. According to village council member Asbjørn Storrusten, 'I did not believe it before I came here and talked to people. These are responsible people and when they look you in the eye and say they have seen something, you cannot disbelieve it. These lakes are less researched than the far side of the moon. Who knows what's there?'

SOUTHERN NORWAY

Places to Stay & Eat

The pleasantly situated *Seljord Camping og Badeplass* (☎ *35 05 04 71)*, beside the lake, is the dock for monster cruises on Seljordvatn (fares vary with the number of passengers). Camping costs Nkr100/110 in a tent/caravan and cabins range from Nkr275 to Nkr375. It's open from 15 May to 15 September. The *Seljord Hotel* (☎ *35 05 10 00, fax 35 05 11 01)*, on the main road, has single/double rooms for Nkr445/690. For quick meals, there's a bright *gatekjøkken* (☎ *35 05 01 02)* in the centre, which provides a bit of nightlife with a dim disco in its basement.

Getting There & Away

Local bus No 301 connects Notodden with Seljord (1¼ hours, Nkr83).

SETESDALEN

Setesdalen, one of Norway's most traditional and conservative regions, makes a secluded and little trodden side-trip off the southern coastal route. This forested and lake-filled mountain valley enjoys some of southern Norway's most beautiful landscapes, thanks mainly to its fabulous geology, and is popular with outdoor enthusiasts: rafters, canoers, hikers and climbers. In Valle, for example, rock climbers will find granite ascents up to 700m high, and the same area also boasts six DNT mountain huts.

Evje

The heart of the action is the village of Evje, which serves as a gateway to the wilder parts of upper Setesdalen and dishes up heavy doses of outdoor recreation. It's also a geologist's paradise, and the ridge east of town is dotted with mines and mineral deposits.

Information The useful Setesdal Informasjonsenter (☎ 37 93 14 00, fax 37 93 14 55, www.setesdal.com) occupies the same building as the bus terminal. For information on mountain hiking and huts in the Setesdalen area, contact the Kristiansand og Oppland Turistforening (☎ 38 02 42 63), Kristian IVs gate 12, Kristiansand.

Evje og Hornes Museum Rock fans will enjoy the Evje og Hornes Museum (☎ 37 93 07 94), 2km from town across the river in Fennefoss, which displays a large collection of minerals found in the surrounding hills, as well as exhibits on local nickel mining and traditional rural life in Setesdalen. It's open mid-June to mid-August from 11 am to 4 pm daily. Admission is Nkr25.

Activities The Setesdal Rafting & Activity Centre (☎ 37 93 11 77, fax 37 93 13 34, troll.mountain@online.no, hotell.nextel.no/troll-mountain), about 7km north of Evje, and Viking Adventures Norway (☎ 37 93 13 03, fax 37 93 15 63, vanevje@online.no, www.viking-adventures.no/), in town, both organise a range of outdoor adventure activities, from white-water rafting, canoeing, kayaking, canyoning and riverboarding to rock climbing, mountain climbing and abseiling. If that's too much adrenalin for your tastes, the Setesdal Rafting & Activity Centre also offers hiking, horse riding and wildlife-viewing safaris in search of beaver, moose and other critters. Alternatively, you can hire a canoe or mountain bike and head off on your own.

On the mountain east of town, a short and easy nature trail for mineral aficionados winds between several mines and mineral deposits. Take the Gautestad road and turn south about 5km from town.

Places to Stay & Eat The convenient *Odden Camping* (☎ *37 93 06 03, fax 37 93 08 20, oddencmp@online.no)* lies only 200m south of town. Without/with a car, tent camping costs Nkr70/80, plus Nkr10 per person; caravans are Nkr130 with two people and five-bed huts range from Nkr300 to Nkr350. *Neset Camping* (☎ *37 93 42 55, fax 37 93 43 93)*, on a beautiful peninsula in Byglandsfjorden, charges Nkr100 for two people in a tent, Nkr250 to Nkr400 for a standard cabin and Nkr600 for a luxury cabin. A steep 1km uphill walk to the south leads to Tjuvhola, the 'thief's cave', which is a legendary hide-out of thieves and outlaws; the route is marked off the highway.

Only 3km north of town is the Christian-oriented *Evjetun Camping* (☎ 37 93 01 63), where tent camping costs Nkr50 per person and rooms and cabins range in price from Nkr350 to Nkr490. Canoe hire is Nkr20 per hour.

The *Evje Vandrerhjem* (☎ 37 93 11 77, fax 37 93 13 34) is run by the Setesdal Rafting & Activity Centre in Surveit, 7km north of town, and is used for its group trips. Here you'll pay Nkr150 for a dorm bed and Nkr140/220 for a single/double room.

The recommended *Revsnes Hotell* (☎ 37 93 43 00), 10 minutes north of town on Byglandsfjord, has rooms with breakfast for Nkr290 per person, while half/full board costs Nkr390/450. At the simple *Grenaderen Motell* (☎ 37 93 04 00, fax 37 93 13 70), 1km south of town, rooms cost Nkr390/550, with breakfast. Its à la carte cafeteria does standard snacks and light meals, including pizza and burgers.

Alternatively, there's the *Pernille Cafeteria*, where the service is a bit slow but there's a good variety of tasty offerings, including pizza baguettes for Nkr29, pizzas for Nkr59 and burgers for Nkr39. The other option is the *China Restaurant*, which of course serves Chinese specialities.

Getting There & Away The daily NorWay Bussekspress bus between Kristiansand (one hour, Nkr59) and Voss (9¾ hours, Nkr430) runs via Evje. It also provides access to Byglandsfjord, Bykle and Hovden.

Getting Around Viking Adventure, opposite the tourist office, hires mountain bikes for Nkr125 per day.

Bykle

A nice short stop for drivers through Setesdalen is distinctive log-built Bykle Kirkje, which dates from 1619 and is one of the smallest churches in Norway. The roses on the front of the galleries and traditional rose paintings on the wall were added in the 1820s, after an 1804 restoration. It's open from 10 am to 6 pm weekdays and noon to 6 pm weekends from 15 June to 15 August. Admission costs Nkr10. There's also a lovely signpost-guided walk past many historical and cultural sites above the Otra River, 5km south of town. The route dates from at least 1770 and was once the main route through Setesdalen. The walk takes about 30 minutes.

Hovden

The ski centre of Hovden lies in a wild open landscape at the very top of Setesdalen. Tourist information is dispensed by Hovdenferie (☎ 37 93 96 30, fax 37 93 97 33, hfas@online.no).

In summer, you can reach the view or start a hiking trip by taking the chairlift to the summit of Mt Nos (1160m), which costs Nkr50. In July, it operates daily from 11 am to 1 pm and two or three days a week at other times in summer. During the ski season, lift tickets cost Nkr190/350/460 for one/two/three days; either alpine or nordic equipment rental is Nkr180/280/340; snowboard rental starts at Nkr170/270/360. In any season, climbers may want to practice on the 6m indoor climbing wall at the G-Sport shop.

The Hovden Jernvinnermuseum (Iron Production Museum) surrounds a reconstructed ancient smelter and presents methods of medieval iron and coal extraction and processing. It's open from 11 am to 5 pm daily from 20 June to 16 August. Admission is Nkr10.

Places to Stay & Eat The *Hovdehytta Vandrerhjem* (☎/fax 37 93 95 52) offers dorm rooms with breakfast for Nkr170. There's also a host of ski huts, flats, chalets and hotels offering good deals in summer. To hire a holiday home (Nkr550 to Nkr750 for five to 12 people) contact the Hovden Hytteformidling (☎ 37 93 97 29, fax 37 93 98 33). You'll find a range of meal options at the *Værtshuset* (☎ 37 93 97 72) restaurant and the affiliated *Furumu Kafé* and *Bamse Gatekjøkken*.

SIRDAL

Sirdal, one of Norway's most important hydroelectric areas, is best known as the access route to the scenic 1000m road descent through 27 hairpin bends to Lysebotn, depicted on dozens of postcards. From the well appointed DNT hut at Ådneram, at the top of Sirdal, hikers can reach Lysebotn in nine hours (you need to follow the road for the last 4km). For tourist information, contact Sirdalsferie (☎ 38 37 13 90).

At Tonstad Kraftverk (power station) in the central part of the valley, there's an interesting 17-tonne glass sculpture entitled *Pure Energy*. Tours of the power station (☎ 38 37 13 90) are conducted daily at 1.30 pm.

Places to Stay

In Sinnes, you can stay at the *Sinnes Fjellstue (☎ 38 37 12 02, fax 38 37 12 05)* for Nkr590 a double.

Getting There & Away

Bus No 470 runs daily except Sunday between Tonstad and Ådneram (one hour, Nkr50) and bus No 475 connects Stavanger and Ådneram (2½ hours, Nkr100), via Sinnes and Tjørhom, daily from 7 June to 26 September.

Central Norway

The central part of Norway, stretching northwards from Oslo to the historic mining town of Røros and westwards across the highland plateaus, takes in Norway's highest mountains and best known national parks. Not surprisingly, it's also one of the most popular outdoor playgrounds for both Norwegians and visitors. Railways create major arteries through the region. The scenic Oslo-Bergen railway climbs through forests and alpine villages to Norway's cross-country skiing paradise, the stark Hardangervidda plateau.

Eastern Central Norway

EIDSVOLL VERK

At the otherwise uninteresting lakeside town of Eidsvoll Verk (not to be confused with Eidsvoll, 8km to the north-east), it's worth visiting the timber manor house Eidsvoll-Byningen. This was the estate of the Ankers family, who'd made their fortune in the local iron works. After the Napoleonic Wars, it served as the venue for Norway's first National Assembly, which was selected from the country's leading citizens. There, on 17 May 1814, they drafted a constitution and created a short-lived independent Kingdom of Norway under King Christian Frederik, a Danish prince, until King Karl Johan of Sweden (formerly one of Napoleon's officers) decided that Norway would unify with Sweden. The manor is open from 10 am to 3 pm daily from May to September (later in mid-summer) and noon to 2 pm the rest of the year. Admission costs Nkr20.

HAMAR

The commercial town of Hamar (population 26,000) sits beside the immense lake Mjøsa and is the capital of Hedmark county. There's little to detain travellers for

HIGHLIGHTS

- Exploring the old copper mines and entering a time warp in the UNESCO World Heritage town of Røros
- Trekking along the extensive hiking routes through the spectacular Jotunheimen and Rondane national parks
- White-water rafting on the Driva or in Heidalen
- Visiting the superb Norsk Skogbruksmuseum (Norwegian Forestry Museum) in Elverum
- Looking for musk oxen in Dovrefjell
- Nordic skiing on the vast Hardangervidda plateau

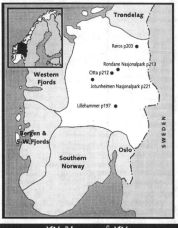

long but it does have a couple of worthwhile sites and many people do stop en route between Oslo, Lillehammer and points north. The tourist office (☎ 62 52 12 17, fax 62 53 35 65), Parkgata 2, is open daily from 16 June to 10 August, and weekdays the rest of the year.

Olympic Sites

Hamar prides itself on having been the site of several Olympic events in 1994. The impressive **Northern Lights amphitheatre**, the world's largest wooden hall, built for the figure skating and short track skating events. The town's landmark, however, is the **sports arena** (☎ 62 51 75 00), a graceful structure with the lines of an upturned Viking ship. The building holds 10,000 spectators and has been described as a 'sports cathedral without equal'. From 1 June to 15 August,

it's open from 8 am to 8 pm weekdays and from 10 am to 6 pm weekends; admission costs Nkr20. Ice skating (Nkr50) is available from 9 am to 9 pm daily between late July and mid-August.

Norsk Jernbanemuseum

The open-air Norwegian Railway Museum (☎ 62 51 31 60, fax 62 52 96 99), on the Mjøsa shore, was established in 1896 in honour of Norway's railway history. In addition to lovely historic stations, engine

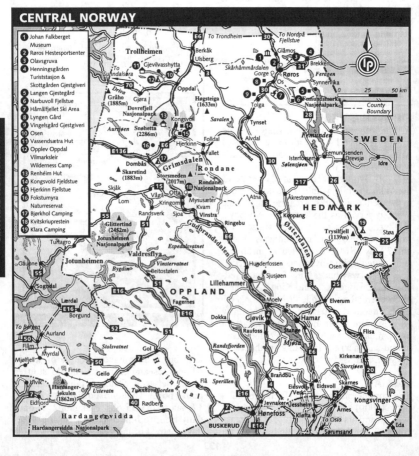

sheds, rail coaches and the 1861 steam locomotive *Caroline*, you'll learn about the extraordinary engineering feats required to construct railways through Norway's rugged terrain. It's open from 10 am to 4 pm daily from 24 May to 30 August (until 6 pm in July). Admission costs Nkr30. In mid-June, you can join the annual tour with the *Caroline* to Elverum, spending two hours at the Norwegian Timber Museum before returning to Hamar. Book well in advance.

Norwegian Emigrant Museum

This museum (☎ 62 57 85 77, fax 62 57 84 59, knut.djupedal@emigrant.museum.no, www.hamarnett.no/emigrantmuseum/) in Stange includes displays on all forms of Norwegian emigration, return migration and immigration, and also provides services and resources for genealogical research in Norway. It's open from 8.30 am to 3.30 pm weekdays and by appointment on weekends. Bus No 403 (30 minutes, Nkr25) runs frequently between Hamar and Stange.

Places to Stay & Eat

The cute two-storey *Vikingskipet Motell og Vandrerhjem (☎ 62 52 60 60, fax 62 53 24 60, Åkervikavegen 10)* offers good value accommodation within 100m of the sports arena. Dorm beds are Nkr125 and singles/doubles Nkr260/360. In town, you can camp at *Hamar NAF Camping (☎ 62 52 44 90, Strandveien 156)*, which charges Nkr80/100 for two people with a tent/caravan and Nkr250 for basic two-bed cabins. *Hedmarktoppen (☎ 62 53 45 11)*, 3km from the town centre, charges Nkr105 for a tent and two people, and has cabins for Nkr195 to Nkr330 and singles/doubles in the summer hotel for Nkr305/505, with breakfast.

The little *Seiersted Pensjonat (☎/fax 62 52 12 44, Holsegata 64)*, in the centre, offers a homy atmosphere for Nkr350/520 in singles/doubles. Some meals are available.

Pizza figures prominently in Hamar: try *Pizzaninni (Torggata 24)* and *Bykjelleren (Torggata 82)*. There's also a lakeside fish restaurant called the *Seaside*.

Getting There & Away

Nor-Way Bussekspress buses between Oslo (two hours, Nkr205) and the Western Fjords call in at Hamar. Trains between Oslo and Hamar (1½ hours, Nkr160) run five or six times daily. Some services continue to Trondheim (five hours, Nkr470) via either Lillehammer or Røros.

The *Skibladner* paddle steamer (☎ 62 52 70 85, fax 62 43 39 23, skibladn@sn.no, www.skibladner.no) offers relaxing transport around lake Mjøsa. From 23 June to mid-August, it plies the lake between Eidsvoll and Lillehammer, but most travellers opt for the route between Hamar and Eidsvoll (2½ hours, Nkr150) which runs on Monday, Wednesday and Friday; or Hamar and Lillehammer (four hours, Nkr150) on Tuesday, Thursday and Saturday. Either of these can be done as a return trip on the same day. Over summer, there are also jazz evenings aboard the steamer for Nkr350.

LILLEHAMMER

Lillehammer (population 23,000) lies at the northern end of Mjøsa, surrounded by farms, forests and small settlements. The town has long been a popular Norwegian ski resort but was catapulted to international renown in 1994, when it successfully hosted the Winter Olympics. Thanks to that distinction, many people expect quite a lot of Lillehammer and, although it's architecturally pleasant and has decent restaurants and nightlife, it's often allotted more time than necessary.

Orientation & Information

There's no denying that Lillehammer's tunnels, one-way streets and convoluted traffic patterns create a nightmare for motorists. For pedestrians, however, the centre is small and readily negotiated. The main shopping street, Storgata (the pedestrianised section is better known as just Gågata), lies just two blocks east of the Skysstasjon (the bus and train stations). The Lillehammer tourist office (☎ 61 25 92 99, fax 61 25 65 85, lillehammer.utvikling@sn.no, www .lillehammerturist.no) is at Elvegata 19, with a branch at the train station. Lille-hammer og Omland DNT (☎ 61 25 08 00), Storgata 82, sells hiking and skiing maps and dispenses mountain hut information.

Olympic Sites

When Lillehammer won its bid for the 1994 Winter Olympics, the Norwegian govern-ment ploughed over two billion kroner into the infrastructure. Most of these amenities remain in use and visitors can tour the main Olympic sites. The **Lysgårdsbakkene ski jump tower** is open from 11 am to 4 pm in winter and from 10 am to 8 pm in sum-mer. Admission is Nkr15. The **ski jump chairlift** ascends to a panoramic view over the town and costs Nkr25, including ad-mission to Lysgårdsbakkene. The shorter cross-country and biathlon events were held at the **Birkebeineren skistadion**, farther up the hill and a nice place for a stroll or ski.

The **Norwegian Olympic Museum** (☎ 61 25 21 00, www.ol.museum.no) is at Håkons Hall, the hockey venue. This worthwhile ef-fort outlines Olympic history in both ancient and modern times. It's open from 10 am to 6 pm daily from mid-May to late September and from 11 am to 4 pm daily, except Mon-day, the rest of the year. Admission costs Nkr50 (for Nkr100 you can also get entry to the Maihaugen Folk Museum).

At Hunderfossen, 15km north of town, you can career down the **Olympic bobsled run** with a professional bobsled pilot. On a taxibob, which takes four passengers and is the real thing, you'll pay Nkr500 per per-son. Bob rafting, aimed at tourists, takes five passengers and costs Nkr125 per per-son. Luge sledding costs Nkr100 per person with a minimum of five people and in sum-mer, when there's a shortage of ice, you can go for the 'wheeled bob' costing Nkr125 per person. Bookings (☎ 61 27 75 50) are advised for these popular rides. If the real thing is too much to handle, back in town there's a **downhill ski and bobsled simula-tor ride** (Nkr35) between Håkons Hall and Kristins Hall.

Lillehammer's two Olympic ski slopes, the **Hafjell Alpine Centre** (☎ 61 27 70 78),

15km north of town, and the **Kvitfjell Alpine Facility** (☎ 61 28 21 05, www.skiinfo .no/kvitfjell/), 50km north of town, offer public skiing between late November and late April. Morning/afternoon/evening lift tickets, which are good for 3½, 4½ and 2½ hours, cost Nkr135/160/110, and one/two/ seven-day tickets are Nkr190/345/900. One/two/seven-day equipment rental costs Nkr180/270/580 for skis; snowboards are Nkr250/350/670. Hafjell is accessible on bus No 186 (15 minutes, Nkr24), which runs six to eight times daily between Lille-hammer, Otta and Skjåk.

Maihaugen Folk Museum

This facility (☎ 61 28 89 00, www.maihaugen .museum.no) is lauded as Norway's premier open-air museum. This collection of 175 buildings, including the transplanted Garmo stave church, traditional Gudbrandsdalen homes and shops and 27 buildings from the farm Bjørnstad, is the life work of local den-tist Anders Sandvig. There are also a num-ber of exhibits, workshop demonstrations by interpreters in period costumes, and a 20th century section featuring Norwegian homes from the 1930s to 1990s. It's open from 10 am to 5 pm daily from May to Septem-ber (9 am to 6 pm in mid-summer). Admis-sion costs Nkr100 (including admission to the Olympic museum). Maihaugen is a 20-minute walk from the train station; go up Jernbanegata, right on Anders Sandvigs gate and left up Maihaugvegen.

Norsk Kjøretøy-Historisk Museum

The Norwegian Museum of Historic Ve-hicles (☎ 61 25 61 65) is a must for auto afi-cionados. It has all sorts of vehicles, from horse-drawn sleighs and wagons to the stars of Norway's short-lived auto industry. Nor-wegian production of the odd-looking 'Troll Car', which appears to be a cousin of the Saab, wound up in the 1950s. There's also a section on railway history. It's open from 10 am to 6 pm daily from 15 June to 19 August, with shorter hours the rest of the year. Admission costs Nkr30.

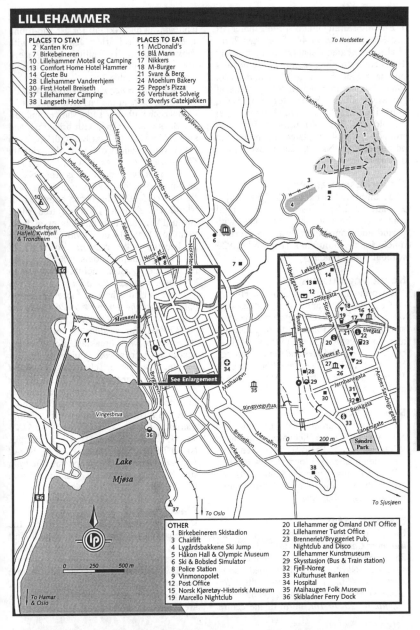

LILLEHAMMER

PLACES TO STAY
2 Kanten Kro
7 Birkebeineren
10 Lillehammer Motell og Camping
13 Comfort Home Hotel Hammer
14 Gjeste Bu
28 Lillehammer Vandrerhjem
30 First Hotell Breiseth
37 Lillehammer Camping
38 Langseth Hotell

PLACES TO EAT
11 McDonald's
16 Blå Mann
17 Nikkers
18 M-Burger
21 Svare & Berg
24 Moehlum Bakery
25 Peppe's Pizza
26 Vertshuset Solveig
31 Øverlys Gatekjøkken

To Nordseter

To Hunderfossen,
Hafjell, Kvitfjell
& Trondheim

To Hamar
& Oslo

See Enlargement

To Oslo

Lake
Mjøsa

Vingesbrua

To Sjusjøen

Søndre
Park

Elvegata

0   200 m

OTHER
1 Birkebeineren Skistadion
3 Chairlift
4 Lygårdsbakkene Ski Jump
5 Håkon Hall & Olympic Museum
6 Ski & Bobsled Simulator
8 Police Station
9 Vinmonopolet
12 Post Office
15 Norsk Kjøretøy-Historisk Museum
19 Marcello Nightclub

20 Lillehammer og Omland DNT Office
22 Lillehammer Turist Office
23 Brenneriet/Bryggeriet Pub,
   Nightclub and Disco
27 Lillehammer Kunstmuseum
29 Skysstasjon (Bus & Train station)
32 Fjell-Noreg
33 Kulturhuset Banken
34 Hospital
35 Maihaugen Folk Museum
36 Skibladner Ferry Dock

0   250   500 m

CENTRAL NORWAY

Lillehammer Kunstmuseum

The architecturally unique Lillehammer Art Museum (☎ 61 26 94 44), Stortorget 2, includes Norwegian visual arts from the early 19th century to the present, with emphasis on the period between 1820 and 1930. Watch for the inspired works by some of Norway's finest artists: Johan C Dahl, Christian Krogh, Edvard Munch Axel Revold and Erik Werenskiold. It's open from 11 am to 4 pm daily in summer and admission costs Nkr30; visiting exhibitions cost extra.

Kulturhuset Banken

The Kulturhuset Banken (☎ 61 26 68 10) is a century-old bank restored as a cultural centre. The interior, richly decorated with period and contemporary art, is worth a quick look. Admission costs Nkr10/25 without/with a guide.

Norsk Vegmuseum

The worthwhile Museum of Road History (☎ 61 27 44 50), sponsored by Statens Vegvesen (Norwegian Highway Department), is at Hunderfossen, 15km north of Lillehammer. You'll get a rundown of the struggle to construct roads, bridges and tunnels through Norway's challenging terrain. It's open from 10 am to 6 pm daily from 18 May to 31 August. Best of all, admission is free.

Special Events

For two weeks around the Christmas and New Year holidays, Lillehammer puts on its White Christmas Festival. This event features sleigh rides, ski tours, Christmas tree felling, Christmas parties, Santa visits and especially appealing winter lighting along the pedestrian shopping street.

Places to Stay

Camping is available at the big new *Lillehammer Camping* (☎ 61 25 33 33, fax 61 25 33 65) on the lakeshore. Tent/caravan sites cost Nkr80/130 and two-bed cabins start at Nkr450. An alternative is the *Lillehammer Motell og Camping* (☎ 61 25 97 10, fax 61 25 90 10), north of the centre.

You'll pay Nkr80/125 for two people in a tent/caravan and Nkr350 for a basic room. These are typical urban camp sites, with cooking and laundry facilities, sports facilities, water sports equipment, children's play areas and cable TV.

The *Lillehammer Vandrerhjem* (☎ 61 26 25 66), upstairs at the bus terminal, has 32 rooms each with four beds, shower and toilet. Beds cost Nkr165, with breakfast, and singles/doubles are Nkr320/450. An even better value budget option is the friendly *Gjeste Bu* (☎ 61 25 43 21, Gamleveien 10), a guesthouse with dorm beds from Nkr60 and simple singles/doubles with shared bath from Nkr175/300. Sheets can be rented for Nkr40. There's a group kitchen, free coffee and a TV room. Reception is open from 9 am to 11 pm. In the Olympic Park, the small country-style *Kanten Kro* (☎ 61 25 03 25) has simple rooms for Nkr150 to Nkr200 per person, including access to kitchen and laundry facilities.

There is also a host of more expensive options. *Birkebeineren* (☎ 61 26 46 00, fax 61 26 47 50), in the Olympic Park, charges Nkr390/690 for doubles in motel/hotel-style rooms, with breakfast. Self-catering apartments start at Nkr1050 for up to four people. The rather charming *Comfort Home Hotel Hammer* (☎ 61 26 35 00, fax 61 26 37 30, Storgata 108) charges Nkr790 for a double room with half-board. A good, more mainstream hotel is the homy *Langseth Hotell* (☎ 61 25 78 88, fax 61 25 94 01, Bakkalykkja 13), which charges Nkr410/520. The central *First Hotell Breiseth* (☎ 61 26 95 00), opposite the train station, has rooms in summer from Nkr550/800.

Places to Eat

Despite its size, Lillehammer offers the same culinary variety as Oslo, which isn't saying much, but most of it is relatively good value.

Nikkers (Elvegata 18), where a moose has apparently walked through the wall, serves international cuisine. Lunch specials are available from 11 am to 3 pm for Nkr49.

Between 3 and 9.30 pm, dinner specials start at Nkr79. Otherwise, for Nkr55 to Nkr95 you'll get burgers, nachos, fajitas, chicken salads and other solid fare.

Svare & Berg (Storgata 83), beneath an enormous brick chimney, has lunch/dinner specials for Nkr65/85, salads from Nkr78 and evening main courses from Nkr143. For Norway, the menu is rather trendy: quesadillas (Nkr48), wraps (Nkr59), salmon soup (Nkr51), chillis with shrimp (Nkr65); there's even a tapas bar. The unpretentious *Vertshuset Solveig* does omelettes, salads and other fast stuff for Nkr48 to Nkr75. At dinnertime the daily specials cost Nkr79, you'll get fish for Nkr79 to Nkr110 and beef dishes with a salad for Nkr150.

The recommended *Blå Mann* does baguette sandwiches from Nkr37, tortillas, burritos and tacos from Nkr90 to Nkr100 and a range of pizza, pasta, beef and fish dishes. And in case you didn't think that wasn't enough choice, you'll also find reindeer (Nkr143), ostrich (Nkr189) and even alligator (Nkr210).

The best place for filling, inexpensive meals is the friendly *Øverlys Gatekjøkken*, which has Mexican-style snacks for Nkr49 to Nkr59, kebabs for Nkr39, burgers from Nkr34 to Nkr63 and pizza starting at Nkr35. The more standard *Peppe's Pizza* offers daily pizza and salad buffets for Nkr89. *M-Burger*, up Lysgårdsvegen from Storgata, has highly lauded burgers for prices commensurate with its low overhead costs, and of course there's a *McDonald's*, but it's out on the highway and aimed at motorists. At the *Moehlum Bakery*, you'll find not only the normal range of bread and pastries but also fine Italian ciabatta.

Entertainment

Bars and night spots are an integral part of the Lillehammer experience, especially in the winter ski season. Most places are clustered around the western end of Storgata and along the river Mesnaelva.

Nikkers (Elvegata 18), the place with the moose and his droppings, is one of the most popular bars; it's open until 1 am from Thursday to Saturday. The *Brenneriet/ Bryggeriet* pub, nightclub and disco appeals to a mixed clientele aged between 20 and 40. Even more universal is the relaxed *Marcello Nightclub*, where patrons range in age from 20 to 60.

Shopping

You'll find beautiful and unique gifts at friendly Fjell-Noreg (☎ 61 26 34 66), Storgata 46, which sells rocks, fossils and minerals, and lovely jewellery made from Norwegian gems and precious stones. You may also want to sample their *rombrød*, flat rum cakes which are unique to central Norway.

Getting There & Away

The main bus terminal, train station and taxi ranks are collectively called the Lillehammer Skysstasjon. For information on bus routes, phone ☎ 177. Nor-Way Bussekspress services between Oslo (3½ hours, Nkr170), the Western Fjords and Trondheim (6½ hours, Nkr400) all pass through Lillehammer several times daily. There are two daily runs to and from Bergen (10½ hours, Nkr538). Rail services on the Dovre line run seven times daily between Lillehammer and Oslo (three hours, Nkr220) and four times daily to and from Trondheim (five hours, Nkr395).

From mid-June to mid-August the *Skibladner* (☎ 62 52 70 85), the world's oldest operating paddle steamer, cruises on Mjøsa and provides a ferry connection between Hamar and Lillehammer (3¾ hours, Nkr210). On Tuesday, Thursday and Saturday, it chugs out of Hamar at 11 am and leaves Lillehammer for the return trip at 3 pm. See also Getting There & Away under Hamar earlier in this chapter.

ELVERUM

Set amid the vast timberlands of southern Hedmark county, Elverum presents a landscape more typical of Sweden or Finland than the classic image of Norway. It enjoys dense populations of moose, beaver and other wildlife. For Norwegians, the area provides abundant timber resources and clear streams brimming with grayling, pike, trout and whitefish.

When the Nazi forces invaded Norway in April 1940, King Håkon and the Norwegian government fled northwards from Oslo and halted in Elverum. On 9 April the parliament met at the folk high school and issued the Elverum Mandate, giving the exiled government the authority to protect Norway's interests until the parliament could reconvene. When the German messenger arrived to impose the Nazi's version of 'protection' in the form of a new puppet government in Oslo, the king issued a pithy 'no' response before heading into exile. Two days later, Elverum became the first Norwegian town to suffer massive bombing by the Nazis and most of the town's old wooden buildings were levelled.

Information

The Elverum Tourist Information office (☎ 62 41 31 16, fax 62 41 00 20) is on the main drag at Storgata 24.

Norsk Skogbruksmuseum

One of Norway's finest and best executed museums is the Norwegian Forestry Museum (☎ 62 41 02 99, norsk.skogbruksmuseum@.no), on the E20, a 2km walk south of the town centre. This large and airy place deals with all facets of Norwegian forests, including hunting, trapping, logging and freshwater fishing from ancient times to the present day. Exhibits feature a nature information centre, geological and meteorological exhibits, wood carvings, an aquarium, nature dioramas with all manner of stuffed native wildlife (including a mammoth) and a 20,000-volume reference library (open from 8 am to 3.30 pm weekdays).

Outdoor exhibits on the museum grounds and across the bridge on the island of Prestøya feature a large arboretum with 80 Nordic tree species, a couple of historic sawmills, an old bog iron plant and riverside freshwater fishponds. It's open from 10 am to 6 pm daily from 10 June to 20 August (until 4 pm the rest of the year). Admission costs Nkr60 and includes entry to the Glomdal Museum.

Glomdal Museum

The large open-air Glomdal Museum (☎ 62 41 18 00) is a collection of 90 historic buildings from along the Glomma valley, including an old apothecary and doctor's surgery. At the period-style restaurant you can sample traditional Østerdalen fare. The museum, accessible from the bridge from the forestry museum, is open between 10 am and 4 pm from 1 June to 31 August (until 6 pm in mid-summer); the farm animals are fed at 11 am and 4 pm. Admission costs Nkr60 and also includes entry to the forestry museum.

Places to Stay & Eat

In a green setting immediately south of the Norwegian Forestry Museum is *Elverum Camping* (☎ 62 41 67 16, fax 62 41 68 17), where tent camping costs Nkr100 and four-bed cabins are Nkr450. To get there, head 2km south of the town centre on the E20, past the forestry museum, and turn west at the first opportunity. A new, larger camp site will soon open across the road. Otherwise the cheapest option is the *Elverum Vandrerhjem & Apartments* (☎ 62 41 55 67, fax 62 41 56 00), which lies 300m west of the town centre, near the train station. Dorm beds are Nkr120 and singles/doubles cost Nkr240/340. Self-catering flats start at Nkr600. The simple *Glommen Gjestehus* (☎ 62 41 12 67, Vestheimgata 2), 500m west of the centre, charges Nkr370/470 for singles/doubles. As its name would suggest, *Hotel Central* (☎ 62 41 01 55, fax 62 41 59 56, Storgata 22) is right in the heart of town, but it's pretty drab. In summer, singles/doubles with breakfast are Nkr590/790.

A nice leafy place for lunch or dinner (summer only) is the fish and game restaurant *Forstmann* (☎ 62 41 59 10), at the forestry museum. The friendly *Oasen* kiosk beside the tourist office serves up relatively good, inexpensive hot dogs, and the Vinmonopolet is just uphill around the corner.

Entertainment

The most popular youth hangout is the *Triangelen* pub, which often stages live concerts. For dancing, try the *Alexis* disco.

Getting There & Away

For visitors, Elverum makes an easy day trip by bus or train from Oslo. The Nor-Way Bussekspress 'Trysil Ekspressen' runs between Oslo (two hours, Nkr140) and Trysil (1½ hours, Nkr83) via Elverum about four times daily. To get from Oslo to Elverum by train (2½ hours, Nkr205), you'll have to make a connection at Hamar. There are about five trains daily.

TRYSIL

The alpine resort town of Trysil sits amid the broad swathe of forest that dominates the Norwegian-Swedish border area. In summer it seems quiet and rather neglected, but come winter its mazes of pistes, more than 24 chairlifts and hundreds of ski chalets hum with the bustle of one of Norway's most popular winter resorts.

The town is in two sections: the town centre, in the valley, and the Trysilfjell Turistsenteret, about 2km up the hill. For tourist information, see the Trysil Turistkontor (☎ 62 45 05 11, fax 62 45 11 65). During the ski season, lift passes cost Nkr165/320/805 for one/two/seven days (about 10% more over the Christmas holidays). Ski equipment can be hired for Nkr160/235/495 and snowboard equipment for Nkr250/405/760.

Hikers may want to attempt the 240km Finnskogleden hiking track, which begins at Osen, south of Trysil, and winds through hills and forests along the border to Eda, south-east of Kongsvinger. The entire hike, part of the historic pilgrimage route between Sweden and Nidaros (Trondheim), takes two to three weeks. For information, contact the Finnskogleden Kulturkontoret (☎ 62 83 72 59, ☎ 62 94 53 33), N-2200 Kongsvinger.

Places to Stay & Eat

Klara Camping (☎ 62 45 13 63), about 1km south of town, has tent/caravan sites for Nkr60/100 and cabins from Nkr200 to Nkr400. They hire out boats for Nkr150 for six hours and canoes for Nkr275 to Nkr375 per day.

At the *Trysil Kro og Camp (☎ 62 45 33 40)*, 10km south of town at Sæteråsen, you can stay in two-bed cabins that are quipped for winter for Nkr200/300 or camp for Nkr100. The cheapest option, however, is to cuddle up on a reindeer skin in the *lavvo* (Sami tepee), which costs just Nkr25 per person.

In winter, the tourist office can organise accommodation in hundreds of huts, apartments and chalets by the day or week for very reasonable prices.

Right in town, the *Norlandia Trysil Hotel (☎ 62 45 08 33, fax 62 45 12 90, trysil@ norlandia.no, Storveien 24)* has standard singles/doubles for Nkr530/660 and seven-bed flats for Nkr430, but sheets are Nkr90 extra and cleaning is Nkr300. On sunny days, the *outdoor café* across the car park is a great place for a light meal. Alternatively, there's *Joffe's Pizza* on the main street near the tourist office.

Getting There & Around

The Nor-Way Bussekspress 'Trysil Ekspressen' runs three or four times daily to and from Oslo (3½ hours, Nkr220) via Elverum (1½ hours, Nkr83).

You can hire bicycles through Jul's Sportshop (☎ 62 45 16 77), in the Turistsenteret, for Nkr145 per day.

RØROS

Røros is a gem. Formerly called Bergstad (mountain city), this historic copper-mining town manages to preserve its past while retaining a welcoming and liveable community atmosphere. Set in a small hollow of stunted forests amid bleak and treeless fells, it also presents a different face of Norway to what most visitors expect. In 1984, UNESCO added the town to its list of World Heritage Sites. Although the town lies within the county of Sør Trøndelag, it definitely belongs to Central Norway.

History

The Røros area has been inhabited for many thousands of years, as evidenced by Stone Age ruins dating back to 8000 BC. There are signs of small-scale smelting of bog iron, as well as seasonal farming, hunting, trapping and herding; it isn't known when the southern Sami first migrated to the region, but it was almost certainly before the 17th century. When Olav Haraldsson was declared a saint after his martyrdom at Stiklestad in 1030, hundreds of pilgrims from Sweden passed through on the Krabatt and Ruten roads.

In 1644, the Røros region landed squarely on the map when local hunter Hans Olsen Aasen shot a reindeer at Storvola (Storwartz). The enraged creature leapt about and pawed up the ground to reveal the first glint of copper ore. In that same year, Røros Kobberverk was established and two years later a royal charter granted it 'circumference rights', or exclusive rights to all minerals, forest products and waterways within a 40km radius of the original discovery.

The location of the mining company headquarters at Røros was largely determined by the availability of wood and the rapids along the river Hyttelva, which provided power for the pumps, hoists, bellows and other machinery used in the smelting process. While there was plenty of power, the surrounding forests were quickly decimated, as wood was needed to heat up and expand the rock, making it easier to chip away (dynamite hadn't yet been invented). It was also used to heat the ore in preparation for smelting and for charcoal to be used in the smelting furnaces.

Røros first burnt to the ground during the Gyldenløve conflict with the Swedes between 1678 and 1679, and the smelter was destroyed by fire again in 1975. For the next two years, the smelting process was done in Sweden, but in 1977, after 333 years of operation, the company went bankrupt. Fortunately, Røros was no longer a one-industry town and managed to continue despite the initial economic hardship. The current population is 3000, roughly the same as during the mid-1600s.

Information

Tourist Office The exceptionally helpful and active Røros Reiseliv Turistkontoret (☎ 72 41 11 65, fax 72 41 02 08, roros.reise liv@ st.telia.no), Peder Hiortsgata 2, is in a historic building just a block from the train station. Staff can provide all the information you'll need to explore the town or set off on a hiking, biking or skiing trip (they've outlined a vast number of possibilities); they have also produced an amazing colour book, the *Turbok for Rørosregionen* (Nkr189), describing the district and its sites of interest in minute detail. This is also the place to go for information on museums and other sites of interest in the neighbouring towns of Tolga, Os, Vingelen and Holtålen. It's open year-round, from 9 am to 4 pm weekdays and 10 am to 2 pm Saturday.

Ask about the Røros Card, which costs Nkr35 and offers discounts on activities and museum admissions.

Emergency Services Local emergency telephone numbers include the following: police ☎ 112 or ☎ 72 41 18 00; fire brigade ☎ 110; medical service ☎ 113 or ☎ 72 41 05 55; and road rescue ☎ 72 41 24 55.

Historic District

Røros' historic district, characterised by the striking log architecture of its 80 protected buildings, takes in the entire central town area. The two main streets, **Bergmannsgata** (its taper from south-west to north-east was intended to create an optical illusion and make the town appear longer and larger than it was!) and **Kjerkgata**, are lined with historical homes and buildings, all under preservation orders. If you follow the river Hyttelva upstream, you'll reach the **historic smelting district** and its tiny turf-roofed miners' cottages, the smelter and other mine company buildings, and protected *slegghaugan* (slag heaps) and other mining detritus which overlook rainbow-coloured earth made barren by chemical residue from the smelting process. Crowning the hill and surrounded by earthen embank-

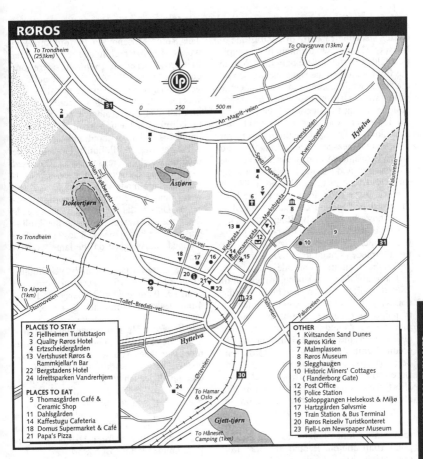

RØROS

To Trondheim
(253km)

To Olavsgruva (13km)

An-Magrit-velen

0   250   500 m

Åstjørn

Doktortjørn

To Trondheim

Johan Falkbergets-vei

Henrik—Grønns-vei

Spelli-Olaveien

Svenskveien

Kvernhuseien

Hyttelva

Falunveien

Kjerkgata

Bergmannsgata

Markisgata

To Airport
(1km)

Stormoveien

Tollef-Bredals-vei

Hyttelva

Olavsveien

To Hamar
& Oslo

To Håneset
Camping (1km)

Gjett-tjørn

PLACES TO STAY
2 Fjellheimen Turiststasjon
3 Quality Røros Hotel
4 Ertzscheidergården
13 Vertshuset Røros &
   Rammkjellar'n Bar
22 Bergstadens Hotel
24 Idrettsparken Vandrerhjem

PLACES TO EAT
5 Thomasgården Café &
   Ceramic Shop
11 Dahlsgården
14 Kaffestugu Cafeteria
18 Domus Supermarket & Café
21 Papa's Pizza

OTHER
1 Kvitsanden Sand Dunes
6 Røros Kirke
7 Malmplassen
8 Røros Museum
9 Slegghaugen
10 Historic Miners' Cottages
   (Flanderborg Gate)
12 Post Office
15 Police Station
16 Soloppgangen Helsekost & Miljø
17 Hartzgården Sølvsmie
19 Train Station & Bus Terminal
20 Røros Reiseliv Turistkontoret
23 Fjell-Lom Newspaper Museum

ments is the **old armoury** which housed the town's defence weaponry.

If it all looks like a film set, you won't be surprised to learn that several films have been made here, including Røros author Johan Falkberget's classic *An-Magrit*, starring Jane Fonda. Flanderborg gate starred in some films of Astrid Lindgren's *Pippi Longstocking* classics and the district even stood in for Siberia in the film of Solzhenitsyn's *A Day in the Life of Ivan Denisovich*. In summer, guided walking tours of the his-

torical district are conducted several times daily (the rest of the year on Sunday only) and cost Nkr40.

Røros Kirke

Røros' first church was constructed on upper Kjerkgata in 1650, but by the mid-18th century it had fallen into disrepair. From 1780 to 1784 a new baroque-style church was built just behind the original at a cost of 23,000 *riksdaler* (the old currency; one riksdaler is the equivalent of Nkr4, and miners earned about 50 riksdaler per year). The church's seating capacity of 1640 is one of Norway's largest. On the main floor, people of wealth and status were permitted to sit in the front – men on the right and women on the left – while poorer and less influential people were relegated to the back. The lower galleries along the sides, with comfortable padded seats, were sold to the wealthiest parishioners. The upper galleries were for the poorest peasants and criminals, who weren't considered worthy to set foot on the church floor and had to climb to their seats directly from outside. The posh King's Gallery at the back, identified by the both the royal and mining company logos, has never hosted a king, as visiting royals have always opted to sit among the people. A particular oddity is the pulpit, which sits over the altarpiece (a rendition of *The Last Supper*) rather than off to one side.

There are also other peculiarities. Until 1865 the building was owned by the mining company, and for this reason the collection of paintings on either side of the altar depicts not saints and angels, but rather such characters as the grizzled Hans Olsen Åsen, credited with the discovery of Røros copper; the first Røros Kobberverk director Lorenz Lossius; and philanthropist Peder Hiort, the company director at the time the church was constructed (he's the one in blue). There are also paintings of the town's first pastor, Peder Ditlevsen (in red); author Johan Falkberget; and the original 1650 church. Behind the altar, well out of sight, hangs a painting of the second mining company director, the unpopular Johannes Irgens, and his harried-looking wife, and a host of attending black-winged angels. The church is open for tours (Nkr15) from 10 am to 5 pm daily (2 to 4 pm on Sunday) between 20 June to 16 August; during the rest of the year, it's open from one to six days a week.

The rose-coloured mausoleum in the churchyard belongs to Peder Hiort, who was embalmed wearing a miner's uniform. At 11.30 am on Thursdays in July, you can tour the mausoleum for Nkr10.

Røros Museum

The Røros Museum, in the old smelting works, is a town highlight. The first smelter in Røros opened in 1646 and operations continued until 1953. Although the building was damaged by fire in the mid-1970s, it was reconstructed in 1988 according to the original plan. The geological and conservation displays in the upper hall are written in the Røros dialect, without translations.

Downstairs you'll find a large balance used for weighing ore, some well illustrated early mining statistics, and a series of brilliant working models of the mines and the water and horse-powered smelting processes. Outside the museum entrance spreads the large open area known as the Malmplassen (Ore Place), where loads of ore were dumped and weighed on the large wooden scale.

The museum is open daily year-round. From 20 June to 15 August, the hours are from 10.30 am to 6 pm weekdays and until 4 pm weekends. Admission is Nkr45.

Fjell-Ljom Newspaper Museum

You'll be especially grateful for your word processor when you see this office full of historic newspaper printing apparatus, including old leaden typesetting equipment. It belongs to the Røros weekly newspaper *Fjell-Ljom*, which has now moved on to more modern production methods. It's open from 10.30 am to 12.30 pm Thursday and 2 to 4 pm Saturday from 23 June to 8 August. Guided tours cost Nkr30.

Olavsgruva Mine

Don't miss the Olavsgruva mine, 13km from Røros (head north-east from the centre of town). The mine tour first passes through the historic Nyberget mine, which dates from the 1650s and invites comparison with the modern Olavsgruva (named for Crown Prince Olav) beyond it, which was begun in 1936 and closed in the 1970s. The ground can get muddy and the year-round temperature in the mine is a steady 5°C, so bring a jacket and good footwear. From 1 June to 10 September, Nkr45 mine tours run from one to six times daily, while the rest of the year they operate on Saturday only. To get to the mine either take a taxi (Nkr160) or the bus (Nkr60 return) which leaves the train station at 1 pm on weekdays (1 July to 9 August) and at 10 am Saturday (year-round), and returns after the tour.

Johan Falkberget Museum

Røros' favourite son, author Johan Falkberget (1879-1967), grew up at Trondalen farm in the nearby Rugel valley. His works (now translated into 19 languages) exposed 300 years of the region's mining history. His most famous work, *An-Magrit*, tells the story of a peasant girl who transported copper ore in the Røros mining district. The museum at Ratvolden, beside the nearby Rugelsjø, has guided tours (Nkr40) from 1 July to 16 August. To get there, take a local train to Rugeldalen station, 20km north of Røros, where a small walking track leads to the museum.

Activities

The **hiking** (and, in winter, **nordic skiing**) possibilities around the Røros plateau are endless, and numerous routes and tracks head out in all directions through hills, valleys and national parks. This semi-forested plateau region is a different side of Norway to the fjords or the high country around Jotunheimen, and hikers can strike out into the high country for an hour or a week. Note, however, that many areas remain snow-covered well into the summer and on the higher fells skiing is possible until July. Håmålfjellet, 16km south of Røros, is the largest downhill area, with two lifts and six slopes up to 300m long.

A short but rewarding walk from Røros will take you to the striking white sand dunes of Kvitsanden, the largest in Scandinavia, which lie 1km north-west of town at the end of a 30km-long esker. They were scoured, transported and deposited there by an ancient glacier.

Another kilometre to the west lies Skårhåmmårdalen, a shallow gorge with sand-lined pools which offers **swimming** on hot days and appears as if it might harbour trolls. You'll find more inviting summer swimming at the Gjett-tjönn pond, at the edge of town.

The tourist office can provide myriad suggestions for longer day hikes and overnight treks, and can also organise canoe hire and advise you on the best places for **canoeing, kayaking** and **angling** and **ice-fishing** for trout.

You can hire horses for Nkr75 per hour from Røros Hestesportsenter (☎ 72 41 29 83) at Sundet, about 6km north of town. Both guided and unguided tours are available.

Organised Tours

In winter you can organise ski tours and excursions by dog-sled (Nkr500/800 for three/six hours) or horse-drawn sleigh (Nkr500 per hour for four people). You can also join a winter day trip to the Southern Sami tent camp at Pinsti-tjønna, 3km from town and 1km off the road, where you'll dine on reindeer and learn such unique skills as ice-fishing and axe-throwing. The three-hour tour costs Nkr335.

Special Events

The biggest event in winter is the Rørosmartnan (Røros Market). It began in 1644 as a rendezvous for hunters and trappers who ventured into town to sell their products to miners and buy supplies. Thanks to a royal decree issued in 1853 stipulating that a grand market be held annually from the penultimate Tuesday of February to the following Friday, it continues today. Nowadays, it's celebrated with cultural programs, street markets and live entertainment.

From early to mid-August every second year (including 2000 and 2002), Røros stages a nightly three-hour rock opera in Swedish entitled *Det Brinner en Eld*, or 'Fiery Call for Peace'. It recounts the invasion of Trøndelag by Swedish soldiers under Lieutenant-General de la Barre. This pointless struggle is followed through the lives and loves of the various players, the eventual occupation of Røros and the subsequent death of thousands of soldiers on their frozen trek homewards to Sweden. The opera was written in 1980 by Arnfinn Strømmevold and Bertil Reithaug and it's enacted on the slag heaps in the upper part of town. If you can manage to get there, don't miss it.

Places to Stay

Camping is available at *Håneset Camping* (☎ 72 41 06 00), about 2km south of town. Two/four-person huts cost Nkr320/420. The good value *Fjellheimen Turiststasjon* (☎ 72 41 14 68, Johan Falkbergetsvei 25), 500m from town, offers camping and has single/double huts for Nkr250/350.

The *Idrettsparken Vandrerhjem* (☎ 72 41 10 89, fax 72 41 23 77, Øra 25) may not be Norway's most pre-possessing hostel, but it's only 300m from the train station. Camping is allowed and there are dorm beds for Nkr160 (with breakfast), private singles/doubles for Nkr260/360 and cabins for Nkr330. The attached hotel has acceptable singles/doubles from Nkr470/680. Head east from the train station, cross the tracks opposite Bergstadens Hotel and follow the signs.

Ertzscheidergården (☎ 72 41 11 94, Spell Olaveien 6), a 15-room guesthouse, lies just a stone's throw from the church and mining museum. It has singles/doubles from Nkr550/690, with breakfast. The cosiest and perhaps best value choice is the *Vertshuset Røros* (☎ 72 41 24 11, Kjerkgata 34), in a historic building in the centre. Singles/doubles start at Nkr575/710, while self-catering units cost from Nkr275 per person.

There are also a couple of business hotels. The *Quality Røros Hotel* (☎ 72 41 10 11, An Magrittsvei 10), on the hilltop, has singles/doubles from Nkr635/870. The cosier and more down-to-earth *Bergstadens Hotel* (☎ 72 40 60 80), near the train station, offers well appointed singles/doubles starting at Nkr640/890. Both these places also feature nightclubs, discos and occasional live music with dancing.

In the village of Brekken, about 30km east of Røros, is the *Henningsgården*

Touriststasjon (☎ 72 41 31 46), which charges Nkr160/300 for single/double self-catering huts. The nearby *Skottgården Gjestgiveri* (☎ 72 41 32 60) charges Nkr320. Unfortunately, they're accessible by bus on Wednesday only in summer. At the small and appealing mountain community of Vingelen, about 40km south-west of Røros, you'll find the *Vingelsgård Gjestgiveri* (☎ 62 49 45 43), which charges Nkr200/360 for singles/doubles. The best out-of-town value, however, is the simple house *Lyngen Gård* (☎ 62 49 81 51), at Dalsbygda, about 25km west of Røros. Accommodation costs Nkr150 per person.

If you want to stay awhile, the tourist office keeps a list of summer cabins, some within walking distance of town, starting at around Nkr2000 per week in the high season. All have self-catering facilities and if you have a group this is certainly the most economical way to go; it's wise to book well in advance. The tourist office can also book rural guesthouses and cabins by the night. These include *Narbuvoll Fjellstue* (Nkr250/450 for a single/double) on Narsjøen lake 40km south of town; *Nordpå Fjellstue* (Nkr260 to Nkr395 for a single and Nkr420 to Nkr580 for a double) about 50km north-west of Røros; and *Langen Gjestegård* (see Fermundsmarka Nasjonalpark later in this section).

Places to Eat

The informal *Kafestuggu cafeteria* (☎ 72 41 10 33, Bergmannsgata 18) offers a good range of coffee, pastries, cold snacks and light meals. The unusual décor in the various rooms is especially interesting. It's open daily for lunch and dinner. Daily until midnight, *Papa's Pizza* (☎ 72 40 60 20), at the end of Bergmannsgata, does pizza and other fast meals, including burgers and chicken dishes. It's also licensed to serve beer and wine.

For formal dining, the finest option is probably the *Vertshuset Røros* guesthouse (☎ 72 41 24 11, Kjerkegata 34), where you'll find a good varied menu including beef and chicken dishes, local reindeer and freshwater fish. On sunny days or when the snow is falling, the conservatory (solarium) is nice and allows you to enjoy the outdoors without facing the elements. The attached *Rammkjellar'n Kjøkken & Bar* *(☎ 72 41 01 88)* has a nice atmosphere and a varied menu. The Quality Røros Hotel and Bergstadens Hotel also have pleasant dining rooms.

There are also many small coffee shops (some attached to crafts and souvenir shops), such as *Dahlsgården (☎ 72 41 19 89)* and *Thomasgården (☎ 72 41 13 65)*, where you can enjoy a quick cuppa and a pastry or slice of pie. Within a block of the tourist office, you'll also find a couple of bakeries and a *Domus supermarket*, with an inexpensive cafeteria. *Soloppgangen Helsekost & Miljø (☎ 72 41 29 55, Kjerkgata 6)* sells health foods.

Shopping

Given its unaffected ambience, it isn't surprising that Røros has attracted over 40 artists and artisans. Of special interest is the Hartzgården Sølvsmie (☎ 72 41 05 50), the silversmith's shop, where you'll find locally hand-crafted silver jewellery with an emphasis on Viking themes, as well as a small historic jewellery exhibit. Also have a look at the unusual indoor water well which dominates the middle of the shop. Another worthwhile place is the Galleri Thomasgården ceramic shop and café (☎ 72 41 13 65), where potter Torgeir Henriksen creates rustic stoneware and porcelain. You'll also find the wonderful nature-inspired wood-carvings of Henry Solli. The player piano is one of only two in Norway and dates back to 1929. The town also has a glass-blower, a copper shop and several general handicraft shops. Guided tours (Nkr40) of the major crafts shops operate on Monday and Wednesday from 20 June to 16 August.

Getting There & Away

Røros, with one or two daily Braathens SAFE flights to and from Oslo and Trondheim, is one of the smallest towns in the world with scheduled flights by jet aircraft. It also lies on the eastern railway line between Oslo (six hours, Nkr430) and Trondheim (2½ hours, Nkr200). There's a daily overnight bus from Oslo which arrives at 4.25 am, then continues to Trondheim. The return bus leaves Trondheim at 10 pm, passes Røros at 12.40 am and arrives at Oslo at 6.45 am. There are also several other daily services to and from Trondheim.

Getting Around

Røros is easily manageable on foot, which is the preferred mode of transport, as parking can be a major headache in summer when the main street is (fortunately) open only to pedestrians. If you have a car, leave it at the edge of town and walk in. For a taxi, phone ☎ 72 41 12 58.

For day trips around town, the tourist office loans bicycles free of charge (but with a deposit). In winter, you can opt for a *spark*, a locally popular kick-sled that resembles a dog-sled without the dogs. For longer summer cycling excursions, you can rent a mountain bike from Røros Sport (☎ 72 41 12 18) on Bergmannsgata.

FEMUNDSMARKA NASJONALPARK

The national park which surrounds Femunden, Norway's second largest lake, was formed in 1971 to protect both the lake and the vast forested area stretching eastwards to the Swedish border. This has long been a source of falcons for use in the European and Oriental sport of falconry and several places in the park are known as Falkfangerhøgda, or 'falcon hunters' height'. You may also see wild reindeer grazing in the heights and in summer a herd of 30 or so musk oxen roams the area along the Røa and Mugga rivers (in winter they migrate to the Funäsdalen area). It's thought that this group split off from an older herd in the Dovrefjell area.

The ferry M/S *Fæmund II* was first launched under steam power in 1905 and was converted to diesel in 1958. Between

14 June and 31 October it sails at least daily between Synnervika (also spelt Søndervika), on the northern shore of lake Femunden, to Buvika (on Tuesday only to Elgå). On Wednesday, it continues all the way to Femundsenden, at the lake's southern tip.

Places to Stay
Camping is permitted anywhere outside developed areas. Alternatively, near Synnervika you can stay at the *Langen Gjestegård* (☎ 72 41 37 18), a cosy turf-roofed farmhouse near the lake, from Nkr305/430 for a single/double with breakfast.

Getting There & Away
From 14 June to 16 August, buses run between Røros and Synnervika at least twice daily. The 8.15 am departure from Røros allows you to cruise around Femunden on *Fæmund II* and return to Røros on the same day. You can reach the southern end of Femunden on the Trysilbussen bus which runs one to four times daily from Hamar (3¾ hours, Nkr208) via Elverum and Trysil.

Northern Central Norway

OPPDAL
Oppdal makes a logical outdoor break between Oslo or Trondheim and the northern reaches of the Western Fjords. This outdoor-oriented town is an activity centre *par excellence* and there's plenty on offer, from winter skiing and snowboarding to summer river rafting, hiking, climbing and canyoning. If you're on a short visit, it's worth heading for the lower gondola station about 600m from the centre, where Nkr50 will take you the lazy way to the view from the Topprestaurant at the summit of Hovden (1125m), which rises 525m over the town. In winter, this gondola provides access to a couple of challenging black diamond ski runs.

Information
The Oppdal Turistkontor (☎ 72 42 17 60, fax 72 42 08 88, post@opp-tur.st.no) is just a block from the train and bus stations.

Activities
White-water Rafting The wild white Driva offers several excellent rafting runs. The outdoor adventure company Opplev Oppdal (☎ 72 40 04 60, fax 72 40 04 65, opplevoppdal@ online.no, www.opplev-oppdal .no) on Høgmoveien organises a range of worthwhile trips. The three-hour Class I family trip (Nkr290/130 for adults/children) is designed more as a wilderness experience than an adrenalin rush, but you can also opt for half/full-day Class III trips (Nkr370/590) which provide substantial thrills. The more daring can opt for the two-day run (Nkr1590), which ranges from Class III to IV and includes a stretch through the steep-walled Gråura canyon. The same company also offers boogie-boarding (Nkr630), canyoning (Nkr590), river kayaking (Nkr590), rock climbing (Nkr590) and a musk ox photo safari on foot in Dovrefjell National Park (Nkr250).

Those on multi-day trips are accommodated at its wonderful Vilmarksleir wilderness camp, west of town, which is also open to casual visitors. Here you can choose between accommodation in mountain huts (Nkr50 per person) and 10-person Sami lavvos (Nkr25 per person). If the rafting hasn't produced enough adrenalin, you can try out the 15m-high circus training equipment.

Skiing & Snowboarding The three-part Oppdal Skisenter climbs the slopes from Hovden, Stølen and Vangslia, all within easy reach of town. Vangslia is generally the easiest, with a couple of beginners' runs, while Stølen offers intermediate skiing and Hovden has three challenging advanced runs. Lift passes for one/two/three-day cost Nkr195/360/495 and a morning/afternoon of skiing is Nkr140/175; or you can opt for six runs for Nkr170 or three days of skiing in five for Nkr560. The season varies, but generally runs from late November to late April.

Places to Stay & Eat

The *Oppdalstunet Vandrerhjem (☎ 72 42 23 11, fax 72 42 23 13)* lies about 1.5km from the centre at the north-eastern edge of town. Dorm beds are Nkr145 and singles/doubles Nkr395/410, including use of kitchen facilities. At the *Quality Hotell Oppdal (☎ 72 42 11 11, fax 72 42 08 24)*, at the bus and train stations, you'll pay from Nkr430/630 for singles/doubles. In summer or the ski season, you'll have a choice of basic four-bed holiday cabins for Nkr200 to Nkr500 per night. The nearest to the centre is the *Vekve Hyttetun (☎ 72 42 12 62)*, which charges Nkr400/500 for two/four-bed huts with shower and toilet. The popular *Café Ludvik* serves a range of inexpensive light meals, including fish and chips, beef dishes and pasta.

Entertainment

If you're over 20, the English-style *George Pub* at the Quality Hotell Oppdal features Mexican pizza and Kilkenny on tap. Oppdal also has a cinema on the main drag which screens a different film every few days (Nkr40).

Getting There & Away

The best access to Oppdal is via the three daily services between Oslo (5¼ hours, Nkr470) and Trondheim (1½ hours, 160). Oppdal lies on the Nor-Way Bussekspress route between Bergen (12½ hours, Nkr650) and Trondheim (2¼ hours, Nkr131), with connections at Otta to and from Oslo.

TROLLHEIMEN

The relatively small Trollheimen range, with a variety of trails through gentle mountains and lake-studded upland regions, is most readily accessed from Oppdal. You can either hitch or hike the 15km from Oppdal up the toll road to **Osen**, which is the main entrance to the wilderness region. The best map to use is Statens Kartverk's *Trollheimen Turkart* (1:100,000), which costs Nkr60 at the tourist office in Oppdal.

A straightforward hiking destination in Trollheimen is the hut and historic farm at

Vassendsætra. From Osen (the outlet of Gjevilvatnet), which lies 3km north of the main road to Sunndalsøra, you can take the boat *Trollheimen II* all the way to Vassendsætra (Nkr120 return). From 1 July to 20 August, it leaves Osen daily at noon and from Vassendsætra at 3.30 pm. Alternatively, you can drive or hike 6km along the road from Osen to the DNT hut, Gjevilsvasshytta, and follow the lakeshore trail for 12km to Vassendsætra. About midway, you'll pass several outstanding sandy beaches, with excellent summer swimming.

Accommodation at Vassendsætra (☎ 72 42 32 20, fax 72 42 34 30) costs Nkr150/200 for DNT members/non-members; breakfast is Nkr60 and other meals are Nkr85 to Nkr140. It's open from 1 July to 30 August. If you're hiking the popular route to the coast at **Sunndalsøra**, you may want to stop at the charming *Sunndalsøra Vandrerhjem (☎ 71 69 13 01, fax 71 69 05 55)*, where you'll find dormitory accommodation for Nkr100 and singles/doubles for Nkr140/250.

RINGEBU

Gudbrandsdalen, the narrow river valley which stretches for 200km between lake Mjøsa and Dombås, has long been a major farming area and also supports a string of small communities. The southernmost is Ringebu, where there's a lovely 13th century stave church 1km west of the E6. The church was extensively restored in the 17th century when the odd red tower was appended to the structure. It's open from 9 am to 6 pm daily in mid-summer, with slightly shorter hours at other times between late May and early September. Admission is Nkr20. The adjacent 1743 vicarage houses the Ringebu Samlingene (☎ 61 28 27 00), a collection of 40 paintings by Jakob Wiedemann. It's open from 10 am to 5 pm Tuesday to Sunday (from 11 am Sunday) from June to September. Admission costs Nkr40.

For information, contact the Ringebu Turistkontor (☎ 61 28 05 33). The low-key *Ringebu Hotel (☎ 61 28 12 50, fax 61 28 12 51, Brugata 27)* has summer single/double rates of Nkr495/630.

KVAM & SJOA

At the riverside chip-boarding town of Kvam, the main attraction is the **Gudbrandsdal Krigsminnesamling** (☎ 61 29 40 33), an exposé of Gudbrandsdalen conflicts beginning with the Sinclair expedition and the Battle of Kringom in 1612 and culminating with the Nazi occupation during WWII. It's open daily from 10 am to 5 pm and costs Nkr30. The Heidalen area between Otta and Vinstra also boasts Norway's largest collection of protected buildings, most of which are still in use.

Sjoa, which in Norway is synonymous with **white-water rafting**, has some of the country's wildest and most popular liquid thrills. The main players are Heidal Rafting (☎ 61 23 60 37, fax 61 23 60 14, heidal.rafting@ online.no or heiraft@online.no) in Sjoa; Sjoa Rafting (☎ 61 23 61 70, fax 61 23 19 00, sjoa@online.no), a few kilometres upstream at Nedre Heidal; and, even farther upstream at Randsverk, Norwegian Wildlife & Rafting (☎ 61 23 87 27, fax 61 23 87 60, sjoaraft@ online.no, www.nwr.no). All four offer half/ full-day trips on the Sjoa's Class II to III white water, for Nkr400/650 to Nkr430/ 750. There are Class I to II family trips on the Otta river (Nkr400) and Class III to IV one/two-day runs (from Nkr790/1890) through the roiling waters of the Åsengjuvet canyon. These companies can also organise other adventure activities, including river-boarding, rock climbing, canyoning, dog-sledding, glacier expeditions and wildlife-viewing safaris.

Most rafting participants stay at Heidal Rafting's hillside *Sjoa Vandrerhjem* (☎ 61 23 62 00, fax 61 23 60 14), in an atmospheric 1747 log farmhouse. Dorm beds cost from Nkr80 to Nkr120 and doubles start at Nkr170/250 without/with showers. Breakfast is an additional Nkr50 and dinners cost Nkr80. An alternative is *Heidal Vertshus*, which charges Nkr400 per person, including breakfast. Norwegian Wildlife & Rafting has its own *wilderness camp*, which costs Nkr600/800 on weekdays/weekends for groups of up to eight people, plus Nkr100 for each additional person.

OTTA

Set deep in Gudbrandsdalen, at the junction of the rivers Otta and Lågen, scenic Otta makes a great jumping off point for hikes in Rondane National Park and also an ideal break along the rail and bus routes between Oslo and Trondheim. The helpful Sel-Rondane Reiselivslag tourist office (☎ 61 23 02 44, fax 61 23 09 60, sel.rondane@online.no), at the Otta Skysstasjon bus and train station, provides a wealth of information on Otta and can also help with trip-planning for Rondane National Park.

Kringom

At Kringom, about 3km south of Otta on the E6 and then a short distance up the hill to the east, a **war memorial** commemorates the 26 August 1612 victory of valley farmers over Sinclair's band of 550 Scottish mercenaries in the employ of the Swedish Kalmar aggressors. On the opposite side of the river rises the hill **Pillarguri**, named for the woman who set the stage for the triumphant and vicious defeat of the Scots (see the boxed text 'Guri Saves the Day').

Kvitskriuprestein

The unusual natural pillar formations of Kvitskriuprestein ('white scree priests') resemble an assembly of priests and were formed by the erosion of an Ice Age moraine. Although much of the moraine material has been washed away by the elements, these pillars were protected by capstones. They lie about 5km east along the road from Selsverket towards Peer Gynt Hytta.

Places to Stay & Eat

You'll find the best value budget accommodation at the convenient and popular *Otta Camping* (☎/fax 61 23 03 09) in Ottadalen. It has tent/caravan sites for Nkr70 for two people, rooms for Nkr300 to Nkr450 and four-bed cabins for Nkr300. It's a 1.5km walk from the train and bus stations. Cross the Otta bridge from the centre, turn right and continue about 1km upstream. The *Sagatun Gjestgiveri* (☎ 61 23 08 14, Ottekra 1) is a decent hostel-style place with

Guri Saves the Day

As you travel around Otta, you're sure to see the image of a young woman blowing a horn triumphantly. You might also notice the monument to her that's been erected on the hill Høgkringom and you may even notice that the local *bunad* (national costume) is a distinctly un-Norwegian tartan. If you're wondering what it's all about, read on for a rollicking Norwegian tale of ambush, bloodshed and vengeance.

The legend of Pillarguri – 'Guri' for short – was inspired by the Battle of Kringom, fought just south of Otta on 26 August 1612. During the Kalmar War between Sweden and Denmark, when Norway was united with Denmark, 550 Scottish mercenaries arrived to aid the Swedish cause. Along their route from the coast to Sweden they had to pass through Gudbrandsdalen. At Høgkringom, south of Otta, the contingent was forced to use a narrow path between the river and a steep hillside, but met with an ambush set up by the resourceful local peasants, whose bravery and ingenuity is remembered by the good folk of Otta to this day.

Having heard of the approach of the mercenaries, the peasants armed themselves with axes, scythes and other farming implements; they stacked up rocks and branches across the track to block the route and, to set up a diversion, placed several older men across the river to fire their rifles at the column, using blanks.

As the Scots approached the narrow path, the heroic Guri dashed up the hill to announce their arrival by sounding her shepherd's birch bark horn. This was the signal for the old farmers to fire; the Scots, confident they'd meet with little resistance, fired back at the old men across the river, then responded to Guri's music by waving their hats and playing their bagpipes, unaware of the trap they were walking into.

As Guri sounded her horn again, more rocks and branches were lowered across the trail behind the column, blocking any hope of a retreat. At this stage, the farmers attacked with their crude weapons, savagely defeating the contingent and making the river flow red with blood.

Only six farmers were killed in the battle, and the victors intended to take the 134 surviving Scots as prisoners to Akershus Fortress. However, during the victory celebrations at Kvam, the farmers, who had to get on with their harvest and couldn't be bothered with a march to Oslo, executed the prisoners one by one. And thus a raggle-taggle band of 450 untrained farmers soundly defeated a professional band of mercenaries.

singles/doubles/triples for Nkr160/250/375. It's open year-round. An alternative inexpensive option is *Killis Overnatting* (☎ 61 23 04 92, Ola Dahlsgata 35), which has singles/doubles for Nkr180/200.

A bit more plush and just as convenient is the *Grand Gjestegård* (☎ 61 23 12 00, fax 61 23 04 62), just behind the bus and train stations. Singles/doubles cost Nkr500/660, with breakfast. The attached cafeteria produces pleasant sit-down meals. The finest in-town choice is the rather nondescript *Norlandia Otta Hotell* (☎ 61 23 00 33, fax 61 23 15 24), which has singles/doubles for

summer rates of Nkr545/695. On Friday and Saturday there's a lively disco which appeals to the 18 to 35 crowd. It's free on Friday but there's a cover charge of Nkr50 on Saturday.

Pizzerina Pizzeria on Mostugugata is open until 1 am and serves wine and beer. There's also the the *Pillarguri Café*, specialising in Norwegian fare. Less pretentious options are on offer at the *Otta Café & Gatekjøkken*, on the corner of Nordmogata and Johan Nygårdsgate. A block to the south, the Chinese niche is filled by *Peking*, which offers inexpensive lunch and dinner specials.

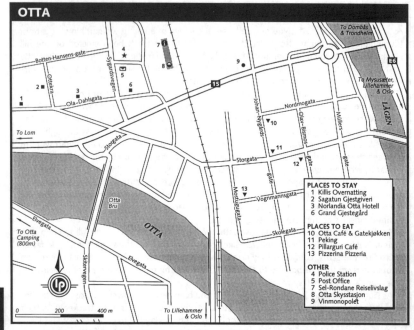

OTTA

PLACES TO STAY
1 Killis Overnatting
2 Sagatun Gjestgiveri
3 Norlandia Otta Hotell
6 Grand Gjestegård

PLACES TO EAT
10 Otta Café & Gatekjøkken
11 Peking
12 Pillarguri Café
13 Pizzerina Pizzeria

OTHER
4 Police Station
5 Post Office
7 Sel-Rondane Reiselivslag
8 Otta Skysstasjon
9 Vinmonopolet

Getting There & Away

Local buses to and from Vågå (45 minutes, Nkr31) and Lom (1¼ hours, Nkr62) leave four or more times daily. There are at least two buses to and from Lillehammer daily (2¼ hours, Nkr130). On Nor-Way Busseks-press, three daily buses between Måløy (5½ hours, Nkr320) and Oslo (5½ hours, Nkr330) pass through Otta. The town also lies on the Dovre rail line between Oslo (3¾ hours, Nkr370) and Trondheim (three hours, Nkr315), with at least three services daily.

RONDANE NASJONALPARK

The 572 sq km Rondane National Park, which Henrik Ibsen described as 'palace piled upon palace', was created in 1962 as Norway's first national park to protect the fabulous Rondane massif, which many regard as the finest alpine hiking country in the country. Ancient reindeer trapping sites

and burial mounds provide evidence that the area has been inhabited for thousands of years. Much of the park's glaciated landscape lies above 1400m and 10 peaks rise to over 2000m; the highest of these are **Rondslottet (2178m)** and **Storronden (2138m)**. Rondane's range of wildlife includes 28 mammal species – from lemmings to reindeer – and 124 bird species.

For hikers, Rondane will provide ample opportunities for high country exploration, and the relatively dry climate makes it all the more appealing. The most accessible route into the park is from the Sprang-haugen car park, near Mysusæter. From there, it's an easy 6km hike to Rondvassbu and then a five-hour return climb to the summit of Storronden. Alternatively, head for the more difficult but also more spectacular view from the summit of Vinjeron-den (2044m), which will take about six hours return from Rondvassbu. If that's not enough, you can also tackle the exposed knife-ridge that leads to the neighbouring peak, Rondslottet (2178m). There are also dozens of other less popular routes.

The best maps to use are Cappelens Kart's *Rondane* (1:100,000) and Statens Kartverk's *Høvringen-Kvamsfjellet Turkart* (1:50,000). Camping is permitted anywhere in the national park except at Rondvassbu, where you're limited to the designated area.

Mysusæter

The easiest Rondane access for hikers is probably via Mysusæter, 13km uphill along a good road from Otta. To proceed past Mysusæter to the Spranghaugen car park at the national park border, 4km farther, there's a toll of Nkr10 per vehicle, but it's also an easy walk and takes you to the best starting point for a mountain hike in Rondane.

Just down the hill from the 'Bom' (toll post) gate is a small shop selling staple provisions. The cheapest place to stay is the hostel-like *Mysusæter Fjellosji* (☎ 61 23 39 17), which has dorm beds for Nkr150 per night. You can also hire mountain bikes here for Nkr25/180 per hour/day. Canoe hire on the nearby lake Furusjøen costs Nkr80/250 per hour/day.

The *Mysusæter Fjellstue* (☎ 61 23 39 25) also provides a roof over your head for Nkr170 for a dorm bed and from Nkr375 per person in a double room. The more plush and upmarket *Rondane Høyfjellshotell* (☎ 61 23 39 33) charges from Nkr740 per person, with full board.

Høvringen

Another popular access to Rondane is via Høvringen; take the east turning about 15km north of Otta on the E6. The Nkr20

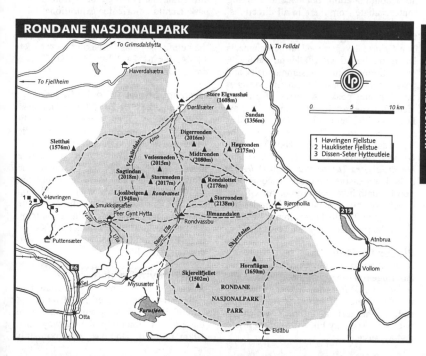

RONDANE NASJONALPARK

To Grimsdalshytta
To Folldal
To Fjellheim
Haverdalsætra

Store Elgvasshøi
(1608m)
Dørålsæter
Sandan
(1356m)

0   5   10 km

Digerronden
(2016m)
Høgronden
(2175m)
Midtronden
(2080m)

1 Høvringen Fjellstue
2 Haukliseter Fjellstue
3 Dissen-Seter Hytteutleie

Sletthøi
(1576m)
Veslesmeden
(2015m)
Sagtindan
(2018m)
Storsmeden
(2017m)
Rondslottet
(2178m)

Ljosåbelgen
(1948m)
Rondvatnet
Smukksjøsæter
Storronden
(2138m)
Bjørnhollia

1
2
Høvringen
Peer Gynt Hytta
Illmanndalen
Rondvassbu
219

3

Puttensæter
Atnbrua

E6
Hornflågan
(1650m)
Vollom

Sel
Skjerelifjellet
(1502m)
RONDANE
NASJONALPARK
PARK

Otta
Furusjøen
Eldåbu

CENTRAL NORWAY

toll to Smukksjøsæter (☎ 61 23 37 19, fax 61 23 37 49), 5km east of Høvringen, is refunded if you stay at the hut. It doesn't belong to the DNT, but offers discounts for DNT members. Dorm beds are Nkr160 and singles/doubles with shower and toilet cost Nkr305/540. There are many other mountain lodges, among them the *Høvringen Fjellstue (☎ 61 23 37 18, fax 61 23 37 47)*, with simple singles/doubles for Nkr235/350, and the beautifully situated *Haukliseter Fjellstue (☎ 61 23 37 17, fax 61 23 37 50)*, with lodge rooms starting at Nkr245 a double. The *Dissen Seter Hytteutleie (☎/fax 61 23 37 15)* accommodates 22 people for Nkr100 per person. The *Høvringen Handel & Kro* sells groceries and serves light meals.

A popular day hike begins at Smukksjøsæter and climbs to Peer Gynt Hytta, where a *café* operates year-round. There's no accommodation, but excellent hiking routes radiate from there in all directions.

Grimsdalsvegen

The Grimsdalsvegen road, which connects Dovre on the E6 with Fallet on the Rv27, passes through a historic summer dairy and pasture area and provides taunting views of the Rondane peaks. A series of plaques identifies sites of interest along the way. From the Fjellheim toll station, the toll is Nkr50 per vehicle. The side route to the Haverdalssetra hut costs Nkr20. DNT's *Grimsdalshytta (☎ 61 23 17 88)* and *Haverdalsetra Turisthytta (☎ 94 19 09 91)* offer inexpensive overnight accommodation for both hikers and motorists. Official *camp sites* are available at Grimsdal and Haverdal for Nkr30, but camping elsewhere along the route is strongly discouraged.

Places to Stay

In addition to the places described under Høvringen and Mysusæter, there are also several *DNT huts* for hikers. The most popular is the staffed hut at Rondvassbu, right in the heart of the park, which lies within an easy day hike of Smukksjøsæter and Mysusæter.

Getting There & Away

Bus access from Otta to Høvringen runs two or three times daily, 20 June to 20 September, stopping at Haukliseter (45 minutes, Nkr33) and Smukksjøsæter (one hour, Nkr34). Buses run twice daily between Otta and Mysusæter (45 minutes, Nkr18).

From Rondvassbu, the ferry *Rondegubben* crosses the lake Rondvatnet to Nordvika (30 minutes, Nkr40) three times daily from early July to late August.

DOMBÅS

The useful road and rail junction of Dombås makes a convenient break for travellers between the highland national parks and the Western Fjords. It's also a popular adventure and winter sports centre. About 90% of the town's commerce is concentrated on a single car park in the centre of town, which includes Dombås' only real attraction, the Dovregubbens Rike Trollpark, a children-oriented exhibition on the trolls of the Dovrefjell mountains. For information on Dombås and Dovrefjell, see the helpful Dombås Turistkontor (☎ 61 24 14 44, fax 61 24 11 90, touristoffice@dovrenett.no).

Dovregubbens Rike Trollpark

The Trollpark (☎ 61 24 12 90) in Dombås' main shopping complex presents a mildly interesting exposé on the legendary trolls which are thought to inhabit much of Norway. According to tradition, the Dovre massif was known as the Realm of the Mountain King, who was the friendliest and most powerful of all trolls. This exhibition provides the lowdown on these elusive creatures and there's also a film explaining a bit of the local natural history. It's open from 10 am to 8 pm daily in summer. Admission is Nkr30.

Fokstumyra Naturreservat

As early as 1816, ornithologists were marvelling over the number and diversity of bird life in the Fokstumyra marshes, west of the E6 and straddling the railway line, 19km north of Dombås. Approximately

Trolls, Wights, Elves & Witches

Norwegian folklore includes references to all sorts of supernatural beings. While many people assume that these creatures, common to most cultures, are simply Jungian archetypes, manifestations of the Id, or alien beings, more traditional folk consider them descendants of the children hidden from God by mother Eve.

Perhaps the most Scandinavian of all these beings is the troll, which is thought to have emerged in Norway at the close of the last Ice Age. Trolls inhabit gloomy forests, moonlit lakes, deep fjords, snowy peaks and roaring waterfalls, but they're predominantly creatures of shadow and darkness. Any troll who makes the mistake of exposing themself to direct sunlight will crack and turn to stone.

Trolls come in all shapes and sizes, some large and some small but nearly all have four fingers and toes on each hand and foot, as well as long, crooked noses and bushy tails. Some have multiple heads, with anything from one to three eyes per head, which of course makes them appear frightening. It's believed that trolls can live for several hundred years and are credited with having produced both Þór's hammer and Oðinn's spear. They also have a penchant for harassing billy goats and despising the sound of church bells. They're known to get irritable on occasion, and even anger easily but, in general, they're kind to humans who remain on their better side.

A larger version of the troll was the giant and, according to the Edda, the world was created from the body of the giant Ymir of Jotunheimen, after his death at the hand of the Norse god Oðinn.

Throughout Europe, a witch has long been the personification of evil. Although most modern witches dabble only in 'white' magic, the traditional view is that anyone accused of being a witch or warlock has sold their soul to the devil and is capable of all sorts of heinous behaviour, including the infliction of unpleasant spells. Norwegian witches are no exception and are still considered evil forces, despite the public relations campaign recently mounted by practitioners of Wicca.

Elves, who normally live stream-side in the deepest forests, also come in both good and bad varieties and only emerge at night, when there is no risk of turning to stone. It's said that the sites of their nighttime festivities and dances are marked by luxuriant rings of grass. Other elusive creatures include mermaids, who do their best to evade Norwegian fisherfolk; the frightening *draugen*, a headless fisherman who foretells drownings with a haunting wail; and the *vetter* (wights), who serve as the guardian spirits of the wildest coastlines.

75 species nest in the area and up to 40 others are occasionally observed. Among the more unusual species breeding near the water are the ruff, the great snipe, Temminck's stint, whimbrel, great northern diver (loon), lapwing, lesser white-fronted goose and hen harrier. Species which breed in the surrounding hills and forests include the snow bunting, ring ouzel, field fare, purple sandpiper, great grey shrike, dipper, brambling, peregrine falcon, dotterel, short-eared owl, raven and shore lark.

The only bus access from Dombås is the twice daily Nor-Way Bussekspress route to and from Trondheim (30 minutes, Nkr30), but both the Dombås Vandrerhjem and the Dovrefjell Activitetssenter offer guided tours. Alternatively, you can rent a bike for Nkr130 or take a taxi for around Nkr200 each way. A 27km portion of the Nidaros Pilgrims' Way provides an easy nature hike between Fokstumyra and the bleak settlement of Hjerkinn, farther north on the E6.

Organised Tours

A good range of adventure tours are offered by the Dovrefjell Activitetssenter (☎ 61 24 15 55, fax 61 24 15 70), in the same building as the tourist office. See Fokstumyra Naturreservat on its canoe moose-viewing safari (Nkr210), where you meet not only moose, but also myriad bird species. Just the birdwatching, with a guide, costs Nkr180. Six-hour musk ox safaris in Dovrefjell are Nkr170, technical climbing trips, with instruction, are Nkr450 per day, rafting trips cost from Nkr230 to Nkr600, glacier and ice-climbing in Jotunheimen is Nkr600, canyoning is Nkr650 and six-hour Snøhetta climbs are Nkr290. Book either directly or through the tourist office. The company also has a climbing wall and hires out mountain bikes for Nkr130 per day.

Places to Stay & Eat

The central *Midtskog Camping* (☎ 61 24 14 29), about 800m down the Raumadalen road from the centre complex, has tent camping for Nkr100 and basic two/four-bed cabins for Nkr230/260.

Norway's best value and probably friendliest camping is *Bjørkhol Camping* (☎ 61 24 13 31), 7km south of Dombås, which has tent camping for Nkr60 and simple four/five-bed cabins starting at Nkr160/275. With a shower and toilet, the four-bed option costs Nkr450. A bus runs several times daily from Dombås.

The popular *Dombås Vandrerhjem* (☎ 61 24 10 45, fax 61 24 11 45), about 1km off the sinuous E6 from the town centre, charges Nkr105 for dorm beds and Nkr200/260 for singles/doubles. Meals are also available. In summer, the hostel organises tours to Fokstumyra and Dovrefjell.

For a plusher night's sleep, the rich-looking *Dombås Hotell* (☎ 61 24 10 01, fax 61 24 14 61, dombas.hotel@riksnett.no), near the tourist office, charges Nkr590/680 in summer, and the nearly adjacent *Dombåstun Motell* (☎ 61 24 12 20, fax 61 24 15 40) has singles/doubles with breakfast for Nkr375/490.

The main commercial complex in the centre includes both the popular *Frich Cafeteria* and the *Senter-Grillen* gatekjøkken and pub, which also serves pizza. The local Chinese restaurant, on the main road towards Otta, is oddly named *Jegerkroa*, the 'hunters' café'.

Getting There & Away

Dombås lies on the railway line between Oslo (4½ hours, Nkr395) and Trondheim (2½ hours, Nkr260). It is also the cut-off point for the spectacular Raumabanen line down Romsdalen to Åndalsnes (1½ hours, Nkr150), which runs two or three times daily in summer. The Åndalsnes line is also served once or twice daily by Togbuss, which spends less time in tunnels and offers better views of the classic vertical scenery. The Nor-Way Bussekspress buses between Bergen (11¼ hours, Nkr570) and Trondheim (3½ hours, Nkr220) also call in at Dombås three times daily in either direction. To get to Oslo, you need to change buses at Otta.

DOVREFJELL NASJONALPARK

The tiny 256 sq km Dovrefjell National Park, established in 1974, exists mainly to protect the dramatic highlands around the 2286m peak Snøhetta and to provide a suitably bleak habitat for Arctic foxes, wild reindeer, wolverines and musk oxen (see the boxed text 'Musk Ox'). The Knutshøene massif (1690m) occupies a small appendage of the park east of the E6 and protects Europe's most diverse intact alpine ecosystem. Although only a small area of the Dovrefjell highlands lies within the park, the vast expanse of wilderness country to the south, west and north provides ample space for hiking in spectacular terrain that's well known only in European climbing circles. There are plans to protect this extended region in a new Skrymtheimen National Park.

Hikers will fare best with the Statens Kartverk map *Dovrefjell* (1:100,000). However, it doesn't include the Knutshø section; for that, you need Statens Kartverk's *Einunna 1519-I* and *Folldal 1519-II* topographic sheets.

Places to Stay

In 1959 the DNT Snøheim hut (formerly called Renheim) was judged to be too near the army's Hjerkinn firing range and was replaced by a new self-service **Renheim hut**, 5km to the north in Stroplsjødalen. DNT also maintains several other self-service huts in the adjacent Skrymtheimen region; keys are available at the tourist office in Dombås.

Park information, maps, meals and accommodation are available at the charming and historic **Kongsvold Fjeldstue** (*☎ 72 42 09 11, fax 72 42 22 72*), 13km north of Hjerkinn on the E6 and the railway line. Intriguing early 18th century timber buildings huddle deep in Drivdalen, half a kilometre from tiny Kongsvoll station. Accommodation costs from Nkr395 per person in a double room, with breakfast and dinner for Nkr95. It's open year-round.

The **Hjerkinn Fjellstue** (*☎ 61 24 29 27, fax 61 24 29 49*), about 1.5km east of Hjerkinn on the Rv29, is the latest in a series of inns on this site, the first of which appeared around 1100. Several fires and reconstructions later, the current building opened in 1992. Cosy single/double accommodation costs Nkr615/720 for the first night and half-price for each night thereafter.

Getting There & Away

There's no public transport into the park, although several tours from Dombås do offer musk ox safaris (see Dombås). The road to Snøheim crosses the Hjerkinn firing range and public access requires permission from the army, which is readily given at the gate unless they're conducting exercises. The only public transport between Dombås and Hjerkinn is by train (30 minutes, Nkr56).

VÅGÅ

Vågå surprises passers-by with its wealth of old log and timber buildings. The original wooden stave church at Vågå was constructed in the 12th century with a single nave and stood 300m west of the present cruciform church, which was reconstructed between 1625 and 1630. On the wall at the entrance, you'll see carved wooden panels from the ancient church, which mostly represent animal subjects. The baptismal font also dates from the original church, and the early Gothic crucifix is from the 13th century. Admission costs Nkr10. For tourist information, contact the Vågå Turistkontor (*☎ 61 23 78 80*).

LOM

Lom, straddling the river Bøvra at the Prestfossen waterfall, may exist for the sake of Jotunheimen tourism, but it still manages to remain picturesque. In addition to a couple of fine attractions, there are plenty of hills and mountain tracks nearby which have excellent views of Ottadalen and Bøverdalen. A popular route is the 3km return loop up Lomseggi to the century-old stone cottage called Smithbue, occupied by a 19th century German artist.

From 15 June to 30 August, the Jotunheimen Reiseliv tourist office (*☎ 61 21 29 90,*

Musk Ox

Although a member of the *Bovidae* family, the musk ox (*Ovibos moschatus*) bears little resemblance to its nearest relations (sheep, goats and cattle) or indeed to any other animal. During the last Ice Age it was distributed throughout much of the northern hemisphere's glaciated areas, but nowadays its range is much more restricted. Wild herds can be found in the North-East Greenland National Park and Kangerlussuaq in Greenland; Arctic Canada; Nunivak Island in Alaska; and Dovrefjell and Femundsmarka national parks in Norway.

The musk ox weighs between 225kg and 445kg, and its anatomy is one of nature's great oddities: in front of its incredibly high shoulders, its enormous, low-slung head has two broad, flat horns that cross the forehead, curving outwards and downwards before twisting upwards and forwards. Its incredibly thick and shaggy coat, with a matted fleece of soft hair (commercially known as *qiviut*) underneath, covers the whole body and hangs down like a skirt to almost reach the ground, and swings from side to side when the animal runs. Below this hair only the bottom part of the legs protrude, giving the animal a solid, stocky appearance reminiscent of a medieval horse dressed for a joust. This analogy is especially appropriate because during the rutting season, when the males gather their harems, they repeatedly charge each other, butting their heads together with a crash that's often heard for miles around. This heated battle continues until one animal admits defeat and lumbers off.

Traditionally, wolves have been the musk ox's main predator, but in high Arctic regions polar bears have also been known to snack on them. Their primary defence is to form a circle with the males on the outside and females and calves inside, trusting in the force of their collective horns to rip open attackers. This defence has proven useless against human hunters, especially the Greenlandic Inuit, who love their beef-like meat and prize their warm qiviut hair. As a result, their numbers have been seriously depleted and only with re-stocking have they been able to thrive again.

In Norway, fossil records show that the musk ox prospered around Dovrefjell during the last Ice Age. In 1931, 10 animals were re-introduced to the area from Greenland. These were joined by two more individuals seven years later. Although the musk oxen all but vanished during WWII, the numbers were augmented when 23 were transplanted from Greenland between 1947 and 1953. The herd has now grown to around 80 animals and some have even split off and shifted eastwards into Femundsmarka National Park to form a new herd. Although musk oxen aren't inherently aggressive toward humans, an animal that feels threatened can charge at speeds of up to 60km/h and woe betide anything that gets in its way. Hikers should stay at least 200m away; if an animal seems agitated or paws at the ground, don't run but back off slowly until it again seems relaxed.

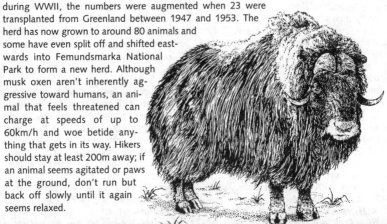

fax 61 21 29 95), in the Norsk Fjellmuseum, is open from 9 am to 6 pm Monday to Saturday (until 9 pm in mid-summer) and noon to 6 pm Sunday (until 7 pm in mid-summer). Visitors can purchase a *Fellesbillet* for Nkr65, which includes admission to the stave church, the Presthaugen Bygdemuseum and the Norsk Fjellmuseum. If you're around for a while, pick up the *Nature and Culture Guide for Lom* by Torgeir Garmo, which contains an exhaustive rundown on local trails and attractions. It's sold at the Fossheim Steinsenter. Hiking maps are sold at the Lom Bokhandel.

Lom Stabkyrkja

This lovely 12th century stave church (☎ 94 39 57 81), in the centre of town, is still the local church. It was constructed in 1170, extended in 1634 and given its current cruciform shape with the addition of two naves in 1663. From 15 June to 15 August, it's open from 9 am to 9 pm for guided tours explaining the interior paintings and Jakop Sæterdalen's carved choir and pulpit. Admission costs Nkr25.

Fossheim Steinsenter

The best attraction in Lom is also one of the most memorable exhibitions in the country. The Fossheim Steinsenter (☎ 61 21 14 60, fax 61 21 17 80) combines Europe's largest selection of rare and beautiful rocks, minerals, fossils, gems and jewellery for sale, but also includes a large museum of Norwegian and foreign geological specimens. (Don't miss the slab of luminescent labradorite, or 'spectralite', which uncannily resembles a computer circuit board!)

The owners of the centre, both avid rockhounds and collectors, travel the world in search of specimens and can answer your questions about Norwegian mineralogy. The local speciality is the Norwegian national stone, Thulite, which was first discovered in 1820 and is now quarried in Lom; the reddish colour is derived from traces of manganese. The shop and museum are open from 9 am to 9 pm daily in summer. Admission is free.

Norsk Fjellmuseum

The Norwegian Mountain Museum (☎ 61 21 16 00) is in fact the visitors centre for Jotunheimen National Park and is filled with mountaineering memorabilia, as well as exhibits on the natural history and cultural and industrial activity in the region. There's also a discussion of tourism and its impact on wilderness. From 15 June to 30 August, it's open from 9 am to 6 pm weekdays (in mid-summer until 9 pm) and from noon to 6 pm Sunday (mid-summer from 11 am to 7 pm). Admission costs Nkr50.

Presthaugen Bygdemuseum

Also in the centre is the Presthaugen Open Air Museum, which is a collection of 19th century farm buildings, several *stabbur* (elevated storehouses), an old hut (it's claimed that St Olav slept here) and an example of a summer mountain dairy. The most interesting feature is the exhibition on early irrigation methods in highland Norway. It's open from 11 am to 6 pm daily from 15 June to 15 August, with guided tours between noon and 5 pm. Admission costs Nkr20.

Places to Stay & Eat

Unfortunately, Lom lacks any sort of inexpensive hostel accommodation; for that you'll have to head up-valley to Bøverdalen (see under Jotunheimen Nasjonalpark later in this chapter). On the Rv55, 400m west of town, is *Lom Motell & Camping* (☎ 61 21 12 20, fax 61 21 12 23, arveen@online.no). Tent or caravan campers with a car pay Nkr130 for up to five people; without a vehicle, you'll pay Nkr75. Single/double motel rooms with breakfast are Nkr425/695 and cabins are Nkr400. It also has a small shop and cafeteria selling groceries, light meals and drinks, including beer and wine.

The *Nordal Turistsenter* (☎ 61 21 10 10, fax 61 21 13 03) in the heart of town offers a wide range of prices for cabins, from Nkr270 for a basic four-bed hut to Nkr950 for a fully-equipped eight-bed cabin. At the eastern end of town is the pleasant *Fossheim Turisthotell* (☎ 61 21 12 05, fax 61 21 15 10), which has been constructed in cosy traditional style. You'll get single/double accommodation with breakfast for Nkr630/835. Don't miss the meals prepared by renowned chef Arne Brimi.

The *Kræmarhuset*, specialising in traditional Norwegian mountain fare, is open daily in summer from 9 am to midnight. The Nordal Turistsenter has a popular *gatekjøkken*, which is a hangout for local youth, and the affiliated *Nordalsfjoset Pub*, in an old two-storey barn, serves up pizza and the usual range of alcoholic beverages. The *Lom Koop*, open from 9 am to 8 pm on summer weekdays (until 6 pm Saturday), has a cafeteria and sells groceries and camping supplies.

Getting There & Around
The thrice daily Nor-Way Bussekspress service between Oslo (6½ hours, Nkr385) and Måløy (4½ hours, Nkr255) passes through Lom. It's also on Ottadalen Billag's summer route between Otta (1½ hours, Nkr70) and Sogndal (3½ hours, Nkr156), which serves the Sognefjellet road.

Lom Motell & Camping hires out mountain bikes for Nkr20/110 per hour/day.

JOTUNHEIMEN NASJONALPARK
The collection of high peaks and glaciers that make up Jotunheimen National Park is far and away Norway's best loved wilderness destination. Jotunheimen was put on the map of favourable climbing destinations by celebrated English mountaineer William Cecil Slingsby in the late 19th century. Since then, its range of possibilities for exploration has attracted throngs of locals and foreigners alike.

While a handful of really popular hiking routes may at times resemble motorways, the park is so vast that it's still not that difficult to find a bit of elbow room. The range of hiking routes lead from ravine-like valleys and past deep lakes, plunging waterfalls and 60 glaciers to the tops of all the peaks in Norway over 2300m, including Galdhøpiggen (the highest peak in northern Europe at 2469m), Glittertind (2452m) and Store Skagstølstind (2405m).

DNT maintains staffed huts along most of these routes and there is a choice of private lodges along the adjoining road system.

For park information, contact the Statskog-Oppland Nasjonalparktjenesta (☎ 61 21 16 99) in Lom.

Sognefjellet Road
The high and scenic Sognefjellet road connects Lustrafjord with Lom and provides easy access to the northern reaches of Jotunheimen National Park. It was constructed in 1939 by unemployed youth and reaches 1434m, making it the highest mountain road in northern Europe. The mountain views can be spectacular, but the snow doesn't normally melt until at least early August, and at higher elevations drivers should prepare for new snow at any time.

From mid-June to late August, Ottadalen Billag runs two daily buses between Otta and Sogndal via Sognefjellet. Westbound, they leave at 7.10 am and 3.30 pm and eastbound at 8.20 am and 1.25 pm.

Spiterstulen The private lodge at *Spiterstulen* (☎ 61 21 14 80, fax 61 21 19 72), an old *sæter* (summer dairy), makes for convenient access to the Galdhøpiggen massif and its tangle of dramatic cirques, arêtes and glaciers. Accommodation in standard singles/doubles with shared bath costs Nkr300/325. Double rooms with a private facilities are Nkr425. Camping is also available for Nkr50 per person.

Note that the toll road to Spiterstulen costs Nkr60 per vehicle, which seems rather steep considering it isn't maintained. On foot, you can approach on the five-hour marked route from Leirvassbu hut, farther west.

Juvvashytta Juvvashytta hut serves as the gateway to the Galdhøpiggen Summer Ski Centre (☎ 61 21 17 50, fax 61 21 21 72) at 1850m on the icy heights of Norway's highest mountain. From Galdesand on the Rv55, follow the Galdhøpiggen road to its end at 1841m. The season runs from June to mid-November.

JOTUNHEIMEN NASJONALPARK

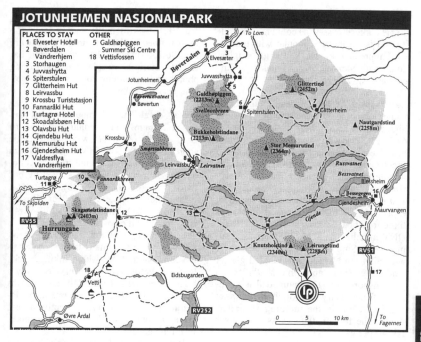

PLACES TO STAY
1 Elveseter Hotell
2 Bøverdalen Vandrerhjem
3 Storhaugen
4 Juvvashytta
6 Spiterstulen
7 Glitterheim Hut
8 Leirvassbu
9 Krossbu Turiststasjon
10 Fannaråki Hut
11 Turtagrø Hotel
12 Skoadalsbøen Hut
13 Olavsbu Hut
14 Gjendebu Hut
15 Memurubu Hut
16 Gjendesheim Hut
17 Valdresflya Vandrerhjem

OTHER
5 Galdhøpiggen Summer Ski Centre
18 Vettisfossen

Bøverdalen Bøverdalen, the valley of the Bøvra river, descends from Sognefjell and mostly follows main road into Lom (although the Sognefjellet road makes a 10km detour into Leirdalen). This scenic and easily accessible area adjoins Jotunheimen and is occupied mainly by a scattering of farms and tourist lodges.

The **Bøverdalen Vandrerhjem** (☎ 61 21 20 64) is open from late May to 30 September and has dorm beds for Nkr75, doubles for Nkr190 and four-bed cabins from Nkr350 to Nkr450. A highly recommended upmarket alternative is the friendly farm **Storhaugen** (☎/fax 61 21 20 69), run by Marit and Magner Slettede. This traditional-style timber farm enjoys views of both the Jotunheimen heights and Bøverdalen. Self-catering accommodation in a transplanted road house costs from Nkr500 to Nkr550 and cabins are from Nkr300 to Nkr1200. At Galdesand, turn south on the Galdhøpiggen road and continue 1.5km to the signposted right turning for Storhaugen.

Elveseter Hotell (☎ 61 21 20 00), one of Norway's most unusual accommodation options, was built up around the Sagasøylen. This 40m-high carved wooden pillar is the result of an abortive attempt in the mid-19th century to create a commemorative monument to trace Norwegian history from unification in 872 to the 1814 constitution. When the Nazis invaded Norway in 1940, the column was still only partially completed and more pressing matters – combined with waning enthusiasm – allowed the project to conveniently die. This white elephant continued to deteriorate for 20 more years until Åmund Elveseter obtained it and, for lack of anything else to do with it, set it up here.

The lodge on the site, a bizarre historic theme park, surpasses the column as an oddity and is particularly popular with tourists who appreciate kitsch. You'll get singles/doubles for Nkr450/650 and breakfasts/dinners are Nkr75/175.

Leirvassbu At 1400m beside lake Leirvatnet, and smack in the middle of all the high country action, *Leirvassbu hut (☎/fax 61 21 29 32)* is a good base in Jotunheimen. From here you can opt for long day hikes to spectacular views or head off on a longer trek through the very heart of Jotunheimen. However, the hut's whopping capacity of 190 people means that it can get crowded, especially in high season. Bunks in a three/four-bed dorm cost Nkr160/110 for DNT members and Nkr175/160 for nonmembers. Singles/doubles with a shower and toilet are Nkr300/500. Guided glacier walks over Smørstabbreen cost Nkr250.

Transport from the main road is available if necessary, although in summer there is a bus in the morning and afternoon. The toll on the access road costs Nkr40 per car.

Krossbu Krossbu, near the head of Bøverdalen, lies at the outset of a tangle of hiking routes, including a short day trip to the Smørstabbreen glacier. The 75-bed *Krossbu Turiststasjon (☎/fax 61 21 29 22)* offers double rooms for up to Nkr440 and larger rooms to Nkr870 Guided glacier hikes and courses are available in summer.

Turtagrø If you're looking for a friendly and laid-back base around Jotunheimen, you couldn't do better than the historic *Turtagrø Hotel (☎ 57 68 61 16, fax 57 68 61 15, turtagro@online.no)*, a mountaineering centre midway between Sogndal and Lom. The hotel, built in 1888, has been run by four generations of mountaineers in the Drægni family, who know how to create an ideal environment for outdoor enthusiasts. They also conduct week-long climbing courses and are active in laying out new hiking routes. Singles/doubles

with breakfast cost Nkr440/660 (doubles are Nkr850 with bath) and beds in the four/two-bed bunk rooms in the annexe are Nkr190/220. There's also a great rustic bar full of historic Norwegian mountaineering photos and the dining room serves excellent, hearty meals.

Øvre Årdal The toll mountain road between Turtagrø and the industrial town of Øvre Årdal is one of Norway's most scenic short drives. It's open in summer only and leads across high, wild and treeless country. In summer, the route is served by bus twice daily (one hour, Nkr35). For tourist information, contact Årdal Reiselivslag (☎ 57 66 11 77). The vehicle toll of Nkr40 is collected at the pass.

From Øvre Årdal you may want to head 12km north-east up the Utladalen valley to the farm Vetti, from where hiking tracks lead to Vettisfossen (275m), Norway's highest free-falling waterfall, and also to the little visited, unstaffed hut at Stølsmaradalen. This is also an alternative access route, via upper Utladalen, to longer hikes in Jotunheimen.

Buses run two to four times daily between Øvre Årdal and Voss (4½ hours, Nkr149), with direct connections to and from Bergen. Local and express buses also run regularly to and from Sogndal (1½ hours, Nkr92) and Lærdal (one hour, Nkr61), and there are express buses to and from Oslo (6½ hours, Nkr315) several times daily.

Gjendesheim & Valdresflya
Between Randen and Fagernes, the Rv51 climbs through the hilly forested Sjodalen country onto a vast wild upland with far-ranging views of peaks and glaciers. It's one of Norway's most scenic mountain routes and is used by the thousands of hikers heading for Jotunheimen's eastern reaches.

The first DNT hut at Gjendesheim was constructed in 1878; the current building dates from 1934, with an extension in the mid-1970s. The current *Gjendesheim hut (☎ 61 23 89 10, fax 61 23 89 65)* now has 115 beds and serves as the main launching point for the popular hike across the Bess-eggen ridge. About 15 minutes south along the road is the *Valdresflya Vandrerhjem* (☎ 22 15 21 85, fax 22 71 34 97), which prides itself on being the highest hostel in northern Europe at 1420m. You'll pay Nkr105 for a dorm bed and Nkr180/240 for singles/doubles.

Between mid-June and mid-September, Ottadalen Billag (☎ 61 23 44 55) runs at least two daily buses between Otta and Gol, via Vågå, Randen, Gjendesheim, Valdres-flya and Fagernes. From Otta, the trip to Gjendesheim takes 1½ hours and costs Nkr75. Valdresflya (Nkr9) is just 15 minutes farther.

Hiking
Jotunheimen's hiking possibilities are prac-tically endless and all are spectacular. The best map by far is Cappelens Kart's *Jotun-heimen* (1:100,000).

The Hurrungane The fabulous Hurrun-gane massif rises darkly above the western-most end of the park. Most experienced mountaineers will be able to pick their way to some of these prominent peaks – and sev-eral are even accessible to skilled scram-blers. For an amenable hiking experience, however, most people would prefer to head eastwards from Turtagrø. From the hotel, a four-hour hike will take you to Norway's highest DNT hut, Fannaråki, on the summit of Fannaråken (2069m), with predictably fabulous views that take in most of the park. To get started, walk about 500m up the road and follow the track up Helgedalen. At Ekrehytta hut, a narrow track starts a steep 800m climb to the staffed DNT hut on the summit of Fannaråken, with improving glacier views all the way.

You can either return the way you came or descend the eastern slope along the well marked track to Keisarpasset and thence back to Ekrehytta. To launch into a multi-day trip, you can also descend Gjertvass-dalen to Skogadalsbøen hut and, once there, choose from literally dozens of routes east-wards through Jotunheimen.

Besseggen No discussion of hiking in Jo-tunheimen would be complete without a mention of Besseggen ridge, which is the most popular hike in Norway. Indeed, it could even be described as over-attended – it sees at least 30,000 hikers in the three months a year that it's passable. If you want to avoid the crowds, choose another route, but if you don't mind sacrificing solitude for one of Norway's most spectacular trips, you probably won't regret it. Henrik Ibsen wrote of Besseggen:

'It cuts along with an edge like a scythe for miles and miles ... And scars and glaciers sheer down the precipice to the glassy lakes, 1600 feet below on either side.'

So daunting did it appear to him, that one of Peer Gynt's mishaps was a plunge down to the lake on the back of a reindeer.

The day hike between Gjendesheim and Memurubu takes about six hours and climbs to a high point of 1743m. From Gjendesheim hut, follow the DNT-marked track towards Glitterheim for about half an hour, where a left fork strikes off up the Veltløyfti gorge, which leads upward onto the level Veslefjel-let plateau. After a short descent from the plateau, the track conducts you onto the Besseggen ridge, which slices between the deep blue lake Bessvatnet and the 18km long glacier-green lake Gjende, so coloured by the 20,000 tonnes of glacial silt dumped into it each year by the Memuru river.

Although there's a lot of hype about its ex-posed nature, Besseggen is never less than 40m wide and only from a distance does it look precarious. After passing the head of Bessvatnet, the route passes a small plateau lake, Bjørnbøltjørn, and shortly thereafter begins its descent to the modern chalet-style Memurubu hut. Once there, you can decide whether to take the boat M/S *Gjende* back to Gjendesheim (30 minutes, Nkr50), continue west to Gjendebu hut, either on foot or on the boat (20 minutes, Nkr50), or hike north to Glitterheim.

FAGERNES

If you're approaching from Lom or Jotunheimen, the descent to Fagernes may disappoint, but for travellers headed north it's a gateway to the high country. The Valdres Folk Museum (☎ 61 36 03 77), occupying a peninsula in the lake south of town, contains exhibitions of Norwegian folk dress, an old village store, an inn from the Filefjell featuring traditional Norwegian cuisine and a shop where musical instruments are made. From mid-June to mid-August, you can watch traditional culture demonstrations: in late June, folk music performances; from 7 to 16 July, day-to-day life on a typical late 19th century Valdres farm; and from 1 July to mid-August, folk dancing programs.

The museum is open from 10 am to 4 pm in summer (9 am to 3 pm the rest of the year). From 8 June to 30 June, admission is Nkr30 (Nkr50 in early July). Musical performances cost extra.

Getting There & Away

The Nor-Way Bussekspress buses between Oslo (3¼ hours, Nkr200) and Sogndal (four hours, Nkr205) pass through Fagernes three to six times daily in either direction.

Drivers between Dokka and Borgund, via Fagernes, may want to watch out for the old milestones along the way (one Old Mile is roughly equivalent to 11km). One of the finest examples is on Grihamar farm at Øye, where a 1687 stone bears the monograms of King Christian V and Governor Ulrik Fredrik Gyldenløve. Distances are calculated from Odnes, near the northern tip of the lake Randsfjorden.

Hardangervidda

The high plateau known as Hardangervidda has long served as a trade and travel route between eastern and western Norway. It remains on the main railway and road routes between Norway's two major cities, Oslo and Bergen. On these high, bleak expanses, old snow lingers until early August and new snow is a possibility at any time of year, but the region is best known for its hiking opportunities and altitude-stretched cross-country ski season.

In 1981, the 3430 sq km Hardangervidda National Park was established to protect the tundra landscape and Norway's largest herd of wild reindeer (caribou). Hikers and skiers will need the Cappelens Kart maps *Hardangervidda Øst* and *Hardangervidda Vest*, both at a scale of 1:100,000.

GEILO

At Geilo, midway between Oslo and Bergen, you can practically step off the train onto a ski lift. In summer there's plenty of fine hiking in the town's mountain backdrop. A popu-lar nearby destination is the expansive plateau-like mountain Hallingskarvet, frosted with several small glaciers.

For tourist information, contact Geilo Turistinformasjon (☎ 32 09 59 00, fax 32 09 59 01, geilo@skiinfo.no, www.geilo .no). The office is open from 1 June to 31 August, with its longest hours from 8.30 am to 9 pm daily between 29 June and 15 August.

Organised Tours

Glacier trekking on Hardangerjøkulen (1860m) is offered by Geilo Activities Guiding (☎ 32 09 59 30). Costs are Nkr395 per person for the standard 10-hour tour and Nkr550 for a more extreme experience. It operates on Tuesday, Thursday and Saturday from 1 July to 15 September.

Places to Stay

For its size, Geilo has a boggling choice of accommodation, most of which is geared towards the outdoor activity crowds. The

Otta Church, central Norway

Midnight sunset, Helgeroa, southern Norway

DNT's highest hut (2069m), Jotunheimen Nat Park

View from Fannaråken, Jotunheimen Nat Park

Geilo Vandrerhjem (☎ 32 09 03 00, fax 32 09 18 96), near the train station, provides convenient inexpensive accommodation. Dormitory beds are Nkr150, with breakfast, and double rooms are Nkr400. The best-value summer hotels are the *Haugen Hotell (☎ 32 09 06 44, fax 32 09 03 87, Gamleveien 16)*, 500m from the centre, which has singles/doubles from Nkr400/500; the commercial *Ro Hotell & Kro (☎ 32 09 08 99, fax 32 09 07 85, Geilovegen 55)*, near the station, with summer rates from Nkr410/ 570; and the no-nonsense *Solli Sportell (☎ 32 09 11 11, fax 32 09 15 60)*, charging Nkr410/ 520. The last option also has four-bed cabins/apartments from Nkr210/350.

Getting There & Around

The only long-distance bus service connects Geilo with Kongsberg (3½ hours, Nkr168) two to five times daily. Of course, most visitors arrive by car or on the train line between Oslo (four hours, Nkr315) and Bergen (three hours, Nkr285). If you wish to cycle the Rallarvegen, cycles can be hired for Nkr130 for the first day and Nkr50 for each subsequent day; you can return them to any of the train stations along the route for an additional Nkr80.

FINSE

Heading west from Geilo, the railway line climbs 600m through a tundra-like landscape of high lakes and snowy peaks to the village of Finse, lying at 1222m near the diminutive Hardangerjøkulen icecap. This bleak region offers nordic skiing through much of the year and lies amid a network of summer hiking routes, including the popular four-hour trek to the Blåisen glacier snout of Hardangerjøkulen. Another frequently trodden track winds from Finse station down to the fjord town of Aurland for a four to five-day trek, with breathtaking mountain scenery along the way as well as a series of DNT mountain huts a day's walk apart. The nearest is the Finsehytte, 200m from Finse station. For more on this route, see Aurland in the Western Fjords chapter.

Rallarmuseet Finse

The Finse Navvies Museum, east of Finse station, reveals the history of the Oslo-Bergen railway and the 15,000 people who engineered and built this hard-won line in 2.5 million worker days. It's open from 10 am to 10 pm daily from 10 July to late September. Admission costs Nkr15.

Rallarvegen

The Rallarvegen, or Navvies' Road, was constructed in the early 20th century as a supply and construction route for workers on the Oslo-Bergen railway, which opened on 27 November 1909. Nowadays, this 80km route of asphalt and gravel extends from Haugastøl and through Finse, Hallingskeid and Vatnahalsen to Flåm, with a 43km branch from the Upsete end of the Gravhals tunnel and down the Raundal valley to Voss. The section from Storurdivatn to Mjølfjell via Finse passes through some lovely highland plateau country and is open only to bicycles and foot traffic, while the bits down the Flåm and Raundal valleys are also open to vehicle traffic. The popular stretch between Vatnahalsen and Flåm descends 865m in 29km, passing through 20 tunnels and 21 hairpin bends.

Cyclists and hikers will find the best conditions between mid-July and mid-September, after the snow has melted from the highland areas. Because of the significant altitude loss, most people do the route from east to west. Bicycles can be hired at the outdoor shop in Finse.

Places to Stay & Eat

Most budget travellers stay at the staffed *Finsehytta DNT hut (☎ 56 52 67 32)*, which charges normal DNT rates, but there's also a hotel, *Finse 1222 (☎ 56 52 67 11, fax 56 52 6717, booking@finse1222.no)*. Accommodation is available in *huts* and *hostels* at Haugastøl, Hallingskeid and Mjølfjell.

Getting There & Away

The only public transport access to Finse is on the railway line between Oslo (4½ hours, Nkr370) and Bergen (2¼ hours, Nkr220).

CENTRAL NORWAY

MYRDAL

Myrdal, west of Finse, is the junction of the Oslo-Bergen railway and the spectacularly steep Flåmbanen railway, where travellers are launched into the excursion that's marketed as part of the 'Norway in a Nutshell' tour. This dramatic line twists its way 20km down to Flåm on Aurlandsfjord, an arm of the Sognefjord. Many people make the descent to Flåm, have lunch and then return to Myrdal to catch the next Oslo-Bergen train. A better option is to transfer to the ferry from Flåm up the lovely Nærøyfjord to Gudvangen, where a connecting bus climbs the steep and dramatically scenic road to Voss. From there, trains to Bergen run almost hourly. For more information, see Flåm and Nærøyfjord in the Western Fjords chapter.

Places to Stay & Eat

The *Vatnahalsen Høyfjellshotell* (☎ 57 63 37 22, fax 57 63 37 67), 820m above Flåm valley, offers a quiet and comfortable summer or winter option. It's accessible only by train or on foot. Singles/doubles with a view cost Nkr550/820.

The handsome *Mjølfjell Vandrerhjem* (☎ 56 51 81 11, fax 56 51 40 00), down the railway line at Mjølfjell, serves as a popular overnight stop on the Rallarvegen cycling and hiking route (see Finse earlier in this section). Dormitory accommodation costs just Nkr95 and singles/doubles are Nkr195/290. Rail travellers wanting to stay at the hostel should disembark at Ørneberget station. By car, it's accessible only on the Raundalen road from Voss.

Bergen & the South-Western Fjords

The southernmost of Norway's fjords, with their relative greenery and amenable landscapes for farming and larger cities and towns, contrast sharply with their more rugged counterparts farther north. Here you'll find not only charming Bergen and the sparkling oil city of Stavanger, but also some of Norway's most interesting landscapes, from the rock-studded farmlands of the south and the bright orchards of Hardangerfjord to the ethereal slopes above spectacular Lysefjord.

Bergen

With 223,000 inhabitants, Bergen is Norway's second largest city. Somehow though, Bergen still manages to retain a pleasantly slow pace of life, and as a university town and cultural centre, it boasts oodles of museums as well as several theatres and a renowned philharmonic orchestra. The greatest fly in the ointment is the weather, and you can reliably expect rain on at least 275 days of the year. However, all this precipitation keeps the place green and flowery, and a low skyline of red-tiled roofs and the early summer explosion of rhododendrons lend it a sense of cheeriness on even the most dismal days.

History

During the 12th and 13th centuries, Bergen served as Norway's capital, and despite the fact that 70% of the population was wiped out by the Black Death in 1359, by the early 17th century it served as the trading hub of Scandinavia and had also become the country's most populous city, with 15,000 people.

Set on a peninsula surrounded by seven mountains, Bergen's history is closely tied to the sea. It became one of the central

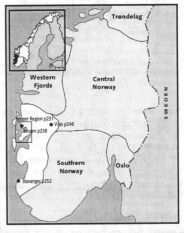

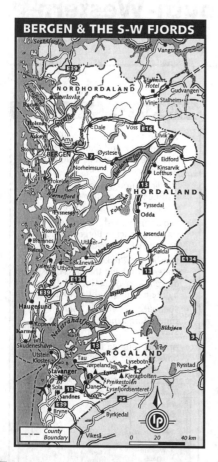

BERGEN & THE S-W FJORDS

sulas and islands, but the central area remains pleasantly compact and easily manageable. The bus and train stations lie only a block apart on Strømgaten, a 10-minute walk from the ferry terminals, and most of the restaurants, hotels, museums, tourist sites and picturesque streets and passages cluster around Vågen, the inner harbour.

Information

Tourist Office The Bergen Reiselivslag tourist office (☎ 55 32 14 80) distributes a free *Bergen Guide* booklet containing a useful city centre map and basic information on tours and sites of interest. The main office, in the 1862 fresco hall of the old Den Norske Bank, is open from 8.30 am to 9 pm daily from May to September, and 9 am to 4 pm Monday to Saturday the rest of the year.'While you're there, take a look at the three fresco panels, which were painted by Axel Revold between 1921 and 1923; they portray fishing in northern Norway, trade activities in Bergen, and human commerce since the industrial revolution. From late May to late August, a branch of the tourist office operates at the train station, open from 7.15 am to 11 pm daily.

Bergen Card The Bergen Card, sold at tourist offices, hotels and the bus terminal, covers transport on local buses, municipal parking, funicular/cable-car rides and admission to most museums and historic sites both in the central area (excluding the Hanseatic Museum and Schøtstuene unless you join a guided Bryggen tour) and farther afield (Gamle Bergen, Ole Bull's Lysøen, Damsgård Manor and Harald Sæverud's Siljustøl). A 24/48-hour Bergen Card costs Nkr130/200.

An alternative option is the Bergens-Pakken, which starts at Nkr325 per person per day and includes a Bergen Card and a bed in a double hotel room (numbers are very limited).

ports of the Hanseatic League, which dominated northern European trade during the late Middle Ages, and its influences are still evident in the Bryggen, the line-up of warehouses that provides modern Bergen with its picturesque waterfront (see the boxed text 'The Bryggen & the Hanseatic League').

Orientation

Greater Bergen may be quite hilly, with suburbs radiating out onto outlying penin-

Money You can change money at the Kreditkassen bank on Christies gate or the nearby post office. The same area also

The Bryggen & the Hanseatic League

By the 13th century, Bergen had developed into a major trading centre for European trade, as well as the episcopal seat of the Christian Diocese of Western Norway and the capital of the Norwegian monarchy. The oldest part of the town and the commercial centre lay on the eastern shore of the Vågen harbour, between the king's residence at Bergenhus, Holmen, and Vågsbotn (or Torget). Here, long parallel rows of buildings run back from gabled fronts facing the wharf, where cargo ships and trading vessels moored and carried on their trade. These ships brought in mostly grain, but also such luxury items as textiles and pottery. In the early 14th century there were about 30 wooden buildings on the Bryggen, each of which was usually shared by several *stuer*, or trading firms. They rose two or three storeys above the wharf and combined business premises with living quarters and warehouses. Each building had a crane for loading and unloading ships, as well as a large assembly room, or *schøtstue*, where employees met and ate. Although cooking fires were hysterically contained and monitored to prevent fires, these convoluted wooden buildings were destroyed by fire at least seven times.

From the mid-11th century in Germany, population growth, land pressure and greater mobility had accelerated the growth of the cities. Some cities were considered 'imperial' and were granted autonomy by crown charter, while others were 'free' cities that had shaken off their clerical rulers. Both types had their own administrations and generally more liberal laws than those of the countryside, and as a result, peasants fled in droves to these urban areas. In order to protect these cities' economic interests, trading leagues were formed. The most significant was the Hanseatic League, which was amalgamated in 1358 from a disparate collection of mercantile guilds and associations. Its trading realm was centred in Lübeck, which controlled a large slice of the European shipping trade.

After the Danes inspired the wrath of this organisation in 1361 by sinking a flotilla of Hanseatic ships off Gotland, the League granted itself a say in the selection of the Danish kings. The resulting Treaty of Stralsund turned the Hanseatic League into northern Europe's most powerful economic and political entity, and at its zenith it had over 150 member cities.

The German Hanseatic *Kontor* at Bergen, established in 1360, was one of the league's four major offices abroad. For over 400 years, the Bryggen was dominated by German merchants and at one stage, it was home to about 1000 permanent German resident traders. In Bergen, the traders formed a tightly-knit sub-community who busied themselves with the import of grain and export of dried fish, among other products, and weren't permitted to mix with, marry or have families with local Norwegians.

By the 15th century, the influence of the Hanseatic League began to decline, due to competition from Dutch and English shipping companies, internal disputes, a shift in the centre of world trade from the North and Baltic Seas to the North Atlantic, and especially, the Black Plague that decimated Europe's population. (However, Hamburg, Bremen and Lübeck are still known as Hanseatic cities, and in fact, Hamburg and Bremen remain separate independent German city-states.) As the League continued its decline through the 17th and 18th centuries, many of the Hanseatic traders opted to take Norwegian nationality and join the local community. Although the Hanseatic League lasted until the late 18th century, the Bryggen continued as an important maritime trade centre until 1899, when the Bergen Kontor (successor to the Norwegian Kontor, which was in turn the successor of the German Kontor) closed down for the last time. In 1980, 58 of the wooden structures along the Bryggen waterfront were added to UNESCO's World Heritage List.

supports a host of other banks and ATMs which change money and dispense cash using your bank card or credit card. The tourist office changes money at 4% less than the bank rates.

Post & Communications The main post office, on Småstrandgaten, is open from 8 am to 5 pm weekdays (to 6 pm Thursday and Friday), 9 am to 3 pm on Saturday. The telephone office, just south of the post office, is open from 9 am to 4 pm weekdays.

Email & Internet Access You can pick up email and access the Internet at the Internet Café Wasteland, south-east of Lille Lungegårdsvann.

Travel Agencies Reise Specialisten, opposite the Galleriet, handles general travel bookings. Kilroy Travel in the university student centre specialises in student tickets.

Bookshops If you're after literature, travel books or just a good read, you can't beat Melvær, Torgallmenningen 8, which has a huge selection of books.

Library The public library, between the bus and train stations, has a good selection of foreign newspapers. It's open to 7 pm on weekdays and 2 pm on Saturday.

Laundry At Jarlens Vaskoteque, 17 Lille Øvregate, it costs Nkr60 per load to wash, or for Nkr85 you can leave your laundry and it will be clean two hours later. It's open from 10 am to 6 pm on weekdays, 9 am to 3 pm on Saturday.

Left Luggage Lockers at the train station cost Nkr10 per day.

Medical & Emergency Services Dial ☎ 112 for police and ☎ 113 for an ambulance. The 24-hour Legevakten medical clinic (☎ 55 32 11 20) at Lars Hilles gate 30 can handle medical emergencies. The pharmacy at the bus station is open daily until midnight.

Historic District

Bergen has lots of quaint cobblestone streets lined with older homes; some of the most picturesque are the winding lanes and alleys above the Fløibanen funicular station.

Torget The waterfront fish market at Torget is a good place to begin exploring. Here, fish odours assault the olfactory senses and spilt effluent turns the quay into a slippery mess, but the market sells more than fish (how about postcards for a bargain Nkr2!) and you'll find a range of tasty seafood snacks at excellent prices. It's also an ideal spot to observe the comings and goings in the harbour area. Adjacent Zachariasbryggen offers a range of restaurants and bars with excellent harbour views.

Bryggen In the 13th century, the Hanseatic League dominated trade between 200 European towns and cities, with major centres in Rostock, London, Bruges, Novgorod and Bergen. From the historic Bryggen waterfront, which was Bergen's main trading zone, Norwegian stockfish, butter, skins and hides were traded for wine, honey and grain, mostly from Britain and Germany. Although much of the league was disbanded in the 16th century, the Bergen office continued to operate up to 1776, when it was taken over by the Norwegian office, comprised of 2000 mostly German traders (and to keep the company pure, no intermarriage – or even fraternising – with Norwegians was permitted). Nowadays the Bryggen is a huddle of timber buildings sheltering museums, restaurants and arty shops. The narrow alleys offer a glimpse of the stacked-stone foundations and reconstructed rough-plank construction of centuries past. They are now on UNESCO's World Heritage List.

The notable tilt of the structures was caused in 1944, when a German munitions ship exploded in the harbour, blowing off the roofs and shifting the pilings. Historically, however, the greatest concern among Bryggen residents was fire; fireplaces were

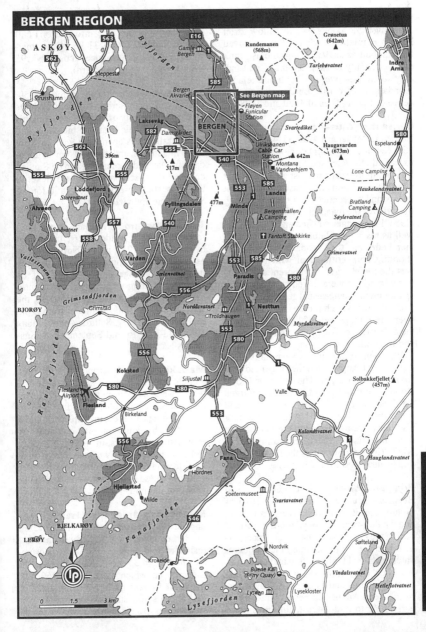

BERGEN REGION

forbidden, barrels of water hung over the stairways, and cooks had to follow strict kitchen regulations. After a fire destroyed the warehouses in 1955, archaeologists took the opportunity to excavate the area. What they found was over one million artefacts, foundations of earlier buildings, and evidence of the big fires of 1170 and 1198.

Hanseatic Museum The worthwhile Hanseatic Museum (☎ 55 31 41 89), in a 16th century rough-timber building, retains its period character and furnishings and offers a glimpse of the austere living and working conditions of Hanseatic merchant sailors and apprentices and the contrasting lifestyles of the management. Highlights include the manager's office and quarters, as well as his private liquor cabinet and summer bedroom; the wooden bird used for shooting competitions, in which its beak was the main target; the apprentices' quarters where beds were shared by two men for spatial rather than sensual reasons; the fish storage room, which pressed and processed over a million pounds of fish a month; and the *fiskeskrue*, or fish press, which extracted cod liver oil.

It's open from 9 am to 5 pm daily from 1 June to 31 August, and the rest of the year from 11 am to 2 pm. The 1½-hour Nkr60 Bryggen tour, which is free with the Bergen Card, is conducted in English at 11 am and 1 pm from 1 June to 31 August. The tour also allows re-admission to the museum on the same day. Otherwise, admission is Nkr35 (it's not covered by the Bergen Card) and is also valid for Schøtstuene.

Bryggens Museum The archaeological Bryggens Museum (☎ 55 31 67 10) was built on the site of Bergen's first settlement, and the 800-year-old foundations unearthed during the construction have been incorporated into the exhibits, which include excavated medieval tools, pottery and skeletons. It's open daily from 10 am to 5 pm from May to August and 11 am to 3 pm the rest of the year. Admission costs Nkr20. From early June to mid-August, folk music and

dance concerts are held on Tuesday and Thursday at 9 pm; for information, call Bergen Folklore (☎ 55 31 95 50). Admission to the performances costs Nkr95 (Nkr80 with the Bergen Card).

Schøtstuene Schøtstuene, Øvregaten 50, houses one of the original assembly halls where the fraternity of Hanseatic merchants once met for their business meetings and beer guzzling. It's open from 9 am to 4 pm daily in summer and from 11 am to 2 pm daily in May and September, and on Sunday only in the off-season. The Nkr35 ticket to the Hanseatic Museum is also valid for the Schøtstuene and vice versa.

Theta Museum This clandestine one-room Resistance headquarters, uncovered by the Nazis in 1942, is now Norway's tiniest museum. Appropriately enough, finding it is still a challenge – it's at the back of the Bryggen building with the unicorn figurehead; pass through the alley and up the stairs to the 3rd floor. It's open from 2 pm to 4 pm on Tuesday, Saturday and Sunday from mid-May to mid-September. Admission is Nkr15.

Mariakirken The stone Mariakirken church, with its Romanesque entrance and twin towers, dates from the early 12th century and is Bergen's oldest building. The interior features 15th century frescoes and a splendid baroque pulpit donated by Hanseatic merchants in 1676. It's open from 11 am to 4 pm weekdays from mid-May to mid-September and from noon to 1.30 pm Tuesday to Friday the rest of the year. Admission is Nkr10.

Rosenkrantztårnet Rosenkrantz Tower, opposite the harbour, was built in the 1560s by Bergen governor Erik Rosenkrantz as a residence and defence post, but incorporates parts of the keep of King Magnus the Lawmender, which dates from 1260, and the 1520 fortress of Jørgen Hansson. You can climb spiral staircases past halls and sentry posts to a nice harbour view from the lookout on top. It's open from 10 am to 4 pm daily, mid-May to mid-September, but from noon to 3 pm only on Sunday in the off season. Admission costs Nkr15.

Håkonshallen This large ceremonial hall, adjacent to the Rosenkrantz Tower, was built by King Håkon Håkonsson in 1261 for his son's wedding. The roof was blown off in 1944 thanks to the explosion of a German munitions boat but extensive restoration has been carried out. It's open daily from 10 am to 4 pm from mid-May to late August, and from noon to 3 pm (3 pm to 6 pm on Thursday) the rest of the year. Entry costs Nkr15.

Fløibanen

For an unbeatable city view, ride the 26° Fløibanen funicular to the top of Mt Fløyen (320m), where well marked hiking tracks lead into the forest; the possibilities are mapped out on the free *Gledeskortet* or *Turløyper På Byfjellene Nord/Øst* maps, which are available at the tourist office. Track 3 makes a 1.3km loop around the lake Skomakerdiket, Track 2 does a figure-eight through hilly woodlands and Track 1 offers a 5km loop over hills, through forests and past several lakes. For a delightful 40-minute walk back to the city from Fløien, follow Track 4 clockwise and connect with Track 6, which switchbacks down to the harbour through neighbourhoods of old timber houses. The funicular runs twice hourly from 7.30 am to 11 pm from early May to the end of August (until midnight in summer) and costs Nkr40 return.

Bergen Kunstmuseum

The three-part Bergen Art Museum (☎ 55 56 80 00, www.bergenartmuseum.no) is housed in two buildings beside the lovely lake Lille Lungegårdsvann at Rasmus Meyers Allé 3 and 7. It exhibits a superb collection of 18th and 19th century international and Norwegian art, including works by Munch and JC Dahl, as well as contemporary European works by Miró, Picasso, Kandinsky, Paul Klee and others.

From 15 May to 14 September, the complex is open from 10 am to 5 pm Monday to Saturday and noon to 6 pm on Sunday, with shorter winter hours. There's a combined entrance fee of Nkr35 (Nkr20 from 15 September to 14 May).

Vestlandske Kunstindustrimuseum

The West Norwegian Museum of Applied Art (☎ 55 32 51 08), in the Permanenten building at 9 Nordahl Burnsgate, attracts a range of visiting art and craft exhibits, and there's also a permanent collection of European handicrafts and Chinese Buddhist temple sculptures. It's open from 11 am to 4 pm Tuesday to Sunday from 15 May to 14 September, and shorter hours at other times. Admission is Nkr30.

Bergen Akvariet

The Bergen Aquarium (☎ 55 55 71 71, www.akvariet.com), at the end of the Nordnes peninsula, has a big outdoor tank with seals and penguins as well as 70 indoor tanks. You'll never forget the lovable steinbit, the hideous anglerfish or the school of herring which seems to function as a single entity. From 1 May to 30 September, opening hours are from 9 am to 8 pm daily, with seal and penguin feedings at 11 am, and 2 and 6 pm. The rest of the year, it's open from 10 am to 6 pm with feeding at 10 am and 4 pm. Admission costs Nkr55. The public park just beyond the aquarium has pleasant shaded lawns and an outdoor heated pool.

On foot, you can get there from the Torget in 20 minutes; alternatively, take bus No 4, marked Nordnes, or the Vågen ferry that runs between the fish market and the aquarium every 15 minutes during business hours from 1 May to 1 September.

University Museums

The university, at the end of Christies gate, has a Sjøfartsmuseet (Maritime Museum; ☎ 55 32 79 80) with models of Viking ships and exhibits tracing Norway's maritime history; a Naturhistorisk Museum (Natural History Museum; ☎ 55 58 29 30) full of stuffed creatures and mineral displays; and, of greater interest, a Historisk Museum (Cultural History Museum; ☎ 55 58 31 40) with Viking weaponry, medieval altars, folk art and period furnishings. There are also sections dedicated to Native American cultures, including Inuit and Aleut. A combination Nkr20 ticket covers the latter two museums, which are open 15 May to 31 August; they're open from 10 am to 3 pm Tuesday to Saturday and 11 am to 4 pm Sunday. There's a separate Nkr20 admission to the Maritime Museum, which is open from 11 am to 3 pm daily from 1 June to 31 August.

Gamle Bergen

The open-air museum Gamle Bergen (☎ 55 25 78 50), 4km north of the city centre, consists of a collection of 35 structures from the 18th and 19th centuries, including a number of historic commercial enterprises. The entertaining guided tours begin on the hour from 9 am to 4 pm, 24 May to 30 August. Admission is Nkr40. It lies just within walking distance (about 30 minutes), but the traffic makes it a hectic walk and most people opt for buses No 1 or 9.

Lepramuseet

For something a bit different, visit the unusual Leprosy Museum at St George's Hospital, Kong Oscars gate 59. Although most of the buildings at St George's date from the 19th century, in medieval times, the site served as a leprosarium which specialised in housing victims of Hansen's disease. Exhibits detail Norway's contributions to leprosy research, including the work of Dr Armauer Hansen, who gave his name to Hansen's disease, the modern name for leprosy. It's open from 11 am to 3 pm daily from late May to late August. Admission costs Nkr20.

Fantoft Stabkirke

The Fantoft stave church (☎ 55 28 0710), in a lovely leafy setting south of Bergen, was built in Sognefjord in the 12th century and moved to the southern outskirts of Bergen

in 1884. It was burned down in 1992 by an irritable Satanist but has now been painstakingly reconstructed. From Bergen take any bus leaving from platforms 19 to 21, get off at the Fantoft stop on Birkelundsbakken and walk uphill through the park for about five minutes. It's open from 10.30 am to 5.30 pm daily, 15 May to 15 September, and admission costs Nkr30.

Troldhaugen

The cottage-style home Troldhaugen (☎ 55 91 07 10), designed by architect Schack Bull and constructed in 1885, occupies an undeniably lovely setting on a lush and scenic peninsula in the coastal lake Nordåsvatnet. Here composer Edvard Grieg and his wife Nina Hagerup spent every summer from 1885 until Grieg's death in 1907. Today the house and grounds are open to the public, a permanent Grieg exhibition has been opened and a 200-seat concert hall constructed. Of particular interest are the Composer's Hut, where Edvard mustered his musical inspiration; the Steinway piano, which was a gift to celebrate Edvard and Nina's 50th wedding anniversary in 1892; and the couple's tombs, which are embedded in a rock face overlooking Nordåsvatnet.

Grieg fans will best appreciate this well conceived presentation, and anyone who's seen *Song of Norway*, the insipid film version of Grieg's life, will probably recognise a few things. It's open from 9 am to 6 pm daily from 18 April to 30 September and admission costs Nkr40. In summer, concerts are held on Wednesday, Saturday and Sunday (tickets are Nkr100 from the tourist office). Take any bus from platforms 19 to 21 to the Hopsbroen stop (or from the stop for the stave church). From there, follow the signs to Troldhaugen; it's a 20-minute walk.

Siljustøl Museum

Another well known Norwegian composer's home lies in a rural area only 3km south of Troldhaugen. Siljustøl (☎ 55 91 07 10), the simple timber home of Harald and Marie Sæverud, was constructed in the 1930s of natural stone and untreated wood in an

Edvard Grieg

Norway's best known and most universally loved composer, Edvard Grieg was born in Bergen on 15 June 1843. At the age of 15 he travelled to Germany to study music at the Leipzig Conservatory, and after four years of intensive study, he graduated as a fully-fledged musician and composer. Until 1866, he lived and worked in Copenhagen, where Niels W Gade encouraged him to compose a symphony, but the result didn't measure up to the Grieg's satisfaction and he scrawled across the score that it must never be performed. His wishes were ignored, however, and he refused to acknowledge it as his own creation!

Grieg's early style strongly reflected his German romantic training but instinctively he realised that it would be his lot to create national music for his homeland, Norway. While in Copenhagen, he met Rikard Nordraak (whose own dedication to Norway resulted in his crowning composition, the Norwegian national anthem). After returning to Christiania (Oslo) in 1866, Grieg became increasingly influenced by Norway's folk music and melodies but he soon realised that the written music represented only a small portion of the effect created by traditional folk musicians.

Through the 1860s Grieg remained in Oslo and struggled to support his family, working not only as a performer, but also as a choral leader, a conductor and a music teacher, often travelling to Germany, Italy and France to garner inspiration. He only indulged himself in composition during the slower summer months, but by 1868, he'd found time to complete his first great work, his *Piano Concerto in A minor*, which has since come to represent Norway as no other work before or since.

In 1869, Grieg travelled to Italy, where he encountered Franz Liszt and found a new sense of enthusiasm. The following year, back in Christiania, he cooperated with author Bjørnstjerne Bjørnson, who had been awaiting a Norwegian composer to set his poetry and writing to music. Their efforts, *Before a Southern Convent*, *Bergliot* and *Sigurd Jorsalfar*, established Grieg as the musical voice of Norway, but their attempt to create a national opera based on the life of Olaf Tryggvason proved too ambitious and never came to fruition. These efforts, however, led Grieg to meet with Henrik Ibsen, who sought a composer for his fantastic novel *Peer Gynt*. Although he struggled with the project, the score of *Peer Gynt* found international acclaim and became his – and Norway's – best remembered classical work.

In 1874, a government grant allowed Grieg to return to his home town of Bergen and set his creative juices flowing; the result was his *Ballad in G minor*, *The Mountain Thrall*, the *Norwegian Dances for Piano* and *The Holberg Suite*. Between 1880 and 1882, he conducted an orchestra in Bergen, but resigned in order to return to his preferred work of composing. In 1885, he and his wife Nina moved into the coastal home Troldhaugen, from which he set off on numerous concert tours of Europe. At Troldhaugen he created the *Sonata for Violin and Piano in C minor*, the *Haugtussa Songs*, the *Norwegian Peasant Dances and Tunes*, and the *Four Psalms* (based on a series of Norwegian religious melodies).

The Psalms would be his last major work, and on 4 September 1907, he died in hospital at Bergen. In the early 20th century, Grieg's music became well known throughout Europe, and although it was somewhat trivialised by its 'coffee house' popularity, modern musicians are again recognising it as a serious force in classical music and a universal voice for the Norwegian nation. In fact, as early as the 1880s, his first biographer, Aimer Grøvald, noted that it was impossible to listen to Grieg without sensing a light, fresh breeze from the blue waters, a glimpse of grand glaciers and a recollection of the mountains of Western Norway's fjords.

attempt to create a unity with the environment. Harald Sæverud was born in Nordnes on 17 April 1897 but moved with his parents to the city at an early age. His first symphony, completed in 1920, launched his career as a composer of orchestral symphonies and later piano pieces and protest music against the Nazi occupation. In 1986 he was made official composer of the Bergen Symphony Orchestra, a position he honoured by creating a symphonic suite to the Ibsen play *Kjeser og Galilæer*. When he died in March 1992 he was given a state funeral and buried at Siljustøl, as he'd requested. The museum in his home is open from 11 am to 4 pm daily from 20 May to 25 August. Admission costs Nkr40. To reach it, take bus No 555 from platform 20.

Damsgården

The 1770 Damsgård Manor (☎ 55 32 51 08), 3km west of town in Lakesvåg, may well be Norway's finest example of 18th century rococo timber architecture. The building's superb (some may say over the top) highlight is the baroque garden, which includes sculptures, ponds and plant specimens which were in common use 200 years ago. Tours are conducted hourly from 11 am to 5 pm, daily except Monday, between 20 May and 31 August. Admission costs Nkr30. Access is on bus No 19, 70 or 71.

Ulriksbanen

The Ulriksbanen cable car (☎ 55 29 31 60), which climbs to the radio tower and café atop Mt Ulriken (642m), offers a panoramic view of the city and surrounding fjord and mountains. The return trip costs Nkr60 and a Nkr90 'Bergen in a Nutshell' ticket includes the cable car and a return bus from the tourist office. Otherwise, it's a 45-minute walk from the centre or a few minutes' ride on bus No 2, 4 or 7 from the post office or bus No 50 from the Bryggen. The cable car operates daily in summer from 9 am to 11 pm.

A popular excursion is to ride up on the cable car and walk three hours north along a well beaten track to the top of the Fløiba-nen funicular railway. Alternatively, you can choose from a tangle of tracks that lace the lovely mountain and lake country behind Mt Ulriken. For route suggestions, pick up a copy of the free map *Turløper På Byfjellene Nord/Øst*.

Lysøen

The beautiful Lysøen estate (☎ 56 30 90 77) on the island of the same name was constructed in 1873 as the summer residence of Norwegian violinist Ole Bull (see the boxed text). This rather quirky and exceptionally talented character had a great deal of influence on other musicians, who visited frequently and used Lysøen as a retreat. In 1973 the estate and its contents were donated to the Norwegian equivalent of the National Trust by Bull's grand-daughter Mrs Sylvea Bull Curtis, who lived in the USA. The grounds are crisscrossed with 13km of leisurely walks and there's a small café serving light refreshments.

It's open 18 May to 30 August from noon to 4 pm Monday to Saturday and 11 am to 5 pm Sunday. In September, it's open Sunday only. Admission, including a guided tour, costs Nkr25. From the centre, take the Lysefjorden bus (No 566 and 567) from platform 20 to Buene Kai, where there's a passenger ferry to Lysøen.

Activities

For maps and information on wilderness hiking and hut accommodation throughout the region, contact the Bergen Turlag DNT office (☎ 55 32 22 30, fax 55 32 81 15) at Tverrgaten 4. It's open from 10 am to 5 pm Monday to Friday (until 6 pm on Thursday).

Organised Tours

A worthwhile tour is the 1½-hour guided stroll around the Bryggen, which includes entertaining and informative descriptions of life during Bergen's trading heyday. The Nkr60 ticket also includes admission to the Bryggens Museum, Schøtstuene and Hanseatic Museums (and allows you to revisit these museums later on the same day). Tours in English begin at the Bryggens

Ole Bull

Ole Bull recognised his affinity for the violin early and by age 25 had already accomplished solo performances with the Paris opera. Born in Bergen in 1810, Bull performed all over the western world for 45 years, bringing Norwegian folk music to a prominence it had never before enjoyed. At one point, he attempted to set up a utopian society near the community of Oleona in Potter County, Pennsylvania, USA, where a lovely state park preserves the remains of his 'castle'. Most of his summers, however, were spent in his native Norway.

During medieval times, the island of Lysøen belonged to the Abbey Lysekloster, founded in 1146 by the Bernardine order. The first modern farm on the island dates from 1670, and its rustic structures are still visible near the pier. After the death of Ole Bull's French-born wife, Felicité Villeminot, he purchased the 70-hectare property, and between 1872 and 1873, he and architect Conrad Fredrik von der Lippe constructed the fantasy villa 'Lysøen'. This 'Little Alhambra' took much of its inspiration from the architecture of Moorish Granada, and integrated not only intricate frets and trellises but also onion domes, romantic garden paths and a high-ceilinged music hall done in Norwegian pine.

When Bull died at Lysøen in August 1880, tens of thousands of mourners accompanied the funeral procession to the Assistentkirkegården near Bergen's old City Gate. Through the following years, his American-born second wife Sara Thorp, daughter of a senator from Wisconsin, and their daughter Olea Vaughan spent their summer holidays at Lysøen. In 1973, Bull's grandchild, Sylvea Bull Curtis, donated the entire property to the Foreningen til Norske Fortidsminnesmerkers Bevaring (the Norwegian Society for Historical Preservation), and since 1984 the site has been a museum dedicated to Norway's best loved violinist. You'll also see a statue and fountain dedicated to the virtuoso on Ole Bulls plass, in the heart of Bergen.

Museum entrance at 11 am and 1 pm. Tours in German start at 10 am and in Norwegian at noon.

Bergen Fjord Sightseeing (☎ 55 25 90 00) operates fjord cruises past Bergen's port and suburban islands, and through several scenic waterways. The four-hour (Nkr250) option leaves at least daily between 1 May and 25 September; at the height of summer, there are also harbour tours (Nkr75) and two-hour cruises (Nkr150). Tours depart from the fish market.

You can also do the popular 'Norway in a Nutshell' tour from Bergen. The Nkr450 day ticket combines a morning train from Bergen to Flåm, a ferry up the spectacular Nærøyfjord to Gudvangen, a bus to Voss and a train back to Bergen in time for a late dinner (or you can continue on to Oslo to arrive around 10 pm).

From early June to early September, another popular excursion is the Sunday tour by veteran steam train between Garnes and Midtun. It begins at 9 am on the historic ferry M/S *Bruvik* from the Bryggen to the railway museum at Garnes (☎ 55 24 91 00) and from there the 18km steam journey to Midtun. From Midtun back to Bergen, the tour uses a historic bus. The whole trip takes four hours and costs Nkr195. The train trip alone costs Nkr100 return.

Any of these tours can be organised through the Bergen Reiselivslag tourist office.

Special Events
The Bergen International Festival (☎ 55 31 21 70), held for 12 days at the end of May, is the big cultural festival of the year, with dance, music and folklore presentations, and other events throughout the city.

Places to Stay
Camping The nearest camping is at *Bergenshallen Camping* (☎ 55 27 01 80), beside the sports hall at the lake Tveitevatnet. It's 10 minutes by bus from the city centre – take bus No 2, 4, 7 or 11 from the train station or post office. Tent/caravan camping costs Nkr60/90 plus Nkr10 per person, and its open from mid-June to mid-August.

BERGEN

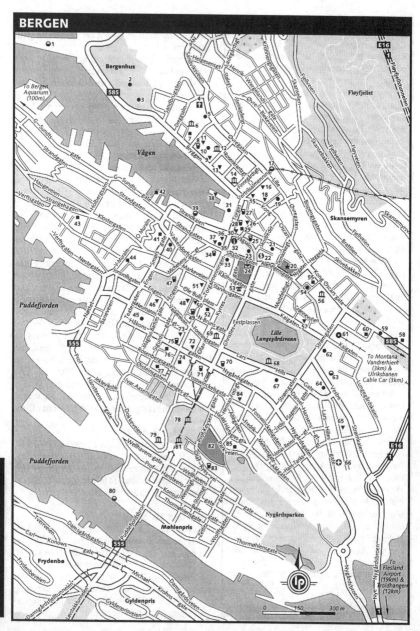

BERGEN

BERGEN

Farther out is the lakeside *Lone Camping* (☎ 55 24 08 20, fax 55 24 43 30), an expanded petrol station between Espeland and Haukeland, about 20km from town. It's overpriced for what's on offer, but this is Bergen, after all, and it's readily accessible by public transport. Bus No 900 runs to and from town approximately every half-hour during the day (30 minutes, Nkr22). Tent camping costs around Nkr60 per tent plus Nkr15 per person, and in summer, bare-bones cabins and rooms start at Nkr300/680 without/with plumbing.

Just 4km south of Lone is *Bratland Camping* (☎ 55 10 13 38), open from 15 May to 10 September. Tent camping is Nkr60 per

tent and Nkr15 per person. Simple cabins cost Nkr290, while self-contained ones cost from Nkr590 to Nkr1200. Use the same bus as for Lone Camping.

Hostels From 15 June to 1 September, a good central place to crash is the friendly 150-bed *YMCA Interrail Centre* (☎ 55 31 72 52, fax 55 31 35 77, ymca@online.no, Nedre Korskirkealmenningen 4). Reception is open from 7.30 am to 1 am, and you can choose between same-sex or co-ed dorms for Nkr100. Kitchen facilities are available and there's a supermarket and a bakery nearby. Best of all, it's near the fish market and a 10-minute walk from the train station.

BERGEN

The other in-town option is *Intermission* (☎ 55 31 32 75, Kalfarveien 5), in a period home near the old town gate. Here the hospitable Christian Student Fellowship provides dorm space for Nkr95, including linen, showers, tea and coffee, and use of the kitchen and laundry facilities. Breakfast costs a bargain Nkr20. It's open from mid-June to mid-August.

The 230-bed *Montana Vandrerhjem* (☎ 55 29 29 00, fax 55 29 04 75, Johan Blyttsvei 30), 5km from the centre near the Ulriksbanen cable car, is open year-round (except over Christmas, from 20 December to 6 January). Dorm beds cost Nkr130/175 without/with breakfast and singles/doubles with bath and breakfast are Nkr350/550. Take bus No 4 from the city centre.

Marken Gjestehus (☎ 55 31 44 04, fax 55 31 60 22, Kong Oscars gate 45) in the town centre charges Nkr170/150 in a four/six-bed dorm and Nkr190 per person in a double room. Breakfast is an additional Nkr40. It's open year-round.

Private Rooms & Pensions The *Kloster Pensionat* (☎ 55 90 21 58, fax 55 23 30 22, Strangehagen 2) is a popular lodge-style guesthouse with 18 clean, simple single/double rooms with shared bath from Nkr320/490, including a continental breakfast. *Myklebust Pensjonat* (☎ 55 90 16 70, fax 55 23 18 01, Rosenbergsgaten 19) has six delightfully comfortable rooms with natural wood floors and tasteful décor from Nkr350/570 with a shared bath and Nkr500/620 with private facilities. An optional continental (Nkr20) or full (Nkr50) breakfast is available.

Kjellersmauet Gjestehus (☎ 55 96 26 08, Kjellersmauet 22) offers rooms with bath and use of the kitchen from Nkr450/500. The *Bergen Gjestehus* (☎ 55 31 96 66, fax 55 23 31 46, Vestre Torggate 20A) is a 23-room hotel with commodious and simple but not cheerless rooms, most of which have kitchenette, TV, phone and private bath. Rates for singles/doubles are Nkr390/490 to Nkr450/650 in summer and Nkr390/490 in winter.

The tourist office books single/double rooms in private homes starting at Nkr160/270, plus a booking fee of Nkr20.

Hotels Bergen's most atmospheric hotel is the *Grand Hotel Terminus* (☎ 55 31 16 55, fax 55 31 85 76), opposite the train station, which has historically been the hotel of choice for the city's better heeled visitors. Never mind that the rooms are cramped by anyone's standards; the décor more than compensates. Single/double rooms, all with bath, cost Nkr510/720 in summer and on weekends, and Nkr920/1150 the rest of the year.

The novel *Hotel Crowded House* (☎/fax 55 23 13 10, 27 Håkonsgaten) presents evidence of the fine line between travellers and tourists. This place charges Nkr340/590 for rooms with breakfast and shared bath, but also offers a pizza bar and both cooking and washing facilities.

Another good choice is *Neptun Hotell* (☎ 55 90 10 00, fax 55 30 68 50, Valkendorfsgate 8), which has well appointed rooms decorated with original artwork. The regular summer and weekend rate is Nkr680/880.

Another relatively inexpensive weekend or summer choice is the delightful 19th century *Steens Hotell* (☎ 55 31 40 50, fax 55 32 61 22, Parkveien 22), where rooms cost Nkr420/580. At other times, they're Nkr580/740.

One of the most elegant places is the *Radisson SAS Hotel Norge* (☎ 55 57 30 00, fax 55 57 30 01), right in the heart of things on Ole Bulls plass. In summer and on weekends, rooms cost Nkr745/990; at other times, they're Nkr1485/1685.

If you prefer the heart of things on the Bryggen, try the affiliated *Radisson SAS Royal Hotel* (☎ 55 54 30 00, fax 55 32 48 08), which charges Nkr100 more across the board. Okay, so you just want a view of the Bryggen? Then try the *Clarion Admiral Hotel* (☎ 55 23 64 00, fax 55 23 64 64, C Sundtsgate 9-13), which charges Nkr690/790 for rooms in summer and a whopping Nkr1100/1345 at other times.

Places to Eat

The bus station harbours a host of cheap stalls serving inexpensive sandwiches and pizza, a fruit stand and a food shop. The *Sol Brød* bakery, on the corner of Vertrilsalmenning and Kong Oscars gate, does oversized pastries for Nkr7. The *Mr Bean Coffee Shop* on Kong Oscars gate brews up enormous cups of coffee for Nkr25. Unfortunately, it doesn't open until 11 am (noon on Sunday), so only late sleepers can use it as a morning kick-start. In the *fish market* at Torget you'll find a choice of fresh fruit and seafood snacks, including tasty open-faced salmon rolls for Nkr15 or a 500g sack of boiled shrimp or crab legs for Nkr50. It's open Monday to Saturday from around 8 am to 3 pm. *McDonald's* and *Burger King* are also represented, and present quick options for filling, inexpensive snacks.

Café Opera (☎ 55 23 03 15, Engen 24) is a trendy place for artists and students, with good, reasonably priced meals. Pastas, salads and vegetarian or beef burritos average Nkr60 to Nkr70. Another inexpensive cafeteria is *Lido (☎ 55 32 59 12, Torgallmenningen 1)*. The unassuming *Pasta Sentralen*, which is on Strømkaien and not all that central, has some of the city's best value for pizza and pasta dishes. At lunchtime, the recommended *Augustus Café (☎ 55 32 35 25)*, in the Galleriet on Torgallmenningen, serves both hot and cold dishes.

The popular *Dickens (☎ 55 90 07 60)* has a sunny dining room overlooking Ole Bulls plass. A lunch special, often steak and potatoes, costs about Nkr80, as do a variety of salads and light dishes that are served any time. In the afternoons, they have a pizza buffet for Nkr59. The bar is quite a lively night spot. *Michelangelo (☎ 55 90 08 25, Neumannsgate 25)*, a dinner restaurant, has authentic Italian food at moderate prices.

The outdoor seating at the richly decorated *Wesselstuen (☎ 55 90 08 20)*, on Ole Bulls plass, offers excellent value in the mid-range, and is especially popular with post-graduate students, philosophers and intellectuals in the local 30 to 40-year-old crowd. In the evening, they use heat lamps to keep it comfortably toasty.

Vegetarians are well served by *Den Gode Klode (☎ 55 32 34 32, Fosswinckelsgata 18)*. Its leafy and airy atmosphere makes it an ideal place to enjoy the vegetarian pizzas, Indian dishes, pasta, salads and sweet snacks. They also do vegan options. It's open Monday to Saturday for lunch and dinner. An odd combination, *India Tandoori & Tapas Tapas Bar (☎ 55 96 22 50, Vertrilsalmenning 15)*, near the Fløibanen terminal, has several vegetarian choices under Nkr100. *Ma-Ma Thai (Kaigaten 20)* is a cosy Oriental place that attracts university students with its good value specials, including a selection of Nkr60 'lunches' that are available throughout the day.

For a splurge, *Ole Bull (☎ 55 57 30 00)* at the Hotel Norge has a pleasant 2nd floor park view and a tempting buffet that includes cold salmon and shrimp, several hot dishes, salads and sweets. The price is Nkr179 from noon to 4 pm and Nkr215 from 7 to 10 pm. An unusual dining experience in Norway is *Louisiana Créole Restaurant (☎ 55 54 66 60)*, opposite the fish market in the Jeppe building. It makes a laudable attempt at Cajun cuisine and serves as a very pleasant mid-range choice.

Bryggeloftet & Stuene (☎ 55 31 06 30, Bryggen 11), in the middle of the historic district, serves traditional Norwegian fare in a pleasant atmosphere. Except in midsummer, they offer generous daily specials from Nkr79; otherwise, dishes start at around Nkr120. It's open from 11 am to 11.30 pm daily (it opens at 1 pm on Sunday). Also in the Bryggen is the cosy *Bryggen Tracteursted (☎ 55 31 40 46)*, housed in a 300-year-old tavern. It's frightfully expensive and mainly caters to tourists and the expense account brigade, but it does offer a dose of Norwegian cuisine and old-style ambience. Similarly popular and upmarket is *Enhjørningen (☎ 55 32 79 19)*, also on the Bryggen, which is fish and seafood from beginning to end (but the name means 'unicorn', and above the door it appears that such a beast is attempting an escape).

The waterfront Zachariasbryggen, at the inner harbour, houses a range of pubs and eateries, including *Kina Kina* (☎ *55 96 18 30*), which serves nine Chinese lunch specials until 6 pm weekdays for Nkr59; *Pasta Basta* (☎ *55 55 96 65*), a mid-range pizza and pasta restaurant; *Skibet* (☎ *55 55 96 50*), which may well put you off Tex-Mex cuisine; the popular *Baker Brun* konditori with pastries (including Bergen's own *shillings-boller* buns) and sandwiches; the *Fiske-krogen* (☎ *55 55 96 60*) game and seafood restaurant; the ubiquitous *Peppe's Pizza* (☎ *55 32 60 10*); an ice cream shop; and the popular *Flaaten Friluftsrestaurant & Bar*, which serves pizza and beer and overflows onto the quay whenever the sun appears.

Supermarkets abound in Bergen. The *Mekka* chain, which has a branch at the bus station, has cheaper prices and longer hours than most. The *Spar* market, opposite the Bryggens Museum, has a takeaway deli with whole grilled chickens for Nkr39. *Kinsarvik Frukt* on Olav Kyrres gate is a food shop with a health-food section. The central *Godt Brød* (*Nedre Korskirkealmenningen 17*) has delicious organic breads and pastries, café tables and long opening hours. Many other bakeries in the centre offer reasonably priced sandwiches. Bergen also brews its own beer, under the Hansa label.

Entertainment

Pubs, Clubs & Discos Among Norway's best beer values is *Torget Music Pub*, near the harbour, where 500ml of lager will set you back only Nkr30. Even better value is *The News*, which uses the Børsen (stock exchange) system for beer prices. At times of low demand, the price can drop to Nkr15 for 500ml, while busy times may cause the price to climb to Nkr45. The disco in the roof garden upstairs imposes a Nkr50 cover charge. Another inexpensive pub, which caters to students, is *Kvartieret*, on Nygårdsgaten. *Garage* (*Christies gate 14*), is Bergen's top rock music venue, and *Hulen Stiftelsen* (*Olaf Ryes vei 47*), behind the student centre, also attracts a university crowd. Their live music performances most

often feature unknown local bands, so expect surprises.

Rick's (☎ *55 55 31 31, Veiten 3*) is a film-themed complex of pubs and eateries which include *Rick's Café*, the *Casablanca* music pub, *Bogarts Nightclub*, the *Piccadilly* English-style pub and *Finnegan's* Irish-style pub. The pubs impose a cover charge of Nkr50 and attract over-25s. The *Banco Rotto* attracts everyone from the ages of 30 to 60 with its weekend live music shows, and the attached *Blue Velvet Bar* puts on live jazz performances for a Nkr60 cover charge.

The *Engelen Nightclub* on the Bryggen caters to patrons in their early 20s with a weekend disco and a special 1950s to 1970s pop music theme on Wednesday. Thursday is 'cheap shots' night, with inexpensive alcohol. The cover charge is Nkr50. Sports-oriented bars include *Scruffy Murphy* on the Torget, *Champions* on the corner of Torgallmenningen and Strandgaten, and the *Brann Football Pub* on Håkons gaten.

Other *Bergen Kino* (www.filmweb.no) on Neumannsgate has 13 cinema screens and first-run movies (Nkr60). The tourist-oriented *Fana Folklore show* (☎ *55 91 52 40*), held in Fana church and Rambergstunet farm south of town, presents a taste of traditional Norwegian music and dancing on Monday, Tuesday, Thursday and Friday between early June and late August. Tickets cost Nkr200, including a bus ride from the Festplassen at 7 pm and back after the show at 10.30 pm. Another group, *Bergen Folklore* (☎ *94 68 46 26*), performs at the Bryggens Museum on Tuesday and Thursday at 9 pm from 5 June to 21 August; tickets are Nkr95.

The Bergen Philharmonic Orchestra stages concerts at *Grieghallen* on Thursday and Friday from September to May for Nkr75 to Nkr200. In summer, classical concerts, recitals and string performances are held at the *Troldhaugen* and *Lysøen* estates, and cost from Nkr100 to Nkr170. The Bergen International Theater and Bergen Operakor holds theatre, dance and opera productions which cost around Nkr100.

For details and schedules, see the summer tabloid newspaper, *Bergen*, which is distributed free at the tourist office. For tickets to any of these performances, contact the Billett Service (☎ 81 03 31 33).

Atop Mt Fløyen, free outdoor pop and rock concerts are held nightly at 8 pm from 21 June to 16 August. Similar action occurs on Ulriken nightly from Monday to Friday between 15 May and 15 September.

Shopping
The broadest selection of handicrafts, wooden toys and traditional clothing is found at Husfliden, Vågsalmenning 3. The Galleriet shopping centre, north-west of the post office, has boutiques, a grocery store and a good bookshop, Melvær. The bus station holds another large shopping complex.

Getting There & Away
Bergen is a main staging point for journeys into the Western Fjords, and numerous buses, trains, passenger ferries and express boats set off daily.

Air Bergen's airport is at Flesland, about 19km south-west of the centre. Both Braathens SAFE (☎ 55 23 55 23, fax 55 23 32 37), Olav Kyrresgata 27, and SAS (☎ 55 99 76 00, fax 55 99 76 35), at the airport, connect Oslo and Bergen many times daily. There are also direct flights to Trondheim, Kristiansand, Stavanger and smaller places around the Western Fjords region, as well as to Copenhagen, Stockholm and London. Widerøe (☎ 55 99 82 20, fax 55 99 82 26), also at the airport, flies to Shetland and Glasgow (see the Getting There & Away chapter) via Stavanger, and to a couple of smaller airports in the Western Fjords.

Bus Daily Nor-Way Bussekspress buses run to Odda (four hours, Nkr200) and to Stryn (6½ hours, Nkr340), Ålesund (9¾ hours, Nkr470) and Trondheim (14¾ hours, Nkr760). Buses to and from Stavanger (five hours, Nkr340) run at least twice daily. The bus trip to Oslo (11½ hours, Nkr580), via Odda, leaves once daily in either direction,

but for most travellers, the train is more convenient.

Train The train line between Bergen and Oslo is deservedly billed as one of the world's most spectacular, climbing from the lush forested coast at Bergen to the high and lonesome Hardangervidda plateau before dropping slowly past lakes and through increasingly green hills to the capital city. The trip (seven hours, Nkr510) departs up to six times daily in mid-summer, including a convenient overnight train with 2nd-class sleepers for Nkr100. Local trains run between Bergen, Voss (one hour, Nkr115) and Myrdal (2½ hours, Nkr170) roughly every hour or two in summer. Seat reservations are required on all rail trips.

Car & Motorcycle The main highway into Bergen is the E16. There's a toll of Nkr5 for vehicles entering the city on weekdays from 6 am to 10 pm.

Boat Daily Fylkesbåtane (☎ 55 32 40 15, fsf@infonet.no) express boats connect Bergen with Balestrand (four hours, Nkr310) and Flåm (5½ hours, Nkr420), in Sognefjord. To Måløy (4½ hours, Nkr435) and Selje (five hours, Nkr470), near the mouth of Nordfjord, they run daily and connect with express boats to and from Ålesund. Flaggruten (☎ 55 23 87 00) has daily runs to and from Stavanger (five hours, Nkr480), via Haugesund (three hours, Nkr290). Hardanger Sunnhordlandske (☎ 55 55 90 70) has daily services to and from Rosendal (2½ hours), Jondal (3¼ hours), Norheimsund (3¾ hours) and Odda (5½ hours), in Hardangerfjord. In Bergen, all these boats use the Strandkaiterminal.

The Hurtigruten coastal steamer leaves from the Frieleneskaien, south of the university, at 10.30 pm daily. See the Getting Around chapter for details. International ferries between Bergen and Britain (Newcastle and Aberdeen), Iceland and Denmark dock at Skoltegrunnskaien, north of Rosenkrantz tower. See the Getting There & Away chapter for more details.

Getting Around

The Airport The airport is in Flesland, 19km by road south-west of central Bergen. The SAS Flybussen (45 minutes, Nkr40) runs at least twice hourly between the airport, the Radisson SAS Royal Hotel, the Radisson SAS Hotel Norge and the main bus terminal. Local bus No 523 also runs between the bus terminal and Flesland airport (45 minutes, Nkr29), with departures more or less hourly.

Bus City buses cost Nkr13, while fares beyond the centre are based on the distance travelled. Route information is available on ☎ 177. There's also a free bus running between the main post office and the bus terminal.

Taxi Taxis (☎ 55 99 70 00) queue up along Ole Bulls plass.

Car & Motorcycle As in most Norwegian towns, it's best to park your car and explore the city centre on foot. Except where there are parking meters, street parking is reserved for residents with special zone-parking stickers; 'P' parking signs accompanied by the word 'sone' indicate a reserved area. In the busiest areas, metered parking is limited to 30 minutes and elsewhere, including the lot west of Grieghallen and on the north side of Store Lungegårdsvann, you get only two hours. Less restricted are the indoor car parks; the largest is Bygarasjen at the bus terminal, which is open 24 hours a day.

Ferry From 1 May to 15 September, the Vågen (☎ 55 30 76 30) harbour ferry runs between the Torget fish market and Tollbodhopen at Nordnes (near the aquarium) approximately every 15 minutes during business hours.

Bicycle In summer, the Bergen Kommune rents bicycles at the kiosk near Husfliden, opposite the post office. You can also hire cycles from Sykkelbutikken (☎ 55 32 06 20) at Østre Skostredet 5.

Hardangerfjord

VOSS

Although it isn't a coastal town, the winter sports centre of Voss is the de facto capital of the Hardangerfjord region and most travellers in southern Norway pass through at least once, even if it's just on the popular 'Norway in a Nutshell' excursion between Oslo and Bergen. For Norwegians, however, it's first and foremost a winter sports venue.

From medieval times, the town served as an agricultural centre and a focus of trade between eastern and western Norway. In 1023 King Olav Haraldson den Heilige (St Olav) stopped by to erect a cross in honour of Voss' conversion to Christianity. In more recent years, the area was used for military training, and Voss became an educational and industrial town. It was levelled by German bombs in 1940, but has now developed into a solid little commercial centre and community of 14,000 people.

Information

The active and helpful Voss Tourist Information office (☎ 56 51 00 51, fax 56 52 08 01, www.voss-promotion.no) is on Utrågata, a 10-minute walk east of the station. From June to August, it's open from 9 am to 7 pm Monday to Saturday and 2 pm to 7 pm Sunday. Anyone who's interested in outdoor activities will want a copy of the Nkr20 *Voss Naturguide – Walks & Adventures in the Voss District*.

Coin laundry is available at the Vaskeri, north of the church.

Vangskyrkja

In 1023 in a field south of the current stone church in Voss, which occupies the site of an ancient pagan temple, St Olav erected a stone cross to commemorate the local conversion to Christianity. The first wooden church on the site was probably constructed of wood, but was replaced with a Gothic-style stone church in the mid-13th century, as evidenced by a congratulatory letter from King Magnus Lagabøte in 1271. In 1277 the church was consecrated in honour of St Michael. Although the original stone altar and the unique wooden spire remain, the Lutheran Reformation of 1536 brought about the removal of many original features. Elias Fiigenschoug's altarpiece, representing the Crucifixion, is done in colour with the exception of Christ on the cross, who appears in black and white. On the ceiling, painted in the late 17th century, a flock of angels flit through a backdrop of sky.

Since the mid-19th century, the structure and its interior have undergone several restorations, and the 1923 stained glass work commemorates the 900th anniversary of Christianity in Voss. Miraculously, the building avoided destruction during the intense German bombings in 1940. It's open between 10 am and 4 pm daily in summer. Admission costs Nkr10. Services are held on Sunday at 11 am.

Prestegardsmoen

The Prestegardsmoen Council recreational and nature reserve, which extends southward from Voss Camping, offers a series of hiking tracks and the chance to observe 140 species of plants and 124 bird species, including waterbirds. It also contains the municipal swimming pool and sports hall.

Voss Folkemuseum

The Voss Folk Museum (☎ 56 51 15 11) takes in three diverse and widely scattered parts. The main portion is the Mølstertunet Museum, which lies at the farm Mølster, on the hillside above town. This collection of historic farm buildings, which date from the mid-17th to mid-19th centuries, displays various facets of life in earlier times. It's open from 10 am to 5 pm daily in May and September, and 10 am to 7 pm from June to August; winter hours are shorter. Admission costs Nkr30.

The other two portions of the museum, the Nesheimstunet Museum and the old wooden Oppheim vicarage, lie 10km and 26km from town respectively, along the Gudvangen road (the E16). They are open by appointment only.

Dagestad Museum & Bordalsgjelet

This museum was opened in 1950 by local woodcarver Magnus Dagestad (1865-1957) and features his lifetime of carvings, drawings and traditional wooden furniture creations, as well as works by his wife, Helena Dagestad. This unusual and worthwhile exhibit is open from 11 am to 3 pm Tuesday to Sunday between 1 June and 31 August (until 5 pm in July). Admission costs Nkr20. It lies about 1.5km from the town centre. On foot, use the 1941 pedestrian bridge from the Prestegardsmoen nature reserve; while you're at it, you may also want to ramble up to the scenic river potholes in Bordalsgjelet gorge, which lie about 20 minutes walk south of the museum. Look for the black and white *fossekallen* (water dipper), Norway's national bird.

Stalheim

In the 1860s, the Nærøydalen valley served as a popular access route for travellers between the coast and the Norwegian interior. Between 1647 and 1909, travellers on the Royal Mail route between Copenhagen, Christiania (Oslo) and Bergen stopped here to rest and change horses. The route climbed up the valley and through the Stalheimskleiva gorge, flanked by the Stalheim and Sivle waterfalls. There has been an inn here since the late 17th century, and the current *Stalheim Hotel* (☎ 56 52 01 22, fax 56 52 00 56), which is the fourth one on the site, was constructed in 1960 and offers an incredible view down spectacular Nærøydalen. Single/double rooms start at Nkr700/990 and the popular restaurant offers a lunch buffet for Nkr160. It's open from mid-May to late September, and the attached shop offers a particularly good range of crafts and souvenirs.

The Stalheim Folkemuseum, near the hotel, includes folk exhibits and 30 log buildings laid out as a traditional farm. Admission costs Nkr20.

To reach Stalheim from Voss (one hour, Nkr47), take any bus towards Gudvangen.

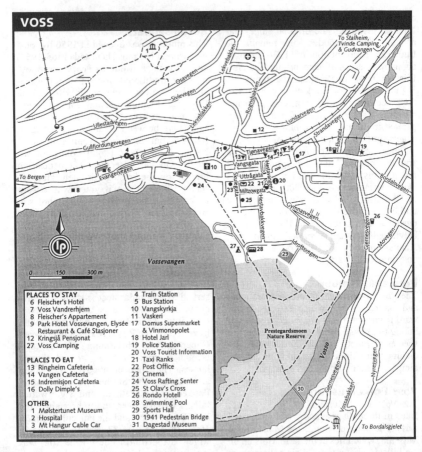

VOSS

To Stalheim,
Tvinde Camping
& Gudvangen

To Bergen

To Bordalsgjelet

Vossevangen

*Prestegardsmoen
Nature Reserve*

Vosso

0   150   300 m

PLACES TO STAY	4 Train Station
6 Fleischer's Hotel	5 Bus Station
7 Voss Vandrerhjem	10 Vangskyrkja
8 Fleischer's Appartement	11 Vaskeri
9 Park Hotel Vossevangen, Elysée	17 Domus Supermarket
Restaurant & Café Stasjoner	& Vinmonopolet
12 Kringsjå Pensjonat	18 Hotel Jarl
27 Voss Camping	19 Police Station
	20 Voss Tourist Information
PLACES TO EAT	21 Taxi Ranks
13 Ringheim Cafeteria	22 Post Office
14 Vangen Cafeteria	23 Cinema
15 Indremisjon Cafeteria	24 Voss Rafting Senter
16 Dolly Dimple's	25 St Olav's Cross
	26 Rondo Hotell
OTHER	28 Swimming Pool
1 Mølstertunet Museum	29 Sports Hall
2 Hospital	30 1941 Pedestrian Bridge
3 Mt Hangur Cable Car	31 Dagestad Museum

Activities

Voss is above all a winter sports centre, and
the ski season runs from mid-December
until April, depending on the snow conditions. The winter action focuses on the
cable-car route up Mt Hangur, which has a
ski school; the lift lies within easy walking
distance of town. Those with vehicles can
opt for Bavallen, 5km due north of the centre, which is used for international downhill
competitions. Lift tickets and equipment
hire are available at either slope (in sum-

mer, the Hangur lift whisks you to the view
every 15 minutes from 11 am to 5 pm for
Nkr50). On the plateau and up the Raundalen valley at Mjølfjell, you'll also find
excellent cross-country skiing. For weather
and snow conditions, phone ☎ 56 51 94 88.

Summer visitors can opt for white-water
rafting (Nkr590), canyoning (Nkr450), waterfall abseiling (Nkr450) and riverboarding
(Nkr650/1500 for one/three days) with the
Voss Rafting Senter (☎ 56 51 05 25, voss
.rafting@online.no, www.bbb.no/rafting/),

located beside the Park Hotel, where the motto is the rather ambiguous 'We guarantee to wet your pants'. Rafters and riverboarders can choose between three very different rivers: the Stranda (Class II to IV), Raundalen (Class II to V) and Vosso (Class II). They also run a riverside wilderness camp with accommodation in Sami-style *lavvos* for Nkr50 per person.

For details on horse riding in Nærøydalen (Nkr180/500 for two/five hours), contact the English-run Stølsheimen Fjellridning/Engjaland Fjellstove (☎ 56 51 91 66, fax 56 51 11 35, www.engjaland.no), a 30-minute drive from town. In the high season, overnight accommodation in this simple lodge costs from Nkr380 to Nkr485 per person. This is also a good base to use for hut-to-hut hiking in the spectacular Stølsheimen mountains. For information, contact the Bergen Turlag DNT office (☎ 55 32 22 30, fax 55 32 81 15) at Tverrgaten 4 in Bergen.

Special Events
In the last week of June, Voss hosts the Extremesport Week, which attracts adrenalin junkies with a range of activities and competitions that few mere mortals will want to attempt.

Organised Tours
The famous 'Norway in a Nutshell' tour, normally done between Oslo and Bergen, also works as a day tour from Voss. It involves rail trips from Voss to Myrdal and Flåm, the boat to Gudvangen and the bus back to Voss. The trip takes five to seven hours and costs Nkr290. Children under 16 pay Nkr145 and seniors over 67 pay Nkr180. You can book through the tourist office, any travel agency, or directly through NSB at the train station.

Places to Stay & Eat
The lakeside *Voss Camping* (☎ 56 51 15 97), 300m south of the tourist office, has tent camping for under Nkr100 and simple cabins from Nkr250 to Nkr350. A scenic alternative is *Tvinde Camping* (☎/fax 56 51 69 19), which lies beside a waterfall about

10km north-east of town. Here you'll pay Nkr65 for tent camping and Nkr250 to Nkr350 for cabins. Without a car, access is on the Voss-Gudvangen bus (20 minutes, Nkr22).

At the pricey *Voss Vandrerhjem* (☎ 56 51 20 17, fax 56 51 08 37), 1km west of the train station, rates start at Nkr165 for dorm beds and Nkr400 for doubles. These include a simple breakfast, but there's no kitchen. For the best lake views, try for a room on the top floor at the back. Bicycles and rowing boats can be hired and there's a free sauna. It's open from January to late October.

A step up in price, atmosphere and elevation is the *Kringsjå Pensjonat* (☎ 56 51 16 27, fax 56 51 63 30) on Strengjarhaugen. It's run by the Ole Bull music academy for its classes and concerts, but rooms are also rented to travellers from Nkr250 per person, with breakfast.

For a bit of historic character, the wealthy can check out the enormous century-old *Fleischer's Hotel* (☎ 56 51 11 55, fax 56 51 22 89, fleischr@sn.no). Singles/doubles cost Nkr925/1290. *Fleischer's Appartement* (☎ 56 51 91 66) has small self-catering units for Nkr350 per person. The other upmarket option, the *Park Hotel Vossevangen* (☎ 56 51 13 22, fax 56 51 00 39), overlooks the lake Vossevangen, 200m from the train station. Rooms cost Nkr725/950.

For pizza, try *Dolly Dimple's* (☎ 56 51 00 40), on Vangsgata at the eastern end of the centre. The *Domus* supermarket has a simple café upstairs, and is also home of the Vinmonopolet. Other cafés include *Vangen Cafeteia*, *Ringheim Cafeteria* (☎ 56 51 13 65) and *Indremisjon Cafeteria* (☎ 56 51 14 08), all along Vangsgata. The finest restaurant option is the *Elysée* (☎ 56 51 13 22), in the Park Hotel Vossevangen; it specialises in French and international cuisine and has a particularly extensive wine list. If you really want to go out on a limb, order the local speciality *smalhove*, which is in fact a singed sheep head. In the same hotel is the popular *Café Stasjonen*, a train-theme café which opens for lunch and in the late afternoon and evening.

Entertainment

The Park Hotel Vossevangen offers a youth-oriented piano bar, the odd *Stallen* pub (where patrons sit on saddles around a fireplace), and the popular *Pentagon* weekend disco. The pub in the *Hotel Jarl (Elvegata 9)* has a cellar disco which attracts the 18 to 21 crowd; anyone older than that may better appreciate the rustic rock-theme disco in the *Rondo Hotell (Gjernesvegen 26)*.

In winter, any sort of outdoor activity may well be followed by a steaming cup of *gløgg*, the *aprés ski* drink of choice around these parts.

There is also a *cinema* in town, which screens a different film every week.

More refined tastes will enjoy the concerts by pianist Åge Kristoffersen, which are held on Wednesday and Saturday at 9.30 pm, from 29 April to 30 September, in the Osa Hall at Fleischer's Hotel. Admission costs Nkr70.

Getting There & Away

Buses stop near the train station, west of the centre. Frequent bus services connect Voss with Bergen (two hours, Nkr115), Norheimsund (two hours, Nkr95) and Aurland (1½ hours, Nkr90), via Gudvangen and Flåm. Buses only run on Tuesday to the hiking and skiing country around Mjølfjell, where there's a hostel.

NSB rail services (☎ 56 52 80 00) on the renowned Bergensbanen to and from Bergen (one hour, Nkr115) and Oslo (six to eight hours, Nkr440) run up to six times daily in summer, and connect at Myrdal (45 minutes, Nkr70) with the steep and scenic line down to Flåm. At the station, have a look at the monument to Knut Rokne (later spelt Knute Rockne in the USA), the Norwegian from Voss who in the early 20th century rose to fame playing American football.

Getting Around

Bicycle hire is available for Nkr30/150 per hour/day from the Voss Rafting Senter (☎ 56 51 05 25), beside the Park Hotel.

For a taxi, phone ☎ 56 51 13 40.

DALE

In the small and scenic town of Dale, between Voss and Bergen, you can visit Dale Kraftverk's unusual Energisenteret (☎ 56 59 65 48), which takes you 400m inside a mountain for a lesson on hydroelectric power. A variety of videos and exhibits contrasts early 20th century hydroelectric power generation with modern methods. From late June to mid-August, guided tours are conducted hourly between 11 am and 4.30 pm. Admission costs Nkr40 per person and Nkr95 per family. All buses using the E13 between Bergen and Voss pass through Dale (1½ hours, Nkr72), and most buses between Bergen and Arna connect with buses on to Dale.

NORHEIMSUND

Norheimsund serves as a main terminal for ferry transport on Hardangerfjord but there's little to detain anyone for long. Most visitors join the daily two-hour Nkr120 scenic cruise on Fyksesund, offered by Fjordtur (☎ 56 55 22 10, fax 56 55 24 82); they depart at noon from Steinstø quay. If for some reason you do want to stay longer, there are a couple of hotels and a camping ground, the *Hardanger Feriesenter (☎ 56 55 13 84)*, with expensive cabins from Nkr480 to Nkr630. The *Norheimsund Fjord Hotel (☎ 56 55 15 22, fax 56 55 15 88)* offers single/double summer rates of Nkr655/855. The more atmospheric *Sandven Hotel (☎ 56 55 20 88, fax 56 55 26 88)*, which dates from 1857, charges Nkr550/820 for incongruously modern accommodation.

ULVIK & OSA

The traditional village of Ulvik lies in the heart of a lovely fruit-growing region and is home to Hjeltnes, Norway's oldest horticultural college (established in 1901). Visitors can stroll around the rose gardens and surrounding Ulvikpollen wetlands, which harbour 80 bird species, including the golden plover.

At the Stream Nest complex (☎ 56 52 68 44) in Osa, 6km away, you can check out the new ecological herb garden and several works of art, including Allan Christensen's *Rambukk* (pile driver) and the odd eponymous stick sculpture, *Stream Nest*, which was originally conceived by Japanese artist Takamasa Kuniyasu for the 1994 Winter Olympics in Lillehammer. Today the sculpture resounds with the tuba music of Geir Løvold, just as it did during the Games. It's open daily from May to September and admission is Nkr40. It's a pleasant 9km walk over the promontory between Ulvik and Osa.

For information, see the Ulvik Turistkontor (☎ 56 52 63 60, fax 56 52 66 23), open daily in summer from 8.30 am to 5 pm Monday to Saturday and 1 to 5 pm Sunday. They also hire bicycles for Nkr100 per day.

Places to Stay
Campers can stay at the convenient *Ulvik Fjordcamping* (☎ *56 52 65 77*), 500m from the centre of town; tent camping costs Nkr60 per tent plus Nkr10 per person and huts start at Nkr250. In summer, you'll find decent singles/doubles at the *Strand Fjordhotell* (☎ *56 52 63 05, fax 56 52 64 10*) for Nkr515/730. The summer-only *Ulvik Fjord Pensjonat* (☎ *56 52 61 70, fax 56 52 61 60*), west along the waterfront from the centre, has rooms for Nkr440/700.

Getting There & Away
Between Voss and Ulvik (1¼ hours, Nkr54), bus No 611 runs two to five times daily. The Hardanger Sunnhordlandske Dampskipsselskap (☎ 55 23 87 80) ferry, M/S *Vøringen*, operates between Norheimsund and Ulvik (1½ hours, Nkr135) at least once daily between mid-June and mid-August. It also connects with the M/S *Hardangerfjord*, which sails between Bergen and Norheimsund (3¼ hours, Nkr220).

Between Ulvik and Osa, your best option is either to walk or take the 11 am daily (except Sunday) tour from the Ulvik tourist office, which costs Nkr160 and includes admission to Stream Nest. It connects with the M/S *Vøringen* ferry to and from Norheimsund.

ODDA
Industrial, iron-smelting Odda is frequently cited as Norway's ugliest town, and while that's not exactly true – there are some pretty dire places in Finnmark – it isn't especially attractive. What Odda's critics fail to mention, however, is that everyone living in its dismal 'workers' dwellings' has a front-row view of some of Norway's finest landscapes. In fact, the backdrop includes not only the uttermost reaches of Hardangerfjord, but also a lake which spills into it through a riotous waterfall and the icy heights of the fabulous Folgefonn glacier.

Information
For information, stop by the Odda Næringsråd tourist office (☎ 53 64 12 97, fax 53 64 42 60), near the Sørfjorden shore, which is open from 10 am to 8 pm weekdays, 10 am to 5 pm Saturday and 11 am to 6 pm Sunday from early June to mid-August. The rest of the year, it's open from 9 am to 3 pm weekdays.

Folgefonn
Folgefonn, mainland Norway's third largest icefield, offers summer skiing, snowboarding and sledding from mid-June to mid-August. Short tours to the ski centre (Nkr80) leave from Jondal quay at noon from mid-June to mid-August, with an additional departure at 10.30 am until early August, and return at 2 and 3.30 pm. The short tours connect with the M/S *Hardangerfjord* ferry to and from Bergen (3¼ hours, Nkr210). From Odda, weekend glacier trips run to Odda Turlag's Holmaskjær mountain hut; in July and August, you can join daily guided overnight hikes for Nkr700, including meals and lodging at the hut. Contact Odda Turlag at PO Box 366, 5751 Odda.

Between 1 June and 31 August, anyone in average physical condition with warm clothing and sturdy footwear can take a guided glacier walk on the Buer arm of Folgefonn. The two daily walks (10 am to 4 pm and 3.30 to 9.30 pm) begin with a one-hour hike up the lovely Buer valley, then proceed onto the ice. The Nkr250 price includes use of crampons and ice axes, but not transport to the start of the tour at Buer, 9km west of Odda. Of course you can forego the tour charge and walk to the glacier face on your own; from town, the return trip is 24km.

Tyssedal

Tyssedal boasts an impressive 1908 hydro-electric power plant, and if you squint a bit, its architecture appears to reveal a hint of in-spiration from Lhasa's Potala Palace. In the structure, which in its day was one of the world's largest powerhouses, the Vestnorsk Industristadmuseum (☎ 53 64 27 44) relates the plant's history. Also of interest is the Tyssedal Hotel (☎ 53 64 69 07), which houses a gallery of fantastic fairy tale and Hardangerfjord landscape paintings by Eidfjord artist Nils Bergslien (1853-1928); his renowned work *Tysso & Tyssen* features two Hardanger caricatures surveying the Tyssedal hydroelectric plant.

To get there from Odda (10 minutes, Nkr14) take local bus No 212.

Places to Stay

The most convenient camping is at *Odda Camping* (☎ 53 64 34 10, fax 53 64 12 92), on the shores of lake Sandvinvatnet at the southern end of town. It's a 20-minute walk uphill from the town centre; it's open from 1 June to 31 August and tent/caravan camp-ing for two people with a vehicle costs Nkr80/100. The *Sørfjordheimen Hotell & Vandrerhjem* (☎ 53 65 14 10, fax 53 65 14 19, oddahot@hardangernett.no), on Buste-tungata near the Sørfjorden shore, offers dormitory rooms for Nkr130 and single/double rooms from Nkr230/420 to Nkr695/835. Another budget option on the Sør-fjorden shoreline is the *Hybo Odda* (☎ 53 64 22 55, Freimsanden 4), where single/double self-catering flats start at Nkr300/450. At the *Hardanger Hotel* (☎ 53 65 14 00, fax 53 65 14 09), you'll pay Nkr790/895 for rooms.

Getting There & Away

Between Odda and Jondal (2½ hours, Nkr95), local bus No 211 operates three to five times daily. Nor-Way Bussekspress buses run daily to and from Bergen (four hours, Nkr200), Voss (2½ hours, Nkr220) and Skien (6½ hours, Nkr310). In summer, the M/S *Vøringen* ferry sails between Odda and Norheimsund (1½ hours, Nkr176) one to three times daily, with bus and ferry con-nections to and from Bergen.

UTNE & KINSARVIK

At the picturesque fruit-growing village of Utne, Hardangerfjord separates into three arms: Granvinfjord, Eidfjord and Sørfjord. The open-air Hardanger Folk Museum (☎ 53 66 69 00) comprises a collection of historic homes, shops, outhouses and a school, plus exhibitions on Hardanger women, weddings, fiddle-making, fishing, music and dance, orchard crops and the woodcarvings of local artist Lars Kinsarvik. It's open from 10 am to 4 pm Monday to Saturday and noon to 4 pm Sunday from 26 April to 31 August (daily until 6 pm in July). Admission and hourly guided tours cost Nkr30.

At Kinsarvik, a short ferry ride away (30 minutes, Nkr20/52 per person/vehicle), you'll see one of Norway's first stone churches. This one, according to legend, was built in Roman style by Scots in 1160, and during medieval times Viking sails and masts were stored in the attic. Chalk paint-ings on the walls depict the weighing of souls by Michael the Archangel. It was re-stored in 1880 and 1961. It's open from 9 am to 7 pm between late May and mid-September.

Kinsarvik and nearby Lofthus also offer appealing access trails up the slopes and onto the network of tracks through the lonely Hardangervidda National Park.

Places to Stay

The *Hardanger Gjestegård* (☎ 53 66 67 10, fax 53 66 66 66) in Utne is housed in a charming 1898 building with atmospheric single/double rooms for Nkr450/600. Also in Utne is the historic wooden *Utne Hotel* (☎ 53 66 67 10, fax 53 66 69 50), built in 1722 after the Great Nordic War, when

Peder Larsson Børsem applied to the king and received permission to set up a guesthouse in Utne; it has been in business ever since. To experience this bit of history – and the hotel's fabulous décor – you'll pay Nkr670/1060 for a room.

Getting There & Away

Nor-Way Bussekspress buses between Bergen (four hours, Nkr200) and Skien pass through Utne, while buses between Voss (2½ hours, Nkr200) and Odda (one hour, Nkr42) stop in Kinsarvik. The M/S *Vøringen* sails between Norheimsund, Odda, Utne and Kinsarvik three to four times daily in summer. Between Norheimsund and Utne/Kinsarvik takes 30 minutes/one hour and costs Nkr76/93. Between Odda and Kinsarvik/Utne takes the same and costs Nkr98/106.

Stavanger & Lysefjord

STAVANGER

Stavanger, Norway's fourth largest city, was a bustling fishing centre at the turn of the century and in its heyday had more than 70 sardine canneries. By the 1960s the depletion of fish stocks stopped the industry cold, but the discovery of North Sea oil spared Stavanger from obscurity. As home to nearly 3000 British and US oil workers and administrators, and the haunt of oil-related business visitors from around the world, it's nearly as cosmopolitan as Oslo. While that affords it dubious value as a tourist attraction, the oil money has also created a visible civic pride, and the city may well be the tidiest and most user-friendly in all of Norway.

Most visitors who arrive on the ferry from Britain make a beeline for Bergen or Oslo, but the city's historic harbour, medieval cathedral, timber architecture, lovely parks, and several good museums will easily absorb a day of strolling and sightseeing, and Lysefjord and Preikestolen make essential day trips.

Orientation

The adjacent bus and train stations lie beside the pond Breiavann, about 10 minutes on foot from the harbour. The modern Kulturhus, a sort of town centre, houses the public library, an eight-screen cinema, an art gallery and several restaurants and cafés. On sunny days the pedestrian streets and pavements behind the Kulturhus bustle with students, street musicians and vendors. Most sites of interest lie within easy walking distance of the harbour.

Information

Tourist Office The Destinasjon Stavanger tourist office (☎ 51 85 82 99, fax 51 85 92 02, info@destinasjon-stavanger.no) at the end of the harbour, is open in summer from 10 am to 8 pm. Information on hiking and mountain huts throughout Rogaland country is available from the Stavanger Turistforening DNT office (☎ 51 84 02 00), in the pedestrian tunnel south of the train station.

Money Most major banks are represented along Olav V's gate and Håkon VII's gate. Den Norske Bank offers competitive rates, but the post office is generally the best value place to change cash or travellers cheques.

Laundry After climbing Preikestolen, you can wash those sweaty clothes at the Stavanger Sentralvaskeriet on Kongsgata, which has coin-operated machines. Alternatively, go to the Fisketorget Guest Harbour, where washing and drying cost Nkr20 each. It's open 24 hours a day.

Gamle Stavanger

A rewarding amble will lead you through Gamle (Old) Stavanger, immediately west of the harbour, where cobblestone walkways pass between rows of early 18th century whitewashed wooden houses. The more than 150 wooden homes in this area comprise what is probably the best preserved timber construction in northern Europe. It's now home to all sorts of artists' studios selling paintings, ceramics, weavings, handcrafted jewellery and other items.

STAVANGER

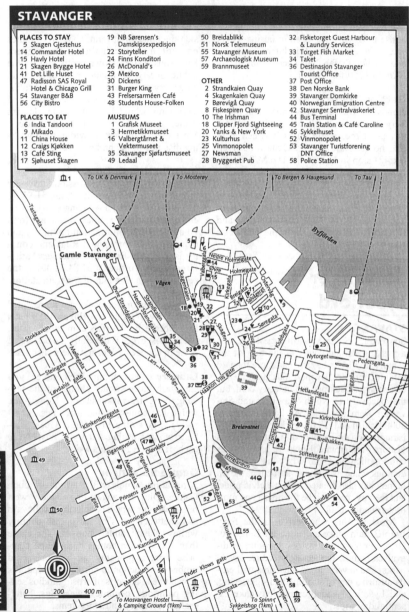

PLACES TO STAY
5 Skagen Gjestehus
14 Commandør Hotel
15 Havly Hotel
21 Skagen Brygge Hotel
41 Det Lille Huset
47 Radisson SAS Royal Hotel & Chicago Grill
54 Stavanger B&B
56 City Bistro

PLACES TO EAT
6 India Tandoori
9 Mikado
11 China House
12 Craigs Kjøkken
13 Café Sting
17 Sjøhuset Skagen

19 NB Sørensen's Damskipsexpedisjon
22 Storyteller
24 Finns Konditori
26 McDonald's
29 Mexico
30 Dickens
31 Burger King
43 Frelsersarméen Café
48 Students House-Folken

MUSEUMS
1 Grafisk Museet
3 Hermetikkmuseet
16 Valbergtårnet & Vektermuseet
35 Stavanger Sjøfartsmuseet
49 Ledaal

50 Breidablikk
51 Norsk Telemuseum
55 Stavanger Museum
57 Archaeologisk Museum
59 Brannmuseet

OTHER
2 Strandkaien Quay
4 Skagenkaien Quay
7 Børevigå Quay
8 Fiskespiren Quay
10 The Irishman
18 Clipper Fjord Sightseeing
20 Yanks & New York
23 Kulturhus
25 Vinmonopolet
27 Newsman
28 Bryggeriet Pub

32 Fisketorget Guest Harbour & Laundry Services
33 Torget Fish Market
34 Taket
36 Destinasjon Stavanger Tourist Office
37 Post Office
38 Den Norske Bank
39 Stavanger Domkirke
40 Norwegian Emigration Centre
42 Stavanger Sentralvaskeriet
44 Bus Terminal
45 Train Station & Café Caroline
46 Sykkelhuset
52 Vinmonopolet
53 Stavanger Turistforening DNT Office
58 Police Station

Norwegian Emigration Centre

The Norwegian Emigration Centre (☎ 51 50 12 67), Bergjelandsgata 30, helps foreigners of Norwegian descent trace their roots. It's open from 9 am to 3 pm Monday to Friday. From 14 to 23 June, it stages a popular Emigration Festival.

Stavanger Domkirke

The Anglo-Norman-style Stavanger Cathedral, on the south end of Kirkegata, is an impressive medieval stone cathedral dating from approximately 1125, but it was extensively renovated following a fire in 1272. As with the famed Winchester Cathedral in the UK, this church is dedicated to St Swithun and, in fact, one of the good saint's arms was brought from Winchester by Stavanger's first bishop, Reinhald. After the Reformation, however, the arm, the original altar and many other icons and relics went missing.

From 15 May to 15 September, the church is open from 10 am to 7 pm Monday to Saturday and 1 to 6 pm Sunday. Admission is free. An atmospheric time to visit is during the organ recital at 11.15 am on Thursday.

Valbergtårnet & Vektermuseet

You can get a good view of the city and the harbour oil rigs from the historic tower Valbergtårnet, at the end of Valberggata, which was constructed as a guards' lookout from 1850 to 1853. Inside is the Vektermuseet, the Guards' Museum, which is open from 10 am to 4 pm Monday to Friday (Thursday to 6 pm) and 11 am to 2 pm Saturday. Admission costs Nkr10.

Stavanger Museum

The five-part Stavanger Museum (☎ 51 52 60 35), with bits scattered around town, is good for the greater part of a sightseeing day. From 15 June to 15 August, the museums are open from 11 am to 4 pm daily (the Seafaring and Canning museums, Tuesday to Friday from 11 am to 3 pm) and the rest of the year, on Sunday only. Admission to all five (on the same day only) is Nkr30.

Stavanger Museum The main museum at Muségata 16 reveals Stavanger's nearly 900 years of history, 'From Ancient Landscape to Oil Town'. Features include evidence of Stone Age habitation, the medieval bishopric, the herring years and the development of the city into a modern oil capital. The Stavanger of the 1880s is described in a series of tableaux focusing on local author Alexander Kielland. In another wing is a pretty standard collection of stuffed birds and wildlife, with exhibits on the migratory patterns of North Atlantic birds.

Hermetikkmuseet A canning museum? Sounds boring, you say? Well, in fact, this appealing little place, housed in an old cannery at Øvre Strandtata 88A, may well be Stavanger's most worthwhile attraction (see the boxed text). Here you'll get the lowdown on Stavanger's main industry between the 1890s to 1960 – canning brisling and fish balls. On Sunday, as well as on Tuesday and Thursday between 15 June and 15 August, the fires are lit and you can sample smoked sardines straight from the ovens.

Ledaal The neoclassical Ledaal, Eiganesveien 45, was constructed between 1799 and 1803 for merchant ship owner Gabriel Schanche Kielland, and now serves as the local royal residence and summer home. Its museum provides a glimpse into the opulent lifestyles of the rich and famous in early 19th century Norway.

Breidablikk The Breidablikk manor and barn at Eiganesveien 40A was also constructed for another merchant ship owner, Lars Berentsen. It dates from 1881 and displays old farming implements, books and knickknacks. This one lets you in on the opulent lifestyles of the rich and famous in *late* 19th century Norway.

Stavanger Sjøfartsmuseet The Stavanger Maritime Museum, in warehouses at Nedre Strandgata 17-19, outlines 200 years of Stavanger's maritime history. There's also a reconstruction of a late 19th century sailmaker's workshop, a shipowner's office and a general store, as well as the merchant's living quarters. The museum also owns two historic sailing vessels, the 1848 *Anna of Sand* and the 1896 *Wyvern*.

Archeologisk Museum

The Archaeological Museum (☎ 51 84 60 00), Peder Klows gate 30A, traces 30,000 years of human and natural history and reveals the parallel relationships between

---

The Lowly Sardine & the Cult of Iddis

Around Stavanger the word *iddis*, derived from the local pronunciation of *etikett* ('label'), has come to apply to the colourfully artistic labels which appear on Norwegian sardine tins measuring precisely 75mm by 105mm. The first of Stavanger's original canneries, Stavanger Preserving, appeared in 1873 and initially produced tinned meat; by the turn of the century, however, the company's attentions had turned to brisling sardines, which had become a mainstay of the local economy. As Stavanger grew into Norway's sardine canning centre, more enterprises took interest and by 1922 the city boasted 70 sardine canneries providing 50% of the town's employment. Each cannery had its own label, ranging from depictions of royalty, wild animals, polar explorers and seafaring scenes to architectural features, zeppelins, sports events and leisure activities. Whatever the theme, however, special care was given to achieving a warming and life-giving quality. No one knows exactly how many designs were actually used, but the best estimates place the figure at between 10,000 and 15,000.

These sardine tin labels created a stir in the local community, which recognised their artistry and collectability. Workers had access to the labels but other collectors had to await a *sjeining*, in which bundles of labels were cast to the wind to be gathered up by the general populace. In fact, these iddis became a form of currency for children, and were traded much the same as baseball cards are today.

Perhaps the most popular and sought-after designs are the Christian Bjelland & Co *Man with a fish* by Kittelsen, and the Skippers' *Sea captain*, which depicts Scotsman William Duncan Anderson dressed in oilskins. The latter was designed by the Scottish artist Angus Watson, who came up with the name 'Skippers'. He purchased the copyright on a photo of Anderson, which he'd selected as the iddis for his brand, and commissioned an artist to come up with a likeness for the label. Unfortunately for poor William Duncan Anderson, the label turned him into a laughing stock and made it impossible for him to secure serious work with any fishing fleet. As a result, he was placed on the Skippers payroll for the rest of his days, and continues to work as an artists' model.

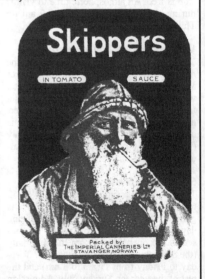

Today, the best of these well appreciated labels can be seen at the Hermetikkmuseet in Stavanger.

them. The emphasis is on the symbiosis between prehistoric humans and their environment. It's open from 11 am to 5 pm Tuesday to Sunday in summer, with shorter hours at other times. Admission is Nkr10.

Ullanhaug Farm Reconstruction
The reconstruction of a 1500-year-old Iron Age farm at Ullanhaug, south of Mosvangen, is affiliated with the Archaeological Museum. It's open daily from noon to 5 pm between 15 June and 17 August. At other times, it's open on Sunday only. Admission is Nkr20. Take the hourly bus No 25 or 26 towards Sandnes and get off at Ullanhaug (15 minutes, Nkr17).

Rogaland Kunstmuseum
The Rogaland Art Museum (☎ 51 53 09 00), on the Mosvangen lakeshore, displays a collection of Norwegian art from the 18th century to the present day, including the works of Stavanger's own Lars Hertervig (1830-1902), whose landscapes hold special significance for the people of Rogaland. Don't miss Hertevig's haunting piece entitled *Gamle Furutrær*. A nine-sided hall houses the Halvdan Hafsten Collection, the largest assemblage of mid-20th century Norwegian art, and includes work by Harald Dal, Kai Fjell, Arne Ekeland and others. It's open Tuesday to Friday from 10 am to 2 pm, Saturday from 11 am and Sunday from 11 am to 5 pm.

Other Museums
There are also several other museums in Stavanger. If you're into phones and other forms of communication right up to the Internet, don't miss the **Norsk Telemuseum** (Norwegian Communications Museum; ☎ 51 76 56 45), Dronningensgata 12. It's open from 11 am to 4 pm daily from 15 June to 15 August (at other times on Sunday only).

Both pyromaniacs and firefighters will enjoy the **Brannmuseet** (☎ 51 50 88 60), in the fire station at Lagårdsvei 32, which is dedicated to fires and firefighting in Norway. It's open by appointment only. The **Vegmuseet** at Lagårdsvei 80 tells the story of

painstaking civil engineering that went into the construction of roads in Rogaland. The **Misjonsmuseet** (☎ 51 51 62 10), Misjonsvei 34, displays items collected by Christian missionaries from the ends of the earth. It's open by appointment only.

For a glimpse into the history of printing in Norway, visit the **Grafisk Museum** (☎ 51 52 88 86), Sandvigå 24. It's open from 11 am to 4 pm on Sunday.

Mosvangen
The large forested park at Mosvangen is a popular destination for strolling, jogging or walking the family dog, but it's also a remarkable wildlife refuge. The lake and its small attached lagoon, which are encircled by footpaths, attract large numbers of nesting and breeding ducks, geese, and sea birds, as well as songbirds. It's a pleasant 3km walk from the centre or 10 minutes on bus No 130 (Nkr17).

Organised Tours
On Sunday from 3 May to 30 August, you can sail from Skagenkaien wharf in Stavanger on the ferry *Riskafjord II* to the island of Mosterøy (5½ hours return, Nkr90), where you can visit Utstein monastery (there's a restaurant here) and the Fjøløy lighthouse.

Stavanger's version of 'Norway in a Nutshell' is actually a self-guided triangle route by rail to Oslo, then to Bergen and back to Stavanger by express boat. The entire route costs Nkr900, and for an additional Nkr235, you can insert the traditional 'Norway in a Nutshell' – via Flåm, Gudvangen and Voss – en route between Oslo and Bergen. Book at the train station.

Places to Stay
Thanks to its petroleum connection, accommodation in Stavanger is often taxed beyond its limit, and finding a room at the last minute – at any time of year – can be an exercise in futility. Book as far ahead as possible, even at the hostel and camping ground.

The lakeside *Mosvangen Vandrerhjem* (☎ 51 87 09 77), 3km from the city centre, charges Nkr135 for a bed in a shared room and Nkr270 for a private single or double. It's technically open year-round, but it doubles as student accommodation so you need a reservation between roughly 1 September and 20 May. Just down the hill lies the *Mosvangen Campground* (☎ 51 53 29 71), open from mid-May to early September, where basic huts cost Nkr255/345 for four/six people. Camping costs Nkr70/95 in a tent without/with a car and Nkr100 with a caravan or camper, plus Nkr10 per person. During the nesting season around the lake, campers are treated to almost incessant birdsong. For either the hostel or camping ground, take bus No 130 (Nkr17) from the corner of Håkon VII's gate and Klubbgata and get off at Henrik Ibsens gate.

A recommended inexpensive place is *Det Lille Huset* (☎ 51 89 40 89, Vaisenhusgaten 40), where the owner Grethe charges Nkr200/300 for a single/double room with access to kitchen facilities. The building dates from 1869. About the same price is the *Stavanger B&B* (☎ 51 56 25 00, fax 51 56 25 01, Vikedalsgata 1A). A decent centrally located guesthouse is the *City Bistro* (☎ 51 53 95 70), which charges Nkr395/495. The *Skagen Gjestehus* (☎ 51 89 55 85, Nedre gate 2) is centrally located at the old Customs House. Summer and weekend rates are Nkr390/525 for singles/doubles; at other times, they're Nkr420/580. Inexpensive private accommodation may be booked through the Destinasjon Stavanger tourist office (☎ 51 85 92 00) for a Nkr20 booking fee.

The recommended *Havly Hotel* (☎ 51 89 67 00, Valberggata 1) and the more standard *Commandør Hotel* (☎ 51 89 53 00, Valberggata 9) both offer comfortable rooms with bath for Nkr400/550 in summer and on weekends.

The large and opulent *Skagen Brygge Hotel* (☎ 51 89 41 00) offers fairly good weekend value at Nkr550/750 on weekends and Nkr650/850 for summer visitors, but low-season business travellers will pay rather excruciating rates of Nkr1045/1245. The similarly upmarket *Radisson SAS*

Royal Hotel (☎ 51 56 70 00), in a quiet spot south-west of the centre, charges Nkr650/750 in summer and on weekends, and Nkr1695/1895 at other times.

Places to Eat

As you'd expect of an oil capital, Stavanger has a plethora of eating establishments offering a range of menus. *Café Caroline*, at the train station, can handle breakfast (a roll or pastry with coffee cost Nkr31), hot dogs and snacks, and the bus terminal has a takeaway sandwich shop. *Finns Konditori*, near the Kulturhus, prepares pastries and sandwiches. The *Students House-Folken* (☎ 51 56 57 67, Olavskleiv 16), a students' cultural hangout, has an inexpensive restaurant. It's open from 11 am to at least midnight Monday to Friday and 3 pm to 1.30 am Saturday. Anyone in need of something really inexpensive can check out the *Frelsersarméen Café*, run by the Salvation Army on Kongsgata.

Dickens (Skagenkaien 6) has a rustic pub atmosphere and serves chips and salsa for Nkr27, lunch specials for around Nkr85, burgers with all the trimmings for Nkr46 and a burrito platter for around Nkr60. Until 5 pm, you can chow down on all the pizza you can eat for a bargain Nkr55.

Until 5 pm daily except Sunday, *China House* (☎ 51 89 18 38, Salvågergata 3) has a Nkr56 lunch special with coffee and an all-you-can-eat dinner buffet for Nkr109. *India Tandoori Restaurant* (☎ 51 89 39 35, Valberggata 14) does authentic Indian dishes starting at around Nkr115. A bit more expensive is the Japanese-oriented *Mikado* (☎ 51 89 33 88, Østervåg 9). Mexican specialities are the forte at the *Mexico Restaurant* (☎ 51 89 15 55, Skagenkaien 12), where full meals average Nkr150.

Not surprisingly, American cuisine, such as it is, features prominently in Stavanger's petroleum circles, and both *McDonald's* and *Burger King* are represented. You'll also find *Craig's Kjøkken* (☎ 51 89 47 76) on Breitorget, which does 'creative American cuisine'; the *Chicago Grill* (☎ 51 56 70 00) at the Radisson SAS Royal Hotel; and *Storyteller*

View over Bergen

Harbour reflections, Bergen

Fish market, Bergen

DEANNA SWANEY

Hello, Hello, Hello, Hello, Hello
Preikestolen & Lysefjord

GLENDA BENDURE

The long and winding road ...
Trollstigen, central Norway

DEANNA SWANEY

The idyllic valley of Grøndalen, Western Fjords

(☎ 51 89 44 11, Skagen 27), which specialises in Cajun fare for all those homesick oil workers from around the Gulf of Mexico.

The seafood spot *NB Sørensen's Damskipsexpedisjon* (☎ 51 84 38 20, Skagen 26) offers a large one-course daily special for Nkr95, but other main courses range from Nkr150 to Nkr180. An even more atmospheric place for fish is the *Sjøhuset Skagen* (☎ 51 89 51 80), in a restored warehouse on the wharf.

Fresh fish is sold at the *Torget fish market* and you'll find wine and liquor at the Vinmonopolet outlets on Olav V's gate and Nytorget.

Entertainment

On Tuesdays at 9 pm, the Stavanger Bluesklubb meets at the *Bryggeriet Pub (Skagenkaien 30)*. For cinema features, see the eight-screen complex in the Kulturhus. Stavanger's Irish pub is *The Irishman* (☎ 51 89 41 81, Hølgebergstata 9), while North Americans may prefer *Yank's* (☎ 51 85 95 50, Skagenkaien 24). On weekends, the adjacent *New York* (☎ 51 89 51 65, Skagenkaien 24) provides youth-oriented fun. Patrons over 22 years of age may prefer the *Taket*, on Strandkaien, which is open nightly until 4 am.

If you're desperate for the latest on international events, the *Newsman* (☎ 51 84 38 80) features constant CNN broadcasts; on weekends, the disco attracts youthful crowds while on Thursday night the clientele is more middle-aged. *Café Sting* (☎ 51 89 38 78, Valberget 3) offers a range of options: meals, a pub, a bar and occasional live performances, with an emphasis on jazz.

Getting There & Away

Air The international airport is at Sola, about 14km south of the city centre. SAS and Braathens SAFE fly between Stavanger and Oslo, Bergen and Trondheim at least once daily, and Widerøe offers especially good value to and from Bergen and Glasgow, Scotland. The city is also served by Air UK/KLM and SAS to and from Aberdeen, Scotland, several times daily.

Bus The daily Nor-Way Bussekspress bus between Stavanger and Oslo (10 hours, Nkr490) leaves Stavanger at 8.45 am and Oslo at 9.30 am. To and from Bergen (5¾ hours, Nkr340), buses leave up to five times daily. The By-til-By bus between Stavanger and Haugesund (2½ hours, Nkr162), via ferry between Mortavika and Arsvågen, leaves five times daily on weekdays and three or four times daily on weekends. Some departures begin from the airport in Sola.

Train Rail services to and from Egersund (one hour, Nkr100) run numerous times daily. Direct trains to Oslo (eight to 10 hours, Nkr580), via Kristiansand and Bø, run three times daily, and two or three more services require a change at Kristiansand. Some services also have connections to Arendal. On weekdays, an overnight train leaves Stavanger at 10.05 pm and arrives in Oslo at 7.12 am; in the opposite direction, it leaves at 10.48 pm and arrives at 7.48 am. However convenient this may be, it would be a shame to miss the landscapes along this remarkably scenic route. Note that all Oslo trains require seat reservations.

Car & Motorcycle The E18, Norway's main south coast highway, terminates in Stavanger, where it becomes the Motorveien. To reach the city centre, follow Madlaveien south.

Ferry From the Børevigå quay, Flaggruten's (☎ 51 86 87 80) express catamaran to Bergen (four hours, Nkr480), via Haugesund (1½ hours, Nkr165), leaves from Stavanger harbour four times daily on weekdays and twice daily on weekends. Spouses and Hostelling International members get a 25% discount, and ScanRail Pass holders get 50%. Ferries to Tau (40 minutes, Nkr81/27 per car/person) sail from Fiskespiren quay. Lysefjord ferries, which also use the Fiskespiren quay, are described under Lysefjord, later in this chapter. For information on ferries between Stavanger and the UK and Denmark, which use the Strandkaien quay, see the Getting There & Away chapter.

Getting Around

The Airport Between 6.30 am and 5 pm weekdays and from 10.45 am to 5.45 pm on weekends, the Flybussen airport buses (☎ 51 52 26 00) run one to three times hourly between the city centre and the airport at Sola (30 minutes, Nkr37). Alternatively, take city bus No 143 (30 minutes, Nkr22), which runs approximately every half-hour between early morning and midnight.

A taxi from the city centre to the airport costs around Nkr220, and between the airport and the Mosvangen Vandrerhjem and camping ground, you'll pay Nkr180 to Nkr190.

Bus Local buses run frequently between the centre and the outskirts, including Sola and Sandnes. Fares start at Nkr15 within the city centre.

Car & Motorcycle The city centre is a combination of narrow streets and pedestrian walkways that are best explored on foot. Drivers will find a host of high-rise parking garages around the post office and bus terminal. Illuminated signs reveal the number of places available (*ledig*).

Bicycle You can hire mountain bikes at the Spinn Sykkelshop (☎ 51 58 55 01), Torgveien 15, for Nkr50/350 per day/week. It's west of Route 44, about 3km south of the centre. The more central Sykkelhuset (☎ 51 53 99 10), Løkkeveien 33, rents bikes for Nkr60/300 per day/week, plus a deposit of Nkr150. For cycle tours around the scenic Rogaland landscape, the tourist office distributes copies of Fjord Norway's *Sykkelkart* cycling map, which outlines three multi-day routes and 30 day-trips.

Avid cyclists may want to make a pilgrimage to the self-proclaimed 'Bicycle Town' of Sandnes (which is also emphatically an oil town), about 20km south of Stavanger. It features tangles of bike trails; bicycle use is free in the city centre; there's an annual Bicycle Blues festival in late June; and even the mayor gets around on a bike. For details, contact the Sandnes Reiselivssenter (☎ 51 60 55 55, fax 51 62 82 14).

AROUND STAVANGER
Utstein Monastery

Utstein monastery (☎ 51 72 47 05), on the island of Mosterøy, hosts a variety of cultural events, including exhibitions and concerts. Regular admission costs Nkr25, while events cost extra. Special classes and religious events are also held throughout the summer season. From Stavanger, take bus No 170 (24 May to 17 August).

Haugesund

Although it's a town of nearly 30,000 people, Haugesund lies well off the beaten routes and is rarely visited by travellers, and that in itself may be a recommendation. The region grew up around the herring fishery in the early 20th century and still relies to some extent on fishing, as well as shipping and copper mining (the nearby Vigsnes mines on Karmøy supplied the copper for the Statue of Liberty in New York harbour).

Information The Haugesund tourist office (☎ 52 72 50 55, eirik.hustvedt@haugesund .online.no, www.haugesund.net), Smedasundet 90, is open from 10 am to 4 pm weekdays.

Things to See Sites of interest include **Haraldshaugen**, the burial site of Viking King Harald Hårfagre, who died of the plague at Avaldsnes, south of Haugesund on Karmøy island. He gained sovereignty over a united Norway after an 872 naval battle which added this region to the realm. The current obelisk was erected in 1872. About 75m to the south is the **Krosshaugen** mound, which bears a stone cross that was erected in celebration of local Christian gatherings around the year 1000. At Avaldsnes itself, you can see King Håkon Håkonsson's **stone church**, which was dedicated to St Olav in 1250. The adjacent 6.5m spire, known as the Virgin Mary's Needle, leans towards the church wall and legend suggests that when it actually falls against the wall, the Day of Judgement is at hand.

Haugesund also claims to be the ancestral home of legendary actress Marilyn Monroe, whose father, a local baker, emigrated to the USA. A monument on the quay commemorates the 30th anniversary of her death.

Places to Stay *Haraldshaugen Camping* *(☎/fax 52 72 80 77)*, near the Haraldshaugen monument, 1.5km north of town, charges Nkr100 per tent or caravan and cabins are Nkr125 to Nkr480. It's open from 1 June to 1 September. The *Hotel Neptun (☎ 52 71 44 55, fax 52 71 16 00, Haraldsgata 207)* offers reasonable single/double summer rates of Nkr445/590. The simpler *Skeisvang Gjestegiveri (☎/fax 52 71 21 46, Skeisvannveien 20)* has year-round rates of Nkr420/520.

On the offshore island of Røvær, 10km west of Haugesund, the *Røvær Vandrerhjem (☎ 52 71 80 35, fax 52 71 80 54)* offers simple dorm accommodation for Nkr85 and doubles for Nkr200. The tiny island of 100 people also supports a boathouse café specialising in Norwegian cuisine. Access from town is by ferry (45 minutes, Nkr20).

Getting There & Away The easiest approach is on the Flaggruten ferry between Bergen (2½ hours, Nkr290) and Stavanger (1½ hours, Nkr165). Nor-Way Bussekspress buses connect Haugesund with Oslo (12 hours, Nkr500) and Bergen (3½ hours, Nkr200) daily and there are also five or six daily buses to and from Stavanger (2½ hours, Nkr162). SAS has five daily flights to Oslo; Braathens SAFE flies three times daily to Bergen; and the Fjord Line ferry (☎ 55 54 86 60) between Bergen and Newcastle (UK) also calls in.

LYSEFJORD

There's little challenge in working out how 42km long Lysefjord ('light fjord') got its name, for even on dull days the granite rock seems to glow with an ethereal – almost ambient – light and even the mist seems luminous. Many people consider it the most unique and beautiful fjord in all of Norway, and whether you cruise from Stavanger, hike to Preikestolen or drive the treacherous road down to Lysebotn, it's a highlight of any trip to Norway.

Lysefjordsenteret

The Lysefjordsenteret (☎ 51 70 31 23), in a fabulous setting north of the ferry terminal at Oanes, provides tourist information and presents the wonders of Lysefjord in natural history exhibits and an audio-visual program. Although this place is rather redundant – the real thing lies just out the window – is a good introduction to this remarkable fjord. It's open from 10 am to 8 pm daily from June to August and costs Nkr50.

Preikestolen

The two-hour trail to the granite slab known as Preikestolen, or 'Pulpit Rock', leaves from the Preikestolhytta Vandrerhjem. It begins along a steep but perfectly manicured route, then climbs past a series of alternating steep and boggy sections to the final climb across exposed granite and along some very windy and exposed cliffs to the end of the trail.

Preikestolen, which is an exposed ledge of rock, appears about to plunge 600m into the fjord below – and there's a hell of a crack to prove it – but that probably won't happen for thousands of years. While looking down can be a bit daunting (and not for anyone who suffers from vertigo), you won't regret the magical view directly up Lysefjord. Although developers have suggested installing a cable car up Preikestolen, there has been vociferous local opposition and thankfully it's unlikely to happen in the near future.

The area also offers several other fabulous walks – the Vatnerindane ridge circuit (two hours), Ulvaskog (three hours), the Refsvatnet circuit (three hours) and summit of Moslifjellet (three hours) – all of which are accessible from the same car park.

Organised Tours If you'd prefer to see Preikestolen from below (far less impressive than from above), the *Clipper* sightseeing boat (☎ 51 89 52 70) has daily cruises (Nkr190 to Nkr275) from Stavanger. Book at the Stavanger tourist office or stop by at sailing time and hope there's space. Alternatively, you'll also have a view on the Lysebotn cruise (see later in this section).

Places to Stay & Eat The turf-roofed *Preikestolhytta (Jöppeland) Vandrerhjem* (☎ 51 84 02 00, fax 51 74 91 11) lies on the lakeshore at the start of the Preikestolen walking track. Dorm beds cost Nkr110, doubles are Nkr270 and meals are available for Nkr60 to Nkr120. Alternatively, in the daytime you can pick up a hot dog or slice of pizza at the kiosk just up the hill. The sauna is ideal for tired bones after the climb to Preikestolen.

Preikestolen Camping (☎ 51 74 80 77) lies on the riverside about 4km back towards Jøssang, and not within easy walking distance. Tent/caravan camping costs Nkr80/ 120, plus Nkr20 per person, with the use of kitchen facilities. Meals are available at the attached shop and restaurant. The site is open from 1 May to 1 October.

Getting There & Away From Stavanger take the 8.30 am ferry to Tau (40 minutes, Nkr25), from where a connecting bus (Nkr38) takes you to the trailhead (late June to early September only), then returns in the mid-afternoon. If you're doing it as a return trip, allow a full day.

If you're driving from Stavanger, the Lauvvik-Oanes ferry (accessed on Route 13 via Sandnes) is considerably shorter and cheaper (10 minutes, Nkr37) than the longer route between Stavanger and Tau (40 minutes, Nkr81). Either way, the trip between Stavanger and Preikestolen takes around 1½ hours.

Lysebotn

A four-hour ferry ride from Stavanger will takes you right to the head of the fjord at Lysebotn, where a narrow and frequently photographed road corkscrews 1000m up towards Sirdal in 27 hairpin turns. The road was opened on 18 October 1984 to service the Tjodan hydroelectric project in Sirdal.

Kjeragbolten After Preikestolen, the most popular Lysefjord walk leads to Kjerag-bolten, which is an enormous oval-shaped boulder, a 'chockstone', lodged between two rock faces about 2m apart. The 10km return hike involves a relatively strenuous 700m ascent from the vast and convoluted Øygardsstølen Café car park, near the highest hairpin bend above Lysebotn.

The route trudges up and over three ridges, and in places, steep muddy slopes make the going quite rough. Once you've reached the view of Kjeragbolten, actually reaching the boulder will require some tricky manoeuvring, including traversing an exposed ledge in a 1000m cliff. From there, you can step (or crawl) directly onto the boulder for one of Norway's finest views, and the photo of you perched on the rock is sure to impress your friends.

Places to Stay & Eat *Lysebotn Camping* (☎ 51 70 34 03, fax 51 70 34 03) occupies an incredible setting at the head of the fjord, and has camping for Nkr80/100 per tent/ caravan plus Nkr10 per person, and cabins for Nkr350 to Nkr450.

For views, you can't beat the *Øygards-stølen Café* (☎ 94 61 77 76), the 'eagle's nest', perched atop the cliff overlooking the hairpin twists down to Lysebotn. However, the prices are equally lofty and most people limit their investment to a cup of coffee to help them contemplate the view.

Getting There & Away From Stavanger, access to Lysebotn is either by ferry or by a boat-and-bus tour combination. The sightseeing boat and return bus (seven hours, Nkr300) run only on Wednesday, Saturday and Sunday from June to August.

Between 1 May and 30 September, Roga-land Trafikkselskap's M/F *Lysefjord* (☎ 51 89 32 12) makes at least one run daily in each direction between Stavanger and Lyse-botn. The four-hour trip leaves daily at 8.30 am from mid-June to mid-August and costs Nkr220 for a car and driver, plus Nkr97 for additional passengers and pedestrians. If you wish to transport a vehicle, be sure to book in advance (☎ 51 89 32 12).

The Western Fjords

For most visitors and armchair travellers, the Western Fjords are Norway's signature landscapes. Amazingly, these formidable, sea-drowned glacial valleys, flanked by almost impossibly rugged terrain, haven't deterred Norwegians from settling and farming their slopes and heights for thousands of years. It goes without saying that this region presents some of the most breathtaking backdrops in Europe. In addition, there's a confounding number of things to see and do in this part of Norway, and the topography is so convoluted that just sorting out an itinerary will prove challenging.

Sognefjord

The Sognefjord, Norway's longest (200km) and deepest (1300m) fjord, cuts a deep slash across the map of western Norway. In places sheer lofty walls rise more than 1000m above the water, while in others, a gentler shoreline supports farms, orchards and small towns. The broad main waterway is impressive but by cruising into its narrower arms, such as the deep and lovely Nærøyfjord (Norway's narrowest fjord) to Gudvangen, you'll have idyllic views of sheer cliff faces and cascading waterfalls.

For information, contact Sognefjord Destination (☎ 57 69 16 17, fax 57 69 14 31, destination@sognefjord.no), Postboks 53, N-5850 Balestrand. Details on major tourist sites, accommodation and transport links are found on www.fjordinfo.no and in the brochure *Sogn og Fjordane*, which is distributed at most tourist offices, train stations and bus terminals. In addition, each district in the region has an exhaustive number of publications detailing accommodation, sites of interest and boggling numbers of hiking possibilities in their respective areas.

HIGHLIGHTS

- Cruising between Geiranger and Hellesylt through the daunting cliffs of Geirangerfjord
- Riding the famously dramatic Flåm railway between the bleak Hardangervidda and the lovely Aurlandsfjorden
- Driving or taking the bus between Åndalsnes and Valldal over the spectacular Trollstigen route
- Visiting a fishing village on a tiny offshore island, such as Ona or Grip
- Photographing, hiking and exploring around the vast Jostedalsbreen icecap
- Re-visiting Art Nouveau in the charming town of Ålesund
- Jazzing it up at the Molde Jazz Festival

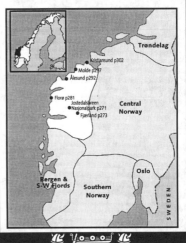

Getting There & Away

From mid-May to mid-September, Fylkesbåtane (☎ 55 32 40 15, fax 55 31 05 76, fsf@infonet.no) operates a daily express

WESTERN FJORDS

THE WESTERN FJORDS

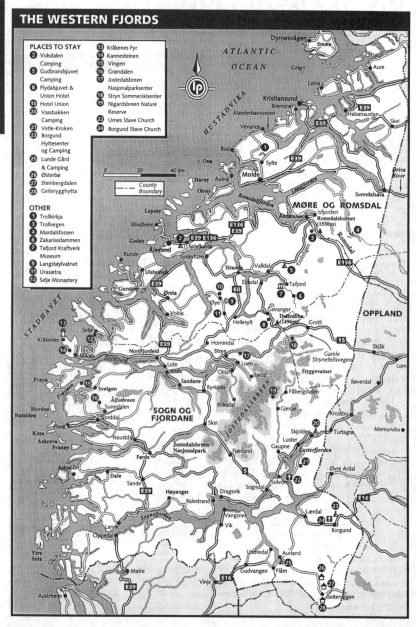

PLACES TO STAY
- ❷ Volsdalen Camping
- ❺ Gudbrandsjuvet Camping
- ❽ Flydalsjuvet & Union Hotel
- ❿ Hotel Union
- ⓴ Vassbakken Camping
- ㉑ Vetle-Kroken
- ㉓ Borgund Hyttesenter og Camping
- ㉕ Lunde Gård & Camping
- ㉖ Østerbø
- ㉗ Steinbergdalen
- ㉘ Geiterygghytta

- ⓭ Kråkenes Fyr
- ⓮ Kannesteinen
- ⓯ Vingen
- ⓰ Grøndalen
- ⓱ Jostedalsbreen Nasjonalparksenter
- ⓲ Stryn Sommerskisenter
- ⓳ Nigardsbreen Nature Reserve
- ㉒ Urnes Stave Church
- ㉔ Borgund Stave Church

OTHER
- ❶ Trollkirkja
- ❸ Trollvegen
- ❹ Mardalsfossen
- ❻ Zakariasdammen
- ❼ Tafjord Kraftverk Museum
- ❾ Langstøylvatnet
- ⓫ Urasætra
- ⓬ Selje Monastery

boat between Bergen and Flåm, near the head of the Sognefjord, stopping at a dozen small towns along the way. It leaves Bergen at 8 am daily and arrives in Flåm (5½ hours, Nkr420) at 1.25 pm. Stops en route include Balestrand (four hours, Nkr310), Vangsnes (4¼ hours, Nkr310) and Aurland (5¼ hours, Nkr420). The return boat leaves Flåm at 3.30 pm, arriving in Bergen at 8.45 pm. Students and rail pass holders get a 50% discount. Numerous local ferries also link Sognefjord towns, and there's an extensive (if infrequent) bus network.

FLÅM

Tiny Flåm, at the head of Aurlandsfjord, occupies a spectacular setting, and as a stop on the popular 'Norway in a Nutshell' tour, it probably sees more foreign tourists than any other village of its size in Norway. The very helpful tourist office (☎ 57 63 21 06) and the post office are both at the train station. You'll find a Mini-Bank ATM just next door.

Undredal

If you're driving, the small goat-cheese producing village of Undredal, midway between Flåm and Gudvangen, makes an interesting short stop. The tiny village church, originally built as a stave church in 1147, is the smallest house of worship in mainland Scandinavia. For Nkr59, you can buy the Undredalskortet (Undredal Card), which provides a guided tour of the church, goat-cheese tasting at Underdalsbui and coffee and waffles at Undredal Brygge.

Also of interest is the farm Stigen, dating from 1603; the access path is so steep that a ladder was required to reach it (the ladder was conveniently removed whenever tax collectors were about). Hikers can follow the steep, one-day route from Langhuso to the DNT mountain hut at Grindafletene, where other walking routes lead to Stalheim, Mjølfjell, Uppsete and Flåm.

You can avoid the crowds in Flåm by camping in Undredal or staying at the *Nedberge Pensjonat*. For meals, there's the small *Undredal Brygge* café (☎ 57 63 17 45) near the harbour.

Organised Tours

Although most visitors do 'Norway in a Nutshell' from either Oslo or Bergen (see Organised Tours in the Getting Around chapter), you can also do a mini version from Flåm. The circle route by boat to Gudvangen, bus to Voss and rail back to Myrdal and Flåm costs Nkr290. Alternatively, you can travel by bus up the historic Aurlandsdalen to Finse and return by rail to Myrdal and Flåm for Nkr330. Book either at the tourist office.

Places to Stay & Eat

Flåm Camping og Vandrerhjem (☎ 57 63 21 21, fax 57 63 23 80), with dorm beds for Nkr85 and doubles for Nkr260, is a few minutes' walk from the station; follow the track up and over the bridge. It's open from 1 May to 1 October. *Heimly Pensjonat (☎ 57 63 23 00, fax 47 63 23 40)* has a great fjord view and straightforward single/double rooms for Nkr450/600, with breakfast. Its cafeteria serves reasonably priced sandwiches with a view. There's also a cafeteria at the *Fretheim Hotel (☎ 57 63 22 00, fax 57 63 23 03)*, which has rooms for Nkr695/990.

The rustic-looking *Furukroa Cafeteria, Restaurant & Bar (☎ 57 63 23 25)*, at the ferry dock, serves all culinary levels from snacks to full meals and you can stay in the guesthouse for Nkr350/600. The novel *Togs Restaurant*, just behind it, is housed in several wooden rail cars.

Getting There & Away

Bus Buses connect Flåm, Gudvangen (30 minutes, Nkr30), some via Undredal, and Aurland (10 minutes, Nkr21), but you won't see much of the spectacular scenery. Most of these routes are inside particularly long tunnels.

Train Flåm is the only Sognefjord village with a rail link, and for many visitors, the 20.2km Flåmbanen railway is a highlight. This engineering wonder descends 865m at a gradient of 1:18 from Myrdal on the bleak and treeless Hardangervidda plateau, past thundering waterfalls (there's a photo stop at awesome Kjosfossen), to the relatively lush and tranquil Aurlandsfjord. It runs up to 10 times daily in summer (one hour, Nkr70), with connections to Oslo-Bergen services at Myrdal and to the Gudvangen ferry and the Sognefjord ferries from Flåm. For information, phone NSB in Flåm (☎ 57 63 21 00) or Myrdal (☎ 57 63 27 00).

Boat At Flåm, boats head out to towns around the Sognefjord. The most scenic trip from Flåm is the ferry up the Nærøyfjord to Gudvangen (Nkr130/165 one-way/return), which leaves daily at 2.45 pm year-round and also at 9 am, 11.15 am and 2 pm from sometime in May until mid-September. At Gudvangen a connecting bus takes you on to Voss. All ferry tickets and the ferry-bus combination from Flåm to Voss (Nkr162) are sold at the tourist office (this is part of the popular 'Norway in a Nutshell' tour).

In addition to the Sognefjord express boat between Flåm and Bergen (5½ hours, Nkr420), the Flåmekspressen boat runs between Flåm and Aurland (10 minutes, Nkr26), Sogndal (1¼ hours, Nkr120), Vangsnes (two hours, Nkr120) and Balestrand (2¼ hours, Nkr135) at least once daily.

Getting Around
The tourist office rents bikes and the hostel rents boats. The docks are just beyond the train station.

NÆRØYFJORD
Nærøyfjord, the 'narrow fjord', lies west of Flåm and provides a vision of archetypal Norway: towering 1000m cliffs, small precariously perched farms, and waterfalls plummeting into a deep blue fjord. It can be easily visited as a day excursion from Flåm; ferries to Gudvangen, via Aurland, leave daily in summer and cost Nkr130/165 one-way/return.

In Gudvangen, you'll find the unusual *Gudvangen Fjordtell* (☎ 57 63 39 29, fax 57 63 39 80), with a modern Viking theme and an impressive glassed-in restaurant. Single/double rooms start at a rather reasonable Nkr470/600.

Ferries between Gudvangen and Flåm (Nkr130/165 one-way/return) leave daily at 11.30 am and also at 12.35, 3.45 and 4.50 pm from late May until mid-September. The car ferry to and from Lærdal costs Nkr230 per car and Nkr65 per adult. Buses run to Flåm (30 minutes, Nkr30), Aurland (45 minutes, Nkr39) and Voss (one hour, Nkr50).

AURLAND
Aurland is best known as the end of the popular and spectacular Aurlandsdalen hiking route. By 2001, the world's longest road tunnel (24km) will connect Aurland and Lærdal, and complete a new ferry-free road connection between Oslo and Bergen. This replaces the incredibly scenic but sinuous Snøvegen (Snow Road), which climbs and twists precipitously up and over the high plateau that separates the two towns, with incredible views all the way. Even after the completion of the tunnel, the road is likely to remain open in the summer months. A side tunnel will emerge at secluded Tynjadalen.

Between Flåm and Aurland lies the early 17th century farm at Otternes, with 27 restored buildings that are now open to tourists. Otternes is open from 30 June to 17 August and admission is Nkr20.

The Aurland og Lærdal Reiselivslag (☎ 57 53 33 13) dispenses tourist information year-round.

Hiking
The famous route down Aurlandsdalen from Hol in Hallingdal to Aurland in Sogn follows one of the oldest trading routes between eastern and western Norway. In summer, you can take this four-day walk from Finse, on the Oslo-Bergen rail line, with overnight stops at Geiterygghytta, Steinbergdalen and Østerbø. However, many people walk only the most scenic section, from Østerbø to Vassbygdi, which can easily be done as a day hike and cuts out a lamentably disagreeable trip down the Aurlandsdalen road past tangles of power lines.

From the rambling Østerbø complex, the route heads down-valley to Holmen, where it splits. The best option (a short cut of sorts) climbs to Bjørnstigen, at 1000m, and continues briefly to the route's signature view down the valley before it begins to descend steeply. An hour later, however, the descent grows more gentle and heads for the river far below; from there to the Vassbygdi power station, the track follows the river, passing waterfalls and sections blasted from sheer rock.

The lower sections of this route are open roughly between early June and late September. From Vassbygdi, buses run to Aurland (15 minutes, Nkr21) at least twice daily.

Places to Stay & Eat
Campers can try the riverside *Lunde Gård & Camping* (☎ 05 63 34 12, fax 57 63 31 65), 1.4km up the valley, which has cabins and camping sites. The modern and comfortable *Aurlandsdalen Hotell* (☎ 57 63 35 05, fax 57 63 36 22), with a lovely sun room, charges Nkr510/700 for singles/doubles with breakfast. The *Vangsgården* (☎ 57 63 35 80) complex consists of the 1772 Vangen Motel, the mid-18th century Aabelheim Inn, five sea cottages and the *Duehuset (Dovecot) Café & Pub*. Rooms start at Nkr250/400.

Getting There & Away
Buses run frequently between Flåm and Aurland (10 minutes, Nkr21) and in summer, the Snøvegen between Aurland and Lærdal (1½ hours, Nkr100) is served by bus daily at 1.55 pm from Aurland and 4.40 pm from Lærdal. Aurland is also connected to other Sognefjord towns by ferry and express boat.

LÆRDAL & BORGUND
Although many pass through en route to the Borgund stave church, about 30km up the valley, Lærdal, at the head of Lærdalfjord, is a small town that sees relatively few visitors. Lærdalsøyri, at the fjord-end of town, makes for pleasant strolling through the collection of intact 18th and 19th century timber homes. The tourist office (☎ 57 66 65 09), Øragata 18, is open from 10 am to 8 pm weekdays from 1 June to 31 August, and from 11 am to 4 pm on weekends.

Norsk Villakssenter
The museum-like Wild Salmon Centre (☎ 57 66 67 71, fax 57 66 66 82, villaks@ vestdata.no) reveals all you'd ever want to know about the Atlantic salmon and its peculiar migration and breeding habits. You can watch wild salmon in the river through viewing windows, see a film about the salmon's life cycle and learn to tie flies which will attract the fish to the angler's hook. It's open daily in summer from 9 am to 9 pm and shorter hours in May, September and October. Admission is Nkr65.

Borgund Stave Church
Most visitors come to see the Borgund stave church, built in the 12th century beside one of the major trade routes between eastern and western Norway. Not only is it one of the best known and most photographed of Norway's stave churches, it's also the best preserved. However, the same can't be said of its furnishings, as the pulpit dates from the late 16th century and the altar, from the early 17th century. It's open from 8 am to 7 pm daily from June to August, and 10 am to 5 pm in May and September. Admission costs Nkr50.

Buses run regularly between Lærdal, Borgund and Borlaug (which has accommodation; see Places to Stay).

Places to Stay
The ordinary but adequate *Offerdal Hotel* (☎ 57 66 61 01, fax 57 66 62 25) in Lærdal charges Nkr550/650 for singles/doubles with breakfast. At Borlaug, 10km up the road from Borgund, sits the less than presupposing *Borlaug Vandrerhjem* (☎ 57 66 87 50, fax 57 66 87 44), which is frequented by hikers. Dorm beds are Nkr100 and rooms are Nkr170/220. Borlaug also has a camping site, *Bjøraker Camping* (☎ 57 66 87 20), with tent and caravan sites for Nkr40 plus Nkr10 per person and 15 cabins starting at around Nkr250. Just 2km east of the Borgund stave church is *Borgund Hyttesenter og Camping* (☎ 57 66 81 71), with tent and caravan sites for Nkr80 with two people and cabins from Nkr300 to Nkr450.

Getting There & Away

The car ferry between Lærdal and Gudvangen runs year-round and costs Nkr230 for a car plus Nkr65 per person. Other ferry services connect Lærdal with other Sognefjord towns. Many people enjoy driving or hiking the 45km Snøvegen between Aurland and Lærdal, which climbs from sea level to 1309m. It's open from 20 May to 15 October and is served by bus from 31 May to 31 August (1½ hours, Nkr100).

VANGSNES

The farming community of Vangsnes, across the fjord from Balestrand, is probably best known for the 12m hill-top statue of saga hero Fridtjof the Intrepid, erected in 1913 by Kaiser Wilhelm of Germany. The statue – and a pretty good view of Sognefjord – lie 1.5km uphill along the road from the ferry landing. Legend has it that Fridtjof is buried in a nearby grave. Ferries frequently shuttle to and from Hella (15 minutes, Nkr18) and Dragsvik (30 minutes, Nkr19).

There's little to detain anyone in the village, but if you're taking a break here, *Solvang Camping (☎ 57 69 66 70)*, a few minutes inland, has tent/caravan sites for Nkr60/80 plus Nkr10 per person, and cabins or rooms cost from Nkr250. *Vangsnes Pensjonat (☎ 57 69 67 22)* has B&B for Nkr220 per person (Nkr190 on weekends), as well as an attached supermarket and café/pub. Otherwise, for meals you're limited to the ferry terminal snack bar, where fish and chips costs Nkr35 and pizzas start at Nkr69.

VIK

The factory village of Vik, which is readily accessed by frequent local buses from Vangsnes (15 minutes, Nkr21), boasts but one attraction: the worthwhile Hopperstad stave church, about 1km above the port area, that was built in 1130. It barely escaped demolition in the late 19th century, and is now one of the country's finest examples of this medieval design. It's open from 10 am to 5 pm daily from mid-May to

mid-September (from 9 am to 7 pm in mid-summer) and admission costs Nkr40 (for an additional Nkr10, you can use the same ticket for the Hove stone church, 1km away, which dates from 1170).

If you have time to spare, drop by Kristianshus, opposite the tourist office, where there's a newly opened (and laboriously collected) assemblage of boats and boat engines.

Tourist information can be obtained from Vik & Vangsnes Reiselivslag (☎/fax 57 69 56 86).

BALESTRAND

Balestrand, the main resort destination on Sognefjord, enjoys a snowy mountain backdrop and a genteel but low-key atmosphere. For information, see the Balestrand tourist office (☎ 57 69 12 55).

Things to See

The road running south along the fjord, lined with apple orchards and ornate older homes and gardens, sees little vehicular traffic and is conducive to quiet strolling. Along the way is the **Church of St Olav**, which was constructed in 1897 by English expatriate Margaret Green of Leeds, who married Norwegian mountaineer and hotel-owner, Knut Kvikne. She insisted that it be built to resemble a medieval stave church.

Less than 1km south along the fjord you'll stumble across two **Viking-age burial mounds**, which revealed remnants of a boat, jewellery and several weapons, as well as the skeletons of a man and woman. One mound is topped by an image of legendary **King Bele**, erected by Germany's Kaiser Wilhelm II, who was obsessed with Nordic mythology and regularly spent his holidays here prior to WWI (a similar monument honouring Fridtjof, the lover of King Bele's daughter, rises across the fjord in Vangsnes).

For those after a longer hike, take the small ferry (Nkr10) across Esefjord to the Dragsvik side, where an abandoned country road forms the first leg of an 8km walk back to Balestrand. There's also the 1km

Granlia forest nature trail, just above the Rv55 tunnel.

Near the ferry dock is the **Sognefjord Akvarium** (☎ 57 69 13 03), which features a saltwater fish exhibit. An audiovisual presentation, accompanied by local folk music, reveals the history of upper Sognefjord. It's open from 10 am to 4 pm daily from 14 April to 31 October (hours are extended in mid-summer, when it's open 9.30 am to 6 pm) and admission costs Nkr40, including a free hour of canoe or rowing boat hire!

Places to Stay

At **Sjøtun Camping** (☎ 57 69 12 23), a 15-minute walk south along the fjord, you can pitch a tent amid apple trees for Nkr70 or rent a rustic four-bunk cabin for Nkr175. The **Balestrand Vandrerhjem** (☎ 57 69 13 03), in the big lodge-style Kringsjå Hotel, has dorm beds/doubles for Nkr160/380, including breakfast; it's open from mid-June to mid-August.

Beside the English Church of St Olav, the **Midtnes Pensjonat** (☎ 57 69 11 33, fax 57 69 15 84) is popular with returning British holiday-makers. In summer, singles/doubles cost from Nkr445/590, including breakfast. **Balestrand Pensjonat** (☎ 57 69 11 38, fax 57 69 19 11), also near the church, is a comfortable, modern place charging Nkr470/590 for rooms.

If money is no object, the pale yellow timber-built **Kvikne's Hotel Balholm** (☎ 57 69 11 01, fax 57 69 15 02), right on the point near the ferry landing, provides a taste of mid-19th century retro luxury. Guests have use of the jacuzzi, billiards room, fitness room and sauna, as well as a boat and fishing gear. Singles/doubles range from Nkr785/1170 to Nkr1420/1770, and if that's not enough, there's a charge of Nkr60/150 per person for a fjord view in the annexe/main building.

Places to Eat

The **Natthuset**, by the shore, fries up burgers and chips starting at Nkr80 and offers a range of main courses for Nkr58 to Nkr125.

It's open until 11.30 pm nightly. Upstairs in the **Joker** supermarket, opposite the ferry dock, a café serves soup and a roll for Nkr28, burgers, chips and salad for Nkr58 and larger main courses from Nkr69 to Nkr109. The hostel serves dinner for Nkr95 and **Kvikne's Hotel** (☎ 57 69 11 01) has an upmarket dining room and the **Balholm Bar og Bistro**. The latter does pasta dishes from Nkr59, fish from Nkr73 to Nkr120, beef from Nkr95, burgers from Nkr82 and other sandwiches, including vegetarian choices, for Nkr37 to Nkr89.

Getting There & Away

Buses travel between Balestrand and Sogndal (1¼ hours, Nkr68) and Bergen (four hours, Nkr200). The latter leaves from Dragsvik, about 10km around Esefjorden from Balestrand, which is reached by bus (15 minutes, Nkr17) at least five times daily. The Bergen bus is not only cheaper than the express boat, but more scenic, passing the Hopperstad stave church in Vik and then climbing over the impressive Vikafjell to Voss. Another scenic route, the Gaularfjellsvegen winds up and over the Gaular mountain to Førde, on Førdefjord, negotiating hairpin bends and skirting Norway's greatest concentration of roadside waterfalls. This route is served by the Nor-Way Bussekspress bus between Oslo (8½ hours, Nkr439) and Førde (two hours, Nkr122), which stops right in Balestrand.

In addition to the Sognefjord express boat to and from Bergen (four hours, Nkr390), local boats connect Balestrand and Sogndal (45 minutes, Nkr88) two to three times daily except Sunday. A popular local ferry runs twice daily, from 30 May to 13 September, up the narrow Fjærlandsfjord to Fjærland (1½ hours, Nkr110/145 one-way/return), which is the gateway to the glacial wonderlands of Jostedalsbreen. You can also add a short glacier tour for Nkr80.

Getting Around

The tourist office hires out bicycles for Nkr20/50/100 per hour/half-day/full day.

Stave Churches

When Norway first converted to Christianity, a series of tiny wooden churches sprang up around the countryside. Although none of these still survives, evidence of their existence remains in the rows of post holes excavated around the country, which reveal that these early churches rotted in the ground and succumbed to the elements. However, it's thought that Norway's 31 remaining timber stave churches reflect the favoured architectural style of that first generation of Norwegian houses of worship while improving on the construction methods, thus increasing the buildings' longevity.

Beginning in the 12th century, this was accomplished by laying down horizontal sill beams above ground level on a raised stone foundation, on which the plank walls rested. At each corner is an upright stave post – hence the name of the style – which ties together the sill beam below and a wall plate above. Walls therefore consist of vertical planks set into grooves in the sill with the tops of the planks fastened into grooves in an upper wall plate.

Most stave church interiors include little more than a small nave and a narrow chancel, although in some, the nave and chancel are combined into a single rectangular space, divided only by a chancel screen. The most elaborate remaining stave church, at Borgund, includes not only a nave and chancel, but also a semi-circular apse at the eastern end. The roof of the nave is supported by freestanding posts spaced about 2m apart and standing about 1m from the walls, although smaller churches had just one interior post right in the centre of the building. In addition to the main sanctuary area, all remaining stave churches are surrounded by outer walls, creating external galleries or passageways.

Another characteristic of the early stave churches is their rich ornamentation. Interior walls are often painted in elaborate designs, including *rosemaling*, or traditional rose paintings, and the complex roof lines are frequently enhanced by scalloped wooden shingles and Viking-age dragon head finials, which surprisingly recall those typically used on Thai wats and other Asian structures. Perhaps the most renowned and intricate enhancements, however, are the wooden carvings on the support posts, door frames and outer walls (especially at Urnes), which represent tendrils of stems, vines and leaves entwined with serpents, dragons and other fantasy creatures. For its creators, this artistry not only promoted an inspired effect, but also successfully meshed Norway's proud pagan past with its new Christian directions. In fact, some scholars even suggest that the stave churches were first conceived as pagan temples and were later adapted to the requirements of the new religion!

SOGNDAL

The modern regional centre of Sogndal is of little note for visitors except as a place to sleep while en route to somewhere else. The tourist office (☎ 57 67 30 83), at the Kulturhus, a five-minute walk east of the bus station, books rooms in private homes from Nkr100 per person. The summer-only *Sogndal Vandrerhjem* (☎ 57 67 20 33, fax 57 67 31 45), a 15-minute walk east of the bus terminal, charges Nkr90 for a dorm room and Nkr160/210 for singles/doubles.

The cheapest eats are at the cafeterias in the adjacent *Domus* and *K-Sentret* supermarkets on Gravensteinsgata.

Sogndal has Sognefjord's only airport. Local buses run between Sogndal, Kaupanger and Hella (Nkr43) and daily buses

Stave Churches

Remaining Stave Churches

The following is a list of the 31 remaining stave churches in Norway (including two that have been moved to folk museums):

Name of Church	Location	Year
Borgund	upper Lærdal	1200
Eidsborg	Dalen, Telemark	around 1354
Fantoft	Bergen	burned 1992 and reconstructed 1997
Flesberg	Numedalen	unknown
Fåvang	Gudbrandsdalen	1630
Garmo	Maihaugen	12th century
Gol Bygdøy Folk Museum,	Oslo	1200
Grip	near Kristiansund	1580
Haltdalen	Trøndelag Folk Museum	unknown
Hedalen	Hedalen, Valdres	12th century
Heddal	Notodden	1250
Hegge	near Fagernes	unknown
Hopperstad	near Balestrand	mid-12th century
Hurum	Valdres	unknown
Høyjord	near Horten	unknown
Kaupanger	Kaupanger, Sogn	1180
Kvernes	near Kristiansund	15th century
Lom	Lom, Gudbrandsdalen	1200
Lomen	near Fagernes	12th century
Nore	Numedalen	unknown
Reinli	Valdres	unknown
Ringebu	Ringebu	unknown
Rollag	Numedalen	unknown
Rødven	near Åndalsnes	1300
Røldal	near Odda	12th century
Torpo	near Gol	12th century
Undredal	near Gudvangen	unknown
Urnes	Urnes, Sogn	1150
Uvdal	Numedalen	13th century
Vågå	Vågå, Gudbrandsdalen	1635
Øye	Øye, Valdres	unknown

also head north-east past Jotunheimen National Park to Lom (3½ hours, Nkr112) and Otta (4¼ hours, Nkr158). Daily boats connect Sogndal and Balestrand (45 minutes, Nkr88) at least twice daily except Sunday.

SKJOLDEN

Novel little Skjolden, on Lustrafjord at the brink of Sognefjord and Jotunheimen, presents a surprisingly pleasant atmosphere, and is gearing itself up as *the* place to stay in the area. One reason may be that nearly everything of interest in Skjolden is arranged in an open plan under a single roof. Here in the Fjordstova, you'll find the tourist office (☎ 57 68 67 50, fax 57 68 12 22), open daily from 9 am to 7 pm; the post office; a café, souvenir shop; library

(Internet access costs Nkr20 per half-hour); swimming pool (Nkr30 per session); and believe it or not, a climbing wall (Nkr40 per day, Nkr40 for equipment and Nkr50 per half-hour of instruction). The bit of industrial-looking junk on display outside is a turbine from the Norsk Hydro power station.

From 1913 to 1914 and from 1936 to 1937, the shore of the turquoise glacial lake Eidsvatnet, 2km east of Skjolden, was the home of philosopher Ludwig Wittgenstein, who loved the place. A monument and flag-pole marks the site of his lakeshore hut.

Organised Tours

Five-hour cruises on Lusterfjord (☎ 57 68 39 30), including a 1½-hour stop at Urnes stave church, operate on Sunday at noon and cost Nkr170. Book through the tourist office.

Places to Stay & Eat

The *Skjolden Vandrerhjem (☎ 57 68 66 15, fax 57 68 66 76)* partly occupies an old bakery, conveniently next door to the Fjordstova complex. For dorm beds, you'll pay Nkr85 and for single/double rooms, Nkr160/200. It's open from June to late August.

Within walking distance east of Skjolden, at the end of the lake Eidsvatnet, is *Nymoen Leirplass*, with inexpensive tents sites and cabins.

Farther up the valley towards Fortun, *Vassbakken Camping (☎ 57 68 61 88)* has very nice tent/caravan sites for Nkr95 with a car and up to four people, or Nkr60 for a tent with one person plus Nkr20 for each additional person. Two-bed cabins with basic cooking facilities are Nkr200, and with a shower and toilet they're Nkr550. Meals are also available.

The *Fjordstova Café* at the Fjordstova complex grills up pretty good burgers for just Nkr25, and in the evening, serves a dinner menu for Nkr65 to Nkr75.

Getting There & Away

Bus No 155 connects Skjolden with Sogndal (1¼ hours, Nkr67) and Fortun (10 minutes, Nkr14) at least six times daily. Skjolden is also on the twice-daily summer bus route between Otta and Sogndal.

Note that the Shell petrol station in Fortun is cheaper than the Statoil in Skjolden, and is the last petrol for 77km.

URNES

Norwegian poet Paal-Helge Hauge wrote of Urnes stave church: 'Someone came here, shouldering a man's load of visions, spread them out over the walls and pillars, gaping beasts angels' wings, dragons out under the knife the hand the brush, tendrils of ochre, red, grey, white, a sinuous short way from paradise to damnation … ' For its unique and elaborate wooden ornamentation, well described by the poet, the stave church at Urnes has been named one of Norway's four UNESCO World Heritage Sites.

This lovely structure overlooking Lusterfjord was probably built around 1150, making it the oldest stave church in Norway. However, there have been several alterations through the ages and it's likely that the unique and elaborate carvings that cover its gables, pillars, doorframes and several strips on the outer wall were transferred from an 11th century building that once stood here.

The church is open from 10.30 am to 5.30 pm daily from 7 June to 24 August and admission costs Nkr40.

Places to Stay

The nearest accommodation is *Vetle-Kroken (☎/fax 57 68 37 50, trips@vetle-kroken.com)*, 8km north-east of the stave church. Accommodation in the *stabbur* bunkhouse costs Nkr300/500 for use of one/two floors of the building, including use of the kitchen facilities.

The main activity here is sea kayaking, and kayak tours (Nkr150 for a sampling; Nkr290 for half-day trips; and Nkr2250 for four-day tours) are available. You can also rent kayaks for Nkr250/1000 per day/week. Pre-booked groups will be picked up in Skjolden or Urnes but individuals must find their own transport.

Getting There & Away

The best public transport access is on the M/F *Urnes* ferry between Solvorn and Urnes. This is also the car ferry. The boat ride takes approximately 20 minutes and costs Nkr19.

The ferry terminal is reached on bus No 155, which calls in at Solvorn on its frequent runs between Sogndal (25 minutes, Nkr27) and Skjolden (one hour, Nkr61). From the ferry landing, it's a 1km uphill walk to the stave church.

Jostedalsbreen

With a total area of 487 sq km, the many-tongued Jostedalsbreen icecap is by far mainland Norway's largest glacial area, and it dominates the highlands of Sogn og Fjordane county. In places, the ice sheet reaches a thickness of 400m and rises to 1950m above sea level. In 1991, the main icecap and several nearby outliers were set aside for protection as the Jostedalsbreen

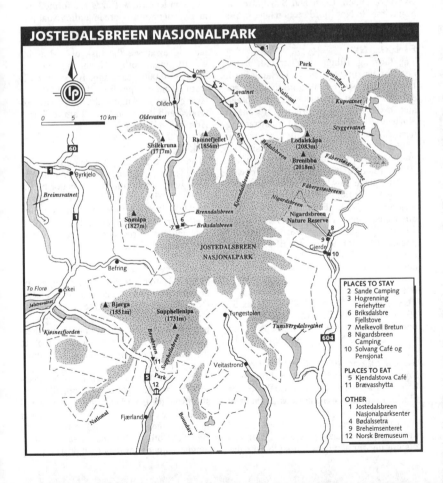

JOSTEDALSBREEN NASJONALPARK

0   5   10 km

PLACES TO STAY
2 Sande Camping
3 Hogrenning Feriehytter
6 Briksdalsbre Fjellstove
7 Melkevoll Bretun
8 Nigardsbreen Camping
10 Solvang Café og Pensjonat

PLACES TO EAT
5 Kjendalstova Café
11 Brævasshytta

OTHER
1 Jostedalsbreen Nasjonalparksenter
4 Bødalssetra
9 Breheimsenteret
12 Norsk Bremuseum

National Park. For national park information, contact Statskog-Vestlandet (☎ 57 65 51 50), Nasjonalparktenesta, N-5840 Hermansverk.

The best hiking map to use for the region is Cappelens Karts *Jostedalsbreen*, at a scale of 1:100,000. You'll also get help at local tourist offices, as well as from the Norsk Bremuseum in Fjærland; the Jostedal Breheimsenteret in Jostedalen and the Jostedalsbreen Nasjonalparksenter above Stryn.

For more details on the gateway towns of Byrkjelo, Olden, Loen and Stryn, see the Sognefjord to Nordfjord section later in this chapter.

FJÆRLAND

The farming village of Fjærland, at the head of narrowly scenic Fjærlandsfjord, lies cradled between two particularly accessible glacial tongues, Supphellebreen and Bøyabreen. For that reason, it's one of Norway's best attended sites, attracting upwards of 100,000 visitors a year. In 1996, however, hoping to diversify its tourist appeal, Fjærland declared itself the 'Book Town' of Norway, and to prove it, this tiny place now boasts at least 14 shops selling a wide range of used books in Norwegian, English, French, German and other languages. A book fair is held annually on the Saturday nearest 23 June. If you're after something specific, contact Den Norske Bokbyen (☎ 57 69 22 10, den.norske.bokbyen@bokbyen.no).

Information

The Fjærland Info (☎ 57 69 32 33, fax 57 69 32 11) tourist office, which doubles as a bookshop, is on the waterfront. It's open during business hours in summer only.

Supphellebreen & Bøyabreen

You can drive to within 500m of Supphellebreen and walk right up and touch the ice. Ice blocks from here were used as podiums at the 1994 Winter Olympics in Lillehammer.

At the creaking blue Bøyabreen, one of the fastest advancing glaciers in Norway, it's not uncommon to witness glacial calving into the meltwater lagoon beneath the glacier tongue. To avoid the crowds, it's wise to get there as early in the morning or as late in the evening as possible.

Norsk Bremuseum

The very well executed Norwegian Glacier Museum (☎ 57 69 32 88) reveals all you'd probably want to know about flowing ice and how it has sculpted the Norwegian landscape. The hands-on exhibits are particularly interesting for children. You can learn how fjords are formed, see an excellent multi-screen audiovisual presentation on Jostedalsbreen, watch a demonstration on the effects of flowing ice and even see the tusk of a Siberian woolly mammoth, which met an icy demise 30,000 years ago. It's open daily from 10 am to 4 pm from April to October (from June to August the hours are extended and it's open from 9 am to 7 pm). Admission is Nkr65.

Hiking

There's no end of hiking possibilities in this area. The essential map of the region, complete with descriptions of 10 major hiking routes, is *Turkart Fjærland*, at a scale of 1:50,000; it sells for Nkr98. After you complete four of these 10 tours, the local sports association will register your achievement and issue a diploma!

Organised Tours

From Balestrand, ferries leave for Fjærland at 8.30 am. There, a bus runs to the glacier (Nkr90), stopping en route at the Norsk Bremuseum and visiting both glacier tongues before returning to the ferry. Alternatively, a taxi from the Fjærland dock to the glacier, with waiting time, costs about Nkr250 return.

From 1 July to 10 August, guided glacier trips (☎ 57 69 32 92) on Supphellebreen start from the Øgard car park, north-east of the Bremuseum, at 9 am on weekdays, but these are more difficult hikes than you'll find at other Jostedalsbreen glacier tongues. Some trips may include a climb up

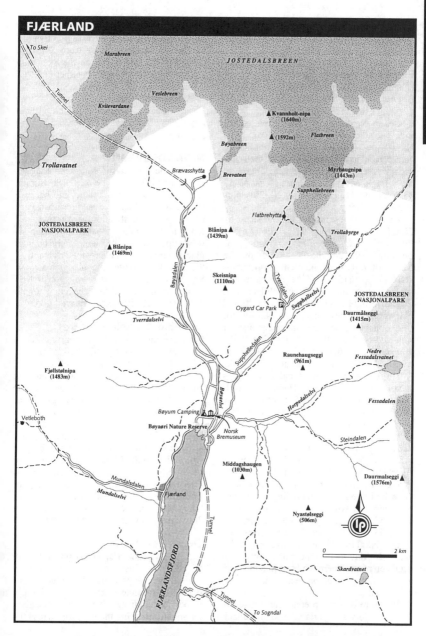

Kvanneholtnipa (1640m). A number of other glacier routes and climbs can also be arranged through the same folks.

Places to Stay & Eat

Hostel-style accommodation is available at *Bøyum Camping* (☎ 57 69 32 52, fax 57 69 29 57), beside the Norsk Bremuseum. Mattresses in the dorm cost Nkr75; tent camping without/with a car is Nkr40/75 plus Nkr10 per person, double rooms are Nkr250 and in the high season, six-bed cabins are Nkr550. Behind the 1861 church in the village, Ms Alma Haugen (☎ 57 69 32 43) rents double *cottages* for Nkr300, plus Nkr40 for sheets and towels.

The upmarket option is the old stand-by *Hotel Mundal* (☎ 57 69 31 01, fax 57 69 31 79, hotelmundal@fjordinfo.no), which was built in 1891 and has been run by the Mundal family ever since. Singles/doubles start at Nkr615/920. The dining room, which sports an evocative 1898 map of Sognefjord, serves laudable traditional Norwegian dishes for around Nkr300 for four courses. Bookings are necessary for non-guests. The other hotel option is the *Fjærland Fjordstue* (☎ 57 69 32 00, fax 57 69 31 61), where rates start at Nkr450/580.

There's also a tourist cafeteria, *Brævasshytta*, at Bøyabreen. Here, filled rolls cost from Nkr15 to Nkr35, light meals are Nkr30 to Nkr83 and dinners range from Nkr89 to Nkr119.

Getting There & Away

An average of five daily buses connect Fjærland and Sogndal (45 minutes, Nkr41). There are also daily buses to and from Stryn (two hours, Nkr115), including a weekday 9.45 am bus with onward connections to Hellesylt and Geiranger. From Balestrand, a local ferry runs to and from Fjærland (1½ hours, Nkr110/145 one-way/return) twice daily, 30 May to 13 September, stopping at Hella en route. There, you can join the glacier tour (Nkr90) and be back in time for the return trip.

If you're driving, prepare for a road toll blow-out to visit Fjærland. The big tunnels on either side of the town cost Nkr400 million to build and there's now a punitive toll of Nkr125 to travel to or from Sogndal. However, the free tunnel on the Skei road enjoys dramatic views from either end.

Getting Around

The S-Marked shop in Fjærland village hires out bicycles for Nkr20/100 per hour/day.

NIGARDSBREEN

Among the Jostedalsbreen glacier tongues which are visible from below, Nigardsbreen is probably the most dramatic, and because it's a minor and easy adventure, it's a very popular visitor destination. If you find it all too touristy and have a vehicle, you can always nip farther up the road past the braided glacial streams at Fåbergstølsgrandane to the dam that creates the big glacial lake Styggevatnet. Along the way you'll find several scenic glacial tongues and a couple of valleys that offer excellent wild hiking.

Jostedal Breheimsenteret

For some odd reason, the incongruous looking Breheimsenteret (☎ 57 68 32 50, fax 57 68 32 40, jostedal@vestdata.no), designed in the form of two ice peaks separated by a crevasse, is also called the 'Glacier Cathedral'. Although there's little religion here, the displays inside do tell the story of the formation and movement of glaciers and how they sculpt the landscape. There's also an exhibit on Jostedalsrypa, the girl who survived the Black Death and thereby became the last person left in Jostedalen. The centre is open from 10 am to 5 pm from 2 May to 1 October (extended summer hours are 9 am to 7 pm from 15 June to 20 August). Admission costs Nkr50.

Organised Tours

Jostedalen Breførarlag (☎ 57 68 31 11, fax 57 68 31 65, josbre@online.no, home.sol .no/~josbre), at the Breheimsenteret, conducts several guided glacier tours. Family walks (minimum age five years) to the glacier snout, including the boat trip across the

Nigardsvatnet and a short walk along the glacier tongue, last 2½ hours and cost Nkr90. Hardy four-hour guided blue-ice walks on the glacier, including instruction and use of technical equipment, are conducted daily at 1 pm from 26 May to 7 September, with an additional departure at 10 am daily from 30 June to 17 August. The meeting place for these walks is the lagoon car park and they cost Nkr280. Shorter sample walks on the ice cost Nkr210 and run at 11.30 am daily in summer, with an additional departure at 3 pm on weekdays from 23 June to 14 August.

More challenging is the climb from Fåbergstølen, 6km up the valley from the Breheimsenteret, to the Fåbergstølsbreen glacier tongue, which licks down the mountainside. From a distance, it's less dramatic and photogenic than Nigardsbreen but it's also more challenging to approach and much less visited. Guided tours run at 10 am on Tuesday, Thursday and Saturday from 7 July to 10 August and cost Nkr325, including equipment rental.

Places to Stay & Eat
Camping and cabins are available at *Nigardsbreen Camping* (☎ 57 68 31 35), at the entrance to the toll road 400m from the Breheimsenteret. Tent/caravan camping costs Nkr70/75 per tent and car plus Nkr15 per person. Reception is open from 9 to 10 am and 5.30 to 9 pm.

Five kilometres down the road from the Breheimsenteret, in the village of Gjerde, you'll find the homy *Solvang Kafé og Pensjonat* (☎ 57 68 31 19, fax 57 68 31 57), where you'll get simple single/double accommodation with breakfast for Nkr270/530. Camping is also available at *Gjerde Camping* (☎ 57 68 31 54), in Gjerde. The Breheimsenteret has a small and rather expensive *café* with a view.

Getting There & Away
From 14 June to 30 August, bus No 158 connects Sogndal and the Jostedal Breheimsenteret (1½ hours, Nkr73) six to eight times daily on weekdays, three times on

Sunday and once on Saturday. For much of the way from the Rv55 at Gaupne, the road to the glacier follows the brilliant turquoise blue Jostedalselva. Watch also for the brilliant red lichen which is splashed across the rocks along the route.

From the Breheimsenteret, a 6km toll road (Nkr20 per vehicle) or a pleasant 6km hike lead to the car park at Nigardsvatnet, the lagoon at the glacial snout. From there, you can take the M/S *Jostedalsrypa* (☎ 94 50 61 67) over the lagoon to the glacier face. From 10 June to 10 September, it runs frequently between 10 am and 6 pm and costs Nkr15/20 one-way/return.

BRIKSDALSBREEN
From the small town of Olden on Nordfjord, a scenic road leads 24km up Oldedalen to the twin glacial tongues of Brenndalsbreen and Briksdalsbreen. The more easily accessible, Briksdalsbreen, attracts hordes of tour buses and has been photographed countless times in conjunction with tourist pony carts crossing the strategically-placed bridge over the river flowing from beneath the ice. The pony carts, operated by two local guesthouses, obviate the easy and pleasant hike to the glacier face.

Organised Tours
Briksdal Breføring (☎ 57 87 38 11, fax 57 87 23 33), at the Fjellstove, and Olden Activ (☎ 57 87 38 88, fax 57 87 59 61), at Melkevoll Bretun, organise a good range of glacier hikes and climbs, and no previous experience is necessary. All rates include use of technical equipment.

Casual visitors can choose between a mini-trip (Nkr130), with half an hour on the ice; a three-hour trip (Nkr130) with an hour on the ice; or a four-hour trip (Nkr200) with two hours on the ice. These depart from the Fjellstove daily in summer at 10 and 11 am and 1, 2 and 5 pm and from Melkevoll Bretun at 11 am, noon, and 2 and 3 pm.

More challenging trips are also available. Briksdal Breføring offers full-day climbs to the cairn on Slingsbyvarden (Nkr350) at

10 am on Wednesday and seven-hour return climbs to Brenndalsbreen (Nkr300), which run year-round by pre-arrangement. Olden Activ teaches introductions to mountaineering for Nkr250 to Nkr300 and rock climbing for Nkr150 to Nkr390 for one to three hours, as well as four hours of ice-climbing instruction and practice for Nkr300.

Places to Stay

The *Briksdalsbre Fjellstove* (☎ 57 87 38 11, fax 57 87 38 61, fbriksda@online.no) has rooms, a camping ground, café, souvenir shop and stables. The attached restaurant specialises in trout and reindeer dishes. For a double room with shared facilities, the charge is Nkr250, and for a four-bed cabin with shower and toilet it's Nkr450. The nearby *Melkevoll Bretun* (☎ 57 87 38 64, fax 57 87 38 90, melkevoll_bretun@ yahoo .com) has a nice green camping ground with cooking facilities, basic camping cabins for Nkr330 and fully-equipped six-bed holiday cabins for Nkr600.

Getting There & Away

The public bus leaves Stryn (one hour, Nkr48) at 10 am and Olden (45 minutes, Nkr33) at 10.15 am daily from mid-June to mid-August, arriving at Briksdal at 11 am (for Melkevoll Bretun, get off 10 minutes earlier). The return bus leaves Briksdal at 1.45 pm. On summer weekdays (mid-June to mid-August), there's also a second departure at 3.45 pm from Stryn and 2 pm and 7.45 am from Briksdal. If you're not up to the easy 6km return walk to the glacier face, Briksdalsbre Fjellstove and Melkevoll Bretun run pony cart rides for Nkr250 per person (advance booking required).

KJENNDALSBREEN & BØDALSBREEN

Lovely Kjenndalsbreen lies 17km by road along a glacial lake (Lovatnet) above the Nordfjord town of Loen. It's probably the least visited of the four glacial tongues, and vies with Nigardsbreen as the most beautiful to approach. Bødalsbreen, in a nearby side valley, provides good hiking possibilities.

Organised Tours

The Stryn Fjell og Breførarlag (☎ 57 87 79 93, fax 57 87 79 61) in Stryn guides five-hour glacier walks on the nearby Bødalsbreen tongue for Nkr300 and more serious 12-hour Saturday trips to the 2083m nunatak Lodalskåpa for Nkr500. These trips begin from Bødalseter, 5km up the Bødalen toll road (Nkr20) from the head of Lovatnet.

Places to Stay

The popular *Sande Camping* (☎ 57 87 76 59, fax 57 87 78 59), near the northern end of Lovatnet, offers scenic lakeside tent and caravan camping, as well as an exhaustive range of cabins from Nkr240 to Nkr800. You'll find four and six-bed cabins for Nkr400 to Nkr600 at *Hogrenning Feriehytter* (☎ 57 87 76 52), overlooking Lovatnet in Lodalen. Tents and caravans are allowed here. *Gjershaugen* (☎ 57 87 76 59) in Bødalen charges Nkr375 to Nkr500 for five-bed cabins with a shower and toilet.

Getting There & Away

Without a vehicle, access is on the M/B *Kjendal* that chugs up Lovatnet from Sande, costing Nkr110 return, including a return bus between Kjendalstova Café, at the end of the lake, and the glacier car park. From here, it's a 2km walk to the glacier face. From 10 June to 1 September, the boat leaves Sande at 10.30 am and from Kjendalstova at 1.30 pm; through most of July, there's an extra departure in the afternoon. Buses leave Stryn at 10 am to connect with this boat and head back from Sande at 2.15 pm.

While you're sailing along, reflect on the huge blocks of stone that dislodged from Ramnefjell and crashed down into the lake in 1905, 1936 and 1950. The first wave killed 63 people and deposited the lake steamer 400m inland and the second wave killed 72, while the third just left a bigger scar on the mountain. You can book the boat trip through the Hotel Alexandra (☎ 57 87 50 50) in Loen.

If you're driving, note that the toll road (Nkr20) above Lovatnet narrows to a single-lane track.

STRYN SOMMERSKISENTER

The Stryn Sommerskisenter (Summer Ski Centre; ☎ 57 87 23 33, fax 57 87 23 71), which is in fact nowhere near the town of Stryn, lies on the Tystigen outlier of Jostedalsbreen. It provides Norway's most extensive and best known summer skiing, and most of those ubiquitous photos of swimsuit-clad skiers were taken here.

The longest alpine run here extends for 2100m with a drop of 518m. The centre also offers miles of cross-country ski tracks. Lift tickets for one/two/seven days cost Nkr200/350/880; alpine equipment can be rented for Nkr180/280/630; cross-country equipment is Nkr140/210/490; and snowboard equipment rental costs Nkr200/320/770. In July, the centre is open daily from 9 am to 5 pm (until 4 pm in June and August).

From the ski centre, the nearest accommodation is *Folven Camping & Strynefjell Turistsenter* (☎ 57 87 53 40). In addition to camping sites, there is a selection of chalet accommodation, ranging from Nkr170 for dormitory beds to Nkr1080 for fully-equipped eight-bed cabins. Typical snacks and light meals are available at the resort's new cafeteria complex.

A ski bus runs from Stryn (one hour, Nkr70) at 9 am and from the ski centre at 5.15 pm from mid-June to mid-August. Drivers will probably enjoy the scenic Gamle Strynefjellsvegen, the back road that connects Grotli with Videsæter. In Stryn you can pick up Statens Vegvesen's informative leaflet on the route.

Sognefjord to Nordfjord

For most travellers the 100km-long Nordfjord is but a stepping stone between the Sognefjord and Geirangerfjord. These two popular fjords are linked by a road that winds around the head of the Nordfjord past the small towns of Byrkjelo, Olden and Loen to the larger town of Stryn.

SKEI

The inland town of Skei, near the head of the lake Jølstravatn, merits a stop for a visit to the worthwhile Astruptunet museum (☎ 57 72 81 05), the former home of artist Nicolai Astrup (1880-1928), which includes a gallery and open-air exhibits. It's open daily from 1 June to 15 August and admission costs Nkr50. The affiliated Midttunet museum, 2km down the road, protects a 17th century west Norwegian farm.

If you want to stick around longer, white-water rafting on the Class II to III Stardal and Class III to V Jølstra rivers is offered by Jølster Rafting (☎ 90 06 70 70, fax 57 72 70 71, jol-raf@online.no, www.jwd.no/rafting/). Day trips range from Nkr450 to Nkr600 and two-day excursions are Nkr950.

On the lakeshore, 5km west of town, is *Haugen Camping* (☎ 57 72 83 85); tent/caravan camping costs Nkr40/50, plus Nkr30 with a car and Nkr10 per person, and basic cabins are Nkr120 to Nkr180. The *Skei Hotel* (☎ 57 72 81 01, fax 57 72 84 23, info@skeihotel.no), near the junction of the Rv5 and the E39, features a swimming pool, sauna, solarium and even a shooting range. The charge is Nkr795/880 for standard singles/doubles and the dining room does solid mid-range fare: fish dishes from Nkr165 and beef from Nkr155. The *Fjøsen Restaurant/Pub* (☎ 57 72 84 00) does light meals from Nkr45 to Nkr79, Norwegian specialities from Nkr39 to Nkr89 and main meals from Nkr89. For good value dinners, try *Audhild Vikens Vevstove*, with main dishes costing Nkr79 to Nkr95.

STRYN

The small town of Stryn likes to consider itself as the de facto capital of upper Nordfjord, and because it lies on several long-distance transport routes, many visitors also see it this way and accordingly break their journeys here. If you need directions or accommodation bookings, the helpful Stryn & Nordfjord Reisemål (☎ 57 87 23 33, fax 57 87 23 71, reisemal@vestdata.no, www.vestdata.no/nordfjord) will happily oblige. Hiking trips are described in its booklet *Guide for Stryn* and cycling routes are outlined in *På Sykkel i Stryn*. It also rents mountain bikes for Nkr20/100 per hour/day. It's open from 9 am to 8 pm daily in July (to 6 pm in June and August).

Jostedalsbreen Nasjonalparksenter

The Jostedalsbreen National Park Centre (☎ 57 87 72 00, fax 57 87 72 01), 15km east of town at Oppstryn, contains glacier-oriented exhibits on natural and cultural history and a garden of endemic vegetation and a decent audiovisual presentation. It also provides information on sites of natural, historical and cultural interest in the immediate area and rents kayaks and rowing boats for pottering around the adjacent lake, Strynsvatn. If you're going on to Fjærland, however, you may want to save your cash for the more interesting Norsk Bremuseum.

The centre is open from 9 am to 8 pm daily in July, until 6 pm in June and August and shorter hours at other times from April to October. Admission is Nkr50.

Places to Stay & Eat

Stryn Camping (☎ 57 87 11 36, fax 57 87 20 25) lies just two blocks uphill from the main drag at the eastern end of town. Tent/caravan camping costs Nkr70/110 plus Nkr10 per person. Without a car, tent camping is only Nkr60 for one person. Cabins range from Nkr300 to Nkr850.

The *Stryn Vandrerhjem (☎ 57 87 11 06, fax 57 87 11 06)*, on the hillside overlooking the town, is open from mid-May to mid-September and charges Nkr150 for dorm beds and Nkr225/385 for single/double rooms.

The historic *Walhalla Gjestgiveri (☎ 57 87 10 72, fax 57 87 18 94, Perhusvegen 13)* was constructed in 1765 as a trading house. Single/double rooms with breakfast cost Nkr275/450. You'll find the best upmarket accommodation at the recently refurbished *Stryn Hotel (☎ 57 87 11 66, fax 57 87 18 02)*, just over the bridge from the centre.

Single/double summer rates start at Nkr545/790.

Tonningstova (☎ 57 87 13 22), on the main street, serves light pizza, salad and pasta meals for under Nkr100, as well as main fish and beef dishes for Nkr100 to Nkr150. It's open weekdays until 6 pm. The smoke-free *Paviljongen Familiesrestaurant (☎ 57 87 22 11)* specialises in burgers and light snacks. The popular *Isehaug Kafeteria & Johans Pub* is open for meals by day and serves drinks until 1 am nightly; and the *Guinness Rock & Roll Pub (☎ 57 87 23 83)* specialises in beer and pizza. The *Scala* disco at the Stryn Hotel *(☎ 57 87 11 66)* is open until 2.30 am on Wednesday, Friday and Saturday and sometimes features live music for the 18 to 21 set. However, the cover charge is rather steep at Nkr80 to Nkr120.

Getting There & Away

Stryn lies on the Nor-Way Bussekspress routes between Oslo (8½ hours, Nkr500) and Måløy (two hours, Nkr115); Ålesund (3½ hours, Nkr164) and Bergen (6½ hours, Nkr340); and Bergen and Trondheim (7½ hours, Nkr450). Coming from Bergen, the latter two call in at Byrkjelo (one hour, Nkr75), Olden (20 minutes, Nkr36) and Loen (15 minutes, Nkr24). The Ålesund route passes Hellesylt (45 minutes, Nkr60), with boat connections to Geiranger.

Self-drivers will probably enjoy the beautiful 27km Gamle Strynefjellsvegen (Rv258) back road to Grotli, which climbs past glacier tongues and stunning views to an altitude of 1130m. It normally opens around 1 June. Bus access along this route to the Stryn Sommerskisenter is described in the Jostedalsbreen section, earlier in this chapter.

BYRKJELO

There's little reason to halt at tiny Byrkjelo, but many travellers do, thanks to the inexpensive accommodation options. For tent camping, the budget-oriented *Byrkjelo Camping (☎ 57 86 74 30)*, at the southern end of the village, charges Nkr30 for hikers and Nkr55 with a vehicle, plus Nkr10 per person. Small four-bed cabins start at Nkr190 and six-bed units with shower and toilet start at Nkr500. The rather ordinary *Byrkjelo Café & Vandrerhjem (☎ 57 86 73 21)* is one of the few centres of action in town. Dorm beds in the hostel cost Nkr85 and single/double rooms are Nkr100/175. Breakfast and lunch cost Nkr55 each and dinner is Nkr10 more. The café also sells staples such as hot dogs and burgers.

OLDEN

For visitors, Olden is used mainly as a staging point for trips to Briksdalen glacier, and perhaps its greatest attraction is the incredible colour of the glacial river that issues from Oldedalen. The main site of interest is the Singersamlinga (☎ 57 87 23 33), which displays the artworks of William Henry Singer of Pittsburgh, Pennsylvania, USA. From 1913 to his death in 1943, he and his wife, Anna Spencer, spent their summers in Olden. His work reflects a touch of pointillism and reveals his affinity for the landscapes of western Norway. For information, contact the Olden Tourist Info (☎ 57 87 31 26), open from 10 am to 6 pm daily from 1 June to 15 August.

Places to Stay & Eat

Alda Camping (☎ 57 87 31 38) has tent sites for campers without/with a car for Nkr40/50 and four-bed huts from Nkr200 to Nkr250. It's open from 1 June to 31 August. There are also 10 other camping grounds in the area, most of which lie along the route to Briksdalsbreen.

The *Olden Krotell B&B*, whose name says it all, charges Nkr200 per person for accommodation and has a steak, chips and salad special for a bargain Nkr70. At the junction of Rv60 and the Oldedalen road is the *Yris Kafé*, which has a meat, spuds and vegetable special plate for Nkr75. Smørbrød costs from Nkr22 to Nkr42, pizzas are Nkr100 and chicken, chips and salad is Nkr80.

The first-class *Olden Fjordhotel (☎ 57 87 34 00, fax 57 87 33 81, post@olden-hotel.no)*

does more plush single/double accommodation starting at Nkr700/800.

LOEN

As with nearby Olden, Loen, at the mouth of dramatic Lodalen, serves as a Jostedalsbreen gateway. The town itself is touristy and unmemorable, but it does provide bus and boat connections along Lovatnet to the Bødalen and Kjenndalen glacial tongues.

A great, but strenuous, five to six-hour hike from Loen will take you to the Skålatårnet tower, which now functions as a self-service DNT hut, on the 1840m summit of Skåla. The route begins from Tjugen farm, north of the river and immediately east of Loen. For information on other excursions from Loen, see Kjenndalsbreen & Bødalsbreen under Jostedalsbreen, earlier in this chapter.

Places to Stay & Eat

Lo-Vik Camping (☎ 57 87 76 19), west of the river, is open from mid-May to mid-September. Here, tent campers without/with a car pay Nkr35/55 per tent plus Nkr15 per person. Cabins cost from Nkr275 for four beds with no facilities to Nkr600 with four beds, a shower, toilet and cooking facilities.

Loen's undisputed centre of action is the *Hotel Alexandra (☎ 57 87 50 00, fax 57 87 50 51, alex@alexandra.no)*, which dominates tourism in the valley with its restaurants, bars, nightclubs, swimming pool, fitness centre, mini-golf and boat and bicycle hire. Although it has been run as a family hotel since 1884, its current architecture approaches the eyesore level. The hotel is also the place to book the Lovatnet boat and other Jostedalsbreen excursions. Single/double summer rates start at Nkr620/940, with breakfast, but you can spend up to an extortionate Nkr2600 for a luxury double suite.

A cosier choice is the more modest *Loen Hotel (☎ 57 87 78 00, fax 57 87 78 30)*, which charges Nkr495/695. The attached café serves hot dogs and chips for Nkr35 and more substantial dishes from Nkr55 to Nkr150.

FLORØ

Florø is not only the westernmost town in Norway, but also one of the most pleasant and surprising. It was founded on 'fishy silver' in 1860 as a herring port, but is now sustained by the 'black gold' of the oil industry. As one of the southernmost ports on the Hurtigruten coastal ferry route, it sees lots of short-term visitors but its gentle seaward ambience probably merits at least a day of exploring and relaxing. For a scenic overview, it's an easy 10-minute climb up the Storåsen hill from the Florø Ungdomsskule on Havrenesveien.

Information

The tourist authority for Florø and the region is the Vestkysten Reiseliv A/S (☎ 57 74 75 05, fax 57 74 77 16, vestkysten@sf.telia.no, www.vestdata.no/infosys). It's open from 8 am to 7 pm on weekdays from 15 June to 15 August, 10 am to 5 pm Saturday and 3 to 7 pm Sunday. For Nkr20 per day, it rents out one-speed 'Bysykkels' for pedalling around the relatively flat town. The booklets *Cycling in Flora* and *On Foot in Flora* are also on sale. Coin-operated laundry services are available at the Guest Harbour, in the centre.

Sogn og Fjordane Kystmuseet

The Sogn og Fjordane Coastal Museum (☎ 57 74 22 33), south-east of the centre, is spread across two islands and several skerries. The two main buildings are chock-full of exhibits on coastal resources, particularly fishing, as well as a model 1900 fishing family's home and a collection of model boats. There are also several old warehouse buildings moved from Florø and Måløy, and the Bataldebua, which was used on the island of Batalden for salting herrings and now contains an exhibit on the herring fishery. The highlight, however, is probably the Snorreankeret oil platform, which is dedicated to the history, exploration and exploitation of the North Sea oil and gas fields. It's open weekdays from 11 am to 6 pm from June to August, and weekends from noon to 4 pm. Admission costs Nkr30.

Offshore Islands

The enigmatic island of Kinn is home to a restored 12th century church, which is believed to have been built by British Celts sheltering from religious persecution. In late June, it's the site of the Kinnespelet pageant (☎ 57 74 37 22), that celebrates the church history on the island. Climbers and hikers also enjoy the dramatic landscapes, particularly the Kinnaklova cleft. Boats between Florø and Kinn run at 2.30 pm daily and return at 3.45 pm, Monday to Friday. Unless you take a tour, you'll probably have to camp or stay overnight at a private cabin on the island.

Ferries also connect the mainland to Svanøy, Batalden, Askrova and Tansøy from Fugleskjærskaia quay. On Svanøy, you can hike, visit the deer centre (☎ 57 74 87 36, svahjort@sf.telia.no) or go horse riding (☎ 57 74 87 66). On Batalden, you can visit the 3500-year-old rock carvings or take a weekend painting course (from Nkr1350) at the pleasant Batalden Havbu fishing cottages (☎/fax 57 74 54 22), which costs Nkr350/500 for single/double accommodation. Askrova has a prehistoric Troll Cave and adjoining Tansøy rises to 233m and affords views over the surrounding archipelago. The major offshore attractions, however, are the lighthouses on Stabben, Kvanhovden and Ytterøyane, which are visited on the tourist office's renowned Friday lighthouse tour (see Organised Tours).

For information on island accommodation, pick up the Florø tourist office brochure *Hytteferie på Kysten*.

Organised Tours

At 10 am on Friday, the tourist office runs a fabulous day tour by boat to the offshore lighthouses at Stabben, Kvanhovden and the remote Ytterøyane, where you're landed in a small tender. This worthwhile trip costs Nkr270 (including lunch) and is extremely popular, so advance bookings are advised. Another good option is the Tuesday and Thursday tours to the islands of Batalden and Kinn. On Batalden, you'll

FLORØ

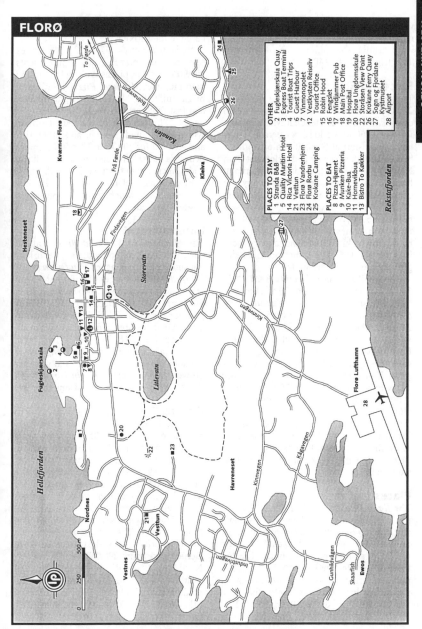

PLACES TO STAY
1 Stranda B&B
5 Quality Maritim Hotel
14 Vesttun
21 Rica Victoria Hotell
23 Florø Vandrerhjem
24 Florø Rorbu
25 Krokane Camping

PLACES TO EAT
8 Pizza-Hjørnet
9 Munken Pizzeria
10 Kaka-Bua
11 Homevikbua
13 Bistro To Køkker

OTHER
2 Fugleskjærskaia Quay
3 Express Boat Terminal
4 Tourist Boat Trips
6 Guest Harbour
7 Vinmonopolet
12 Vestkysten Reiseliv
   Tourist Office
15 Robin Hood
16 Fengslet
17 Windjammer Pub
18 Main Post Office
19 Hospital
20 Florø Ungdomsskule
22 Storåsen View Point
26 Krokane Ferry Quay
27 Sogn og Fjordane
   Kystmuseet
28 Airport

visit a converted herring salting house, then continue to Kinn, where there's a two-hour walk around the major sites of interest. This trip costs Nkr240.

Places to Stay

The friendly *Krokane Camping* (☎ 57 74 22 20, fax 57 74 75 70), on a peninsula 2km east of town, offers tent/caravan camping for Nkr30/60 plus Nkr10 per person. Four-bed cabins start at Nkr240 while two/four-bed units with a shower and toilet cost from Nkr280/380. From the centre, buses run at least hourly on weekdays and Saturday; get off at Solheim. The *Florø Vandrerhjem* (☎ 57 74 06 89, fax 57 74 38 20, Havrenesveien 32B), at the Åsgården Motell, offers dorm rooms with two to three beds, bath, shower, kitchenette and laundry facilities for Nkr155. The same rooms as singles/doubles cost Nkr250/345.

The small and homy *Stranda B&B* (☎ 57 74 06 26) charges Nkr330/550. The turf-roofed Russian-style huts at *Vesttun* (☎ 90 69 77 04) cost Nkr450 to Nkr650 per hut. *Florø Rorbu* (☎ 57 74 81 00, fax 57 74 32 90) at Krokane Kai has double shorefront flats for Nkr400 to Nkr700 in the high season. One upmarket option is the *Rica Victoria Hotell* (☎ 67 75 10 00, Markegata 43), which charges Nkr625/750. The tourist office can also book holiday cabins in secluded seaside or fjordside locations. Alternatively, try the appealing *Quality Maritim Hotel* (☎ 57 75 75 75, Hamnegata 1) on the waterfront. Rooms cost Nkr950/1100 during the week and Nkr595/750 at weekends.

Places to Eat

The *Kake-Bua* (☎ 57 74 22 42), in the centre, combines a pastry shop, pub, café and rustic and wonderful 'museum' of nautical artefacts. It's open from 8.30 am to 4 pm on weekdays and to 2 pm on Saturday. The 2nd floor of the *Hornevikbua* (☎ 57 74 01 22) pub and restaurant, with its ship-like interior, serves lunches from Nkr49, fish soup for Nkr60, fish dishes from Nkr152 to Nkr172 and meat dishes from Nkr155 to

Nkr200. Outdoor seating is available on a barge in the harbour.

Pizza-Hjornet (☎ 57 42 23 18) serves fast food and pizza; a 30cm pizza costs Nkr90 and 40cm pizzas are Nkr145. In the daytime, the *Munken Pizzeria* offers a pizza buffet for Nkr75. For light lunches and fast food, see *Bistro To Køkker* (☎ 57 74 24 87), 50m east of the tourist office, which does squid, salmon and other fish and seafood for Nkr76 to Nkr99. For more pedestrian tastes, fish and chips costs Nkr39 and burgers range from Nkr36 to Nkr64.

Florø is particularly happy with its new Vinmonopolet, which recently opened on Fugleskjærsgata.

Entertainment

The *Morilden* (☎ 57 74 10 00) pub at the Rica Victoria Hotell provides a quiet drinking spot while the attached *Fru Olsen* (☎ 57 74 10 00) disco charges Nkr50 after 11 pm and attracts everyone in town between 20 to 50 years old. On weekends, the *Windjammer Pub* (☎ 57 74 29 88) is divided into a pub which features live music, and a disco for patrons over 18. The rest of the week, it's just a drinking den. The *Fengslet* or 'Prison' bar attracts a rougher and younger crowd while the calmer *Robin Hood* (☎ 57 74 29 88) is popular with patrons over 21.

Getting There & Away

Widerøe flies at least daily between Oslo and Florø for Nkr585, although a few seats are available for just Nkr375; book early.

Florø lies at the end of a very long Nor-Way Bussekspress route from Oslo (10½ hours, Nkr570), which runs three times daily. Express boats run two or three times daily between Bergen (3½ hours, Nkr370) and Måløy (1¼ hours, Nkr125), stopping in Florø en route. The town is also a stop on the Hurtigruten coastal steamer between Bergen (7¼ hours, Nkr398) and Kirkenes. Northbound, it calls in at 4.45 am and southbound at 8 am. Stops farther north include Måløy (2¾ hours, Nkr126), Ålesund (7¼ hours, Nkr370) and Trondheim (25¼ hours, Nkr897).

AROUND FLORØ
Vingen Petroglyphs

The 1500 incredible early Stone Age petroglyphs at Vingen, facing the sea from the slopes of Vingenfjellet, constitute the largest field of petroglyphs in northern Europe. They're thought to be the work of early Stone Age hunters and date back to between 6000 and 4000 BC. There's no road to the paintings and the only way to reach them is by boat with the Hotel Svelgen (☎ 57 79 33 01, fax 57 79 31 62 or 57 79 41 13) in the bizarre industrial town of Svelgen. The tours operate weekly through July and the first half of August and cost Nkr150 per person. A combined walk and boat tour runs on Sunday from 28 June to 16 August and costs Nkr50. For further information, contact the tourist office in Svelgen (☎ 57 79 33 37). From Florø, you can reach Svelgen (1½ hours, Nkr67) on bus No 653 five to eight times daily.

Grøndalen

A large region north and east of Florø and west of the Ålfotbreen glacier presents a quite different face of Norway than surrounding areas. Here the geology consists of a predominantly pinkish sandstone formation, and the landscape is characterised by bare and rocky peaks with superb hiking potential. One of the loveliest spots is the hidden Shangri-la valley of Grøndalen, east of Norddalsfjord, which is known as the rainiest spot in Norway. The road here comes to a dead end in a magical spot, where you can leave your car and strike off up the hill. It's a rather steep 2km walk up to Grøndalsstølen hut, and three hours to Blåbrebu hut, where there's easy access to the Ålfotbreen ice. In summer, buses run between Florø and Sunndalen (1¾ hours, Nkr51), about 4km from the road's end, at 8.30 am Monday, Wednesday and Friday from Sunndalen and 1.20 pm from Florø.

MÅLØY

The dramatically located fishing town of Måløy, at the mouth of Nordfjord, lies on Vågsøy island beneath twin hills and is connected to the mainland by its landmark, the graceful S-curve Måløybrua bridge. There's little of major interest in the town itself but the island is laced with sea-view hiking routes (you can pick up a photocopied map at the tourist office) and boasts two worthwhile destinations, the Kråkenes Fyr lighthouse and the bizarre seaside rock, Kannesteinen. The Vågsøy Reiseliv tourist office (☎ 57 85 08 50, fax 57 85 07 97), on Sjøgata, is open on weekdays between mid-May and mid-August only.

Kannesteinen

The wave-tortured 'balanced' rock Kannesteinen, which rises from the sea like a stone mushroom, makes a great destination for a day trip. It may not exactly live up to expectations – there's a lot of hype – but the trip out there is lovely on a sunny day and it's ideal for a seaside picnic. From Måløy, take the Oppedal bus (No 853) to the end of the line (30 minutes, Nkr21). It runs five times daily on weekdays and twice on Saturday.

Kråkenes Fyr

Kråkenes lighthouse (☎/fax 57 85 55 27), perched precariously on a rock shoulder above a potentially wicked sea, was first opened in 1906 and automated in 1986. Even on a sunny day, it fulfils most romantics' expectations, but this German-run operation is also open for overnight guests and the very lucky will be able to hole up there on enigmatically stormy nights. This unusual hostel accommodates up to seven people and costs Nkr300 per person per night, or Nkr2760 per week, with shared facilities and use of the kitchen; groups of at least six can book the whole thing. Day visitors are also welcome on the point but can't enter the building. To get there, take bus No 852, which runs to and from the lighthouse (one hour, Nkr33) on Thursday from 14 June to 15 August. On other days (except Sunday), you'll only get as far as Kvalheim (45 minutes, Nkr34), about 10km away.

Places to Stay & Eat

The nearest camping ground is Gerd and Oddbjørn Nygård's friendly and recommended *Steinvik Camping* (☎/*fax 57 85 10 70*), at Deknepollen, over the bridge. Tent camping with a car costs Nkr70 with no per person charge, use of the kitchen and free hot showers; caravans stay for Nkr80; two-bed cabins cost Nkr200; four-bed cabins with a shower and toilet are Nkr450 and Nkr550; and four-bed self-catering flats cost Nkr400 to Nkr500. From town, take any bus east over the bridge to the sign-posted turn-off and walk the 1.2km to the camping ground.

The large glass-fronted *Nordlandia Måløy Hotel* (☎ *57 85 18 00, fax 57 85 05 89*) is the centre of most tourist activity in town, and shares the building with the recommended *Aquarius* dining room and its novel 3000L marine aquarium. Single/double rooms cost Nkr550/750, with breakfast. Set lunches cost Nkr135 and three-course dinners average Nkr235.

The covered *Galeåsen* pub (☎ *57 85 22 40*), at the harbour opposite the hotel, serves full meals from 6 to 10 pm in summer and lay on a taco buffet for Nkr69. There is also dancing here on weekend evenings. For something faster, try the unfortunately-named *Midtgaard's Mat i Farten* gatekjøkken (the name means 'food on the run'), beside the tourist office, which does burgers, hot dogs, chicken and chips. *Mama Rosa* specialises in pizza and pasta and is open from 2 to 11 pm Monday to Thursday and from noon to 11 pm Friday to Sunday.

Getting There & Away

Måløy is reached on three daily Nor-Way Bussekspress buses from Oslo (10½ hours, Nkr590) via Stryn (two hours, Nkr115), with several additional runs between Stryn and Måløy by Nordfjord og Sunnmøre Billag. The express boat from Bergen (4½ hours, Nkr435) to Florø continues on to Måløy, and the Hurtigruten coastal steamer passes daily (7.30 am northbound and 5.30 am southbound).

SELJE

Few visitors traipse all the way out to Selje, which is one of the northernmost outposts of Sogn og Fjordane country on the western edge of Norway, but those who do find a very pleasant small town and one of the finest beaches in the country, just outside the door of the tourist office. You may also want to make the trek out to Vestkapp, about 27km by road from Selje, which isn't Norway's westernmost point but still provides superb sea views.

Many travellers to the area want to visit the lovely ruins of Selje monastery and church of St Sunniva on Selja island, which date from the 11th and 12th centuries, respectively. From 29 June to 2 August, ferries (☎ 91 80 74 14) leave the mainland at 10.15 am and 1 and 3.30 pm, and there are one or two daily departures at other times between 25 May and 30 August. Pick up tickets (Nkr90 return) from the tourist office (☎ 57 85 66 06) at the beach, which is open from 11 am to 5 pm from 25 May to 23 August (extended summer hours of 10 am to 8 pm occur from 20 June to 9 August).

Places to Stay & Eat

Although it gets a bit soggy after rain, the only viable camping place is *Selja Camping & Hytter* (☎ *57 85 62 43*), about 2km east of town. Tent camping for two people with a car costs Nkr70 and huts range from Nkr350 to Nkr450.

The well heeled *Selje Hotel* (☎ *57 85 61 07, fax 57 85 62 72, posta@seljehotel.no*), back in the trees near the centre of town, charges from Nkr700/980 to Nkr915/1300 for singles/doubles. The less pretentious annexe, the *Selje Sjøhus* at the harbour, has rooms for Nkr350/500 and serves fish dishes from Nkr130 to Nkr190.

The rustic *Frimannsbua Kro* serves up traditional specialities, including *speke* (wind-dried meat) with potato salad and flatbread for Nkr100, herring and flatbread for Nkr30 and dried cod for Nkr70. If that doesn't appeal, pizzas range from Nkr65 to Nkr129.

Getting There & Away

Buses run between Måløy and Selje (one hour, Nkr58) three times daily on weekdays. It's also the end of the Nordfjord express-boat route from Bergen (4¾ hours, Nkr470).

The Northern Fjords

ÅNDALSNES

Most people approach Åndalsnes along the spectacularly scenic Raumabanen, the rail route from Dombås, which follows a deeply cut glacial valley flanked by sheer walls and plummeting waterfalls. During WWII, Åndalsnes was the last port with a railway to be occupied by the Germans, and was used by the Allies as a supply depot and access to the interior. It was to here that the Norwegian royal family was evacuated before they were spirited out of the country. Shortly thereafter, however, the Germans got wise and bombed it to the ground before setting up a major base. As a result, the modern town is rather nondescript, but the surrounding landscapes remain top notch.

Information

The useful Åndalsnes og Romsdal Reiselivslag tourist office (☎ 71 22 16 22, fax 71 22 16 82) is at the train station.

Trollveggen

Approaching from Dombås, the road and rail lines follow the dramatic 1800m high Trollveggen, or Troll's Wall, whose ragged and often cloud-shrouded summit is considered the ultimate challenge among Norwegian mountaineers. It was first climbed in 1965 by a joint Norwegian and English team. Since 1980, when a Finnish man leaped off it with a parachute, Trollvegen has also been a venue for now-illicit base jumping.

Trollstigen

The Trollstigen (Troll's Path), south of Åndalsnes, is a thriller of a road with 11 hairpin bends, a 1:12 gradient and, to add a daredevil element, it's one lane practically all the way. Bus passengers get a photo stop at the thundering 180m Stigfossen waterfall and a quick halt at the top for a dizzy view down the valley. If you have a car, however, you'll probably also want to pause for photos of the dramatic 1500 to 1600m peaks of Karitind, Dronningen, Kongen and Bispen, as well as Norway's only 'Troll Crossing' road sign. You may also enjoy the Vegmuseum, at the pass, which tells the engineering history of this awesome road.

Activities

Hiking The tourist office has 14 leaflets (Nkr5 each) describing a range of excellent hiking tracks and routes around the Romsdalen Alps, but the best map for extensive exploration is *Romsdals-alpene* 1:80,000, which it sells for Nkr79. An excellent day hike begins in town, 50m south of the Esso petrol station, and climbs to the summit of Nesaksla (715m), the prominent peak that rises above the town (to fully appreciate it, get there soon, because a cable car is planned for 2000). While the path is quite steep, at the top you'll be rewarded with a terrific view of the surrounding fjords and mountains. In fine weather, the view extends down Romsdalsfjord and up Romsdalen and Isterdalen (to Trollstigen), and easily rivals any in Norway.

From the shelter at the top, it's a straightforward climb to the summit of Høgnosa (991m) and beyond to Åkesfjellet (1215m). In summer the ascent can be hot in the midday sun, so get an early start and carry water. Alternatively, you can traverse along the marked route 5km eastward and descend to the town of Isfjorden, at the head of the Isfjord, or attempt the multi-day hike to the famous 1150m Romsdalshornet (only accessible to hikers via Isfjorden and Venjedalen).

Climbing Serious climbers may want to contact the Aak Fjellsportsenter (☎ 71 22 64 44), Postboks 238, N-6301 Åndalsnes, 4km from town along the Dombås road. It runs mountaineering courses, sells topographic maps, rents skis and mountain-climbing equipment, and also has a few rooms to rent. Mountaineers may also enjoy the Norsk Tindemuseum, on the road to Åndalsnes Camping, with exhibits on the expeditions of renowned mountaineer Arne Randers Heen.

Fishing Four-hour fishing tours on Romsdalsfjorden are available through the tourist office for Nkr250 per person; they run three times daily in summer.

Places to Stay

Åndalsnes Camping (☎ 71 22 16 29, fax 71 22 62 16), less than 2km from town at the mouth of Raumadalen, enjoys a dramatic riverside setting. Tent/caravan camping costs Nkr64/70 plus Nkr15 per person, and heated cabins range from Nkr220 to Nkr400. Canoes can be hired for Nkr40 per hour and mountain bikes for Nkr90 per day. *Trollveggen Camping (☎ 71 22 37 00, fax 71 22 16 31)*, at the foot of the Trollveggen wall, has tent camping without/with a car for Nkr50/75 and caravan camping for Nkr90. The scenic *Trollstigen Camping (☎ 71 22 68 99)* doesn't allow tenting, but caravanners pay Nkr105 and huts cost from Nkr400 to Nkr500. The new *Trollstigen Gjestegård (☎ 71 22 11 12)* has five-bed cabins with cooking facilities for Nkr450 and the adjoining farm rents double cabins for Nkr250.

A good choice for budget travellers is the sod-roofed *Setnes Vandrerhjem (☎ 71 22 13 82)*, 2km from the train station on the Rv9. Pleasant single/double rooms cost Nkr260/395 and dorm beds are Nkr100. Don't miss the famous pancakes-and-fried-fish breakfast (Nkr60). Most people walk here from town, but if you have a lot of luggage, you can hop on the Ålesund bus which meets the train and passes right by it. It's open from 15 May to 15 September.

If the hostel is full – and it often is – try the nearby *Romsdal Gjestegård (☎ 71 22 13 83)*, with plain rooms for Nkr320/490 with breakfast, and rustic two-bedroom cabins with kitchens for Nkr500. Alterna-

tively, the tourist office keeps a list of eight to 10 private homes offering accommodation from Nkr250 to Nkr350 for a single or double, with linen.

The *Grand Hotel Bellvue (☎ 71 22 75 00, fax 71 22 60 38)*, which caps a hillock in the centre of town, is the choice of most tour groups. It offers adequate single/double rooms, most with fine views, for Nkr695/850 to Nkr795/980. For the best views and least traffic noise, ask for a room at the back, and as high up as possible. An alternative is the *Hotel Rauma (☎ 71 22 12 33)*, right in the centre, which has rooms for Nkr350/450 without bath and Nkr650/795 with bath.

Places to Eat

The train station shop sells fruit and sandwiches and there are a couple of supermarkets and cafeterias in the centre. For sandwiches and sweet treats, locals like the *Måndalen Bakeri*, on the waterfront near the train station. The nearest cafeteria to the hostel is *Vertshuset Rauma*, on the E69 on the west bank of the river. More formal and expensive dining is available in the basement of the *Grand Hotel Bellevue* and at the Italian-oriented *Buona Sera*, right in the centre, which predictably specialises in pizza and pasta.

Getting There & Away

Trains to and from Dombås run three times daily (1½ hours, Nkr135), in sync with Oslo-Trondheim trains (twice daily, the Dombås-Åndalsnes route is also served by Togbuss), and the sleeping cars on the overnight train are linked up with the Oslo-bound train. Trains also connect in Åndalsnes with Togbuss services to Ålesund (Nkr142) and Molde (Nkr142).

Buses along the 'Golden Route' to Geiranger (three hours, Nkr117), via the Trollstigen, the Eidsdal ferry and the scenic Ørnevegen, operate from 15 June to 31 August. The Trollstigen pass is cleared and open by at least 1 June, and early in the season it's an impressive trip through a popular cross-country ski field, between high walls of snow. The buses leave Åndalsnes at 6.45 am and 5.15 pm daily (the early bus tacks on a return excursion to Langvatn and Dalsnibba for an extra Nkr25), and from Geiranger at 1 and 6.10 pm.

Getting Around
Those who just want to spin up to Trollstigen or along the Trollvegen can rent a car for Nkr550 per day at either Åndalsnes Camping or Hertz (☎ 71 22 14 24) at the Hydro station. By taxi, you'll pay around Nkr400 for the return trip to the Trollstigen pass.

VALLDAL & TAFJORD
Lots of visitors pass through the 'strawberry town' of Valldal, over the famous Trollstigen pass from Åndalsnes, but few linger. There are, however, several sites of interest in the region, not to mention an annual Strawberry Festival. For details contact the Norddal Reiselivslag tourist office (☎ 70 25 77 67, fax 70 25 70 44, norddalr@online.no), which is open from 9 am to 9 pm daily from 20 June to 20 August, with shorter hours the rest of the year.

Tafjord
At 3 am on 7 April 1934, an enormous chunk of rock 400m high and 22m long – a total eight million cubic metres – broke loose from the hillside and crashed into Korsnæsfjord, creating a 64m tidal wave that washed 700m inland and claimed 41 people in Fjorrå and Tafjord. The disaster is now commemorated in the newly-opened Tafjord Geosenter. Displays also include geological exhibits on the two-billion-year-old gneiss and granite formations dominating the region.

The Tafjord Kraftverk Museum (☎ 70 25 80 00), in the village of Tafjord, reveals the history and purposes of the Tafjord hydro-electric schemes and the 96m high dam, Zakariasdammen, that dates from 1967. It's housed in a defunct power station that operated from 1923 to 1989. It's open daily from noon to 5 pm from 20 June to 20 August. Admission is free. The road that climbs from the village up to the Zakarias reservoir passes through a bizarre corkscrew tunnel and a couple of kilometres higher up, a short walking route leads down to the decrepit bridge at the narrow base of the dam, where you can imagine at close range what sort of stresses the structure tolerates.

Stordal
If you're travelling between Valldal and Ålesund, be sure to stop at the amazing Rose-Kyrkja (☎ 70 27 81 40), or Rose Church, in Stordal. This unassuming building, constructed in 1789 on the site of an earlier stave church, contains perhaps the most incredible baroque interior of any church in Norway, thanks to the 1799 efforts of Andreas Reinholt and Vebjørn Halling in the employ of local parishioners. Some elements, including the baptismal font, the pulpit base and the crucifix, came from the original stave church. It's open from 11 am to 4 pm daily from 15 June to 15 August.

Activities
A good reason to halt in Valldal is to join a four-hour white-water rush down the Valldøla river (Nkr390). Contact Valldal Naturopplevingar (☎ 70 25 70 75, www.graficonn.no/valldal.natur/).

Places to Stay & Eat
For a treat, stop at *Gudbrandsjuvet Camping* (☎ 70 25 86 31), 15km up the valley from Valldal. It sits beside the hellbound river just upstream from the canyon and several of the cabins have great watery views. Camping in a tent costs Nkr60 plus Nkr10 per person, while cabins start at Nkr250. The adjoining kiosk has pizza for Nkr22 and burgers for Nkr28. Four kilometres up the valley from Valldal is *Valldal Camping (☎ 70 25 79 93)*, which has tent/caravan camping for Nkr60/90 plus Nkr10 per person, and one very simple cabin for Nkr250.

There's also a hostel right in the centre. At the *Valldal Vandrerhjem (☎ 70 25 70 31, fax 70 25 75 11)*, dorm beds are Nkr90 and single/double rooms are Nkr180/230. The simple, compact and rather charming *Fjellro Turisthotell (☎/fax 70 25 75 13)* charges Nkr495/690, with breakfast. In the attached restaurant, beef or seafood dishes cost from Nkr75 to Nkr120.

The large *Fjordheim Turistsenter* (☎ *70 25 80 48, fax 70 25 81 33)*, right at the head of the fjord in Tafjord, has dorm beds for Nkr100, rooms from Nkr295/490, two/four-bed cabins with a shower and toilet for Nkr390/490 and a self-catering flat for Nkr300.

The *Severinhuset* (☎ *70 25 70 08)* pub and restaurant, in a historic home, specialises in fish and beef dishes. The less formal *Mercur Bistro* serves burgers from Nkr40 to Nkr60 and chicken from Nkr80 and a Nkr75 special, pork with cheese and broccoli sauce. The *Muritunet/Lupinen Café* (☎ *70 25 84 10)* is open daily and specialises in pizza. On Sunday from noon to 9 pm, it puts on an inexpensive buffet. About 4km up the valley, the new *Jordbærstova* (☎ *70 25 75 89)* honours the valley's mighty strawberry. Stop in for a slice of strawberry cheesecake or the local pancake speciality known as *svele*, served with strawberries and cream. Light meals are also available.

Getting There & Away

Valldal lies on the 'Golden Route' bus service between Åndalsnes (one hour, Nkr66) and Geiranger (2¼ hours, Nkr109). Don't miss the spectacular Rv63 approach via the Trollstigen pass. If you're driving, you may want to pause at Gudbrandsjuvet, 15km up the valley from Valldal, where the river slots through a 5m wide, 20m deep canyon.

Buses between Valldal and Tafjord (20 minutes, Nkr26) run twice daily on weekdays and once on Saturday.

GEIRANGER

The towering walls of twisting, 20km-long Geirangerfjord are lined with scattered cliffside farms, some abandoned, and a line-up of breathtaking waterfalls with names such as De Syv Søstre (The Seven Sisters), Friaren (the Friar), the Suitor and Brudesløret (Bridal Veil). Geiranger, at the head of the fjord, may have only 300 residents but its fabulous views attract hordes

of visitors on frantically rushed sightseeing trips. In the evening, however, after the cruise ships and tour buses have moved on, things get more appropriately serene. The tourist office (☎ 70 26 30 99) is in the post office complex near the pier.

Flydalsjuvet

After even a few days in Norway, you're sure to see photos of the overhanging rock Flydalsjuvet, which invariably features a figure gazing down at a cruise ship in Geirangerfjord. The car park signposted Flydalsjuvet, about 5km uphill from town on the Stryn road, overlooks a great view of the fjord and the frightfully green river valley, but doesn't provide the postcard view. For that, you'll have to trot about 150m down the hill, then descend a slippery and rather indistinct track to the edge. Your photo subject will have to scramble down onto to the overhang from about 50m farther along.

Ørnevegen

The Ørnevegen route into Geiranger from Åndalsnes and Valldal, constructed in 1954, twists down the almost sheer slope in 11 hairpin bends and affords incredible views down the narrow fjord. The vistas take in the Preikestolen rock outcrop and the lovely De Syv Søstre waterfall.

Hiking

All around Geiranger you'll find great hiking routes to abandoned farmsteads, waterfalls and vista points. The tourist office distributes maps featuring 11 short hikes from town. The most popular longer hike begins on the fjord sightseeing boat (see Organised Tours). On the way back, the boat will stop at the start of the walking route. Climb from the landing for 45 minutes to the precariously perched hillside farm known as Skageflå. From there, it's a gradual 2¼-hour hike back along the mountain to Geiranger. Another recommended hike follows a normally muddy path to the Storseter waterfall, where the track actually passes behind the cascading water. This one takes about 45 minutes each way.

Organised Tours

Geiranger Fjordservice (☎ 70 26 30 07, fax 70 26 31 41) sightseeing boat tours are organised at the tourist office for Nkr70 per person. From 1 June to 1 September, they run five times daily, with an extra evening departure daily from 25 June to 31 July. Geiranger Fjordservice is also recommended for the popular Skageflå hike.

Places to Stay

Hotels in Geiranger can be quickly booked out by package tours, but a dozen or so camping possibilities skirt the fjord and hillsides, including *Geiranger Camping* (☎ 70 26 31 20), right in town at the head of the fjord. *Fjorden Camping* (☎ 70 26 30 77), 2km from town, has four-bed cabins with a hotplate for Nkr200.

Visitors have long lamented the lack of an official hostel in Geiranger, but then an enterprising local woman, Ms Liv-Ida Bjørnstad, decided to turn her spacious but cosy home, which has a convenient location and super views, into the *Vinjebakken Hostel* (☎ 70 26 32 05). Dorm beds cost Nkr120 with your own sleeping bag or Nkr160 with sheets, and breakfast is available for Nkr50. It's open in July and August only. Head up the hill to the octagonal church, look to the left and you'll see it there on the hill.

The incongruous imposition at the head of the fjord is actually the *Hotel Geiranger* (☎ 70 26 30 05, fax 70 26 31 70), which is where the big tours stay. Single/double rooms start at Nkr660/860, but rooms with a view cost Nkr800/1140. The more charming and spectacularly situated *Union Hotel* (☎ 70 26 30 00, fax 70 26 31 61), high on the hill above town, has summer rates of Nkr620/940. The *Grande Fjord Hotell* (☎ 70 26 30 90, fax 70 26 31 77), about 1km north-east of the village, offers tent camping, cabins from Nkr150 to Nkr650, and motel-style rooms from Nkr590/680.

Around the village, you'll also find plenty of *Rom* signs, indicating private rooms for rent, or you can pay Nkr20 at the tourist office and a booking will be made for you. Rooms average Nkr200/300.

Places to Eat

Naustkroa (☎ 70 26 32 30), near the pier in the centre, serves inexpensive fare, including fish soup for Nkr39, fish dishes from Nkr90, and beef or chicken from Nkr85 to Nkr155. The attached *gatekjøkken* manages takeaway hot dogs, burgers and chips. The *Olebuda Café-Pub* (☎ 70 26 31 60) does salads and seafood dishes, kebabs for Nkr105, tacos for Nkr118 and an all-you-can-eat pizza buffet from 9 pm to midnight for an incredible Nkr49. Otherwise, pizzas cost from Nkr105 to Nkr155. The *Friaren Pizza Pub* (☎ 70 26 45 55), just a few metres away, serves pizzas for Nkr75, Nkr110 and Nkr140.

If you're feeling really hungry, head uphill to the *Union Hotel*, where a blowout evening buffet costs Nkr200. You can pick up groceries at the *Daglivarer Maråk* supermarket in the Hotel Geiranger basement, which is one of the only supermarkets in Norway that's open on Sunday.

Getting There & Away

In summer, daily buses to Åndalsnes leave Geiranger (three hours, Nkr117) at 1 and 6.10 pm. The morning bus from Åndalsnes and Valldal arrives in Geiranger at 9.50 am. It then continues to Langvatn and en route back to Geiranger, does a 10km return tourist run to the 1500m summit of Dalsnibba and stops at Flydalsjuvet. If you're travelling from Langvatn to Geiranger (two hours, Nkr60), the Dalsnibba side trip costs an additional Nkr25; from Geiranger, the entire return trip is Nkr100. If you're driving, the toll road up Dalsnibba costs Nkr40 per car.

For Molde, you'll have to change buses in Åndalsnes; for Ålesund, change at Hellesylt.

The popular Møre og Romsdal Fylkesbåtar ferry between Geiranger and Hellesylt (1¼ hours, Nkr32/95 for passengers/cars; Nkr16 with a ScanRail pass), which probably represents the most spectacular scheduled ferry route in Norway, shuttles up and down the fjord four to 10 times a day from 1 May to 29 September. The latest schedules are available from MRF (☎ 71 21 95 00).

Every 11 days in summer, the Hurtigruten coastal steamer *Richard With* sails into Geiranger on its north-bound run, between stops in Ålesund (four hours, Nkr284 each way).

HELLESYLT

The old Viking port of Hellesylt may be calmer and less breathtaking than Geiranger, but it's still spectacular, and is lulled by a roaring waterfall that cascades through the centre. The dockside tourist office (☎ 70 26 50 52) dispenses information and also rents rowing boats and fishing rods. It's open from 9 am to 5.30 pm daily from June to August.

Places to Stay & Eat

The fine *Hellsylt Vandrerhjem* (☎/*fax 70 26 51 28)*, perched on the hillside overlooking the town, offers dorm beds for Nkr100 and single/double fjord-view cabins for Nkr200/250. It's on the road towards Stranda, about 200m from the junction. There's also the convenient but rather exposed *Hellesylt Camping* (☎ 70 26 51 04), right in the centre, which charges Nkr65 per tent (without a vehicle) and Nkr75 for caravans, plus Nkr10 per person.

The rustic old 1875 *Grand Hotel* (☎ 70 26 51 00, fax 70 26 52 22) has fjord-view rooms starting at Nkr370/550 and its dining room, the *Grand Hotel Pub & Kro*, is the most formal restaurant in town. Soup costs Nkr35, fish dishes average Nkr125 and beef dishes, from Nkr95 to Nkr130. For quicker and cheaper meals, there are the *Hellesylt Gatekjøkken* and the *Fossetun Bistro*, which are opposite and affiliated with the camping ground.

Getting There & Away

The spectacular MRF ferry ride to and from Geiranger (1¼ hours, Nkr32/95 for passengers/cars; Nkr16 with Scanrail) runs four to 10 times daily in summer. Some of these services connect with buses to and from Stryn (50 minutes, Nkr61) and Ålesund (2¾ hours, Nkr120). The daily Nor-Way Bussekspress buses between Bergen (8¼ hours, Nkr390) and Ålesund (2¾ hours, Nkr117) also pass through Hellesylt.

NORANGSDALEN

One of the most inspiring yet little visited parts of the Western Fjords is Norangsdalen, the hidden valley that connects Hellesylt with the Leknes-Sæbø ferry, on the scenic Hjørundfjorden, via the village of Øye. If you have a car, it's not to be missed, but the partially untarred Rv665 is also served by daily buses.

As the scenery unfolds past towering snowy peaks, ruined old farmsteads and haunting mountain lakes, you may experience a sense of passing through some alternative reality. In the upper part of the valley at Urasætra, beside a dark mountain lake, you'll see the ruins of several stone crofters' huts. Hikers and climbers will find plenty of scope in the dramatic peaks of the adjacent Sunnmørsalpane and you can still see the foundations of ruined farmhouses beneath the surface of the pea-green lake Langstøylvatnet, created in 1908 when a rockslide crashed down the slopes of Keipen.

For information on hiking, climbing and mountain huts in this majestic region, contact the local DNT organisation, Ålesund-Sunnmøre Turistforening (☎ 70 12 58 04, fax 70 12 95 60), Postboks 250, Kaiser Wilhelmsgata 22, N-6001 Ålesund.

Places to Stay & Eat

There's little choice of accommodation in Norangsdalen but that's not really a problem. If you splash out on one night in a Norwegian hotel, make it the historic and surprisingly affordable 1891 *Hotel Union* (☎ 70 06 21 00, fax 70 06 21 16) in Øye, which has attracted mountaineers, writers, artists and royalty for over a century. Although the period artwork, subdued classical music, wooden panelling and original furnishings might be considered excessive, there's little to suggest that you're inhabiting the present day, and you can choose from rooms named for celebrities who have occupied them: Sir Arthur Conan Doyle, Karen Blixen, Kaiser Wilhelm, Edvard Grieg, Roald Amundsen, Henrik Ibsen, a host of kings and queens, and even Coco

Chanel. Also take a look at the monument to CW Patchell, the English mountaineer who lost his heart to this valley.

Double rooms with shared facilities cost Nkr305, while basic twin or bunk rooms are Nkr505 and rooms with a fjord view cost Nkr555. It's open from 1 May to 1 October. The dining room serves two-course lunches for Nkr175 from noon to 3 pm and two/three-course dinners for Nkr205/255. The especially popular Sunday buffet, which includes lunch, cake and coffee, costs Nkr185 and is served from 1 to 4 pm.

Getting There & Away
From 14 June to 15 August, bus No133 runs through Norangsdalen between Hellesylt and Leknes (45 minutes, Nkr37) daily on weekdays. There are also four weekday services and one Sunday service between Øye and Leknes (20 minutes, Nkr14).

RUNDE
The island of Runde, 67km south-west of Ålesund, has just 160 inhabitants but plays host to half a million sea birds of 230 to 240 species, including 100,000 pairs of migrating puffins that arrive in May and stay until late July. You'll also see colonies of kittiwakes, gannets, fulmars, storm petrels, razor-billed auks, shags, guillemots and other sea birds, and 70 other species that nest here. The best birdwatching sites – as well as offshore seal colonies – are accessed on half-day boat tours that depart at 11 am from 1 May to 31 August, and cost from Nkr100 per person (with a minimum of four people). In fine weather, the tour also passes through the 'green lagoon' to the Branden sea caves. HI members get a 10% discount on these trips.

Alternatively, a four-hour tour around Runde on the yacht *Charming Ruth* (☎ 70 01 30 00) departs from the Ulstein Hotell at Ulsteinvik, on the neighbouring island of Hareidøya, at 11 am on Wednesday, Saturday and Sunday between 20 June and 16 August. The tour costs Nkr175.

For tourist information, contact the Runde Reiselivslag (☎ 70 01 37 90, fax 70 01 37 91), in Ulsteinvik.

Places to Stay & Eat
The harbourside *Runde Vandrerhjem & Camping* (☎ 70 08 59 16, fax 70 08 58 70, vadset@mimer.no) has dorm beds for Nkr95, single/double cabins for Nkr180/230 and tent space for Nkr50 per tent plus Nkr10 per person, all including use of the guest kitchen. The *Runde Café* (☎ 70 08 59 15), about 300m from the hostel, is open from 1 May to 31 August.

Getting There & Away
Runde is connected by bridge to the mainland. A ferry-bus combination departs from Ålesund (2½ hours, Nkr104) daily in summer. On weekdays, this combination is available as a day trip; a catamaran ferry sails from Ålesund to Hareid (30 minutes, Nkr43) at 8.30 am where it connects with a bus to Runde (two hours, Nkr59), via Ulsteinvik (20 minutes, Nkr20). To return to Ålesund on the same day, you'll have to leave Runde on the 5.05 pm bus. For cruises on the *Charming Ruth*, get off the Hareid-Runde bus at Ulsteinvik (Nkr20).

ÅLESUND
The agreeable coastal town of Ålesund, crowded onto a narrow fishhook-shaped peninsula in the sea, is considered by many to be even more beautiful than Bergen, and it's far less touristy. The town's characteristic Jugendstil Art Nouveau buildings, adorned with turrets, spires and gargoyles, emerged after the sweeping fire of 23 January 1904, which left 10,000 residents homeless. So tightly packed is the town centre that expansion would be impossible, and today most of the town's 38,000 people (there are 150,000 in the district) live scattered across surrounding islands and peninsulas.

Information
The Ålesund Reiselivslag tourist office (☎ 70 12 12 02, fax 70 12 66 06, office@alesund-tourist.mr.no) is in the town hall, diagonally opposite the bus station. In summer, it's open weekdays from 8.30 am to 7 pm, Saturday from 9 am to 5 pm and

Sunday from 11 am to 5 pm. The rest of the year, it's open weekdays from 9 am to 4 pm.

You can do laundry downstairs in the Guest Harbour service building near the head of Brosundet.

Art Nouveau Architecture

In 1908, Ålesund won the Houens National Memorial Prize for the preservation of Art Nouveau architecture, and you'll see some of the best examples along Apotekergata, Kirkegata, Løvenvoldgata and especially Kongensgata. After the great fire of 1904, the German emperor Kaiser Wilhelm II sent shiploads of provisions and building materials and the city was rebuilt in the typically German Jugenstil, or Art Nouveau style, that was popular in that era. Ålesund's particular version of that theme features a number of Norse influences, including figures and scenes from Norse mythology. The tourist office distributes the free booklet *On Foot in Ålesund*, detailing the town's architectural highlights in a walking tour.

ÅLESUND

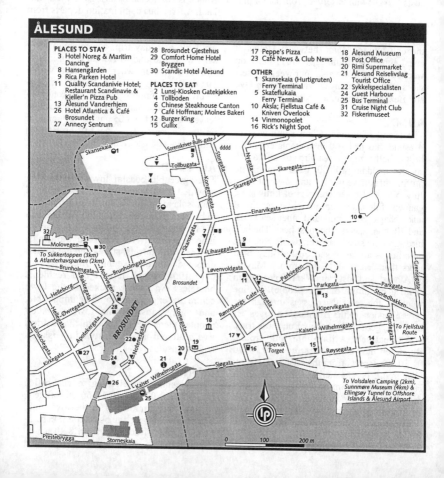

PLACES TO STAY
3 Hotel Noreg & Maritim Dancing
8 Hansengården
9 Rica Parken Hotel
11 Quality Scandanivie Hotel; Restaurant Scandinavie & Kjeller'n Pizza Pub
13 Ålesund Vandrerhjem
26 Hotel Atlantica & Café Brosundet
27 Annecy Sentrum
28 Brosundet Gjestehus
29 Comfort Home Hotel Bryggen
30 Scandic Hotel Ålesund

PLACES TO EAT
2 Lunsj-Kiosken Gatekjøkken
4 Tollboden
6 Chinese Steakhouse Canton
7 Café Hoffman; Molnes Bakeri
12 Burger King
15 Gullix
17 Peppe's Pizza
23 Café News & Club News

OTHER
1 Skansekaia (Hurtigruten) Ferry Terminal
5 Skateflukaia Ferry Terminal
10 Aksla; Fjellstua Café & Kniven Overlook
14 Vinmonopolet
16 Rick's Night Spot
18 Ålesund Museum
19 Post Office
20 Rimi Supermarket
21 Ålesund Reiselivslag Tourist Office
22 Sykkelspecialisten
24 Guest Harbour
25 Bus Terminal
31 Cruise Night Club
32 Fiskerimuseet

Ålesund Museum

The town museum (☎ 70 12 31 70, aalesund .museum@telia.no), Rasmus Rønnebergs gate 16, concentrates on the history of sealing, fishing, shipping and industry in the Sunnmøre region, the fire of 1904, the German occupation from 1940 to 1945 and the town's distinctive Jugendstil architecture. You'll also see a collection of boats and ships, including the *Uræd* lifeboat piloted across the Atlantic in 1904 by Ole Brude, and an 1812 barn which has been converted into an old-time grocery. Opening hours are from 11 am to 3 pm Monday to Saturday from 15 June to 15 August, and from noon to 3 pm on Sunday. Admission costs Nkr20.

The affiliated Ålesund Fiskerimuseet, or Fishery Museum, in the 1860 Holmbua warehouse at Molovegen 10, contains exhibits on fishing through the ages and a special exhibit on the drying stockfish and processing of cod liver oil.

Sunnmøre Museum

Ålesund's most celebrated museum, the Sunnmøre Museum (☎ 70 15 40 24), is housed at the site of the old Borgundkaupangen trading centre, 4km east of the centre. The main open-air exhibit consists of 50 old buildings, visiting displays on traditional crafts and textiles, and a collection of 30 historic boats, including replicas of Viking-era ships and a commercial trading vessel from around 1000 AD. It's open from 10 am to 5 pm Monday to Saturday from 15 June to 31 August and from noon to 5 pm on Sunday, with shorter hours the rest of the year.

There are also archaeological excavations and a reproduction of the 10th century town of Borgundkaupangen. These exhibitions reveal the history, trade, art, industry and religion of the west Norwegian coastal folk and their hunting and fishing cultures in medieval times.

It's open from 11 am to 4 pm Monday to Saturday from 15 June to 31 August, and from noon to 4 pm on Sunday. Admission to both sections costs Nkr40.

Aksla

The 418 steps up the hill Aksla lead to the splendid Kniven overlook over Ålesund and the surrounding mountains and islands. Follow Lihauggata from the pedestrian shopping street Kongensgata to the start of the 15-minute puff to the top of the hill. There's also a road to the top; take Røysegata east from the centre, and then follow the Fjellstua signposts up the hill.

The *Fjellstua Café* (☎ 70 12 65 82) and souvenir shop, on the top, are open from 10 am to 10 pm daily from 15 May to 1 September.

Atlanterhavsparken

The new Atlantic Ocean Park (☎ 70 12 82 00), Tueneset, 3km from the centre at the western extreme of the fishhook peninsula, introduces visitors to the North Atlantic's undersea world with glimpses into the submarine life around ferry harbours and piers, in main ocean currents, around offshore islands, and deep in the fjords. The most interesting feature is an enormous four-million-litre aquarium where human divers and the largest ocean fish are integrated into the underwater scene.

The grounds also offer superb coastal scenery, bathing beaches and hiking trails. The park is open from 10 am to 6 pm daily from June to August and from 11 am to 4 pm in September and May. Admission costs Nkr75.

Sukkertoppen

A more challenging hike for an even wider ranging view leads to the summit of Sukkertoppen. It begins on the street Sukkertoppvegen, on the 'hook' of Ålesund's fishhook peninsula. The track follows the easiest route, right up the east-pointing ridgeline. Take bus No 13 from town.

Offshore Islands

The offshore islands of Valderøy, Vigra, Giske and Godøy make nice day trips from Ålesund. Ytterland on Valderøy (20 minutes, Nkr32) and Vigra (30 minutes, Nkr44) are reached on buses No 61, 62 and 63, and

Giske (45 minutes, Nkr38) and Godøy (30 minutes, Nkr41) are accessed on bus No 64.

Giske is best known as the historic seat of the Viking-age ruling family, Arnungate, which ruled feudally from 990 to 1582. The island was also the home of Gange-Rolv (known as Rollon in France; he's also claimed by Vigra), the Viking warrior who founded the Duchy of Normandy in 911 and was an ancestor of England's William the Conqueror. In 1911, when Normandy celebrated its millennium, a copy of the Rollon statue in Rouen was presented to Ålesund, where it now stands in the Byparken.

Worthwhile sites on the islands include the Skjonghellaren caves on north-western Valderøy and the Blindheimssanden (also called Blimsand) white sand beach on north-western Vigra. Giske's 12th century marble church (admission Nkr10), which was restored in 1756, is open daily from 11 am to 4 pm, and the Makkevika marshes, also on Giske, offer fine birdwatching. The picturesque Alnes lighthouse (☎ 70 18 50 90) and fishing station, at the northern tip of Godøya, has a café and art exhibit that are open daily, noon to 6 pm, from 1 June to 31 August. Buses from Ålesund cost Nkr44. Valderøy and Godøy also offer some excellent short mountain hikes.

There are also a number of fully-equipped fishing cottages where you can stay for Nkr550 to Nkr625: *Alnes Rorbuferie* (☎ 70 18 51 96) on Giske, *Alnes Rorbuutleie Peggy* (☎ 70 18 53 73) on Godøy, *Farstad Rorbu* (☎ 70 12 93 10) on Valderøy and *Godøy Chalets* (☎ 70 18 50 26) on Godøy.

Organised Tours

On summer weekdays, you can do a day trip to Runde island. Start with the scheduled ferry M/S *Hjørungavåg* from the Skateflukaien quay to Hareid (30 minutes, Nkr43), and then connect with the bus to Ulsteinvik and Runde (two hours, Nkr59). Boat tours around the bird cliffs are available on weekdays from Runde and three days a week from Ulsteinvik. For details, see Runde, earlier in this chapter.

Also on summer weekdays, you can make scenic bus-ferry day trips (Nkr290) that include a cruise down the Geirangerfjord, three hours in Geiranger and a return to Ålesund via the Ørnevegen. This complicated route involves a lot of connections: a bus from Ålesund to Magerholm (weekdays at 8.50 and 11.15 am), ferry to Ørsneset, bus to Hellsylt, ferry to Geiranger, bus to Eidsdal, ferry to Linge and bus back to Ålesund.

A Monday, Wednesday and Friday day tour to Hjørundfjord on public transport begins with a bus from Ålesund to Ørsta (Nkr90) at 10 am; a bus from Ørsta to Sæbo (Nkr35) at 1.40 pm; a ferry from Sæbo to Standal (Nkr22) at 2.45 pm; a bus from Standal to Festøy (Nkr26) at 3.45 pm; and a ferry from Festøy back to Ålesund (Nkr47) at 4.55 pm. Unfortunately, it misses out Norangsdalen.

MRF boat tours to the lovely fishing community on Ona island are available four times each season (see the tourist office for details) but the island is more readily accessed from Molde. You can also take a return day trip to Molde (Nkr189) on the MRF express ferry (see Getting There & Away later in this section).

Places to Stay

Volsdalen Camping (☎ 70 12 58 90), above the shore about 2km east of the centre, is the friendliest camping option and also the nearest to town. Tent camping costs Nkr75/90 without/with a car, plus Nkr10 per person. Simple cabins for two to six people cost from Nkr300 to Nk450. It's open from 1 May to mid-September and is accessed on buses No 13, 14, 18 and 24, but at a pinch, you can also walk from town. If you want a more luxurious cabin, you can try *Prinsen Strandcamping* (☎ 70 15 52 04), about 2km farther east, but it's overpriced – tent camping costs a whopping Nkr130 – and the ambience seems almost comically sour.

The centrally located *Ålesund Vandrerhjem* (☎ 70 12 04 25, fax 70 11 58 59, Parkgata 14), has dorm beds for Nkr165, with breakfast and the use of cooking and laundry facilities. Single/double rooms cost Nkr250/400. It's open from 1 May to 30 September. The simple *Annecy Sentrum* (☎ 70 12 96 30, Kirkegata 1) lets out self-contained student rooms in summer. Dorm beds cost Nkr165 and doubles range from Nkr270 to 300. *Hansengården (☎ 70 12 10 29, Kongensgata 14)* offers student lodgings from 15 June to 15 August. Rooms cost from Nkr200/300 to Nkr220/ 330, plus Nkr30 for linen.

You'll find a more formal guesthouse atmosphere for Nkr500/570 at the *Brosundet Gjestehus (☎ 70 12 10 00, fax 70 12 12 95, Apotekergata 5)*. The tourist office also keeps lists of private rooms that start at around Nkr200 per person. It also keeps a list of *rorbu* (fishing hut) accommodation, some of which is quite plush, on the offshore islands (see Offshore Islands, earlier in this section).

The *Hotel Atlantica (☎ 70 12 91 00)*, near the bus station, has modern rooms and summer rates of Nkr510/680. A well located alternative is the *Hotel Noreg (☎ 70 12 29 38, Kongensgata 27)*, with summer and weekend rates from Nkr550/750. There are also a host of other upmarket choices charging an average of Nkr600/800, including the *Comfort Home Hotel Bryggen (☎ 70 12 64 00, fax 70 12 11 80, Apotekergata 1-3)*; the Art Nouveau-style *Quality Scandinavie Hotel (☎ 70 12 31 31, fax 70 13 23 70, Løvenvoldgata 8)*; the *Rica Parken Hotel (☎ 70 12 50 50, fax 70 12 21 64, Storgata 16)*; and the *Scandic Hotel Ålesund (☎ 70 12 81 00, fax 70 12 92 10, Molovegen 6)*.

Places to Eat

The all-you-can-eat pizza and salad lunch buffet at *Peppe's Pizza (☎ 70 12 82 22, Kaiser Wilhelmsgata 25)*, operates from noon to 3 pm and costs Nkr89. *Café Hoffmann (☎ 70 12 37 97, Kongensgate 11)* has a fine harbour view and serves simple meals, such as fish soup with bread for about Nkr35. It's open until 6 pm (4 pm on Saturday). *Molnes Bakeri (☎ 70 12 19 95)*, in the same complex, does the usual line of bread and pastry. The *Café News (☎ 70 12 28 00)* stocks the daily paper and serves up 28 menu options for just Nkr49.

Oddly enough, the locally named *Restaurant Scandinavie (☎ 70 12 91 26, Løvenvoldsgata 8)*, in the Quality Scandinavie Hotel, specialises in Chinese cuisine. Another odd Chinese hybrid is the *Chinese Steakhouse Canton (☎ 70 12 44 46, Kongensgata 7)*. Lunches range from Nkr65 to Nkr70 and in the evening, main dishes average Nkr96. It's open Monday to Saturday.

The *Café Brosundet (☎ 70 12 20 85)*, in the Hotel Atlantica, specialises in local seafood. Bacalao, which is Iberian-style dried cod, costs Nkr80 and steinbit with wild rice is Nkr105. If fish isn't your thing, lasagne with bread and salad costs Nkr69. If you don't mind paying for its rustic atmosphere, *Gullix (☎ 70 12 05 48)* is good for fish, pasta, and Mexican and Spanish dishes. A three-course fish dinner will cost around Nkr350, but lunch-time snacks start at around Nkr60 to Nkr90 and from noon to 7 pm, a tourist 'fish special' for Nkr123 is available.

A solid upper range place with a great harbourside location is the *Tollboden (☎ 70 12 86 70)*, right near the Hurtigruten quay. Across the street, you'll find the *Lunsj-Kiosken (☎ 70 12 31 83)* gatekjøkken, which offers what's probably the best deals in town on decent quick and light meals. Hot dogs start at Nkr15, burgers cost up to Nkr50 and chicken and chips goes for Nkr68. More familiar fast food is grilled up at the *Burger King*.

The best value supermarket is the *Rimi*, downstairs in the Kremmergården behind the tourist office. At Brosundet, you can buy the catch of the day directly from the fishing vessels.

Entertainment

The *Cruise Nightclub* on Molovegen, immediately west of the centre, has a weekend disco as well as an English-style pub. Another recommended pub is the popular *Club News (☎ 70 12 28 00, Notenesgata 1)* at the Café News. *Rick's Night Spot*, on Kiperviktorget, appeals mainly to the 18 to

20 gang, while a slightly older crowd frequents *Maritim Dancing* (☎ 70 12 29 38) at the Hotel Noreg.

The *Kjeller'n Pizza Pub* (☎ 70 12 31 31), in the Quality Scandinavie Hotel, has a dart board and pool table, and sometimes hosts live bands.

Getting There & Away

Air Ålesund is served by both Braathens SAFE (☎ 70 11 49 16) and Color Air (☎ 70 11 49 50, fax 70 18 50 02, www.colorair.no). The latter has Oslo fares from Nkr399.

Bus You'll find the main bus terminal on Kaiser Wilhelmsgata, diagonally opposite the tourist office. There are daily Nor-Way Bussekspress buses to and from Hellesylt (2¾ hours, Nkr120) and Bergen (8½ hours, Nkr390), and Ålesund Bilruter Togbuss services to and from Åndalsnes (2½ hours, Nkr142) at least three times daily. The Nor-Way Bussekspress Vestlandekspressen runs daily on weekdays between Ålesund, Molde (two hours, Nkr105) and Kristiansund (3¾ hours, Nkr206). There's also a direct daily run between Ålesund and Oslo (11¾ hours, Nkr600), via Stryn (3½ hours, Nkr165).

Boat The MRF express boat M/S *Fjørtoft* links Ålesund with Molde (2¼ hours, Nkr145) from Skateflukaia two or three times daily on weekdays. Hurtigruten coastal steamers arrive/depart at noon/3 pm northbound and at 11.45 pm/12.45 am southbound; on its northbound run, the Hurtigruten steamer *Richard With* makes a popular detour via Geiranger.

Getting Around

The Ålesund airport is on Vigra island, which is connected to the town by the undersea tunnels to Ellingsøy (3600m) and Valderøy (4200m). Flybuss bus services (☎ 70 13 68 00) depart from Skateflukaia in town one hour before the departure of domestic flights (25 minutes, Nkr50). The cheaper city buses No 61, 62 and 63 also pass within easy walking distance of the airport, and several detour right to the terminal.

Drivers to the airport and the offshore islands pay tunnel tolls totalling Nkr60 one-way for a car and driver plus Nkr15 per additional passenger.

Sykkelspecialisten (☎ 70 12 28 20), on Notenesgata, hires out bicycles for Nkr100 per day, plus Nkr20 for insurance.

MOLDE

Molde, scenically situated beside the sea at the wide mouth of Romsdalsfjorden, calls itself the 'Town of Roses' but is best known for its annual jazz festival in July. In April 1940, Molde suffered almost utter destruction at the hands of the Nazis. The Luftwaffe had heard that King Håkon was holed up in a red house, and set about destroying every red building. In fact, the king personally witnessed the bombing from beneath a birch tree now called Kongebjørka, at Glomstua; the last thing he saw of the town before heading for exile in Britain was the collapsing spire of the burning church. On a happy note, one local hero saved the old altarpiece painting, Axel Ender's *Resurrection*, by ripping it out with a knife as the bombs fell, and the Norwegian resistance managed to smuggle out 36 tonnes of royal gold on the HMS *Glasgow*.

As a result of the wartime destruction, modern Molde has little of architectural interest, but it's still a friendly and pleasantly compact little place and the unique coastal landscapes more resemble New Zealand or Seattle's Puget Sound than the rest of Norway. For a fine overview, drive or trek up to the Varden overlook, 400m above the town.

Information

The friendly Atlantic Safari tourist office (☎ 71 25 71 33) is in the Rådhus. From 15 June to 15 August, it's open from 9 am to 6 pm weekdays and from 10 am to 4 pm on Sunday. The rest of the year, it's open from 8.30 am to 3.30 pm on weekdays. For hiking and mountain hut information, see the Molde og Romsdals Turistforening (☎ 71 25 18 66), Storgata 56.

You can do laundry at the Guest Harbour, near the western end of town.

Romsdalsmuseet

The Romsdalen Folk Museum (☎ 71 25 25 34), founded in 1912, sprawls across a large open area north-west of the centre. It includes 40 homes that have been shifted to this spot from around the entire Romsdalen region. As much as possible, their original furnishings have been left intact, and reveal aspects of life in this region from the 14th to 20th centuries. From 23 June to 10 August, it's open from 11 am to 6 pm Monday to Saturday, and from noon to 6 pm on Sunday, closing an hour earlier at other times from 1 June to 31 August. A two-day admission ticket costs Nkr30 and also includes the Fiskerimuseet.

Fiskerimuseet

A short ferry ride from the Torget terminal is the Fishery Museum (☎ 94 66 16 01), on Hjertøya. This open-air museum brings to life the coastal fishing cultures around the mouth of Romsdalfjorden from the mid-19th century to the present day. It's open from noon to 5 pm daily (except Thursday) from 16 June to 17 August. During the same period, ferries (☎ 94 78 00 74) run daily except Thursday from Molde at noon and 2 and 4 pm and from Hjertøya at 12.45, 2.45, 4.45 and 6.30 pm. The two-day admission ticket costs Nkr30 and is also good for the Romsdalsmuseet.

Special Events

Undoubtedly the pre-eminent event is the renowned Molde Jazz Festival, which is held from Monday to Saturday in the 29th week of the year (every seven years, it's held on week 28), placing it around mid-July. It attracts both Norwegian and international names, as well as at least 60,000 fans, who pay from Nkr100 to Nkr200 for

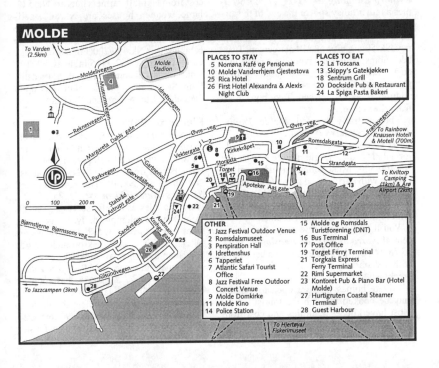

MOLDE

To Varden (2.5km)

Molde Stadion

PLACES TO STAY
5 Norrøna Kafé og Pensjonat
10 Molde Vandrerhjem Gjestestova
25 Rica Hotel
26 First Hotel Alexandra & Alexis Night Club

PLACES TO EAT
12 La Toscana
13 Skippy's Gatekjøkken
18 Sentrum Grill
20 Dockside Pub & Restaurant
24 La Spiga Pasta Bakeri

To Rainbow Knausen Hotell & Motell (700m)

To Kviltorp Camping (1km) & Åro Airport (2km)

To Jazzcampen (3km)

Bjørnstjerne Bjørnssons veg

0   100   200 m

OTHER
1 Jazz Festival Outdoor Venue
2 Romsdalsmuseet
3 Perspiration Hall
4 Idrettenshus
6 Tapperiet
7 Atlantic Safari Tourist Office
8 Jazz Festival Free Outdoor Concert Venue
9 Molde Domkirke
10 Molde Kino
14 Police Station
15 Molde og Romsdals Turistforening (DNT)
16 Bus Terminal
17 Post Office
19 Torget Ferry Terminal
21 Torgkaia Express Ferry Terminal
22 Rimi Supermarket
23 Kontoret Pub & Piano Bar (Hotel Molde)
27 Hurtigruten Coastal Steamer Terminal
28 Guest Harbour

To Hjertøya/ Fiskerimuseet

the big events. Traditional jazz concerts take place in the Perspiration Hall, the big concerts are held outdoors near the Romsdalsmuseet, indoor concerts take place at the Idrettenshus (sports hall) and free events are held nightly in front of the Rådhus. For information, contact the Molde International Jazz Festival (☎ 71 21 60 00, fax 71 25 36 35, moldejazz@moldejazz.no, www.moldejazz.no). Credit-card ticket sales are available for a Nkr10 surcharge through BillettService (☎ 81 53 31 33).

Molde's other festival is the Bjørnsonfestivalen, the Norwegian Festival of International Literature, which is held in Molde and Nesset from early to mid-August to honour home-grown author Bjørnstjerne Bjørnson. It attracts literary and theatrical figures from around the world.

Places to Stay

Kviltorp Camping (☎ 71 21 17 42) occupies a rather noisy spot at the end of the airport runway but fortunately, there's little air traffic. Without/with a car, tent campers pay Nkr50/80, plus Nkr10 per person. Two-bed cabins, which are available year-round, cost Nkr250 and four-bed cabins with a shower and TV are Nkr450. Sheets cost an additional Nkr50 per bed. Take bus No 20 from the centre.

The centrally located *Molde Vandrerhjem Gjestestova* (☎ 90 82 77 32, fax 71 21 61 80), on Romsdalsgata, has dorm beds for Nkr150 and single/double rooms for Nkr300/500. Most rooms include a mini-kitchen with a fridge and hotplate but guests may also use the communal kitchen. After mid-August, inexpensive accommodation is limited to only a couple of rooms.

You'll find decent mid-range digs at the central *Norrøna Kafé og Pensjonat* (☎ 71 25 18 24, fax 71 25 10 20), which has rooms with TV starting at Nkr395/595, including breakfast.

Private homes that are open to visitors may be booked through the tourist office. Most have kitchen facilities and cost from Nkr150 to Nkr200 per person. During the Molde Jazz Festival, hundreds of local households also offer private accommodation, and a large temporary camping ground, *Jazzcampen*, is set up 3km west of the centre and costs Nkr40 per person.

The *Rica Hotel* (☎ 71 20 35 00, fax 71 20 35 01, Storgata 8) has summer rates starting at Nkr620/750 and the *First Hotel Alexandra* (☎ 71 25 11 3, fax 71 21 66 35, Storgata 1-7) charges from Nkr590/790 on weekends and Nkr750/895 at other times in summer. At the eastern end of town, towards the airport, is the *Rainbow Knausen Hotell & Motell* (☎ 71 25 15 77), which has summer rates of Nkr750/850 in the hotel section, with breakfast, and Nkr450 for a double in the motel part, without sheets or breakfast.

The elaborate *Skarstua Turistsenter* (☎ 71 26 56 22, fax 71 226 50 06) holiday centre, in a relatively wild setting at Skaret, about 12km north of town on the Rv64, offers a range of accommodation: motel rooms cost from Nkr450, farmers huts are Nkr575, large wooden houses are Nkr800, self-catering huts are Nkr426, *stabbur* are Nkr700 and simple singles/doubles with breakfast cost Nkr500/700. From Molde, take bus No 252F or 252G (15 minutes, Nkr19), which run via Skaret two to three times daily. From Skaret, it's a popular 5km walk up to the Langdalsbu self-service DNT hut.

Places to Eat

The *Sentrum Grill* gatekjøkken, rising from the town square, is open from 11 am to 6 pm on weekdays and 2 to 10 pm on weekends. Burgers cost from Nkr39 to Nkr55 and fish and chips are Nkr49. The recommended *Skippy's Gatekjøkken* (☎ 71 25 22 30), which doubles as a café, serves fast meals from 8 am to midnight daily. Burgers cost from Nkr38 to Nkr53, fish sandwiches are Nkr42, schnitzel costs Nkr66 and the odd Hawaiian pork special is Nkr83.

At lunch time, the cosy *Dockside Pub & Restaurant* (☎ 71 21 50 33) has soup for Nkr29 and daily specials for Nkr79, as well as a menu of à la carte choices for Nkr55 to Nkr70. Pizzas range from Nkr90 to Nkr20, salads from Nkr50 to Nkr60 and beef dishes from Nkr100 to Nkr125.

Fast-food Italian specialities are available at the small and clean *La Spiga Pasta Bakeri*, with pasta dishes for Nkr60 to Nkr68 and small/large pizzas for Nkr35/95. Italian cuisine, albeit more formal, is also the speciality at *La Toscana* (☎ *71 25 64 11*), east of the centre. Daily specials cost Nkr95, pizzas are Nkr85, meat dishes range from Nkr165 to Nkr205, fish plates are Nkr175 to Nkr205 and pasta from Nkr79 to Nkr 125.

The upmarket dining room at the *First Hotel Alexandra* specialises in fish and game dishes, including reindeer, roe deer and ptarmigan, which start at Nkr250.

The inexpensive *Rimi* supermarket is found right in the centre at Storgata 24.

Entertainment

In the Hotel Molde, the *Kontoret Pub & Piano Bar* stays open until 1.30 am on Friday and Saturday. For cultural information, see the kommune website www.molde .kommune.no. The *Alexis Nightclub* at the First Hotel Alexandra has live music at weekends and appeals mainly to those over 30. The cover charge averages Nkr50. The disco at the *Dockside* puts on live performances every second week or so and attracts the over 20 crowd. The younger 18 to 25 student set will probably enjoy the *Tapperiet*, run by the student association. Cover charges apply only when there's live music.

The *Molde Kino* (cinema) is on Romsdalsgata, immediately east of the river.

Getting There & Away

Molde's Arø airport lies on the shore just 4km east of the city centre; it's accessed on bus No252 (10 minutes, Nkr19) or the Flybuss (10 minutes, Nkr25). Braathens SAFE (☎ 71 21 97 00 or ☎ 71 21 47 00) has at least four daily flights to and from Oslo.

The Nor-Way Bussekspress Vestlandekspressen runs daily on weekdays between Ålesund (two hours, Nkr105) and Kristiansund (1¼ hours, Nkr109), via Molde. The express ferry *Fjørtoft* between Ålesund and Molde's Torgkaia terminal (2¼ hours, Nkr145) sails two or three times daily on weekdays. Northbound, the Hurtigruten

coastal steamer leaves Storkaia in Molde at 6.30 pm and southbound, at 9.15 pm.

If you're driving towards Åndalsnes, you'll pay Nkr50 to pass through the Fanafjorden tunnel, plus Nkr20 per passenger. The Tassentunnelen shortcut, on the northbound Rv64, costs Nkr15, but can be easily circumvented by following the main road via Skaret.

AROUND MOLDE

Ona

The beautiful outer island of Ona, with its bare rocky landscapes and picturesque lighthouses, represents the epitome of an offshore fishing community. Gazing out to sea, you can probably imagine the enormous tidal wave that washed over it in 1670. It's an excellent walking and cycling venue, and makes a popular day or overnight trip from Molde. En route, WWII buffs may want to stop off at the Gossen Krigsminnesamling (☎ 71 17 30 52) on the low island of Gossa/Aukra, which is an exhibit on the Nazi wartime airstrip built by Russian POWs. It's open from noon to 5 pm daily in summer and costs Nkr30.

Self-catering accommodation is available at *Ona Rorbu* (☎ *71 27 71 77*) and the recommended *Ona Sjøhus* (☎ *71 27 60 74*). The latter has simple huts for Nkr150 per person plus Nkr50 for sheets.

If you'd rather visit Ona on a day trip, take the 8.15 am bus from Molde to Hollingsholm (30 minutes, Nkr26), which connects with a ferry to Aukra (15 minutes, Nkr17), a bus to Småge (20 minutes, Nkr20), and then a ferry No 32 to Ona (1½ hours, Nkr28), via Finnøy and Sandøy. It arrives in Ona at 11.35 am. You can then begin the return route at either noon or 3.35 pm. On Saturday from 20 June to 8 August, ferries also run between Harøysund (near Bud) and Ona (1½ hours, Nkr140 return), via Bjørnsund (30 minutes, Nkr50). They leave at 11 am from Harøysund and 3.30 pm from Ona. En route, you may want to visit the abandoned summerhouse village of Bjørnsund, where a café and shop operate in summer only.

Mardalsfossen

If you have a car and a day to spare, it's about a two-hour drive up Langfjorden and the dramatic lake, Eikesdalsvatnet, to what was once northern Europe's highest waterfall, Mardalsfossen. How could it have lost this status, you might ask? Well, in the 1970s, this two-level 655m waterfall (the greatest single drop is 297m) was extinguished by a hydroelectric project. Although environmentalists chained themselves together to prevent the construction, it went ahead and Mardalsfossen now flows only during the tourist season, between 2 June and 20 August.

Bud

Along the coastal route between Molde and Kristiansund lies the rustic little fishing village of Bud, which huddles around a compact little harbour. In the 16th and 17th centuries, it was the greatest trading centre between Bergen and Trondheim but is better known for its role in more recent history. The Ergan Kystfort (Ergan Coastal Fort), which serves as a WWII museum (☎ 71 26 15 18) and memorial, was hastily erected by Nazi forces in May 1940 and dismantled between May and November 1945. Around the hill are dispersed various armaments and a network of bunkers and soldiers' quarters. It's open from 10 am to 6 pm daily from 1 June to 30 August; guided tours are available at 11 am and 1, 3 and 5 pm. Admission costs Nkr40.

The rustic old fish restaurant *Bryggen i Bud* (☎ 71 26 11 11) serves up the local catch in a harbourfront warehouse with well ventilated floorboards. However, it attracts a lot of coach tours and the boat-shaped tables near the windows may be a tad touristy for some. Fish soup costs Nkr65, salmon is Nkr95 and other main courses range from Nkr70 to Nkr100.

If you want to stay the night, the *Blåhammer Camping* (☎ 71 26 17 03) has tent camping for Nkr90 per tent and basic four-bed cabins for Nkr225. *Bud Camping* (☎/fax 71 26 10 23) has tent sites for Nkr150 and four/six-bed huts for Nkr250/600. For supplies and fast food, there's a *Spar* market and *gatekjøkken* just inland from the harbour.

On weekdays, bus No 252 between Molde and Bud (50 minutes, Nkr55) leaves up to 10 times daily, while there are two departures on Saturday and one on Sunday.

Trollkirkja

If you're heading towards Bud and the Atlanterhavsveien, it's worth making a short side trip to the mystical cave Trollkirkja, the 'Trolls' Church'. This series of three white marble grottoes is connected by subterranean streams, and one contains a fabulous 14m waterfall. The entrance is a 2.5km, 1½-hour, uphill walk from the road, and you'll need a torch and good boots to explore it fully. From Molde, bus No 241 runs five times daily past the Trollkirkja car park.

Atlanterhavsveien

The eight storm-lashed bridges of the Atlanterhavsveien between Vevang and the island of Averøya connect 17 islands. On calm days, you may wonder what the big deal is, but in a storm, you'll experience nature's wrath at its most dramatic. Highlights include the frightfully exposed Hestskjæret Fyr lighthouse, north of Averøya, and the tongue-in-cheek 'Fish Crossing' road sign near the toll booth at Vevang. There's also a chance of observing whales and seals offshore along the route, and rock fans can check out the rather odd Steinbiten stone exhibition, at the Statoil petrol station in Bremsnes. The vehicle toll to pay for construction of all these bridges is Nkr40 per car and driver, plus Nkr10 per passenger (however, the toll is scheduled to disappear in 1999).

For accommodation, try the novel *Håholmen Havstuer* (☎ 71 61 24 12, fax 71 51 25 02), right in the middle of the route, which is run by explorer Ragnar Thorseth and his wife, Kari. Single/double rooms here cost Nkr500/800 and the 'Saga Siglar' exhibit, which concentrates on Viking voyages, is open daily in summer.

Access from the main road is by Viking ship (or at least a decent replica); from mid-June to mid- August, it leaves hourly from 11 am to 8 pm.

Another overnight option is the simple little *Sjøbua* (☎ *71 51 21 78*) cabin, which comes with a small rowboat and costs Nkr500. It's on the shore at Randøy, north of the main road and about 10km from the eastern end of the Atlanterhavsveien. There's also the appealing little *Skjerneset Camping & Rorbuer* (☎ *71 51 18 94, fax 71 61 18 15)*, in a warehouse at Skeggevika on Ekkilsøya, west of Bremsnes. This sea-oriented place has tent camping for Nkr90 and traditional three/four/six-bed rorbuer for Nkr330/450/550.

The only bus that uses this route is No 305 between Molde and Bremsnes (1¾ hours, Nkr95), which runs four times on weekdays and twice daily on weekends. From Bremsnes, there are ready ferry connections to Kristiansund (20 minutes, Nkr18).

KRISTIANSUND
Built on a series of hills across three islands, the historic cod-fishing and drying centre of Kristiansund lacks any unmissable attractions, but this little town's friendly ambience makes it a pleasant stop for a day or two, and both the new church and the offshore island of Grip are unforgettable.

Information
From 15 June to 15 August, the Kristiansund Reiselivslag (☎ 71 58 63 80, fax 71 58 63 84, destination.kristiansund@eunet.no), Vågaveien 5, is open weekdays from 8 am to 8 pm and on weekends from 10 am to 6 pm. The rest of the year, it's open weekdays from 8 am to 4 pm. The Kristiansund og Nordmøre DNT office (☎ 71 67 69 37) is found at Storgata 8/10. For books and maps, see Sverdrup Libris bookshop (☎ 71 67 17 11, www.boknett.no/sverdrup), on the corner of Kaibakken and Nedre Enggate.

At the Guest Harbour, laundry costs Nkr30 to wash and Nkr30 to dry. You can also take a shower for Nkr10.

Things to See
Kristiansund's **Gamle Byen**, or old town, occupies the island of Innlandet, where you'll find clapboard buildings dating from as early as the 17th century. The opulent Lossiusgården, at the eastern end of the historic district, is the distinguished home of an 18th century merchant. The best access from the centre is on the Piren/Sundbåt ferry (five minutes, Nkr10). Other interesting structures include the 1786 Christie-gården house; the monumental 1914 Art Nouveau-style Festiviteten, which is used for theatrical and opera productions; and the *Klippfiskkjerringa* statue by Tore Bjørn Skjøsvik, which represents a fishwife carrying cod to the drying racks. The Mellemværftet, which to many resembles a nautical junkyard, includes the remnants of Kristiansund's 1867 shipyard, an 1872 forge and workshop and 1887 workers' quarters. You can stroll through at any time, but from 8 am to 3 pm on weekdays, guided tours are available from the tourist office for Nkr10.

Milnbrygga & Norsk Klippfiskmuseum
The Norwegian Klippfish museum, in the 1749 Milnbrygga warehouse on the Gomalandet peninsula, presents the 300-year history of the dried-cod export industry in Kristiansund, and the setting is as interesting as the subject matter (it's all very fishy). It's open from noon to 5 pm Monday to Saturday and 1 to 4 pm Sunday from 21 June to 16 August. Admission is Nkr25. The easiest access from the centre is on the Piren/Sundbåt ferry (15 minutes, Nkr10).

Hjelkrembrygga
This lovely old klippfish warehouse, dating from 1835, presents an exhibit of historic sepia photographs from around Kristiansund's harbour area. It's open from 1 to 4 pm on Sunday from 21 June to 16 August. Admission costs Nkr20. The neighbouring Woldbrygga (☎ 71 67 15 78) displays a collection of wooden boats and rope-manufacturing equipment in an old 1875 barrel factory, but it's only open by appointment.

Kirkelandet Kirke

One Kristiansund building that can't be ignored is architect Odd Østby's Kirkelandet Church, which was built in 1964 to replace the one bombed by the Nazis in 1940. From the exterior, this utterly bizarre building, which was intended to expand on the theme 'Rock Crystal among Roses', appears to have taken a hell of a karate chop, but inside, the 320 panes of stained glass create an inspiring effect. Moving upward from the earthy colours at the base, they lighten

and at the top, attempt to admit the 'celestial light of heaven'. Behind lies the large Vanndammene Park area, with plenty of greenery and walking tracks. The church is open from 10 am to 7 pm from 1 May to 31 August, and from 10 am to 2 pm the rest of the year. Admission is free.

Nordmøre Museum The worthwhile Nordmøre Museum, near the Atlanten camping ground, includes regional archaeological artefacts from as early as 7000 BC, as well

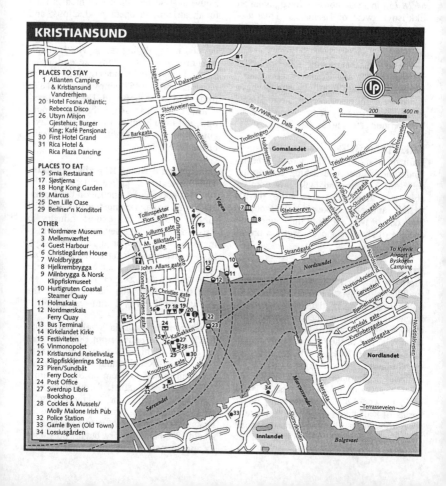

KRISTIANSUND

PLACES TO STAY
1 Atlanten Camping & Kristiansund Vandrerhjem
20 Hotel Fosna Atlantic; Rebecca Disco
26 Utsyn Misjon Gjestehus; Burger King; Kafé Pensjonat
30 First Hotel Grand
31 Rica Hotel & Rica Plaza Dancing

PLACES TO EAT
5 Smia Restaurant
17 Sjøstjerna
18 Hong Kong Garden
19 Marcus
25 Den Lille Oase
29 Berliner'n Konditori

OTHER
2 Nordmøre Museum
3 Mellemværftet
4 Guest Harbour
6 Christiegården House
7 Woldbrygga
8 Hjelkrembrygga
9 Milnbrygga & Norsk Klippfiskmuseet
10 Hurtigruten Coastal Steamer Quay
11 Holmakaia
12 Nordmørskaia Ferry Quay
13 Bus Terminal
14 Kirkelandet Kirke
15 Festiviteten
16 Vinmonopolet
21 Kristiansund Reiselivslag
22 Klippfiskkjerringa Statue
23 Piren/Sundbåt Ferry Dock
24 Post Office
27 Sverdrup Libris Bookshop
28 Cockles & Mussels/ Molly Malone Irish Pub
32 Police Station
33 Gamle Byen (Old Town)
34 Lossiusgården

as an old *stabbur*, a historic smokehouse and an early waterwheel. It's open from 10 am to 2 pm Tuesday to Friday and from noon to 3 pm on Sunday. Admission costs Nkr20.

Grip

Crowded onto a tiny rocky island, the colourful village of Grip sits amid an archipelago of 80 islets and skerries, and makes a wonderful day trip from Kristiansund. In the period between 1780 and 1820, a drop in the cod fishery and two powerful storms (1796 and 1804) left the village crushed and practically abandoned. Although it eventually bounced back to become Norway's smallest municipality, in 1964 it was appended to Kristiansund.

The stave church on the island was originally constructed in the late 15th century, the current structure was built in 1621 (opening hours correspond with the arrival of the ferry), and on an offshore skerry rises the lovely 47m Bratthårskollen lighthouse, built in 1888.

From 15 May to 30 August, the ferry M/S *Gripskyss* (☎ 71 68 26 16 or ☎ 92 28 65 58) plies the 14km between Kristiansund and Grip (30 minutes, Nkr140 return) twice daily from Monday to Saturday and three times on Sunday. Accommodation bookings are available through the Kristiansund tourist office.

Places to Stay

The recommended *Atlanten Camping* (☎ 71 67 11 04, fax 71 67 24 05), which lies within reasonable walking distance of the centre, charges Nkr60/80 per tent/caravan and Nkr10 per person. Best of all, these rates include hot showers and the use of kitchen facilities. Cabins range from Nkr270 to Nkr490. The same complex is also the home of the *Kristiansund Vandrerhjem*, which charges Nkr125 for dorm beds and Nkr200/300 for single/double motel-style rooms.

Near Kjevik airport on Nordlandet island is pleasantly-located *Byskogen Camping* (☎ 71 58 40 20), which offers tent camping amid the trees for Nkr30 per person, cara-

van camping for Nkr100 per vehicle (including electricity), dorm beds for Nkr125, and cabins with varying amenities for Nkr280 to Nkr570. From the centre, take the Vikan bus that runs about half-hourly from Monday to Saturday and from 3.30 to 10.30 pm on Sunday (15 minutes, Nkr13).

The hotel scene in Kristiansund is fairly standard. The cheapest deal is the *Utsyn Misjon Gjestehus* (☎ 71 67 33 05, Kongens Plass 4), which charges Nkr285/385 for basic single/double rooms. It has an attached café. Next up the scale is the *Hotel Fosna Atlantic* (☎ 71 67 40 11), with rooms for Nkr545/740 in summer and on weekends. The best choice, however, is probably the *First Hotel Grand* (☎ 71 67 30 11), with summer and weekend rates from around Nkr590/790. The similar *Rica Hotel* (☎ 71 67 64 11, Storgata 41) charges from Nkr565/710 on weekends and Nkr625/750 on summer weekdays.

Places to Eat

Den Lille Oase (☎ 71 67 14 80, Kongens Plass) is a popular place that has been around for decades and is known for its inexpensive fare and agreeable outdoor seating. Hot dogs cost from Nkr18 to Nkr23, *lapskaus* (Norwegian beef stew) sausage is Nkr30 to Nkr35, chicken or schnitzel costs Nkr55 and burgers are up to Nkr35. Local youth and families frequent the *Burger King* and the *Kafé Pensjonat* upstairs is a popular hang-out for local seniors.

The atmospheric *Smia Restaurant* (☎ 71 67 11 70, Fosnagata 30), in an old waterfront boathouse, predictably specialises in seafood. Its famous fish soup costs Nkr56, assorted fish dishes cost around Nkr225, and landlubbers' steak and lamb dishes are Nkr160 to Nkr180. For seafood, you can also try *Sjøstjerna* (☎ 71 67 87 78), with outdoor seating right in the shopping district. Mussels or salmon cost Nrk90, main fish courses range from Nrk118 to Nkr178, paella is Nkr128 and it also serves pasta dishes, lamb and steak for mid-range prices.

Chinese specialities are the forte at the adjacent *Hong Kong Garden* (☎ 71 67 55 60).

The *Marcus* (☎ *71 67 84 35)* specialises in Mexican and Italian fare, with nachos for Nkr98, fajitas for Nkr138, excellent small/large pizzas for Nkr79/98, salads for Nkr49 to Nkr69 and fish from Nkr112.

For a quick breakfast of coffee and pastry, visit the *Berliner'n Konditori*. The Vinmonopolet is on the corner of Langveien and Helsingsgata.

Entertainment

For intensive drinking action, try the rough and smoky *Cockles & Mussels/Molly Malone Irish Pub*, which is open daily from noon to 1 am. The *Rebecca* disco appeals to ages 23 to 35, the *Rica Plaza Dancing* (☎ *71 67 64 11)* is aimed at everyone over 30 and the *Tropicana*, just opposite, caters to the 18 to 25 crowd.

Getting There & Away

Air The Kjevik airport is on Nordlandet island. Braathens SAFE has at least eight flights daily to and from Oslo, as well as direct flights to and from Bergen, Ålesund, Molde and Trondheim.

Bus The main bus terminal lies immediately north of the Nordmørskaia quay. The Nor-Way Bussekspress Vestlandekspressen runs daily on weekdays between Kristiansund and Ålesund (3¾ hours, Nkr206), via Molde (1¾ hours, Nkr109). A Mørelinjen bus has least three daily services between

Kristiansund and Oppdal (4¾ hours, Nkr223), which connect with trains to Oslo and Trondheim. The same company also has several daily bus departures to Trondheim (5½ hours, Nkr281).

Car & Motorcycle For drivers on the E39, the Krifast toll tunnel between Gjemnes and the island of Frei costs Nkr55 per car and driver plus Nkr20 per passenger.

Boat For day trips to the eastern end of the Atlanterhavsveien, the 1771 Bremsnes church and the Bremsneshatten cave, you can take the Bremsnes ferry (20 minutes, Nkr18) from Holmakaia quay. Express boats connect Kristiansund with Trondheim (3½ hours, Nkr370) two or three times daily from Nordmørskaia and the Hurtigruten coastal steamer also calls in daily at Holmakaia. Southbound, it departs at 5 pm and northbound, at 11 pm.

Getting Around

Town buses cost Nkr13 per ride, and there are frequent Flybuss services to Kjevik airport (20 minutes, Nkr35). The Piren/Sundbåt ferry circulates from the town centre to the islands of Innlandet and Nordlandet, and the peninsula, Gomalandet. It runs constantly from Monday to Friday, 6.45 am to 4.35 pm, and on Saturday from 8.40 am to 1.30 pm. The full circuit takes 20 minutes and any portion of it costs Nkr10.

Trøndelag

TRONDHEIM

The lively university town of Trondheim (population 144,000) is Norway's third-largest city and its first capital (some purists still refer to it by its early name, Trondhjem). The town has had a rich medieval history, and most visitors find it a surprisingly agreeable place to explore on foot.

History

The site of Trondheim was determined by the Christian King Olav Tryggvason, who, in 997, selected this broad sandbank at the river Nid estuary (Nidaros) to moor his longboat. The town's natural harbour and strategic position at the river mouth made it especially useful for defence against the warlike pagan chiefs of Lade, who were a perceived threat to Christianity – and to stability – in the region. It is believed that Leifur Eiríksson visited the king's farm two years after its founding and, over the following winter, was converted to Christianity. By the spring, he'd set sail for Iceland, from where he went on to settle in Greenland and, in turn, became the first European to set foot in North America.

Until 1217 Nidaros served as the capital of Norway and ruled an empire extending, for a time, from what is now western Russia to the shores of Newfoundland. After King Olav Haraldsson was martyred in battle at Stiklestad in 1030 and canonised the following year, Nidaros became a pilgrimage centre for people from all over Europe. When Norway became a separate bishopric in 1153, Nidaros also emerged as the ecumenical centre over all of Norway, as well as Orkney, the Isle of Man, the Faroe Islands, Iceland and Greenland. The cult of St Olav continued until the Reformation in 1537, when Norway was placed under the Lutheran bishopric of Denmark.

After a fire razed most of the city in 1681, Trondheim was redesigned with wide streets and a Renaissance flair by General

HIGHLIGHTS

- Touring the Nidaros Cathedral, Norway's most sacred building
- Visiting the medieval battlefield at Stiklestad, where St Olav met his untimely fate
- Widening your musical horizons at Trondheim's Ringve Musikkhistorisk Museum (Ringve Museum of Music History)
- Being able to honestly claim that you've been to Hell and back
- Joining the students of Trondheim hiking through the wilderness of Bymarka, right in the city's backyard
- Sailing out to the charmingly preserved fishing village of Sør-Gjæslingan, near Rørvik

Caspar de Cicignon. Today, the Nidaros Cathedral spire remains the highest point in town.

TRØNDELAG

Orientation

Central Trondheim is easy to explore on foot, occupying a triangular peninsula bordered by the river Nidelva to the south and east, and Trondheimsfjorden to the north. The train station, bus terminal and Hurtigruten coastal steamer quay are over the canal, immediately north of the centre.

Activity focuses on the Torvet (also spelt Torget), or central square, which bustles with fruit vendors and enjoys a well framed view of Nidaros Cathedral. Around it, you'll find the tourist office, a fine statue of the saintly King Olav, and the 13th century stone church, Vår Frue Kirke (Church of Our Lady). In June, July and August, the church is open from 10 am to 1 pm Tuesday to Friday.

Maps The map in the tourist office's free Trondheim Guide usually suffices for most visitors, but the tourist office also distributes the more detailed public transport map produced by Trondheim Trafikkselskap.

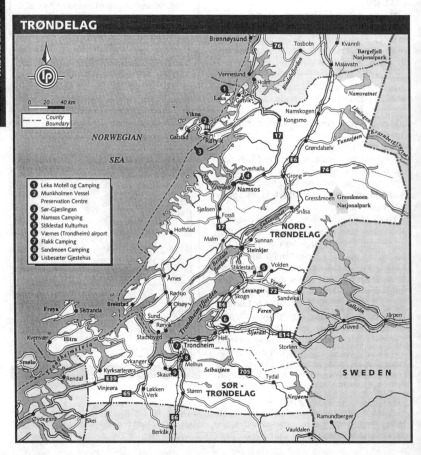

TRØNDELAG

1 Leka Motell og Camping
2 Munkholmen Vessel Preservation Centre
3 Sør-Gjæslingan
4 Namsos Camping
5 Stiklestad Kulturhus
6 Værnes (Trondheim) airport
7 Flakk Camping
8 Sandmoen Camping
9 Lisbesæter Gjestehus

Information

Tourist Office The helpful Trondheim Aktivum tourist office (☎ 73 92 93 94, fax 73 51 53 00, firmapost@taas.no, www.taas .no), Postboks 2102, N-7001 Trondheim, located on the Torvet, is open from late June to early August, from 8.30 am to 10 pm on weekdays and 10 am to 8 pm on weekends. For most of May, June and August, it opens until 8 pm on weekdays and 6 pm on weekends. The rest of the year it's open weekdays from 9 am to 4 pm. There's also a desk at Trondheim Sentralstasjon (☎ 72 57 20 20) which is open daily, year-round, from early morning until 11.30 pm.

Post & Communications You'll find the main post office at Dronningens gate 10 and the telecommunications office at Kongens gate 8. Internet access at the public library on Kongens gate is available until 4 pm on weekdays and until 2 pm Saturday, and at the Vitensenteret (for hours and admission, see later in this section).

Emergency Services Emergency numbers are the same as in most places in Norway: fire ☎ 110, police ☎ 112 and ambulance ☎ 113. The hospital emergency room number is ☎ 73 52 25 00 and the 24-hour chemist/pharmacy is St Olav Vakt-apotek (☎ 73 52 66 66) on Kjøpmannsgata, near the Bakke Bru.

Laundry The Elefanten Vaskeri self-service laundrette at Mellomveien 20 charges Nkr30 per load to wash. It's open from 10 am to 6 pm weekdays and 11 am to 4 pm Saturday.

Nidaros Domkirke & Erkebispegården

The grand Nidaros Cathedral, Trondheim's most dominant landmark and Scandinavia's largest medieval building, was first constructed as the Kristkirken, or Christ's Church, under the orders of King Olav Kyrre in 1070. The altar was placed over the original grave of St Olav, the Viking king who replaced the Nordic pagan religion with Christianity (see History in the Facts about Norway chapter). When Norway became a separate archbishopric in 1153, a larger cathedral was begun. The current transept and chapter house were constructed between 1130 to 1180 and reveal Anglo-Norman influences, while the Gothic-style nave, choir and octagon were completed around the early 14th century.

The church has been damaged by fire five times, most seriously in 1531, when only a few walls were left and intensive reconstruction was required. Some of the original gargoyles and carved stones from the early church were recycled into the new building but weren't discovered until major renovation work began in 1869. Many of the bits left intact have been rejoined and are now on display in the Archbishop's Palace (see later in this section).

From mid-June to mid-August, the cathedral is open weekdays from 9 am to 6.15 pm; from 1 May to 21 June and 17 August to 14 September it's open from 9 am to 3 pm; and the rest of the year from noon to 2.30 pm. It always closes at 2 pm on Saturday and is open from 1 to 4 pm (to 3 pm in winter) on Sunday. Admission is Nkr20 (except for Sunday services, which are held at 11 am and 6 pm; the 6 pm service on the third Sunday of the month is in English). Especially worth noting are the vibrantly coloured modern stained-glass work and the ornately embellished exterior west wall, which is lined with statues of biblical characters and Norwegian bishops and kings. For information on special cathedral musical programs, phone ☎ 73 94 52 69.

Norwegian coronations take place here and visitors can view the crown jewels on summer weekdays (except Friday) and on Saturday from 9 am to 12.30 pm and on Sunday from 1 to 4 pm. The rest of the year they can be seen on Friday only from noon to 2 pm. From mid-June to mid-August, you can climb the cathedral tower for a rooftop view over the city (Nkr5).

Admission to the cathedral also includes the adjacent 12th century Erkebispegården (Archbishop's Palace). It was commissioned by Archbishop Øystein Erlandsson

TRØNDELAG

Along the Pilgrims' Way

Nidaros Cathedral was built on the site of the grave of St Olav, who was canonised and declared a martyr after his death at the battle of Stiklestad on 29 July 1030. Since then, the cult of St Olav has grown in popularity and 340 churches have now been dedicated to St Olav in Scandinavia, Britain, Russia, the Baltic States, Poland, Germany and the Netherlands. As a result, pilgrims from all over Europe have journeyed to his grave at Nidaros, making it the most popular pilgrimage site in all of northern Europe. Historically, both the rich and poor journeyed from Oslo for up to 25 days, while others braved longer sea voyages from as far away as Iceland, Greenland, Orkney and the Faroe Islands. In fact, the grave of St Olav became the northern compass point for European pilgrims, whose other spiritual cornerstones were Rome in the south, Jerusalem in the east, and Santiago de Compostela in the west.

The routes taken by these pilgrims as they travelled from church to church and village to village acted as arteries for the spread of the cult of St Olav. During medieval times, the journey itself was considered an exercise in unity with God, and the early pilgrimage routes, with wild mountains, forests and rivers to cross, provided the pilgrims with time to reflect, and ultimately, insights into the hardships of life's journey into eternity. Most pilgrims thus chose to travel on foot, while the better off journeyed on horseback. Those without means were forced to rely on local hospitality along the way and, in Norway, travelling pilgrims were always held in high esteem and openly welcomed.

In 1994, the Pilgrims' Way project of the Norwegian Ministry of Environment revived the ancient pilgrimage route between Oslo and Trondheim. The rugged way, which consists mainly of mountain tracks and gravelled roads, has now been marked and St Olav devotees are officially encouraged to follow the ancient pilgrimage routes, not only for religious purposes, but also for outdoor enjoyment and participation in Norwegian history and cultural awareness. The present Pilgrims' Way, which follows ancient, documented trails and is marked by posts bearing the Pilgrims' Way logo, provides modern wanderers with the opportunity to relive the experiences of the historic pilgrims. All along the way, the path is marked with place names and monuments linked to the life and works of St Olav, as well as a number of ancient burial mounds and other historic monuments.

If you're interested in further information, contact the Pilegrimskontoret (Pilgrim Office; ☎ 22 11 19 05), Kristian IVs gate 15, N-0164 Oslo. The office also sells the best English-language publication about the route, *On the Pilgrim Way to Trondheim*.

around 1160 and is the oldest secular building in Scandinavia. The new wings, which were rebuilt after a fire in 1983, now house a museum. The displays on the 1st and 2nd floors focus on the history of the cathedral and include the recycled carvings from the original cathedral. You'll see everything from kings, queens and saints (including St Denis, with head in hand) to fantasy gargoyles and a spouting toad from the cathedral fountain. In the basement are excavations from the original palace, which include the drinking horn of Archbishop Bolt, who served from 1428 to 1450; the tile floor of the original armoury, which dates from around 1500; a royal mint used from 1500 to 1520; and an array of early coinage. The history of the cathedral construction is recounted in an audiovisual program entitled 'To the Glory of God'.

If antique swords, armour and cannons sound interesting, you can also visit the adjoining Rustkammeret military museum, which recounts the days from 1700 to 1900, when the Archbishop's Palace served as a Danish military installation. Also attached is the Hjemmesfront Museum, which tells of Trondheim's role in the resistance movement during the WWII Nazi occupation of Norway. From June to August, the museums are open from 9 am to 3 pm weekdays and 11 am to 4 pm on weekends. They're open weekends only from February to May and September to November. Admission to both costs Nkr5.

Old Trondheim

The older sections of Trondheim are great places to stroll and imagine how life was in medieval times and in the great trading periods that followed. The cobblestoned streets of the Hospitalsløkkan area, immediately south of the canal, are lined with wooden buildings dating from the mid-19th century. Note especially the octagonal 1705 timber church known as Hospitalskirken in the grounds of the historic hospital founded in 1277.

The picturesque Gamle Bybro (Old Town Bridge) was originally constructed in 1681 but the current structure dates from 1861. A stroll across it offers a superb view of the Bryggen, a line-up of 18th and 19th century riverfront warehouses reminiscent of their better known counterparts in Bergen. Immediately to the east, at the foot of Kristiansten Festning (Kristiansten Fort), lies the revived working-class neighbourhoods of Møllenberg and Bakklandet, which are now full of trendy shops, bars and cafés.

You may also want to have a look at the renowned Ravnkloa fish market, beside the canal at the northern end of Munkegata; you'll smell it before you see it.

Kristiansten Festning

For an overall view, climb 10 minutes from the Gamle Bybro to the Kristiansten Fort, constructed after the great fire of 1681 to protect the city from conquests, such as the one attempted by the Swedish in 1718. During WWII, the Nazis used the fort as a prison and execution ground for members of the Norwegian Resistance movement. It's open daily, June to August, from 10 am (11 am on weekends) to 3 pm. Admission to the dungeon, including a guided tour, costs Nkr10.

Tyholt-Tårnet

The prominent 74m telecommunications tower on the hill about 1km north-east of Kristiansten Fort contains the rotating *Galaksen Restaurant* (☎ 73 51 31 66) and presents a fine overall view of Trondheim and surroundings. A trip to the top costs Nkr25, but it's refunded if you have a meal at the restaurant. Both the restaurant and tower are open from 11.30 am to 11 pm Monday to Saturday and noon to 6 pm Sunday. From the centre, take bus No 20 or 60.

Medieval Church Ruins

During excavations for the new library, archaeologists found the ruins of a medieval church, thought to be part of the 12th century church, Olavskirken. You can see part of the ruins and some well preserved skeletons in the courtyard during library opening hours. In the basement of the bank Sparebanken, Søndre gate 4, are the ruins of the medieval **Gregorius Kirke**, which were also discovered during excavations for the new building. They're open to the public during banking hours.

Stiftsgården

The lovely old timber mansion, Stiftsgården (☎ 73 52 24 73), on Munkegata, was constructed between 1774 and 1778 and is now the official royal residence in Trondheim. From 1 June to 20 August, it's open from 10 am to 5 pm Tuesday to Saturday (until 3 pm from 1 to 19 June) and on Sunday from noon to 5 pm (however, it's closed when the king is in residence). Admission is Nkr30.

Trøndelag Folkemuseum

The open-air Trøndelag Folk Museum (☎ 73 89 01 00), west of the centre at Sverresborg, adjoins the ruins of King Sverre's castle and opens up onto fine hilltop views of the city. It contains over 60 period buildings, including a collection of 18th to early 20th century structures arranged around an old-town market square; numerous farm buildings from rural Trøndelag; and the small Haltdalen stave church, which dates back to 1170. There's also a ski museum featuring the history of skiing in Trøndelag and the achievements of local skiers. It's open daily from 11 am to 6 pm from 20 May to 31 August. It makes a nice 40-minute stroll from the centre, or you can take bus No 8 or 9 (direction Stavset or Byåsen Heimdal) from Dronningens gate. Admission is Nkr40.

Ringve Botaniske Hage & Ringve Musikkhistorisk Museum

The Ringve Botanical Gardens (☎ 73 92 24 11), 2km north-east of the centre, provide a quiet green setting for strolling. Set in the middle at Lade Allé 60 is the 18th century estate Ringve Gård, which houses the Ringve Museum of Music History. This highly worthwhile museum displays collections of musical instruments from around the world and is a highlight of Trondheim. The requisite tours are led by music students who demonstrate the an-

tique musical instruments on display. From 14 June to 10 August, tours are held in English at 11 am and 12.30, 2.30 and 4.30 pm daily. In late August they drop the 4.30 pm tour; from mid-May to mid-June there are tours at 11.30 am and 2.30 pm; and the rest of the year, they run either once daily or on Sunday only. Admission costs Nkr50.

Ringve is a pleasant 2km walk from the bus terminal and train station, but you can also take bus No 3 or 4 from Munkegata. While you're in the area, it's also worth strolling along the coastal track that fringes the Ladé peninsula.

Vitenskapsmuseet NTNU

The Museum of Natural History & Archaeology (☎ 73 59 21 45), Erling Skakkes gate 47, belongs to NTNU, the Norwegian University of Science & Technology. This comprehensive museum contains a hotch-potch of exhibits on the natural and human history of the Trondheim area: reconstructions of old-town streets and homes; a rundown of Norway's ecclesiastical history; archaeological excavations from the Stone Age through medieval times; the Southern Sami culture; and the natural history of all major Norwegian environments. From 2 May to 14 September, opening hours are from 10 am to 5 pm weekdays (weekends from 11 am). Admission is Nkr25.

Nordenfjeldske Kunstindustrimuseum

The eclectic Museum of Applied Art (☎ 73 52 13 11), Munkegata 5, exhibits a fine collection of contemporary arts and crafts ranging from Japanese pottery by Shoji Hamada to tapestries by Norway's highly acclaimed tapestry artist, Hannah Ryggen. It's open from 10 am to 5 pm weekdays and noon to 5 pm on Sunday from 20 June to 20 August, but closes earlier the rest of the year. Admission is Nkr30.

Trondhjems Kunstmuseum

The Trondheim Art Museum (☎ 73 52 66 71), Bispegata 7, houses a collection of modern Norwegian and Danish arts from

1800 on, including a hallway of Munch lithographs. From 1 June to 30 August, it's open daily except Tuesday and Saturday from 10 am to 4 pm (Thursday until 6 pm). Admission is Nkr30. Free guided tours run on Sunday at 1 pm.

Trondheims Sjøfartsmuseum

The cosy Trondheim Maritime Museum (☎ 73 52 89 75), housed in an old prison at Fjordgata 6A, is an appealing little place full of relics from 18th century whaling ships and frigates; navigational instruments; and models, paintings and photos of historic sailing ships. It's open from 8.30 am to 5 pm weekdays, 9 am to 3 pm Saturday and 11 am to 3 pm Sunday from 1 June to 31 August. Admission costs Nkr25.

Special Interest Museums

If you're around on the first Sunday of the month, from noon to 3 pm, you may want to visit Det Jødiske Museum (The Jewish Museum; ☎ 73 52 20 30), which is housed in the Synagogue at Arkitekt Christies gate 1B. It's also open for groups by pre-arrangement. Another special interest museum is the Norsk Døvehistorisk Museum (Museum of Norwegian Deaf History; ☎ 73 52 62 06), Bispegata 9B. It reveals the challenges, technical aids and accomplishments of deaf people through the ages. Entry is by pre-arrangement only.

Children will probably enjoy the Vitensenteret (☎ 73 59 61 23), the Science Centre in the old Norges Bank building at Kongens gate 1. Here you can conduct hands-on experiments and learn more about how the world works. It's open 1 June to 31 August from 10 am to 6 pm on weekdays (except Monday) and 11 am to 6 pm on weekends (shorter hours the rest of the year).

Munkholmen

At the time Trondheim was founded, the islet of Munkholmen – the Monks' Island – served as the town execution ground. That distinction notwithstanding, in the early 11th century it became the site of a Benedictine monastery, which stood until the

Days Out in Trondheim

The following recommendations were provided by a reader who has lived in Trondheim for several years:

Boats run between Trondheim (Pirterminalen) and Kristiansund, as well as the islands of Hitra, Frøya, Ulvøya and Fjellværøya. A few days of biking and camping on these outer islands can be a great experience if the weather is fine. However, bicycles are necessary to get around on the islands, as buses run only infrequently.

Begin at Fjellværøya (take your bike on the boat) and cycle or catch the local bus out to Ulvøya, where you can rent a *hytte* (cabin), or just put up a tent somewhere near the water (the *allemannsretten* dictates that you must be more than 150m from a structure). The little fishing community of Ulvøya is a pearl, and you can buy inexpensive cod from the docks where the fishing boats moor, on the Fjellværøya side of the bridge. Alternatively, you can hire a motorboat and catch the fish yourself. At the same place you'll also find a convenience store where you can weigh the fish you've caught or chosen to buy.

From Ulvøya and Fjellværøya you can bike to Hitra, where you're sure to see deer, as the island is crowded with them. The tourist office in Trondheim can provide advice about places to stay.

Tone Dragland

mid 17th century when the island began a series of stints as a prison, a fort and a customs house. Today, it's a popular picnicking and sunbathing venue. From late May to late August, ferries leave on the hour between 10 am and 6 pm (and more frequently on sunny weekends) from the harbour east of the Ravnkloa fish market. The fare is Nkr30 return. Guided tours of the island are available for Nkr14.

TRONDHEIM

PLACES TO STAY
3 Trondheim Bo-Bil Camp
7 Trondheim Vandrerhjem
9 Radisson SAS Royal Garden Hotel
10 Clarion Grand Olav Hotel &
    Olavshallen
18 Chesterfield Hotel
19 Rainbow Gildevangen Hotel
29 Hotel Norrøna
40 Britannia Hotel & Queens Pub
45 Pensjonat Jarlen
46 Munken Hotel
49 Rainbow Trondheim Hotell
66 Gammeldagshuset
68 Ila Privat Pensjonat
77 Singsaker Sommerhotel
78 Trondheim Inter Rail Centre,
    Edgar Café & Studentersamfundet
79 Elgeseter Hotell

PLACES TO EAT
11 Bakeri Teatret
13 Athene
14 Café Dalí
15 Grønn Pepper
16 Det Lille Franske
17 Akropolis
22 Banzara Curry House
24 Big Horn Steakhouse
27 Abelone Mat & Vinkjeller
31 Egon
37 Peppe's Pizza
41 Café Erichsen
44 Restauranthuset & Danseklubb
    Posepilten & Smoke Filmcafé
55 Benitos/Zia Teresa
58 Havfruen
60 Café Dromedar &
    Bakklandet Skydsstasjon
62 Café Gåsa
63 Bryggen Restaurant
76 Grenaderen

ENTERTAINMENT
12 Café 3-B
20 Norsk Rock Café Trondheim
23 Astoria Dansotek &
    Alex Musikkafé
28 Frakken
32 Café Replikken
33 Nova Kino (Cinema)
36 Bakke Bydelshus
43 Sake Pub
51 Dirty Nelly's
57 Café Remis
59 Briefklubben & Slarvhus
70 Prinsen Kino (Cinema)

47 Hospitalkirken
48 Police Station
50 Rema 1000 Supermarket
52 Torvet
53 Trondheim Aktivum
    Tourist Office
54 Vår Frue Kirke
61 Kristiansten Festning
64 Gamle Bybro
73 Nidaros Domkirke
80 Hospital

MUSEUMS
8 Trondheims Sjøfartsmuseum
42 Stiftsgården
56 Vitensenteret
65 Nordenfjeldske
    Kunstindustrimuseum
67 Vitenskapsmuseet NTNU
69 Det Jødiske Museum
71 Norsk Døvehistorisk
    Museum & Café Ni Muser
72 Trondhjems Kunstmuseum
74 Erkebispegården
75 Ruskammeret &
    Hjemmesfront Museum
81 Trøndelag Folkemuseum;
    Vertshuset Tavern

OTHER
1 Hurtigruten Coastal
   Steamer Quay
2 Pirterminalen Quay;
   Express Boats to Kristiansund
4 Trondheim Sentralstasjon
5 Rutebilstasjon
6 Elefanten Vaskeri
21 Hardangerfrukt Health Foods
25 Ferries to Munkholmen
26 Ravnkloa Fish Market &
    Trondheim Turistforening
    DNT Office
30 Post Office
34 St Olav Vakt-Apotek
35 Vinmonopolet
38 Library & Olavskirken Ruins
39 Sparebanken &
    Gregorius Kirke Ruins

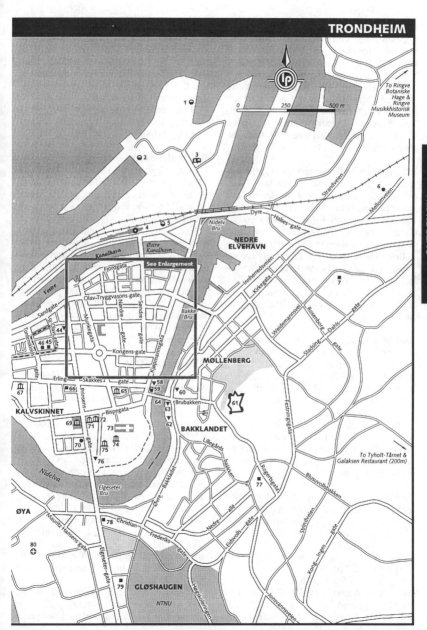

TRONDHEIM

Activities

For information on outdoor activities, contact the Trondheimsregionens Friluftsråd (☎ 72 54 65 79, trondheimsregionens-friluftsrad.postuttak@trondheim.kommune .no), Holtermannsveien 1. It also distributes the free *Friluftsliv i Trondheimsregionen* (Outdoor Life in the Trondheim Region) map showing all nearby outdoor recreation areas. The map is also available from the tourist office.

Hiking West of Trondheim spreads the Bymarka, a green woodland area laced with wilderness footpaths and ski trails. The easiest access is by bus No 11, 75 or 76 west towards Trolla, bus No 10 to the Gråkallen Skistua, or the Gråkalbanen train from St Olavsgata station to Lian, which has excellent views over the city and a good swimming lake, Kyvannet. The rather upmarket Lian Restaurant serves coffee, snacks and full meals, or you can head for the basic student coffee shops at Elgsethytta and Rønningen.

Skiing The Vassfjellet mountains, 20km due south of town, are the place to go for cross-country skiing. Take a bus or train to Melhus and walk 2km east to Løvset, where a well maintained trail heads into the hills. On weekends in the ski season, a ski bus runs directly from the Trondheim terminal to the Vassfjellet Skisenter. The Bymarka also offers excellent cross-country skiing, as does the Trondheim Skisenter Granåsen, which boasts the world's largest plastic-surfaced ski jump.

Fishing The Gaula and Orkla rivers offer good salmon fishing within an hour's drive of town. Guided sea-fishing trips are available from Trondheim Aktivum (☎ 73 92 93 94), on the Torvet.

Organised Tours

Daily at noon from 20 June to 15 August, Trondheim Aktivum (☎ 73 92 93 94) runs two-hour guided city tours (Nkr120), taking in the Trøndelag Folkemuseum, the cathedral and Archbishop's Palace, the Kristiansten Fort and the university. On Tuesday, Thursday and Saturday from 30 June to 30 July, 2½-hour guided tours (Nkr155) to the Trøndelag Folkemuseum and the Granåsen ski jump leave from the Torvet tourist office at 3 pm.

If you want to have a go at winter dog-sledding through the Bymarka, contact Fagerlund Hundesport (☎ 72 56 02 96).

Special Events

Olavsfestdagene (☎ 73 92 94 70, fax 73 50 38 66), a cultural festival in celebration of St Olav, takes place during the week around 29 July and includes a working medieval market.

Every second year, Trondheim's 25,000 university students stage the three-week ISFiT UKA ('the week') celebration (isfit@ isfit.ntnu.no, www.uka.ntnu.no), an international students' festival which amounts to a continuous party with concerts, plays, and other festivities held at the round red Studentersamfundet (student centre) on Elgesetergate. It will be held in the spring of 2001 and 2003.

Places to Stay

Camping The nearest camping ground is *Sandmoen Camping (☎ 72 88 61 35, fax 72 84 82 11)*, near Heimdal, 10km south of the city along the E6. Simple self-catering cabins for three or four people cost Nkr475 while Nkr975 will get you a large cabin with indoor facilities and space for six to eight people. Tent camping costs Nkr100/ 130 without/with a car and caravanners pay Nkr150. Take bus No 44 or the Klæbu bus and get off at the Sandmoen Camping stop.

Flakk Camping (☎ 72 84 39 00), on the beach front at Flakk, 10km west of town, has tent sites for Nkr90, caravan sites for Nkr125 and cabins (no water) from Nkr300 for four people to Nkr500 for five people. It's open from 1 May to 1 September. Take bus No 75 or 76.

If you're driving a recreational vehicle (not a caravan/trailer), you can park at the *Trondheim Bo-Bil Camp* at the Shell petrol station just north of the train station, which has a septic tank dump station.

Hostels From around 26 June to 18 August, the Samfundet organisation of university students operates the *Trondheim InterRail Centre* (☎ 73 89 95 38, tirc@ stud.ntnu.no, Elgesetergate 1), in an unusual round building known as the 'Casa Rossa' ('red house' in Italian). It's not only convenient (five minutes' walk south of the cathedral), but it's also one of Norway's friendliest and best value places at Nkr95 with breakfast and free Internet access. Best of all, there are no curfews. The attached *Edgar Café* serves good value meals (dinner costs Nkr39) and beer. In the off-season, it becomes a student hangout and informal music venue. If you hear strange noises after the nightly partying subsides, it's just the ghost of S Møller, a student who mysteriously disappeared in the 1930s.

Trondheim Vandrerhjem (☎ 73 53 04 90, fax 73 53 52 88, Weidemannsvei 44), 2km east of the train station, has dorm beds for Nkr185, with breakfast. It's open from 5 January to 22 December. Take bus No 63. More central is *Pensjonat Jarlen* (☎ 73 51 32 18, fax 73 52 80 80, Kongens gate 40), which has rooms with TV, shower and kitchenette. You'll pay Nkr150 for a dorm bed and Nkr350/450 for singles/doubles.

The good value *Singsaker Sommerhotel* (☎ 73 89 31 00, fax 73 89 32 00, Rogertsgata 1), near the Kristiansten Fort, is open from 6 June to mid-August. Dorm beds cost Nkr125/ 190 in a large/small dorm, and single/ double rooms are Nkr255/400. All rates include breakfast.

B&Bs *Gammeldagshuset* (☎/fax 73 51 55 68, Hvedingveita 8), in a beautiful old house near Leutahaven, charges Nkr420 per person, including breakfast. If you don't mind staying out of town, *Ms Inger Stock* (☎ 72 88 83 19), at Porsmyra 18 in Tiller (10km south of the centre), has single/double rooms for Nkr280/360. Take bus No 46 to Tonstadgrenda. *B Abraham*

(☎/fax 73 91 29 90), at Sildedråpsveien 4D in Angelltrøa, has simple B&B accommodation for Nkr250 per person. Take bus No 24 east from the station and get off at the Sildedråpsveien stop. A bit more central is the *Ila Privat Pensjonat* (☎ 73 51 18 80), Berglisgata 17 in Ila, 1km west of the centre. Here you'll pay Nkr250/350 for single/ double rooms. Take bus No 3 or 5 west from Kongens gate.

The tourist office also books single/ double rooms in private homes for Nkr200/ 300, plus a Nkr20 booking fee.

Self-Catering Flats If you really want to get away from it all, take a ferry to the remote archipelago of Sula (with 200 people and two cars), where you can stay in the *Sula Rorbuer* self-catering flats (☎ 73 53 34 00, fax 73 53 34 60, knuttf@online.no). In summer you'll pay Nkr2750/1000 per person for a week/weekend with two people and Nkr1400/440 per person with four people. Rates include motorboat transfers from the mainland.

Hotels The *Rainbow Trondheim Hotell* (☎ 73 50 50 50, fax 73 51 60 58, Kongens gate 15) and the turn-of-the-century *Rainbow Gildevangen Hotell* (☎ 73 51 01 00, fax 73 52 38 98, Søndre gate 22), both in the Tulip Inn-Rainbow group, have summer and weekend rates of Nkr450/690 for singles/doubles, as well as 'economy doubles' for Nkr570 on weekdays and Nkr400 on weekends.

The spartan but pleasantly central *Munken Hotel* (☎ 73 53 45 40, fax 73 53 42 60, Kongens gate 44) has single/double rooms with bath for Nkr495/595 and with shared bath for Nkr450/550. The *Elgeseter Hotell* (☎ 73 94 25 40, fax 73 93 18 73, Tromodsgata 3), three blocks south of the Elgeseter bridge, offers comfy single/double rooms for Nkr590/750 during the week and Nkr490/650 on weekends.

The *Chesterfield Hotel* (☎ 73 50 37 50, Søndre gate 26) has commodious rooms with private baths, and some rooms even have cooking facilities at no extra cost. If you want to bask in the midnight sun, ask for one of the corner rooms on the 7th floor which have huge skylights and broad city views. Rates are Nkr850/995 on weekdays and Nkr550/650 on weekends, except in July, when they're Nkr600/700.

At the elegant (some would say pretentious) and well located *Britannia Hotel* (☎ 73 53 53 53, fax 73 51 29 00, Dronningens gate 5), you'll get British-style attention to detail for the single/double summer rates of Nkr625/800. The *Hotel Norrøna* (☎ 73 80 23 00, fax 73 80 23 01, norrona .trondheim@sn.no, www.norrona.no, Thomas Angellsgata 20) is Norway's first Internet hotel, with web access for guests. Standard single/double rooms cost Nkr695/820 on weekdays and Nkr500/650 at weekends.

The *Radisson SAS Royal Garden Hotel* (☎ 73 53 22 00, fax 73 52 11 75) is a fine first-class hotel in a good central location, with all the usual amenities. The summer and weekend single/double rates of Nkr790/890 are about 60% of the normal rate. The modern and central *Clarion Grand Olav Hotel* (☎ 73 53 53 10, fax 73 53 57 20, Kjøpmannsgata 48), near the river, offers high-rise luxury over a light and airy shopping complex. Single/double rooms start at Nkr650/780.

For an out-of-town treat, you may want to head 45km south of Trondheim to Skaun, where you'll find the historic *Lisbesæter Gjestehus* (☎ 72 86 42 10, fax 72 50 47 00). In 1867, Dr Eyvind Kraft signed onto a sailing ship to America and eventually wound up in Hawaii, where he became the personal physician to the king of those islands. As fate would have it, one of the princesses fell in love with him but the king had no interest in a Norwegian son-in-law and paid Eyvind a large sum of money to go home. With this windfall he returned to Skaun and in 1890 built this lovely log structure as a sanatorium and hydrotherapy spa on the site of a medieval mountain dairy farm. It now operates as a guesthouse. Singles/doubles are good value at Nkr395/595, with breakfast. The guesthouse is open from 17 May to 5 October.

Places to Eat

Travellers stumbling off the night train can head to *Det Lille Franske* (Søndre gate 25), which opens at 8 am on weekdays and serves coffee and pastries at pavement tables. *Bakeri Teatret* in the Olavskvartalet cultural centre has hearty sandwiches and pizza slices from Nkr25. One of the best deals is *Peppe's Pizza* (☎ 73 50 73 73), in a historic building on the Bryggen waterfront, which has pizza and salad lunch buffets for Nkr74.

An inexpensive student haunt is the popular *Café Dalí* (☎ 73 50 34 90, Brattørgata 7). *Café ni Museer*, in a period house at the art gallery at Bispegata 9, is a casual spot with inexpensive light meals and an arty crowd – it's busiest on sunny afternoons when the outdoor terrace doubles as a beer garden. Trondheim's first coffee bar, the *Dromedar*, near the Bakklandet end of the Gamle Bybro, is a longstanding local favourite. A well established café and restaurant that attracts clientele of all ages is the *Café Erichsen* (☎ 73 52 52 23, Nørdre gate 8).

Grønn Pepper, a Mexican restaurant with two outlets (☎ 73 51 66 44, Søndre gate 17; and ☎ 73 53 26 30, Fjordgata 7), has a lunch special of four tacos with rice and salad for Nkr55 until 4 pm Monday to Saturday. *Egon* has a good Nkr65 pizza-and-salad buffet served until 6 pm daily. For Greek cuisine, try the *Athene* (☎ 73 53 50 53, Brattørgata 5) or the *Akropolis* (☎ 73 51 67 51, Fjordgata 9). The *Banzara Curry House* (☎ 73 52 21 08, Ørjaveita 4), behind the Astoria Hotel, serves up Indian food, but is also known as a good place for a beer. *Benitos/Zia Teresa* (☎ 73 52 64 22, Vår Frue Strete 4), a cosy Italian bistro, does Nkr65 pasta and salad-bar specials on weekdays from noon to 3 pm. At other times, main dishes start at around Nkr75. The gregarious owner, who bears a striking resemblance to Luciano Pavarotti, is often asked to provide operatic accompaniment.

For a thoroughly Norwegian experience try the *Vertshuset Tavern* (☎ 73 52 09 32) in Sverresborg, an 18th century inn, near the folk museum, which serves traditional Norwegian meals from Nkr100. The **Grenaderen** (☎ 73 51 66 80), near the Archbishop's Palace, offers typical Norwegian cuisine and outside seating. The homy and recommended **Café Gåsa** (☎ 73 51 58 36, Øvre Bakklandet 8), just south-east of the Gamle Bybro, offers an original international menu and strolling geese.

The cosy Viking-style **Abelone Mat & Vinkjeller** (☎ 73 53 24 70, Dronningens gate 15) specialises in large hunks of meat (for Norway, anyway). Another steakhouse of note is the American-style **Big Horn Steakhouse** (☎ 73 50 94 90, Munkegata 14), near Ravnkloa. For fish dishes, your best options are the **Havfruen** (☎ 73 53 26 26, Kjøpmannsgata 7) and the **Bryggen Restaurant** (☎ 73 52 02 30, Bakklandet 66), just over the Gamle Bybro.

The **Restauranthuset & Danseklubb Posepilten** (☎ 73 50 27 05, Prinsens gate 32) specialises in Turkish, Bosnian, Palestinian, Greek and Norwegian cuisine. Kebabs cost from Nkr69 to Nkr89, falafels are Nkr69 and vegetarian pitas cost Nkr59. Moussaka is Nkr135; lamb, beef and fish dishes range from Nkr149 to Nkr169; and chicken costs from Nkr110.

There's a small health food store, **Hardangerfrukt**, at Fjordgata 62. For more standard fare, **Rema 1000** at Torvet has good prices on groceries and bakery items – or you can munch on inexpensive fish cakes from the Ravnkloa fish market.

Entertainment

Nightlife As a student town, Trondheim offers a heaping serving of nightlife. **Studentersamfundet** (Elgesetergate 1) is a student centre featuring a lively pub, cinema and alternative music performances. During the school year the main party night is Friday, but in summer most activities gear down and the centre converts into a travellers' crash pad (see Places to Stay, earlier).

Fans of English footy will love the **Queens Pub** (☎ 73 53 53 53) in the Britannia Hotel, where you'll see all the home matches on TV. A less specialist sports café

is the **Dockers Bar**, near the northern end of Nørdre gate. The lively Irish pub **Dirty Nelly's**, near the Torvet, is especially popular with tourists. A louder venue is the large **Norsk Rock Café Trondheim**, near the corner of Fjordgata and Nørdre gate, with live rock bands. If you just want to drink, try the **Bakke Bydelshus** or the **Bakklandet Skydsstation** (☎ 73 92 10 44), both in the historic Bakkland area east of the river.

The **Briefklubben & Slarvhus**, near the west end of the Gamle Bybro, is a great pub with live music at weekends. If you prefer to dress in black and discuss Karl Marx, check out **Café 3-B** on Brattørgata. For a Japanese spin, there's the **Sake Pub**, near the corner of Olav Tryggvasons gate and Prinsens gate. Ballroom dancing is the speciality at the **Astoria Dansotek** (Olav Tryggvasons gate 26), and the attached **Alex Musikkafé** is known for live jazz music. The **Frakken**, on Dronningens gate, is a nightclub and piano bar featuring both Norwegian and foreign musicians. The cosy **Café Replikken**, on Olav Tryggvasons gate, is known for its quiet nature and frequent poetry readings. The most popular gay bar, **Café Remis** (☎ 73 52 05 52, Kjøpmannsgata 12), is often regarded as the best disco in town.

Cultural Events & Cinema The main concert hall, Olavshallen, at the Olavskvartalet cultural centre, hosts a range of performers from the Trondheim Symphony Orchestra to international rock and jazz musicians. Most performances are held between September and May.

The local theatre group **Avant Gården** (☎ 73 52 08 98, Olav Tryggvasons gate 44) presents popular works, some in English, and there are also two **cinemas**, Nova Kino and Prinsen Kino (☎ 73 52 15 52).

Getting There & Away

Air The Værnes airport, 32km east of Trondheim, is served by both SAS and Braathens SAFE to and from all major Norwegian cities, as well as to and from Stockholm and Copenhagen. Widerøe flies between Værnes and Sandefjord (near Oslo), Namsos, Rørvik, Brønnøysund and all of northern Norway. This is not only the best value way to go, but the smaller aircraft also provide the most scenic flights in the country.

Bus The new city bus terminal (Rutebilstasjon) adjoins the Trondheim Sentralstasjon (also known as Trondheim S).

As the main link between southern and northern Norway, Trondheim is a bus transport crossroads, of sorts, and Nor-Way Bussekspress services run at least daily to Oslo (9¼ hours, Nkr495), Bergen (14¾ hours, Nkr760), Ålesund (eight hours, Nkr405) and Namsos (3¾ hours, Nkr230). For bus access to Narvik and points north you first need to travel by train to Fauske or Bodø.

Train For train information, phone ☎ 72 57 20 20.There are half a dozen daily trains to Oslo (6¾ hours, Nkr590) and two to Fauske (9¼ hours, Nkr670) and Bodø (10 hours, Nkr680). If you're in a rush to head north, consider taking the overnight train from Oslo, drop your luggage in a locker and spend a day exploring Trondheim before continuing on an overnight train to Bodø (which passes through Hell just before midnight). Between Trondheim and Oslo you can also travel via Røros (two hours, Nkr210) and Hamar (six hours, Nkr470). Most journeys necessitate a change in Hamar.

Trains also run from Trondheim to Storlien in Sweden (two hours, Nkr130) at 7.50 am and 3.49 pm daily, with onward connections to Stockholm.

Car & Motorcycle The E6, the main north-south motorway, passes through the heart of the city. On weekdays between 6 am and 6 pm, drivers entering the city must pay a toll of Nkr12 (the motorway toll into town also covers the city toll, so keep your receipt). For car hire, Avis (☎ 73 52 69 15) is at Kjøpmannsgata 34 and Budget (☎ 73 51 89 00) is at Kjøpmannsgata 73.

Boat On its northbound journey, the Hurtigruten coastal steamer arrives in Trondheim at 6 am and departs at noon heading for Rørvik (9¼ hours, Nkr557), Bodø (24½ hours, Nkr1117), Tromsø (50¾ hours, Nkr1668) and points farther east. Southbound, it arrives at 6.30 am and departs at 10 am for Kristiansund (seven hours, Nkr411) and Bergen (28½ hours, Nkr1159).

Fossen Trafikklag's Kystekspressen boats (☎ 72 57 20 20) between Trondheim and Kristiansund (3½ hours, Nkr370) depart from the Pirterminalen quay.

Getting Around

To/From the Airport
Airport buses, or Flybussen (Nkr45), leave from the Leutahaven terminal on the corner of Erling Skakkes gate and Kalvskinnsgata, in conjunction with SAS, Braathens SAFE and Widerøe flights. They also stop at the train station and the Britannia and Royal Garden hotels.

Taxis (☎ 73 50 50 73 or ☎ 74 83 75 00) to the airport cost from Nkr400 to Nkr500. If you're on a budget you can request a shared taxi, which costs Nkr200 per person. Also, trains run eight times daily between Trondheim and the Værnes airport station (40 minutes, Nkr47).

Bus The centre of Trondheim is easily explored on foot, but to reach some attractions – for example, the Trøndelag Folkemuseum at Sverresborg or the Ringve Museum of Music History – most people prefer to take a bus. The city bus service, Trondheim Trafikkselskap (☎ 72 57 20 20), has its central transit point on the corner of Munkegata and Dronningens gate, and all lines stop here. Bus and tram fare costs Nkr17 per ride (or Nkr45 for a 24-hour ticket), and you must have exact change.

Tram Trondheim's only tram line, the Gråkalbanen, runs west from St Olavs gate to Lian, in the heart of the Bymarka. On Saturdays in summer antique trolleys run along this route. Transfers are available from city buses.

Car & Motorcycle Drivers and motorcyclists should note that metered parking zones are marked *P Mot avgift* or *P Avgift*. Green meters cost Nkr3 per hour and red meters are Nkr5 for 15 minutes, with a 30-minute maximum.

Boat Fossen Trafikklag (☎ 72 57 20 20) runs car ferries between Flakk and Rørvik and passenger ferries from the Pirterminalen quay to the Rissanes peninsula and the offshore islands, calling in at Vanvikan, Brekstad, Hitra, Frøya, Sula and even faraway Halten.

Bicycle Trondheim has around 200 green bicycles available to tourists and locals free of charge (locals use them mainly as shopping trolleys). You'll find them locked in bicycle racks conveniently located around the city centre. To release one, insert a Nkr20 coin, which will be returned when you re-lock the bike.

Cyclists heading from the Gamle Bybro up the Brubakken hill to Kristiansten Fort can avail themselves of Trampe, the world's only bike lift. Lift cards are available free at the tourist office, or you can buy one from the Bybroen or Bruhjørnet kiosks near the bottom of the lift.

The Route North

HELL
Home of the Hell Senter shopping complex (look for the devilishly red sign), the Rica Hell Hotel (which serves as Trondheim's Værnes airport hotel), Hell Bil auto sales (you can buy the car from Hell) and a railway stop, Hell has little to offer but its name, which roughly translates as 'prosperity' in Norwegian.

Still, lots of travellers stop here for a cheap chuckle or at least to snap a photo of the well graffitied sign at the train station. And for ever after, whenever someone suggests you make a destination of this place, you can honestly say you've already been there and it wasn't all that bad.

STIKLESTAD
At Stiklestad on 29 July 1030, an army of around 100 men, led by the Christian King Olav Haraldsson, was defeated by the larger and better equipped forces under the command of local feudal chieftains. King Olav, who was descended from King Harald Harfågre, had been forced from the Norwegian throne by King Knut of Denmark and England. He briefly escaped to Sweden but, on his return, was met with the resistance of local chieftains who'd apparently taken exception to his tendency to destroy pagan shrines and execute anyone who persisted with heathen practices.

The Battle of Stiklestad is generally regarded as Norway's passage between the Viking Age and the medieval period, and between pre-history and modern times. The fall of King Olav is generally lauded as a victory for Christianity in Norway as the slain hero has since been remembered as a martyr and, eventually, as a saint. St Olav developed a following around Norway and all of northern Europe and his grave in Trondheim's Nidaros Cathedral became the destination of pilgrims from all over the continent. The battlefield at Stiklestad continues to attract pilgrims and Norwegian holiday-makers and is now one of the best attended tourist attractions in Trøndelag.

Stiklestad Kulturhus
The Stiklestad Cultural Centre (☎ 74 07 31 00) is a sort of theme park, which includes exhibits on the Battle of Stiklestad, a folk museum and the 12th century Stiklestad church.

The rather haunting (and over-the-top) walk-through 'Stiklestad 1030' exhibit, housed in a visitors' centre shaped like a Viking ship, is imperative for Norwegians in search of their own history. It certainly invokes some strong emotions, but foreigners will probably need more background to fully appreciate what it means to locals. A good source is the English translation of the booklet *St Olav – King of Norway*, by Father Olav Müller, sold at the centre for a reasonable Nkr35. You'll also need the

TRØNDELAG

Historic Exhibition pamphlet, which is free at the information desk.

The attached folk museum reveals aspects of life in the region from the 17th century and, over the road, you can visit the lovely Stiklestad church, which Snorre Sturluson tells us was raised between the years 1150 and 1180 over the stone where St Olav leaned before he died. The original stone reportedly had healing powers, but it was removed during the Reformation and hasn't been seen since. The only original item which remains is the soapstone baptismal font.

From 1 June to 14 August, the centre is open daily from 9 am to 8 pm; the rest of the year it's open from 9 am to 5 pm weekdays and 11 am to 6 pm weekends. Admission is Nkr50.

Special Events
Every year during the week leading up to St Olavs Day – 29 July – Stiklestad hosts an outdoor pageant recreating the original battle scene. The text by Olav Gullvåt and music by Paul Okkenhaug conjure up the past conflicts between King Olav den Hellige (St Olav, or Olav the Holy) and the local farmers and chieftains.

Places to Stay & Eat
Campers can stay at *Stiklestad Camping* (*☎/fax 74 04 12 94*), west of Stiklestad in Verdal. Tent/caravan camping costs Nkr60/100, plus Nkr10 per person, and the fairly well appointed cabins cost from Nkr530. The centre is open from 1 June to 31 August. The overpriced *cafeteria* at Stiklestad offers snacks and a range of standard fare, but nothing special.

Getting There & Away
The nearest train to Stiklestad stops at Verdalsøra, which is 6km from Stiklestad, and from there any Vuku bus passes within 2km of the site (15 minutes, Nkr22).

STEINKJER
The mid-sized town of Steinkjer, on the rail and bus lines north of Trondheim, serves as the administrative centre of Nord Trøndelag and the southern anchor of the fabulous Kystriksveien coastal route to Bodø. The medieval saga author Snorre Sturluson mentions it as a major trading centre and seat of the Jarls (Earls) Eirík and Svein Håkonsson, who briefly ruled over Norway following the battle of Svolder. For tourist information, see the Steinkjer Servicekontor (*☎ 74 16 67 00, fax 74 16 10 88*).

The *Guldbergaunet Sommerhotel & Camping* (*☎ 74 16 20 45, fax 74 16 47 35*) charges Nkr110/120 for tents/caravans, Nkr370/790 for rooms and Nkr300 to Nkr790 for cabins. A good upmarket choice is the *Tingvold Park Hotel* (*☎ 74 16 11 00, fax 74 16 11 17, Gamle Kongeveien 47*), which charges from Nkr550/660 for singles/doubles. Steinkjer is probably the smallest place in Norway to have a *McDonald's* (*☎ 74 16 07 40*), but there are also several finer and more expensive places to eat, most of which are associated with hotels.

SNÅSA
On the E6 north of Steinkjer, you'll follow the northern shore of the narrow, 45km-long lake Snåsavatnet, while the Rv763 follows the more lethargic southern shore. The village of Snåsa, at the eastern end of the lake, is best known to travellers for its exceptional hostel, which makes a good base for visits to the forests and uplands of Gressåmoen National Park, farther east.

At the *Snåsa Vandrerhjem* (*☎ 74 15 10 57, fax 74 15 16 15*) you'll pay Nkr115/155 for a dorm bed without/with breakfast and Nkr230/310 for a single or double room without/with breakfast. The same place also functions as a hotel, with single/double rooms for Nkr680/780, with breakfast, and cabins for Nkr325 to Nkr500. At the opposite end of the lake, near Sunnan, is *Føllingstua* (*☎/fax 71 14 71 90*), with tent/caravan camping from Nkr50/100 and four-bed cabins for Nkr300. For information on accommodation at the six-bed *Seisjø Jaktstue*, at Gressåmoen, contact Statskog Trøndelag/Møre (*☎ 74 14 49 92*), at Høvdingveien 10 in Steinkjer. You'll pay around Nkr350 for two people.

The boat *Bonden II* (☎ 90 99 27 16 or ☎ 74 14 46 64) sails up and down the lake between Sunnan and Snåsa (Nkr170 return, including a meal) daily between 1 June and 15 August. You can also reach Snåsa by bus or rail from Trondheim or Steinkjer.

NAMSOS

Namsos, the first scenic port town on the northbound coastal route between Trondheim and Bodø, may be the sort of place where teens drive around screeching their tyres, but it's a pleasant overnight stop and has a couple of interesting diversions. For further information, contact the Namsos Turistkontor (☎ 74 27 09 88, fax 74 27 09 59), at the library. If you're hankering after Internet access, check out the Nerí Gata Internett Kafé, a block from the harbour.

Things to See & Do

A scenic and easy 20-minute walk up Kirkegata from the centre will take you to the lookout atop the prominent loaf-shaped rock **Bjørumsklumpen** (114m), which affords a view over the town and its environs as well as Namsfjorden. About a third of the way up, a sign identifies a side track which leads to some impressive WWII-era German bunkers hewn from solid rock. Inside, placards (in Norwegian only) describe the history of these shelters.

If you're interested in wood chopping and chipping, check out the **Norsk Sagbruksmuseum** (☎ 74 27 60 56), over the bridge 4km east of town, which commemorates Norway's first steam-powered sawmill, the 1853 Stiftelsen Spillum Dampsag og Høvleri. From 1 May to 30 August, the museum is open from 9 am to 5 pm daily. Admission costs Nkr30. The more culturally-oriented **Namdalsmuseet** (☎ 74 27 40 72), Kjærlighetsstien 1, emphasises the history of the Namsos area. It's open from 9 am to 5 pm daily from June to August, and costs Nkr20.

Once you've done all that, drop by the 28°C pool at the novel **Oase swimming hall**

(☎ 74 27 11 55), built deep inside a mountain about 1km east of town. It's open from 11 am to 9.30 pm Monday to Friday and 9.30 am to 4 pm on weekends. Admission costs Nkr50.

Places to Stay & Eat

At *Namsos Camping* (☎ 74 27 53 44, fax 74 27 53 93), east of town near the airport, tent/caravan camping costs Nkr70/110 and cabins are from Nkr275 to Nkr700. The best accommodation value is the bright and friendly *Borstad Gjestgiveri* (☎ 74 27 21 31, fax 74 27 14 48), where the single/double summer rates start at Nkr450/680. It has large sunny rooms and you can also enjoy the pleasant outdoor seating in the garden. The more traditional *Hotel Central* (☎ 74 27 10 00, fax 74 27 11 22) charges Nkr465/700 on weekends and from 1 July to 31 August, and Nkr780/995 at other times.

The *Kafeverten* (☎ 74 27 25 26), beside the cinema, and the *Café Rothe* (☎ 74 27 44 48), upstairs in the Spar market, serve traditional cafeteria fare. On weekdays between 10 am and 3 pm and on Saturday from 10 am to 2 pm, the former puts on warm lunch buffets for Nkr65, including coffee or tea. The *Namsos Bistro*, near Tino's Hotel, is open every day for light meals. A good place for seafood is the *Kai Kanten* (☎ 74 27 27 73), at the harbour, and just down the street you'll find the *Big Buffalo Argentinian Steakhouse*.

The requisite pizza hangout in Namsos is *Numero Uno* (☎ 74 27 52 66), which redefines the words 'thin crust'. Still, Nkr60 or so will get you a pizza large enough for two people who aren't too hungry. Alternatively, you can opt for pasta or a range of salads from Nkr45 to Nkr60.

Getting There & Away

Between Namsos and Trondheim (3¾ hours, Nkr230), the Nor-Way Bussekspress Inherredsekspressen bus runs twice daily. Buses also run between Namsos and Brønnøysund (six hours, Nkr219), farther up the Kystriksveien.

RØRVIK

Charming little Rørvik struggles to be considered a tourist destination, but it's just too far off the beaten track for most visitors. Nevertheless, the Hurtigruten coastal steamer calls in daily, from both directions, and the town accommodates arrivals with proud tours of its historic museum (☎ 74 39 04 41) in the Berggården Trading House (admission Nkr30). This museum also has several components, including the **historic boatyard** protected as the Munkholmen Vessel Preservation Centre, on the islet of Munkholmen just 1km from town, and the offshore Sør-Gjæslingan **fishing village**. The *Namdalingen* ferry runs to Sør-Gjæslingan from Namsos (3¾ hours, Nkr79) and Rørvik (30 minutes, Nkr38) on Wednesday, Friday and Sunday, and day tours to this interesting site are available on Saturday from Namsos and Sunday from Rørvik. Students, military personnel and seniors pay half price.

Currently under construction is the ultramodern **Norveg Senter for Kystkultur og Kystnæring** (☎ 74 39 04 41, sialsake@sn .no), which will function as a museum covering 10,000 years of coastal culture and industry; it should be open by the summer of 2000.

Places to Stay & Eat

Camping and cabins are available at the *Sæternes Hyttegrend* (☎/fax 74 39 38 14), at Austafjord, 10km west of town. The cabins cost from Nkr250 to Nkr325. The well appointed *Kysthotellet Rørvik* (☎ 74 39 01 00, fax 74 39 02 50, Storgata 20), in the centre, has summer single/double rates of Nkr485/590.

A more basic and considerably more interesting option is the museum *Woxengs Samlinger Kystmuseet* (☎ 74 39 04 41, fax 74 39 22 72), which rents out historic

rorbuer (fishing huts) in Sør-Gjæslingan fishing village, on an island south of Rørvik, for Nkr150 plus Nkr70 per person. It's open from 15 May to 1 September.

For pizza and burgers, the best option is *Kystgrill'n* (☎ 74 39 12 34, Skippergata 8). More sophisticated meals, particularly seafood, are served at the *Vertshuset Galeåsen* (☎ 74 39 00 88), on Strandgata near Fossåvegen.

Getting There & Away

Buses between Rørvik, the Grong train station (2¾ hours, Nkr186) and Namsos (three hours, Nkr192) run several times daily. Ferries between Namsos and Rørvik (1¾ hours, Nkr129) leave twice daily. When the northbound and southbound Hurtigruten coastal steamers call in for an hour at the same time, this normally sleepy little place springs to life. The southbound boat leaves at 9.30 pm and the northbound at 9.15 pm.

LEKA

You won't regret a short side-trip to the wild and beautiful red serpentine island of Leka, and for hikers, the desert-like Wild West landscapes will be particularly enchanting. Not only is this prime habitat for the white-tailed sea eagle, but it also has several Viking Age burial mounds and Stone Age rock paintings. For tourist information, contact the Leka Turistkontor (☎ 74 39 96 90) in Leka village. Accommodation is available at *Leka Motell og Camping* (☎ 74 39 98 23, fax 74 39 98 99), with tent and caravan camping from Nkr80 and cabins from Nkr250 to Nkr550.

Leka is accessed by ferry from Gutvik (20 minutes, Nkr18/48 per person/car and driver), which lies about 20 minutes off the main Rv17 coast road; from Rørvik, buses run to Gutvik (2¾ hours, Nkr94) on weekdays.

Nordland

Drivers heading north on the Arctic Highway enter Nordland through the obtrusive Nord Norge arch, which represents the aurora borealis, and as one moves northward through this long narrow county, the fields give way to lakes and forests, vistas open up, the peaks sharpen and the tree line descends ever lower on the mountainsides. In summer, this is where northbound travellers get their first taste of the midnight sun and visitors can't fail to be impressed by the razor-sharp peaks and fabulous Caribbean-coloured seas of Lofoten. If you're travelling by car, you may also want to check out the fruits of the novel Artscape Nordland project, which has commissioned artists from around the world to enhance the boreal landscapes with works which range from the inspired to the inaccessible.

This chapter includes not only the Nordland regions of the Arctic Highway and the Kystriksveien (Coastal Route), but also the north-eastern section of Vesterålen, which belongs to the county of Troms. If you need general travel info for the region, contact the Nordland Reiseliv (☎ 75 54 52 00, fax 75 52 83 28, ntravel@online.no, www.nordlandreiseliv.no).

The Arctic Highway

MOSJØEN

The aluminium-producing town of Mosjøen is scenically situated astride the mouth of the river Vefsna, where it empties into lake-like Vefsnafjorden. It's a charming place to break your journey for a couple of hours, and the friendly Indre Helgeland Reiseliv tourist office (☎ 75 17 61 20, fax 75 17 79 93, ihr@hnett.no) can provide good direction. If you want to stay longer, they can also suggest several worthwhile hiking routes, including a trip to Kvannligrotta, a 900m deep cave on the farm Kvannligård, which can only be accessed with an underwater

HIGHLIGHTS

- Exploring charming fishing villages and marvelling at the peaks around Å, Reine and Hamnøy in Lofoten

- Becoming mesmerised by the Saltstraumen maelstrom south of Bodø

- Following the spectacular Kystriksveien route between Steinkjer and Bodø

- Spending a day at the Norsk Luftfartsmuseum (Norwegian Aviation Museum) in Bodø

- Heading out to the revived ghost village of Nyksund or charming Andenes to watch sperm whales in the Arctic seas

- Hiking the historic Rallarveien (Navvies' Trail) between Abisko or Riksgrensen and Narvik

dive. For information on fishing in the river Vefsna, contact Erling Karlsen (☎ 75 18 94 23) or Åsbjørn Stimo (☎ 75 18 94 13).

NORDLAND

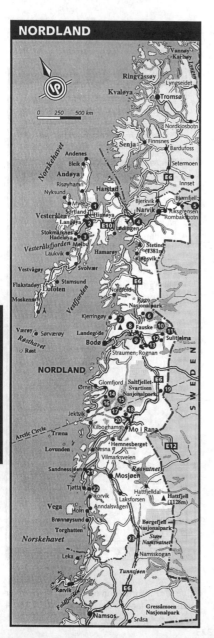

NORDLAND

1   Jennestad Handelssted
2   Sortland Camping og Motell
3   Kinnarps Turist og Kurssenter
4   Evenes airport
5   Rallarvegen (hiking route)
6   Lakshol
7   Steigtind
8   Lundhøgda Camping
9   Fauske Camping
10 Blåmannisen (icefield)
11 Sulitjelmaisen (icefield)
12 Jakobsbakken Fjellsenter
13 Saltdalen Historical Village &
    Blood Road Museum
14 Svartisen Turistsenter &
    Engebreen (glacier tongue)
15 Ostisen (icefield)
16 Vestisen (icefield)
17 Pikhaugsvatnet
18 Setergrotta, Grønligrotta
19 Polarsirkelsenteret
20 Røssvoll Airport
21 Syv Søstre (Seven Sisters) Range
22 The Skier of Røøya
23 Nord Norge Arch

Vefsn Dolstad Museum

The Dolstad district, over the river Skjerva
north of the centre, features 12 buildings
from the 18th and 19th centuries. It's open
from 8.30 am to 3.30 pm on weekdays and
from 11 am to 3.30 pm on Sunday. The adjacent octagonal cruciform Dolstad Kirke,
which dates from 1735, occupies the site of
a medieval church dedicated to St Michael.

Sjøgata

An obligatory stroll in Mosjøen will take
you past the galleries, coffee shops and private homes which are housed in the **historic
warehouses and boatsheds** along Sjøgata.
In the Jakobsensbrygga Warehouse at Sjøgata 31B is the **Vefsn Museum annexe**,
which recounts the history of Mosjøen from
the early 19th century to the present day. It's
open daily except Sunday from 10 am to
3.30 pm (until 2 pm on Saturday). At
Wenche's ceramic workshop, visitors can
create their own pottery, which will be
available for collection the following day.

Laksforsen

The roaring 17m Laksforsen waterfall, about 30km south of Mosjøen, is best known for its leaping salmon and the fishing possibilities in the broad river pool below it. Perched over the river and lost in the waterfall's ample spray is the overpriced *Laksforsen Turist-Café* (☎ 75 18 21 82) and shop where you can stay dry while viewing the impressive chute.

Places to Stay & Eat

The convenient *Mosjøen Camping* (☎ 75 17 79 00, fax 75 17 49 93) is on the banks of the Skjerva, about 500m south-east of the centre. Tent/caravan camping costs Nkr70/ 120, rooms are from Nkr390 to Nkr495 and cabins cost Nkr280 for a basic unit and Nkr650 for a considerably more plush option. At the *Skaugum B&B* (☎ 75 11 39 00, fax 75 11 39 01), near the train station 300m north of the centre, single/double rooms start at Nkr395/525. The only cheaper option is *Fru Haugans Hotel* (☎ 75 17 04 77, fax 75 17 05 34), opposite the tourist office, which charges from Nkr350/500.

The well known *Heimebakeriet* (☎ 75 17 20 90), in Sjøgata, occupies a shop dating from 1842; the current décor is little changed from the shop which operated there in 1879. Also in Sjøgata is the *Egon Restaurant* (☎ 75 17 49 00), which serves a hotch-potch of fast foods – burgers, pizza, kebabs, tacos, lasagne, salads – as well as full steak and seafood dinners. The incongruous but refreshing *El Paso* (☎ 75 17 00 43, Christian Qvalesgata 1-3) specialises in Tex-Mex cuisine.

Getting There & Away

Mosjøen lies on the rail line between Trondheim (5½ hours, Nkr440) and Fauske (3¾ hours, Nkr230); there are two daily services along the entire route, and one between Mosjøen and Bodø. Buses run several times daily except Saturday between Mosjøen and Brønnøysund (3½ hours, Nkr166); there are also connections via Sandnessjøen (1¾ hours, Nkr78).

For drivers from either the north or south, a lovely detour follows the wild and scenic Villmarksveien route, which runs parallel to the E6 east of Mosjøen and approaches the bizarre 1128m *moberg* peak, Hatten (or Hattfjell); from the road's end, the hike to the top takes about two hours. For through travellers, however, this route does cut out Mosjøen itself.

MO I RANA

In the spruce forests and snow peaks around Mo i Rana, northbound travellers get their first sense of the northern wilderness. At first glance, you may not be charmed by industrial Mo i Rana, where the architecture was greatly affected by the socialist notions of the 1950s. Look a bit deeper, however, and you'll probably support its reputation as Norway's friendliest town. This is often chalked up to the fact that with the construction of the steel plant, its population grew from just 5000 to its current 25,000. As a result, nearly everyone in town knows how it feels to be a stranger, and treats visitors accordingly!

Information

The exceptionally active and helpful Polarsirkelen Reiseliv (☎ 75 13 92 00, fax 75 13 92 09, adm@arcticcircle.no) occupies an unassuming building near the Sørlandsveien roundabout. No question or problem is too great and they'll do all they can to help you enjoy the area. From 15 June to 9 August it's open 9 am to 8 pm on weekdays, 9 am to 4 pm on Saturday and 1 to 7 pm on Sunday. During the rest of the year its open on weekdays from 10 am to 3 pm.

Nordlands Naturmuseum

The Nordland Natural History Museum (☎ 75 15 25 55), west of the rail line, concentrates on the geology, ecology, flora and wildlife of the Arctic Circle region, and features several hands-on exhibits which will appeal to children. It's open year-round on weekdays from 9 am to 3 pm, and from 15 June to 15 August it's also open from 7 to 10 pm. Admission is Nkr10.

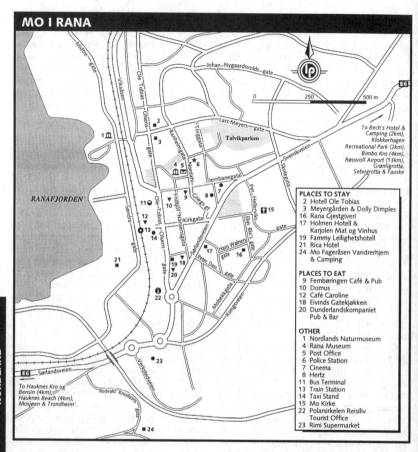

MO I RANA

RANAFJORDEN

Talvikparken

To Bech's Hotel &
Camping (2km),
Klokkerhagen
Recreational Park (2km),
Bimbo Kro (4km),
Røssvoll Airport (13km),
Grønligrotta,
Setergrotta & Fauske

To Haukines Kro og
Bensin (4km),
Hauknes Beach (4km),
Mosjøen & Trondheim'.

PLACES TO STAY
2   Hotell Ole Tobias
3   Meyergården & Dolly Dimples
16 Rana Gjestgiveri
17 Holmen Hotell &
    Karjolen Mat og Vinhus
19 Fammy Leilighetshotell
21 Rica Hotel
24 Mo Fageråsen Vandrerhjem
    & Camping

PLACES TO EAT
9   Fembøringen Café & Pub
10 Domus
12 Café Caroline
18 Eivinds Gatekjøkken
20 Dunderlandskompaniet
    Pub & Bar

OTHER
1   Nordlands Naturmuseum
4   Rana Museum
5   Post Office
6   Police Station
7   Cinema
8   Hertz
11 Bus Terminal
13 Train Station
14 Taxi Stand
15 Mo Kirke
22 Polarsirkelen Reisiliv
    Tourist Office
23 Rimi Supermarket

Rana Museum

The Rana Museum (☎ 75 15 13 84), beside
the post office, deals with the local southern
Sami culture and the history of Nordic
settlement in southern Nordland. In summer
it's open weekdays from 10 am to 3 pm and
7 to 9 pm and on Saturday from noon to
3 pm. Admission costs Nkr15.

Grønligrotta & Setergrotta

The limestone and marble country north-
west of Mo i Rana is riddled with caves

and sinkholes which were formed by river
water dissolving layers of marble between
layers of mica schist. Grønligrotta and
Setergrotta are currently open to the public
on guided tours conducted by Svartisen
Grotte-guiding (☎ 75 13 92 00).

Grønligrotta (☎ 75 16 23 05) has electric
lighting and the 30-minute guided tour
takes you along an underground river,
through a rock maze and past a granite
block torn off by the glacier and deposited
in the cave by the brute force of moving

water. From mid-June to mid-August, tours leave hourly between 10 am and 7 pm.

Considerably more adventurous is the trip through Setergrotta, which is unlit and requires the use of headlamps, hardhats, gumboots (Wellingtons) and coveralls. Highlights include a couple of extremely tight squeezes and a thrilling shuffle between rock walls while straddling a 15m gorge. From 1 June to 3 August, the two-hour tours run at 11.30 am, with an additional departure at 3 pm between 21 June and 3 August.

Access can be a problem, as there's no public transport. If you don't have a car, phone Svartisen Grotte-guiding and see if someone is going out there from town. Alternatively, the tourist office will try to help you organise a shared taxi.

Places to Stay
The very convenient *Mo Fageråsen Vandrerhjem & Camping* (☎ 75 15 09 63, fax 75 15 15 30) is unfortunately slated to move in the near future and no one yet knows where it will go. If that situation changes and it stays put, you'll pay Nkr100 for dorm beds, Nkr150/200 for singles/doubles and nominal rates for camping.

Campers can also head for *Bech's Hotel & Camping* (☎ 75 13 02 11, fax 75 13 15 77), 200m off the E6, 2km north-east of town. Single/double rooms cost Nkr450/550. At the nearly adjacent Klokkerhagen recreational park, you'll find picnic sites, sports fields, jogging tracks and cycle paths, as well as canoe hire. The *Fammy Leilighetshotell* (☎ 75 15 19 99, fax 75 15 19 90, Ole Tobias Olsens gate 4) has bright, four-bed self-catering flats from Nkr495 to Nkr645.

The *Rana Gjestgiveri* (☎/fax 75 15 22 11, Hans Wølners gate 10), about 200m from the church, charges Nkr350/450 for singles/doubles. The railway-themed *Hotell Ole Tobias* (☎ 75 15 77 77, fax 75 15 77 78), on Ole Tobias Olsens gate, was named after the local teacher and priest who convinced the government to build the Nordlansbanen railway connecting Trondheim with Fauske and Bodø. In summer, singles/doubles cost

Nkr550/690. There are three other upmarket options charging from Nkr450/550 to Nkr550/720 for singles/ doubles: the *Meyergården* (☎ 75 13 40 00, fax 75 13 40 01, Ole Tobias Olsens gate 24); the *Rica Hotel* (☎ 75 15 28 00, fax 75 15 43 70, Søndre gate 9); and the *Holmen Hotell* (☎ 75 15 14 44, fax 75 15 18 76), on the corner of Sørlandsveien and TV Westens gate.

At the caves, you can stay at *Grønligrotta Lodge* (☎ 75 16 23 44, fax 75 16 23 66), which is open from 20 June to 20 August and charges Nkr350 for simple doubles.

Places to Eat
The *Dolly Dimples*, at the Meyergården Hotel, makes a good choice for pizza and beer. The expensive *Karjolen Mat og Vinhus* (☎ 75 15 14 44), at the Holmen Hotell, is recommended for its traditional Norwegian cuisine and extensive wine list.

You'll find simple cafeteria snacks at the *Domus* (☎ 75 15 16 33) supermarket on Fridtjof Nansensgata and the *Café Caroline*, at the train station. *Eivinds Gatekjøkken* (☎ 75 15 04 33) fries up even faster snacks – burgers, chips and the like – and on weekends, stays open until 4 am. The cheapest groceries are at the Langneset *Rimi* (☎ 75 15 40 01), south of the centre.

On Sørlandsveien, 6km towards Trondheim, is the friendly truck-stop style *Hauknes Kro og Bensin* (☎ 75 14 07 50), which dishes up hearty fish or beef specialities for between Nkr60 and Nkr100. It's very popular in summer, thanks especially to the sandy Hauknes bathing beach over the road. Take bus No 402, which runs hourly, Monday to Saturday, and once on Sunday.

If you're heading north, the unfortunately named *Bimbo Kro* (☎ 75 15 17 77), at Selfors, offers excellent value, and the name doesn't suggest any sort of peripheral enterprise. Rather, it honours a nearby elephant-shaped rock formation – perhaps a case of Dumbo jumbo mistaken identity? They offer steaks for a bargain Nkr99 and a good solid 'truck drivers' special' with eggs, bacon, beans and potatoes for Nkr60.

Entertainment

In addition to the hotel bars, you can enjoy a drink at the *Fembøringen Café & Pub* (☎ *75 15 09 77*) and the *Dunderlandskompaniet Pub & Bar*. Mo i Rana also has a *cinema*, on Jernbanegata.

Getting There & Away

By air, Mo i Rana's Røssvoll airport is served by Widerøe at least daily from Trondheim and Brønnøysund, and it's a fabulous trip with excellent views of the Svartisen icecaps.

Most visitors arrive at Mo i Rana's unique octagonal train station (☎ 75 15 01 77) on the two or three daily trains from Trondheim (seven hours, Nkr530) or Fauske (2¼ hours, Nkr140). By bus, your options are fairly limited. There are services daily except Saturday between Mo i Rana and Sandnessjøen (3¼ hours, Nkr125). From Sunday to Friday, there's at least one daily Rana-ekspressen bus to and from Mosjøen (two hours, Nkr93).

Self-drivers can stop by the friendly tourist office and pick up a free tourist parking permit. This novel idea is unique in Norway and proves that Mo i Rana is serious about promoting tourism!

Getting Around

For a taxi, phone the local operator (☎ 75 15 23 33), at OT Olsensgata. Car hire is available through Hertz (☎ 75 15 22 55, fax 75 15 36 52), Gjennomgangen 9.

SALTFJELLET-SVARTISEN NASJONALPARK

The 2105 sq km Saltfjellet-Svartisen National Park combines the high and rolling moorlands of the Salfjellet massif with the rugged peaks surrounding the two-part Svartisen icecap (Norway's second largest icefield, with a combined area of 369 sq km).

Information

Three DNT offices cover the Saltfjellet-Svartisen National Park. For hiking and hut information on the Saltfjellet section,

contact the Sulitjelma og Omegn Turistforening (☎ 75 64 04 01), at the Tourist & Course Centre in Sulitejelma. For the eastern side of Svartisen, see the Rana Turistforening (☎ 75 15 04 21), at the tourist office in Mo i Rana. If you're heading for the western end of Svartisen, contact the Bodø og Omegn Turistforening (☎ 75 52 14 13), at Storgata 44 in Bodø. For national park information, see Statskog Helgeland (☎ 75 15 79 50) in Mo i Rana.

The best map to use is Statens Kartverk's *Turkart Saltfjellet*, at a scale of 1:100,000.

Svartisen

The two Svartisen icecaps, which are separated by the valley Vesterdalen, straddle the Arctic Circle between Mo i Rana and the Meløy peninsula. In its heights, the icecap averages about 1500m altitude, but some of its tongues lick the lowlands to become the lowest-lying glaciers in Europe, outside of Iceland and Svalbard. Svartisen can be visited from either the east or the west, but to travel between the two main access points would amount to a major technical expedition on foot and a one or two-day detour in a car. In fact, most visitors to the glacier just make a quick hop across Holandsfjorden by boat from the Kystriksveien, but hikers will find more joy approaching from the east.

Østisen From the end of the Svartisdalen road, 20km up the valley from Røssvoll (the airport for Mo i Rana), ferries (☎ 75 16 23 79) across Svartisvatnet (20 minutes, Nkr60) operate between 20 June and 31 August. From 10 July to 10 August they run hourly from 10 am to 4 pm and at other times at 10 am, noon and 2 and 4 pm. Alternatively, it's a tedious 4km walk along the lakeshore, plagued by rocks and stream crossings. From the ferry landing at the western end of the lake, it's a 3km hike to the snout of the Austerdalsisen glacier tongue, which has receded about 1km in the past two decades due to warming temperatures. It's hoped that increased snowfall higher up will eventually reverse that process and preserve this lovely feature. There's a kiosk and camp site at the lake.

From the end of the road you can also trek up to the hut on the shore of Pikhaugsvatnet, a mountain lake surrounded by peaks and ice. This is an excellent base to use for day hikes up the Glomdal valley or to the Flatisen glacier. Experienced technical climbers will find excellent challenges on Nordre Kamplitinden (1532m) and Skiptinden (1591m).

Vestisen The estranged Vestisen icecap is best accessed from the Kystriksveien route and probably attracts more visitors than any other part of the park. Kystriksveien travellers will catch glimpses of the Svartisen icecap from the Kilboghamn-Jektvik and Ågskardet-Forøy ferries, and good views from the highway along Holandsfjorden. From Holand and Brasetvik quays, the Engen Skyssbåt (☎ 94 86 55 16) ferries *Engebreen* and *Isprins* shuttle across Holandsfjorden to the snout of Engebreen (15 minutes, Nkr40). From 1 June to 31 August they sail 12 times between 7.20 am and 8 pm on weekdays and 10 times on weekends between 9.50 am and 8 pm.

A 15-minute walk from the Enganeset ferry landing takes you to the Svartisen Turistsenter (☎ 75 75 00 11), which entails a café and shop; it's open from May to September. Guided glacier walks (☎ 75 75 00 32) from the end of Engabrevatnet are available for Nkr200 per hour plus Nkr100 for equipment. Independent hikers can slog up the steep route along the glacier's edge to the Tåkeheimen hut, near the summit of Helgelandsbukken (1454m).

Northbound travellers on the Hurtigruten coastal steamer can incorporate a visit to Engabreen with their journey. They disembark at Ørnes, visit the glacier and then travel by bus to Bodø to reconnect with the Hurtigruten (Nkr510 for the whole tour). On weekdays, anyone can do the return trip to Engebreen from Bodø by taking the Hurtigruten to Ørnes steamer (3¼ hours, Nkr176) at 4 am and connecting with bus No 907 from Ørnes to Holand

(45 minutes, Nkr49). After visiting the glacier tongue, you return from Holand to Bodø (2½ hours, Nkr169) on bus No 900 (Glomfjordbussen) at 4.30 pm.

Saltfjellet

Along the Arctic Circle, the landscape is characterised by the high broad plateaux of the Saltfjellet massif. These plateaux connect the high peaks surrounding the Svartisen icecap and the Swedish border. Dotted around this relatively inhospitable wilderness are numerous fences and sacrificial sites attributed to the Sami people; some sites date from as early as the 9th century AD, and evidence suggests reindeer-herding activities as early as the 16th century.

From the *Global Hotell Polarsirkelen* (☎ 75 69 41 22, fax 75 69 41 27), at Lønsdal, 20km south of the Arctic Circle, you can begin a high-country hike through a relatively desolate and little known landscape. In summer, single/double rooms in this rather luxurious mountain hotel cost Nkr490/790, cabins cost Nkr300 and camping is available. DNT members may prefer the club's simpler *Lønsstua* (☎ 75 69 41 25); you can pick up keys at the Lønsdal train station.

A 15km walk to the east leads to Graddis, near the Swedish border, where you'll find the amenable *Graddis Vandrerhjem* (☎ 75 69 43 41, fax 75 69 43 88), which was established in 1867 and has been run by the same family ever since. At this cosy little place, you'll have an excellent base to launch yourself into one of Norway's least attended hiking venues. Here you'll pay Nkr100 for a dorm bed and from Nkr200/300 to Nkr250/480 for private single/double rooms. Camping is also available. (Have a look at their 1000-year-old pine tree, which lies 200m from the hostel and has been named Methuselah.) Alternatively, you can head west over the moors to several unstaffed *DNT huts*: Saltfjellstua, Bukkhaugsstua, Bjellåvasstua and Krukkistua.

If you prefer an easier route, one of the area's best short hikes leads through the wildly twisting Junkerdalsura gorge, which is recognised as a rich botanical reserve. From the Junkerdal (Saltdal) Turistsenter at Storjord, head east and cross the swinging bridge over the Junkerdal river. After 200m, you'll reach an information notice board. From there, a hiking path follows an old cart track for 4km up the gorge to the Junkerdalen bridge, near the village of Solvågli.

Getting There & Away

Rail travellers can disembark at Lønsdal en route between Fauske (45 minutes, Nkr60) and Trondheim (8½ hours, Nkr630), but you may have to request a stop, as only three daily trains schedule halts here. For drivers, access to Saltfjellet is either along the E6 or the Rv77, which follows the southern slope of the valley Junkerdalen. On Wednesday and Friday, bus No 791 runs between the Junkerdal Turistsenter, Bodø (3¼ hours, Nkr155) and Fauske (1¼ hours, Nkr93).

ARCTIC CIRCLE

Along the Arctic Highway between Mo i Rana and Fauske, a big deal is made of the Arctic Circle – the 66°33' line of latitude which marks the southernmost extent of the midnight sun on the summer solstice and the ragged edge of the polar night on the winter solstice. Here, the bleak moors adjoining Saltfjellet-Svartisen National Park provide the appropriate polar illusion, but the effect is more a factor of the 600m altitude than the latitude, and northbound travellers quickly descend into the relatively lush, well vegetated environment that's more typical of northern Norway.

At the **Polarsirkelsenteret**, which straddles the 66° 33' parallel, visitors can pay Nkr45 to learn the significance of the Arctic Circle, peruse a collection of stuffed wildlife specimens and watch an audio-visual presentation on the Arctic regions. Afterward, they can scour a gift shop selling all manner of boreal kitsch, have postcards stamped with a special Arctic Circle postmark, drink a bottle of Arctic Ice and pick up a certificate verifying that they've actually crossed the magic line. Perhaps the most worthwhile feature is the memorial to

the forced labourers who, during WWII, constructed the Arctic Highway for the occupying German forces.

From 30 June to 31 August, one daily train between Trondheim and Bodø and another between Mosjøen and Fauske stop at the Arctic Circle station. The fare from Trondheim is Nkr610.

FAUSKE

Fauske, with 10,000 people, is known mainly for marble quarrying, and has contributed stone for numerous monumental structures, including the Oslo Rådhus and the UN building in New York. Fauske also serves as a travellers' hub of sorts: it's a jumping-off point for Sulitjelma and the Rago National Park, and is also the place where northbound ScanRail passengers must forego the rails and get on the bus to reach Lofoten or Tromsø. Unless you're pressed for time, however, it's worth making the trip west to Bodø, where you'll find several interesting sites and ready ferry access to southern Lofoten. The Salten Reiselivslag tourist office (π 75 64 33 03, fax 75 64 32 38, salten.turistkontor@no) can provide the information you'll need for your visit.

Things to See

Sites in town include the marble-theme **town square**; the **Fauske Bygdemuseum** (π 75 64 46 98), which is open weekdays from 7.30 am to 3 pm and costs Nkr15; and the free **Norsk Vegmuseum** (Road Museum; π 75 64 64 99), 2km north of town, which features Nordland's hard-won highways and byways. It's open weekdays from 7.30 am to 3 pm.

If you like Fauske's streaky salmon-coloured marble, visit **Ankerske** (π 75 64 33 06), 500m south of the centre, where you can buy a range of locally-produced marble products.

Places to Stay

Fauske has two campgrounds. *Fauske Camping* (π 75 64 84 01, fax 75 64 84 13) lies 4km south of the centre on the E6. Tent/caravan camping costs Nkr60/90 and spartan cabins cost Nkr200. The other – and perhaps better – choice is *Lundhøgda Camping* (☎ *75 64 39 66)*, 3km west of town, which enjoys a superb view of the fjord and surrounding peaks. Camping in a tent or caravan costs Nkr100, while four-bed cabins of varying standards cost from Nkr230 to Nkr450. Take bus No 1 from the centre, or follow the Rv80 towards Bodø and turn south on Erikstadveien, towards Øynes.

The cosy and basic old *Fauske Vandrerhjem* (☎ *75 64 67 06, fax 75 64 59 95, Nyveien 6)*, 250m west of the centre, has dorm beds for Nkr100 and single/double rooms for Nkr200/250. The other options are the *Fauske Hotell* (☎ *75 64 38 33, fax 75 64 57 37, Storgata 82)*, which charges a rather steep Nkr875/1050 for summer-rate singles/doubles, and the better value *Brygga Best Western* (☎ *75 64 63 34, fax 75 64 59 95, Sjøgata 86)*, with summer and weekend singles/doubles for Nkr595/775.

Getting There & Away

Bus The popular Nord-Norgeekspressen between Bodø (1¼ hours, Nkr70) and Narvik (4¾ hours, Nkr270) passes through Fauske at least three times daily in either direction and on the especially scenic Narvik route allows substantial discounts for holders of ScanRail, InterRail and Eurail passes. You can also travel directly to Lofoten from Fauske on the Fauske-Lofoten Ekspressen, which operates daily between Fauske, Sortland (5¼ hours, Nkr263) and Svolvær (8½ hours, Nkr363).

There's also a daily bus between Fauske and Å i Lofoten (13 hours, Nkr321); the fare includes the ferry between Svolvær and Skutvik. It leaves Å at 7.45 am and Fauske at 9.30 am. To and from Harstad, on the Vesterålen island of Hinnøya, you can take the daily Togbussen (six hours, Nkr293). The Saltens Bilruter local bus between Fauske and Bodø (1¼ hours, Nkr70) runs at least three times daily.

Train Trains ply the Nordlandsbanen between Trondheim (9½ hours, Nkr670) and Bodø (45 minutes, Nkr90), via Fauske, at least twice daily.

Car & Motorcycle In fine weather, the drive between Fauske and Narvik, characterised by naked granite peaks and cloud-girt heights, is one of the most spectacular in the world. However, drivers and motorcyclists should be wary of their speed within a 100km radius of Fauske (especially south of Rognan), as the region derives a healthy income from creative radar traps; even 5km over the posted limit nets an on-the-spot fine of Nkr1000 or more.

AROUND FAUSKE
Saltdalen Historical Village & Blood Road Museum

At Saltnes, 1km north of Rognan, the Saltdal Historical Village consists of a collection of rural buildings on the site of the 1750 Skippergården farm. More interesting is the Blood Road Museum, which is housed in an old German barracks and reveals conditions for Allied prisoners of war between 1942 and 1945. The name commemorates the Yugoslav prisoners who died building the highway between Saltnes and Saksenvik. From 20 June to 20 August it's open from 9 am to 5 pm weekdays, 1 pm to 4 pm on Saturday and on 1 pm to 6 pm Sunday. Admission costs Nkr20. From Fauske, take any bus headed south along the E6.

Sulitjelma

Along the Rv830, south-east of Fauske, lies the community of Sulitjelma. In 1860, a Sami herder discovered copper ore in the forested country north of Langvatnet and suddenly the Sulitjelma region was attracting all sorts of opportunists from southern Norway. By 1876, large ore deposits were discovered, and the Sulitjelma Gruber mining company was founded in 1891. By 1928, the wood-fuelled smelter had taken its toll on the surrounding birch forests, as did high concentrations of CO_2 (a by-product of the smelting process), and subsequent erosion ensured that reforestation would be ineffective. The environmentally conscious Sameting (Parliament) closed down the smelter in 1990, but the land immediately surrounding the settlement has yet to recover.

NORDLAND

Things to See & Do Despite the environmental degradation caused by the mining, the country east and south of Sulitjelma still enjoys especially scenic glacial surroundings and ample hiking opportunities, and as evidence, the area has its own DNT chapter, the Sulitjelma og Omegn Turistforening (☎ 75 64 04 01), Postboks 87, N-8230 Sulitjelma. Hikers can choose from several routes past nine major huts (pick up DNT keys from the Sulitjelma Hotel).

For technical climbers, favoured destinations are the the **three nunataks** (mountain peaks protruding through a glacier or icecap), Vardetoppen (1722m), Stortoppen (1830m) and Sulistoppen (1930m), all in the Sulitjelmasisen icecap. The 123 sq km **Blåmannsisen icecap** (1571m), farther north, is also popular. The topo sheets to use are *Låmivatnet* (sheet 2229-III), *Sulitjelma* (sheet 2129-II) and *Balvatnet* (sheet 2128-I), all at a scale of 1:50,000.

Visits to the **Giken mines** (☎ 75 64 06 95) involve a two-hour guided tour and a rail ride through the copper tunnels. Tours run from 9 am to 4 pm between 20 June and 15 August, and cost Nkr50. For details, contact the Sulitjelma Besøksgruve (☎ 75 64 06 95).

You'll also want to peruse the **Sulitjelma Gruvemuseum** (☎ 75 64 02 40), which reveals the area's 100 years of mining history. It's open weedays from 11 am to 3 pm (and Tuesday in July from 6 to 8 pm), and admission costs Nkr10. The 11km **Okshola cave system** at Hjemgam can be visited with a guide from the Salten Reiselivslag in Fauske; tours cost Nkr100 per person.

Places to Stay The *Jakobsbakken Fjellsenter* (☎/fax 75 64 02 90), at the end of the Jakobsbakken road, has dormitory accommodation for Nkr100 to Nkr300 and the *Sulitjelma Hotel* (☎ 75 64 04 01, fax 75 64 06 54, Andr Quales vei 15) charges Nkr510/ 720 for single/double rooms. At the lake Dajavatn you'll find the *Sulitjelma Camping og Fritidsenter* (☎ 75 64 04 33), which offers inexpensive camping and cabins from Nkr400.

Getting There & Away Buses between Fauske and Sulitjelma (one hour, Nkr49) run at least three times daily Monday to Saturday and once on Sunday.

Rago Nasjonalpark

The small 167 sq km Rago National Park comprises an incredibly rugged chunk of forested granite mountains and moorlands, riven with deep glacial cracks and capped by great icefields. Rago, together with the large adjoining Swedish parks, Pakjelanta, Sarek and Stora Sjöfjallet, belongs to a protected area of 5500 sq km. Wildlife includes not only beavers in the deep Laksåga river valley, but also wolverines in the higher areas. Rago is best known, however, for the series of foaming cascades and spectacular waterfalls in the relatively lush Storskogdalen valley; from bottom to top, they include Værivassfoss (200m), Trollfoss (43m) and Storskogsfoss (18m).

For serious hikers hoping to escape the crowds, hotel-like huts and highway-like tracks typical of some Norwegian national parks, scarcely-visited Rago is the place to go. From the main trailhead at Lakshol, it's a three-hour, 7km walk up the valley to the free Storskogvasshytta hut and thence a stiff climb up and over the ridge into Sweden to connect with the well established trail system over the border. The maps to use for the park are the topo sheet *Sisovatnet* (sheet 2129-I), at a scale of 1:50,000, or *Sørfold*, at a scale of 1:75,000. To reach Lakshol, turn east off the E6 at the Trengsel bridge and continue about 6km to the end of the road.

The nearest bus access is No 841 between Fauske and Megården (one hour, Nkr32) which runs at least twice daily, but from there, it's still 7km up the valley to Lakshol.

NARVIK

Narvik was established a century ago as an ice-free port for the rich Kiruna iron mines in Swedish Norrland, and the current city is bisected by a monstrous transshipment facility where the ore is off-loaded from rail cars onto ships bound for industries around the world.

History

The earliest inhabitants of the Narvik region were present during the Stone Age, as evidenced by the very distinct rock carving of a moose found at Vassvik, north-west of the centre.

During WWII, this strategic ice-free port became an obvious target for the Nazis, who were intent upon halting iron supplies to the Allied war machine and usurping the steel bounty for its own purposes. In a blizzard on 9 April 1940, 10 German destroyers entered the port and sank the Norwegian battleships *Norge* and *Eidsvoll*. The following day five British destroyers arrived to defend the port. A fierce naval battle resulted in the loss of two ships on each side and on 12 April, British aircraft-carrier based planes attacked. By late May, British, Norwegian, French and Polish troops disembarked and took back the town in a single day – the first major Allied victory in the Norwegian campaign – proving that the Nazi forces weren't invincible.

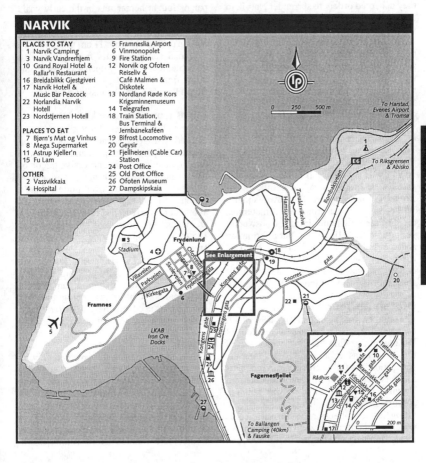

NARVIK

PLACES TO STAY
1 Narvik Camping
3 Narvik Vandrerhjem
10 Grand Royal Hotel & Rallar'n Restaurant
16 Breidablikk Gjestgiveri
17 Narvik Hotell & Music Bar Peacock
22 Norlandia Narvik Hotell
23 Nordstjernen Hotell

PLACES TO EAT
7 Bjørn's Mat og Vinhus
8 Mega Supermarket
11 Astrup Kjeller'n
15 Fu Lam

OTHER
2 Vassvikkaia
4 Hospital
5 Framneslia Airport
6 Vinmonopolet
9 Fire Station
12 Norvik og Ofoten Reiseliv & Café Malmen & Diskotek
13 Nordland Røde Kors Krigsminnemuseum
14 Telegrafen
18 Train Station, Bus Terminal & Jernbanekaféen
19 Bifrost Locomotive
20 Geysir
21 Fjellheisen (Cable Car) Station
24 Post Office
25 Old Post Office
26 Ofoten Museum
27 Dampskipskaia

But the Germans didn't retreat. Between 28 May and 8 June, Narvik wasn't just bombed into submission; it was decimated, as evidenced by the remains of soldiers in the cemeteries and 34 ships of five nations (Norway, Britain, France, the Netherlands and Germany) in the harbour. Some ships actually sunk themselves to avoid destruction by bombing, and were later re-floated and/or salvaged.

Escalating conflicts in France prevented the Allies from dedicating sufficient resources to defending the port and on 8 June they accepted orders to surrender Narvik to the occupying forces. The Germans remained in control until 8 May 1945.

Although the town was admirably rebuilt, modern Narvik is less than prepossessing (and indeed, some would say it's ugly). Fortunately, this port city remains a major iron ore railhead, and the surrounding fjord, forest and mountain country borders on the spectacular in all directions.

Information
The Narvik og Ofoten Reiseliv tourist office (☎ 76 94 33 09 or ☎ 90 12 55 46, fax 76 94 74 05, www.narviknett.no), Kongens gate 44, is hidden away in a little glass-fronted shop opposite the town square. While it's short on promotional materials, the staff are very helpful and can answer all your questions. Hiking and hut information is dispensed by the Narvik og Omegns Turistforening (☎ 76 94 37 90), Postboks 615, N-8501 Narvik. DNT cabin keys are available from the fire station (☎ 76 92 26 83).

Ofoten Museum
The unique Ofoten Museum (☎ 76 96 00 50) occupies the NSB's wonderfully colourful 1902 administration building, which served the Germans as a command base during the occupation. It's full of character and contains a diverse collection of paraphernalia from Narvik's fishing, farming, railway building and ore transshipment heritage. Most interesting is the collection of historic photos which are contrasted with modern photos taken from the same angles. In July it's open

on weekdays from 11 am to 3.30 pm and on weekends from noon to 3 pm. At other times, it's open weekdays from 10.30 am to 3.30 pm. In the park just down the road, you can also see the restored (1991) 19th century Ofoten office, which served as the Viktoriahamn post office from 1888 to 1988.

Nordland Røde Kors Krigsminnemuseum
The Norwegian Red Cross War Museum (☎ 76 94 44 26), on the town square, does an admirable job of exposing the military campaigns fought hereabouts in the early years of WWII, and it's likely to leave you feeling rather stunned. From 1 March to 30 September it's open daily from 11 am to 3 pm, with extended summer hours from 10 June to 20 September when it's open Monday to Saturday from 10 am to 10 pm and on Sunday from 11 am to 5 pm. Admission costs Nkr25.

LKAB Iron Ore Docks
In the valley between Narvik's two commercial districts lies the vast LKAB iron ore transshipment complex and the railway line that feeds it. This impressive tangle of rusty industrial machinery, conveyors, ovens and heaps of iron pellets has a strange intimidating appeal, and says it all about Narvik's *raison d'être*. Interestingly, an average tanker-load of ore weighs in at 125,000 to 175,000 tonnes, and takes an entire day to load.

Tours of the LKAB facility lasting one hour are available daily at 1 pm and cost Nkr30 per person, with a minimum of eight participants; don't miss seeing the first locomotive used on the harbour railway, which now has a bear for an engineer.

Geysir
This 85m plume of water, powered only by the heat created when gravity conducts water from the mountains through the Norsk Energi hydroelectric plant, is of interest especially on warm days when children come to cool off in the simulated rainfall. It's fired up daily in summer at 1 and 9 pm, and spews for about 30 minutes before winding down.

Fjellheis

Behind the town, the Fjellheisen cable car (☎ 76 94 16 05) climbs 656m up Fagernesfjellet for incredible views over the surrounding peaks and fjords. It operates from 10 am to 1 am daily between 15 June to 15 August. The return fare costs Nkr60.

Rallarveien

The incredible Ofotbanen railway was constructed by migrant labourers at the end of the 19th century to connect the port of Narvik with the iron ore mines at Kiruna, in Sweden's far north. The railway was opened by King Oscar II in 1903, and it currently transports 12 to 14 million tonnes of iron ore annually.

If there's one reason to visit Narvik, it's to follow the beautiful Rallarveien, the old navvies' trail which runs parallel to the rail line between Sweden's Abisko National Park and the sea. Few people actually walk the entire route, however, and most just opt for the descent from Bjørnfjell or Riksgrensen (spelt Riksgränsen in Swedish), on the Swedish border, to either Katterat, on the road, or all the way to Rombaksbotn, at the head of Rombaksfjord. At Riksgrensen, where there's the very well appointed Swedish *Riksgränsen Turiststation* hotel *(Sweden ☎ 0980 400 80, fax 0980 431 25)*, don't miss the free Apoteket gallery of mountain photos by Sven Hörnell.

Between 15 June and 15 August, guided hikes are offered by the Narvik Turistkonteret, including rail transport to the upper trailhead and a boat back from Rombaksbotn. If you want to do the trip independently, pick up the booklet *Hikes Along the Navvy Road*, which includes a good map of the entire route from Abisko to Rombaksbotn and costs Nkr30 from the tourist office. Self-organised boat trips (Nkr75) leave Rombaksbotn at 7 pm on Saturday and Sunday from 4 to 31 July (from Vassvikkaia in Narvik to Rombaksbotn, they leave at 5 pm on the same days). On other days, the Narvik tourist office can arrange private boat transport back to town starting at around Nkr200 for two people.

Svartabjørn

It isn't known whether or not there actually was a cook named Svartabjørn who dished up meals for the navvies of the Ofoten line, but her name certainly lives on in legend. In his *Malm* trilogy, published in 1914, novelist Ernst Didring recounted stories told to him by the navvies who built the railway, and prominent among these tales were accounts referring to a cook they called Svartabjørn, the 'black bear'.

It's said that this dark and beautiful woman walked the tracks with the workers between Ofotenfjord and the Swedish border, and although she was too young to be away from her home, she got on well with the workers and cooked their evening meals. It's said that she fell in love with the same man as another woman, and was subsequently beaten to death with a laundry paddle and taken by the navvies to be buried at the Tornehamn cemetery. Today, the grave is marked *Anna Norge*, but the date of her death has been changed at least three times to fit different women who are thought to have been the real Svartabjørn.

Over the Swedish border, several long-distance routes radiate out from the Rallarveien, including the connecting route with Øvre Dividal National Park, in the Norwegian county of Troms, and the world-renowned Kungsleden, which heads south from Abisko into the heart of Sweden.

Activities

Extreme hiking, climbing and glacier trekking with local mountain guides are available from Höjdpunkten (☎ 76 95 94 87). If you've always wanted to dive in Arctic seas, you couldn't do better than Narvik, where the harbour is chock-a-block with sunken ships from WWII. The Narvik Dykkesenter (☎ 76 94 60 00) offers dives, instruction and certification. At Skjomen, about 20km south of town, you can tackle the world's northernmost 18-hole golf course, the Narvik Golf Club (☎ 76 95 12 01), which has a par of 72; you'll pay Nkr180 per person for a full round.

Organised Tours

The most popular guided tour is the NSB (☎ 76 92 31 21) return excursion along the incredible Ofotbanen railway between Narvik and Riksgrensen, on the Swedish border. This feat of engineering features 50 tunnels and snowsheds, as well as the views of the impressive Norddal trestle which was used from 1902 to 1988, when the line was shifted to the north. Ironically, it was built by a German engineering firm, MAN, and during WWII, the Germans were unable to destroy it. From 20 June to 10 August, the train departs daily at 4.05 pm and costs Nkr130, including admission to the Årromsadje audiovisual program and a stop at the Apoteket display of Hörnell's photography at Riksgrensen. Book through the tourist office.

Sightseeing, fishing and whale-watching on the boat *Delphin Senior* can be arranged through Skipper Ivar Hågensen (☎/fax 76 95 71 51, mobile ☎ 94 86 97 62); during the herring runs between October and December you may see orcas (killer whales). In October and November, Per Ole Lund, at the Tysfjord Nature Cruise (☎ 75 77 32 55, mobile ☎ 94 85 33 86), runs five-hour orca-watching cruises from Storjord, about 90km south of Narvik on the E6.

Special Events

Each year in March, the navvies who built the railway are commemorated in the annual Ofotbanen festival.

Places to Stay

The nearest campground is *Narvik Camping* (☎ 76 94 58 10), an easily walkable 2km north-east of the centre on the E6. Tent/caravan camping costs Nkr80/100 and four/six-bed cabins are Nkr425/550, plus Nkr55 for sheets. If you don't mind staying well out of town, the lovely *Ballangen Camping* (☎ 76 92 83 97, fax 76 92 81 50), 40km south of town at Ballangen, is a well

organised site right beside the fjord. Camping costs Nkr110 per tent or caravan and simple four-bed huts cost Nkr250, while more opulent options range from Nkr350 to Nkr625. The route between Narvik and Ballangen is served by numerous buses (one hour, Nkr52).

Since the historic old hostel on Havnegata became a refugee centre, the *Narvik Vandrerhjem* (☎ 76 94 25 98, fax 76 94 29 99, Tiurveien 22) has relocated to the Jaklamyra student housing complex and now opens only from mid-June to mid-August. Dorm beds cost Nkr140 and singles/doubles are Nkr240/360, with breakfast. Reception is open from 7 am to noon and 6 to 8 pm.

More central is *Breidablikk Gjestgiveri* (☎ 76 94 14 18, fax 76 94 57 86, Tore Hunds gate 41), a pleasant pension with a hillside view. Dorm beds cost Nkr150 and singles/doubles are Nkr300/400. The optional breakfast costs Nkr50. The central *Astrup Kjeller'n* (☎ 76 96 04 02, Kinobakken 1), which is better known as a restaurant, has basic doubles for Nkr300. The least expensive hotel option is the *Nordstjernen Hotell* (☎ 76 94 41 20, fax 76 94 75 06, Kongens gate 26), which charges Nkr495/595 for singles/doubles.

The top-range accommodation is the *Grand Royal Hotel* (☎ 76 94 15 00, fax 76 94 55 31, Kongens gate 64), which enjoys a commanding view over the fjord. In summer, single/double rooms with breakfast and dinner cost Nkr630/860. Other upmarket options include the *Norlandia Narvik Hotell* (☎ 76 94 75 00, fax 76 94 28 65, Skistuaveien 8), with summer single/double rates of Nkr545/745 and the *Narvik Hotell* (☎ 76 94 70 77, fax 76 94 67 35, Kongens gate 36), with summer rates of Nkr600/900, including half-board.

Places to Eat

The large *Jernbanekaféen* (☎ 76 94 17 45) at the train station serves standard cafeteria fare as well as burgers, fish and chips and even light meals. *Astrup Kjeller'n* (☎ 76 94 40 80, Kinobakken 1), beside the Rådhus, has pizza, daily specials and late hours.

There's very good pizza, as well as pasta and other light meals, at the *Rallar'n* restaurant on the ground floor of the Grand Royal Hotel. Chinese specialities are served up at the *Fu Lam (☎ 96 94 40 35, Dronnings gate 58)*.

Over the bridge in Frydenlund is the more upmarket *Bjørn's Mat og Vinhus (☎ 76 94 42 90)*, which serves full meals from Nkr120 and also has a bar. In the same area, there's a cheap cafeteria at the *Mega* supermarket at Frydenlundsgata 15. The Vinmopolet is at the western end of Frydenlundsgata.

Entertainment

The most popular local hangout is the *Telegrafen (☎ 76 95 43 00, Dronningens gate 56)*, which is open nightly and attracts the 20 to 35 crowd. It shows the latest sports matches on wide-screen TV. When there's no band it has a cloakroom charge of Nkr20; for live bands, you'll pay a cover charge of Nkr50 to Nkr100.

At the two-part *Café Malmen & Diskotek (☎ 76 94 20 00)*, with seating both above and outside the tourist office, you'll find the world's most expensive Cokes at Nkr28 a glass – you may as well pay another Nkr20 and have a beer! The weekend disco attracts mostly students from 18 to 20.

The *Music Bar Peacock*, in the Narvik Hotell, offers a relatively mellow scene for patrons from 20 to 35. In winter, the bar at the *Nordlandia Narvik Hotel (☎ 76 94 75 00)* is renowned as Narvik's most atmospheric *aprés ski* venue.

Getting There & Away

Air The Framneslia airport, on the Framnes peninsula about 3km west of the centre, is readily accessed by town buses. Widerøe flies between Bodø and Tromsø via Narvik and five other airports in Nordland, but larger planes use the Evenes airport, which Narvik shares with Harstad.

Bus Narvik's former bus terminal has been gutted and, until further notice, buses will leave from and arrive at the train station. Several express buses between Fauske and

the far north make an overnight break in Narvik. The Nor-Way Bussekspress buses between Bodø and Narvik (6¾ hours, Nkr332), via Fauske (4¾ hours, Nkr270), run at least twice daily. The fares include the ferry trip between Bognes and Skarberget and holders of ScanRail or InterRail passes get a 50% discount.

Between Narvik, Sortland (3¾ hours, Nkr207) and Svolvær (5¾ hours, Nkr308), you can take the Narvik-Lofoten Ekspressen, which runs daily; fares include the ferry between Melbu and Fiskebøl. On weekends, it travels only from Sortland to Narvik, and on Saturday, from Narvik only as far as Sortland.

The Nord-Norgeekspressen buses between Narvik and Tromsø (4¼ hours, Nkr279) leave at least three times daily. There's also the daily, except Saturday, Lofotbussen service, which connects Narvik with Å i Lofoten (8½ hours, Nkr436), on Moskenesøy. It leaves Narvik at 10.10 am (with an additional departure at noon on Sunday) and from Å at 1.15 pm.

From 15 June to 31 August, the popular Nordkappekspressen between Narvik and Nordkapp (13½ hours, Nkr700/1050 one-way/return), via Abisko and Karesuando, Sweden, and Enontekiö, Finland, leaves Narvik daily at 8.45 am. Holders of ScanRail and InterRail passes get a 50% discount. Additional charges include the Honningsvåg ferry (Nkr34) and admission to Nordkapp (Nkr175). A range of combination return trips are also available in conjunction with this route. To return from Nordkapp to Harstad with the Hurtigruten and thence by bus to Narvik costs Nkr1595 return; to return with the Hurtigruten from Nordkapp to Sortland, the bus to Å i Lofoten, and then the ferry to Bodø is Nkr1870 return. For details, contact Ofotens Bilruter (☎ 76 92 35 00, fax 76 92 35 30, ob@ ofotens-bilruter.no, www.ofotens-bilruter .no), Postboks 223, N-8501 Narvik.

Train There are two daily services between Narvik and Kiruna (2¾ hours, Nkr127), in Sweden, via Katterat (30 minutes, Nkr55),

NORDLAND

Bjørnfjell (45 minutes, Nkr55) and Riksgrensen (50 minutes, Nkr52; there's a discount for crossing the border), with connections to Gallivåre, Boden and Luleå. This route takes you up the spectacular Ofotbanen and past Abisko National Park (1½ hours, Nkr56), which offers excellent hiking and lovely Arctic scenery; if you're headed east, don't miss it!

Ferry From 7 June to 26 September, the M/S *Bortind* express boat (☎ 75 54 17 41) to Svolvær (four hours, Nkr255) leaves the Dampskipskaia on weekdays at 3 pm and on Sunday at noon. The dock is on Havnegata, 2km south of the centre along Kongens gate.

Getting Around
Narvik's Framneslia city airport lies pretty much within walking distance of the centre; Flybussen buses between Narvik and Harstad's Evenes airport run six to 10 times daily (two hours, Nkr95). For a taxi, phone (☎ 76 94 65 00). Hertz Car Hire (☎ 76 94 48 00) has an outlet at the Framneslia airport. Mountain bikes are hired out by Midnight Sun Adventures (☎ 90 72 10 91) for Nkr200 per 24 hours.

Kystriksveien – The Coastal Route

At Steinkjer, road travellers must choose between the relatively well travelled Arctic Highway to Bodø and Narvik, or the lesser-known and more expensive – but incredibly beautiful – E17 Kystriksveien, or 'Coastal Route'. There's magic around every bend here, and if you have a vehicle and enough cash for the ferries – or enough time to take the buses – you won't want to miss it. Every view along this route presents a photo opportunity and many Norwegians agree that this is the best of mainland Norway – or very close to it.

For information on the southern reaches of the route, see the Trøndelag chapter, earlier in this book; you'll also want to pick up a copy of *The Coastal Route*, a free brochure distributed by Kystriksveien (☎ 74 16 36 17, fax 74 14 56 35, post@rv17.no, www.rv17.no) or any of the tourist offices hereabouts.

BRØNNØYSUND
Set amid an archipelago of islets and skerries in a tropical-looking sea, the regional centre of Sør-Helgeland, Brønnøysund, comes as a pleasant surprise. In July you can stop by the Rådhus and check out the daily audiovisual program on the Sør-Helgeland coast. Tourist information is provided by the Sør-Helgeland Turistkontor (☎ 75 01 12 10, fax 75 01 12 19), which is open year-round.

Hildur's Urterarium
The herb, rose and cactus gardens at Hildur's Herbarium (☎ 75 02 51 34, fax 75 02 51 07) make a worthwhile stop, and the attached 'Viking Hall' and café provide the opportunity to learn about the Viking era in northern central Norway, taste the local herbal mead and sample soups and breads seasoned with locally produced herbs. The gardens include 400 types of herbs, 100 varieties of roses and around 1000 different species of cacti. It's on the Tilrem estate, along the Rv17 6km north of Brønnøysund. From 15 June to 15 August it's open from 11 am to 6 pm daily. Admission costs Nkr25 and with a three-hour guided program and a light meal it's Nkr185.

Torghatten
The most bizarre site on the coastal route has to be the Torget island peak, Torghatten, the 'market hat', which the Sagas relate was pierced through with an arrow shot by the Hestmannen, the 'Horse Man' (the Hestmannen himself is a very distinctive knobbed peak on the island of Hestmanna, seen from the Kilboghamn-Jektvik ferry, farther north). This was an attempt to kill the woman Lekamøya, but a local, Sømnafjellan, intervened and threw down his hat to distract the archer. With the sunrise, the whole scene turned to stone. Scientific

The Kystriksveien Ferries

The main element that puts budget or time-strapped travellers off taking the fabulous Kystriksveien between Steinkjer and Bodø is the cost and inconvenience of the minimum of six ferry crossings along the way. If you want to have a go anyway, the following table may help you work it into your budget:

route	ferry	passengers	car & driver	campers/ caravans	time	frequency (daily)	status
Holm-Vennesund	M/S Lysningen	Nkr18	Nkr48	Nkr90	20 minutes	10-15	Obligatory
Horn-Ånddalsvåg	M/F Torghatten	Nkr18	Nkr45	Nkr83	15 minutes	8-10	Obligatory
Forvik-Tjøtta	M/F Tjøtta	Nkr28	Nkr84	Nkr158	1 hour	8-10	Obligatory
Levang-Nesna	Peter Dass	Nkr20	Nkr56	Nkr103	20 minutes	15-18	Obligatory
Kilboghamn-Jektvik	M/F Rødøy	Nkr32	Nkr99	Nkr186	1 hour	6	Obligatory
Ågskardet-Forøy	M/F Bogøy	Nkr16	Nkr37	Nkr69	10 minutes	15-20	Obligatory
Ørnes-Vassdalsvik	M/F Landego	Nkr22	Nkr63	Nkr117	30 minutes	5	Optional

types, however, like to claim that the hole is the result of aeons of wind and water erosion on weak rock.

This particular hole, which measures 160m long, 35m high and 20m wide, is accessed by a good 20-minute walking track from the base. The peak lies only 15km south of Brønnøysund and is accessed over the Brønnøysund bridge from town, but the hole is best seen from the south. In fine weather the southbound Hurtigruten coastal steamer provides the optimum views.

Places to Stay & Eat
Conveniently located *Solli Camping* (☎ 75 02 20 09, Laukholmveien 4) offers tent camping from Nkr60/90 without/with a car, caravan camping for Nkr100 and two/four-bed cabins from Nkr250/350. Farther afield on the Torghatten road is *Mosheim Camping* (☎ 75 02 13 73), with tent/caravan camping for Nkr50/60 and good value cabins for Nkr200 to Nkr300.

The budget option is the *Corner Motel* (☎ 75 02 08 77, fax 75 02 09 41, Storgata 79), which has summer rates of Nkr465/625 for singles/doubles. The posh choice here is the *Galeasen Hotell* (☎ 75 02 14 44, fax 75 02 13 35, Havnegata 34-36) in town, which

charges summer single/double rates starting at Nkr530/715 and climbing to Nkr565/780.

If you want to stay at Torghatten, try the *Torghatten Kurs- og Feriesenter* (☎ 75 02 06 50, fax 75 02 05 40), with cabins for Nkr375 to Nkr500 and single/double rooms for Nkr500/650; it also has a basic restaurant. The atmospheric waterfront *Hotell Kystferie* (☎ 75 02 31 20, fax 75 02 01 16, kystferi@eunet.no), on the island of Nordøya west of town, offers fully-equipped seaview rooms for Nkr600/770, with lower rates on weekends.

The well known ice cream sold at the quayside *gatekjøkken* includes (believe it or not), a locally harvested seaweed agent!

Getting There & Away
For the best possible view of Torghatten, fly with Widerøe (☎ 75 01 81 20) into Brønnøysund from either Bodø or Mo i Rana; the approach route passes right over the mountain and improves on the traditional sea level view. The colour of the seas around these parts is normally associated with warmer and more southerly climes.

If you're bussing the coastal route, Helgeland Trafikkselskap links Brønnøysund and Sandnessjøen (three hours, Nkr124) three

NORDLAND

times daily on weekdays, twice on Saturday and once on Sunday; fares include the Horn-Anddalsvåg and Forvik-Tjøtta ferries.

The M/S *Vegtind* ferry from Brønnøy-sund to Sandnessjøen (two hours, Nkr139) sails on Wednesday at 8.30 am. The same boat sails to and from the large and scenic island of Vega (45 minutes, Nkr57) at least daily. The Hurtigruten coastal steamer calls in at Brønnøysund daily at 1 am northbound and 5 pm southbound.

TRÆNA & LOVUND

If you have time for just one offshore island along the Kystriksveien, Træna, Norway's oldest fishing settlement, is a good bet. In fact, Træna is an archipelago of over 1000 small, flat skerries, five of which are inhabited. Most people live on Husøy, but the adjacent island of Sanna, which measures just over 1km in length, has an amazing miniature mountain range culminating at the northern end in the 336m spire, Træna-staven. The little village at the foot of this peak enjoys a white sand beach, and when the ferry arrives on Husøy from Stokk-vågen, a local guide frequently meets visitors to offer guided climbs of this steep and impressive summit. If you have some time on the island, also check out the Kirkehelleren Cave, where archaeologists have discovered Stone Age and Iron Age artefacts.

The steep-sided island of Lovund, with 240 people, rises 623m above the sea and is home to prolific bird colonies. Every 14 April the island celebrates Lundkommer-dag, the day 200,000 puffins return to the island to nest until mid-August. You need not bring a car, as the island is tiny and easily managed on foot.

Places to Stay

Træna's accommodation options are on the island of Husøy. The *Træna Gjestegård* (☎ 75 09 52 28) has single/double rooms for Nkr450/550, as well as a restaurant, and the *Træna Rorbuferie* (☎/fax 75 09 51 67, mobile ☎ 94 85 43 96) has four-bed fishing cottages for Nkr500 to Nkr700. On Lovund, the *Lovund Rorbuhotell* (☎ 75 09 45 32,

fax 75 09 46 50) offers single/double cabins for Nkr575/750.

Getting There & Away

The M/S *Helgeland* express catamaran ferry (☎ 75 06 41 00) connects Sandnessjøen and Træna (2¾ hours, Nkr135) at least twice daily (once on Saturday), via Lovund (2¼ hours, Nkr101). The M/F *Haarek*, operated by the same company, makes the same run from Sandnessjøen to Træna (6¼ hours, passengers/cars Nkr79/290) on Tuesday and Sunday at 10 and 11.30 am, respectively, also via Lovund (three hours, passengers/cars Nkr58/189). The trip back to Sandnessjøen from Træna departs at 6.30 pm on Monday and Friday.

SANDNESSJØEN

Sandnessjøen is the main commercial centre of coastal Helgeland, and in its scenic backdrop rises the imposing Syv Søstre (Seven Sisters) range, which reaches an altitude of 1072m. All seven summits can be reached by hardy hikers without technical equipment and there's an annual competition taking in all the peaks. The record for setting foot on all seven is three hours, 54 minutes – think you can break it?

The Polarsirkelen Reiseliv (☎ 75 04 41 30, fax 75 04 41 30) has details on the town and surrounding area. They also hire bicycles for Nkr10/50/300 per hour/day/week.

The Skier of Røøya

On the island of Tro, east of Tjøtta, you can see the readily recognised rock carving, the *Skier of Røøya* (☎ 75 04 65 28), which dates from 3000 to 4000 years ago; this figure was seen around the world as the symbol of the Lillehammer Winter Olympics in 1994. From Tjøtta (30 minutes, Nkr19), south of Sandnessjøen, Tro is accessible daily on one morning ferry to Forvik (except on Sunday), and by request on several other daily sailings. Tours can also be arranged through Mindland Boat Charters (☎ 75 04 65 67, mobile ☎ 94 81 13 43) at Mindland, but they're quite expensive unless you have a group.

Places to Stay & Eat

There's no hostel, but that niche is filled by the friendly Czech-run *Sandnes Overnatting* (☎ *75 04 10 29, Haral Hårfagres gate 35)*, which offers tent camping in the garden for Nkr60, dorm beds for Nkr120 and private single/double rooms from Nkr250/350. A more sophisticated choice is the *Rica Hotel Sandnessjøen* (☎ *75 04 00 77, fax 75 04 01 86, Torolv Kveldulvsons gate 16)*, with summer single/double rates from Nkr545/790.

The charming *Tjøtta Gjestegård* (☎ *75 04 64 40, fax 75 04 55 06)*, at the northern end of the Forvik-Tjøtta ferry, is a good distance out of town but offers a super blend of mountain and sea. For singles/doubles, it's good value at Nkr375/575, and the restaurant is also deservedly renowned.

Jante's Pizza, on the waterfront near the large Prix supermarket, serves pizza, kebabs, chicken, snacks and beer. On sunny days they provide harbour-view outdoor seating. A good sit-down choice is the rustic and fully-licenced *Buri's Bistro* (☎ *75 04 40 40, Torolv Kveldulvsons gate 71)*.

Getting There & Away

Buses run a couple of times daily except Sunday between Sandnessjøen and Brønnøysund (three hours, Nkr124); in summer, a ferry between the two (two hours, Nkr139) sails on Wednesday. Drivers to and from the north have to grin and bear the toll on the imposing but inordinately expensive 1073m Helgelandsbrua bridge. It's Nkr72 for a car and driver.

RØDØY

On the one-hour ferry ride between Kilboghamn and Jektvik, in the Rødøy district, you'll pass a tiny island where a globe marks the Arctic Circle, and every sailing comes with an announcement and celebratory toot as you cross the magic line. The 440m red serpentine mountain Rødøløva makes an especially intriguing landmark.

ØRNES

Ørnes, one of the smallest ports of call on the Hurtigruten coastal steamer route, lies amid very pleasant surroundings and presents lots of hiking opportunities. For information on visiting Svartisen, see Vestisen, in the Svartisen-Saltfjellet National Park section earlier in this chapter. In summer, the *Ørnes Hotell* (☎ *75 75 45 99, fax 75 75 47 69, Havneveien 12)* charges Nkr670 for doubles.

Several times daily, buses connect Bodø with Ørnes (2½ hours, Nkr131), and most of these continue on to the Engebreen ferry terminal at Holand (one hour, Nkr61). The Hurtigruten leaves northbound at 9.30 am and southbound at 7.15 am.

BODØ

Bodø, at a latitude of 67°17', is not only Nordland's largest town with 40,000 people, but also serves as the northern terminus for the Nordlandsbanen railway. Founded in 1816 as a trade centre, it turned to fishing in 1860 during an especially lucrative herring boom. Because it was levelled on 27 May 1940 and completely rebuilt in the 1950s, the town itself looks rather ordinary – it's a bit shabby and smells strongly of the fish that sustain it – but its open backdrop of distant rugged peaks and vast skies make it one of Norway's most interestingly-positioned towns. The seas north of Bodø feature a number of dramatic islands which support the world's densest concentration of sea eagles and you'd be unlucky not to spot one gliding across the sky.

Bodø may only be 63km west of Fauske but many northbound travellers give it a miss in their rush to reach the far north, which is too bad because it's a great place to spend a couple of days. What's more, the hinterlands hold a couple of top-notch attractions and it's an easy four-hour ferry ride to the most spectacular bits of Lofoten.

Information

Tourist Office Destinasjon Bodø (☎ 75 52 60 00, fax 75 52 21 77, destinasjon.bodo@nl.telia.no, www.bodoe.com), Sjøgata 21, is just five minutes on foot from both the train station and bus terminal. This very active office not only provides information on what to see in Bodø, but also books inexpensive private accommodation, organises day excursions and can help get you to and around Lofoten, whether by bus, ferry or plane. From June to August, it's open from 9 am to 8.30 pm Monday to Friday, 10 am to 4 pm and 6 to 8 pm on Saturday and noon to 4 pm and 6 to 8 pm on Sunday. The rest of the year, you can stop by on weekdays from 9 am to 4 pm. There's also a small information desk at the Bodø airport.

Hiking, climbing and other outdoor information is the speciality of DNT's Bodø og Omegn Turistforening (☎ 75 52 14 13), Storgata 44, which is open on Tuesday from 11 am to 2.30 pm and Thursday from 11 am to 7 pm. For cabin keys, visit Berg Sport (☎ 75 52 48 90), Torvgata 4.

Bookshops If you're looking for something to read on the Lofoten ferry, check out the relatively well stocked Odds Interbok, on the corner of Storgata and Professor Schyttesgata, or Bokmiljø Bodø at Dronningens gate 13. A large selection of used books is sold by Ludvig's Bruktbokhandel at Dronningens gate 42.

Laundry You can do your laundry at the Firkanten Vasketeria (☎ 75 52 28 90), Gamle riksvei 1-5, which is open weekdays from 10 am to 4 pm and on Saturday from 10 am to 2 pm. Washing, drying and detergent costs Nkr75 per load.

Norsk Luftfartsmuseum

The Norwegian Aviation Museum (☎ 75 50 85 50) is the one Bodø attraction that shouldn't be missed, and if you have even a passing interest in flight and aviation history, allow at least half a day to see it all. The well conceived exhibits begin with a simulated (and technically functional) control tower and proceed through an exhaustive exposé of Norwegian aviation history. Note that the structure itself is built in the shape of an aeroplane propeller. Other worthwhile features include hands-on demonstrations on the theory and dynamics of flight; the logistics behind commercial aviation (including what happens to checked baggage!); examples of historic military and civilian aircraft from the Gloster Gladiator and Tiger Moth to the De-Havilland Otter and the U2; and the chance to pilot an F16 or a Harrier in a flight simulator (alas, at an extra charge).

The museum is open weekdays year-round from 10 am to 4 pm and on weekends from 10 am to 5 pm. It's extended summer hours from June to August are from 10 am to 8 pm weekdays and Sunday and 10 am to 5 pm on Saturday. Admission costs Nkr65. It's less than a 2km walk from town, but on weekdays, you can also catch city bus No 12.

Nordlandmuseet

The mildly interesting Nordland Museum (☎ 75 52 16 40), Prinsens gate 116, contains an assortment of exhibits, from background on the indigenous Sami culture, the historic lot of women in northern Norway, the regional fishing culture and even a few odd natural history displays. It's open weekdays from 9 am to 3 pm year-round and in summer its also open on weekends from 10 am to 3 pm. Admission costs a token Nkr15.

The museum has an open-air component, the Bodøsjøen Friluftsmuseum, 3km from town near Bodøsjøen Camping. Here you'll find 4 hectares of historic homes, farm buildings, boat sheds, WWII German bunkers and the square-rigged sloop *Anna Karoline af Hopen*. Admission to this section is free. The museum is also the start of a long-distance walking track up the river Bodøgårdselva, which eventually leads to the wild and scenic Bodømarka woods.

Bodø Domkirke

When you're out wandering around town, you may want to stop into the 1956 modern Gothic-style Bodø Cathedral, which sports an unusual detached spire and two stained glass windows, one a rosette and the other 12m high. The building replaced the previous church, which was destroyed during the bombings of May 1940. Admission is free.

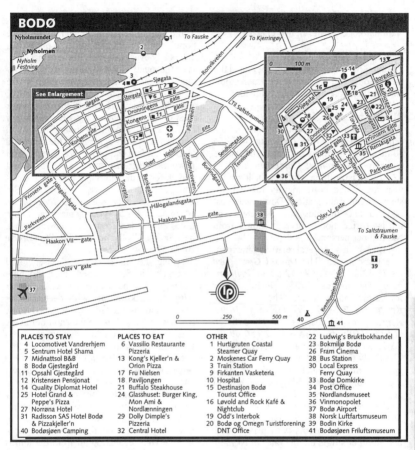

BODØ

PLACES TO STAY
4   Locomotivet Vandrerhjem
5   Sentrum Hotel Shama
7   Midnattsol B&B
8   Bodø Gjestegård
11 Opsahl Gjestegård
12 Kristensen Pensjonat
14 Quality Diplomat Hotel
25 Hotel Grand &
    Peppe's Pizza
27 Norrøna Hotel
31 Radisson SAS Hotel Bodø
    & Pizzakjeller'n
40 Bodøsjøen Camping

PLACES TO EAT
6   Vassilio Restaurante
    Pizzeria
13 Kong's Kjeller'n &
    Orion Pizza
17 Fru Nielsen
18 Paviljongen
21 Buffalo Steakhouse
24 Glasshuset: Burger King,
    Mon Ami &
    Nordlænningen
29 Dolly Dimple's
    Pizzeria
32 Central Hotel

OTHER
1   Hurtigruten Coastal
    Steamer Quay
2   Moskenes Car Ferry Quay
3   Train Station
9   Firkanten Vasketeria
10 Hospital
15 Destinasjon Bodø
    Tourist Office
16 Løvold and Rock Kafé &
    Nightclub
19 Odd's Interbok
20 Bodø og Omegn Turistforening
    DNT Office

22 Ludwig's Bruktbokhandel
23 Bokmiljø Bodø
26 Fram Cinema
28 Bus Station
30 Local Express
    Ferry Quay
33 Bodø Domkirke
34 Post Office
35 Nordlandsmuseet
36 Vinmonopolet
37 Bodø Airport
38 Norsk Luftfartsmuseum
39 Bodin Kirke
41 Bodøsjøen Friluftsmuseum

NORDLAND

Bodin Kirke

Less than 1km south-east of the Aviation Museum sits the small and quite intriguing Bodin Kirke, a little onion-domed stone church dating from around 1240. The Lutheran Reformation brought about substantial changes to the exterior, including the addition of a tower, and a host of lively 17th and 18th century Baroque elements grace the interior. From June to August, it's open from 10 am to 7 pm daily. Admission is free.

Organised Tours

Bodø Sightseeing (☎ 75 56 30 00, fax 75 56 30 01) conducts short informal town tours by sightseeing train for Nkr50 to Nkr75 from the tourist office at 11 am and 1 pm. If you'd like a taste of the Hurtigruten coastal steamer, you can take the half-day 'mini-cruise', which costs Nkr320 and entails the 7.15 am bus to Ørnes and the Hurtigruten cruise at 9.30 am back to Bodø. For information on day trips to the Engebreen glacier tongue in Svartisen-Saltfjellet National Park, see Vestisen under Svartisen-Saltfjellet National Park, earlier in this chapter.

Special Events

For a unique experience, why not attend the world's only festival honouring grand mothers and their role in society worldwide?

Places to Stay

Within reasonable walking distance of the centre is the *Bodøsjøen Camping* (☎ 75 56 36 80), 3km from town on bus No 12. The 25-room *Locomotivet Vandrerhjem* (☎ 75 52 11 22) is nothing special, but it's open year-round and conveniently located upstairs at the train station. Dorm beds cost Nkr140 and doubles cost Nkr280. The tourist office books private rooms from Nkr150 per person.

There are also several relatively inexpensive guesthouses. The *Opsahl Gjestegård* (☎ 75 52 07 04, fax 75 52 02 28, Prinsens gate 131) charges Nkr350/590 in summer for single/double rooms. The good value *Kristensen Pensjonat* (☎/fax 75 52 16 99, Rensåsgata 45) charges just Nkr290/470 and the *Midnattsol B&B* (☎ 75 50 49 00, fax 75 50 49 10) has rooms for Nkr350/550. The *Bodø Gjestegård* (☎ 75 52 04 02, Storgata 90) makes a relatively quiet option at the edge of the centre. Singles/doubles cost approximately Nkr350/550.

The friendly *Norrøna Hotel* (☎ 75 52 55 50, Storgata 4), opposite the bus station, has comfortable rooms with private bath and summer single/double rates of Nkr340/550. The Indian-run *Sentrum Hotel Shama* (☎ 75 52 48 88, fax 75 52 58 90, Storgata 39) is nothing special, but offers reasonable value at Nkr450/550 for singles/doubles.

The big chain hotels include the *Hotel Grand* (☎ 75 52 00 00, fax 75 52 27 09) and the *Radisson SAS Hotel Bodø* (☎ 75 52 41 00, fax 75 52 74 93), both on Storgata. They charge from Nkr550/750 to Nkr670/820 for singles/doubles. The top of the line is the deluxe business-class digs, the *Diplomat Hotel* (☎ 75 54 70 00, fax 75 54 70 55, Sjøgata 23), charging Nkr1095/1370.

Places to Eat

You'd be forgiven for thinking that the entire population of Bodø has joined a pizza cult, and nearly every eatery makes sure that pizza is on the menu. Good value pizza choices include the old stand-by *Peppe's Pizza* (☎ 75 52 22 25), in the Hotel Grand at Storgata 3; *Kong's Kjeller'n & Orion Pizza*, a block west of the train station; and *Pizzakjeller'n* (☎ 75 52 41 11) in the Radisson SAS Hotel. The last also does a range of Mexican and Norwegian fare and fish dishes. The *Vassilio Ristorante Pizzeria* (☎ 75 52 02 50) is best known for its delicious and inexpensive calzone, as well as its Greek specialities. Believe it or not, there's also a *Dolly Dimples* (☎ 75 52 53 85, Storgata 1) pizzeria. If your tastes run to large hunks of cowboy-style beef, try the US-themed *Buffalo Steakhouse* (☎ 75 52 15 40, Havnegata 1).

Along the Glasshuset, a glass-enclosed portion of the Storgata pedestrian shopping street, you'll find a supermarket, a *Burger King* and a konditori with decent sandwiches and discounted day-old bread. *Mon Ami* (☎ 75 52 06 00), on the 2nd floor in the Glasshuset, offers outdoor seating, continental cakes and pastries and light and healthy French-style cuisine for very reasonable prices. It's open until 8 pm. The *Paviljongen* (☎ 75 52 01 11), on the Torget, is a great outdoor spot for the Bohemian crowd; they serve not only coffee, but also light and inexpensive continental-style lunches. Another very popular daytime and evening spot is *Fru Nielsen*, just uphill from the tourist office; when the sun is shining, you'll be hard-pressed to find a seat. On the quay, *Løvold's Café* (☎ 75 52 02 61, Tollbugata 9) prepares filling Norwegian specialities for good prices.

The nearby *Central Hotel* serves more elaborate Norwegian fare, including fish and reindeer, for around Nkr110. At the Indian-oriented *Shama Restaurant* (☎ 75 52 48 88), in the Sentrum Hotel Shama, simple meat/fish lunch specials cost Nkr85/75.

At the docks, you can buy inexpensive fresh shrimp; the Vinmonopolet is just a couple of blocks farther west.

Entertainment

The town's largest disco is the very animated *Rock Kafé & Nightclub* (☎ 75 70 46 30), on Tollbugata, which serves up Tex-Mex bar snacks, burgers, steaks and sports on a large-screen TV. At the *Bonsak Piano Club*, you get fine keyboard entertainment and a cosy intimate atmosphere for drinking and chatting. It's open Monday to Thursday until 2 am and on Friday and Saturday until 3 am. The *Nordlænningen* (☎ 75 52 06 00, Storgata 16) restaurant, in the Glasshuset, is best known for its pub and disco, but also serves pizza and beef dishes.

Bodø's *Fram Cinema* (☎ 75 52 30 23), on Storgata near the entrance to the Glasshuset, has several showings daily; admission costs Nkr60.

Getting There & Away

Air Bodø's airport, right in town, lies within fairly easy walking distance of the youth hostel and hotels. The city is served by SAS, Braathens SAFE and Widerøe.

Bus Although most visitors to Bodø drive or use the train, there are still several bus services worth noting. Along the Kystriksveien, there are one or two buses daily between Bodø and Halsa (3¾ hours, Nkr180), via Ørnes (2½ hours, Nkr131), Glomfjord (three hours, Nkr139) and Holand (3½ hours, Nkr169).

The Nor-Way Bussekspress bus to and from Narvik (6¾ hours, Nkr332), via Fauske (45 minutes, Nkr70), averages three services daily; ScanRail and InterRail pass holders get a 50% discount. To reach Sortland or Svolvær by bus, take the 7.30 am bus from Bodø and change in Fauske.

Train Trondheim trains arrive in Bodø at 9.35 am and 6.35 pm. If you're continuing north by bus, get off at Fauske, where daily express buses continue to Narvik, with connections to Tromsø and Alta. Southbound trains to Fauske (45 minutes, Nkr90) and Trondheim (10 hours, Nkr680) leave Bodø at 11.30 am and 9 pm daily from 7 June to 26 September.

Ferry The northbound Hurtigruten coastal steamer arrives in Bodø at 12.30 pm and departs at 3 pm; southbound, it's in port from 1 to 4 am. The Hurtigruten quay and Lofoten car ferry docks are a five-minute walk north of the train station, while express catamaran boats dock beside the bus station.

The ferry M/S *Røst* (☎ 76 96 76 00) sails at least once daily between Bødo and Moskenes in Lofoten (3¾ hours, Nkr108/380 for passengers/car and driver), and most days also calls in at the southern Lofoten islands of Røst (Nkr119) and Værøy (Nkr99), either before or after landing in Moskenes. If you're taking a car, it's extremely wise to book in advance, which costs an additional Nkr100.

Getting Around

Buses within the city centre cost Nkr13 per ride. The tourist office rents bikes for Nkr60/110/160 for one/two/three days, plus a deposit.

AROUND BODØ
Landegode

The distinctive profile of the island of Landegode is a familiar landmark along the road north of Bodø. Its original name was Gygrøy, the 'giantess' island', but the local fishing crowd renamed it 'Good Land' lest the island's mountain giantess take offence. Legend has it that one day this temperamental landlord grew lonely and shouted across the water to Blåmann, on the mainland, and asked him to marry her and keep her company. He agreed, provided she'd bring the island along with her and thereby elevate him above the troublesome trolls of Sulitjelma. By the time she'd packed up the island, however, the sun rose and she turned to stone, as did Blåmann, who'd stayed out too long waiting for her.

The classic 40m lighthouse on the islet of Eggløysa, north of the main island, was built in 1900 and the keepers' quarters are now used for accommodation and conventions. Contact *Landego Fyr* (☎/fax 75 52 90 92) or the *Skagen Hotel* (☎ 75 52 24 00, fax 75 52 59 30), at Nyholmsgata 11 in Bodø.

You can reach the island by ferry from the Hurtigbåtkaia in Bodø (30 minutes, Nkr47) on Tuesday, Thursday, Friday and Saturday.

Kjerringøy

On a sunny day, you certainly won't regret a visit to the lovely 19th century trading station Kjerringøy, 40km north of Bodø, which lies on a sleepy peninsula beside luminescent turquoise seas with a backdrop of soaring granite peaks. Here, the entrepreneurial Erasmus Zahl trading family provided local fishing families with supplies in exchange for their catches, and after making their fortune, expanded into mining, banking and steam transport concerns.

Most of the timber-built historic district has been preserved as an open-air museum contrasting the spartan quarters and kitchens of the fishing families with the sumptuous décor and living standards of the merchants. The historical displays have been augmented by a café and audiovisual presentation. From 23 May and 23 August its open from noon to 5 pm daily, with extended hours from 20 June to 9 August when it's open daily from 11 am to 7 pm. Admission to the museum costs Nkr30 and guided tours of the main building are Nkr25. You can stay overnight at the old rectory, which is now the *Kjerringøy Prestegård* (☎ 75 58 34 60, fax 75 50 07 10, fax 75 50 77 33), with hostel-style beds for Nkr100 and doubles in the adjoining stable for approximately Nkr450.

Buses from Bodø to Kjerringøy (1½ hours, Nkr65) leave on summer weekdays at 1.35 and 4.15 pm, on Saturday at 2.10 pm and on midsummer Sundays at 2.15 pm. Fares include the Festvåg-Misten ferry. Return buses generally leave Kjerringøy about two hours after they arrive; on weekdays, there's also a morning bus back to Bodø at 8.25 am. The Festvåg-Misten ferry (15 minutes, Nkr16/37 for passengers/cars) runs on weekdays between 6.30 am to 10.30 pm, with shorter hours on the weekend. Along the way, take note of the distinctive profile of **Landegode** island, the white sandy beaches at **Mjelde** (but you'll need a car to reach them) and the beautiful and dramatic peak **Steigtind**, which rises a few kilometres south of Festvåg.

Saltstraumen

The 3km-long and 150m-wide Saltstraumen Strait connects Saltenfjord and Skjerstadfjord, and here, the tides cause one fjord to drain into the other and create the equivalent of a waterfall in the sea. The result is a swirling, churning, 20-knot watery chaos which shifts over 400 million cubic metres of water every six hours. This maelstrom, which is claimed to be the world's largest, is impressive to say the least, and can be readily viewed from the arching Saltstraumbrua bridge which spans the strait. Visitors have mixed reactions to this place – they're either awestruck and cathartic or utterly bored – but if you're the sort of person who can be mesmerised by water in turmoil and distant views of impossible peaks, you won't regret the effort of getting there.

All this water action creates an ideal environment for plankton, which attracts an abundance of both fish and anglers. In the spring, you can also see the squawking colonies of gulls which nest on the midstream island of Storholmen. The Saltstraumen Opplevelsessenter (☎ 75 56 06 55), on the northern shore, presents a multimedia show and explains everything you'd want to know about tidal bores – and perhaps even more. It's open daily from 1 May to 30 September and costs Nkr50. Perhaps allow time for a light meal or snack at the lively *Sjøbua* outdoor café (☎ 75 58 71 38), which overlooks the roiling waters.

From Bodø, bus No 19 frequently travels the 33km from Bodø to Saltstraumen (50 minutes, Nkr39). The Bodø tourist office keeps tide tables and can tell you exactly when to expect the best shows. If you're approaching Saltstraumen from the south (that is, you'll reach Saltstraumen before Bodø), the tourist office is happy to fax or email this information (see Information under Bodø, earlier in this chapter).

Lofoten

The rather unearthly glacier-carved peaks of the islands of Lofoten, separated from the mainland by tapering Vestfjorden, rise straight out of the sea and, from a distance, this so-called Lofoten Wall appears as an unbroken mass. The rich fishing grounds here have been created by the meeting of the Gulf Stream and the icy Arctic Ocean, which draws spawning arctic cod from the Barents Sea southward each winter. This in turn draws migrating north coast farmers who favour the open landscapes and rich soils of Vestvågøy and for centuries have relied on this seasonal boon. Although cod stocks have dwindled dramatically in recent years, fishing remains Lofoten's largest industry, as evidenced by the innumerable wooden drying racks which lattice every village.

The sensational main islands, Austvågøy, Vestvågøy, Flakstadøy and Moskenesøy, boast sheltered bays, sheep pastures and

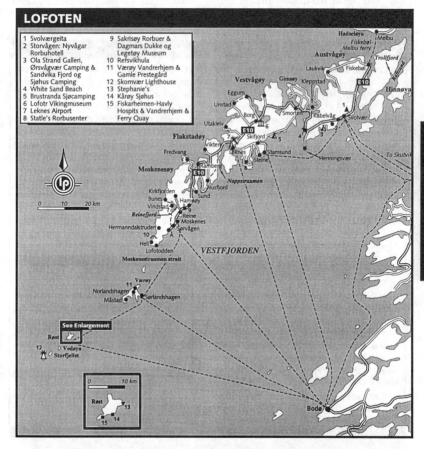

LOFOTEN

1 Svolværgeita
2 Storvågen: Nyvågar Rorbuhotell
3 Ola Strand Galleri, Ørsvågvær Camping & Sandvika Fjord og Sjøhus Camping
4 White Sand Beach
5 Brustranda Sjøcamping
6 Lofotr Vikingmuseum
7 Leknes Airport
8 Statle's Rorbusenter
9 Sakrisøy Rorbuer & Dagmars Dukke og Legetøy Museum
10 Refsvikhula
11 Værøy Vandrerhjem & Gamle Prestegård
12 Skomvær Lighthouse
13 Stephanie's
14 Kårøy Sjøhus
15 Fiskarheimen-Havly Hospits & Vandrerhjem & Ferry Quay

NORDLAND

picturesque villages where the backdrops, dominated by looming crags, might be mistaken for painted Hollywood film sets. Both this overwhelming scenery and the mystical Arctic light have long attracted artists who are represented in galleries at Svolvær, Kabelvåg and the trendy little fishing village of Henningsvær.

Because the islands see so much tourism, there's a range of accommodation possibilities, but most people opt for either *rorbuer* or *sjøhus*. The name of the former means literally 'rowers' dwelling', and originally, they were small red-painted fishing huts which lined the fishing harbours and were occupied by visiting fisherfolk. Nowadays, the name is applied to a range of structures, from historic cottages formerly occupied by fishing folk to dire little pre-fab camping cabins to simple holiday homes and fully-equipped modern self-catering units. There are few real bargains – most visiting Norwegians are happy to pay for any semblance of nostalgia or rusticity – but some are quite atmospheric and it's worth spending at least a night in one of the more traditional ones.

Sjøhus, on the other hand, are normally bunkhouse-style buildings on the docks where fishery workers processed the catch, and for convenience, they also ate and slept

Glory Be to Cod

In Lofoten, cod have been caught (using long lines or nets) on a large scale since the early 17th century. In the past, large numbers of fishermen travelled to the islands, living in shacks called *rorbuer*, which were built on stilts at the edge of the sea.

In 1854 at Å i Lofoten, the pharmacist Peter Møller decided it was time to introduce more people to the healthy properties of cod liver oil, which was rich in vitamin D and successfully assuaged the winter depression brought on by the lack of sunlight in the Arctic regions. The oil was also used to light lamps all over northern Europe, hence its local name *lysi*, or 'light'. Møller constructed a cauldron, filled it with water and cod livers, and steam-boiled them down into a potent oil. This medicinal concoction was honoured at trade fairs in Europe and abroad. Even after the oil was skimmed off, the livers were steamed in large oak barrels and then pressed to yield every last drop of the commercially profitable oil. Every summer, thousands of barrels of oil were shipped from Lofoten to Bergen and on to Europe. The smell, however, pervaded the entire village and local people liked to comment that in Å, one could smell the scent of money.

The Lofoten Cod Fishery continues to be a major Lofoten economic force and reaches its height from January to April when cod come to Vestfjorden to spawn. Around the end of March each year the unofficial World Cod Fishing Championship is held in Svolvær and can involve up to 300 entrants. Nowadays, cod numbers have been diminished by overfishing, but the overall catch is still substantial, at 50,000 tonnes annually (30,000 tonnes without the heads). One in 20,000 of these fish is a king cod and bears a distinctive lump on the forehead, which indicates intelligence and is supposed to bring good luck to the fishing family that catches it. These unique fish are often hung on a string from the ceiling and used to forecast the weather, hence the name 'weather cod'.

Traditional methods of preserving the fish are still used today, namely drying in the open air on large racks, and 15,000 tonnes are now hung out each year. The fish are normally prepared in three different ways: as *saltfish*, which is cut into fillets, salted and dried for about three weeks; *klipfish*, which is saltfish that's cleaned, re-salted and dried in large heated plants; and *stockfish*, which is unsalted fish dried on large racks in fresh cold air (note that 1kg of stockfish has the same nutritional value as 5kg of fresh fish!).

there. Some of these have now been converted into summer tourist lodges and apartments, and they can be quite nice. Tent and caravan camping are available at Unstad, Kabelvåg, Kleppstad, Laukvik, Ramberg, Strandslett (Stamsund) and Svolvær.

For independent travellers, getting around isn't too difficult, as the four main islands are linked by bridge or tunnel, and buses run the entire E10 from the Fiskebøl-Melbu ferry in the north to Å at road's end in the south-west. Note that bus fares are half-price for holders of InterRail and ScanRail passes.

Information is available at the website www.lofoten.com.

History

The history of Lofoten is in effect the history of its fishing industry, and numerous battles have been fought over these seas, which became exceptionally rich in spawning cod after the glaciers retreated about 10,000 years ago. The best known entanglement in northern Norway was the Battle of Stiklestad (near Trondheim) in 1030, in which the largely inexperienced army of the northern Norwegian king, Tore Hund, prevailed over the southern king, St Olav. In later conflicts, however, the north lost the right to its own resources and in 1120, King Øystein set up the first church and for visiting fisherfolk, he

Glory Be to Cod

The dried and/or salted fish stays edible for years, and dried cod is often eaten raw (it's a trifle chewy!), smoked, salted or reconstituted with water and boiled. Ling is also salted, dried and occasionally smoked. A small proportion of the cod and ling catch is used domestically (cod tongue is a local delicacy) and the roe is salted in enormous German wine vats, but most of the dried stockfish is exported to Italy, Spain and Portugal, and the heads are sent to Nigeria to form the basis for a popular and spicy West African dish.

In order to get children involved from an early age, they're assigned the task of removing the cod tongues, and are paid for the number they can extract. The tongues are then packed in water and frozen in plastic bags for later use. The normal method of serving them is to boil them in salt water and serve them up with gravy as *stekte torsketungur*, simply 'boiled cod tongues'.

Modern fishing folk of Nordland and Troms are quite vociferous in their opposition to the EU. If Norway joined the EU, the Spanish fishing fleet would be allowed access to Norwegian inshore waters and that prospect is none too welcome. This helps explain votes of around 90% against the EU in certain northern districts. In recent times, there have even been skirmishes with Icelandic trawlers over territorial fishing rights.

The latest news from the world of cod involves their fishy mating calls; it seems that the grunts they use to attract mates are so loud that submarines' sonar devices are blocked, making underwater navigation almost impossible!

built a number of rorbuer, 4m by 4m wooden cabins with a fireplace, earthen floor and small porch area. Thereby, he took control of the local economy and ensured rich tax pickings for himself.

In the 13th century the German Hanseatic League moved in and utterly usurped power from the local aristocracy. The general populace, which remained at the mercy of the sea, were left in abject poverty, despite an increase in export trade. By 1750, however, the trade monopoly lost its grip, locals again took control of their own economic ventures and opportunists migrated in from the south. Through the 19th century, power over the trade fell to local *nessekonger*, or 'merchant squires' who'd bought up property, and through the rorbu system, this new aristocracy forced tenants to deliver their entire catch at a price set by the landlords. Fortunately, the Lofoten Act of 1857 greatly diminished the power of the nessekonger, but not until the Raw Fish Sales Act of 1936 did they lose the power to set prices. By the end of WWII, trade was again freed up and Lofoten fishing families could finally conduct their own trade, set prices and export their resources with a relative minimum of outside interference.

AUSTVÅGØY

Many visitors make their aquaintance with Lofoten on Austvågøy, the northernmost island in the group and the one with most people and visitor facilities. Arriving from Melbu, in Vesterålen, they're greeted by craggy, impossible peaks, while those arriving by sea at Svolvær are greeted by Lofoten's finest hotels and restaurants, as well as most of its cultural attractions.

Raftsund & Trollfjorden

The narrow Raftsund channel, which separates the Lofoten island of Austvågøy and the Vesterålen island of Hinnøya, emerges as a highlight for through-passengers on the Hurtigruten coastal steamer route. The most memorable section of the trip is the short jaunt into constricted 2km long Trollfjorden; while its dark waters and towering walls are admittedly quite scenic, if you have to choose between a Trollfjorden excursion or a visit to southern Moskenesøy, the latter may well prove more interesting and unusual. For access information, see Organised Tours under Svolvær, later in this section.

Svolvær

By Lofoten standards, the modern and busy port town of Svolvær is as exciting as it gets. The town once sprawled across a series of skerries, but the in-between spaces are now being filled in to create a largely reclaimed peninsula with a bit of room for growth.

There's a choice of banks, shops, accommodation and eateries, and a bookshop, Rødsand Libris (☎ 76 07 05 33). The helpful Destinasjon Lofoten tourist office (☎ 76 07 30 00, fax 76 07 30 01, tourist@post.lofotposten.no), Postboks 210, N-8301 Svolvær, can provide information on the entire archipelago.

Svolvær Krigsminnemuseum The Svolvær War Memorial Museum (☎ 76 07 00 49) is one of the best such museums in Norway. It's known for its large collection of original military uniforms, including both Allied and German examples, as well as its largely unpublished WWII-era photos and details on the June 1940 bombing of Svolvær.

Svolværgeita (The Goat) Daredevils like to scale The Goat, a distinctive two-pronged peak visible from the harbour, and then jump from one horn to the other. The ascent begins at a churchyard (which awaits those who leap and miss ...) on the left as you leave Svolvær on the E10 towards Narvik. The route climbs steeply from the Innstadviak road behind the churchyard. It isn't easy, however, and requires some scrambling. While nearly anyone can get to the base of Svolværgeita, reaching the horns, Storhornet and Lillehornet, requires a 40m technical climb. After that, the jump between them may seem a piece of cake – but is emphatically not recommended. If your detemination is unswayed but you haven't brought your climbing gear, see the Nord Norsk Kaltreskole in Henningsvær, who can set you up with a guide and equipment; see Henningsvær, later in this section.

Skrova The offshore island of Skrova makes an amenable day visit from Svolvær, and offers a couple of short walks. The ferry from Svolvær (30 minutes, Nkr23) runs two or three times daily in summer, then continues on to Skutvik (two hours, Nkr53), on the mainland, to connect with ferries to Bodø.

Organised Tours The M/S *Lofotcruise* and M/S *Trollfjord* excursion boats sail daily in summer into the constricted confines of Trollfjord, which is just 2km long but spectacularly steep and narrow. The tours run five to 10 times daily between

about 10 June and 20 August and cost Nkr250 per person. The coastal steamer also makes a jaunt into the fjord, practically scraping the rock walls before doing a three-point (Y) turn and heading off. If you prefer sticking close to the water, informal Zodiac (inflatable raft) tours (☎ 90 79 38 47 or ☎ 90 68 92 06) to Trollfjorden and Skrova are conducted for Nkr450 per person, with a minimum of six people.

Special Events Every second year for three weeks in June, Svolvær hosts the Lofoten Arts Festival, which alternates with the Composers' Week festival in April of other years.

Places to Stay The *Svolvær Sjøhus-camping* (☎ 76 07 03 36) is a rustic dockside beachhouse with beds from Nkr150 and singles/doubles for Nkr300/480. Turn

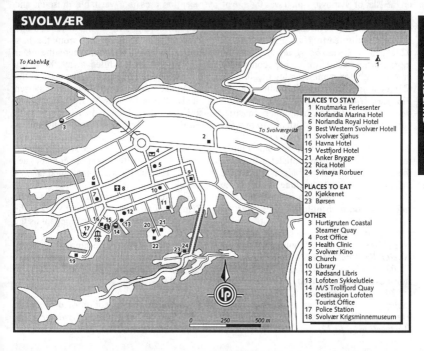

SVOLVÆR

To Kabelvåg

To Svolværgeita

PLACES TO STAY
1 Knutmarka Feriesenter
2 Norlandia Marina Hotel
6 Norlandia Royal Hotel
9 Best Western Svolvær Hotell
11 Svolvær Sjøhus
16 Havna Hotel
19 Vestfjord Hotel
21 Anker Brygge
22 Rica Hotel
24 Svinøya Rorbuer

PLACES TO EAT
20 Kjøkkenet
23 Børsen

OTHER
3 Hurtigruten Coastal
  Steamer Quay
4 Post Office
5 Health Clinic
7 Svolvær Kino
8 Church
10 Library
12 Rødsand Libris
13 Lofoten Sykkelutleie
14 M/S Trollfjord Quay
15 Destinasjon Lofoten
  Tourist Office
17 Police Station
18 Svolvær Krigsminnemuseum

0   250   500 m

NORDLAND

right on the first road past the library, five minutes east of the harbour. Alternatively, you can try the lakeside *Knutmarka Feriesenter* (☎ *76 07 21 64, fax 76 07 26 32, Leirskoleveien 10)*, 3km from Svolvær. Tent or caravan camping costs Nkr65 plus Nkr15 per person. For well appointed cabins with showers and toilets, you'll pay Nkr375 to Nkr775. It's open from 19 June to 16 August and amenities include a sauna and canoe hire.

The beautiful *Anker Brygge* (☎ *76 06 64 80, fax 76 06 64 70)* apartments occupy a modernised 1880 fish processing plant, salting house and barrel factory. Guests have access to the lovely rustic sauna. The very amenable top-floor room, complete with cooking facilities, holds five people and costs Nkr2000 while a smaller self-catering flat above the sauna costs Nkr1500. The similarly appealing and even more rustic *Svinøya Rorbuer* (☎ *76 07 06 23, fax 76 07 21 11)* is on the islet of Svinøya, which was the site of the first settlement in Svolvær. Two to six-bed cottages go for Nkr650 to Nkr1100.

The down-to-earth *Havna Hotel* (☎ *76 07 10 55, OJ Kaarbøesgata 5)*, near the tourist office, has comfortable rooms with private bath for summer rates of Nkr550/650 for singles/doubles. The oddly coloured *Vestfjord Hotel* (☎ *76 07 08 70, fax 76 07 08 54, Fiskergata 46)*, in a rather industrial part of town, has comfortable rooms for Nkr480/620. At the *Rica Hotel* (☎ *76 07 22 22, fax 76 07 20 01)*, which is built on pilings over the water on the islet of Lanholmen, some suites have balconies, but the most unusual actually includes a hole in the floor so the occupants can fish without leaving their room. Singles/doubles start at Nkr550/810.

Other upmarket choices charging from Nkr550/690 for singles/doubles include the *Norlandia Royal Hotel* (☎ *76 07 12 00, fax 76 07 08 50, Siv Nilsensgata 21)*; the very non-descript *Norlandia Marina Hotel* (☎ *76 07 07 77, fax 76 07 22 15)*, on Repslagergata; and the *Best Western Svolvær Hotell* (☎ *76 07 19 99, fax 76 07 09 09, Austnesfjordgata 12)*.

Places to Eat The *Havna Hotel*'s attached café serves pizza for Nkr55 and daily specials for Nkr75. The restaurant at the *Vestfjord Hotel* specialises in Chinese cuisine.

For a treat, check out the acclaimed *Kjøkkenet* (☎ *76 06 84 80)*, which is affiliated with the Anker Brygge apartments. The dining room, made up like an old-time kitchen, comes complete with a spinning wheel, a stuffed cat under the stove and kitchen words of wisdom on the wall samplers. The bar is a lifeboat from a WWII Polish troop ship which washed up in Svolvær in 1946. Best of all, it's real (except for the cat) and not just a tourist mock-up. The recommended menu choice is of course fish.

Another unusually appealing choice is the *Børsen* (☎ *76 07 08 80)*, the name of which means 'stock exchange'. It's housed in the restored *Krambua* general store; the reception area is a veritable museum and the dining room, with its cracked and bowed flooring, still smells of tar and cod liver oil. The name comes from the harbourfront bench outside, where the older men of the town whiled away the hours discussing the price of fish, the state of the world and other pertinent topics. It's often cited as the best lamb restaurant in Norway, and the fillet of lamb in rosemary with *diable* sauce, brussels sprouts and mushrooms costs Nkr195. You can also sample a reindeer starter for Nkr78, *steinbit* in pastry with saffron for Nkr168, cod tongues for Nkr155 and the much-maligned *lutefisk* for Nkr170.

The elegant boat-shaped restaurant in the *Rica Hotel* affords an excellent view of the harbour and the prices are as elegant as the fish-dominated meals.

There's a pub-style restaurant, a bakery and a couple of other eateries on the square and a *Rimi* supermarket a block inland on Torggata.

Entertainment In addition to the hotel bars, there's a cinema, the *Svolvær Kino*, which screens recent films nightly.

Remember to pack sunscreen and sunnies ... Midnight sun, Vesterålen Islands

NED FRIARY

Warehouses of Trondheim, Trøndelag

NED FRIARY

An island of the Great Barrier Reef? No, it's Brønnøysund, Nordland

The most scenic town in Norway? Reine, Lofoten Islands, Nordland

Shopping Those in search of Lofoten-theme art may well find something at the Ola Strand Galleri (☎ 76 07 74 61), whose graphic prints reveal the nature and culture of this island. It's in Ørsnes, 10km west of town. From 1 June to 31 August, it's open weekdays from 10 am to 9 pm and on Saturday from 10 am to 6 pm.

Getting There & Away Flights between Bodø and Svolvær (or Leknes) cost Nkr630/755 one-way/return. If you're heading for or coming from Vesterålen, bus No 512 between Svolvær and the Fiskebøl ferry quay (3¼ hours, Nkr43) runs at least daily in each direction. Buses to Leknes (two hours, Nkr79) leave Svolvær at least four times daily and a car ferry runs between Svolvær and the mainland town of Skutvik (two hours, Nkr50/174 for passengers/cars). Express boats ply the waters between Bodø and Svolvær (3½ hours, Nkr213) and between Narvik and Svolvær (3¼ hours, Nkr255) daily except Saturday. There are no sailings on Saturday and no Monday sailing from Svolvær to Narvik.

Northbound, the Hurtigruten coastal steamer leaves Bodø at 3 pm daily, arriving in Svolvær (six hours, Nkr271), via Stamsund (2½ hours, Nkr90), at 9 pm. Southbound, it arrives from Tromsø (17 hours, Nkr627), Finnsnes (15¾ hours, Nkr492), Harstad (10½ hours, Nkr325), Risøyhamn (7½ hours, Nkr266), Sortland (5¼ hours, Nkr189) and Stokmarknes (three hours, Nkr157) at 6.30 pm and heads for Stamsund and Bodø at 7.30 pm.

Getting Around The Svolvær area is ideal for cycling, and you can hire bikes at Lofoten Sykkelutleie (☎ 76 07 24 80, mobile ☎ 91 15 04 90), Parkgata 8. Those who'd prefer to potter around Lofoten in a car can hire from the private Rent-a-Car agency (☎ 95 05 35 66) for a bargain Nkr300 per day, with unlimited mileage. All the main agencies are also represented: Hertz (☎ 76 07 07 20), Budget (☎ 76 07 00 00), Avis (☎ 76 07 11 40) and InterRent (☎ 76 06 61 40).

Kabelvåg

Quiet Kabelvåg, which is essentially a suburb of Svolvær, presents a more intimate face than its larger neighbour to the east. A few old timber buildings remain, there are several visitor attractions (including a worthwhile trio of museums at nearby Storvågen) and the hostel ensures that lots of independent travellers wind up here.

The small town square wraps around the harbour and features an informal outdoor market. While you're there, watch for Jack Berntsen, a colourful retired teacher who writes and sings his own songs and once won *Dagblådet*'s 'messiest office in Norway' competition.

Vågan Kirke The 1898 Vågan Church (☎ 76 07 82 90), one of Norway's largest wooden houses of worship, rises over the main road outside the town. Built a century ago to minister to the influx of seasonal fisherfolk, its seating capacity of 1200 far surpasses Kabelvåg's current population.

Storvågan Behind the old prison, a trail climbs to the statue of King Øystein, who in 1120 ordered the first rorbu to be built to house fishermen who had been sleeping in their overturned rowing boats. It was more than an act of kindness, however, as the tax on the exported dried fish was the main source of the king's revenue. Some of these original rorbuer have recently been excavated as part of the Lofoten Museum (☎ 76 07 82 23), and contrast the lifestyles of the commoners and that of the Lofoten squires. It's open from 9 am to 3 pm, with extended hours between 16 May and 31 August, when its open from 9 am to 6 pm. These hours are further extended from 15 June to 15 August when it's open daily from 9 am to 9 pm. Admission costs Nkr35.

The sea-front Lofoten Aquarium (☎ 76 07 86 65), beside the Lofoten Museum, brings to the surface some of the faces which made Lofoten great, mainly cod but also other fish and even some sea mammals. From 15 June to 15 August, it's open from 10 am to 9 pm daily, and shorter hours the rest of the year. Admission costs Nkr60. If you prefer to observe them in their natural environment you can opt for the Nkr150 submarine experience aboard the *Captain Nemo* (☎ 76 07 07 03), a submarine-style boat with a glassed-in keel to permit underwater viewing. For even more of a hands-on experience contact Lofotdykk (☎ 76 07 82 71, mobile ☎ 94 18 64 32), at Kaiveien 15 in town, which offers Arctic scuba diving.

Gallery Espolin (☎ 76 07 84 05) features artist Kaare Espolin-Johnson's works, which reveal the lives and hardships of the Lofoten fisherfolk. It's undoubtedly one of Norway's most worthwhile galleries and you won't soon forget the haunting quality of his monochrome themes. From 15 June to 14 August, it's open daily from 10 am to 8 pm with shorter hours the rest of the year. Admission costs Nkr35.

Places to Stay & Eat The institutional-looking – and often fully-booked – *Kabelvåg Vandrerhjem* (☎ 76 07 88 00, fax 76 07 80 03) is housed in a school building about 1km from the centre. Dorm beds are Nkr130 and singles/doubles cost Nkr240/350. In summer advance booking is essential. *Kabelvåg Sjøhuscamping* (☎/fax 76 07 25 60, mobile ☎ 90 52 06 75, Rækøyveien 62), 900m from town, offers sjøhus rooms with a fridge and cable TV for Nkr300 to Nkr450.

At Storvågan, you can stay at the shore-side *Nyvågar Rorbuhotell* (☎ 76 07 89 00, fax 76 07 89 50), which also has an acclaimed restaurant. Fully-equipped modern rorbuer with four beds start at Nkr980. Just off the E10, 3km and two inlets west of Kabelvåg, you can camp at *Ørsvågvær Camping* (☎ 76 07 81 80, fax 76 07 83 37) for Nkr70/100 in a tent/caravan. Huts can be rented for Nkr330 to Nkr790. Next door (you have to use the Ørsvågvær entrance) is the beautifully located *Sandvika Fjord og Sjøhus Camping* (☎ 76 07 81 45, fax 76 07 90 10). Here, you'll pay Nkr110 per tent or caravan and Nkr610 for relatively plush cabins. To reach either of these places, you can take the bus from Svolvær (15 minutes, Nkr16) along the E10 to the bus stop about 900m from Sandvika; it runs about 15 times on weekdays and four to six times on the weekend.

The popular *Præstenbrygga Restaurant* (☎76 07 80 60) is another fishy place with character. Check out the old photo of the fishing community attending church, which says a lot about the historic demographics here!

Getting There & Away From Svolvær you can walk the 5km to Kabelvåg or catch the hourly town bus (15 minutes, Nkr16).

Henningsvær

Although it's somewhat preposterously called the 'Venice of Lofoten', few people would disagree that bohemian Henningsvær is the lightest, brightest and of course, trendiest place in the archipelago. It's also the region's largest and most active fishing village, but these days the harbour bustles with as many pleasure craft as fishing boats and especially on weekends, the outdoor seating at the waterside bars and restaurants is great for hours of observing the lively scene. On sunny summer days, the white sand beach near the E10 turnoff also attracts lots of local people for picnics and Arctic swimming.

Lofoten House Gallery The art gallery at Lofoten House, in a former fish-processing house, displays a fine collection of theme paintings from around northern Norway, and upstairs, you can peruse a selection of antique paintings which are for sale, as well as a series of professional turn-of-the-century photos. Downstairs, a 17-minute slide show of art photos reveals the people and landscapes of Lofoten in all kinds of weather. It runs hourly, on the hour. Admission to the gallery and slide show costs Nkr40.

Nord Norsk Klatreskole The North Norwegian Climbing School (☎ 76 07 49 11, fax 76 07 46 46), N-8330 Henningsvær, offers a wide range of technical climbing, kayaking and skiing courses all around northern Norway (as well as the Himalaya),

Nordland Boats

No visitor to northern Norway will fail to notice the uniquely shaped Nordland boat, which takes its inspiration from the early seafaring Viking ships and has served the local fishing community from the earliest days of settlement in this region. In fact, these boats have now come to symbolise the earthy and self-sufficient lifestyles followed by the hardy coastal folk of the northern regions. Today, they remain in use from Namsos, in Nord Trøndelag, right up to the Kola Peninsula in Arctic Russia, but the greatest concentrations are found in the tiny villages of Lofoten.

The smallest versions are known as *færing*, which measure up to 5m, while the progressively larger ones are called *hundromsfæring* (6m), *seksring* (7m), *halvfjerderomning* (7.5m), *firroing* (8m), *halvfemterømming* (9m), *åttring* (10 to 11m) and *femboring* (11 to 13m). Traditionally, the larger the boat, the greater the status of its captain, or *høvedmann*. However, all boats of this construction are renowned for being excellent for both rowing and sailing, even in rough northern seas, and historically, the fishing communities took great pride in joining sailing competitions against their neighbours. A good place to see museum-quality examples is in the harbour at Å i Lofoten.

including the challenging Stetind, south of Narvik, which WC Slingsby called 'the ugliest mountain I ever saw'.

If you want to tackle Svolværgeita or any other Lofoten peak, climbing with an experienced guide, including equipment, costs Nkr900/1000 per day for one/two people; you must book one day in advance. For ideas, you can check out their own publication, the 320-page *Climbing in the Magic Islands*, by Ed Webster, which is the last word on climbing in Lofoten; it's sold at their attached mountaineering shop. The school also rent single kayaks for Nkr150/250 per half/full day and double kayaks for Nkr250/400.

Places to Stay & Eat Henningsvær lacks a hostel, but *Den Siste Viking* (☎ 76 07 49 11, fax 76 07 46 46), run by the climbing school, crosses a Lofoten rorbu with an English pub and a Himalayan trekkers' lodge. Dorm beds cost Nkr120.

Of the several rorbu complexes, the least expensive is the *Giæver Trading* (☎ 76 07 47 19, fax 76 07 49 00), right in town, which belongs to the fish plant. In summer it hires out workers' accommodation to

tourists; simple rorbuer cost from Nkr400 to Nkr600 and a room in the *Handelshuset* sjøhus is Nkr300 to Nkr400.

The most economical hotel, the *Henningsvær Hotell* (☎ 76 07 49 99, fax 76 07 49 35, Dreyers gate 8), has single/double rooms from Nkr350/550. Henningsvær's quayside hotel, the *Henningsvær Bryggehotel* (☎ 76 07 47 50, fax 76 07 47 30) is a nice atmospheric place with single double rooms, most with water views, from Nkr700/850.

Henningsvær's culinary claim to fame is the fish soup at the *Fiskekrogen* (☎ 76 07 46 52) at the colourful harbour. As a young girl Queen Sonja visited on a backpacking trip and the soup remains a royal favourite. She now makes a point of returning whenever she's in town. The *Klatrekafeen* (☎ 76 07 49 11) at the climbing school serves up light meals and hearty snacks, as well as coffee and sweets.

Getting There & Away Bus No 510 shuttles between Svolvær (35 minutes, Nkr35), Kabelvåg (30 minutes, Nkr29) and Henningsvær at least four times daily from Monday to Saturday and once on Sunday.

NORDLAND

VESTVÅGØY
Vestvågøy may be known as the 'flattest' of the Lofoten islands, but it's far from flat and holds several interesting surprises, especially around the edges.

Unstad & Eggum
Those with a car may enjoy driving over the steep, untarred road to the wild and isolated west coast village of Unstad. There you can follow the 9km coastal track past several headlands, a solitary lighthouse and superb sea views, to the equally isolated village of Eggum, which is known for its views of the midnight sun. At Unstad, you can camp at *Unstad Camping* (☎ 76 08 33 91, fax 76 08 54 42) for Nkr70 per tent or stay in their cabins for Nkr350 to Nkr700. At Eggum, the *Eggum Sjøhus* (☎ 76 08 62 00) has dorm beds for Nkr125. It's open from 1 June to 31 August.

On Monday, Wednesday and Friday, the 11.45 am bus No 407 from Leknes to Borg makes a run to Eggum (1¼ hours, Nkr35) and on Tuesday and Thursday it runs via Unstad (1¼ hours, Nkr32). On the same days it leaves Eggum or Unstad at 1 pm and continues to Borg.

Lofotr Vikingmuseum
It was in 1981 at Borg, near the centre of the island, that local farmer Frik Harald Bjerkli inadvertently ploughed up the remains of the 83m-long dwelling of a powerful Viking chieftain, which turned out to be the largest yet discovered anywhere in Scandinavia.

The site's new and very worthwhile Lofotr Viking Museum (☎ 76 08 49 00, lofotr@ lofotposten.no) offers a glimpse of life in Viking times, complete with a full-scale reconstruction of the building, costumed interpreters and a Viking ship replica. Best of all is the dim interior where, according to their brochure, 'light flickers from the hearths and gleams from cod liver oil lamps, the smell of wood tar fills your nostrils and the humming from cooking activities rises the 9m up to the roof.' Visitors can enhance the experience with such culinary specialities as a chieftain's lunch, a chieftain's feast (evenings only) or just a peasants' bowl of lamb broth stew. Around Christmas, they dish up the seasonal pagan feast known as *jølblot* (yule blood), which features mead, fish stew and the meat of various beasts.

From 23 May to 31 August, the museum is open daily from 10 am to 7 pm. Admission and guided tours cost Nkr70; guided tours include a glass of mead and cost Nkr80, while tours and a light lunch are Nkr95 to Nkr120. The Svolvær-Leknes bus passes the entrance.

Leknes
Leknes, the modern municipal centre of Vestvågøy exists mainly for it's airport, where you'll find direct flights to Oslo, via Bodø, but other than to change buses or catch a flight, there's little reason to visit. Leknes has an economy restaurant at the bus station and a bakery across the street. Next door in the Rådhus you'll find the Leknes Turistkontor tourist office (☎ 76 08 97 92), post office and taxi stand.

Stamsund
The traditional fishing village of Stamsund makes a fine destination largely because of its dockside hostel, which is a major magnet for independent travellers, and some have loved it so much that they've lingered for weeks on end. In the town centre, inasmuch as Stamsund has one, you'll find a bakery, food shop, post office and bus stop – and very little else.

Places to Stay & Eat At *Justad Vandrerhjem/Rorbuer* (☎ 76 08 93 34), bunks in the old beachhouse cost Nkr75, doubles start at Nkr190, and great four-bed cabins cost Nkr390. The unique and friendly manager, Roar Justad, can tell you all about local hiking routes; he also rents old bicycles and mopeds and loans out rowboats free of charge. In the evening around high summer, he also offers boat and bus trips to see the midnight sun. Laundry and cooking facilities are available to guests and the hostel is open from mid-December to mid-October.

The socialist-era architecture of the *Stamsund Hotel* (☎ *76 08 93 00, fax 76 08 97 26)* has little character, but this place does offer fine sea views and a restaurant serving hearty and filling fare from around Nkr150, including a lunchtime buffet. Single/double rooms cost Nkr690/910. About 300m down the road towards Leknes, you'll also find a couple of places renting cheap and nasty rooms for Nkr75 to Nkr80 per person.

The only camping in the area is at *Brustranda Sjøcamping* (☎ *76 08 71 00, fax 76 08 71 44)*, at Strandslett on the Rv815, 15km north of town. Tent/caravan camping is Nkr50/80 plus Nkr10 per person and basic cabins start at Nkr200.

Getting There & Away Buses run every hour or two between Leknes and Stamsund (25 minutes, Nkr26). The coastal steamer stops at Stamsund at 7.30 pm northbound and 9.15 pm southbound en route between Bodø (Nkr245) and Svolvær (Nkr87).

Mortsund

Scenic little Mortsund rates a mention mainly because it's home to the friendly *Statle's Rorbusenter* (☎ *76 08 75 55, fax 76 08 71 11)*, where the 40 cabins and 28 rooms sprawl across a rocky promontory. Pleasant double rooms start at Nkr600 and the equally fine restaurant serves both local dishes and light meals. Bicycle hire and hiking routes are available. The bus between Leknes and Stamsund calls in only on Saturday.

FLAKSTADØY

For information on the island of Flakstadøy, visit the tourist counter at Flakstad Brunestrand (☎ *76 09 34 50)*, in Ramberg. It's open daily between 10 am and 7 pm from 15 June to 31 August.

Nusfjord

The secluded village of Nusfjord, arranged around a constricted little south coast harbour, makes a superb day trip or overnight stop. In addition to an excruciatingly picturesque waterfront and a lovely restored

general store, you'll find a selection of rorbuer. To stay in the real thing, albeit restored, contact *Nusfjord Rorbuer* (☎ *76 09 30 20, fax 76 09 33 78)*. Four/10-bed rorbuer with showers and toilets cost Nkr520/920. The only restaurant is the acclaimed *Oriana Kro* (☎ *76 09 30 20)*.

Ramberg

If you're tempted to skip Ramberg, you may want to think again. Imagine a vast arch of white sand along a sparkling blue-green bay – that should, by all rights, be about 50° of latitude farther south – against a backdrop of snow-capped Arctic peaks. It all makes more sense when you succumb to the temptation to test the water temperature, but if you're there on a sunny day, no one at home will believe that your holiday snaps of this place were taken north of the Arctic Circle.

You'll also want to check out the red onion-domed Flakstad Kirke, which was built in 1780; most of the wood used in its construction was ripped out of the ground by the Arctic-bound rivers of Siberia and washed up here as driftwood.

The recommended *Ramberg Camping & Gjestegård* (☎ *76 09 35 00, fax 76 09 31 40)*, right on the beach, gives you the chance to camp within spitting distance of the sand. With a tent/caravan, you'll pay Nkr60/85 and for a two/three/four-bed cabin, Nkr450/550/650. They also have a reasonable restaurant and hire kayaks and bicycles for Nkr20 per hour.

Viknes

With a car, you can make a side trip to Viknes to visit the Glasshytta (☎ 76 09 44 42) and watch a glassblower at work on Lofoten-theme glassware. From 15 June to 15 August, it's open Monday to Saturday from 10 am to 7 pm, with shorter hours the rest of the year.

Sund

The only reason to make a detour to Sund might be the Stiftelsen Sund Fiskerimuseum (☎ 76 09 37 90), which has a rather desultory collection of shacks containing displays on fishing, smithing, and boat propulsion. While it may be interesting for someone with a particular interest – and the smithy has gained a reputation for his iron cormorant sculpture – the Å museums are friendlier and better organised. From 2 June to 16 August it's open 10 am to 6 pm daily and admission costs Nkr35.

Getting There & Away

Flakstadøy lies on the main bus routes between Leknes and Å, but Nusfjord and Sund are considerable detours off the main route. For drivers, the tunnel between Flakstadøy and Vestvågøy costs Nkr60.

MOSKENESØY

The 34km-long glaciated island of Moskenesøy is like no place else on earth – a series of pinnacled igneous ridges rising directly from the sea, separated by deep lakes and fjords, and indeed, it would make an ideal location for the film version of a Tolkien fantasy.

While these formations amount to a paradise for mountaineers, there are also a few places where non-technical hikers can reach the incredible heights of this tortured island, including the high point, Hermannsdalstind (1029m).

Information

You'll find tourist information at the Fiskeværsferie Lofoten Turistkontoret (☎ 76 09 15 99, fax 76 09 24 25, tour-off@ lofoten-info.no, www.lofoten-info.no), at the harbour at Moskenes. From 19 June to 13 August, hours are daily from 10 am to 7 pm; at other times between 1 June and 31 August, it's open weekdays from 10 am to 5 pm.

Reine

Delightful Reine, which sits beside a calm turquoise lagoon backed by pinnacled peaks, has recently been voted the most scenic place in all of Norway, and visitors won't fail to be impressed. The best way to get the measure of the place is to climb the precipitous track from the village to the summit of Reinebringen (670m). The obvious track starts from the E10, about 1.2km south of the Reinehalsen junction, and climbs very steeply to the ridge, where the route bears to the right and leads to the 448m top. Here, you'll have an exceptional view of Reine and the road lacing the islands in the turquoise waters. Experienced hikers who want to keep going can continue to the peak of Reinebringen for spectacular views of Reinevatnet, then steeply down a very exposed route to the col (pass) of Navaren and on to Navaren's 730m summit.

Dagmars Dukke og Legetøy Museum

On the island of Sakrisøy, 4km east of Reine, a local woman has collected over 1500 dolls, antique teddy bears and historic toys from 1860 to 1965 into Dagmar's Museum of Dolls and Toys (☎ 76 09 21 43). Opening hours from June to August are daily from 10 am till 8 pm, during the rest of the year weekends only from noon to 5 pm. Admission is Nkr35.

Places to Stay & Eat Along the road, you'll see *Sjøhus* signs indicating private rooms. The least expensive option is the relatively authentic *Sakrisøy Rorbuer* (☎/fax 76 09 22 39) complex, on the islet of Sakrisøy, where you'll get an ochre-coloured overwater cottage for Nkr450 to Nkr850. The fully-equipped modern four-bed cottages at *Reine Rorbuer* (☎ 76 09 22 22, fax 76 09 22 25) cost from Nkr800 to Nkr1000. Bicycles are available for rent. Diagonally over the road is a well stocked supermarket with an attached bakery.

The *Gammelbua Restaurant & Loftet Pub*, with a woody maritime ambience, is a nice place to sample Lofoten's contribution to haute cuisine – boiled cod tongues – for Nkr135, or you can spend Nkr58 and opt for the considerably less daring fish soup. Afterwards, you can wash it all down with a brew.

Getting There & Away All buses between Leknes and Å stop near the post office in Reine.

Hamnøy

Reine may be considered the most beautiful place in Norway, but Hamnøy shares a similar backdrop and adds the charming elements of a colourful fishing harbour and traditional timber buildings.

It's a great place to stay and a couple of rorbu complexes offer appealing accommodation. *Eliassen Rorbuer* (☎ 76 09 23 05, fax 76 09 24 40) charges Nkr450 to Nkr650 and *Wulff-Nilsen Rorbuer* (☎ 76 09 23 20, fax 76 09 21 65), Nkr350 to Nkr750. For quality seafood meals, try the *Krambua Pub & Restaurant*, housed in a shop which dates from 1880.

Moskenes & Sørvågen

The sprawling and relatively uninteresting twin villages of Moskenes and Sørvågen offer little but a ferry landing, tourist office and a few convenient rorbu complexes. The most interesting excursion is a hike up to DNT's Munkebu hut on the Djupfjordheia moor; overnight stays cost Nkr60/120 for members/non-members of DNT. There's a stove and cooking implements, but you need a sleeping bag. It's also accessible from the Reinefjord settlement of Vindstad.

On the E10 in Sørvågen, you can also stop into the Norwegian Telecommunications Museum (☎ 76 09 14 88), which advertises itself as a study in 'cod and communications', surely a winning combination. If you're keen on radio communications, it's probably a must-see. It's open daily from 20 June to 20 August from 2 to 4 pm and admission costs Nkr30.

Å

At the tail-end of Moskenesøy, the fair village of Å (appropriately, the last letter of the Norwegian alphabet!), often referred to as Å i Lofoten, is truly a living museum – a preserved fishing village with a shoreline of red rorbuer, cod drying racks and picture-postcard scenes at almost every turn.

Norsk Fiskeværs Museum Most of Å's 19th century buildings – and that includes most of the buildings in the history centre –
have been compiled into the Norwegian Fishing Village Museum (☎ 76 09 14 88, lte@lofotposten.no, www.lofotposten/home/lte/lofotour.htm), taking in boathouses, storehouses, fishing cottages, farmhouses and commercial buildings. Highlights include the cod-liver-oil factory, where you'll be treated to a taste of the wares; the smithy, who still makes cod-liver-oil lamps; the still-functioning bakery from 1844; the old rorbuer, complete with period furnishings; and a couple of traditional Lofoten fishing boats. Guided tours cost Nkr35.

Norsk Tørrfiskmuseum The must-see Lofoten Stockfish Museum (☎ 76 09 12 11) will reveal all you ever wanted to know about Lofoten's mainstay, which is catching and drying cod for southern European markets – Italy, Spain and Portugal – where this staple is called *barcalao*, *bacalao* and *bacalhau*. They even provide information on how to prepare these Mediterranean specialities. The cod heads, on the other hand, are exported to Nigeria, where they're boiled with peanuts and red hot peppers into a lively West African dish.

The museum displays take you through every step of the truly fascinating production process, which begins with hauling the fish out of the sea, and progresses through drying, grading, sorting and exportation. In fact, the enthusiasm of the museum proprietor and curator may well have you considering a simpler life and a change of career! From 2 to 19 June, it's open weekdays from 11 am to 4 pm, and from 20 June to 20 August, daily from 11 am to 5 pm. At other times, phone for special openings. Admission costs Nkr30.

Moskenesstraumen Beyond the campground south of the village, you'll have an excellent hillside view of Værøy island, across the Moskenesstraumen strait. This formidable expanse of water is exceptionally rich in fish and therefore attracts large numbers of sea birds and marine mammals. The mighty maelstroms created by tidal flows between the two islands were first described 2000 years ago by Pytheas and later appeared as fearsome adversaries on fanciful early sea charts. More recently, they've inspired tales of maritime peril by the likes of both Jules Verne and Edgar Allen Poe.

Places to Stay & Eat *Moskenesstraumen Camping* (☎ 76 09 11 48) has simple cabins for Nkr300. For tent camping, you'll pay Nkr60 for a tent with one person and Nkr10 for each additional person. Caravans cost Nkr80/100 without/with electricity and two/four-bed cabins are Nkr290/490.

The *Å Vandrerhjem* (☎ 76 09 11 21), open year-round, offers accommodation in some of the historic museum buildings for Nkr125 per person. They serve breakfast for Nkr50, lunches from Nkr75 and dinners from Nkr100. However, your best option in Å is the friendly *Hennumgården Sjøhus* (☎ 76 09 12 11, fax 76 09 11 14), where you'll get a charming room in a historic building for just Nkr80 per person. The building dates from the 1860s. The affiliated *Å-Hamna Rorbuer* offers 18 restored fishing huts from the last century; 12 of these are in Å and the rest, in nearby Sørvågen. For traditional Lofoten accommodation, you're unlikely to find anything more genuine than this place. For four to eight-bed units, you'll pay from Nkr400 to Nkr900.

Apart from the over-water restaurant at the Norsk Fiskeværsmuseum, meal choices in Å are limited, and your best bet is probably to use the kitchen where you're staying. You can buy fresh fish straight off the boats and pick up other supplies at the small food shop behind the vandrerhjem office. You can also get coffee and waffles at the Lofoten Stockfish Museum.

Vindstad & Bunes
In summer, ferries run between Reine and Vindstad (40 minutes, Nkr21) through the scenic Reinefjord. From Vindstad, it's a one-hour hike across the ridge to the abandoned beachside settlement of Bunes, where you'll see the amazing 610m Helvetestind rock slab which soars up from the beach. If you

take the morning ferry from Reine, you can return on the afternoon ferry. Alternatively, you can keep hiking from Bunes to reach the Helvetestinden summit.

Hermanndalstind
The challenging 12km return hike and scramble to the summit of Hermanndalstind (1029m) begins at Vindstad and takes at least 10 hours. Perhaps unfortunately, the ferry schedules (see Vinstad & Bunes, earlier, or Getting Around at the end of this section) won't allow this as a day trip, so you'll probably have to camp at Vindstad.

Refsvikhula
The Refsvika Cave, which lies west of Å, on the northern side of the headland, is a 115m-long and 15m-high natural rock cathedral. Around mid-summer, the midnight sun shines directly into the mouth of the cave and illuminates a panel of Stone Age stick figures marching across the walls. They're thought to have been painted at least 3000 years ago. The cave lies 30 minutes on foot above the lovely white sand beach at Refsvika, but you're not permitted to enter it without a guide and the only viable access is on a boat tour. See Organised Tours for details.

Organised Tours
From Reine, you can choose between several worthwhile boat tours which run from 1 June to 31 August. The most popular – and rightfully so – is the six-hour midnight sun excursion to the cave Refsvikhula, which departs from Reine on Friday at 9 pm and costs Nkr390, including a snack. There's also a daytime departure at noon on Monday. A two-day version of this trip including a guided hike, camping and meals, costs Nkr1000.

Alternatively, you can take a bird and marine mammal-watching safari into the wild and fish-rich Moskenestraumen maelstrom. These five-hour tours cost Nkr290 and leave Reine on Wednesday and Sunday at noon.

You can also head off on a traditional fishing trip and learn some of the time-tested local techniques; these three-hour trips leave at noon daily from Reine and Å and cost Nkr260.

A guided tour of Å, followed by a spin in a traditional Nordland boat and a meal of traditionally-prepared cod, begins at the Norsk Fiskeværsmuseum in Å at noon daily and costs Nkr350. Four-hour midnight sun cruises between the incredible peaks of Reinefjorden cost Nkr250 and leave from Reine on Tuesday, Thursday and Sunday at 10 pm from 27 May to July 15 and at 6 pm at other times from 1 May to 30 August.

All these tours may be booked through the tourist office in Moskenes (☎ 76 09 15 99).

Getting There & Away

Daily in summer, about five buses connect Leknes and Å (two hours, Nkr76). The first one southbound runs between 10 am and 1.35 pm and northbound between 7.45 and 11.15 am.

Lofotens og Vesterålens Dampskibsselskab (☎ 76 15 14 22) runs car ferries between Bodø to Moskenes (3¾ hours, Nkr102/380 for a passenger/car), with at least one daily connection to Værøy (1¼ hours, Nkr42) and Røst (3¾ hours, Nkr79). In summer, it operates several times daily on a rather complicated schedule.

Getting Around

Buses connect Å and Hamnøy (30 minutes, Nkr23), via Sørvågen, Moskenes and Reine, about six times daily in summer. The Reinefjorden ferry sails between Reine and Vindstad each morning and afternoon or evening. If you want to take a hike from Vindstad, your best bet is on Friday between 22 June and 23 August, when the first run leaves Reine at 7 am and the last one leaves Vindstad at 10.15 pm.

SOUTHERN ISLANDS

Lofoten's southern islands of Værøy and Røst have some of the finest birdwatching in Norway. Most people come for the clumsy little puffins but, as a result of dwindling herring stocks, their numbers have dropped by more than 50% in the past

decade. Although Værøy is mainly high and rugged and Røst is flat as a pancake, both islands offer good hiking and you'll also find a rare measure of relative solitude in well touristed Lofoten.

Værøy

Craggy Værøy, with 1000 people and 100,000 nesting sea birds – fulmars, gannets, Arctic terns, guillemots, gulls, sea eagles, puffins, kittiwakes, cormorants, eiders petrels, and a host of others – makes an unusual getaway from the more touristed main islands. But there's more; from the white sand beaches, soaring ridges, granite-gneiss bird cliffs and sparkling seas combine to make it one of Norway's finest gems. The tourist office (☎ 76 09 52 10) lies about 200m north of the ferry landing at Sørland and from 15 June to 15 August, it's open on weekdays from 10 am to 2 pm, as well as other times when the car ferry is in port.

Hiking The best way to get around Værøy is on foot, and hiking routes lead to most of the larger sea-bird rookeries. The most scenic and popular hike begins at the end of the road, about 300m beyond the airstrip, and heads southward along the west coast and over the Eidet isthmus to the abandoned fishing village of Måstad, on the east coast, where meat and eggs from the puffin colonies once supported 150 people.

Note that the route is exposed in places and shouldn't be attempted in poor weather. Really keen hikers may also want to attempt the steep climb from Måstad to Måhornet (431m), which takes about an hour each way. Alternatively, you can follow the road (or perhaps the more interesting ridge scramble) up to the NATO installation at Håen (438m). This hike begins from the quay at Sørland.

Places to Stay & Eat The *Værøy Vandrerhjem* (☎ 76 09 53 52), about an hour on foot north of the Sørland ferry landing, offers some of the most authentic rorbu accommodation in Lofoten. You'll pay Nkr85 in the dormitory, Nkr170/235 in single/double

NORDLAND

rooms and Nkr500 to Nkr900 for a four-bed, self-catering rorbu. The hostel has a kitchen, but there's also a nearby café. The hostel will arrange three-hour boat tours for a sea-level view of the most impressive bird cliffs for around Nkr250. It's open from 15 May to 15 September.

The alternative is the nearby *Gamle Prestegård* (☎ *76 09 54 11, fax 76 09 54 84*), housed in the old vicarage, which charges Nkr300/550 for single/double rooms.

Getting There & Away The ferry between Bodø (4¼ hours, Nkr99) and Moskenes (1¾ hours, Nkr79) makes at least one daily call into Værøy, and also provides access to Røst (2¼ hours, Nkr52). You can also purchase a return ticket routed Bodø-Værøy-Røst-Bodø for Nkr170.

Røst

The 356 islands and skerries of Røst comprise the ragged southern edge of Lofoten. Røst stands in sharp contrast to its rugged neighbours to the north, and were it not for a small pimple in the middle, the main pond-studded island of Røstlandet would be dead flat. Thanks to its location in the heart of the Gulf Stream, this rather enchanting little place basks in one of the mildest climates in Norway and attracts 2.5 million nesting seabirds to some serious rookeries on the cliffs of the outer islands.

An unusual account of medieval life on the island is provided in the accounts of the shipwrecked merchant of Venice called Pietro Querini, who washed up on Sandøy in 1432 and eventually introduced *lutefisk* to Italy. The tourist office distributes a photocopied sheet outlining the amusing tale.

Organised Tours The Røst Vandrerhjem arranges all-day tours for Nkr125, which cruise past several bird cliffs, hoping to also show you an orca and a seal or two. Stops include the 1887 Skomvær lighthouse, once inhabited by artist Theodor Kittelsen, and the Vedøy kittiwake colonies, where Italian sculptor Luciano Fabro's placed his monument to its avian population and entitled it

The Nest. You'll also have a short leg-stretcher up to a fine panoramic view. Upon completion of this tour, you'll have exhausted Røst's organised activities and will be on your own until the ferry leaves.

Places to Stay & Eat The bland but friendly *Fiskarheimen-Havly Hospits & Vandrerhjem* (☎/fax *76 09 61 09*) charges Nkr100 in the dormitory and Nkr130/230 for single/double rooms, and has an attached café, as well as a sauna for guests and rowing boats for hire. It's open from 1 May to 30 August. The *Kåroy Sjøhus* (☎ *76 09 62 38*) has three sjøhus for Nkr90 per bed. For meals, your best choice is *Stephanie's* (☎ *76 09 64 80*), which is open in the evening on Wednesday, Friday, Saturday and Sunday.

Getting There & Away There are scheduled flights to Røst from Bodø and Leknes on Widerøe airlines, but only private flights to Værøy, as the government considers the landing strip rather dodgy. The ferry between Bodø (4¼ hours, Nkr99) and Moskenes (1¾ hours, Nkr79) makes at least one daily call into Værøy, and also provides access to Røst (2¼ hours, Nkr52). Sailing times given are for direct ferries, but note that not every service is direct. You can also purchase a return ticket routed Bodø-Værøy-Røst-Bodø for Nkr170.

Vesterålen

The islands of Vesterålen, which are the northern continuation of the archipelago which includes Lofoten in the south, are divided between the counties of Nordland and Troms, but for convenience, the entire area is covered in this chapter. Although the landscapes here aren't as dramatic as those in Lofoten, they tend to be much wilder and the forested mountainous regions of Hinnøya represent a unique element in Norway's largely treeless northern coast.

A good source of information in English is the book *An Encounter with Vesterålen –*

Culture, Nature & History, which outlines the history, sites and walking routes in the region. It's sold at tourist offices for Nkr117.

HADSELØYA

Vesterålen's link to Lofoten is the island of Hadseløya, which is connected by ferry to Fiskebøl on Austvågøy. It's best known around Norway for the Summer-Melbu festival, held in Melbu in June, which repesents one of northern Norway's liveliest cultural festivals, with seminars, lectures, concerts, theatrical performances and art exhibitions.

Melbu

If you have a free hour in Melbu, on the Vesterålen end of the Fiskebøl ferry, visit the Norsk Fiskeriindustrimuseum (☎ 76 15 98 25), which traces the life of a fish from the deep sea to the kitchen table. There's also a children's exhibition about the goings-on at the sea floor. Between 15 June and 15 August it's open weekdays from 11 am to 5 pm and on weekends from 11 am to 4 pm. Admission costs Nkr25. You may also want to stop by the Vesterålen Museum, at the northern end of town.

Places to Stay A fine place to stay is the simple but character-filled *Melbu Vandrerhjem* (☎ 76 15 71 06, fax 76 15 83 82), where you'll pay Nkr100 for a dorm bed and Nkr200/300 for a single/double room with a toilet. The hostel can organise guided mountain hikes, bird cruises and whale-watching trips.

Getting There & Away The ferry between Fiskebøl and Melbu (25 minutes, Nkr22/63 for passengers/cars) sails at least 12 times daily between 6.40 am and 1.40 am the next night. Buses between Melbu and Stokmarknes (45 minutes, Nkr35) run several times daily on weekdays and twice daily on weekends.

Alternatively, you can follow the 22km hiking route across the relatively low island of Hadseløya between Melbu and Trolldalen, near Stokmarknes. The Ørnheihytta hut makes a good lunch stop and offers a superb view of the northern reaches of Lofoten. Strong hikers can complete the trip in about six hours.

Stokmarknes

In his book *Vagabonds*, author Knut Hamsun described the Torvet market in Stokmarknes:

'The market place was busy and noisy ... there were tight rope walkers, organ grinders, wild animals, nine-pins, peddlers, a carousel and fortune tellers. You could buy soft drinks, see the fattest lady in the world and a calf with two heads.'

Despite its folksiness, this quiet little market town is renowned as the birth place of Vesterålen Dampskipsselskab's popular Hurtigruten coastal steamers between Bergen and Kirkenes. This vital link, which was founded in Stokmarknes in 1881 by Richard Bernhard With, began with the service of a single ship, the S/S *Vesterålen* between Trondheim and Hammerfest, with nine ports of call. It now boasts 11 ships and serves 35 towns and villages. It once carried the post, passengers and vital supplies, and now provides transport for local people and a scenic cruise-like experience for tourists. Look for the monument to With near the Hurtigruten quay.

The tourist office (☎ 76 15 29 55), which is less than active, is open only on weekdays.

Hurtigrutmuseet You can learn all about Hurtigruten history at the appealing Hurtigrutmuseet (☎ 76 15 28 22). From June to September, it's open from 10 am to 6 pm daily; admission costs Nkr35. For a sample of the real thing, from Stokmarknes you can take the coastal steamer south to Svolvær (three hours, Nkr158) at 3.30 pm, then get back on the northbound Hurtigruten at 10 pm and be back in Stokmarknes by 1 am.

Places to Stay & Eat Camping is available at the *Kinnarps Turist og Kurssenter* (☎ 76 15 29 99, fax 76 15 29 95), east of town along the main road, where tent camping

NORDLAND

costs Nkr30 per person and caravan camping is Nkr90. Single/double rooms cost Nkr660/780 and rorbuer start at Nkr700. A good place for a meal is the **Rødbrygge Pub** near the Hurtigruten quay. In the centre, a **Rimi** supermarket dispenses all the staples and it's even open on Saturday.

Getting There & Away The Nor-Way Bussekspress buses between Svolvær (1¾ hours, Nkr109), Narvik (five hours, Nkr230) and Fauske (6¼ hours, Nkr283) also stop at Stokmarknes. The ferry between Svolvær (1¾ hours, Nkr83) and Sortland (35 minutes, Nkr37) calls in at Stokmarknes a few times daily. Daily except Monday and Saturday, you can also take the M/S *Ofoten* ferry to Svolvær (1¼ hours, Nkr137) and Bodø (4¾ hours, Nkr308); northbound, it sails daily except Saturday and Sunday.

Many people visit Stokmarknes only on the southbound Hurtigruten coastal steamer, which leaves at 3.30 pm, after pausing long enough for passengers to have a quick look at its namesake museum. Northbound towards Harstad (5¾ hours, Nkr271) and Tromsø (13¾ hours, Nkr583), it stops at 1 am.

LANGØYA
Sortland
The modern and rather unappealing town of Sortland has little to offer but an overnight stop or a petrol station to help you move on. It is, however, the commercial capital of south-western Vesterålen and you'll find tourist information on much of the region at the Vesterålen Reiselivslag (☎ 76 12 15 55, fax 76 12 36 66, vestreg@online.no).

Jennestad Handelssted The 19th century trading post at Jennestad (☎ 76 12 12 11), 8km west of Sortland, recalls the era of heavy direct trade between the fishing grounds of Nordland and the markets of mainland Europe. From 15 June to 15 August, it's open weekdays from 11 am to 5 pm and weekends from noon to 5 pm. Admission costs Nkr30.

Special Events The annual 240km Arctic Sea Kayak Race is one of the ultimate challenges in competitive sea kayaking, but lesser beings can also opt for a 150km option or an introductory course in sea kayaking, to get you geared up for the race the following year. For information and dates, contact the Arctic Sea Kayak Race (☎ 76 12 12 44, fax 76 12 33 88, karl-einar.nordahl@tin.no), Postboks 287, N-8401 Sortland.

Places to Stay The only camping option is **Sortland Camping og Motell** (☎ 76 12 13 77, fax 76 12 25 78), 1km from the centre on Vestmarkveien. The rather odd-looking **Strand Hotell** (☎ 76 12 28 88, fax 76 12 29 18, Strandgata 34) charges Nkr580/900 for single/double rooms and isn't worth it. A more interesting option is the **Sjøhus Senteret** (☎ 76 12 37 40, fax 76 12 00 40) at Ånstadsjøen, where you'll pay Nkr600 to Nkr800 for a room with toilet and shower.

Getting There & Away Sortland is certainly the transport hub of Vesterålen, and you have a choice of buses. In summer, one to four daily buses connect Sortland with Risøyhamn (1¼ hours, Nkr61) and Andenes (2½ hours, Nkr111). Buses run two to four times daily between Sortland and Lødingen (one hour, Nkr67).

The long-distance bus between Å (5¾ hours, Nkr240) and Narvik (4¼ hours, Nkr207) also calls in daily except Saturday (on Sunday, the southbound bus doesn't continue to Å). Buses to and from Harstad (two hours, Nkr99) run one to four times daily. Finally, you can take the Nor-Way Bussekspress: the Narvik-Lofoten Ekspressen between Narvik (3¾ hours, Nkr207) and Svolvær (2½ hours, Nkr109) operates daily except Saturday and the Fauske-Lofoten Ekspressen between Fauske (5¼ hours, Nkr263) and Svolvær runs daily.

Ferries sail between Sortland and Svolvær (2¼ hours, Nkr109), via Stokmarknes (35 minutes, Nkr37), one to four times daily in summer. The Hurtigruten coastal steamer stops by at 3 am northbound and 1.15 pm southbound.

Myre

Along the way to Nyksund, you'll pass the sprawling and strangely un-Norwegian looking town of Myre, which would look more at home in the Colorado Rockies than beside the Arctic seas. Information on the entire Øksnes area, which takes in Nyksund and Stø, is found at Øksnes Turistinformasjon (☎ 76 13 44 44, fax 76 13 42 23).

Oppmyre Camping (☎ 76 13 36 55), which lies about 2km south of the town, is the area's only tent campground. If you're arriving by bus, ask the driver to drop you off. Alternatively, you can stay at the *Myre Turisthotell (☎ 76 13 44 10, fax 76 13 41 61)*, which charges Nkr440/700 for singles/doubles, with breakfast. It also has a restaurant and nightclub.

About 15km east of Myre on the coast near Alsvåg is *Tøftenes Sjøhuscamping (☎ 76 13 14 55, fax 76 13 14 55)*, housed in an old 1909 trading station, which has simple rooms, tent and caravan camping and a basic restaurant. Spartan single/double cabins or rooms in the sjøhus cost Nkr350/450.

You'll find buses between Sortland and Myre (50 minutes, Nkr49) three to five times daily; some of these continue on to Stø (30 minutes, Nkr26).

Nyksund

No one will regret a visit to fabulous Nyksund, an abandoned fishing village which is now re-emerging as an artists' colony and whale-watching centre. From the crumbling and collapsing old structures to the faithfully renovated commercial buildings, everything here is picture-perfect and the lively youthful atmosphere belies the fact that only recently Nyksund was considered a ghost village. Tourist information is handled by Whale Tours (☎ 76 13 11 66). For information on the circular hiking route to Stø, see Stø, later in this section.

History In 1874 the struggling fishing village of Nyksund improved its harbour and built a mole to protect ships and buildings from the wrath of the open seas. A church was built in 1880, when Nyksund boasted a telegraph station, bakery and a selection of shops as well as a steamboat. In 1934, a fire destroyed the harbour side on Nyksund island, the government determined it was too expensive to rebuild and in 1939 the school closed. Because the harbour was too small for the new motorised fishing vessels, which permitted people to live farther from the fishing grounds, many Nyksund residents relocated to Myre.

Some people, however, opted to stay, and after WWII concerted local efforts rebuilt much of the town in stone, improved the mole and dynamited and enlarged the harbour. In the 1960s, however, economic factors caused the closure of the bakery and post office, and most remaining families relocated to Myre. Nearly everyone else left after the mole was destroyed in a storm in 1975, and the last inhabitant, blacksmith Olav Larsen, went to Myre in 1977.

Sheep and vandals ruled the site until 1984, when an international growth project imported youth from around Europe to again renovate Nyksund. Homes were rebuilt, electricity was installed and prospective residents began envisioning utopia. Although political problems arose, tourism became an issue in 1994 and the following year, a café, guesthouse and whale-watching operation started up. Nyksund now boasts a summer population of 30 to 40 people. Four or five remain even through the harsh winters.

Whale Watching Whale Tours (☎ 76 13 11 66, fax 76 13 14 08) is probably the most recommended whale-watching operator in Vesterålen. Over the squid-rich banks off Andenes, you're almost certain to see sperm whales lounging and sounding, but with a bit of luck, you'll also spot minke and pilot whales. The all-day cruises, which begin with a quick tour of Nyksund and include a light lunch on board, cost Nkr550. On the way back, you chug past a small island which is abuzz with squawking sea birds and lounging seals. If you don't see whales, which is very rare, you can choose between another trip free of charge or a 50% rebate.

NORDLAND

The Queen's Route A worthwhile activity is the walk over the headland along the fabulously scenic hiking route to Stø and back. Most people start out along the three-hour route via 517m Sørkulen and return via the considerably easier two-hour sea level route. The name is derived from a hike taken by Queen Sonja in 1994. A photocopied map of the circular return route, detailing sites of interest along the way, is free from Whale Tours in Nyksund and Whale Watch Stø in Stø.

Places to Stay & Eat The main accommodation is the lovely and authentically renovated *Nyksund Gjestehus (☎ 76 13 11 66)*, where you get a dorm bed for Nkr120 and basic singles/doubles for Nkr175/275. A set breakfast at the café next door costs Nkr75 and traditional fish, whale and pizza meals cost from Nkr80 to Nkr150. An alternative place to stay is the *Kunsthåndverksted Gjestehus (☎/fax 76 13 43 81)* in 'Det Gamle Posthuset', the old post office.

Getting There & Away There's no public transport to Nyksund, but if you get to Myre and are booked onto a whale-watching cruise, phone Whale Tours (☎ 76 13 11 66) and they'll find a way to get you there in time.

Stø

At the northernmost tip of Langøya clings the small and distinctive fishing village of Stø, where Whale Watch Stø (☎ 76 13 44 99, www@alpha1.nndata.no, www.whale-watch.no) offers five to eight-hour whale-watching cruises for Nkr550. In summer you're almost certain to see sperm whales, and from 15 October to 15 November, they run Nkr550 orca and pilot whale tours from Lødingen. In Stø, they also operate seal and seabird tours for Nkr350 and a marine mammal and seabird display and slide show.

The *Stø Bobilcamp (☎ 76 13 25 20, fax 76 13 25 31)* has caravan sites and the *Stø Rorbuer (☎ 76 13 44 99)* charges Nkr200

for a dorm bed and Nkr450 for a three to five-bed cabin.

Buses connect Sortland (1½ hours, Nkr64), Myre (30 minutes, Nkr26) and Stø two to four times daily.

ANDØYA

Andøya may not be as high or rugged as most of Vesterålen, but this long, narrow island has a charm all its own, and thanks to the 1000m deep waters off its north-western shore, it still receives a good share of the region's tourist trade. These deep, dark and cold waters attract abundant stocks of squid – including some very large specimens – which in turn attract squid-loving sperm whales. The result is a rather reliable whale-watching venue.

Risøyhamn

Risøyhamn, the only Hurtigruten port of call on Andøya, is known for its 2km dredged channel, which allows shipping through the otherwise very shallow approach to the harbour. The Andøy Museum in the town presents the history and natural features of the entire island. You'll find basic accommodation at the *Risøyhamn Gjestehus (☎ 76 14 76 25)*, with summer single/double rates of Nkr325/450.

The Hurtigruten coastal steamer pauses briefly at 4.30 am northbound and 11.15 am southbound.

Andenes

Andenes, at the northern end of Andøya, is the northernmost town in Nordland county and also one of Norway's most exposed communities. Despite its remoteness, however, the town has enjoyed a rich fishing history and has now become a major tourist destination, thanks to the whale-watching potential immediately to the west. The town itself, especially its jumble of wooden harbourfront boat sheds and nautical detritus, also exudes a charmingly nostalgic atmosphere.

When you arrive, it's worth dropping by the Andøy Reiseliv (☎ 76 11 56 00, fax 76 11 56 10), at the Andenes Whale Centre.

Andenes Hvalsenter & Hisnakul The Andenes Whale Centre (☎ 76 11 56 00, post@whalesafari.no, www.whalesafari.no) is nothing special, but does provide a perspective for whale watchers, with displays on whale research, whaling and whale life cycles, as well as daily lectures in Norwegian, English and German. It's open between 25 May and 16 September from 8 am to 4 pm, with extended hours from 15 June to 15 August when it's open until 8 pm. Admission costs Nkr40.

The affiliated but considerably better Hisnakul Natural History Centre, in a restored wooden warehouse, concentrates on the natural history of northern Norway, with exhibits on seabirds, landscape topography, marine mammals, farming, fisheries, local cultures, and the aurora borealis. Whatever you do, don't miss the bird beaks or the Northern Lights slide show featured at the 1994 Winter Olympics at Lillehammer.

Polar Museum This Arctic-themed museum (☎ 76 14 20 88) includes displays on local hunting and fishing traditions, with extensive coverage of Hilmar Nøis' 38 winter hunting expeditions in Svalbard. It's open daily from 10 June to 31 August between 10 am to 6 pm. Admission costs Nkr25.

Andenes Fyr Andenes' landmark red lighthouse, opened in 1859, has now been automated but still presents a classic form. Guided tours, which require a climb up 40m and 148 steps, are available through the Polar Museum (☎ 76 14 20 88) for Nkr15 per person.

Organised Tours Whale Safaris' (☎ 76 11 56 00, fax 76 11 56 10) popular whale-watching cruises operate from Andenes between 25 May and 15 September and guarantee sightings of sperm whales. There's also a chance of spotting minke and pilot whales. The tour begins with a spin through the Andenes Hvalsenter, followed by a three to five-hour boat trip. Trips depart at 10.30 am and cost Nkr595. They also do two-hour cruises to the seabird rookeries on the pyramid-shaped island of Bleiksøya (Nkr120); two-hour fishing trips from Bleik (Nkr250); and seal and seabird safaris to the islands and skerries around Andøya, from the village of Stave (Nkr150).

Places to Stay & Eat At Andenes Camping (☎ 76 14 12 22, fax 76 14 19 33), you'll pay Nkr70/90 for a tent/caravan. There are no cabins. The timber-built Andenes Vandrerhjem (☎ 76 14 28 50, fax 76 14 28 55), in the Lankanholmen Sjøhus, is a real treat and makes a great base for a couple of days. For dorm beds, you'll pay Nkr125, while single/double rooms are Nkr190/300, including the use of cooking facilities. It's open from 1 June to 1 September.

Single/double rooms at the equally charming Den Gamle Fyrmesterbolig (☎ 76 14 10 27, fax 76 14 40 87), in the old lighthouse keepers' cottage, cost Nkr300/400. Even less expensive is the basic Sjøgata Gjestehus (☎ 76 114 14 51, fax 76 14 14 53), which charges Nkr250/300 for singles/doubles without bath. At the warehouse-like Grønnbua (☎ 76 14 14 99, fax 76 14 21 33), which is built right over the water, you'll pay Nkr200 for a single or double room.

Your posh choices are the exceptionally ugly Norlandia Andrikken & Viking Hotells (☎ 76 14 12 22, fax 76 14 19 33), which belong to the same chain and charge Nkr795/1045 for single/double rooms. They're about 1km from the harbour.

Down the west coast of the island, at Bleik, you'll find Bleik Camping (☎ 76 14 57 40, fax 76 14 55 51), which charges Nkr50/100 for tents/caravans and the simple Bleik Rorbu (☎ 76 14 57 17), where you'll get a single/double room for Nkr200/250, including use of the kitchen.

For meals, you can choose between the lodgings or try the Moby Dick Kafé, at the Hvalsenter.

Getting There & Away One of the finest ways to approach Andenes is on Widerøe airlines from Narvik or Bodø, which provides spectacular aerial views of the landscapes,

NORDLAND

seas and agricultural patterns on and around the island of Andøya. The Widerøe route between Andenes and Tromsø, however, is a contender for the world's most scenic flight, but don't just take my word for it.

By bus, you can travel to and from Sortland (2½ hours, Nkr111) and Risøyhamn (one hour, Nkr61) one to four times daily. As you approach the town along the Rv82, you'll cross a vast and soggy moorland that contrasts sharply with the panoramas of distant ragged peaks. Alternatively, you can travel between Risøyhamn and Andenes (1½ hours, Nkr70) via Bleik (15 minutes, Nkr20), on the west coast of Andøya, twice daily on weekdays and once on Saturday.

From 1 June to 31 August, a special ferry link connects Andenes with Gryllefjord (1¾ hours, Nkr80), and passes what is certainly the most incredible coastal scenery in Norway south of Svalbard. This little-seen coastline will not disappoint. From Andenes, it runs at 8 am and 12.30 and 5.30 pm and from Gryllefjord, at 10 am and 3 and 7.30 pm. For information and bookings, contact Andøy Reiseliv (☎ 76 11 56 00).

HINNØYA

The island of Hinnøya, the largest island off mainland Norway, is fairly evenly divided between the counties of Troms and Nordland and consists largely of a forested green upland punctuated with bleak snow-caps and deeply indented by fjords. Between Hinnøya and Austvågoy, Vesterålen is divided from Lofoten by the narrow Raftsund strait and its renowned offshoot, Trollfjorden.

Lødingen

While there's little for the tourist in Lødingen, it does sit squarely on the highway routes between the mainland, Vesterålen and Lofoten, and the only museum, the Lødingen Pilots' Museum & Norwegian Telecom Museum, which chronicles 130 years of communications and the work of northern Norway's ship pilots, opens only on Saturday. The Lødingen Turistkontor (☎ 76 93 11 00, fax 76 93 17 12) is open from 15 June to 20 August.

If you're here for a night, the least expensive digs is *Sentrum Overnatting (☎ 76 93 12 94, fax 76 93 19 92)*, which has beds for Nkr150 and doubles for Nkr400. The *Lødingen Hotel (☎ 76 93 10 05, fax 76 93 20 70, Rådhusveien 11)* charges Nkr430/590 for singles/doubles and has a decent restaurant.

The express ferry M/S *Børtind* between Svolvær (1¾ hours, Nkr155) and Narvik (1¼ hours, Nkr127) calls in daily except Saturday. It's also a stop on most of the bus routes between Narvik (3¼ hours, Nkr155) or Fauske (four hours, Nkr214) and Harstad (1¼ hours, Nkr92), Sortland (one hour, Nkr59), Svolvær (3½ hours, Nkr167) and Å (seven hours, Nkr299).

Harstad

Like an orphan, Harstad sits in a detached corner of Troms county, near the northern end of Hinnøya. This heavily industrial and defense-oriented city of 23,000 people, with its docks and tanks and warehouses, seems rather unappealing, but it enjoys a nice hillside setting above Vågsfjord and it's the largest and most active place in the Vesterålen region.

Information The Harstad Turistkontor (☎ 77 01 89 89, fax 77 01 89 80, hoarr@online .no), at the bus station, is open 16 June to 17 August on weekdays from 7.30 am to 6.30 pm, on Saturday from 7.30 am to 3 pm and on Sunday from noon to 7 pm.

Trondenes Most of Harstad's sites of interest are scattered around the Trondenes peninsula, north of town. Hourly buses connect Trondenes with the central bus station (10 minutes, Nkr14).

The **Trondenes Historiske Senter** (☎ 77 02 83 40, trondeneshs@online.no) brings home the Viking history of Hinnøya and nearby Bjarkøy, from where chieftains controlled most of Troms and Vesterålen. It also outlines the transition between the Viking and Christian ages, and the bloody battles that marked it. This rather impressive production is a must for anyone remotely interested in Scandinavian medieval history. From 2 June to 16 August it's open daily from 10 am to 7 pm and the rest of the year on weekends from 11 am to 5 pm.

The WWII relic known as the **Adolf Kanonen** is often boastfully cited as the world's largest land-based big gun, and with a calibre of 40.6cm and a recoil force of 635 tonnes, it may well be. In the bunker, you can also see a collection of artillery, military equipment and instruments used by German coastal batteries during WWII. Because it lies in a military area, you're obliged to take a guided tour of the site; they run daily at 11 am and 1, 3 and 5 pm and cost Nkr50.

Around 1150, after the Viking chieftains lost the battle against the unification of Norway under a Christian regime, King Øystein built **Trondenes Kirke**, which was at the time the northernmost church in Christendom. Originally constructed as a timber building, the current – and modern-looking – stone structure replaced it around 1250 and quickly came to double as a fortification against Russian aggression. On Monday, Nkr20 guided tours run at 10 am, noon and 2 and 4 pm and from Tuesday to Friday and on Sunday, they run at 2, 4 and 6 pm.

Organised Tours On Thursday from 2 June to 9 August, the tourist office organises historical sightseeing tours around Trondenes. They leave the tourist office at 6 pm and visit the Trondenes Church, the Adolf Kanonen and the Trondenes Historical Centre for Nkr110. You must book before 2 pm on Wednesday.

At noon daily from the Kulturhuskaia, you can take a fjord cruise for Nkr200 aboard the historic 36m 1868 schooner, *Anna Røgde* (☎ 77 06 11 53, mobile ☎ 94 85 48 68), which may well be the oldest active sailing schooner in Norway.

Places to Stay The *Harstad Vandrerhjem* (☎ 77 06 41 54, fax 77 06 56 33), 2km north of town near the base of Trondenes, charges Nkr150/190 for dorm beds without/with breakfast and Nkr190/260 for single/double rooms. *Harstad Camping* (☎ 77 07 36 62,

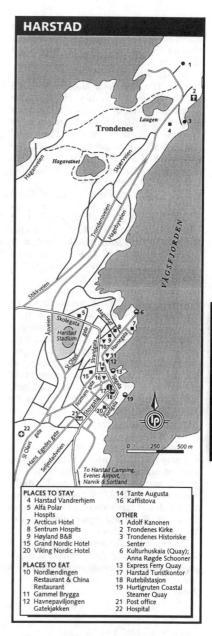

HARSTAD

PLACES TO STAY
4 Harstad Vandrerhjem
5 Alfa Polar Hospits
7 Arcticus Hotel
8 Sentrum Hospits
9 Høyland B&B
15 Grand Nordic Hotel
20 Viking Nordic Hotel

PLACES TO EAT
10 Nordlændingen Restaurant & China Restaurant
11 Gammel Brygga
12 Havnepaviljongen Gatekjøkken
14 Tante Augusta
16 Kaffistova

OTHER
1 Adolf Kanonen
2 Trondenes Kirke
3 Trondenes Historiske Senter
6 Kulturhuskaia (Quay); Anna Røgde Schooner
13 Express Ferry Quay
17 Harstad Turistkontor
18 Rutebilstasjon
19 Hurtigruten Coastal Steamer Quay
21 Post office
22 Hospital

fax 77 07 35 02), about 5km south of the centre at Nesseveien 55, has tent or caravan sites for Nkr100 plus Nkr15 per person and cabins for Nkr290 to Nkr600.

Harstad also claims several mid-range choices. The *Alfa Polar Hospits (☎ 77 06 34 46, Skolegata 6)* has single/double rooms for Nkr250/350 and the *Sentrum Hospits (☎ 77 06 29 38, Magnusgata 5)* charges Nkr250/350 without bath and Nkr350/450 with a shower and toilet. The *Høyland Bed & Breakfast (☎ 77 06 49 60, Magnusgata 4)* offers bed-only for Nkr260/320 and B&B for Nkr300/400.

The relatively plush *Arcticus Hotel (☎ 77 06 50 00, fax 77 06 52 00, Havnegata 3)* has summer rates of Nkr680/890 (at other times Nkr1150/1435), while the slightly simpler *Viking Nordic Hotel (☎ 77 06 40 80, fax 77 06 40 60, Fjordgata 2)* and *Grand Nordic Hotel (☎ 77 06 21 70, Strandgata 9)* charge Nkr590/680.

Places to Eat For quick greasy snacks, see the *Havnepaviljongen Gatekjøkken (☎ 77 06 73 00, Sjøgata 8)*. The *Nordlændingen Restaurant (☎ 77 01 87 50, Strandgata 30)* specialises in local fish and meat dishes prepared in the typical northern Norwegian manner, but those with less refined tastes can fall back on the pizza. The adjoining *China Restaurant (☎ 77 06 24 00)* is the local Chinese specialist and, for hard-core carnivores, also sizzles up a decadent Mongolian grill.

Tante Augusta (☎ 77 06 94 40) serves not only pizza and snacks, but also a good seafood and grill menu. Opposite the express boat quay is the very amenable *Kaffistova (☎ 77 06 12 57, Rikard Kaarbøsgata 6)*, which was established in 1911. It's open for lunch, dinner and through the afternoon for coffee and snacks.

The very nice *Gammel Brygga (☎ 77 06 75 11, Havnegata 23B)* enjoys a bright café and bistro, as well as a piano bar. A disco operates on Wednesday, Friday and Saturday.

Getting There & Away The Harstad-Narvik airport is at Evenes, one hour by bus east of town. Harstad is served by both SAS and Braathens SAFE.

Buses to and from Sortland (two hours, Nkr99) run one to four times daily; the fare includes the ferry between Flesnes and Revsnes. The bus to and from Narvik (2½ hours, Nkr134), via Evenes airport (one hour, Nkr58), operates two or three times daily. Between Harstad and Fauske (5¾ hours, Nkr293), the Togbussen runs daily.

If you're heading for Tromsø, the easiest and most scenic option is by boat. The M/S *Fjordkongen* express ferry sails once to three times daily between Harstad and Tromso (2¾ hours, Nkr345), via Finnsnes (1½ hours, Nkr85). There are also two or three daily Fergesambandet Harstad (☎ 77 01 89 89) ferries between Harstad and Skrolsvik (1½ hours, Nkr85), at the southern end of Senja island, where you'll find bus connections to Finnsnes and thence on to Tromsø. Directly to and from Finnsnes, Troms Fylkes Dampskipsselskap (☎ 77 64 81 00) express ferries sail once or twice daily.

The Hurtigruten coastal steamer chugs out at 8.15 am northbound, headed for Finnsnes (3¾ hours, Nkr198), Tromsø (6½ hours, Nkr366) and beyond. At 8.45 am it heads southbound towards Risøyhamn (2½ hours, Nkr121), Sortland (4½ hours, Nkr203) and Stokmarknes (6¾ hours, Nkr271).

Drivers should be aware that parking in Harstad can be a nightmare; it's not only expensive, but finding a space can prove an exercise in futility. You may want to park well away from the centre and hoof it into town.

Getting Around The Flybussen (50 minutes, Nkr70) shuttles back and forth between the town's centre and the Evenes airport several times daily, and often continues on to Narvik. Alternatively, you can take the regular Narvik bus to Evenes (one hour, Nkr58). For trips out to Trondenes, you can hire bikes at the Sykkel og Motor (☎ 77 06 63 67), Tordenskjoldsgata 6.

The Far North – Troms & Finnmark

Norway's northern counties of Troms and Finnmark, which arc across the top of Europe, represent the last frontier of European civilisation on the mainland, and most travellers consider the effort of getting there an appropriate part of the experience. From the dramatic island of Senja to the animated town of Tromsø, the tourist cul-de-sac at Nordkapp and the Sami cultures of Finnmarksvidda, this lovely and varied end of Norway contains some of the country's most exotic attractions and broadest horizons.

Troms

This section covers the northern two-thirds of Troms county; the Troms portions of Hinnøya island are included in the Nordland chapter.

SENJA & FINNSNES

Senja may be best known as the second largest island off mainland Norway, but that fact belies its incredible landscapes. The Innersida, the eastern coast that faces the mainland, consists of a broad agricultural plain while the interior is occupied by vast virgin forests, and along the western coast, the Yttersida, a convoluted series of knife-ridged peaks, rises directly from the Arctic Ocean. The best views are from the air, but parts of this wild coastline are also accessible on tiny back roads leading to such colourful and isolated fishing villages as Skrolsvik, Gryllefjord, Hamn, Skaland, Mefjordvær, Husøy and Botnhamn. The scenery here rivals that of Lofoten but it attracts a fraction of the visitors and remains considerably more traditional in character.

Camping and cabins are available near the gateway town of Finnsnes as well as at several villages: *Fjordbotn Camping* (☎ 77 84

93 10) in Botnhamn; *Draugen Kro & Camp* (☎ 77 85 59 70) in Kaldfarnes; *Senja Camping* (☎ 77 85 32 55), at Silsand near Ånderdalen National Park; *Skatvik Camping*

THE FAR NORTH

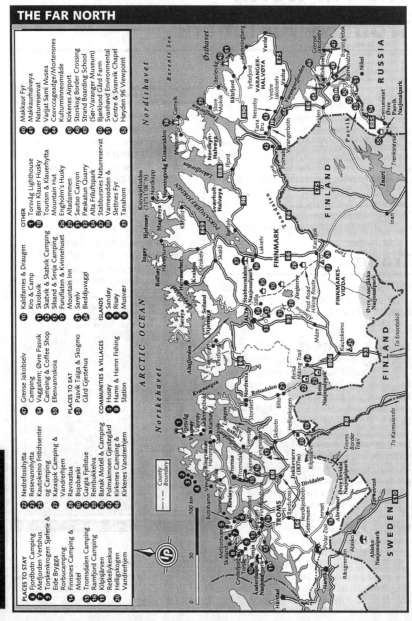

(☎ 77 85 35 30) at Skatvik; and *Eide Brygga Rorbucamping (☎ 77 85 53 43)* at Torsken. You'll find more expensive formal accommodation at the *Mefjorden Vertshus (☎ 77 85 86 00, fax 77 85 87 69)* in Mefjordvær; the beautiful *Hamn Fishing Station (☎ 77 84 01 20, fax 77 84 04 10)* at Hamn; and the *Torskenkrogen Sjøferie (☎ 77 85 54 00, fax 77 85 54 31)* in Torsken.

Finnsnes

As the gateway to Senja island and a stop on the Hurtigruten coastal steamer route, the mainland town of Finnsnes sees a bit of tourist traffic. It also enjoys the distinction of being one of Norway's two designated residences of Santa Claus (the other is in Drøbak), who has homes in most Arctic countries. For tourist information on the town and the island of Senja, see the Finnsnes Turistkontor (☎ 77 84 18 28), opposite the harbour on Bernhard Lundsveien.

Visitors can choose between the lively *Finnsnes Camping & Motel (☎ 77 84 21 20)*, Finnfjordbotn, 5km south of town (take bus No 40 or 41, or any bus towards Tromsø or Bardufoss), or the upmarket *Finnsnes Hotell (☎ 77 84 08 33, fax 77 84 04 44)*, right in the centre. The former has tent and caravan sites as well as cabins, motel rooms and a Chinese restaurant. Rooms at the latter start at Nkr670/860 for singles/doubles.

Getting There & Away Local buses leave from the Senja Rutebilstasjon (☎ 77 85 35 09), opposite the lovely lake Finnsnesvatn, and serve Bardufoss (one hour, Nkr61), Tromsø (2¾ hours, Nkr179) and, in summer, most villages on Senja island: Skrolsvik (1¼ hours, Nkr86), Skaland (30 minutes, Nkr32), Mefjordvær (1¾ hours, Nkr89), Gibostad (30 minutes, Nkr39), Botnhamn (1½ hours, Nkr70), Husøy (two hours, Nkr77), Hamn (one hour, Nkr67), Gryllefjord (1½ hours, Nkr83) and Torsken (1¾ hours, Nkr86).

In summer, Troms Fylkes Dampskibsselskap (☎ 77 64 82 00) express ferries connect Finnsnes with Tromsø (1¼ hours, Nkr160) and Harstad (1½ hours, Nkr185)

at least twice daily. The southbound Hurtigruten coastal steamers call in at 4.45 am and the northbound, at noon.

SETERMOEN

Nondescript Setermoen serves as a shopping centre for the Bardu district and a staging point for visits to Øvre Dividal National Park. It's worth popping into the Bardu Kirke, on the main road through town, which was built between 1825 and 1829 after repeated petitions for a church by local parishioners; the bell dates from 1698. Note the anachronistic heating system, which involves wood stoves and hot water pipes running beneath the pews. It's open from 10 am to 5 pm Monday to Saturday from 22 June to 2 August. Organ concerts are held at 8.30 pm on Wednesday. You may also want to stop by the Troms Forsvarsmuseum (☎ 77 18 56 50), the military museum, which also serves as the tourist office.

Polar Zoo

The Polar Zoo (☎ 77 18 41 14, www.polarzoo .no), features wildlife of the boreal taiga in relatively natural-looking enclosures. Here you can watch and photograph those enigmatic but elusive faces that beam from postcards all over Norway: moose, brown bears, deer, musk oxen, reindeer, wolves, lynx, wolverines, badgers and foxes. It's open between 10 am and 6 pm daily from June to August (until 8 pm in July), and admission costs Nkr90. Feeding time is between noon and 2 pm daily. The zoo lies about 2km east of the E6, about 20km south of Setermoen.

Places to Stay

In Setermoen, you can stay at the *Annekset Gjestegård (☎ 77 18 20 63, fax 77 18 24 00, Altevannsveien 20)*, which charges Nkr400/600 for singles/doubles, or the *Bardu Best Western Hotell (☎ 77 18 10 22, fax 77 18 14 01, Toftakerlia 1)*, with summer rates starting at Nkr610/750. For tent or caravan camping or cabins, see the *Bardu Camping og Feriesenter (☎ 77 18 15 58)*, one block east of the E6 near the northern end of town.

Getting There & Away

The bus terminal occupies a car park just east of the E6/Altevannsveien junction. The Nor-Way Bussekspress Nord-Norgeekspressen between Narvik (1½ hours, Nkr108) and Tromsø (three hours, Nkr185) calls in one to three times daily and the Narvik bus passes within 2km of the Polar Zoo. The bus between Narvik and Alta (8½ hours, Nkr477) also calls in daily in summer.

ØVRE DIVIDAL NASJONALPARK

A wild, roadless and lake-studded 750 sq km chunk of Norway between Setermoen and the Swedish and Finnish borders comprises Øvre Dividal National Park. While it lacks the spectacular steep-walled scenery of coastal Norway, this remote semi-forested upland wilderness still enjoys lots of alpine peaks and views.

The most popular hike is the eight-day Troms Border Trail, which laces seven unstaffed DNT huts. The route begins along the northern shore of the artificial lake, Altevatn, about 3km east of Innset, and twists north-eastward, passing several times into Sweden before winding up near the point where Sweden, Finland and Norway meet. At the easternmost hut, Galdahytta, the track splits and you can head for either Helligskogen in Norway or better equipped Kilpisjärvi in Finland. Many hikers also use the linking trail between the western end of Altevatn, in Øvre Dividal, and Abisko National Park, in northern Sweden, where you'll find the start of Sweden's world-famous Kungsleden hiking route.

The map to use for the Troms Border Trail and the Abisko Link is Statens Kartverk's *Turkart Indre Troms*, at a scale of 1:100,000. In summer, hikers cannot underestimate the mosquito nuisance in this area; use a head net and carry plenty of repellent!

Organised Tours

Winter visitors will have the unique opportunity to join a dog-sled trip through Arctic Norway led by renowned and resourceful musher, Bjørn Klauer. In addition to tours through nearby Øvre Dividal National Park, he runs expeditions into Finnmark, northern Sweden, Finland, and even Svalbard. With two people, seven/10/12-day tours, including meals and hut or tent accommodation, cost Nkr14,500/21,000/25,500 per person. For further information, contact Bjørn Klauer (☎/fax 77 18 45 03), Innset, N-0250 Bardu.

Places to Stay

A series of seven unstaffed *DNT huts* run the length of the main hiking route through Øvre Dividal: Gaskashytta, Vuomahytta, Dividalshytta, Dærtahytta, Rostahytta, Gappohytta and Galdahytta. Keys and bookings are available from the Troms Turlag DNT office in Tromsø (see Information under Tromsø).

In the village of Innset, near the western end of the hiking route, you have two options. The basic *Altevann Villmarkssenter* (☎/fax 77 18 21 92), right in the village, charges Nkr150 per person. About 300m farther along the road towards Setermoen, dog musher Bjørn Klauer has opened the lovely and rustic *Klauerhytta* (☎ 77 18 45 03) to hikers and other travellers. He also charges Nkr150 per person, including the use of a well equipped kitchen.

Near the eastern end of the park, on the E8 in upper Skibotnsdalen, is the *Helligskogen Vandrerhjem* (☎/fax 77 71 54 60), a rural hostel surrounded by wild open highlands. It's handy for travel between Norway and Finland, and serves hikers finishing the Troms Border Trail. Dorm rooms cost Nkr90 and singles/doubles are Nkr160/220.

Alternatively, you can stay at the friendly and inexpensive *Kilpisjärven Retkeilykeskus (Finland ☎ 358-16 537 771)*, which anchors the eastern end of the Troms Border Trail, just over the Finnish border in Kilpisjärvi. Simple four-bed rooms with use of cooking facilities cost around Nkr300; there's also a good value café. From here, you can arrange boat trips across the lake Kilpisjärvi and choose between a number of scenic hikes through Finland's highest mountains.

Getting There & Away

Access to Innset is by private vehicle, taxi (Nkr150 each way) or weekly shopping bus from Setermoen. In summer, the bus runs on Thursday (one hour, Nkr47); it leaves Innset at 9 am and Setermoen at 1 pm.

Between Tromsø and the Kilpisjärven Retkeilykeskus hotel in Kilpisjärvi, Finland (2¾ hours, Nkr250), at the eastern end of the hiking route, you can catch the Lapin Linjat bus, which runs daily between 1 June and 30 September. Northbound, it leaves Kilpisjärvi at 6.25 pm daily and southbound, it leaves Tromsø at 7.10 am. You can also board at the Helligskogen hostel, about 12km north of the Finnish-Norwegian border.

TROMSØ

Tromsø (population 58,000), the main town of Troms county and the largest in northern Norway, claims lots of northernmost titles – the world's northernmost 18-hole golf course, botanical garden, university, Protestant cathedral, brewery (they seem to ignore the one in Murmansk) and even the most boreal Burger King, among other things.

Although Tromsø lies beside an arm of the Arctic Ocean at nearly 70°N latitude – almost 400km north of the Arctic Circle – the climate is pleasantly moderated by the Gulf Stream and the long winter darkness is offset by round-the-clock activity through the perpetually bright days of summer.

In contrast to some of the more sober communities in the region, this spirited town boasts cultural bashes, street buskers, a lively street scene, a midnight sun marathon, the hallowed Mack brewery and more pubs per capita than any other town in Norway. For visitors and locals alike, the backdrop, scenically dominated by snow-topped peaks, provides excellent hiking in summer and great skiing and dog-sledding in winter.

Tromsø received its municipal charter in 1794 when the city was developing into a trading centre, but its history actually goes back to the 13th century, when the first local church appeared on Prostneset. In more recent times, the city has become known as a launching point for northern polar expeditions and, thanks to that distinction, it's nicknamed 'The Gateway to the Arctic' (which is probably more appropriate than the rather absurd moniker 'Paris of the North', which was suggested by an apparently myopic German visitor in the early 1900s).

Orientation

Tromsø's central area and the airport occupy the island of Tromsøya, with the

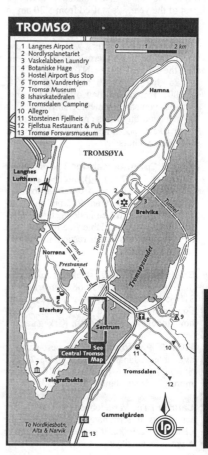

TROMSØ

1 Langnes Airport
2 Nordlysplanetariet
3 Vaskelabben Laundry
4 Botaniske Hage
5 Hostel Airport Bus Stop
6 Tromsø Vandrerhjem
7 Tromsø Museum
8 Ishavskatedralen
9 Tromsdalen Camping
10 Allegro
11 Storsteinen Fjellheis
12 Fjellstua Restaurant & Pub
13 Tromsø Forsvarsmuseum

university at the southern end of the island, but the city also spills onto the mainland and the suburbs sprawl onto Kvaløya island. The three sections are linked by two delicately arching bridges.

Information

Tourist Office From 1 June to 15 August, the Tromsø Arrangement tourist office (☎ 77 61 00 00, fax 77 61 00 10, info.tromsoe@ tos-arr.no), Storgata 61, is open from 8.30 am to 6 pm on weekdays, 10 am to 5 pm on Saturday and 10.30 am to 5 pm on Sunday. The rest of the year, it's staffed from 8.30 am to 4 pm on weekdays (in May, it's also open from 10 am to 5 pm on Saturday).

Long-distance hikers who plan to use DNT cabins in northern Norway can contact the Troms Turlag DNT office (☎ 77 68 51 75, fax 77 68 40 50), PO Box 284, N-9001 Tromsø. At their office at Grønnegata 32, you can pay membership fees, pick up keys and buy maps and books. It's open from 10 am to 2 pm on Tuesday and 10 am to 6 pm on Thursday.

Post & Communications The main post office (☎ 77 62 40 00), hidden away at Strandgata 41, is open from 8 am to 5 pm on weekdays and 10 am to 2 pm on Saturday. The parcel office is downstairs. Internet services are available free to patrons at the Amtmandens Datter restaurant and pub at Grønnegata 81.

Bookshops The best stocked bookshop is the Sentrum Libris (☎ 77 68 35 40), Sjøgata 31/33; upstairs you'll find a stationery shop. For used books, see the Tromsø Bruktbokhandel (☎ 77 68 39 40), Kirkegata 6.

Film & Photography The best value is available at Japan Photo (☎ 77 65 71 27), Storgata 91. The purchase of 10 rolls or more yields substantial discounts.

Laundry The Vaskelabben (☎ 77 67 58 55) laundry is at Terminalgata 86, north of the centre in Breivika. It's open from 10 am to 6 pm on weekdays.

Churches

In the city centre you'll find several period churches, including the **Tromsø Domkirke**, one of Norway's largest wooden churches, and a **Catholic church**, both built in 1861. However, Tromsø's most striking church is the **Ishavskatedralen** (Arctic Ocean Cathedral), on the mainland, which is designed to reflect the nature of the Arctic regions. Its 11 spires, which suggest glacial crevasses and auroral curtains, are said to represent the 12 apostles, minus poor, despicable Judas. It's open from 10 am to 8 pm in summer; Sunday services are held at 11 am and organ recitals on the ship-shaped pipe organ are at 5 pm on Wednesday, Thursday and Friday from 25 June to 8 August. Admission costs Nkr15 (for recitals add Nkr10).

Historic Buildings

You'll still see quite a few early 19th century timber buildings around the central area. In 1898, the **Aagaard House**, Søndre Tollbugate 1, built for merchant Andreas Aagaard in 1838, was the first building in town to be electrically lit. You'll also see a lineup of **1830s shops and merchants' homes** along Sjøgata, a block south of the Stortorget (main square). At Skippergata 11, you can see the 1833 home which adjoins Tromsø's only remaining **town garden**. Also notable is the home of merchant Peder Figenschou at Storgata 84, which was built in the early 19th century in accordance with the town development plan of 1788 and established Storgata as the centre of Tromsø. The 1835 home of merchant Thomas B Holst at Storgata 94 served as a vicarage; the truncated corner was a concession to early fire safety regulations.

For a complete rundown of historic buildings in Tromsø, pick up the booklet *Town Walks*, which costs Nkr50 from the tourist office.

Tromsø Museum

The Tromsø Museum (☎ 77 64 50 00, www.imv.uit.no/homepage.htm), Lars Tøringsvei 10 near the southern end of Tromsøya, is northern Norway's largest museum,

CENTRAL TROMSØ

PLACES TO STAY
18 Kongsbakken Gjestehus
23 Rica Ishavshotel Tromsø
24 Radisson Sas Hotel Tromsø & Rorbua Pub
27 Hotell Nord
28 Rainbow Polar Hotel
29 Grand Nordic Hotel & Papagena Bar

PLACES TO EAT
1 Pizzahuset
2 Hong Kong Village
3 Café Parus
9 Pedersen's Bakeri
13 Domus Supermarket
14 Peppe's Pizza
16 Fokus Complex; Amtmandens Datter,
  Victoria Fun Pub, Football Pub & Subsirkus
17 Burger King
33 Paletten Kafé
40 Skarven
41 Le Mirage
42 Meieriet
44 Indigo
45 Blå Rock Cafe

OTHER
4 Skippergata 11
5 Aagaard House
6 Polarmuseet
7 Skansen Brygge
8 Japan Photo
10 Sportshuset
11 Catholic Church
12 Thomas B Holst House
15 Sentrum Libris; Bus No 26 Stop
19 Fokus Kino
20 Peder Fischengau's House
21 Mack Kjeller'n; Compagniet
22 Bus No 28 Stop
25 Tromsø Domkirke
26 Trygg Underground Car Park
30 Collosseum
31 Tromsø Arrangement Tourist Office
32 Tromsø Bruktbokhandel
34 Tromsø Jernbanestasjon – Altitude 3.48m
35 Main Post Office
36 Prostsnet; Main Bus Terminal
37 Hurtigruten Quay
38 Café; Lockers;
  Hurtigruten Waiting Room
39 Express Ferry Terminal
43 Troms Turlag DNT Office
46 Mack Ølhallen; Main Taxi Stand
47 Mack Ølbryggeri
48 Nordnorsk Kunstmuseum
49 Polaria

To Ishavskatdralen &
Tromsdalen Camping

To Tromsø,
Vandrerhjem
& Airport

Stortorget

Kongsparken

Richard
Withs
plass

Strandtorget

Tromsøysundet

0   100   200 m

THE FAR NORTH

and has well presented displays on Arctic birds, Sami culture and regional history, as well as general archaeological and natural history exhibits. It's open from 9 am to 9 pm daily from 1 June to 31 August. Admission is Nkr20. Take bus No 28 from the Torget or bus No 42 from southern Sjøgata.

Polarmuseet

The harbourside Polar Museum (☎ 77 68 43 73), housed in a restored customs house on Søndre Tollbugata, concentrates on polar research and exploration – particularly Roald Amundsen – but also ventures into less universally agreeable issues such as the hunting and trapping of fuzzy Arctic creatures. Opening hours are from 11 am to 8 pm daily from 15 June to 31 August, with shorter hours the rest of the year. Admission is Nkr30.

Nordnorsk Kunstmuseum

The city also has a regional art museum, the North Norwegian Art Museum (☎ 77 68 00 90), Muségata 2, which features the sculpture, photography, painting and material arts of northern Norway. It's open from 11 am to 5 pm daily except Sunday, and admission is free.

Mack Ølbryggeri

Okay, it isn't really the world's northernmost brewery – the Russians cook up their 12% *pivo* as far north as Murmansk – but Macks (☎ 77 62 45 00, fax 77 65 86 77), on the corner of Strandveien and Muségata, is the northernmost brew that sticks to the Reinheitsgebot, the German standard of beer purity. Established in 1877, it now produces Macks Pilsner, Arctic Beer, Haakon, Helmachs and several dark beers. Public visits may be arranged by appointment but a good place to sample all the wares is the Ølhallen Pub at Storgata 4, which oddly enough is open only during the day: from 9 am to 5 pm on weekdays and 9 am to 1 pm on Saturday.

Nordlysplanetariet

One thing summer visitors seem to love is the opportunity to complement the 24-hour daylight with a visit to the Northern Lights Planetarium (☎ 77 67 60 00) for a simulated glimpse of a winter-only phenomenon, the aurora borealis. In summer, English-language shows begin at 1.30 and 4.30 pm on weekdays and at 4.30 pm on weekends; German programs are given at 6 pm on weekdays and noon on weekends. At 11 am daily, an audiovisual presentation on the aurora is also screened. Admission costs Nkr50. To get there, take bus No 37 from the Svaneapoteket chemist or bus No 20 from Fr Langes gate.

Polaria

If you're wondering what the hell all those toppled dominoes are doing marching up from the harbour near the Mack Brewery, you need wonder no more. You're looking at the new and architecturally daring Polaria

---

The Tromsø Palm

In and around Tromsø, you're bound to encounter the ubiquitous *Heracleum laciniatum*, which is known elsewhere by the pedestrian name of 'cow parsnip' and hereabouts by the euphemistic moniker, the 'Tromsø palm'. Although it bears a striking resemblance to edible angelica, don't mistake this poisonous beast for that tasty treat, or you're sure to regret it!

This plant, which has yellow-green flowers arranged in broad 'starburst' clusters, arrived from Asia via Britain in 1850, when it was introduced as an ornamental plant in the mining community of Kåfjord. The climate there proved too dry, however, and the seeds were transferred to Tromsø, where the plant took root, thrived and quickly spread across the island. Eventually, it took root all over northern Norway, and its enormous 2 to 3m high clusters have proven impossible to eradicate. What's more, because they're toxic, not even cows will eat them, and people who touch them may suffer an itchy rash.

(☎ 77 60 69 00), which is a museum dedicated to Arctic phenomena, human habitation, marine environment and wildlife. The highlight, Ivo Caprino's well produced audiovisual program on Svalbard, may well have you clamouring to buy a ticket to Longyearbyen. Summer opening hours are from 11 am to 8 pm daily; the rest of the year, it's open from 11 am to 5 pm. Admission costs a rather steep Nkr70 but family rates are available.

Tromsø Forsvarsmuseum

The southern end of Tromsø, on the mainland, was first developed by the Germans in 1940 as a coastal artillery battery, complete with six big guns. The cannons have now been restored as the basis of the Tromsø Defence Museum (☎ 77 62 88 36), which also includes a restored commando bunker, an old searchlight and an old ammunition dump with a display on the 52,600-tonne German battleship *Tirpitz*, which was sunk by British air forces at Tromsø on 12 November 1944. The museum is open from 11 am to 7 pm daily from June to August; admission costs Nkr20.

Botaniske Hage

The world's northernmost botanical gardens (☎ 77 64 50 00), on Breivika near the university, comprise less than two hectares of landscaped gardens featuring Arctic and alpine species. It was established in 1994, in honour of Tromsø's bicentennial. It's open all day between May and September and admission is free. Take bus No 20 from Fr Langes gate or bus No 32 from the Svaneapoteket chemist.

Storsteinen Fjellheis

You can get a fine city view by taking the cable car 420m up Mt Storsteinen. It runs from 10 am to 5 pm daily from 1 April to 30 September, and until 1 am on clear nights from 20 May to 20 August, when the midnight sun is visible. From the top, you can choose from a network of highland hiking routes. At the top, the *Fjellstua Restaurant & Pub* (☎ 77 63 86 55) serves lunch, dinner

and drinks until the cable car stops running. The return trip costs Nkr60. Take bus No 26 from Havnegata at the Stortorget waterfront.

Special Events

A popular annual event is the Midnight Sun Marathon, which features a full marathon, half marathon and mini-marathon, as well as a children's race. It normally takes place on a Saturday in early July. For information and bookings, contact the organising committee, Midnight Sun Marathon (☎ 77 68 40 54, fax 77 65 56 35, post@msm.no, www.msm.no).

Places to Stay

Most campers head for *Tromsdalen Camping* (☎ 77 63 80 37, fax 77 63 85 24), on the mainland 2km east of the Ishavskatedralen, which features leafy green sites beside a slow-moving stream. Tent/caravan camping costs Nkr100/120, plus Nkr10 per person, and simple cabins start at Nkr250, but they also have self-catering units for up to Nkr800. A small shop and cafeteria is open in summer from 8 am to 11 pm. To get there, take bus No 36 from the town centre. Those with a vehicle may prefer the nicely-situated *Ramfjord Camping* (☎ 77 69 21 30, fax 77 69 21 30), which lies 30km from town on the E8 and is open year-round. Tent/caravan camping is Nkr70/100 and basic cabins range from Nkr200 to Nkr400.

The friendly *Tromsø Vandrerhjem* (☎ 77 68 53 19, fax 77 06 63 03, Gitta Jønsonsvei 4) occupies a school dormitory 2km west of the centre in the Elverhøy district. It's normally reached on bus No 24 from the town centre, but the slog up the hill is only unpleasant if it's raining or you're carrying all your luggage. It's open from 20 June to 19 August and charges Nkr100 for dorms and Nkr200/250 for singles/doubles. Reception is closed from 11 am to 5 pm.

The tourist office books rooms in private homes from Nkr150 per person (most charge around Nkr450 for double or family rooms), plus a booking fee of Nkr25.

On the hillside just a few minutes walk from the centre is the *Kongsbakken Gjestehus* (☎ 77 68 22 08, fax 77 68 80 44,

Skolegata 24), which charges Nkr390/505 for single/double rooms with shared facilities and Nkr510/620 with bath. The front rooms offer superb city views. The *Hotell Nord (☎ 77 68 31 59, fax 77 61 35 05, Parkgata 4)*, which is more of a guesthouse or *pensjonat* than a hotel, charges the same rates.

The popular *Skippershuset Pensjonat (☎ 77 68 16 60, fax 77 65 62 92, Storgata 112)* has simple but comfortable rooms with shared bath for Nkr398/498.

There's also a selection of pricey chain hotels. One of the nicest, thanks to its relative simplicity, is the *Rainbow Polar Hotel (☎ 77 68 64 80, fax 77 68 91 36, Grønnegata 45)*, with modern rooms and a cheery breakfast room with a city view. Summer rates start at Nkr615/770 and non-residents can pay Nkr80 and enjoy the excellent buffet breakfast. Other choices include the *Grand Nordic Hotel (☎ 77 68 55 00, fax 77 68 25 00, Storgata 44)*, which starts at Nkr625/850; the *Rica Ishavshotel Tromsø (☎ 77 66 64 00, fax 77 66 64 44, Fr Langes gate 2)*, where summer rates range from Nkr675/850 to Nkr745/890; and the *Radisson SAS Hotel Tromsø (☎ 77 60 00 00, fax 77 65 61 10, Sjøgata 7)*, with summer rates from Nkr795/995.

Places to Eat

If simple pastry and coffee are enough for breakfast, try *Pedersen's Bakeri*, in a historic timber building on Storgata near Skanckesmuget.

Tromsø's fast-food scene is led by *Burger King (Storgata 84)*, where you'll get a burger, chips and coke from Nkr49. However, serious burger lovers should head for the *Blå Rock Café (☎ 77 61 00 20, Strandgata 14/16)*, where you'll find a selection of monster burgers for Nkr70 to Nkr90 and other simple but filling meals. Pizza is also a local institution and *Peppe's Pizza (☎ 77 61 11 66)*, on the Stortorget, offers good value with its Nkr89 pizza and salad lunch buffet, including a soft drink. Alternatively, the popular student hangout *Pizzahuset (☎ 77 68 44 10, Skippergata 44)*, in the Studenthuset near the bridge,

does decent pizza from 3 pm (from 1 pm on weekends) to at least midnight daily. Another pizza variation is available from *Allegro (☎ 77 68 80 71, Turistveien 19)*, near the foot of the cable car, which bakes up Italian-style pizzas in a birch-fired oven.

Trendy spots in the centre include the *Paletten Kafé (☎ 77 68 05 10, Storgata 51)*, where sandwiches start at Nkr30 and meals at Nkr85; occasionally, the atmosphere is enhanced by live music. The casual *Le Mirage (☎ 77 68 52 34)* does Nkr25 sandwiches and also cobbles together tacos, omelettes and spaghetti starting at Nkr70. Both are near the intersection of Storgata and Strandskillet. The *Meieriet (☎ 77 61 36 39, Grønnegata 37/39)* combines a cake shop, café and pub and is open from lunch time until late every day. Its all-you-can-scoff taco buffet costs only Nkr85.

The *Amtmandens Datter (☎ 77 68 49 06, Grønnegata 81)* restaurant and pub serves fairly good value lunches and dinners in a nice pub-like atmosphere, and patrons may use its newspapers, books, and chess and backgammon sets, as well as enjoy Internet access. Meals are available until closing time. For Chinese takeaways, see the *Hong Kong Village (☎ 77 61 14 88, Storgata 132)*, which is open until 11 pm Monday to Saturday and to 10 pm on Sunday. Indian is the speciality at the mid-range *Indigo (☎ 77 61 10 50, Storgata 36)*.

For more upmarket dining, try the three-part *Skarven (☎ 77 61 01 01, Strandtorget 1)*, which specialises in beef, reindeer, seagull eggs, seafood, and if you aren't put off, dishes featuring marine mammals (ever tried seal lasagne?). Main dishes start at around Nkr180.

Self-caterers will find the largest selection at the *Domus* supermarket, on the Torget. The upstairs cafeteria features a fine harbour view. It's open weekdays from 9 am to 8 pm and Saturday until 6 pm. For groceries after hours, try any of the petrol station convenience shops.

You'll find fresh boiled shrimp from fishing boats at the Stortorget waterfront and can combine them with a loaf of bread from the nearby bakery for a picnic at the dockside tables. You'll also find hot dogs and fried titbits for sale at stands around the Stortorget market.

For something different, especially if you're heading for Russia, drop by the *Café Parus* (☎ 77 68 48 88, Skippergata 6), which is run by the Kirkens Bymisjon Tromsø as a wholesome Russian-Norwegian gathering spot. It's open on Tuesday, Friday and Sunday afternoons.

Entertainment

The main cinema is the *Fokus Kino*, on Grønnegata, which screens films nightly for Nkr60 admission. Thanks to its university crowd, Tromsø also enjoys a thriving nightlife, in spite of its summer dearth of night time, and on Friday and Saturday, most night spots stay open until 4 am.

Le Mirage (☎ 77 68 52 34) offers a pleasant and relatively gentle atmosphere for the 20 to 30 crowd. The lively and hip *Blå Rock Café* (☎ 77 61 00 20, Strangata 14/16) features massive burgers, theme evenings, 75 types of beer, a jukebox and disco music at weekends. For live performances, you'll pay a cover charge of Nkr80; it caters for over 18s. The *Skarven* (☎ 77 61 01 01, Strandtorget 1), with its popular outdoor seating, offers fine bar meals, including seafood dishes, and a quiet waterfront hangout mainly for adults over 25. For more serious drinking, try the seedier *Tromsø Jernbanestasjon – Altitude 3.48m* (☎ 77 61 23 48), on Strandgata, where Tromsø's nonexistent railroad happenings are announced to the mainly over-30 patrons. The rock bottom in the centre, however, is the *Rorbua Pub* (☎ 77 60 00 00) at the SAS Hotel, which is mainly a hangout for Russian and Norwegian sailors in port.

The normally quiet *Mack Kjeller'n* (☎ 77 68 20 85, Sjøgata 12) is known for its fondue and attracts good live music shows; the adjacent *Compagniet* (☎ 77 65 57 21) offers 80s rock music and dancing mainly for patrons from 25 to 40 years of age. In the complex known as *Fokus* (☎ 77 68 49 06), on

Grønnegata, you'll find a choice of four pubs. The *Amtmandens Datter*, where the name is derived from an 1830s novel by Camille Collett, caters to those between 25 and 35 with drinking and bar meals from Nkr50 to Nkr100; beneath is the English-themed *Victoria Fun Pub*, the *Football Pub* and the nightclub, *Subsirkus*. The relatively sophisticated *Skansen Brygge* attracts folks over 25 or so with its higher prices and emphasis on northern Norwegian cuisine.

The main meat market is the *Collosseum* (☎ 77 68 44 00, Storgata 46), which draws the 18 to 30 crowd with its loud techno music and tendency towards bare flesh. The *Papagena* (☎ 77 68 55 00), next door at the Grand Nordic, is good naturedly referred to as the 'second-hand market', where the over-40 crowd heads with a similar purpose in mind – but the music and dress are a bit mellower. Although there's no specific gay venue, most gays and lesbians frequent either Le Mirage or Amtmandens Datter.

Getting There & Away

Air Tromsø has the main airport in the northern region, and is served by SAS, Braathens SAFE and Widerøe. Direct flights connect the city with Oslo, Bergen, Bodø, Trondheim, Alta, Hammerfest, Honningsvåg, Kirkenes and Longyearbyen.

Bus Nor-Way Bussekspress has at least two daily express buses to and from Narvik (five hours, Nkr279) and one or two daily services to and from Alta (6¾ hours, Nkr312). In summer, it also runs a twice daily Tromsø-Nordkapp Ekspressen bus to and from Nordkapp (13 hours, Nkr627), with one daily connection to Kautokeino from Alta (2½ hours, Nkr158) and to Hammerfest from Skaidi (1¼ hours, Nkr69). Passengers to Nordkapp must pay an additional fee of Nkr175 for admission to the Nordkapp tourist complex.

There are also local buses between Tromsø and outlying areas, including Belvik (45 minutes, Nkr36) and Summarøy (two hours, Nkr80).

Car & Motorcycle The best way to nego-
tiate the far northern reaches of Norway is
clearly by car, as there's plenty of wild
scenery to appreciate and buses run relatively infrequently. Car hire isn't cheap but
it's available at Avis (☎ 77 61 58 50, fax 77
61 58 52, runeku@barentsnett.no), Vestregata 16; Europcar (☎ 77 67 56 00, fax 77 67
04 16), at the airport; Hertz (☎ 77 62 44 00,
fax 77 68 45 41), Richard Withs plass 4; and
Budget/Nord (☎ 77 68 54 11, fax 77 65 78
87), Fridtjof Nansens plass 3.

Boat In summer, Troms Fylkes Dampskibsselskap (☎ 77 64 82 00) express ferries connect Tromsø (1¼ hours, Nkr160) and Harstad
(1½ hours, Nkr185), via Finnsnes, at least
twice daily. The northbound Hurtigruten
coastal steamer arrives at 3.15 pm and departs
at 6.30 pm for Hammerfest (11 hours,
Nkr537), Honningsvåg (22½ hours, Nkr723)
and Kirkenes (40¾ hours, Nkr1234). Southbound, it arrives at 11.45 pm and departs at
1.30 am for Finnsnes (3¼ hours, Nkr167),
Bodø (23½ hours, Nkr781), Trondheim (53
hours, Nkr1668) and points south to Bergen
(85 hours, Nkr2374). Phone the office
(☎ 77 64 82 00) for information and bookings.

Getting Around

To/From the Airport The Langnes airport lies about 5km from the centre, on the
western side of Tromsøy island. From the
Radisson SAS Hotel in the centre, the Flybuss (☎ 77 67 02 33) runs to the airport
(15 minutes, Nkr36) more or less hourly to
connect with arriving and departing flights;
it also stops at the Grand Nordic Hotel and
is happy to pick up or drop passengers at the
Tromsø Vandrerhjem bus stop, a five-
minute walk from the hostel. Alternatively,
you can take the city bus for just Nkr18; arriving air passengers can wait for it on the
road opposite the airport entrance.

Taxis between the airport and the centre
charge around Nkr75.

Bus To thoroughly explore the city will
take time, as most of the worthwhile sites
lie outside the central area. City buses cost
Nkr18, or you can buy a 24-hour bus pass
starting at Nkr50.

Car & Motorcycle Tromsø has ample
parking in the centre. There's also the huge
Trygg underground car park east of the harbour on Vestregata, but it's not open to trailers or caravans.

Taxi The main taxi stand (☎ 77 60 30 00) is
at Strandveien 30.

Bicycle You can hire bicycles from the
Sportshuset (☎ 77 68 36 68), right in the
centre at Storgata 91.

AROUND TROMSØ
Belvik Ferry
An excellent short ferry cruise will take
you past the lovely little islands and communities of Vengsøy, Musvær, Laukvik,
Mjølvik, Risøy and occasionally, Sandøy.
The trip begins with a bus from Tromsø to
Belvik (45 minutes, Nkr36), where you
board the M/F *Kjølva* ferry for the return
cruise (4½ hours, Nkr75) before returning
to Belvik and connecting with a bus back
to Tromsø.

Although the ferry runs every day, it's
possible to do the entire trip on public transport only on Friday and Sunday. On these
days, the bus leaves the Prostneset terminal
in Tromsø at 4.03 pm and the ferry sails at
5.10 pm, calling in at all ports and islands
where passengers are boarding or disembarking. The boat then arrives back in
Belvik at 9.35 pm to connect with the return
bus to Tromsø, which arrives at Prostneset
at 10.10 pm.

Sommerøy
A beautiful beach that's popular with
Tromsø people is on Sommerøy island,
where lots of locals also have holiday cottages. For a pleasant escape, you can book
private double accommodation through the
Tromsø tourist office for around Nkr450. To
reach Sommerøy, take the Hillesøy bus
from the Prostneset terminal in Tromsø (1¾
hours, Nkr80); it runs once or twice daily.

Karlsøy

The island of Karlsøy is probably one of the most interesting places in all of Troms county, but it's well known only by Norwegians. Its history closely reflects that of most other north Norwegian fishing communities but after WWII, the population began to decline. By 1970, there remained only 45 people on the island, most of whom were elderly.

Although authorities accepted the eventual de-population of the district, the trend switched dramatically when an emergent counterculture recognised the appeal of this remote island. Over the next decade, young people from elsewhere in Norway and abroad began moving to the island to create a sort of Arctic utopia, complete with communes, 'flower power', an artists' colony, the cultivation of soft drugs and generally anarchistic tendencies. The population eventually climbed to 80, new farmland was cultivated and a new economy emerged, based on the arts, tourism and production of goats' milk. It's still a unique community and makes an interesting visit.

For the full story on Karlsøy, see the Nkr50 booklet *Among Church Cottages & Goats in Alfred Eriksen's Kingdom*, from the tourist office in Tromsø.

Places to Stay At the *Karlsøy Brygge og Sjøsportell* (☎ 77 74 93 99, fax 77 74 93 85), you can camp or stay in seaside cabins. It also has a shop and pub and rents horses, bicycles and water sports equipment. It's open from May to October.

Getting There & Away One or two daily buses connect the Prostneset terminal in Tromsø with the Hansnes ferry quay (1¼ hours, Nkr80), on Ringvassøy island. From there, you can take the M/F *Fløytind* ferry to Karlsøy (15 minutes, Nkr27) several times daily.

While you're in the area, you may also want to visit nearby Vannøy island, with its sandy beaches, classic staffed lighthouse and wild Arctic-looking coastlines. You can reach Skåningsbukt by car ferry daily from

Hansnes (40 minutes, Nkr27) and several times weekly from Karlsøy. There, occasional buses connect the quay with Torsvåg (near the lighthouse) in the north and Kristoffervalen in the east.

Lyngen Alps

Some of the most rugged alpine peaks in all of Norway form the spine of the heavily glaciated Lyngen peninsula, east of Tromsø, and you'll have the best views from the eastern shore of 150km-long Lyngenfjord. The peaks, the highest of which is Jiekkevarre (1833m), offer plenty of opportunities for mountaineers but for hikers, the challenging glacial terrain is suitable only for the experienced. The most accessible and popular hiking area is the Lyngsdalen valley, above the industrial village of Furuflaten. The usual route begins at the football pitch south of the bridge over the Lyngdalselva and climbs up the valley to the snout of the glacier Sydbreen, 500m above sea level (don't approach the ice as it's rotten and meltwater has created dangerous patches of quicksand).

The map to use for hiking in Lyngsdalen (and other areas of Lyngen) is Statens Karverk's *M711 Storfjord*, sheet 1633IV. For information, contact the tourist offices in Furuflaten (☎ 77 71 06 92), open from 1 June to 19 September; Svensby (☎/fax 77 71 22 25), open from 20 May to 20 August; and Lynseidet (☎ 77 71 17 00, fax 77 71 00 49), open year-round.

Places to Stay The *Kvinnehuset* (☎ 77 71 06 92) in Furuflaten is the best base to use for hiking in the Lyngsdalen valley. This small mountain inn has single/double rooms for Nkr175/275, as well as a pub serving basic meals. Guided glacier hikes are available.

The *Svensby Tursenter* (☎ 77 71 22 25), near the ferry landing, offers rooms and cabins and can organise all sorts of outdoor activities for guests, including fishing, glacier hiking, mountaineering and dog-sledding. Cabins accommodating up to six people cost Nkr600.

Getting There & Away The twice-daily Nor-Way Bussekspress bus between Tromsø and Alta travels via Svensby (1¼ hours, Nkr64) and Lyngseidet (1¾ hours, Nkr86); times and fares are from Tromsø. At least once daily except Saturday, bus No 11 travels between Tromsø and Nordkjosbotn (1¾ hours, Nkr89), which connects with bus No 2 to Furuflaten (1½ hours, Nkr65) and Lyngseidet (1¼ hours, Nkr79).

Coastal Finnmark

Norway's northernmost mainland county, Finnmark, has been inhabited for 10,000 to 12,000 years, first by the Komsa hunters of the coastal region and later by the Sami fishing cultures and reindeer pastoralists, who settled on the coast and in the vast interior, respectively.

Landscape-wise, the county enjoys a distinctly dual character. Its wild northern coast, dotted with fishing villages, is deeply indented by grand fjords while the relatively expansive interior is dominated by the broad Finnmarksvidda plateau, a stark wilderness with only two major settlements, Karasjok and Kautokeino.

Virtually every Finnmark town was decimated at the end of WWII by retreating Nazis, whose scorched-earth policy intended to delay advancing Soviet troops. They were soon rebuilt but unfortunately, the most efficient architectural style was boxy and uninspiring and most of the modern towns are somewhat less than memorable.

Tourist information is available from the Finnmark Travel Association (☎ 78 43 54 44), Postboks 1223, 9501 Alta.

ALTA

The beautifully sheltered fishing and slate quarrying town of Alta (population 17,000) has two main centres, Sentrum and Bossekop, 2km apart, but the town's various other shopping centres, business districts and residential developments actually stretch for at least 15km along the E6. Although it lies at 70°N latitude, it enjoys a relatively mild climate and less precipitation than the Sahara. Despite its uninspiring architecture and elongated nature, it holds a certain 'frontier' charm and the ancient Hjemmeluft petroglyphs at its western end make it a 'must-see' in northern Norway.

The river Altaelva, which slices through the town, was once a traditional Sami fishery and a popular haunt of sporting 19th century English dukes and lords, but is now also one of the most contested waterways in northern Europe. In the late 1970s, despite strong local opposition, a 100m-high dam was built and this rich salmon-spawning stream was developed for hydroelectric power. The issue still riles local sentiments, which remain vociferously opposed to the dam.

Information

The Destination Alta tourist office (☎ 78 43 77 70, fax 78 43 51 84) is in the shopping centre near the bus stop in Bossekop. It's open from 10 am to 6 pm on weekdays, 10 am to 4 pm on Saturday and noon to 4 pm on Sunday from 15 June to 16 August, with shorter hours at other times between 2 June and 31 August.

Hjemmeluft Petroglyphs & Alta Museum

Alta's big attraction is the concentration of prehistoric rock art at Hjemmeluft, at the western end of town, which was named a UNESCO World Heritage Site in December 1985. The area holds an estimated 2500 to 3000 individual Stone-Age and Iron-Age carvings, which are thought to date from between 6200 and 2500 years ago. As sea level decreased after the last Ice Age, carvings were made at lower and lower altitudes; therefore the oldest carvings are now found highest on the hillside. The most prominent and accessible works have now been enhanced with red-ochre paint (which is thought to have been the original coloration) and connected by a 3km network of boardwalks. Popular themes in this area include hunting scenes, fertility symbols, bears, moose, reindeer and crowded boats (amazingly, one boat has a crew of 32 people!).

Aerial view of central Spitsbergen, Svalbard

Coastal village, Finnmark

Look out, polar bear behind you!

Prehistoric tourists on a fjord cruise at Alta

Not-so-prehistoric tourists on a fjord cruise on Magdalenefjord

Too lazy to go on a fjord cruise

The Nkr40 admission fee includes the adjacent Alta Museum (☎ 78 45 63 30), which features exhibits on Sami culture, the military history of Finnmark, the Alta hydroelectric project and observations of the aurora borealis. It's open from 8 am to 11 pm daily from 15 June to 15 August; until 8 pm from 1 to 15 June and 15 to 31 August, and from 9 am to 6 pm at other times from 2 May to 30 September.

Sautso-Alta Canyon

For tourists, the Altaelva hydroelectric project has had little effect on the most scenic stretch of river, which slides through 400m deep Sautso, northern Europe's grandest canyon. The easiest way to see this impressive forested gorge is on a four-hour tour organised by the Destination Alta tourist office. Tours leave from the tourist office daily at 4 pm between 24 June and 16 August and cost Nkr295 per person, with a minimum of five people. In addition to views of the canyon, they also include a pass through the Alta Power Station dam and a snack of coffee, Sami máze cake and dried reindeer meat in a traditional *lavvo*. Trips run from late June to mid-August.

If you have your own vehicle, you can follow the river upstream to the Gargia Fjellstue mountain lodge, 25km from town, where a very bad road (passable to sturdy vehicles only – 4WD and high clearance are recommended) continues for 4km to end at a signpost and dust bin. From this point, you'll have to walk the remaining 7km to the canyon. The route is marked in red blazes but it involves two river crossings and a bit of swamp-slogging so bring strong footwear. Most of all, don't forget your mosquito repellent!

Pæskatun

South of town at Pæskatun, the Alta Skiferprodukter (☎ 78 43 33 45) operates the slate quarry which is one of Alta's economic mainstays. Visitors are welcome to stop by to see the quarry, the historical exhibits and a fine view over the Altaelva. It also serves snacks and sells a range of

Finnmark minerals as well as souvenirs made of slate products. Admission is free but guided tours must be booked in advance and cost Nkr50 per person, with a minimum of 10 participants.

Activities

Plenty of long-distance hiking trails trace historic routes across the Finnmarksvidda. Among them is the five-day, 120km, post road hike between Alta and Karasjok, which begins at Bjørnstad in the Tverrelvdalen valley, climbs to 500m and passes through upland birch forests to wind up at Assebakti, on Rv92, 14km west of Karasjok. The Alta og Omegn Turlag, PO Box 1129, N-9501 Alta (it doesn't have an office but the tourist office can put you in touch with the current club leaders), maintains self-service mountain huts at the Reinbukkelva river and Bojobæski, 16km apart. About 35km farther south is another hut, the Ravnastua mountain lodge (☎ 98 80 06 88), which lies just four hours from the trail's end. Note that you need a tent for the third night of the route. For maps, see the Alta Bok og Papirhandel (☎ 78 43 58 77) in the Parksentret, Sentrum.

Organised Tours

From Alta Friluftspark (☎ 78 43 33 78, fax 78 43 34 65), beside the Altaelva 16km south of town, you can choose from several riverboat rides, which last from 20 minutes to three hours and cost from Nkr95 to Nkr325 per person. They leave at 1 and 3 pm daily from June to August. From 15 July to 15 August, you can also join organised half-day and full-day sea-kayaking trips on Altafjord with AKU Finnmark (☎ 78 43 48 40, fax 78 44 04 80, ulf.thomassen@eunet.no).

Places to Stay

There are three main camping options in Øvre Alta, a 3.5km walk south of the E6 on the Kautokeino road. The first is *Alta River Camping* (☎ 78 43 43 53, fax 78 43 69 02), followed by *Wisløff Camping* (☎/fax 78 92 43 03) and *Alta Strand Camping* (☎ 78 43 40 22, fax 78 43 42 40).

THE FAR NORTH

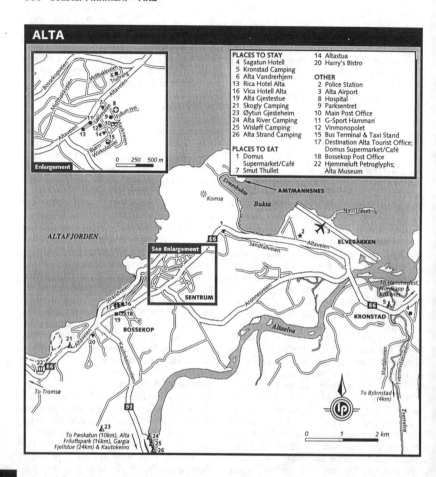

ALTA

PLACES TO STAY
4 Sagatun Hotell
5 Kronstad Camping
6 Alta Vandrerhjem
13 Rica Hotel Alta
16 Vica Hotell Alta
19 Alta Gjestestue
21 Skogly Camping
23 Øytun Gjesteheim
24 Alta River Camping
25 Wisløff Camping
26 Alta Strand Camping

PLACES TO EAT
1 Domus
   Supermarket/Café
7 Smut Thullet

14 Altastua
20 Harry's Bistro

OTHER
2 Police Station
3 Alta Airport
8 Hospital
9 Parksentret
10 Main Post Office
11 G-Sport Hammari
12 Vinmonopolet
15 Bus Terminal & Taxi Stand
17 Destination Alta Tourist Office;
   Domus Supermarket/Café
18 Bossekop Post Office
22 Hjemmeluft Petroglyphs;
   Alta Museum

More convenient are the rather informal *Skogly Camping* (☎ 78 43 56 03), just north of the E6 and east of the museum, and the popular *Kronstad Camping* (☎ 78 43 03 60, fax 78 43 11 55), on the river Tverrelva near the eastern end of town. Generally, you'll pay around Nkr60/100 for tent/caravan sites (Kronstad charges only Nkr40/70), plus Nkr10 per person. All these places offer a range of cabins but the cheapest option for doubles is at Alta Strand Camping, which charges Nkr220,

and the best for four-bed rooms is Alta River Camping, charging Nkr350. Alta Strand Camping also has self-catering apartments for Nkr450 to Nkr730.

The *Alta Vandrerhjem* (☎ 78 43 44 09, Midtbakken 52), a 10-minute walk from the Sentrum bus stop, charges Nkr115 for dorm beds and Nkr230/260 for single/double rooms. However, it's often booked out by bus tours so reservations are essential. It's open from 15 June to 20 August. Note that reception is closed from noon to 5 pm.

The large *Alta Gjestestue* (☎ 78 43 55 66, fax 78 43 50 80, Bekkefaret 3) in Bossekop, has single/ double rooms starting at Nkr490/ 650; a bit cheaper is the *Øytun Gjestheim* (☎ 78 43 55 77, fax 78 43 60 40), 6km from the centre in Øvre Alta, which charges Nkr400/550 with breakfast; it's housed in the folk high school and is open in summer only. The more upmarket *Rica Hotel Alta* (☎ 78 48 27 00, fax 78 48 27 77, Løkkeveien 61) charges from Nkr675/850; the timber-built *Vica Hotell Alta* (☎ 78 43 47 11, fax 78 43 42 99, Fogdebakken 6) charges Nkr845/ 995; and the *Sagatun Hotell* (☎ 78 43 09 99, fax 78 43 00 50), Nkr540/840. Of these choices, the Vica Hotell Alta, housed in a former farmhouse, is probably the most interesting, as it has a free sauna and the owner is commendably hospitable and helpful.

The *Gargia Fjellstue* (☎ 78 43 33 51, fax 78 43 33 36) mountain lodge, 25km south of Alta, offers a great forest getaway and a range of outdoor activities, including the best foot access to the Sautso-Alta Canyon, as well as several other fine day hikes. Rooms cost Nkr190 per person, four-bed cabins are Nkr250 and lavvos are Nkr400, plus Nkr125 per person for linen, showers/ saunas and breakfast. Additional amenities include an open-air hot tub, sauna, river excursions, horse-riding and fishing. You can hire fishing equipment for Nkr50 per day and mountain bikes for Nkr150 per day.

Places to Eat

The *Domus* supermarkets in Bossekop and Elvebakken both have overpriced cafeterias but the best options are in the Sentrum. The town's finest dining is found at the *Altastua* (☎ 78 44 55 54, Løkkeveien 2) bar and restaurant, which features such local ingredients as ptarmigan, reindeer, moose, halibut, salmon and cloudberries, as well as more questionable options. The Rica Hotel Alta has a dining room, pizza restaurant, bar and disco. There's also a restaurant and bar at the Vica Hotell Alta in Bossekop (see Places to Stay, above). A good lunch or dinner option is the unfortunately named *Smut Thullet* (☎ 78 44 05 11, Løkkeveien 35)

in Sentrum. A more down-to-earth choice is *Harry's Bistro* (☎ 78 43 65 30) on Gakoriveien, in the Gakori district at the western end of town.

Getting There & Away

Alta's Elvebakken airport is served by SAS and Widerøe; the latter offers particularly great deals and scenic flights to and from Tromsø, Hammerfest, Båtsfjord and Kirkenes.

One or two daily Nor-Way Bussekspress services run between Tromsø and Alta (6¾ hours, Nkr312). If you're heading for Finnmarksvidda, buses run to and from Kautokeino (2½ hours, Nkr158) three times daily on weekdays and twice daily on weekends. To and from Hammerfest (three hours, Nkr165), buses run twice daily in summer.

The Wednesday and Saturday Express 2000 bus between Hammerfest and Oslo, via Finland and Sweden, passes through Alta at 2 pm southbound and 12.25 pm northbound. The summer express buses between Tromsø, Narvik and Nordkapp also pass through Alta; see Nordkapp, later in this chapter.

Getting Around

Fortunately, this sprawling town has a local bus to connect its dispersed ends. On weekdays, buses run more or less hourly between Hjemmeluft and Kaiskuru (35 minutes), via Bossekop, Sentrum and the Elvebakken airport; some run via the inland district of Aronnes. Services are less frequent on Saturday and don't run at all on Sunday. For optimum flexibility, you can hire bicycles from G-Sport Hammari (☎ 78 43 61 33), Løkkeveien 10 in the Sentrum district.

LAKSELV

The small and plain fishing village of Lakselv (population 2250) lies at the head of the great Porsangerfjord (also called Porsangen) and is the largest town of Norway's third largest municipality. The rather generic name means 'Salmon Stream', which reflects its main appeal to most Norwegian holiday-makers.

THE FAR NORTH

As a stopover, it has all the usual tourist amenities: banks, restaurants, supermarkets, camping facilities, hotels and petrol stations. For information on the region, contact the Porsanger Arrangement tourist office (☎ 78 46 22 99, fax 78 46 19 97). It can also organise a range of activities in the region.

Bio Nordkapp

Lakselv also claims to be the site of the world's northernmost winery, Bio Nordkapp (☎ 78 46 27 20, fax 78 46 27 22), which produces its own special vintages from wild Arctic berries. It's open from 10 am to 3 pm weekdays and admission costs Nkr50, including tasting.

Stabbursnes Naturreservat

The Stabbursnes Nature Reserve occupies an expanse of wetlands and mudflats on the western shore of Porsangen, 4km north of Lakselv. It's especially popular with birdwatchers who come to observe the many species of ducks, geese, divers and sandpipers that rest in the area while migrating between the Arctic and more temperate zones. Rare species to watch for include the lesser white-fronted goose, the bar-tailed godwit, the knot and the dunlin. Note that the coastal marshes are closed to visitors in the nesting season, between 1 May and 30 June.

Stabbursdalen Nasjonalpark

Although compact, the 98 sq km Stabbursdalen National Park offers a scenically forested slice of Finnmark as well as a spectacular glacial canyon and the world's most northerly pine forest. This little visited park makes an excellent walking venue and hikers are accommodated in two mountain huts, Rurkulphytta and Ivarstua, as well as the turf shelter, Gamma.

Unfortunately, since the bridge over the Stabburselva was destroyed in a flood, hikers no longer have the option of making a loop circuit and must return the way they came. The northern track, which passes all the huts but actually lies outside the park, departs from near the visitors centre. The shorter but more diverse southern track begins at the car park about 7km west of the main road, 12km north of Lakselv. Both, however, are worthwhile, and offer keen hikers an opportunity to venture well off the touristed track. The topographic sheets to use are Statens Kartverk's sheet 1935II and 2035III, in the 1:50,000 series.

For the latest information, stop by the museum and visitors centre (☎ 78 46 47 65), 15km north of Lakselv on the E6. It's open daily from 9 am to 8 pm from 16 June to 8 August, and from 10 am to 5 pm at other times from 1 June to 31 August. Information is free but admission to the museum, which features Sami exhibits and a slide show, costs Nkr25. It also sells field guides and topographic maps, and over the road is the official camping site, the *Stabbursdalen Camp & Fritidspark*.

From Lakselv, take the Honningsvåg bus (No 305), which departs at least twice daily in summer, and get off at the Stabbursdalen Naturhus & Museum (20 minutes, Nkr16).

Places to Stay & Eat

Just 1km west of town on the E6 lies the convenient *Solstad Pensjonat og Camping* (☎ 78 46 14 04, fax 78 46 12 14), where campers pay Nkr85 per tent or caravan. Basic huts cost from Nkr200 to Nkr300 and self-catering cabins, from Nkr400 to Nkr500. The rather institutional-looking *Porsanger Vertshus* (☎ 78 46 13 77, fax 78 46 13 95), in the centre, charges Nkr695/895 for singles/doubles, with a 10% discount on weekends. The attached *Åstedet Café & Bistro* is one of the best eateries in town and also has a pub and dancing on weekends.

The simpler *Banak Motell & Camping* (☎ 78 46 10 31, fax 78 46 13 76), about 1km out the Karasjok road, has rooms and cabins with shared facilities for Nkr530/650, as well as caravan sites for Nkr100.

On the main drag in the centre, the *Lakselv Gjestestue* has a great new pizza restaurant, and you'll find decent fast snacks at *Lorre's*, just opposite.

Getting There & Away

Lakselv lies in a crossroads position in northern Norway. Buses between Nordkapp and Inari (Finland), pass two to four times daily in summer. It also lies on the bus route between Kirkenes (7¼ hours, Nkr443) and Hammerfest (3¼ hours, Nkr165), with services daily except Friday and Sunday in summer.

Also in summer, buses to and from Karasjok (1½ hours, Nkr89) operate twice daily on weekdays and once on Saturday. To and from Honningsvåg (four hours, Nkr202, including the ferry), you can travel at least twice daily on weekdays and once daily on weekends.

HAMMERFEST

Hammerfest, with a population of 10,000, is another predominantly fishing and fish processing community – with a bit of oil drilling for good measure. It was founded in 1789 and for over two centuries, proudly claimed to be the northernmost town in the world. Unfortunately for Hammerfest, nearby Honningsvåg was recently designated a town and thereby summarily usurped those honours. Its remaining – and fortunately more lasting – legacy is Europe's first electrical street lighting, which dates from 1890 and has since proved a blessing in the long winter nights.

Despite its long history, Hammerfest has suffered various ignominies: it was decimated in a gale in 1856, burned in 1890 and bombed into ruins in 1944, and all that remains of its original structures is a small chapel. Today, the main employer is the Findus fish processing plant.

If you're arriving on the Hurtigruten coastal steamer, you'll have only two hours to race around, pick up an Arctic souvenir or two and scoff some fresh shrimp at the harbour, but for most people, that will suffice. As Bill Bryson noted of Hammerfest in *Neither Here nor There*, on a trip north to see the aurora borealis: 'I began to feel as if a doctor had told me to go away for a complete rest ... Never had I slept so long and so well.'

Information

Hammerfest Turist (☎ 78 41 21 85, fax 78 41 19 00), on Corn Moes gate, provides tourist information and books local activities.

Royal & Ancient Polar Bear Society

The Hammerfest Rådhus (town hall) houses the renowned Royal & Ancient Polar Bear Society, which features exhibits on Arctic hunting. However, it's best known for the silver bear outside, which has posed for photos with decades of keen boreal tourists. Admission is free but membership in the club – and a smart certificate, sticker and pin to prove it – costs Nkr150. The displays are open from 7 am to 8 pm on weekdays and 10 am to 5 pm on weekends.

Gjenreisningsmuseet

Hammerfest's Reconstruction Museum (☎ 78 42 26 30) celebrates the reconstruction period that followed the decimation of the town after the German bombings of 1944, and reveals the hardships that people endured through the following winter. It also discusses the 'Norwegianisation' of the indigenous Sami culture in northern Norway. In summer, it's open from 8 am to 9 pm daily. Admission is Nkr40.

Hammerfest Kirke

On Kirkegata, a five-minute walk from the harbour, lies Hammerfest's contemporary church. It's unusual in that it lacks an altarpiece, which has been replaced by a large stained glass window. You may find reindeer grazing in the churchyard and the adjacent chapel is the only building in town to survive the 1944 bombings.

Salen

For panoramic views over the town, coast and mountains, climb Salen Hill (86m) which is topped by a small Sami turf hut. The 10-minute trail begins at the small park uphill behind the Rådhus. For Nkr220, the tourist office organises a Sami-style meal there at 5 pm each Saturday in July.

Fuglenes

On the Fuglenes peninsula, across the harbour from the centre, is the Meridianstøtta, the marble column commemorating the first survey (1816-52) to determine the arc of the global meridian and thereby calculate the size and shape of the earth. At the end of the same peninsula lie the rather nondescript ruins of the Skansen fortress, which date from the Napoleonic Wars.

Organised Tours

Nightly in July, you can make a return midnight-sun cruise to Honningsvåg. It departs at 7 pm and arrives in Honningsvåg at 9 pm, where buses leave for Nordkapp and arrive at 10 pm. After a quick tour, the buses return to Honningsvåg to connect with the return cruise to Hammerfest, which arrives at 3.40 am. The Nkr620 price includes a light dinner but not the Nkr175 admission

to Nordkapp. Book through the FFR (☎ 78 40 70 00) or the tourist office.

Åttringen Nordlandsbåt (☎ 78 41 00 16, mobile ☎ 94 13 45 38) charges Nkr190 per person (with a minimum of three people) for three-hour fishing and sailing tours on Sørøysundet in a traditional Nordland boat.

Places to Stay

NAF Camping Storvannet (☎ 78 41 10 10), 2km east of the centre on Storvannsveien, is open from 1 June to 15 September and offers tent sites for Nkr50/100 without/with a car and caravan sites for 100, plus Nkr15 per person, and cabins for Nkr300. Cooking facilities are available.

There's also a hostel, the *Hammerfest Vandrerhjem* (☎/fax 78 41 36 67, Idrettsveien 52), which is also near the lake Storvannet. Here you'll pay Nkr100 for dorm

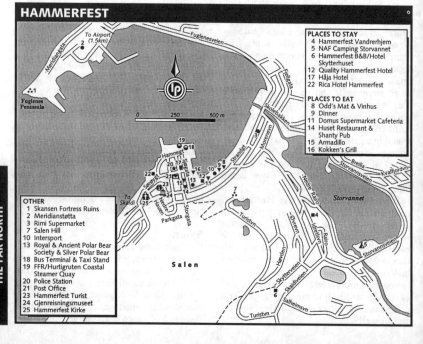

HAMMERFEST

PLACES TO STAY
4 Hammerfest Vandrerhjem
5 NAF Camping Storvannet
6 Hammerfest B&B/Hotel
    Skytterhuset
12 Quality Hammerfest Hotel
17 Håja Hotel
22 Rica Hotel Hammerfest

PLACES TO EAT
8 Odd's Mat & Vinhus
9 Dinner
11 Domus Supermarket Cafeteria
14 Huset Restaurant &
    Shanty Pub
15 Armadillo
16 Kokken's Grill

OTHER
1 Skansen Fortress Ruins
2 Meridianstøtta
3 Rimi Supermarket
7 Salen Hill
10 Intersport
13 Royal & Ancient Polar Bear
    Society & Silver Polar Bear
18 Bus Terminal & Taxi Stand
19 FFR/Hurtigruten Coastal
    Steamer Quay
20 Police Station
21 Post Office
23 Hammerfest Turist
24 Gjenreisningsmuseet
25 Hammerfest Kirke

THE FAR NORTH

beds and Nkr250 for doubles. The *Hammerfest B&B/Hotel Skytterhuset (☎ 78 41 15 11, fax 78 41 19 26, Skytterveien 24)* has summer rates of Nkr520/720.

A popular central hotel is the *Håja Hotel (☎ 78 41 18 22, fax 78 41 43 98, Storgata 9)*, which is now best known as the site of Bill Bryson's long winter naps (and drinking exploits) in *Neither Here nor There*. In summer, singles/doubles with shared bath cost Nkr550/700. The *Quality Hammerfest Hotel (☎ 78 41 16 22, fax 78 41 21 27, Strandgata 2)* has similar summer rates, and the more posh *Rica Hotel Hammerfest (☎ 78 41 13 33, fax 78 41 13 11, Sørøygata 15)* charges from Nkr580/860 in summer and Nkr995/1095 at other times.

Places to Eat
Probably the finest restaurant in town is *Odd's Mat & Vinhus (☎ 78 41 37 66, Strandgata 24)*, which is open in summer for lunch and dinner. Although rather expensive, it's considered a gourmet option and features meat and seafood concoctions. Considerably more pedestrian is the well known *Kokken's Grill (☎ 78 41 15 50)* between the harbour and the town hall, which cooks up traditional and international fast fare. Believe it or not, Hammerfest also has Chinese and Mexican options, *Dinner (☎ 78 41 38 78, Strandgata 22)*, and *Armadillo (☎ 78 41 07 20, Storgata 23)*, respectively.

For pizza, beer and billiards, the place to go is *Shanty*, at the *Huset Restaurant (☎ 78 41 49 00, Storgata 27)*.

The *Domus* supermarket on Strandgata, east of the town hall, has an inexpensive cafeteria, but the *Rimi* supermarket is cheaper for groceries.

Getting There & Away
The Express 2000 bus leaves Hammerfest at noon on Wednesday and Saturday and travels to Oslo (29½ hours, Nkr1750), via Finland and Sweden, arriving at 5.30 pm the following day. From Oslo, it leaves at 10.30 am on the same days. Daily except Friday and Sunday, there's also a bus between Hammerfest and Kirkenes (10 hours, Nkr597), via Karasjok (4¾ hours, Nkr248) and Tana Bru (6¾ hours, Nkr446).

The FFR (☎ 78 41 10 00) express boat to Honningsvåg (two hours, Nkr300) leaves Hammerfest daily at 7 pm from mid-June to mid-August. You can also get a return ticket that includes a bus to Nordkapp to see the midnight sun (see under Organised Tours earlier in this section). The Hurtigruten coastal steamer also stops in Hammerfest for approximately two hours in either direction. It departs at 7.45 am northbound, towards Honningsvåg (9¼ hours, Nkr280) and Kirkenes (27½ hours, Nkr885), and 1.15 pm southbound, towards Tromsø (10½ hours, Nkr537).

Getting Around
Bicycles may be hired at the Intersport shop at Strandgata 16 for Nkr50 per day.

HONNINGSVÅG
Honningsvåg (population 2900) is the only real settlement on the island of Magerøy and is also the main service centre for the entire Nordkapp area. Much to the dismay of its neighbour Hammerfest, it recently declared itself a *by* (town) and consequently usurped the title of the world's northernmost town.

Unfortunately for Honningsvåg, it's bypassed by the main road and most visitors – save those tour passengers who require upmarket accommodation – whiz past on day tours without stopping or stay at the inexpensive accommodation at Skipsfjorden.

Information
The enthusiastic Nordkapp Reiseliv tourist office (☎ 78 47 25 99, fax 78 47 35 43, nctravel@online.no), midway between the bus station and quay, provides information on the town and the Nordkapp area and also organises local tours, including birdwatching in summer and snow machine tours in winter. The Nordkapp Safari company (☎ 78 47 27 94, fax 78 47 37 45) runs deep-sea fishing trips by Zodiac for Nkr700 plus Nkr50 per person per hour.

Things to See

Honningsvåg has the small and locally-oriented **Nordkapphuset Museum**, near the bus terminal, with displays concentrating on the Arctic fishing culture. It's open from 9 am to 8 pm weekdays and Saturday from 15 June to 15 August, and from 1 am to 8 pm on Sunday. Admission is Nkr20. There's also the **19th century church**, which was the only structure to survive the Nazi bombs in 1944. The real tourist destination, however, is Nordkapp, 35km away.

Places to Stay & Eat

Nordkapp Camping & Vandrerhjem (☎ 78 47 33 77, fax 78 47 11 77), open from 1 May to 30 September, occupies a stark site at Skipsfjorden on the Nordkapp road, 8km north of Honningsvåg. Tent or caravan camping costs Nkr80 per unit plus Nkr20 per person, dorm rooms are Nkr120, doubles cost Nkr400 and cabins, Nkr440 to Nkr800. Unfortunately, the nearby 'Sami Cultural Centre' is little more than a trap for bus tours.

If you're getting into the 'northernmost' spirit which pervades this part of Norway, you can always pitch your tent at *Kirkeporten Camping* (☎ 78 47 52 33, fax 78 47 52 47), at the tiny village of Skarsvåg 20km from Honningsvåg, which claims to be the world's northernmost camping ground. In fact, it has been beaten hands down by the camping grounds in Longyearbyen and Ny Ålesund, Svalbard, but that's immaterial for most visitors, and it can still legitimately claim the world's northernmost camping cabins, which cost from Nkr400 to Nkr900.

Thanks to the burgeoning tourist trade that revolves around Nordkapp, Honningsvåg's hotels are expensive. The cheapest is the *SIFI Sommerhotell* (☎ 78 47 28 17, fax 78 47 35 11, Kobhullveien 12), with single/double rooms in student quarters for Nkr400/500. It's open from 20 May to 20 August. The *Hotel Havly* (☎ 78 47 29 66, Storgata 12) charges Nkr690/940 and meals are served between noon and midnight.

The upmarket choices, the *North Cape Hotel* (☎ 78 47 23 33, fax 78 47 33 70), *North Cape Hotel Bryggen* (☎ 78 47 28 88, fax 78 47 27 24), *Honningsvåg Brygge* (☎ 78 47 24 24, fax 78 47 24 25), and *Rica Hotel Nordkapp* (☎ 78 47 33 88, fax 78 47 32 33), all charge Nkr500 to Nkr780 for singles and Nkr900 to Nkr1195 for doubles. All are in town (and rather nondescript) except the Rica Hotel Nordkapp, which adjoins the Vandrerhjem at Skipsfjorden.

The fish restaurant *Corner* (☎ 78 47 27 01), behind the tourist office, features a café, seafood, pizza and a bar. It's open until midnight Sunday to Thursday and until 2 am on Friday and Saturday, when it doubles as a disco. There are two supermarkets, the *Rema 1000*, on the road from the ferry terminal, and the cheaper and more convenient *Rimi*. The best bar in town is undoubtedly the *Nøden Pub* (☎ 78 47 27 11), near the North Cape Hotel.

Getting There & Away

The Valan airport lies about 3km from town, but most arriving passengers are on tours and there are no public bus connections with the town centre.

From early June to mid-August a daily express bus travels between Alta and Honningsvåg (5½ hours, Nkr242). The road approach from the E6 is via Olderfjord, where it connects with the Rv69 north-west to Kåfjord. The Kåfjord-Honningsvåg car ferry (☎ 78 41 10 00) runs every hour or two (45 minutes, Nkr34/107 for passengers/cars), but soon (ostensibly in mid-1999, but due to delays, the final opening date is uncertain), it will be eliminated by the new 28km, Nkr930 million Fatima road route, which includes the world's northernmost (and Europe's longest) undersea road tunnel. The only advantage, however, will be convenience, as the tunnel toll will match the ferry fare.

The Hurtigruten coastal steamer stops at Honningsvåg at 1 pm northbound and 6.45 am southbound. The 4½-hour northbound stop allows a quick buzz up to Nordkapp, and the Hurtigruten offers passengers a moderately priced tour. See Hammerfest for information on the express boat services and tours from that town.

For information on Nordkapp buses, see Nordkapp, below.

Getting Around
If you want to make a quick excursion to Nordkapp, Hertz (☎ 78 47 35 28) has a special four-hour deal on car hire for Nkr600, including petrol. If that seems a bit steep, you've never hired a car or bought petrol in Norway!

NORDKAPP
Nordkapp (North Cape) is a high rugged coastal plateau at 71°10'21"N and the main destination for most travellers in far northern Norway, but it would be more appropriately regarded as a nice view at the end of long and scenic tour. The sun never drops below the horizon from mid-May to the end of July and the steep cliffs and stark scenery emanate a bleak and rather ethereal Arctic ambience. Indeed, long before other Europeans took an interest in the area, Nordkapp was considered a power centre and sacrifice site by the Sami people.

It was named North Cape by Richard Chancellor, the English explorer who drifted this way in 1553 on a search for the North-East Passage. Following a much-publicised visit by King Oscar II in 1873, Nordkapp became a pilgrimage spot of sorts – and continues to be one – but don't let anyone tell you it's the northernmost point in Europe. Those honours go to the promontory Knivskjelodden, a few kilometres to the north-west (see later in this chapter).

Nordkapphallen Tourist Centre
Nowadays there's a tourist complex, Nordkapphallen (☎ 78 47 68 60, fax 78 47 68 61), with various polar exhibits, the posh Compasset restaurant and Grotten bar, a Thai museum (of all things), the St Johannes chapel, a post office (tourists love the Nordkapp postmark) and various souvenir shops. The five-screen 225° theatre runs a decent audiovisual program but it's a bit repetitive – there are only so many views of Nordkapp – and to really appreci-

ate the place, you need to take a walk out along the cliffs. In fair weather, perched on the edge of the continent, you can gaze down at the wild surf 307m below, watch the mist roll in and perhaps even dream of Svalbard, far to the north.

It's open from 10 am to 2 am daily from 8 June to 10 August, with shorter hours at other times from 6 April to 5 October. Unfortunately, it imposes an extortionate and rather unpopular admission fee of Nkr175 per person, and the only way to avoid it is to walk to Nordkapp (access to the nature reserve is free) and forego visiting the tourist complex (alas, no embossed certificate ...) However, the nearest car park lies about 2km back along the road and bus passengers are discouraged from disembarking there, so you'll need your own vehicle and enough energy for a short slog.

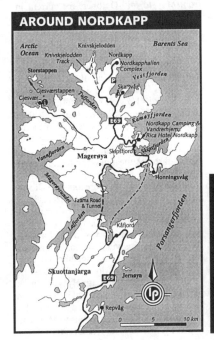

AROUND NORDKAPP

Gjesvær

Those with some spare time may also enjoy riding the twice-daily bus from Honningsvåg out to the remote fishing village of Gjesvær (45 minutes, Nkr49), which lies well off the touristed route. The tourist office in Honningsvåg can organise boat tours to the fabulous offshore bird cliffs at Gjesværstappen, where you can observe puffins, guillemots, kittiwakes, skuas, razorbills, cormorants and gannets, among other seabirds (you need a minimum of five people). Simple hut accommodation is available at the Gjesvær Turistsenter (☎ 78 47 57 73, fax 78 47 57 07) for Nkr300 to Nkr600.

Getting There & Away

The asphalted road to Nordkapp winds across a rocky plateau, past herds of grazing reindeer, to the northern edge of Europe. Depending on snow conditions, it's open from May to mid-October; for current information, contact the National Road User Information Centre (☎ 22 65 40 40).

In summer, Nor-Way Bussekspress has a twice daily service between Tromsø and Nordkapp (13 hours, Nkr627), with one daily connection to Kautokeino from Alta (2½ hours, Nkr158) and to Hammerfest from Skaidi (1¼ hours, Nkr69). Students, seniors, children and InterRail and Scan-Rail pass holders receive a 50% discount. Note that passengers for Nordkapp must pay the Nkr175 admission fee, plus the Nkr34 fare for the ferry (or tunnel, as the case may be).

An alternative is the more tour-like Ofotens Bilruter Nordkapp Expressen (☎ 76 92 35 00, fax 76 92 35 30, ob@ofotens-bilruter.no, www.ofotens-bilruter.no), which does a return trip between Narvik and Nordkapp (Nkr1050). It runs via Sweden, Finland and Finnmarksvidda on the northbound route (13½ hours) and via Alta and the E6 on the return (13 hours). Alternatively, you can return on the Hurtigruten coastal steamer from Honningsvåg to Sortland, then travel by bus to Narvik (Nkr1755), or by bus to Moskenes (Lofoten) and ferry to Bodø (Nkr1870).

From mid-May to the end of August, local buses run daily at 11.50 am between Honningsvåg and Nordkapp (one hour, Nkr50), with an additional service at 8.20 pm between 2 June and 16 August and another at 10.55 pm between 2 June and 9 August. Between 2 June and 9 August, the last bus departs Nordkapp at 1.10 am, allowing views of the midnight sun. If you're on a budget, avoid any ostensible 'tours', that charge considerably more for similar services.

KNIVSKJELODDEN

From an unassuming car park about 9km south of Nordkapp, you can hike the marked 9km track to the lovely Knivskjelodden promontory. Thanks to an apparently unspoken agreement with Nordkapp promoters, the signpost there doesn't identify it as such, but at 71°11'08"N latitude, Knivskjelodden is the real northernmost point in Europe. It's not a difficult walk but does require a few ups and downs and takes about five hours return.

MEHAMN & GAMVIK

The old whaling village of Mehamn, at the end of the Nordkyn peninsula, was the site of one of Norway's earliest environmental movements. In 1903, troops were brought in to subdue a revolt by the local fishing community when they decided the whaling industry was exterminating the whales which had historically made fishing easy by driving cod towards the shore.

Although there's little reason to make the long slog up to Mehamn or neighbouring Gamvik, at the end of the Nordkyn peninsula, those who collect 'northernmosts' may be interested to know that nearby Kinarodden is the northernmost point of *mainland* Europe (Knivskjelodden, above, is on an island) and Slettnes Fyr, on Varnesodden, is the northernmost mainland lighthouse in the world. A birdwatchers' trail has recently been constructed through the Slettnes Naturreservat, which is frequented by nesting and migrating ducks and wading birds, but the area is accessible only on foot or by private vehicle.

After checking those sites off the list, pop into the Latitude 71 Museum (☎ 78 49 61 18) at Gamvik (yes, it's Europe's northernmost museum ...), which reveals the local fishing cultures in this far-flung corner of the world. It's open from 11 am to 5 pm daily from 20 June to 20 August, with shorter hours the rest of the year. Admission is Nkr20.

In Gamvik, you can stay at the basic *Gamvik Gjestehus (☎ 78 49 61 12, Strandveien 22)* for Nkr350/500 and in Mehamn, at the *Mehamn Hotell (☎ 78 49 71 57)*, which charges Nkr390/600 in summer. Buses run daily except Saturday between Lakselv and Mehamn (4½ hours, Nkr254) but you can travel between Mehamn and Gamvik (30 minutes, Nkr33) on weekdays only. Mehamn is also a brief stop on the Hurtigruten coastal steamer.

BERLEVÅG

If for some reason you find yourself in Berlevåg, take three hours and hike to the Sami sacrificial site atop 269m Tanahorn for a wonderful view over the Arctic Ocean. The 8km return walk begins 8km west of town, along the gravel road towards the equally interesting abandoned fishing village of Store Malvik (20km west of Berlevåg). There's also a Havnemuseum (Harbour Museum) that contains the usual maritime displays, as well as an unusual old expedition dory, the *Berlevåg II*. It's open from 11 am to 5 pm daily from 15 June to 15 August and admission costs Nkr15.

The accommodation option here is *Berlevåg Camping & Appartement (☎ 78 98 16 10)*, which charges Nkr80 for tent or caravan camping and Nkr335/370 for single/double rooms. Buses run from Tana Bru (2½ hours, Nkr155) and Båtsfjord (1¾ hours, Nkr109) at least once daily, except Saturday. It's also a stop on the Hurtigruten coastal steamer route.

BÅTSFJORD

Locals are proud to point out that Båtsfjord is Norway's largest fishing port, and if you like scruffy little harbour towns with all their attendant industrial maritime paraphernalia, it does have a certain charm. You'll find the Båtsfjord Turistinformasjon desk (☎ 78 98 31 00) at the Båtsfjord Nye Hotell. It's open from 1 June to 1 September.

Båtsfjord Kirke

The main site of interest is the church, which was constructed in 1969. Fortunately, its less than inspiring (some would say ugly) exterior is unique in Norway and contrasts sharply with the wonderful 85 sq m of stained glass by Jardar Lunde, which is visible from inside. It's open daily in summer and admission is free.

Makkaur

From town, a 25km hike eastward along the fjord's southern shore leads to Makkaur, an abandoned fishing village that dates from medieval times and escaped bombing during WWII. As a result, there's all sorts of interesting junk left over, including a German POW camp from WWII. Makkaur's only remaining resident is the attendant at the 1928 lighthouse.

The 113 sq km Makkaurhalvøya Naturreservat immediately to the east was established in 1983 to protect the 4km-long and 200m-high Syltefjordstauren bird cliffs. In summer, it attracts around 250 breeding pairs of gannets, as well as sea eagles, cormorants, razorbills, puffins, both common and Brunnichs guillemots and 150,000 breeding pairs of kittiwakes. You can arrange boat tours through the tourist office in Båtsfjord.

Places to Stay

The cheapest accommodation is the seamen's mission, the friendly *Havly Fiskarheim (☎ 78 98 42 05, fax 78 98 34 81, Havnegata 31)*, which has an attached cafeteria and charges from Nkr350 for a single room. At the comfortable but dreary and overpriced *Båtsfjord Nye Hotell (☎ 78 98 31 00, fax 78 98 39 18, Valen 2)*, you'll pay Nkr875/1100 for singles/doubles.

Fridtjof Nansen

Anyone looking for a modern hero need not look further than the Norwegian explorer, Fridtjof Nansen (1861-1930), who not only exceeded many of the frontiers of human endurance, but also of human compassion. Nansen grew up in the rural area of Store Frøen, at the edge of the Nordmarka woods outside Oslo, and enjoyed a privileged childhood thanks to his family's relative wealth. Perhaps his interest in exploration was derived from this setting, as well as the influence of his father, Hans Nansen, who had once served as the mayor of Copenhagen and explored the shores of Russia's White Sea.

As a young man, he was an excellent skier and ice skater, winning the national Nordic skiing championships 12 times and breaking the world record for the one-mile skating course. When he entered the University of Christiania, his interests were in physics and mathematics, but he elected instead to study zoology, as he thought it would allow him to spend more time out of doors. At the suggestion of one of his tutors, in 1882 he took passage aboard the sealing ship, *Viking*, to sail to the Arctic Ocean and study ocean currents, ice movements and wildlife. During this voyage, he had tantalising glimpses of the eastern coast of Greenland, and he was seized with the desire to undertake a journey across the central icecap of that continent-like island.

Between 18 June and 19 September 1888, after six more years of study in Bergen, these dreams came to fruition when he led a six-man expedition from the east to the west coasts of Greenland. He chose to walk from the wild east coast to the more populated west because there could be no retreat, and although he was only 27 years old, the expedition was completed without mishap. As there was no ship to take them back to Norway that year, Nansen remained in Greenland through the winter, observing the Inuit peoples and gathering material for his 1891 book, *Eskimo Life*.

In order to mount his next expedition, which would observe Arctic Ocean currents and the westward flow of ice, he commissioned shipbuilder Colin Archer to design a ship that would survive being frozen fast in pack ice. The result was the 400-tonne vessel *Fram*, which had a three-layered oak hull reinforced with steel. He selected Otto Sverdrup, who'd accompanied him to Greenland, to captain the ship and in June 1893, the expedition left Christiania with provisions for six years and fuel for eight. Nansen also left his wife Eva and six-month old daughter Liv, with no idea when he'd return.

After several monotonous months on the ship, Nansen decided to make a bid for the North Pole, and on 14 March 1895, he and Hjalmar Johansen left the *Fram* and its mission in the hands of Otto Sverdrup. After a five-month, 550km journey on foot over the ice, the two men holed up on an island where they sheltered for nine winter months in a tiny stone hut they'd built. The following May they set off southward and in June, ran into British explorer Frederick Jackson (for whom Nansen later named the island where they'd spent the winter). Having given up on reaching the Pole, Nansen and Johansen headed south with Jackson, and arrived back in Vardø, just a week before *Fram* arrived in Skjervøy.

By 1905, Sweden and Norway faced a political crisis that stemmed from Norway's bid for independence from the union, and Nansen, who was by then perceived as a national hero, was dispatched to Copenhagen and Britain to represent the Norwegian cause.

When Norway did achieve its independence, Nansen was asked to act as the prime minister of the new country (there are rumours that he'd turned down offers of the job of king or president), but declined, wishing only to continue as a scientist and explorer, and eventu-

Fridtjof Nansen

ally mount an expedition to the South Pole. However, he did accept the offer of King Håkon, who asked him to serve as the Norwegian ambassador to Britain. In 1907, however, after the sudden death of his wife, he permitted fellow Norwegian explorer Roald Amundsen to use the *Fram* on an expedition north of Siberia, which meant that he had to abandon any hopes of reaching the South Pole.

After WWI, Nansen worked tirelessly for the newly organised League of Nations, and took up the cause of half-a-million German soldiers who'd been imprisoned in the Soviet Union and no longer had a homeland. Although the USSR would not recognise the League of Nations, Nansen set off in April 1920 to plead the case of these dispossessed soldiers. By September 1922, he'd successfully repatriated over 400,000 men or found countries willing to accept them.

Even before this project was finished, a failed grain crop in Russia threatened 20 million people with famine and pestilence and the International Red Cross asked Nansen to lead an aid project. He soon discovered, however, that the League of Nations was unwilling to help a communist country, and resorted to private fundraising missions to help as many Russians as possible. At the same time, he identified that two million Russians who had fled the 1917 Bolshevik revolution remained stateless; the result was the 'Nansen Passport', which enabled thousands of stateless Russians and Ukrainians to travel and settle in other countries.

Nansen's greatest diplomatic achievement, however, was probably the resettlement in their home countries of several hundred thousand Greeks and Turks who had been displaced after the defeat of the Greek Army by the Turks in 1922. As a result, in 1922 he was awarded the Nobel Peace Prize, and donated his prize money to international relief efforts. After 1925, his work concentrated on international disarmament and lobbying the League of Nations to provide a non-Soviet homeland for Armenian refugees in Turkey, Syria and other countries. Although this latter project failed, his name is still revered among Armenians around the world.

On 13 May 1930, Nansen died quietly at his home in Polhøgda, near Oslo, and was buried in a quiet garden nearby. If you want to learn more about the life of this extraordinary man, look for the biography *Nansen*, by Roland Huntford, published in the UK in 1997, or the earlier book of the same title, by EE Reynolds, which was first published in 1932.

Getting There & Away

The airport, 5km from town, is served by Widerøe from Alta and Kirkenes. These are certainly among the most novel flights in Norway, as you have excellent views of the Arctic landscapes, complete with grazing reindeer.

Otherwise, bus services connect Båtsfjord with Tana Bru (two hours, Nkr125) and Berlevåg (1¼ hours, Nkr109) daily except Saturday. Båtsfjord is also a stop on the Hurtigruten coastal steamer.

TANA BRU

Tana Bru, on the great Tana River, is well known for its picturesque bridge (for which it's named) and its reputation as a sport fishing paradise. This is one of Europe's best salmon streams, and anglers use the odd technique of constructing barrages to obstruct the upstream progress of the fish. In fact, the natural barrage at Storfossen falls, about 30km upstream, is one of the finest fishing spots around.

You'll find tourist information at the Tana tourist office (☎ 78 92 86 27, fax 78 92 82 11); it's open from 10 am to 6 pm daily from 10 June to 29 August.

The *Tana Turisthotell (☎ 78 92 81 98, fax 78 92 80 05)* has cabins and rooms for Nkr680/880, as well as a restaurant, bar and weekend disco. At *Polmakmoen Gjestegård (☎ 78 92 89 90)*, 20km upstream, you can stay in Sami-style *gamma* (turf huts) or guesthouse rooms from Nkr350/400. It also conducts 1½-hour riverboat cruises for Nkr75.

The Nor-Way Bussekspress bus between Hammerfest (7¼ hours, Nkr446) and Kirkenes (2¼ hours, Nkr165) crosses the bridge at Tana Bru, and local buses run daily except Saturday to and from Berlevåg (2½ hours, Nkr155) and Båtsfjord (two hours, Nkr125) and daily to and from Vadsø (1¼ hours, Nkr82).

If you're travelling towards Båtsfjord or Berlavåg, note the spectacular and colourful folded sedimentary layers in the Gamasfjellet cliffs, along the eastern shore of Tanafjord.

VADSØ

As the administrative centre of Finnmark, Vadsø has a rather stable population these days, but historically, it was the site of large-scale immigration from Finland and during the 1830s and 1840s, the town's population was 50% Kvæn (as the Finnish were known). In the centre, a 1977 monument honours this cultural heritage.

The cemetery on Vadsø island also provides evidence of the Pomor culture, the Russian trading and fishing community from the White Sea area, which prospered here in the 17th century.

Vadsø Museum

The three-part Vadsø Museum (☎ 78 95 29 55) includes the Tuomainen-Gården estate, a Finnish farmhouse dating from the 1840s; the merchant's home, Esbensengården *Sletten*, which dates from the 1850s; and the restored Kjeldsen fish plant at Ekkerøy, 14km east of town.

The town sites are open from 10 am to 5.30 pm on weekdays and 10 am to 2 pm on weekends between 20 June and 1 September, with shorter hours at other times. Kjeldsen, which has a summer café, is open from 11 am to 6 pm on weekdays and Sunday and from 11 am to 4pm on Saturday. Admission to all three properties costs Nkr25.

Vadsø Kirke

Vadsø has what is surely one of the most bizarre churches in Norway. Built in 1958 to replace the 1861 church, which was destroyed during WWII, this is Vadsø's fourth church (the first two were constructed in 1575 and 1710). In this one, architect Magnus Poulsson intended to recall an arching iceberg floating in the Arctic Ocean, but it seems more reminiscent of a Jesuit mission in the wilds of South America. Just as odd is the Orthodox-inspired altarpiece, in which artist Gretha Thiis created a sort of unisex Christ figure, and the stained glass work, in which Ragna Thiis Helland depicts the divinity of water and the seasons.

Luftskipsmasta

The odd mast on Vadsø island was built in the mid-1920s as an anchoring and launch site for airships on their way to the polar regions. It was first used in April 1926 by the Roald Amundsen, Umberto Nobile and Lincoln Ellsworth expedition, which flew via the North Pole to Teller, Alaska, in the airship *Norge N-1*. In 1928, it was used to launch Nobile's airship, *Italia*, which attempted to repeat the journey but crashed in the ice on the north-west coast of Spitsbergen. Amundsen joined the rescue expedition and disappeared in the attempt, thereby becoming a martyr as well as a hero.

The area also boasts numerous ruins of protected pre-historic turf huts; you can pick up a map of the main sites at the museum in town. If you're visiting in early summer, also watch for the rare Stellar's duck, which nests in this area.

Ceavccageadge/Mortensnes Kulturminneområde & Varjjat Sami Musea

If you have a vehicle, it's worth stopping at Mortensnes to stroll though the remnants of 11,000 years of Sami history, from the Stone Age into the Bronze and Iron Ages. From the small visitors centre (☎ 78 95 82 55, info@varanger-Samiske.museum.no), a track winds past ancient burial sites and home ruins, as well as a reconstructed turf hut that was typical of coastal Sami settlements. The Sami name 'ceavccageadge' means 'fish oil stone' and refers to the prominent standing pillar, which was smeared with cod liver oil to ensure luck while fishing.

East of the main site, a nature trail leads down to the shore past several ancient burial mounds. Also note the Bjørnstein ('bear rock'), atop the hill east of the site, which resembles a bear from every angle and was revered by early Sami inhabitants. The site is open from 11 am to 6 pm daily from 15 June to 21 August. Admission is Nkr30.

At Varangerbotn, at the head of Varangerfjord, there's also the affiliated Varjjat Sami Musea (Varangerbotn Museum) a museum of the history, religion and traditions of the coastal Sami cultures of northern Norway. It's open the same hours and admission also costs Nkr30.

Places to Stay

Unfortunately, there's no longer a camping ground in Vadsø; the nearest is at Vestre Jakobselv (☎ 78 95 60 64), 17km west of town, where four/six-bed cabins cost Nkr210/250. Apart from that, the least expensive options are the private guesthouses of *Ragnhild Schetne* (☎ 78 95 25 83), who charges Nkr250 per person, and *Anne Grethe Mathisen* (☎ 78 95 38 23 evening, ☎ 78 95 11 58 daytime, Grønnliveien 6), who has doubles for Nkr400. The *Rica Hotel Vadsø* (☎ 78 95 16 18, fax 78 95 10 02, Oscars gate 4) has summer single/double rates of Nkr500/700 to Nkr675/850 and the simpler *Lailas Hotell* (☎ 78 95 33 35, fax 78 95 34 35, lailas.hotell@vadso.online.no), Brugata 2 on Vadsøya island, charges Nkr450/500 to Nkr595/695.

Getting There & Away

Vadsø is a stop on the northbound Hurtigruten coastal steamer route (it calls in at 9.30 am). You can also get there by bus from Tana Bru (1¼ hours, Nkr82) at least once daily, but that means you can't stop at Mortensnes en route and continue your journey on the same day. Between Vadsø and Vardø (1½ hours, Nkr92), buses run at least once daily, except Sunday.

VARDØ

Vardø, Norway's easternmost town, crowds onto a butterfly-shaped portion of Vadsøya island and is linked to the mainland by the 2.9km Ishavstunnelen (Arctic Ocean tunnel) under the Barents Sea. With a sort of skewed logic, Vardø is proud to point out that technically, it's the only mainland Norwegian town lying within the Arctic climatic zone, which means that the mean monthly temperature never exceeds 10°C. Once a stronghold of the Russian Pomor trade, it's now a major fishing port and is home to a number of Russian and Sri Lankan immigrants.

THE FAR NORTH

The Vardø tourist office (☎ 78 98 82 70, fax 78 98 74 77), at the Vardøhus Festning, is open from 10 am to 6.30 pm weekdays and from 11 am to 6.30 pm on weekends. In summer, it can organise short cruises with Vardø Havnevesen (☎ 78 98 72 75) to see the teeming bird cliffs on the island of Hornøya, the easternmost point in Norway, which has a picturesque lighthouse.

Things to See

The main attraction is the star-shaped **Vardøhus Festning** (fortress) – yes, it's the world's most northerly – which was constructed in 1737 by King Christian VI to define the 'end of Norway'. On a nice day, it's pleasant to stroll around its flower-covered bastions and ramparts and past its turf-roofed buildings and Russian cannons (which were captured by the Germans during WWII). Note that the well house inspired the design of Vardø's town hall. The admission fee of Nkr10 can be paid either at the tourist office or by dropping it into the sinister-looking WWII-era sea mine that guards the entrance.

Between 1621 and 1692, 80 Vardø women were accused of witchcraft and burned to death; on the 156m hill, **Domen**, south of town on the mainland, you can see the cave where they were supposed to have held their 'satanic' rites.

In the centre, the **Pomor Museum** recaps the historic trade between Russia and Norway, which lasted until the Bolshevik Revolution in 1917. It also reveals the natural history of the region, as well as the expeditions of Fridtjof Nansen and William Barents. It's open from 9.30 am to 6 pm weekdays from 15 June to 15 August, and from 11 am to 6 pm on weekends; admission costs Nkr20.

The 1958 **Vardø Kirke** is open from 5 to 6 pm, when the southbound Hurtigruten coastal steamer is in port.

Places to Stay & Eat

The only budget option is *Svartnes Camping* (☎ 78 98 71 60), which cannot, in good faith, be recommended. Those with

tents would probably be happier hiking off into the hills or finding a spot along the beach. For anyone prepared to tolerate the grime and the scowls, exposed tent sites cost Nkr80 and rooms in a dreary pre-fab unit are Nkr150 per person. The ostensible café hasn't functioned any time in recent history.

In the centre, you can choose between the *Gjestegården* (☎ 78 98 75 29, Strandgata 72), or the strictly functional *Vardø Hotell* (☎ 78 98 77 61, fax 78 98 83 97, Kaigata 8). The former charges a reasonable Nkr250/300 for single/double rooms, plus Nkr50 for breakfast, while the latter has more institutional rooms for Nkr550/650, including breakfast.

For meals, there's little choice, but most people go to *Naustet* (☎ 78 98 74 74), on Strandgata, which has a café, pub and restaurant.

Getting There & Away

Vardø is a stop on the Hurtigruten coastal steamer route, but otherwise, it's well off the beaten track for all but the most die-hard travellers. Buses do the scenic seaside run between Vadsø and Vardø (1½ hours, Nkr92) at least once daily, except Sunday.

HAMNINGBERG

The tiny and utterly charming settlement of Hamningberg amply rewards the efforts required to get there. The road in from Vardø is lined with some of the most fascinating geology in northern Norway, including lichen-covered forests of eroded stone pillars, the remnants of sedimentary layers turned on end. For visitors, this may seem like the uttermost end of Norway but residents maintain that this is in fact where Norway begins!

For most visitors, a highlight is a stay at Mr Edvald Svensen's *Hamningberg Gjestehus*, a very traditional *rorbu* (fishing cabin) with basic three-bed rooms for Nkr100 per person. The same building also houses a small fishing museum brimming with maritime paraphernalia from Hamningberg's past. For bookings, contact the Svensens via Mr Sven Knudsen, at the town shop (☎ 78 98 81 54).

During Vardø's Pomordagene festival in early August, throngs of people set out to walk the scenic 37km from Vardø to Hamningberg, and those who make it are treated to a barbecue at the church. Visitors are welcome to join in. Otherwise, you need a private vehicle to get there.

KIRKENES

During WWII, the industrial and iron ore mining port of Kirkenes probably suffered the worst bombings of any town in Norway. In spite of its remote northerly location, its rock and forest-studded surroundings are surprisingly lush and not at all bleak. Although it's not yet a major tourist destination, Kirkenes is the northern terminus of the Hurtigruten coastal steamer line and a staging point for trips into Arctic Russia, just over the border. The current population is around 4500.

History

Until 1846, when the Finnish border was surveyed, the Sør-Varanger district was jointly occupied by Norway and Russia. The modern history of Kirkenes began in 1906, when iron ore was discovered at nearby Bjørnevatn, and during WWI the town became a major supplier of raw materials for artillery. Although the industry subsequently suffered a series of industrial disputes, WWII brought a new boom and Kirkenes found itself in a key position, thanks mainly to its proximity to the free Russian port of Murmansk. Early in the war, it was occupied by the Nazis, who recognised its resources and strategic position, and 30,000 troops were posted there. As a result, the town suffered at least 300 devastating air raids by Soviet bombers.

When Kirkenes was finally liberated by Soviet troops in October 1944, it was burned to the ground by the retreating Nazis. Although it was subsequently rebuilt and continued to supply iron ore to much of Europe, costs were too high to sustain the trade, and in 1996 the mines closed down.

Information

Tourist Office The helpful Grenseland Tourist Office (☎ 78 99 25 01, fax 78 99 25 25, grenseland@online.no), in the centre, is open from 8.30 am to 6 pm weekdays from 10 June to 21 August, and from 10 am to 6 pm on weekends. The rest of the year, it's open from 8.30 am to 4 pm weekdays only.

Laundry You can do your washing at the coin-operated Rens og Vask, beside the Vinmonopolet at the western end of Kirkegata.

Dangers & Annoyances If you're approaching the Russian border, don't even think about popping across for a quick photo. Both Norwegian and Russian sentries are equipped with surveillance equipment and the current fine for illegal crossings, even momentary ones, starts at Nkr5000. What's more, 'any attempts at violations will be punished as if they had been carried out'. You may not even greet people you see on the other side or toss anything across the line, and although photography is permitted along most of the border area, you may not use telephoto or zoom lenses. Other fussy rules and regulations are outlined in the pamphlet, *Conduct and Travel at the Norwegian-Russian Border*, which is available at the tourist office or from the Norwegian border commissioner (☎ 78 99 31 20) in Kirkenes.

Things to See & Do

Kirkenes' few in-town attractions include the **Hagenes Monument** which is dedicated to the Soviet Red Army troops who liberated the town in 1944, and an underground cave, the **Andersgrotta** bunker, which was used as an air-raid shelter during the war. A short video retells the tale at 10 am and 2 and 6.15 pm on weekdays, and at 2 and 6.15 pm on weekends, from 10 June to 16 August. There's also a particularly friendly looking **bear sculpture** outside the post office.

The well done **Sør-Varanger Grenseland Museum** (☎ 78 99 48 80), about 1km from the centre, deals with the geography, culture, religion and especially WWII history

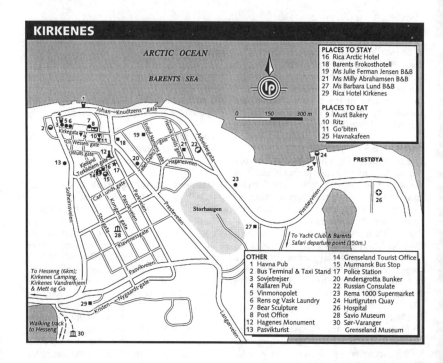

KIRKENES

ARCTIC OCEAN

BARENTS SEA

PRESTØYA

Storhaugen

To Hesseng (6km);
Kirkenes Camping,
Kirkenes Vandrerhjem
& Mett og Go

Walking track
to Hesseng

To Yacht Club & Barents
Safari departure point (350m.)

PLACES TO STAY
16 Rica Arctic Hotel
18 Barents Frokosthotell
19 Ms Julie Ferman Jensen B&B
21 Ms Milly Abrahamsen B&B
27 Ms Barbara Lund B&B
29 Rica Hotel Kirkenes

PLACES TO EAT
9 Must Bakery
10 Ritz
11 Go'biten
25 Havnakafeen

OTHER
1 Havna Pub
2 Bus Terminal & Taxi Stand
3 Sovjetrejser
4 Rallaren Pub
5 Vinmonopolet
6 Rens og Vask Laundry
7 Bear Sculpture
8 Post Office
12 Hagenes Monument
13 Pasvikturist
14 Grenseland Tourist Office
15 Murmansk Bus Stop
17 Police Station
20 Andersgrotta Bunker
22 Russian Consulate
23 Rema 1000 Supermarket
24 Hurtigruten Quay
26 Hospital
28 Savio Museum
30 Sør-Varanger
   Grenseland Museum

of the Norwegian, Finnish and Russian border regions. It also includes a library, shop and café. In summer, it's open daily from 10 am to 6 pm.

Also worthwhile is the **Savio Museum** (☎ 78 99 25 01), Kongensgate 10B, which is dedicated to the Sami-inspired work of artist John A Savio (1902-38). It's open from 10 am to 6 pm daily from 20 June to 20 August; admission costs Nkr20.

Visiting Russia

If you're intending to enter Russia independently at Storskog, which is the only official border crossing, be sure to have your Russian visa (preferably from your home country) before arriving in Kirkenes. Unless you have an official pre-arranged invitation, the Russian consulate in town (☎ 78 99 37 37), Arbeidergata 6, does not issue independent tourist visas, and no amount of charm or

begging will sway them. Some nationalities may be issued visas at the Russian consulate in Oslo, but US citizens in particular shouldn't count on it. Note that your visa must specify which Russian cities and towns you intend to visit. Without permission to visit Nikel (which is surely the most horrible spot on earth, and deserves a visit for that reason alone), Zapolyarny, Murmansk or another Pechenga or Kola-area town, you may not be allowed to cross the border.

Those who already have a visa can just hop on the Murmansk Shipping Company's public bus to Murmansk (seven hours, Nkr400), which travels via Nikel and Zapolyarny. It leaves Kirkenes on Wednesday, Friday and Sunday at 3 pm from the Rica Arctic Hotel and from the Hotel Polyarny Zory in Murmansk at 9 am on the same days (thanks to more efficient border crossings, the return trip takes only four hours).

Due to military exercises along the route, it's only open to foreigners from 7 am to 9 pm Norwegian time (9 am to 11 pm Russian time) on Monday, Wednesday, Friday and Sunday. For further information on independent travel, see Lonely Planet's *Russia, Ukraine & Belarus*.

If you're happy with just a quick hop across the border, you can pop over with a local travel agent (see Organised Tours in this section), who can organise your visa locally. However, your itinerary will be rather limited and without a great deal of creativity, you probably won't be permitted to continue further into Russia.

For tour participants, visa fees are determined by nationality and also vary according to what sort of urgency is required; all applications require three passport photos and for the best rates, you'll have to wait a minimum of 10 days. Citizens of Canada, the UK, Italy, Japan and India pay just Nkr50 while Norwegians pay Nkr245, other Scandinavians Nkr200, other EU citizens Nkr280 and US citizens Nkr350. In addition, everyone pays a servicing fee of Nkr50. If you need a visa the next day, you'll pay anywhere from Nkr1000 to Nkr2500. Naturally, this is all subject to change on a whim.

Organised Tours

Many visitors who have travelled as far as Kirkenes want to visit Russia – or at least sally up to the border – and several local agencies are happy to accommodate them.

Sovjetrejser (☎ 78 99 19 81, fax 78 99 11 42) organises day trips to the hell-hole, Nikel, for Nkr480 to Nkr600 per person, including a lunch and guide, and to Zapolyarny for Nkr1100. Day trips to Murmansk run daily except Sunday and Wednesday, 1 June to 31 August, and cost Nkr1000, while weekends in Murmansk cost Nkr1650 per person plus Nkr400 per night. Straight minibus transfers between Kirkenes and Murmansk are Nkr550.

The other main player offering Russia trips is Pasvikturist (☎ 78 99 50 80, fax 78 99 50 57), which runs adventure tours, including canoeing and camping in the Pechenga wilderness, and longer tours of north-western Russia. An eight-day all-inclusive trip visiting Murmansk, the Pomor trading centre of Solovki and Archangelsk costs Nkr5950 per person.

For those who can't wait for a visa, Barents Safari (☎ 90 19 05 94, fax 78 99 80 69, hhatle@online.no) offers another option: a boat trip up the Bøkfjorden to the Russian border at Boris Gleb (Borisoglebsk in Russian), with stops at the Trifons cave and the photographic exhibition at the border (you won't, however, see the distinctive 16th century timber church in Boris Gleb). There are daily departures at 11.30 am and 3, 6 and 9 pm from the yacht club in Kirkenes; the cost is Nkr300 per person. The same company also organises custom tours around the Pasvik region, as does the Grenseland tourist office. So how about an overnight tour on a reindeer sledge for Nkr1650?

Places to Stay

Kirkenes Camping (☎ 78 99 80 28) is in Hesseng, 6km west of town. You can camp in a tent without/with a vehicle for Nkr55/75 and caravan camping is Nkr85. Very basic double cabins cost Nkr150 and four-bed cabins with minimal cooking facilities are Nkr250 to Nkr320.

Also in Hesseng, just off the E6, the friendly *Kirkenes Vandrerhjem (☎ 78 99 88 11)* actually doubles as a hotel and is the cheapest and nicest budget option. Hostel beds cost Nkr130 and single/double rooms, from Nkr275/400 to Nkr450/600. It's open in summer only.

Other mid-range choices in town include the *Barents Frokosthotell (☎ 78 99 32 99, Presteveien 3)*, where you'll pay Nkr450/650 for rooms without bath and Nkr550/700 with bath (rates include breakfast) and three private B&Bs. *Ms Julie Ferman Jensen (☎ 78 99 11 44, Fritjof Nansens gate 6)* charges Nkr200/400 for singles/doubles; *Ms Barbara Lund (☎ 78 99 32 07, Henrik Lunds gate 13)* has rooms for Nkr200 per person; and *Ms Milly Abrahamsen (☎ 78 99 12 48, Prestøyveien 28A)* charges Nkr250/400.

The **Sollia Gjestehus** (☎ 78 99 08 20, fax 78 99 08 15) lies about 15km from Kirkenes and 300m from the Storskog border. It's not an opulent option but it's still fairly good value. Single/double rooms cost Nkr300/500, basic double cabins are Nkr350 and plusher four-bed cabins are Nkr450 to Nkr500.

The two big hotels, **Rica Arctic Hotel** (☎ 78 99 29 29, Kongensgate 1) has summer room rates of Nkr675/850 and the **Rica Hotel Kirkenes** (☎ 78 99 14 91, fax 78 99 13 56, Pasvikveien 63), 500m from the centre, charges Nkr625/750. The former has a pool and sauna and the latter, a view.

Places to Eat

Kirkenes isn't really a gourmet's paradise (for that you'll have to get to Pasvik Taiga, in Pasvik), but you will find sustenance. In addition to the dining rooms and bars at the two Rica hotels, you'll find a very nice little pizza place, the **Ritz** (☎ 78 99 34 81, Dr Wessels gate 17), which also has an attached café, the **Go'biten** (☎ 78 99 34 80), a disco and a sports pub.

The imperative-sounding **Must Bakery** (Kirkegata 2) does sweet breakfasts and coffee, as well as light lunches, or you can go for the simple cafeteria meals at the **Havenkafeen** (☎ 78 99 22 68), on the Hurtigruten pier. A more diverse cafeteria and grill menu is available at the **Mett og Go**, next door to the Kirkenes Vandrerhjem in Hesseng. For self-catering, there's a **Rema 1000** supermarket (☎ 78 99 21 74) on Prestøyveien.

Entertainment

As you can imagine, Kirkenes' entertainment scene revolves around pubs. The most popular hangout is the **Ritz** (Dr Wesselsgata 17), which has a disco, pub and Saturday nightclub. The Saturday pub and disco at the Rica Arctic Hotel attracts mainly the 18 to 21 crowd. A fun and fairly raucous place that attracts local people of all ages is **Ral-laren**, in the centre. The sailors' hangout is the **Havna Pub**, which is also the place to play pool or darts.

Getting There & Away

Daily at 9.15 am (on Saturday in summer only), a bus leaves Kirkenes for Karasjok (five hours, Nkr363) and Hammerfest (10¼ hours, Nkr597), with a 6.25 pm connection at Skaidi to Alta (1¾ hours, Nkr102). The Murmansk bus (five to seven hours, Nkr400) leaves Kirkenes at 3 pm on Wednesday, Friday and Sunday (for more information, see Visiting Russia, earlier in this section).

Kirkenes is the end of the line for the Hurtigruten coastal steamer, which arrives at 11.15 am and departs at 2.30 pm on its long southbound cruise to Tromsø (35 hours, Nkr1234), Trondheim (88¾ hours, Nkr2665), Bergen (120¾ hours, Nkr3685) and points in between.

Getting Around

The airport is served by a Flybuss (25 minutes, Nkr45) which connects the hospital, bus terminal, two big hotels and Hesseng (12 minutes, Nkr23) with all arriving and departing flights. Buses run between the centre and Hesseng (15 minutes, Nkr16) every hour or two on weekdays, at least five times on Saturday and once on Sunday. There's also a pleasant walking route to Hesseng, which follows the lakeshore part of the way.

ØVRE PASVIK NASJONALPARK

Even when the diabolical mosquito swarms make life hell for warm-blooded creatures, the remote lakes, wet tundra bogs and Norway's largest stand of virgin taiga forest lend a strange appeal to odd little Øvre Pasvik National Park. Indeed, this is the last corner of Norway where wolves, wolverines, lynx and brown bears still roam freely, and it seems more like Finland or Siberia than anywhere else in Norway (in fact, it strongly reminds me of my lakeside cabin in Alaska). The park is also home to moose and a host of relatively rare birds, including the Siberian jay, pine grosbeak, cedar waxwing, black-throated diver, red-breasted merganser, capercaillie, rough-legged buzzard, spotted redshank, hawk owl, great grey owl and even osprey.

The Stone Age Komsa hunting culture left its mark here in the form of hunters' pitfall traps around the lake Ødevann and elsewhere in the region; some date from as early as 4000 BC.

Information

You'll find the most reliable information at the coffee shop in Vaggatem, where you can also pick up the pamphlet *Bears in Pasvik*, which outlines hopeful directions on what to do should you encounter a testy bruin. You'll also find it at the tourist office in Kirkenes and most tourist facilities in the Pasvik region.

Hiking

If you can manage it, douse yourself in mozzie repellent and head off on a hike into the wilds. The most accessible route is the poor road that turns south-west 1.5km south of Vaggatem and ends 9km later at the car park near the north-eastern end of the lake Sortbrysttjørna. There, a marked track leads south-westward for 5km, passing several scenic lakes, marshes and bogs to end at the Ellenvannskoia hikers' hut, beside the large lake, Ellenvatn. To extend the hike by two days, you can walk all the way around the lake, but there are no marked tracks.

Also from the Ødevasskoia car park, it's about an 8km walk due south to 145m Krokfjell and the Treriksrøysa, the monument marking the spot where Norway, Finland and Russia meet. Although you can approach it and take photos, you may not walk around the monument, which would amount to an illicit border crossing! Note also that hikers may not walk around the lake Grenseparvann, which would require crossing the Finnish border.

The topographic sheet to use is Statens Kartverk's *Krokfjellet 2333-I*, which conveniently covers the entire park.

Places to Stay & Eat

There are several hunting and fishing huts scattered around the park but the only one that's practical for casual hikers is Ellenvannskoia, which is free. With a licence,

you can also fish in the lake (which contains perch, grayling and pike).

The coffee shop in Vaggatem is the best source of park information and the only choice for coffee and snacks. *Øvre Pasvik Camping* (☎/fax 78 99 55 30) next door has cabins for Nkr200/250/350 for one/two/four people. It also rents canoes and bicycles.

The highly acclaimed *Pasvik Taiga* restaurant (☎ 78 99 54 44, fax 78 99 54 99), Skogfoss, presents a range of gourmet fish and game dishes. You may, however, want to forego any menu items of dubious provenance, such as bear. Prices for a three-course dinner start at Nkr300. At the attached *Skogmo Gård* guesthouse, single/double rooms cost Nkr500/800, with breakfast. The catch is that guests are required to eat at the restaurant and full board costs Nkr1000/1800.

Getting There & Away

If you have a car, there are several things to see en route to the park, including the Strand branch of the Sør-Varanger Museum, which preserves Norway's oldest public boarding school and reveals the region's ethnic mix; the timber-built Svanvik chapel, dating from 1934; the 19th century Bjørklund Gård farm, which demonstrates the lives of early settlers in the Pasvik region; and the Svanhøvd Environmental Centre (☎ 78 99 50 37, fax 78 99 51 22, svanhovd.miljosenter@svanhovd.no), which monitors the considerable environmental concerns in the Barents Sea region. You can also call in at the viewpoint known as Høyden 96 for a view eastward to the Russian mining town of Nikel, which could resolve any notions you may have about visiting there.

If you don't have a car, however, all is not lost. On Monday, Wednesday and Friday, buses leave Kirkenes for Vaggatem (2¼ hours, Nkr112) at 1.20 pm and from Vaggatem, at 7.05 am. This means you'll have to stay the night at Vaggatem and then hike the 10.5km along the road to the park trailhead (there's little traffic, so it's wise not to rely on hitching).

GRENSE JAKOBSELV

The first settlement at Grense Jakobselv probably appeared around 8000 years ago, when the sea level was 60m lower than it is today. Here only a small stream separates Norway and Russia, and along the road, you can see the border obelisks on both sides. The only real attraction here – apart from the chance to gaze over the magic line – is the 1869 stone church. It was constructed within sight of the sea to cement Norway's territorial claims after local people complained to the authorities that Russian fishing boats were illegally trespassing into Norwegian waters; it was thought that the intruders would respect a church and change their ways. When King Oskar II visited in 1873, he gave the church his name.

The only accommodation is *Grense Jakobselv Camping* (☎ 78 99 65 10), which allows tent camping and has two and four-bed cabins for Nkr 100 to Nkr400.

During school holidays, you can make a return trip between Kirkenes and Grense Jakobselv (1½ hours, Nkr72) on Monday, Wednesday and Friday; the bus leaves at 9 am and returns at 11.30 am, allowing an hour in the village. On Sunday, the bus leaves at 4.20 pm but allows only 10 minutes in the village before it heads back at 5.45 pm. By taxi (☎ 78 99 13 96), the return trip from Kirkenes takes 3½ hours and costs Nkr800.

Finnmarksvidda

KAUTOKEINO

The desultory settlement of Kautokeino (Guovdageainnu in Sami), with its decidedly non-European ambience, is the heart of the 'big sky country' of northern Scandinavia and the cultural heart of Norway's portion of the semi-political entity known as Sápmi, the 'land of the Sami'.

Settlement in the area can be traced back to the last Ice Age, 5000 years ago; from as early as 1553, during the gradual transition between nomadism and stationary lifestyles, records reveal evidence of permanent settlement at Guovdageainnu. Christianity took hold early on and the first church appeared here in 1641. While tidier Karasjok has made concessions to both prevailing cultures – Sami and Scandinavian – Kautokeino remains emphatically Sami, and resembles no other town in Norway. As evidence, take a look at the sculpture *Flyvesjamanens Fugl* ('flying shaman's bird'), at the entrance to the secondary school.

Information

The Kautokeino tourist office (☎ 78 48 65 00), in the Siva Kafeen on the main road, is open from 9 am to 7 pm from 6 June to 31 July, with gradually shortening hours from 1 August to 26 August.

Guovdageainnu Gilišillju

The fascinating Kautokeino Outdoor Museum (☎ 78 48 60 43) presents a traditional Sami settlement, complete with an early home, temporary dwellings, a trapping exhibit and several agricultural and pastoral outbuildings. These include a fish storage hut, potato hut, lichen hut (lichen, or 'reindeer moss', is considered prime reindeer fodder), kitchen hut, equipment hut, a sauna, and sheds for sheep, cattle, goats and reindeer. There's also an indoor museum containing a complement of Sami handicrafts, farming and reindeer herding implements, religious icons and artefacts, and winter transport gear.

It's open from 9 am to 7 pm weekdays from 15 June to 15 August, and from noon to 7 pm on weekends. The rest of the year, it's open from 9 am to 3 pm on weekdays. Admission costs Nkr20.

Kautokeino Kirke

The timbered Kautokeino church, which dates from 1958, presents a colourful bastion of Christianity in the village. It's open from 10 am to 8 pm daily from late June to mid-August.

Organised Tours

The main player in the area is Cávzo Safari (☎ 78 48 75 44, mobile ☎ 94 80 26 20, fax 78 48 75 75), in Máze village (which

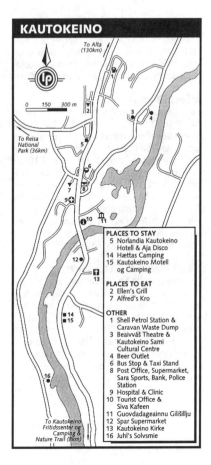

KAUTOKEINO

To Alta
(130km)

0   150   300 m

To Reisa
National
Park (36km)

PLACES TO STAY
5 Norlandia Kautokeino
   Hotell & Aja Disco
14 Hættas Camping
15 Kautokeino Motell
   og Camping

PLACES TO EAT
2 Ellen's Grill
7 Alfred's Kro

OTHER
1 Shell Petrol Station &
   Caravan Waste Dump
3 Beaivváš Theatre &
   Kautokeino Sami
   Cultural Centre
4 Beer Outlet
6 Bus Stop & Taxi Stand
8 Post Office, Supermarket,
   Sara Sports, Bank, Police
   Station
9 Hospital & Clinic
10 Tourist Office &
   Siva Kafeen
11 Guovdadageainnu Gilišillju
12 Spar Supermarket
13 Kautokeino Kirke
16 Juhl's Solvsmie

To Kautokeino
Fritidssenter og
Camping &
Nature Trail (8km)

narrowly escaped drowning by the late 1970s hydroelectric project in Alta), north of Kautokeino. From 26 June to 16 August, it conducts five-hour riverboat trips to the Altaelva dam for Nkr295, including a Sami-style meal and cultural instruction and entertainment.

Places to Stay & Eat
The *Kautokeino Motell og Camping* (☎ 78 48 54 00, fax 78 48 53 01) offers 25 fully-equipped cabins and 17 basic cabins, with access to a common kitchen. In the centre of the complex is a large Sami *lavvo*, which provides a warm and cosy spot to relax by a wood fire. Tent or caravan camping costs Nkr100 per unit, cabins are Nkr280 and Nkr300, and motel rooms cost from Nkr480 to Nkr850.

Alternative camping options are *Hætta's Camping*, just next door, or the *Kautokeino Fritidssenter og Camping* (☎ 78 48 57 33), 8km south of town. Both places charge Nr65/85 for tent/caravan camping, plus Nkr10 per person, and Nkr200 to Nkr800 for cabins. The latter is also the start of an interesting 4km nature trail. The more elite *Norlandia Kautokeino Hotell* (☎ 78 48 62 05, fax 78 48 67 01) charges Nkr595/840 in summer and higher rates at other times.

For meals, you can opt for the Norwegian standard, *Ellen's Grill*, or sample the reindeer steaks at *Alfred's Kro* (☎ 78 48 61 18), which also does more usual grilled fare. There's a small café, the *Siva Kafeen*, at the tourist office. The *Spar* supermarket, near the river, offers a limited range of supplies.

Entertainment
The world's only professional Sami theatre, *Beaivváš* operates through the Kautokeino Sami Cultural Centre, which also houses the Nordic Sami Institute. For information on performances, contact the Kautokeino Kommune (☎ 78 48 58 00). More pedestrian tastes are served at the *Aja Disco* in the Norlandia Kautokeino Hotell.

Shopping
The highly acclaimed Juhl's Solvsmie (☎ 76 48 61 89), run by Frank and Regine Juhls, creates traditional and modern silver and gold jewellery and Sami handicrafts. The results may not be cheap but they are original and beautiful. In summer, it's open from 8.30 am to 10 pm daily. In addition, you'll find several less sophisticated shops along the main road through town, which offer competitive and negotiable prices on authentic but often non-traditional Sami crafts. There's also a nice souvenir shop adjoining the tourist office, in the centre.

THE FAR NORTH

Getting There & Away

Buses connect Kautokeino with Alta (2½ hours, Nkr158) at least once daily. To and from Karasjok (1¾ hours, Nkr148), buses run on Monday, Wednesday, Friday and Sunday. You can also travel on the Lapin Linjat bus between Kautokeino and Rovaniemi, Finland (6¼ hours, Nkr252) on Monday, Wednesday, Saturday and Sunday, with a change at Enontekiö.

Getting Around

You can hire bicycles from Sara Sports at the rather steep cost of Nkr180 per day. Alfred's Kro hires out canoes to potter around on the river for Nkr200 per day.

REISA NASJONALPARK

Although it's technically in Troms county, Reisa National Park is most readily accessible by road from Kautokeino. For hikers, the 50km route through this remote Finnmarksvidda country is one of Norway's wildest challenges. The northern trailhead at Sarelv is accessible on the Rv865, 47km south of Storslett, and the southern end is reached on the gravel route to Reisevannhytta, 4km west of Bieddjuvaggi on the Rv896, north-west of Kautokeino.

Most people walk from north to south. From Bilto or Sarelv, you can either walk the track up the western side of the anomalous cleft that channels the Reisaelva river or hire a riverboat for the three-hour 27km trip upstream to Nedrefoss, where there's a DNT hut. En route, notice the 269m Mollesfossen waterfall, east of the track on the tributary stream Molleselva. From Nedrefoss, the walking route continues for 35km south to the Reisavannhytta hut on the lake Reisajävri, near the southern trailhead.

KARASJOK

Although Kautokeino is the most Sami settlement in Norway, Karasjok (Kárášjohka in Sami) is the home of the recently established Sametinget, the Sami Parliament, as well as the NRK Sami Radio, the Sami Library, the Sami School of Advanced Studies and the Sami Art Centre, making it the in-disputable capital of Sami Norway. Karasjok is also the site of Finnmark's oldest timber church, Gamlekirke, which dates from 1807 and was the only Karasjok building to survive the WWII bombings and fires.

Information

The Karasjok Opplevelser tourist office (☎ 78 46 73 60, fax 78 46 69 00) has a desk in the Samelandsenteret, at the junction of the E6 and the Rv92. It's open from 8.30 am to 6.30 pm Monday to Saturday and 10 am to 7 pm on Sunday from 10 June to 4 August, with shorter hours the rest of the year. In the same hall, you can also check out the 15-minute Sameland audiovisual program, which includes traditional Sami music and scenes about nomadic reindeer herding. It runs daily on the hour and costs Nkr30.

Sámiid Vuorká Dávvirat

The worthwhile Sami Museum provides an easily digestible rundown of Sami history and culture from ancient times to the present day. Highlights include the practical reindeer sledges used in former days and a display on the colourful blue and red traditional dress which has come to represent the Sami culture to the outside world. The outdoor exhibits feature a simple homestead and reveal simplicity of life in the olden times. Opening hours are from 9 am to 6 pm, Monday to Saturday, and from 10 am to 6 pm on Sunday, from 6 June to 16 August, with shorter hours the rest of the year. Admission is Nkr25.

Organised Tours

At Engholm's Husky (☎ 78 46 71 66, fax 78 46 71 76, se.engholm@online.no), 6km from town on the Kautokeino road, Sven Engholm (☎ 78 46 71 66) presents Alaskan sled dog demonstrations in summer at 10 am and 1 pm daily (Nkr30). He also offers great winter dog-sled and cross-country skiing tours, as well as summer dog-packing tours. All-inclusive week-long dog-sled tours range from Nkr8000 to Nkr12,000. If you just want a taste of dog mushing, you can take a short spin around the premises for Nkr150.

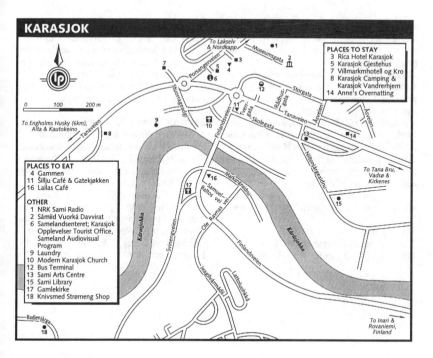

KARASJOK

PLACES TO STAY
3 Rica Hotel Karasjok
5 Karasjok Gjestehus
7 Villmarkmhotell og Kro
8 Karasjok Camping &
   Karasjok Vandrerhjem
14 Anne's Overnatting

PLACES TO EAT
4 Gammen
11 Šillju Café & Gatekjøkken
16 Lailas Café

OTHER
1 NRK Sami Radio
2 Sámiid Vuorká Davvirat
6 Samelandsenteret; Karasjok
  Opplevelser Tourist Office,
  Sameland Audiovisual
  Program
9 Laundry
10 Modern Karasjok Church
12 Bus Terminal
13 Sami Arts Centre
15 Sami Library
17 Gamlekirke
18 Knivsmed Strømeng Shop

Places to Stay & Eat

Karasjok Camping (☎ 78 46 61 35, fax 78 46 66 23) has tent or caravan camping for Nkr60 per unit (Nkr40 for a tent with no vehicle) plus Nkr10 per person. Simple two/four-bed cabins are Nkr200/400 and larger five-bed cabins cost Nkr550. For luxury five/seven-bed units with a shower and toilet, you'll pay Nkr650/850. The one five-bed cabin with a sauna costs Nkr650. This place also serves as the ***Karasjok Vandrerhjem***, with dorm beds for Nkr115.

The ***Villmarksmotell og Kro*** (☎ 78 46 74 46, fax 78 46 64 08) has cabins for one/two/four people for Nkr190/230/360, without linen, and single/double motel rooms for Nkr390/460. Breakfast costs an additional Nkr50 per person.

Anne's Overnatting (☎ 78 46 64 32, Tanaveien 40) charges Nkr320/420 for rooms and Nkr275/350 for two/four-bed

cabins; with linen, you'll pay Nkr420/650. All rooms have TV and guests have access to the kitchen.

At the friendly ***Engholm's Husky*** (☎ 78 46 71 66, fax 78 46 71 76), 6km from town along the Kautokeino road, you'll have a range of very atmospheric accommodation choices. Cosy and well designed log cabins with two/three/five beds cost Nkr250/450/525, while *lavvo* camping costs just Nkr100 per person. Breakfast is an additional Nkr50 per person. Substantial lunches/dinners cost Nkr200/350. For guests, pickup from town is free.

The premier lodging in Karasjok is the ***Rica Hotel Karasjok*** (☎ 78 46 74 00, fax 78 46 68 02), off Porsangerveien, with decent rooms for Nkr745/940 in summer, including breakfast. With a Rica or Norlandia discount pass, the rates decrease to Nkr545/780. Ask for something on the main floor,

THE FAR NORTH

as the basement is rather drab. The attached *Karasjok Gjestehus* (☎ *78 46 74 46, fax 78 46 64 08)* has more basic rooms for Nkr350/450.

The *café* at the Samelandsenteret and *Lailas Kafé*, over the bridge on Markangeaidnu 1, have moderately priced meals. For less sophisticated grill meals, there's the *Šillju Café & Gatekjøkken*, on Finlandsveien. The underground *Gammen* (☎ *78 46 74 00)*, on the Rica Hotel grounds, dishes up traditional Sami food and atmosphere, with an emphasis on reindeer and *biddus*, or 'wedding stew'. It isn't cheap but it's a good communal eating experience and you won't regret spending the money.

Shopping

The Knivsmed Strømeng (☎ 78 46 71 05, fax 78 46 64 40), in the Samelandsenteret, creates unique and original handmade Sami knives, calling on four generations of local experience. Several other worthwhile crafts shops are under the same roof, including a silversmith and a couple of handicraft vendors. Knivsmed Strømeng also has an outlet south of the centre at Badjenjárga.

Getting There & Away

On Monday, Wednesday, Friday and Sunday, afternoon buses run to and from Kautokeino (1¾ hours, Nkr148). There's also a service to and from Lakselv (1¼ hours, Nkr89) daily except Sunday. The buses between Hammerfest (4¾ hours, Nkr238) and Kirkenes (five hours, Nkr363) pass through daily in summer. The Finnish Lapin Linjat bus between Lakselv, Norway, and Rovaniemi, Finland (6¾ hours, Nkr267), also passes through Karasjok.

Svalbard & Jan Mayen

The Arctic archipelago of Svalbard and the tiny mid-Atlantic island of Jan Mayen present a side of Norway that isn't present anywhere on the mainland. While the Arctic magic of Svalbard attracts increasing numbers of tours and cruise ships, storm-lashed Jan Mayen remains largely neglected by both Norwegians and visitors.

Svalbard

Svalbard is an assault on the senses. This wondrous archipelago, Norway's toehold in the high Arctic, is not only the world's most readily accessible bit of the polar north, but also one of the most spectacular places imaginable. Here, vast icebergs and floes choke the surrounding seas and icefields and glaciers frost the lonely heights, but under close scrutiny, the harsh Arctic conditions reveal tiny gems. The Arctic desert soil, however barren-looking, still produces lichens, miniature grasses and delicate little flowers, and the seemingly harsh environment supports larger creatures: whales, seals, walrus, polar bears, Arctic foxes and Svalbard caribou (or reindeer). Add to that some of the most haunting scenery anywhere on earth and you have a dream destination for an unusual and unforgettable holiday.

History
The first mention of Svalbard occurs in an Icelandic saga from 1194. Officially, however, the Dutch voyager Willem Barents, in search of a north-east passage to China, is credited with the first European discovery of the archipelago (1596). He named the islands Spitsbergen, or 'sharp mountains'; the Norwegian name, Svalbard, comes from the old Norse for 'cold rim' or 'cold coast', as cited in the sagas, which referred to 'a land in the far north at the end of the ocean'.

At the time of Barents' discovery, the archipelago was uninhabited, as the early

HIGHLIGHTS

- Cruising around ice floes in search of seals, walrus and polar bears
- Spending a sunny morning surrounded by the brilliant glaciers and turquoise waters of Magdalenefjord
- Searching for plant fossils around Longyearbreen
- Taking a Russian cultural lesson at Barentsburg or Pyramiden
- Running the Arctic tern gauntlet to appreciate Ny Ålesund's hauntingly beautiful backdrop
- Trekking through some of the most intense wilderness on earth

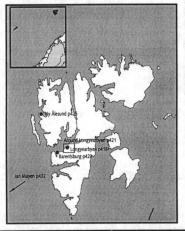

Inuit migrations eastward from Siberia and Alaska halted in Greenland. There's archaeological evidence of Russian over-wintering around the turn of the 17th century but the first confirmed European activities in Svalbard didn't begin until a decade later. From 1612 to 1720, English,

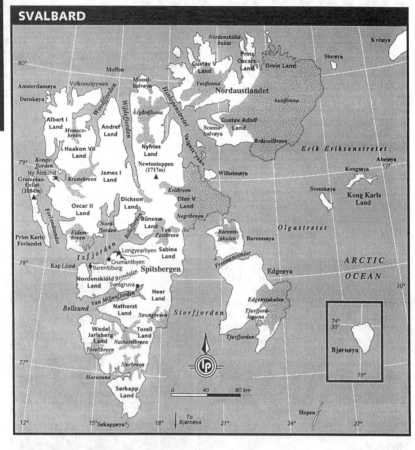

SVALBARD

Dutch, French, Norwegian and Danish ships engaged in whaling for bowhead and Greenland right whales off the western coast of Spitsbergen Island, and it's estimated that the Dutch alone took 60,000 whales.

The first known over-wintering took place at Bellsund in 1630 by an English group, which was followed by a Dutch group at Smeerenburg in 1633; the following winter, however, scurvy took its toll and the entire settlement perished. From the early 18th century, Russian Pomor hunters

and traders focused their attentions on Svalbard and began hunting walrus, caribou, seals and belugas, and from 1795, Norwegians began taking notice of the islands' wildlife resources and began hunting both polar bears and Arctic foxes.

In the late 19th and early 20th centuries, a series of explorers attempted to reach the North Pole using hydrogen balloons, and most met with failure. Although Roald Amundsen and Umberto Nobile were successful in 1926, two years later Nobile made a solo attempt and disappeared, as did Amundsen on a flight north to search for Nobile.

Perhaps as early as 1612, whalers had discovered coal at Ny Ålesund, but the first modern mine wasn't opened until 1906, when the Arctic Coal Company (ACC) began extracting coal from a rich seam. The settlement that grew up around this mine was named for the ACC's US owner, John Munroe Longyear. In 1916, ACC sold out to the Store Norske Spitsbergen Kull Compani (SNSK). Over the next few years, two other Norwegian companies set up operations on the archipelago's southernmost island, Bjørnøya, and the Kings Bay Kull Compani opened a mine at Ny Ålesund.

Meanwhile, in 1920 the Svalbard Treaty was signed, which granted Norwegian sovereignty over the islands, restricted military activities, and granted business and mineral extraction rights to all 42 signatories of the treaty (subject to Norwegian conservation laws).

During WWII, mining activities were halted, and on 3 September 1941 the islands were evacuated. Although a few Norwegians remained, in September 1943 the Germans bombed Longyearbyen and Barentsburg, and the following year, Sveagruva. When the Germans surrendered in 1945, Norwegian civilians returned, Longyearbyen was rebuilt and the Russians resettled in Pyramiden and Barentsburg.

Ny Ålesund also re-opened, but was closed down after a mine explosion in 1962 and converted into a scientific post. It's expected that the remaining mines around Longyearbyen will close down before 2003 and that the centre of operations will be transferred to the apparently more durable Sveagruva seams, 44km from Longyearbyen. Already, this is the most active mine in Svalbard and workers – who are based in Longyearbyen – are flown into Sveagruva for one-week shifts.

Geography & Climate
The Svalbard archipelago, which is about the size of Ireland, consists mainly of glaciated and eroded sedimentary layers laid down beneath the sea up to 1.2 billion years ago (although remnants of material up to three billion years old have been found in the rock). Between 300 million and 60 million years ago, Svalbard lay in the lush warm tropics, where rich layers of organic matter built up on the surface and eventually metamorphosed under great heat and pressure into the coal seams that now drive the islands' economy. Thanks to continental drift, however, it has migrated northward to its current polar location, and most of its present-day landforms were created during the ice ages of the past two million years. Currently, the highest points are Newton-toppen (1713m) and Perriertoppen (1712m).

Svalbard's latitude range extends from 74°N at Bjørnøya in the south to over 80°N on northern Spitsbergen and Nordaustlandet. In Longyearbyen the midnight sun lasts from 20 April to 20 August while the polar night lasts from 28 October to 14 February.

Climatically, the archipelago enjoys a brisk polar desert climate, and receives only 200 to 300mm of precipitation annually. Although the west coast remains ice-free for most of the summer, pack ice hovers just north of the main island year-round and vast sheets and rivers of ice cover approximately 60% of the land area. Snow and frost are possible at any time of year; the mean annual temperature is -4°C, and in July, it's only 6°C. On occasion, however, you may experience temperatures of up to 20°C or higher. In January, on the other hand, the mean temperature is -16°C, but temperatures of -30°C aren't uncommon.

Books
The Svalbard section in this book is intended for tourists and casual independent travellers only. Those who are interested in more background information, or who wish to mount a longer expedition, may want to check out one of the three books which are dedicated only to Svalbard. The German-language *Spitsbergen Reisehandbuch*, by longtime Svalbard resident Andreas Umbreit, is the most comprehensive. An

Independent Expeditions in Svalbard

The easiest way to visit Svalbard and enjoy its wilderness is with a pre-organised tour, which will take care of the logistics and provide access to the islands' finest sites with a minimum of fuss.

Virtually everything in Svalbard is controlled by the office of the governor, the Sysselmann (☎ 79 02 31 00), and independent travellers are not only discouraged, but they also face a host of rules and regulations aimed at protecting this fragile environment from the ravages of mass tourism (tourism operators are subject to the same regulations). As a result, only a relatively small portion of the archipelago (mainly Nordenskiöld Land, in the vicinity of Longyearbyen, Bünsow Land and Dickson Land) is open to independent travellers without expedition credentials, comprehensive rescue insurance and specific government approval.

Even in those open areas, logistics are complicated and hikers and boaters must carry firearms to protect themselves from polar bears, and permission and insurance may be required for mountain climbing or sea kayaking trips. Transport can also be a problem, as tourist-chartered helicopters may not land outside of settlements and public transport is limited to boats between the Isfjord settlements and flights between Longyearbyen and Ny Ålesund. Tour operators are reluctant to sell partial passages (except at the last minute) as it means losing a full fare and, similarly, they prefer not to commit to picking up groups at remote places, as access may be made inaccessible by drift ice, weather or other factors. If you're headed for a remote area, therefore, you'll probably have to get there on foot or skis, or use private charter boats or sea kayaks.

If you're set on a remote trekking or boat trip, or wish to independently visit a national park or reserve in Svalbard, contact the Sysselmann's office well in advance (around six months) and post or fax a detailed description of your plans, itinerary, equipment and the experience of the participants, and apply for permission. In most cases, the Sysselmann will then fix a maximum coverage sum required for search and rescue insurance (this may require coverage of up to Nkr300,000) or a bank guarantee, which must also amount to the recommended total to cover possible rescue costs.

Once the Sysselmann's office has received proof of this insurance or bank guarantee, the issuer may be required to sign a no-fault agreement guaranteeing payment in any case required by the Norwegian regulations for Svalbard. Norwegian insurance companies selling special comprehensive insurance for Svalbard are Europeiske Reiseforsikring (☎ 23 11 90 00, fax 23 11 90 10) and Gjensidige Forsikring (☎ 22 96 80 00, fax 22 96 92 00), both in Oslo. You may also need proof that you have the required equipment and firearms, including a rifle with a minimum calibre of 7.62mm. You can import your own weapon with a special licence or hire one in Longyearbyen. Although it's possible to organise all this on site (that is, at the Sysselmann's office in Skjæringa, Longyearbyen), insurance companies may equate such lack of preparation with expedition incompetence and respond accordingly.

abridged English translation of this book has been published by Bradt Publications as the *Guide to Spitsbergen*. Lastly, the French tour agency Grand Nord Grand Large has published the French-language *Spitzberg – L'Archipel du Svalbard*.

Organised Tours

Thanks to government regulations, logistics and the uncertainties governing independent travel in Svalbard (see the boxed text above), most visitors to this part of the world will want to book a place on an

Independent Expeditions in Svalbard

Note also that all cultural remains in Svalbard dating from prior to 1945 (including rubbish tips!) are protected by law and other relics, such as the Taubane cableway in Longyearbyen and various animal traps and hunting sites, are protected regardless of age. Modern visitors, on the other hand, may not leave any evidence of their own visit, nor can they pick flowers, trample vegetation, or feed, chase or otherwise disturb wildlife.

Also – and this is very important – you may only shoot a bear as a last resort, when there is a clear attack and the animal cannot be frightened away by other means – screaming, flares, sound grenades, and a number of warning shots (accordingly, you should have a rifle with a sufficient magazine capacity). A bear standing nearby or destroying non-vital equipment is no excuse for shooting it and if you do, the fines will be severe.

As an aside, it's worth noting that government, economic and scientific interests enjoy a lot more latitude than tourists and tour operators. In the interests of the environment, visitors should not only follow the rules closely, but they should also take note of any violations or unwise practices by other factions and duly report them to the Sysselmann in Longyearbyen.

For further direction, look for the pamphlets *Responsibilities & Resources*, *Regulations Relating to Tourism and other Travel in Svalbard* and *Take the Polar Bear Danger Seriously!*, which are available at the airport, tourist office and Sysselmann's office, all in Longyearbyen.

organised tour, and several reputable companies offer a range of options. Most of the following companies can also book a range of day tours from Longyearbyen (see Organised Tours under Longyearbyen, later in this chapter).

Svalbard Polar Travel Svalbard Polar Travel (☎ 79 02 34 23, fax 79 02 34 01, spot@svalbard-polar.no, www.svalbard-polar .com), Næringsbrygget, Postboks 540, N-9171 Longyearbyen, locally known as 'SPOT', conducts a range of worthwhile cruises and excursions, which include a maximum number of landings and/or hikes in sites of interest. The five-day Svalbard Adventure Cruise (with three days of actual cruising) departs twice weekly in summer from Longyearbyen and heads northward to 80°N, with two to four landings daily, including Barentsburg, Magdalenefjord, Ny Ålesund and Blomstrandhalvøya. For a single/ double cabin with a shared shower and no porthole, you'll pay Nkr11,540/ 17,580. The most expensive option, a cabin with private facilities on the upper deck, costs Nkr17,290/27,380.

An alternative cruise includes a wondrous eight-day circumnavigation of Spitsbergen, which includes all the landings of the Adventure Cruise, plus a cruise along the western coast of Nordaustlandet and a possible visit to the face of Austfonna glacier. This option also greatly increases your chances of spotting polar bears and walrus. The cheapest rates for singles/doubles are Nkr33,690/ 51,980. If you don't mind sharing a basic triple/quadruple cabin, you'll pay Nkr22,490/20,490 per person.

The company also offers a 13-day option called Trekking at the North Pole Rim, which includes a series of fascinating day hikes from the Raudfjord and Blomstrandhalvøya base camps. All-inclusive single/ double rates are Nkr18,590/31,180. In summer, you can also do a 13-day nordic ski trek on north-western Spitsbergen for Nkr19,390/ 32,780, while four-day winter snow machine trips through Nordenskiöld land cost Nkr16,590/28,380. The really adventurous can opt for a 15-day expedition to the summit of Svalbard's highest peak, Newtontoppen (1713m). This one is for keen mountaineers only and costs Nkr19,350/ 34,700 for singles/doubles, not including skis or camping gear.

Spitsbergen Tours Spitsbergen Tours (☎ 79 02 10 68, fax 79 02 10 67, info@ spitsbergen-tours.com, www.spitsbergen-tours.com), Postboks 6, N-9171 Longyearbyen, has operated since 1987 and was the first registered tour operator in Svalbard.

Run by Andreas Umbreit, who has written a couple of books on the area, it specialises in small group arrangements (normally fewer than 10 people). The company cooperates closely with the WWF and emphasises environmental considerations and limits the use of snow machines, which damage the tundra.

There are a range of adventurous options; note that all rates include return flights from Tromsø. An Arctic Week, based in Longyearbyen, Barentsburg and Pyramiden is offered over the New Year (during the long, dark polar night), in the wintry springtime, and also during the summer high season, for Nkr8100 to Nkr18,000 per person, including day excursions from the settlements (two days of dog-sledding, a snow machine tour, boat cruises and walks, during the applicable seasons). For a straight week-long dog-sledding tour in the spring, you'll pay Nkr16,000, while 11-day ski tours cost Nkr13,300, including accommodation in a remote trapper's cabin. Cruises on ice-worthy research vessels start at around Nkr21,000 for an 11-day circumnavigation of Spitsbergen Island, with numerous landings. On a simpler sailing ship, you'll pay just Nkr13,500. In summer, a 15-day hiking and trekking tour around Longyearbyen and Barentsburg or Pyramiden costs Nkr13,020, while a more demanding 22-day trek involving an inland crossing with pre-arranged food caches and two fjord cruises costs Nkr16,500.

Spitsbergen Travel Spitsbergen Travel (☎ 79 02 24 10, fax 79 02 10 10, spitra@ mail.link.no), in conjunction with Troms Fylkes Dampskibsselskap, runs Hurtigruten ferry trips between Troms and Longyearbyen (see Getting There & Away under Longyearbyen). The boat arrives in Longyearbyen on Tuesday around noon, then at 7 pm heads north towards 80°N, stopping at Magdalenefjord and Moffen Island (ice conditions permitting) before turning south to land in Ny Ålesund on Thursday morning. En route back to Longyearbyen, it calls in at Barentsburg for a short tour on Thursday afternoon, then sails back to Tromsø, via Nordkapp, to arrive on Friday night. The entire return cruise, including accommodation in a single/double cabin with shared facilities, costs Nkr10,700/15,140. More upmarket cabins are available for considerably higher rates; the most expensive option is a private single/double suite with a shower and toilet for Nkr19,640/26,180.

Alternatively, you can fly between Tromsø and Longyearbyen and only join the Svalbard portion of the cruise for Nkr9485/16,390 in basic single/double cabins. If you join the cruise in Longyearbyen, the minimum cost is Nkr3350/5200 for singles/doubles. All rates include meals and landings.

Svalbard Wildlife Service The Svalbard Wildlife Service (☎ 79 02 10 35, fax 79 02 12 01, wildlife@mail.link.no, www .svalbard.com/wildlife) offers some of the usual and several unusual trips. In addition to booking the day tours listed under Longyearbyen, they operate a week-long wilderness camp around Isfjorden (Nkr14,875); a week of trekking on Ekmanfjorden (Nkr13,940), and a three-day cruise to Ymerbukta (Nkr4400), which includes kayaking and hiking.

LONGYEARBYEN

With a population of around 1200, Longyearbyen is the capital and 'metropolis' of Svalbard. This very practical-looking community on Adventfjorden (a branch of Isfjorden) had its beginnings as the main export site for the rich coal seams which characterise the island.

The modern town, which is strewn with all sorts of abandoned coal mining detritus from mines No 1a, 1b, 2a, 2b and 4, also enjoys a superb backdrop which includes two glacier tongues, Longyearbreen and Lars Hjertabreen. Construction methods here must reflect the Arctic climate, and most structures are built on pilings to prevent the heated buildings from melting permafrost and sinking into the resulting muck. For the same reason, the heavily-insulated plumbing pipes also run above ground.

Local decorum dictates that people remove their shoes upon entering any building in town, including homes, offices and hotels. Exceptions include most shops and eateries.

Information

Tourist Information The friendly and helpful Info-Svalbard tourist office (☎ 79 02 23 03, fax 79 02 10 20, infos@ssd.no), on the pedestrian street, is open from 8 am to 6 pm weekdays, 9 am to 4 pm Saturday and noon to 4 pm Sunday.

Post & Communications Postal services and payphones are available at the post office (☎ 79 02 16 04) on the main street. It's open Monday to Wednesday and on Friday from 10 am to 4 pm, on Tuesday to 5 pm and Saturday to 2 pm. The Telenor telephone office is on the hill near the Sysselman's office.

Money You can change cash and travellers cheques at the Sparebanken Norge (☎ 79 02 18 01), in the post office building.

Bookshops & Libraries The public library is in the Lompen Senteret, open on Monday and Thursday from 5 to 8 pm and on Wednesday from 10 am to 2 pm. The local newspaper, *Svalbardposten*, comes out on Friday and costs Nkr10. The Norwegian Polar Institute in the Næringsbrygget sells Arctic books, maps and posters.

Film & Photography Film and one-hour film processing are available at the Konica Photo Express in the Lompen Senteret.

Emergency Services For emergencies and medical prescriptions, see the Longyearbyen Hospital (☎ 79 02 17 05).

Firearm Hire For hiking and other independent expeditions, it's naturally best to bring your own firearm to Svalbard, mainly because you're more likely to be comfortable with it and familiar enough with its workings to use it in an emergency.

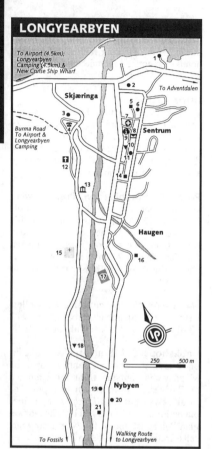

LONGYEARBYEN

LONGYEARBYEN

PLACES TO STAY
5   Svalbard Polar Hotel, Restaurant Nansen & Barents Pub
14 Svalbard Kro og Motell & Restaurant Fredheim
16 Funken Hotel
21 Nybyen Gjestehus

PLACES TO EAT
10 Lompen: Café, Busen, Svalbard Matsenter Supermarket, Konica Photo Express & Public Library
18 Huset Restaurant, Bar, Nightclub & Convenience Shop; Cinema

OTHER
1   Svalbard Snøscooterutleie
2   UNIS University
3   Sysselmann's Office
4   Telephone Office
6   Svalbard Polar Travel
7   Longyearbyen Hospital
8   Post office & Sparebanken Norge
9   Næringsbrygget: Info-Svalbard Tourist Office, Spitsbergen Travel & Norwegian Polar Institute
11 Svalbardbutikken Supermarket & Nordpolet Off-licence
12 Church
13 Svalbard Museum
15 Historic Graveyard
17 Sports Hall & Swimming Pool
19 Gallery Svalbard
20 Svalbard Wildlife Service

However, because very few visitors actually own such weapons, it is possible to hire one at either Svalbard Safari (☎ 79 02 13 22) or Svalbard Wildlife Service (☎ 79 02 10 35); insist that they provide enough ammunition to allow you to practice and get a feel for the gun before heading off.

Museum

Longyearbyen's little museum (☎ 79 02 13 84), at Skjæringa, occupies a former pig sty, which is one of the oldest buildings in town.

Exhibits cover not only the history, climate, geology, wildlife and exploration of the archipelago, but also include some detail on the mining activities that form Svalbard's current economic basis. The highlight is probably the sculpted miner, who readily illustrates how uncomfortable it is to lie in low and narrow mine shafts. If you're inspired, you can don *lompen* (miners' coveralls) and crawl in to experience it for yourself. A small shop at the entrance sells local-theme books and maps.

Graveyard

The haunting little graveyard on the hillside above the town dates from the early part of this century and is worth a quick look. In a few days in October 1918, seven young men in Longyearbyen were struck down by the Spanish flu, a virus which killed 40 million people in Europe, Asia and North America. Very little is known about it, but because the graves of these seven men lie in permafrost, Canadian scientist Dr Kirsty Duncan believes that the virus may remain frozen there and may yet hold enough genetic material to be cultured and studied – and that it may perhaps aid in the development of a vaccine to prevent a re-emergence. In 1997, a study was launched and research is ongoing.

Gallery Svalbard

The nearest thing Longyearbyen has to an art museum is Gallery Svalbard (☎ 79 02 11 80), which features historic maps and books, the mainly Svalbard-theme works of artist Kåre Tveter, temporary exhibits and Thomas Widerberg's short slide show on the magic of the polar light. It's open daily except Monday from 3 to 6 pm (on Wednesday until 8 pm).

Organised Tours

The travel and tour companies organise a range of day tours from Longyearbyen: town tours (Nkr300); fossil hunting at Longyearbreen (Nkr300); mine No 3 tours (Nkr550); day tours to Barentsburg (Nkr870); kayak tours (Nkr450); boat tours to Pyramiden and Nordenskiöldsbreen glacier (Nkr70); hiking in Bjørndalen (Nkr350); fossil-hunting hikes to the Rieperbreen and Scott Turnerbreen glacier tongues in Bolterdalen (Nkr480); hikes (Nkr350) or horsepacking tours (Nkr550) onto the Platåberget; day tours to Tempelfjord and Von Postbreen glacier (Nkr800); and wilderness barbecues in Bolterdalen (Nkr395). They also do three-day 'mini-expeditions' to Ymerbukta, on the northern shore of Isfjorden (Nkr4400).

For information on longer tours, see Organised Tours at the beginning of this chapter.

Courses

Those interested in Arctic meteorology, geology, biology, geophysics and other pursuits may want to look into courses offered by the local university, UNIS. For details, contact the university offices (☎ 79 02 33 00).

Places to Stay

Your cheapest option is *Longyearbyen Camping* (☎ 79 02 14 44), near the airport, where a nice marshy bit of turf for your tent and use of the service building, washing rooms and heated toilets costs Nkr70 per person. It's about an hour walk from town on the main road and slightly longer on the Burma Road. You can also hire tents and/or sleeping bags for Nkr100 per night each (for sleeping bags, each subsequent night after the first costs Nkr50). Showers cost Nkr10 and laundry, Nkr40. Soft drinks and very basic snacks are also available on the site. From late June to early September, the kitchen and reception are open daily from 8 to 10 am and 7.30 to 9.30 pm.

In town, the budget choice is the *Nybyen Gjestehus* (☎ 79 02 24 50, fax 79 02 10 05), in the Nybyen suburb. Single/double rooms cost from Nkr350/490 to Nkr495/795, but cheaper rooms are sometimes available at late notice, so it may be worth stopping by to check. The *Funken Hotel* (☎ 79 02 24 50, fax 79 02 10 05), between the centre and Nybyen, has comfortable singles/doubles for Nkr1045/1345, plus Nkr175 for extra beds.

The poshest digs in Longyearbyen is the well appointed new *Svalbard Polar Hotel* (☎ 79 02 35 00, fax 79 02 35 01), near the centre. Singles/doubles cost Nkr1060/1320, plus Nkr50 for a room with a view. Also in the centre, the *Svalbard Kro og Motell* (☎ 79 02 24 50, fax 79 02 10 05) charges Nkr725/940 for singles/doubles, plus Nkr175 per extra bed. However, it's currently under renovation and a change of management, so check in advance for the latest information. All the hotel rates include breakfast.

Places to Eat

Although it's away from the centre, a good choice for meals is *Huset* (☎ 79 02 25 00), which also houses a popular pub, bar and convenience store. The restaurant portion is open daily from 7 pm to midnight.

For lunch, the main local meeting place is the *Kafé Busen* (☎ 79 02 17 07), in the Lompen Senteret, which has daily specials as well as typical cafeteria fare. It's open Monday to Saturday from 10 am to 6 pm and on Sunday from 1 to 6 pm.

Another lunch and dinner option is the acclaimed *Restaurant Fredheim* (☎ 79 02 13 00), at the Svalbard Kro og Motell. It also has a bar and is open daily from noon to 2 am.

The *Restaurant Nansen* (☎ 79 02 35 00) at the Svalbard Polar Hotel offers fine dining at commensurate prices. Their buffet breakfast is a real treat.

The supermarket in the *Svalbardbutikken* has a good selection of groceries, and there's also a sophisticated little grocery, the *Svalbard Matsenter*, in the Lompen Senteret.

Entertainment

Longyearbyen has two main entertainment institutions, and appreciation of the nightlife can seem fairly universal in this small town. On Friday night, the place to see and be seen is the *Barents Pub* at the Svalbard Polar Hotel, and on Saturday, everyone goes to the *Huset*, which imposes a cover charge of Nkr50. To prevent drunken driving, on Saturday, buses leave the centre for Huset in the early evening and return to the centre when the pub closes at 4 am.

There's also a bar at the *Svalbard Kro & Motell*, but if you prefer a rowdier scene, try the one at the *Funken Hotel*.

The *Longyearbyen Cinema*, at Huset, screens films on Sunday at 8 pm.

For healthier activities, squash and swimming are available at the *Sports Hall*, near the school, on Tuesday, Thursday and Sunday from 6 to 9 pm.

Although alcohol is duty-free in Svalbard, it's rationed for locals, and visitors must present a valid airline ticket off the archipelago in order to buy it. The Nordpolet beer, wine and spirits outlet is at the back of Svalbardbutikken.

Getting There & Away

Air In clear weather, the worthwhile flight between Tromsø and Longyearbyen provides otherworldly views of Svalbard's Arctic mountains and glaciers. SAS (☎ 79 02 16 50) flies this route on Monday and Friday and Braathens SAFE (☎ 79 02 19 22) flies daily. The full price return fare is Nkr3930, but you can also get special midprice and mini-price deals for Nkr2955 and Nkr2360, respectively. Discounts are also available in Braathens SAFE's no-frills Braathens Back class, which eliminates meal-and-drink service. For information on flying to Ny Ålesund, see Ny Ålesund, later in this chapter.

Those who are flush with cash can charter a helicopter from Airlift (☎ 79 02 10 00, fax 79 02 14 30), which costs Nkr10,000 per hour for up to five people and Nkr15,500 per hour for five to nine people. Note that visitors may land only in official settlement landing sites, and nowhere in the national parks. With a minimum of four people, you can get transfers to Kap Linné for Nkr1500 per person return.

Ferry The Troms Fylkes Dampskibsselskap, in conjunction with Spitsbergen Travel (☎ 79 02 24 10, fax 79 02 10 10), runs the M/S *Nordstjernen* ferry between Tromsø and Svalbard on Sunday from 22 June to 28 August. The boat arrives in Longyearbyen on Tuesday around noon and returns from its cruise around northern Spitsbergen at 10 pm on Thursday. It then sails back to Tromsø, via Nordkapp, to arrive on Friday night.

The entire return cruise, including accommodation in a single/double cabin with shared facilities, costs Nkr10,700/ 15,140 (these rates include the entire Spitsbergen cruise). Classier cabins are available for considerably higher rates; the most expensive option is a private single/ double suite with a shower and toilet for Nkr19,640/ 26,180.

If there's space from Tromsø, you may also be able to opt only for return transport to Longyearbyen.

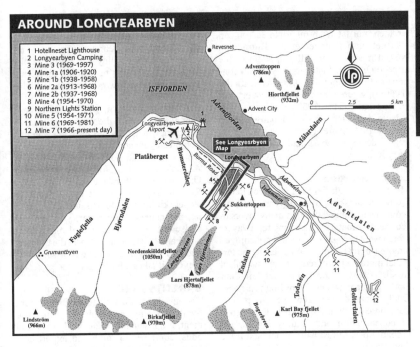

AROUND LONGYEARBYEN

1 Hotellneset Lighthouse
2 Longyearbyen Camping
3 Mine 3 (1969-1997)
4 Mine 1a (1906-1920)
5 Mine 1b (1938-1958)
6 Mine 2a (1913-1968)
7 Mine 2b (1937-1968)
8 Mine 4 (1954-1970)
9 Northern Lights Station
10 Mine 5 (1954-1971)
11 Mine 6 (1969-1981)
12 Mine 7 (1966-present day)

Getting Around

Norwegians and foreigners who wish to live in Svalbard aren't permitted to do so until they have secured employment, and several have fulfilled this requirement by applying to drive a taxi. The Longyearbyen Buss & Taxi (☎ 79 02 13 75 or 79 02 13 05) charges Nkr75 between the town and the airport in a taxi. The airport bus (Nkr35) runs between the airport and the Nybyen Gjestehus, via the Svalbard Polar Hotel, the Svalbard Kro og Motell and the Funken Hotel, to connect with arriving and departing flights.

Bicycle hire is available for Nkr50/85/210/380 per half-day/full-day/weekend/week from the Nybyen Gjestehus, the Funken Hotel and Longyearbyen Camping, and is probably the best way to explore the limited road system. You can hire a car from Avis (☎ 79 02 11 75) or Longyearbyen Bil-

utleie (☎ 78 02 11 88, fax 79 02 10 83) – and you'll get the cheapest petrol in Norway (under Nkr5 per litre) – but there's only 45km of road and not much to see from a vehicle. In winter, you can hire snow machines from Svalbard Safari (☎ 79 02 32 20, fax 79 02 18 10, safari@svalbard.com) and Svalbard Snøscooterutleie (☎ 79 02 16 66, fax 79 02 17 71) starting at Nkr650/3900 per day/week; note that you need a driving licence from home to operate a snow machine in Svalbard.

AROUND LONGYEARBYEN
Platåberget & Bjørndalen

The vast upland region overlooking Longyearbyen to the west is known as Platåberget (commonly called The Plateau), and it makes a popular day hike. You can either ascend from near the Sysselmann's office in town, which is a steep and scree-covered route, or preferably, sneak up Bloms-terdalen, not far from mine No 3. You can also get onto Platåberget via Bjørndalen (yes, it means 'bear valley'), south of the airport. Once on Platåberget, you can con-tinue to the summit of Nordenskiöldsfjellet (1050m), where a Swedish observatory op-erated from 1931 to 1932.

Note that bears do occasionally wander onto the plateau area (there was a well pub-licised death in 1996) and hikers need to carry a firearm.

Longyearbreen

The prominent glacier tongues which lick at the upper outskirts of Longyearbyen have scoured and gouged through many layers of sedimentary material, including fossil layers which were created when Svalbard enjoyed a more tropical climate. As a result, the ter-minal moraine is littered with unusual plant fossils – leaves and twigs that left their marks between 60 and 40 million years ago. Oddly enough, there aren't yet any restric-tions on collecting them but in the interest of conservation and future visitors, it's probably best to just have a look and leave them where they lie.

To get there, pass the Huset and head up the right side of the river, past the aban-doned mine buildings, and onto the rough track. After the remains of a bridge (on your left), you'll approach the terminal moraine and cross a stream which flows down from your left. The track then traverses some steep slopes, crosses the river (sometimes there's a bridge) and continues upstream to its end at the fossil fields. The 5km return hike from Huset takes about 1½ hours.

Burma Road

The Burma Road, which is now a walking track, follows the old coal mine Taubanen cableway to the processing plant and mine No 3, near the airport. It makes an easy half-day hike and doesn't require a firearm.

Adventdalen

The stark and open landscapes of Advent-dalen beckon visitors holed up in town and,

indeed, these wild landscapes are the Arc-tic you came to see. Most people want a photo of the polar bear crossing sign at the town end of the valley and hiking is also pleasant, but if you're heading more than 1km or so from town, a firearm is highly recommended.

After leaving town, you'll pass the pun-gent husky kennels; the freshwater lake, Is-dammen, which provides drinking water for Longyearbyen; and a northern lights station which is linked to similar facilities in Alaska and Tromsø. Note also the mountain Operafjellet north of the valley; in 1996 a Russian Tupelev aircraft crashed into its slopes, killing the 140 Russian and Ukrain-ian passengers. With a car, you can also cruise out to the defunct coal mines No 5 and 6 and have a look at No 7 (the only one that still functions) in an hour or so. With a bicycle, it takes a bit longer.

BARENTSBURG

The anachronistic village of Barentsburg, Svalbard's only remaining Russian settle-ment, is a fascinating place and, against all odds, continues to mine and export coal. Despite the Norwegian currency in use and the Norwegian postal icon over the post of-fice, this now decaying community is a very different world than modern Long-yearbyen and you may well find it difficult to believe you're still in Norway. If you've never visited modern Russia, you'll have a taste of it here, complete with plenty of Soviet-era relics, and it will surely be an unforgettable experience.

History

Barentsburg, on Grønfjorden, was first identified as a coal producing area around 1900, when the Kullkompaniet Isefjord Spitsbergen started operations. They were followed in 1905 by the US-based Arctic Coal Company and in 1908 by several Nor-wegian companies, most of which were col-lectively bought out in 1916 by the ACC and the new Store Norske Spitsbergen Kull Compani. In 1920, the town was founded by a smaller player, the Dutch company

Nespico, and 12 years later was passed to the Soviet Trust Arktikugol.

As with Longyearbyen, Barentsburg was partially destroyed by the British Royal Navy in 1941 (to prevent it falling into Nazi hands), and in 1941, the job was completed by the German navy. In 1948, however, it was rebuilt by Trust Arktikugol and embarked on a period of growth, development, scientific research and Soviet social programs that lasted until the fall of the Soviet Union.

Since 1993, about 30% of Trust Arktikugol's coal shipments have gone directly to the west while the rest are shipped to Murmansk and Archangelsk, but of late, the operations have been neglected and the situation continues to worsen. Paychecks are now being eaten up by Russian inflation, there are no longer flights to or from Murmansk and obsolete mining equipment is breaking down. The scientific community is now gone and the population has dwindled to fewer than 900 people. Predictably, supplies are sparse, but Barentsburg has responded by becoming more self-sufficient. On what is certainly the world's northernmost farm, they grow greenhouse tomatoes, onions, potatoes, cabbages and other Russian staples, and raise chickens, pigs and cattle for meat and milk. For most people, conditions here are preferable to those at home in Russia (or the Ukraine, which many Barentsburg people call home) and they do what they can to remain beyond their standard initial two-year contracts.

Pomor Museum

The simple and appealing little Pomor Museum on ulitsa Ivana Starostina outlines (in Russian only) the Pomor trade and Russian coal mining in Svalbard, and also has exhibits on the natural element and Russian history of Svalbard. Especially worthwhile are the excellent geological exhibit and the collection of artefacts which suggests Russian activity in Svalbard even prior to its accepted European 'discovery' by Willem Barents. Admission costs Nkr20 and the ticket heartily thanks you for your visit.

Places to Stay & Eat

At the charmingly rustic *Barentsburg Hotel* (☎ 79 02 10 80 or ☎ 79 02 18 14), on ulitsa Ivana Starostina, you'll pay Nkr440 for a double room and traditional Russian breakfasts (Nkr60), lunches (Nkr80) and dinners (Nkr90) are also served. The meals are surprisingly good and feature such specialities as boiled pork with potatoes and Arctic sorrel, parsley and sour cream. In the shop, they sell a selection of overpriced Russian souvenirs, but in the bar, you can enjoy a

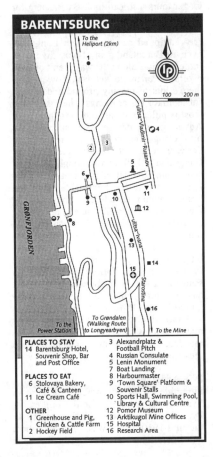

BARENTSBURG

To the Heliport (2km)

GRØNFJORDEN

ulitsa Vladimir Rusanov

ulitsa Ivana Starostina

0   100   200 m

To Grøndalen (Walking Route to Longyearbyen)

To the Power Station

To the Mine

PLACES TO STAY
14 Barentsburg Hotel, Souvenir Shop, Bar and Post Office

PLACES TO EAT
6 Stolovaya Bakery, Café & Canteen
11 Ice Cream Café

OTHER
1 Greenhouse and Pig, Chicken & Cattle Farm
2 Hockey Field
3 Alexandrplatz & Football Pitch
4 Russian Consulate
5 Lenin Monument
7 Boat Landing
8 Harbourmaster
9 'Town Square' Platform & Souvenir Stalls
10 Sports Hall, Swimming Pool, Library & Cultural Centre
12 Pomor Museum
13 Arktikugol Mine Offices
15 Hospital
16 Research Area

deliciously affordable shot of Stolichnaya vodka for a bargain Nkr10.

In another building near the 'Town Square', there's also the *Stolovaya* bakery, café and workers' canteen. For meals at the café, visitors must pay at the hotel. A small *ice cream café*, around the corner from the Pomor Museum, opens occasionally.

Getting There & Away

The easiest way to reach Barentsburg is on a tourist cruise, and day trips are available from Longyearbyen for Nkr870. Most longer tours also call in at Barentsburg for a quick look around.

In summer, strong hikers who are properly equipped can walk from Longyearbyen to Barentsburg in at least five days (note that huts along the way aren't open to hikers). Prepare to get wet, however, as there's lots of marshy ground and several substantial river crossings. The easiest and most popular route ascends Todalen (from Adventdalen), crosses Gangskardet pass into Gangdalen to the emergency hut Sørhytta. The route then crosses the river Gangselva, which can be tough, and descends into Reindalen. It then ascends the fairly level valley Semmeldalen to the small Semelbu hut before climbing past the face of the Tavlebreen glacier and crossing the pass into Grøndalen. From there, it's a fairly straightforward descent along Grøndalen to the road's end south of Barentsburg. The map to use is the Norsk Polarinstitutt map *Nordenskiöld Land*, at a scale of 1:200,000, but be sure to seek local advice before you set out. A firearm is required for this trip.

Alternatively, you can travel by snow machine in winter but this isn't recommended, due to the environmental damage these machines cause.

PYRAMIDEN

Pyramiden, Russia's other settlement in Svalbard, was named for the impressive Pyramiden mountain which rises nearby. In the mid-1910s, coal was discovered here and operations were set up by the same Swedish interests with holdings at Sveagruva. In 1926, they were taken over by a Soviet firm, Russkiy Grumant, which sold out to another Soviet company, Trust Arktikugol, in 1931. In the 1950s, it counted 1100 residents, and during its heyday in the early 1990s it boasted 60km of shafts, 130 homes, agricultural enterprises similar to those in Barentsburg and the world's most northerly hotel and swimming pool.

In the late 1990s, it became apparent that the complex geology in this region wasn't yielding enough coal to make the operation profitable and Russia was no longer willing or able to subsidise the mine. As a result, operations ceased on 31 March 1998 and the settlement was abandoned in October of the same year. Until 2001, however, Trust Arktikugol funding during the summer months will maintain a basic infrastructure for workers cleaning up the site and the mining detritus.

Despite the demise of the mine, the surrounding area continues to offer superb hiking opportunities, and Trust Arktikugol, in conjunction with Spitsbergen Tours, is currently considering a joint management scheme which will involve both eco-tourism and the establishment of a small international community for people who want to spend three months to several years in the high Arctic. Whether this ambitious project will succeed remains to be seen, but it would be the northernmost settlement in the world without direct government or mining subsidies and would also offer the chance to study the transition of Pyramiden from an ecologically destructive mining operation into an environmentally-conscious community. The intent is to cooperate with the WWF to resurrect abandoned buildings and pipeline routes as tourist accommodation and walking tracks. One can only wish them well.

Organised Tours

In addition to the day tours offered by various Longyearbyen agencies, Spitsbergen Tours runs longer hiking tours based at the Pyramiden Hotel and in remote cabins.

NY ÅLESUND

At 79°N, the scientific post of Ny Ålesund, founded in 1916 by the Kings Bay Kull Compani, isn't the most hospitable spot – as a concession to the climate and permafrost, all the pipes in town run above ground inside insulated wooden conduits – but you'd be hard pressed to find a more awesome backdrop anywhere on earth. Ny Ålesund likes to claim that it's the world's northernmost permanently inhabited civilian community and it may be if you can ignore the fact that it lacks both children and pensioners. In fact, a similar case could be made for any of the three places that lie farther north: the Krenkel scientific post in Franz Josef Land, Russia, and the meteorological station of Eureka and the Alert military post, both on Canada's Ellesmere Island.

Through much of the 20th century, Kings Bay extracted coal from the low-altitude coalfields beneath Zeppelinfjell. At the height of activity, 300 people lived and worked here, but due to frequent explosions (one particularly bad one in November 1962 resulted in 21 deaths), mining activities ceased in 1963. Since then, Ny Ålesund has emerged as a prominent scientific post with a year-round population of about 25. In summer, however, as many as 100 researchers from Norway, Germany, Britain, France, Italy, Japan and other places descend on the place to work on their own projects.

Information

There's no tourist office, but for novelty value, visitors can buy a postcard at the world's northernmost gift shop and drop it off at the world's northernmost post office.

It's worth noting that because Ny Ålesund doesn't rely on tourism, the scientific community may not accord visitors the sort

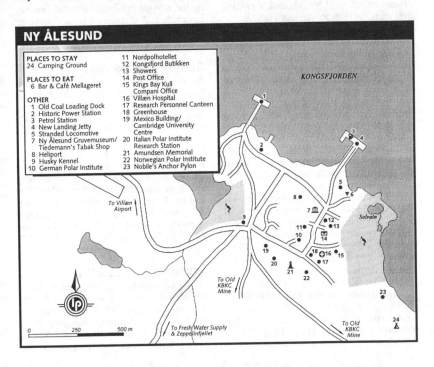

NY ÅLESUND

PLACES TO STAY
24 Camping Ground

PLACES TO EAT
6 Bar & Café Mellageret

OTHER
1 Old Coal Loading Dock
2 Historic Power Station
3 Petrol Station
4 New Landing Jetty
5 Stranded Locomotive
7 Ny Ålesund Gruvemuseum/
  Tiedemann's Tabak Shop
8 Heliport
9 Husky Kennel
10 German Polar Institute
11 Nordpolhotellet
12 Kongsfjord Butikken
13 Showers
14 Post Office
15 Kings Bay Kull
  Compani Office
16 Villæn Hospital
17 Research Personnel Canteen
18 Greenhouse
19 Mexico Building/
  Cambridge University
  Centre
20 Italian Polar Institute
  Research Station
21 Amundsen Memorial
22 Norwegian Polar Institute
23 Nobile's Anchor Pylon

KONGSFJORDEN

Solvain

To Villæn
Airport

To Old
KBKC
Mine

To Fresh Water Supply
& Zeppelinfjellet

To Old
KBKC
Mine

0   250   500 m

of warm reception they often come to expect. While this local indifference does suggest a rather limited perspective – after all, most everyone has once been a tourist somewhere – some of the coolness is probably warranted, as careless visitors can unwittingly affect instrument readings, alter the environment being studied or damage sensitive equipment. About all I can recommend is that you stay aware, watch where you tread and make known any plans you may have to strike out into the wilds.

Unfortunately, you'll also receive a less than friendly reception from the Arctic terns which nest in town, so it's wise to pick up a tern stick (available free at the dock) to hold over your head and prevent a vicious pecking by a paranoid mother.

Things to See
In the early 20th century, several polar explorers set off from Ny Ålesund, including the likes of Roald Amundsen, Lincoln Ellsworth, Admiral Byrd and Umberto Nobile. The **anchor pylon** was used by Nobile and Amundsen to launch the airship *Norge* on their successful flight over the pole to Alaska in 1926 and was again used two years later, when Nobile returned to launch the *Italia* on his ill-fated attempt to repeat the feat. Amundsen himself went missing during an attempt to rescue his friend's expedition. As a result, you'll see a number of **memorials** around town, which commemorate Amundsen, the mining disasters, the loss of the *Italia* and the Ellsworth-Amundsen expedition.

Perhaps the most unusual sight in town is the **stranded locomotive** near the dock. In 1917, a 90cm-gauge railway was constructed to connect the coalfields with the harbour, and it remained in use until 1958. The restored locomotive is naturally the world's northernmost railway relic.

The town also supports a very nice little **Gruvemuseum**, in the old Tiedemann's Tabak (tobacco) shop, which concentrates on the coal mining history of this area. Admission costs US$1 (yes, it's posted in US$!), which translates into about Nkr7.

Places to Stay & Eat
Technically, Ny Ålesund does have a hotel, the Nordpolhotellet. It opened on 3 September 1939, then WWII came along and it closed the following day. There's talk that it may someday re-open, but that's unlikely. Currently, the only place to stay is the *camping ground* (the world's northernmost, of course), near Nobile's airship pylon. However, the only facilities are a long-drop toilet and a trash can.

Near the locomotive is the *Bar & Café Mellageret*, but watch for terns, as the ground here is a favoured nesting site. Basic snacks are sold at the *Kongsfjord Butikken*, but there's no supermarket, so bring your groceries from elsewhere. The local scientific community mainly eats at the town canteen.

Shopping
At the Kongsfjord Butikken, you can buy postcards and a range of polar souvenirs, but the T-shirts seem to be the most popular items.

Getting There & Away
As with many other places in Svalbard, most visitors arrive in Ny Ålesund on tourist cruises and only linger for an hour or two. Alternatively, in July and August, Lufttransport (☎ 79 02 16 60, fax 79 02 17 28) has a 25-minute scheduled daily air service between Longyearbyen and Ny Ålesund. From 1 May to 30 June and 1 to 30 September, it operates on Monday, Wednesday and Thursday. The return fare is Nkr2500 and the 20kg baggage allowance is strictly enforced. You can either book through Lufttransport or the Kings Bay Kull Compani (☎ 79 02 71 11, fax 79 02 71 13), N-9173 Ny Ålesund.

AROUND NY ÅLESUND
Kongsfjorden
Ny Ålesund's spectacular backdrop, Kongsfjorden (the namesake for the Kings Bay Kull Compani), contrasts bleak grey-brown shores with the expansive white Kongsbreen, Kronebreen and Kongsvegen ice-

fields. The distinctive Tre Kroner peaks, Dana (1175m), Svea (1226m) and Nora (1226m) (in honour of Denmark, Sweden and Norway, respectively), which rise from the ice, are among the most recognised landmarks in all of Svalbard.

Blomstrandhalvøya

Gravelly Blomstrandhalvøya was once a peninsula, hence its name, but in the early 1990s, it was released from the icy grip on its northern end and it's now an island. In summer, the name Blomstrand, 'flower beach', would be appropriate, but it was in fact named for a Norwegian geologist. At Ny London, at the southern end of the island, Ernest Mansfield of the Northern Exploration Company unsuccessfully attempted to quarry marble in 1911. Only too late did he discover that the stone had been rendered worthless by aeons of freezing and thawing. Only a couple of buildings and some decrepit machinery remain.

ELSEWHERE AROUND SPITSBERGEN
Kap Linné

Kap Linné, at the entrance to Isfjorden, consists of little more then the Isfjord Radio installation, but the enterprising facility also offers remote tourist accommodation (☎ 79 02 27 90, fax 79 02 17 82). Here you'll pay Nkr890/1380 for a single/double room, including full board. Transport is by boat, snow machine or helicopter from Longyearbyen or Barentsburg, and both independent hiking and guided day tours are available in the area. Note, however, that much of the surrounding area lies within a bird reserve and is off-limits for most of the summer.

Sveagruva

Coal was first discovered at Sveagruva, at the north-eastern end of Van Miljenfjorden, in the early 1910s. In 1917, the Swedish company, Aktiebolaget Spetsbergens Svenska Kolfält, established the first mine, which changed hands several times, passed through a fire and yielded 400,000 tonnes of coal before it was taken over by SNSK

in 1934. The operations were levelled by a submarine attack in 1944, but activity snapped back after the war and by the late 1970s Sveagruva had grown into a well appointed settlement of 300 workers and enjoyed nearly as many amenities as Longyearbyen.

Over the following years, increased production around more-accessible Longyearbyen resulted in declines at Sveagruva, and by the mid-1990s it had dwindled to just a handful of miners and administrators. Currently, with just one working mine around Longyearbyen, Sveagruva is the only hope for continued coal mining in this area, and new buildings have been constructed to handle its anticipated resurrection. The workforce is currently increasing and SNSK hopes to profitably increase production to around 700,000 tonnes of coal annually by the time Longyearbyen's mine No 7 is closed in 2003. Current calculations suggest that will be possible, but it depends on the coal prices remaining static.

From March to May, hikers, skiers and snow-machiners have access to the *Polartun Gjestehus* (☎/fax 79 02 5112), which has single/double rooms for Nkr525/700.

Prins Karls Forlandet

As you're cruising north along the west coast of Spitsbergen, it's worth noting the oddly-shaped 86km-long island of Prins Karls Forlandet, which is a national park set aside to protect breeding pinnipeds. The alpine northern reaches, which rise to Grampianfjellet (1084m), are connected to Saltfjellet (430m), at the southern end, by a long flat plain called Forlandsletta.

Krossfjorden

Thanks to its grand tidewater glacier, Lillehöökbreen, and several cultural relics, Krossfjorden also attracts quite a few cruise ships. At Ebeltoftbukta, near the mouth of the fjord, you can see several whalers' graves as well as a heap of leftover junk from a 1912 German telegraph office that was shifted wholesale to Ny Ålesund in 1914 and kicked off that town's reputation

Roald Amundsen

If Fridtjof Nansen had the biggest heart of any polar explorer, fellow Norwegian Roald Amundsen had the most determination and grit. Born in 1872 at Borge, near Sarpsborg, he dreamed from an early age of becoming a polar explorer and spent his early days devouring every bit of literature he could find on the subject of polar exploration. He was especially enthralled by the journals from the ill-fated 1845 expedition of Sir John Franklin, who had sought the North-West Passage. In deference to his mother's wishes, Amundsen dutifully studied medicine, but when she died in 1893 he returned to his polar dreams and never looked back.

Applying the same methodical approach he'd taken all his life, Amundsen decided that most failed polar expeditions stemmed from captains' errors, and decided to study for his masters' licence. In 1894 he went to sea and three years later, sailed to the Antarctic as first mate on the Belgian *Belgica* expedition led by Adrien Gerlache de Gomery. However, the ship froze fast in the ice near Peter I's Island where it remained for 13 months. When the captain fell ill with scurvy, Amundsen took over command and displayed his ability to handle a crisis. Although there wasn't much choice, this became the first expedition to over-winter in the Antarctic.

Having gained a reputation as a captain, Amundsen set his sights on the North-West Passage, and decided to justify the expedition with scientific studies of the Magnetic North Pole. After a period of study in Hamburg, to learn about the earth's magnetic field, he selected a 47-tonne sloop, the *Gjøa*. Fully loaded, the expedition set out from Oslo in June 1903 and passed Greenland, Baffin Island and Lancaster Sound. The crew chose to over-winter in a natural harbour on King William Island, which they named Gjøahavn. Here they remained for two years, building observatories, taking magnetic readings, establishing the position of the Magnetic North Pole, studying the lives of the Inuit and learning how to drive their dog teams. By August 1905 they'd completed their studies and they continued westward, eventually emerging into waters that had been charted from the west, sighting a whaling vessel from San Francisco. Having been the first vessel to navigate the North-West Passage, the *Gjøa* froze fast in the ice and in October, Amundsen and an American companion set off by dog-sled to the telegraph station at Eagle, Alaska, over 900km away. There he announced the news of his success.

Amundsen's next goal was to be the first man to reach the North Pole, and he asked his friend Fridtjof Nansen if he could borrow the ship *Fram* (meaning 'forward') for the expedition. Nansen agreed, but his hopes were dashed in April 1909 when Robert Peary announced that he'd reached the Pole overland. That goal apparently lost, Amundsen decided to change directions and head for the South Pole. In 1910, he set out, only to learn that Britain's Robert Falcon Scott's *Terra Nova* expedition was setting out from New Zealand with the same idea in mind (Scott had already failed at one attempt on the Pole).

In January 1911, the *Fram* dropped anchor at Roosevelt Island, which was 60km closer to the South Pole than Scott's Ross Island base. With four companions – Olav Bjåland, Helmer Hanssen, Sverre Hassel and Oscar Wisling – and four light sleds pulled by 13 dogs each, Amundsen set out overland on 19 October. Although they met with some resistance passing the crevasses of the vast Axel Heiberg glacier, the expedition reached the South Pole on 14 December 1911. Famously, Robert Scott arrived on 17 January 1912, only to discover the Norwegian flag already there. Many historians feel that the hardy Amundsen had made the trip look too easy, especially because Scott's expedition met its end when five members –

Roald Amundsen

Edgar 'Teddy' Evans, Lawrence Oates, Henry Bowers, Edward Wilson and Scott himself – died of cold and starvation on the Ross Ice Shelf while en route back to civilisation.

After two abortive attempts to make further oceanographic, meteorological and geophysical studies in the Arctic aboard the ship *Maud*, which involved three winters frozen into fast ice, Amundsen decided to be the first man to successfully fly over the North Pole. On a lecture tour in North America, he met American Lincoln Ellsworth, who was interested in purchasing two flying boats and sponsoring the expedition, in exchange for taking part in the journey. On 21 May 1925, the two planes took off from Svalbard bound for Alaska but, thanks to a leaking fuel tank on one and engine trouble on the other, they were forced to land on sea ice about 150km from the Pole. After using hand tools to hew out a runway, the pilot Hjalmar Riiser-Larsen managed to take off with all six crew members and return one plane to Nordaustlandet, in Svalbard, where they ditched in the sea and had to be rescued.

Having decided that fixed-wing aircraft were unsuitable for polar exploration, the following year Amundsen tried again, this time aboard the airship *Norge* with Lincoln Ellsworth, Italian Umberto Nobile and pilot-navigator Hjalmar Riiser-Larsen. They left northern Spitsbergen on 11 May 1926 and, 16 hours later, dropped the Norwegian, American and Italian flags on the North Pole. On 14 May they landed triumphantly at Teller, Alaska, having flown 5456km in 72 hours and completing the first flight between Europe and North America. They also determined that the Arctic Ocean area was all water, with no land masses embedded in it. (Note: Robert Peary's claim to have been the first at the North Pole, and subsequent claims by Dr Frederick Cook and Robert Byrd, have since been disputed, and it hasn't yet been determined who was the first. In fact, the Amundsen expedition was the first one with indisputable evidence of its success.)

In May 1928, Nobile attempted another expedition in the airship *Italia*, but it crashed in the Arctic. Amundsen volunteered to join the rescue expedition and took off from Tromsø. Although Nobile and his crew were rescued on 22 June, Amundsen's last signals were received three hours after his take-off and he was never seen again.

as a scientific post. On the opposite side of the entrance rise some crowded bird cliffs, which overlook one of the most verdant spots in all of Svalbard. Here grow a variety of flowers, mosses and even grasses.

Magdalenefjord

The lovely blue-green bay Magdalenefjord, flanked by towering alpine peaks and intimidating tidewater glaciers, is the most popular anchorage along the western coast of Spitsbergen and for most visitors, it's also the most inspiring. In the 17th century, this area saw heavy Dutch whaling activities and at Graveneset, near the mouth of the fjord, you can still see the remains of two stoves used to boil down the blubber. Between the early 17th and mid-18th centuries, numerous whalers were buried at this site, which is now protected as a cultural monument and marked with a 1930 memorial honouring these early adventurers.

For better or worse, this site is extremely popular and if you're there with (or at the same time as) a large cruise ship, your enjoyment of the place will probably be affected. In fact, be warned that cruise-line crew members frequently enhance their beach barbecues by dressing up as polar bears or penguins (clearly lost ones) and dancing on a convenient ice floe.

Danskøya

One of the most intriguing sites in northwestern Spitsbergen is Virgohamna, on the bleak and gravelly island of Danskøya. This was the site of several historical enterprises, and ample remains of several broken dreams now lie scattered across the lonely beach. Among them are the ruins of three blubber stoves from the old 17th century whaling station, as well as eight stone-covered graves from the same era. There's also the remains of a cottage built by English adventurer Arnold Pike, who took a notion to sail north in the yacht *Siggen* and spend a winter subsisting on polar bears and reindeer.

The next adventurer at Virgohamna was Swedish engineer Salomon August Andrée, who in the summer of 1897 set off from Virgohamna in a balloon, hoping to reach the North Pole. The fate of this expedition, which also included his colleagues Frænkel and Strindberg, wasn't known until 1930, when their crash site was discovered on the island of Kvitøya. It's thought that they survived the crash, but died of food poisoning after eating undercooked bear meat.

Then in 1906, journalist Walter Wellman, who was sponsored by a US newspaper, attempted to reach the North Pole in a zeppelin but failed. He returned to try again the next year, when his ship was damaged in a storm. On his third attempt, in 1909, he floated to within 60km of the pole, where he met with technical problems and gave up for good, mainly because he'd heard that Robert Peary had already reached the pole anyway. Most of the junk that now litters the beach are the remains of these four attempts, and it's all protected as a historical monument (including dozens of rusted 44-gallon fuel drums).

Amsterdamøya & Fairhaven

The offshore island of Amsterdamøya was the site of the large Smeerenburg whaling station, which was co-founded in 1617 by Dutch and Danish concerns, but all that remains are seven ovens and some graves. All around the nearby sound, Fairhaven, which lies between the mainland and the four small offshore islands, are scattered numerous whalers' graves.

Moffen

Known for its walrus population, most tourist cruises attempt to approach flat and gravelly Moffen Island, but most are turned back by pack or drift ice. In any case, between 15 May and 15 September, boats can't approach within 300m of the island, lest they disturb the walruses' breeding activities.

OUTER ISLANDS
Bjørnøya

Svalbard's southernmost island, 178 sq km Bjørnøya, is visited mainly by the curious crews of private yachts and cruise ships. There's little to see but a tiny museum, the

Norwegian Bjørnøya Radio meteorological station and a couple of historic buildings. The most interesting is a former pig sty known as Hammerfesthuset, which was constructed in 1823 and is the oldest surviving building in Svalbard. The island's name is derived from an errant bear who inhabited the island when Willem Barents first landed there.

Hopen

In 1942, the narrow and lonely island of Hopen saw the wreck of the Soviet freighter *Dekabrist* ('Decembrist') and only three of the 80 passengers and crew members survived the near-impossible winter conditions. The following year, the island was occupied by a German meteorological station, which was later rebuilt by the Norwegians to monitor climatic conditions and later, to study ice movements and the aurora borealis. It's now home to a handful of scientific personnel.

Nordaustlandet

Vast Nordaustlandet, Svalbard's second largest island, takes in over 14,700 sq km, about 75% of which is covered with ice. The lonely eastern coast is dominated by the vast Austfonna ice sheet, which forms the longest tidewater glacial face in the Arctic region.

Although the island is currently uninhabited, it's littered with the ruins of past activities, including the former German weather station at Rijpfjorden and the once unsightly Kinnvika weather station on Murchisonfjorden. Fortunately, the Sysselmann's office cleaned up the mess left at this installation and now maintains a helicopter fuel depot there.

Kvitøya

The 700 sq km island of Kvitøya, or 'white island', is aptly named, as only three tiny headlands are free of ice and it's almost perpetually surrounded by either pack ice or drift ice. Not surprisingly, it's uninhabited, but there is an unstaffed radio transmitter and the odd icebreaker does call in from time to time. Its 15 minutes of fame,

however, came when the Swedish balloon expedition of Andrée, Frænkel and Strindberg crashed here after a failed attempt on the North Pole. All three died, probably of food poisoning from eating infected polar bear meat.

Jan Mayen

Norway's 'other' Arctic territory, the island of Jan Mayen, lies in the Norwegian Sea 600km north of Iceland, 500km east of Greenland and 1000km west of the Norwegian mainland. It sits squarely on the northern end of the mid-Atlantic ridge and at its northern end, known as Nord-Jan, rises Norway's only active volcano, Beerenberg (2277m). The island measures 54km long by up to 16km wide, and covers 380 sq km. This includes a 3.5 sq km slice called Nylandet, which was added by an eruption of Beerenburg in September 1970.

In 1614, English captain John Clarke stumbled upon the island and named it Isabella, but didn't stay. Later the same year, the Dutch captain Jan Jakobs May van Schellinkhout stumbled upon Jan Mayen in a fog so dense that he couldn't even see the length of his own ship, and the island only gave itself away in the sound of the waves breaking on its barren shores. As he approached, the looming peak of Beerenberg came into view and he realised he'd discovered an uncharted island. His first mate did some mapping and named the place after the captain.

Around 1633, the Dutch began whaling in the area and sent seven sailors to overwinter and thereby establish a Dutch presence and a place to boil down the blubber. Naturally, scurvy took its toll and when the ships returned in the spring, everyone was dead. That didn't stop the whaling activities, however. Over the following years, the Greenland right whale was nearly exterminated in these waters and commercial whaling ended in 1640.

From that time, the island was used only as a staging point for polar expeditions, and

JAN MAYEN

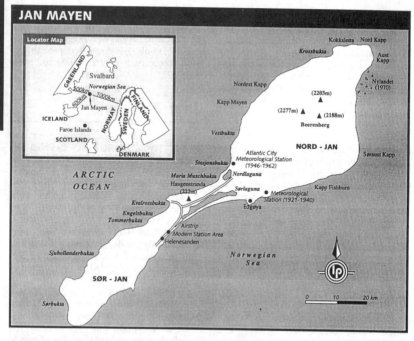

as a meteorological post. During WWII, it was never occupied by the Germans and was operated by Norwegian forces in exile. In 1943, the Americans established a radio installation called Atlantic City, and after the war, Norway and the USA set up a joint Loran (long-range navigation) station. Nowadays, all that remains is a small Norwegian meteorological post.

A dispute between Norway and Denmark regarding the fishing exclusion zone between Jan Mayen and Greenland was settled in 1988 by the international court in The Hague, granting the greater area of sovereignty to Denmark. Jan Mayen was formerly administered by the Sysselmann of Svalbard, but is now administered by the county of Nordland, from Bodø.

Visiting Jan Mayen

Although Arctic cruise ships call in occasionally and a couple of specialist tourism operators offer fleeting visits to the island, independent travel is all but non-existent.

In any case, prospective visitors must obtain permission from the Ministry of Defence in Oslo. If you're intent on visiting Jan Mayen, check with Spitsbergen Tours in Longyearbyen, which may be able to arrange something.

Language

NORWEGIAN

Norway has two official languages – Bokmål and Nynorsk – but differences between the two are effectively very minor. In this language guide we have used Bokmål – it's by far the most common language that travellers to Norway will encounter. For a more detailed description of these languages and their usage see Language in the Facts about Norway chapter. For a more comprehensive list of Norwegian words and phrases, get a copy of Lonely Planet's *Scandinavian Europe phrasebook*.

The Norwegian alphabet has 29 letters, those used in English, plus the vowels æ, ø and å (which are listed at the end of the alphabet). While the consonants c, q, w, x, and z are included, they are used mainly in foreign words. On many Norwegian place names, the definite article 'the' – which may be masculine (-en), feminine (-en or -a) or neuter (-et) – is appended to the end, eg *Jotunheim* becomes *Jotunheimen*, and *Horningdalsvatn* becomes *Horningdalsvatnet*. Plurals are usually formed by adding -e or -er.

Pronunciation

Norwegian pronunciation is a complex affair for native English speakers. These guidelines only approximate the sounds of the language as you'll hear them in the everyday speech of Norwegians – the best way to improve your pronunciation is to employ the 'listen and learn' method.

Vowels

As in English, Norwegian vowels can have many permutations. The length of vowels is a very important feature in the pronunciation of Norwegian. When occurring in a stressed syllable every vowel has both a (very) long and a (very) short counterpart. Generally, a vowel is short when followed by one consonant, and when followed by two or more consonants, it's long.

a	long, as in 'father'; short, as the 'u' in 'cut'
å	long, as in the 'o' in 'lord'; short, as the 'o' in 'pot'
e, æ	long, as in posh British 'day'; short, as in 'bet'; before r, as in British 'bad'. When in unstressed syllables it's always as the 'u' in 'lettuce'.
i	very short, as the 'ea' in 'beat'; long as the 'ee' in 'seethe'
o	short, as in British 'pot'; long as in American 'zoo'; short, as the 'u' in put; long, as in 'lord'
ø	as the 'e' in 'her'
u	long, as the 'oo' in 'soon'; short, as in 'put'
y	a bit like German 'ü'; try pursing your lips and saying 'ee'

Diphthongs

ai	as the word 'eye'
ei	as the 'ay' in 'hay'
au	similar to the word 'owe'
øy	like 'er-y' in the expression 'her year', with no 'r' sound

Consonants & Semivowels

d	often silent at the end of a word, or when between two vowels
g	as in 'go' except before ei, i, j, øy and y when it's pronounced as the 'y' in 'yard'; in the combination gn it's pronounced as the 'ng' of 'sing' followed by an 'n'
h	as in 'her'; silent before v and j
j	always as the 'y' in 'yard'
k	a hard sound, as in 'kin'; before the letters or combinations ei, i, j, øy and y it's mostly pronounced as the 'ch' in 'chin'. (In many areas, these combinations are pronounced as the 'h' in 'huge', or as 'ch' in Scottish *loch*.)
l	pronounced thinly, as in 'list', except after 'ah', 'aa', 'o' and 'or' sounds, when it's like the 'll' in 'all'

ng	in most areas, as the 'ng' in 'sing'
r	trilled, like Spanish 'r'; in south-west Norway the **r** has a guttural pronunciation, as in French *rien*. The combinations **rd, rl, rn, rt** sound a little as they do in American 'weird', 'earl', 'earn' and 'start', but with a much weaker 'r'. The combination **rs** is pronounced 'sh' as in 'fish'.
s	as in 'so'. The combination **sk** followed by **ei, i, j, øy** and **y** is pronounced as 'sh', eg the Norwegian word *ski* sounds like English 'she'.
t	as in 'top', except in two cases where it's silent: in the Norwegian word *det* (it, that) – roughly pronounced like British English 'dare' – and in the definite singular ending *-et* of Norwegian neutral nouns
v	mostly as English 'w' but without rounding the lips

Basics

Hello.	*Goddag.*
Goodbye.	*Morna.*
Yes/No.	*Ja/Nei.*
Please.	*Vær så snill.*
Thank you.	*Takk.*
You're welcome.	*Ingen årsak.*
Excuse me. (Sorry)	*Unnskyld.*
Do you speak English?	*Snakker du engelsk?*
How much is it?	*Hvor mye koster det?*
What's your name?	*Hva heter du?*
My name is ...	*Jeg heter ...*

Getting Around

What time does the ... leave/arrive?	*Når går/kommer ...?*
boat	*båten*
bus (city)	*bussen (bybussen)*
bus (intercity)	*bussen (linjebussen)*
tram	*trikken*
train	*toget*
I'd like a ...	*Jeg vil gjerne ha ...*
one-way ticket	*enkeltbillett*
return ticket	*tur-retur*

1st class	*første klasse*
2nd class	*annen klasse*
left luggage	*reisegods*
timetable	*ruteplan*
bus/tram stop	*buss/trikkhaldeplass*
train station	*jernbanestasjon*
ferry terminal	*ferjeleiet*

Where can I rent a car/bicycle?	*Hvor kan jeg leie en bil/sykkel?*
Where is ...?	*Hvor er ...?*
Go straight ahead.	*Det er rett fram.*
Turn left.	*Ta til venstre.*
Turn right.	*Ta til høyre.*
far/near	*langt/nær*

Around Town

bank	*banken*
chemist/pharmacy	*apotek*
embassy	*ambassade*
market	*torget*
my hotel	*hotellet mitt*
newsagency	*kiosk*
post office	*postkontoret*
telephone centre	*televerket*
tourist office	*turistinformasjon*

Accommodation

hotel	*hotell*
guesthouse	*gjestgiveri/pensjonat*
youth hostel	*vandrerhjem*
camping ground	*kamping/leirplass*

Do you have any rooms available?	*Har du ledige rom?*

Signs

INNGANG	**ENTRANCE**
UTGANG	**EXIT**
OPPLYSNINGER	**INFORMATION**
ÅPEN	**OPEN**
STENGT	**CLOSED**
FORBUDT	**PROHIBITED**
POLITISTASJON	**POLICE STATION**
TOALETTER	**TOILETS**
HERRER	**MEN**
DAMER	**WOMEN**

Emergencies

Help!	*Hjelp!*
Call a doctor!	*Ring ein lege!*
Call the police!	*Ring politiet!*
Go away!	*Forsvinn!*
I'm lost.	*Jeg har gått meg vill.*

Does it include breakfast?	*Inklusive frokosten?*

How much is it ...?	*Hvor mye er det ...?*
per night	*pr dag*
per person	*pr person*

I'd like a ...	*Jeg vil gjerne ha ...*
single room	*eit enkeltrom*
double room	*eit dobbeltrom*

one day	*en dag*
two days	*to dager*
one week	*en uka*

Time, Days & Numbers

What time is it?	*Hva er klokka?*
today	*i dag*
tomorrow	*i morgen*
yesterday	*i går*
in the morning	*om formiddagen*
in the afternoon	*om ettermiddagen*

Monday	*mandag*
Tuesday	*tirsdag*
Wednesday	*onsdag*
Thursday	*torsdag*
Friday	*fredag*
Saturday	*lørdag*
Sunday	*søndag*

0	*null*
1	*en*
2	*to*
3	*tre*
4	*fire*
5	*fem*
6	*seks*
7	*sju*
8	*åtte*
9	*ni*
10	*ti*
100	*hundre*
1000	*tusen*

one million	*en million*

SAMI

Although written Fell Sami includes several accented letters, it still doesn't accurately represent the spoken language – even some Sami people find the written language difficult to learn. For example, *giitu* (thanks) is pronounced 'GHEECH-too', but the strongly aspirated 'h' is not written.

Here are a few Sami phrases; to learn the correct pronunciation, it's probably best to ask a local to read the words aloud.

Hello.	*Buorre beaivi.*
Hello. (reply)	*Ipmel atti.*
Goodbye. (to person leaving)	*Mana dearvan.*
Goodbye. (to person staying)	*Báze dearvan.*
Thank you.	*Giitu.*
You're welcome.	*Leage buorre.*
Yes.	*De lea.*
No.	*Li.*
How are you?	*Mot manna?*
I'm fine.	*Buorre dat manna.*

1	*okta*
2	*guokte*
3	*golbma*
4	*njeallje*
5	*vihta*
6	*guhta*
7	*cieza*
8	*gávcci*
9	*ovcci*
10	*logi*

Glossary

You may encounter some of the following terms and abbreviations during your travels in Norway. See also the Language chapter and the Food section in the Facts for the Visitor chapter.

Note that the letters æ, ø and å fall at the end of the Norwegian alphabet.

allemannsretten – 'every man's right'; a tradition (now a law) allowing universal access to private property (with some restrictions), public lands and wilderness areas
apotek – pharmacy
automatisk trafikkontrol – speed camera

bakke – hill
bekk – creek, stream
berg – mountain
bibliotek – library
bil – car
billett – ticket
bird cliffs – sea cliffs inhabited by colonies of nesting birds
bokhandel – bookshop
bru, bro – bridge
brygge – quay, wharf
bryggeri – brewery
bukt, bukta – bay
bunad – the Norwegian national costume; each region has its own version of this colourful affair
by – town
børsen – stock exchange
båt – boat

col – mountaineering term for a hollow or pass between peaks

dagskort – 'day card', a daily bus pass
dal – valley
DNT – *Den Norske Turistforening* (The Norwegian Mountain Touring Club)
domkirke – cathedral

elv, elva – river
etasje – floor, storey

ferje – ferry
festning – fort, fortress
fjell, fell, fjall – mountain
fjord – drowned glacial valley
fonn – glacial icefield
forening – club, association
foss – waterfall
fylke – county
fyr, fyrtårn – lighthouse

galleriet – gallery or shopping arcade
gamma, gammen – Sami turf hut, sometimes partially underground
gamle, gamla, gammel – old
gamlebyen – the 'old town'; the historic portion of a city or town
gate, gata – street (often abbreviated to just **gt**)
gatekjøkken – literally 'street kitchen'; street kiosk/stall/grill selling greasy fast food
gjestehavn – 'guest harbour', the area of a port town where visiting boats and yachts moor; washing and cooking facilities are normally available
gjestehus – guesthouse
gravlund – cemetery
grense – border
grotta – grotto, cavern
gruve, gruva – mine
gård, gard – farm or courtyard

hage – garden
halvøya – peninsula
hamn – northern Norwegian word for harbour
hav – ocean
havn – harbour
hule, hula – cave
Hurtigruten – literally 'the Express Route'; system of coastal steamers plying the route between Bergen and Kirkenes

hus – house
hytte – cottage, hut

iddis – colourful sardine tin label; Stavanger dialect for *'etikett'* or label
innsjø – lake
is – ice
isbjørn – polar bear
isbre – valley glacier

jernbanestasjon – train station
jul – Christmas
juvet – gorge

kai, kaia – quay
kapp – cape
kart – map
kirke, kirkja, kirkje, kerk – church
klokken – o'clock; the time
koldtbord – cold buffet or smorgasbord
kong – king
kort – card
krone – Norwegian currency unit
kunst – art
kyst – coast

lavvo, lavvu – tepee; Sami tent dwelling
legevakten – clinic
libris – books; indicates a bookshop
lompen – miners' coveralls, used in the Svalbard coal mines
lufthavn – airport

magasin – department store
mark – woods
mat – food
MOMS – Value Added Tax/sales tax
M/S – *mesterskap* or mastership, used to designate ship names
museum, museet – museum
mush – to drive a dog-sled (word of Alaskan origin)
myntvaskeri – coin laundry

nasjonalpark – national park
naturreservat – nature reserve
navvy – railway worker
nedre – lower
nord – north
nordlys – northern lights, aurora borealis

Norge – Norway
Norsk – Norwegian
NORTRA – Norwegian Tourist Board
'Norway in a Nutshell' – a range of tours which give high-speed travellers a glimpse of the best of Norway in one or two days
NSB – *Norske Statsbanen* (Norwegian State Railways)
ny – new

og – and

pensjonat – pension or guesthouse
plass – plaza, square
polarsirkelen – Arctic Circle; 66°33'N latitude
Pomor – the Russian trading and fishing community from the White Sea area, which prospered in northern Norway in the 17th century
postkontor – post office
påske – Easter

reker – shrimp
rorbuer – cabin/fishing hut
rosemaling – painted floral motifs
rutebilstasjon – bus terminal
ruteplan – transport timetable
Rv – *Riksvei*; national highway
rådhus – town hall

selskap – company
sentrum – town centre
sjø – sea
sjøhus – fishing bunkhouse on the docks; many are now available for tourist accommodation
skerries – offshore archipelago of small rocky islets
skog – forest
skål! – cheers!
slott – castle, palace
snø – snow
spark, sparky – a kicksled that's popular in winter
stabbur – raised storehouse
stabkirke – stave church
stasjon – station
Statens Kartverk – State Mapping Agency
stokkfisk – 'stock fish'; dried cod

storting – parliament
strand – beach
sund – sound, strait
Sverige – Sweden
svømmehall, svømmebad – swimming pool
sykehus – hospital
sykkel – bicycle
sør – south
søyle – column, pillar

teater – theatre
telekort – telephone card
tog – train
togbuss – bus services in Raumadalen and Nordland run by NSB to connect railheads with other popular destinations
torget, torvet – town square
torsk – cod
turistkontor – tourist office
tårn – tower

utleie – hire company, as in *bilutleie* (car hire), *sykkelutleie* (bicycle hire), *kano-utleie* (canoe hire) or *hytteutleie* (hut hire)

vandrerhjem – youth hostel
vann, vatn, vannet, vatnet – lake
vaskeri – laundry
vei, veg – road (often abbreviated to **vn**)
vest – west
vidde, vidda – plateau
vinmonopolet – 'wine monopoly shop'; government-run shop selling wine and liquor
værelse – room

Zodiac – small inflatable boat powered by outboard engine

øl – beer
ølutsalg – beer sales outlet
øst – east
øvre – upper
øy – island

Date Abbreviations
f. Kr – før Kristi fødsel – BC
e. Kr – etter Kristi fødsel – AD

FREE Lonely Planet Newsletters

We love hearing from you and think you'd like to hear from us.

Planet Talk

Our FREE quarterly printed newsletter is full of tips from travellers and anecdotes from Lonely Planet guidebook authors. Every issue is packed with up-to-date travel news and advice, and includes:

- a postcard from Lonely Planet co-founder Tony Wheeler
- a swag of mail from travellers
- a look at life on the road through the eyes of a Lonely Planet author
- topical health advice
- prizes for the best travel yarn
- news about forthcoming Lonely Planet events
- a complete list of Lonely Planet books and other titles

To join our mailing list, residents of the UK, Europe and Africa can email us at go@lonelyplanet.co.uk; residents of North and South America can email us at info@lonelyplanet.com; the rest of the world can email us at talk2us@lonelyplanet.com.au, or contact any Lonely Planet office.

Comet

Our FREE monthly email newsletter brings you all the latest travel news, features, interviews, competitions, destination ideas, travellers' tips & tales, Q&As, raging debates and related links. Find out what's new on the Lonely Planet Web site and which books are about to hit the shelves.

Subscribe from your desktop: www.lonelyplanet.com/comet

LONELY PLANET

Mail Order

Lonely Planet products are distributed worldwide. They are also available by mail order from Lonely Planet, so if you have difficulty finding a title please write to us. North and South American residents should write to 150 Linden St, Oakland, CA 94607, USA; European and African residents should write to 10a Spring Place, London NW5 3BH, UK; and residents of other countries to Locked Bag 1, Footscray, Victoria 3011, Australia.

(Bombay) • Nepal • Nepali phrasebook • Pakistan • Rajasthan • Read This First: Asia & India • South India • Sri Lanka • Sri Lanka phrasebook • Tibet • Tibetan phrasebook • Trekking in the Indian Himalaya • Trekking in the Karakoram & Hindukush • Trekking in the Nepal Himalaya
Travel Literature: The Age of Kali: Indian Travels and Encounters • Hello Goodnight: A Life of Goa • In Rajasthan • A Season in Heaven: True Tales from the Road to Kathmandu • Shopping for Buddhas • A Short Walk in the Hindu Kush • Slowly Down the Ganges

ISLANDS OF THE INDIAN OCEAN Madagascar & Comoros • Maldives • Mauritius, Réunion & Seychelles

MIDDLE EAST & CENTRAL ASIA Bahrain, Kuwait & Qatar • Central Asia • Central Asia phrasebook • Dubai • Hebrew phrasebook • Iran • Israel & the Palestinian Territories • Istanbul • Istanbul City Map • Istanbul to Cairo on a shoestring • Jerusalem • Jerusalem City Map • Jordan • Lebanon • Middle East • Oman & the United Arab Emirates • Syria • Turkey • Turkish phrasebook • World Food Turkey • Yemen
Travel Literature: Black on Black: Iran Revisited • The Gates of Damascus • Kingdom of the Film Stars: Journey into Jordan

NORTH AMERICA Alaska • Boston • Boston City Map • California & Nevada • California Condensed • Canada • Chicago • Chicago City Map • Deep South • Florida • Hawaii • Hiking in Alaska • Hiking in the USA • Honolulu • Las Vegas • Los Angeles • Miami • Miami City Map • New England • New Orleans • New York City • New York City City Map • New York City Condensed • New York, New Jersey & Pennsylvania • Oahu • Out to Eat – San Francisco • Pacific Northwest • Puerto Rico • Rocky Mountains • San Francisco • San Francisco City Map • Seattle • Southwest • Texas • USA • USA phrasebook • Vancouver • Virginia & the Capital Region • Washington, DC City Map • World Food Deep South, USA
Travel Literature: Caught Inside: A Surfer's Year on the California Coast • Drive Thru America

NORTH-EAST ASIA Beijing • Cantonese phrasebook • China • Hiking in Japan • Hong Kong • Hong Kong City Map • Hong Kong Condensed • Hong Kong, Macau & Guangzhou • Japan • Japanese phrasebook • Korea • Korean phrasebook • Kyoto • Mandarin phrasebook • Mongolia • Mongolian phrasebook • Seoul • South-West China • Taiwan • Tokyo
Travel Literature: In Xanadu: A Quest • Lost Japan

SOUTH AMERICA Argentina, Uruguay & Paraguay • Bolivia • Brazil • Brazilian phrasebook • Buenos Aires • Chile & Easter Island • Colombia • Ecuador & the Galapagos Islands • Healthy Travel Central & South America • Latin American Spanish phrasebook • Peru • Quechua phrasebook • Read This First: Central & South America • Rio de Janeiro • Rio de Janeiro City Map • Santiago • South America on a shoestring • Santiago • Trekking in the Patagonian Andes • Venezuela
Travel Literature: Full Circle: A South American Journey

SOUTH-EAST ASIA Bali & Lombok • Bangkok • Bangkok City Map • Burmese phrasebook • Cambodia • Hanoi • Healthy Travel Asia & India • Hill Tribes phrasebook • Ho Chi Minh City • Indonesia • Indonesian phrasebook • Indonesia's Eastern Islands • Jakarta • Java • Lao phrasebook • Laos • Malay phrasebook • Malaysia, Singapore & Brunei • Myanmar (Burma) • Philippines • Pilipino (Tagalog) phrasebook • Read This First: Asia & India • Singapore • Singapore City Map • South-East Asia on a shoestring • South-East Asia phrasebook • Thailand • Thailand's Islands & Beaches • Thailand, Vietnam, Laos & Cambodia Road Atlas • Thai phrasebook • Vietnam • Vietnamese phrasebook • World Food Thailand • World Food Vietnam

ALSO AVAILABLE: Antarctica • The Arctic • The Blue Man: Tales of Travel, Love and Coffee • Brief Encounters: Stories of Love, Sex & Travel • Chasing Rickshaws • The Last Grain Race • Lonely Planet Unpacked • Not the Only Planet: Science Fiction Travel Stories • Lonely Planet On the Edge • Sacred India • Travel with Children • Travel Photography: A Guide to Taking Better Pictures

Index

Text

Bold indicates maps.
Italics indicates boxed text.

Bold indicates maps.
Italics indicates boxed text.

Boxed Text

MAP LEGEND

BOUNDARIES

————·—·—·—·—·· ....International
—··—··—··—·· ....State

HYDROGRAPHY

................................Coastline
........................River, Creek
➤——————————— ....River Flow
................................Lake
..................Intermittent Lake
.... Salt Lake
⊙ ——➤➤—— ....Spring, Rapids
........................Swamp
—✦—◄◄◄◄◄ ....Waterfalls

○ **CAPITAL** ....National Capital
◉ **CAPITAL** ....State Capital
● **CITY** ....City
● **Town** ....Town
● **Town** ....Small Town
○ ....Point of Interest

■ ....Place to Stay
▲ ....Camping Ground
⊞ ....Caravan Park

▼ ....Place to Eat
⬛ ......Pub, Entertainment
▨ ....Picnic Area

ROUTES & TRANSPORT

================= ....Freeway
================= ....Highway
================= ....Major Road
————————— ....Minor Road
====== ....Unsealed Road
————————— ....City Highway
————————— ....City Road
================= ....City Street, Lane

.......................Pedestrian Mall
➔====== ....Tunnel
⊢⊢⊢⊢—●—⊢ ....Train Route & Station
—··—-Ⓜ—·· ....Metro & Station
................................Tramway
⊢–⊢–⊢–⊢–⊢– ....Cable Car or Chairlift
————————— ....Walking Track
————————— ....Ferry Route

AREA FEATURES

.............Aboriginal Land
.........................Beach
+ + + + ...Cemetery

[⌐ ─ ─ ─ ¬] ....Marine Park
✿ ..National Park, Gardens
.............................Urban Area

MAP SYMBOLS

✈ ....Airport
✝ ....Airfield
❶ ....Bank
ﾎ ....Beach
⌒ ....Cave
🏛 🛆 ....Church
⌒⌒⌒ ......Cliff or Escarpment
ⵑ ....Golf Course
✛ ....Hospital
⌖ ....Lighthouse
❋ ....Lookout
✕ ....Mine
⚑ ....Monument
▲ ....Mountain
🏛 .....Museum, Art Gallery

🅿 ....Parking
)(.........Pass, Chasm, Gap
★ ....Police Station
✉ ....Post Office
❖ ....Shopping Centre
🏛 ....Stately Building
⚡ ....Surf Beach
⛆ ....Swimming Pool
☎ ....Telephone
⊙ ....Toilet
❶ ......Tourist Information
⊖ ....Transport
⬛ ....Trekking Hut
⚘ ....Winery
⚒ ....Zoo

Note: not all symbols displayed above appear in this book

LONELY PLANET OFFICES

Australia
Locked Bag 1, Footscray, Victoria 3011
☎ 03 9689 4666 fax 03 9689 6833
email: talk2us@lonelyplanet.com.au

USA
150 Linden St, Oakland, CA 94607
☎ 510 893 8555 TOLL FREE: 800 275 8555
fax 510 893 8572
email: info@lonelyplanet.com

UK
10a Spring Place, London NW5 3BH
☎ 020 7428 4800 fax 020 7428 4828
email: go@lonelyplanet.co.uk

France
1 rue du Dahomey, 75011 Paris
☎ 01 55 25 33 00 fax 01 55 25 33 01
email: bip@lonelyplanet.fr
www.lonelyplanet.fr

World Wide Web: www.lonelyplanet.com *or* AOL keyword: lp
Lonely Planet Images: lpi@lonelyplanet.com.au